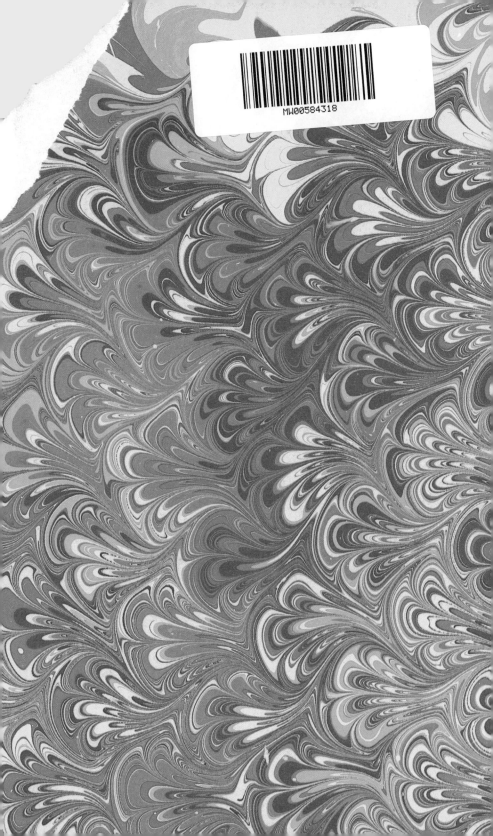

SCORCHED EARTH
PAUL CARELL

Also by Paul Carell
THE FOXES OF THE DESERT
INVASION! THEY'RE COMING
HITLER MOVES EAST
OPERATION BARBAROSSA IN PHOTOGRAPHS

PAUL CARELL
SCORCHED EARTH

THE RUSSIAN-GERMAN WAR 1943-1944

Schiffer Military History
Atglen, PA

ACKNOWLEDGEMENTS

I should like to express my warmest thanks to all those without whose collaboration and help I could never have written this book. To list them all is impossible – the list would include over a thousand names.

It would include not only the Field-Marshal, the army commander, and the corps commander, but equally the ordinary ranker; it would include the Chief of the General Staff and the assault-party commander, the division commander and the humble corporal, the tank commander and the pilot, the artillery commander and the ordinary gunner, the railway engineer, the radio operator, the truck driver, the medical orderly, and the Red Cross nurse.

Without the vast number of reports by these voluntary helpers I should not have been able to shape the difficult military-historical material into a piece of living history.

Particular thanks are due to the expert support given me with the drafting and finalizing of this book. A factual account, aiming at truth and truthfulness, must stand or fall on the care that goes into the collection and interpretation of facts and figures. The processing of the sources required a good deal of laborious research: thousands of letters were needed; German and Soviet units in the text and in the maps had to be painstakingly identified in the face of frequently conflicting records; the index and the reading of the manuscript and proof demanded a great deal of dedicated work.

My special thanks are due to my helpers who did all these things.

PAUL CARELL

Dust jacket photo courtesy of Richard Wilson.

Translated from the German by Ewald Osers.
Courtesy of George G. Harrap & Co., Ltd., London

This book originally published under the title *Verbrannte Erde*, by Verlag Ullstein.

Copyright © 1994 by Schiffer Publishing Ltd.
Library of Congress Catalog Number: 93-87471

Printed in the United States of America.
ISBN: 0-88740-598-3

We are interested in hearing from authors with book ideas on related topics.

Published by Schiffer Publishing Ltd.
77 Lower Valley Road
Atglen, PA 19310
Please write for a free catalog.
This book may be purchased from the publisher.
Please include $2.95 postage.
Try your bookstore first.

Preface • 1994

Has the collapse of the Soviet Union, and the subsequent access to numerous documents from Moscow's secret archives resulted in any new findings concerning the history of the German-Soviet war? As far as the course of military events is concerned, no. The account presented in this edition of *Scorched Earth* remains valid.

The secret documents of the Soviet High Command which are now available do, however, substantiate something which is historically significant. Namely this: the long-accepted view of the German-Soviet war, that on June 22, 1941 a peace-loving Soviet Union, organized only for defense, was attacked without cause by Germany, can no longer be supported. In 1941 Stalin and his high command had completed preparations for an offensive against Germany, but Hitler beat them to it.

Since 1990-1991, high ranking members of the Russian military have stated that the Red Army was preparing for an offensive war in 1941 and that, objectively, the German attack had all the features of a preventive war. Colonel Petrovin wrote in the May 8, 1991 edition of PRAVDA that, "Unrealistic plans of an offensive nature were drawn up before the war as a result of an overestimation of our own possibilities, and an underestimation of the enemy. In accordance with these plans we began grouping forces on the western frontier. But the enemy beat us to it."

The high point of the opening of the secret Russian archives occurred in early 1993, when Russian Colonel General Danilov published the complete war plan of the Soviet General Staff for 1941 in the renowned Austrian Military Journal. This document came from the central archives of the General Staff of the Russian Armed Forces and its authenticity is beyond doubt. Colonel Danilov quoted a memorandum written by Marshall Vassilevski, which reveals that Stalin had approved the plan in May 1941.

Stalin's decision to prepare for war grew out of the Wehrmacht's quick and overwhelming victory over France, which frustrated his hopes for a long, drawn-out war with the western powers which would wear down Hitler's Germany. Stalin's attack preparations began with the fall of France. Another key piece of evidence is the secret speech given by Stalin to the graduates of the military academy in 1941 at the Kremlin.

According to an account by Colonel General Volkoganov, Stalin declared that war was unavoidable. They must be ready to smash German fascism unconditionally. Immediately after this speech Stalin issued a directive: "The entire personnel complement of the Red Army must be aware that the increased political, economic and military strength of the Soviet Union allows us to pursue an offensive foreign policy, decisively defeat military powers on our borders and expand our territory."

When Stalin made this speech in early 1941, the Red Army's buildup on the western borders of the USSR (opposite Germany's eastern frontier and the Romanian oil fields) was in full swing. The 1st Strategic Echelon, in the western part of Russia had 14,700 tanks in position. There was also a massed artillery force of 34,695 guns and 9,000 combat aircraft on airfields near the frontier. This 1st Strategic Echelon, positioned on the Polish border and in the bend of the Bialystok, comprised more than 20 armies with 2.9 million soldiers. According to recently released documents, the 2nd Strategic Echelon consisted of 1.4 million men, so that in early 1941 the two strategic echelons stood ready to attack with a total of 258 divisions, including 58 tank and 30 motorized, with 14,700 battle ready tanks. This was a tremendous offensive concentration of forces in forests, field positions and crowded airfields, just beyond the Polish and Romanian borders. It was a buildup which, according to military principles, could not have been maintained beyond the winter.

The Wehrmacht launched its attack on June 22, 1941 with about three-million soldiers, of which 600,000 were from allied nations, 3,468 tanks and assault guns, and 2,510 combat aircraft. The German artillery and tanks were inferior in quality and quantity to those of the

Russians. The tremendous success which Germany enjoyed in the initial weeks was due to the fact that the German attack was launched into the midst of a buildup by the Red Army, which led to the great encirclements and the tremendous losses. Nevertheless, by December 31, 1941, the Wehrmacht's total losses in the eastern campaign already stood at 830,000 men killed, wounded or missing. A total of 509,000 soldiers were available to replace them. The winter months brought further cold related losses in the order of 400,000 men.

The summer offensive of 1942 resulted in further huge territorial gains by the Wehrmacht: the German divisions raced across the arid Kalmuck Steppe in panzer-blitzkrieg tempo, crossed passes of the High Caucasus and fought their way through subtropical valleys leading to the Black Sea. But the result was a greatly overextended front stretching to the Volga and the Black Sea, for which there were insufficient numbers of troops. The tragedy of the Sixth Army in Stalingrad was the result. The German forces always lacked the decisive last battalion, whether in Stalingrad or in the battle for the Caucasian oil.

The writings of Soviet historians allow us to see today just how desperate, how critical, the situation was on the Soviet side during the German summer offensive, including Stalingrad. They reveal what decisive lessons Stalin and the Soviet High Command had learned from the German blitzkrieg strategy, how and with what means young, hard-as-steel Russian generals mastered operational crises, and how the Russian soldier fought on under desperate conditions in spite of tremendous losses. The Red marshals won at Stalingrad, and they forced the weakened, overtaxed German armies of the Caucus Front into a desperate retreat.

But the Wehrmacht once again gathered itself for a decisive battle, hoping to employ new armored weapons (Tiger, Panther and large-caliber assault guns) to force a decision in the Kursk salient in July 1943 (Operation "Citadel"). It was an unbelievably bloody battle, which for a time stood on the razor's edge. But the defensive forces of the Red Army, mightily strengthened by deliveries of materiel from the United States, were stronger than the offensive forces of the German Wehrmacht.

The loss of the Battle of Kursk was the turning point in the war in the east, and ushered in the German defeat.

Paul Carell
January 1994

Preface to the Original English Edition

Hitler Moves East ended with Stalingrad. But, contrary to common belief, the disaster of the Sixth Army on the Volga was not the starting-point of the German defeat. Stalingrad was the final halt of the German campaign of conquest; the crucial turning point of the Russian war, on the other hand, was the battle of Kursk in the summer of 1943. That is why I have placed this operation at the beginning of *Scorched Earth,* so that the two great phases of the war in Russia should emerge more clearly. The German victorious advance ended at Stalingrad – the German defeat began at Kursk.

The intervening operations, from the end of 1942 until July 1943, are described in flashback form. This arrangement, admittedly, means a break in the chronology, but it provides the reader with a better understanding of the situation, as well as of the importance and dramatic character of the fighting during the period from Stalingrad to Kursk. Stalin intended to decide the outcome of the war in this battle between Don and Donets, but he failed in the face of Field Marshal von Manstein's outstanding generalship. Once more the German Command was offered an opportunity to save the situation by going over from a campaign of conquest to a war of attrition.

But Hitler refused to see what the commanders in the field kept urgently explaining and demonstrating to him. He continued to gamble, he staked everything on one card, and he hoped that Operation Citadel – which was the code name for the battle of Kursk – would bring about the great turning-point.

Thus the war in the East was moving towards its climax in the Kursk salient. With a tremendous military effort the opponents clashed – spirited German attack against vigorous Russian defense. The latest weapons, fanatical determination, skillful generalship, ruses, and betrayal – all these reached their peak in this great encounter. The Soviet war historians are right to call Operation Citadel the most important battle of the entire war.

Kursk was followed by a string of German defeats. What makes this phase of the war so gripping to the chronicler and the reader alike is the performance of the bled-white troops, the devotion to duty, and the discipline of the men in difficult and indeed hopeless situations.

In handling the material I have kept to the method which proved successful in *Hitler Moves East* – the fusion of factual accounts by surviving witnesses with the documentary evidence of history.

A technique of questionnaires, developed in the course of the work, made it possible for exceedingly busy men, who in the war held commands or were in action at certain focal points, to pass their information on to me. The numerous unpublished or specially written essays which were put at my disposal contained exceptionally valuable material and have enriched the present account by a great many interesting and hitherto unknown pieces of military information.

Particularly important was the fact that I was able to make use of the specialized Soviet literature on the war, published during the post-Stalin era, as well as the personal memoirs of Soviet Army commanders and staff officers. Equally important was the fact that I had access to the microfilms of German war diaries now in American archives.

I have again dispensed with footnotes referring to sources but would like to point out, for the sake of order, that every character in this account is genuine, and every fact and description based on reliable historical evidence.

Paul Carell

Photographic Acknowledgments

CONTENTS

PART ONE: The Battle of Kursk

PART TWO: Manstein

PART THREE: Battles on the Northern Wing

PART FOUR: Last Chance

PART FIVE: To the Dnieper

PART SIX: Between Kiev and Melitopol

PART SEVEN: Disasters on the Southern Wing

PART EIGHT: The Cannae of Army Group Centre

MAPS

PART ONE:
The Battle of Kursk

1. Hitler stakes Everything on One Card

*Mission in Bucharest–Conference at the Wolfsschanze
tea-room–An oak wood near Oboyan–5th July, 0330
hours: start of Operation Citadel–Ferdinand the Giant–
Duel by the Ponyri schoolhouse.*

THE heat haze of a Rumanian summer hung over Bucharest. The
noon-day air of Walachia was like a stifling hot breath in the city.
It lay heavily over the massive castle, over the white churches, and
over the empty hotels. The Strada Victor Emanuel was deserted. The
first building on it, No. 1, was the German Embassy.

"Fancy having to dress up in this damned heat," Herr von Killinger
grumbled. He was standing by his office desk, wearing his diplomatic
uniform. The blinds had been let down. The large room was in semi-
darkness. The electric fan hummed softly as it pushed the cool, stale
air around the room.

Three hours previously the telegram had arrived from Berlin. "For
the eyes of the Ambassador only." He had decoded it. And he had at
once asked for an appointment with Marshal Antonescu. He was now
being expected at the small villa on the outskirts, at 1600. It was time
to leave.

On the dot of 4 P.M. Killinger drove into the forecourt of the heavily
guarded residence of the Rumanian Head of State.

Antonescu received the German Ambassador in his salon on the first
floor. As always, the short, wiry general was in uniform.

"Well, Mr Ambassador, is the Führer granting Field-Marshal von
Manstein leave to pay us a visit?" he asked with a smile.

Killinger pulled the telegram from his pocket. And in a deliberately
solemn voice he read out: "The Führer requests you to call on the
Head of State at once to inform him that Field-Marshal von Manstein
will arrive in Bucharest tomorrow afternoon to present to him, on the
Führer's behalf, the Gold Crimea Shield on the occasion of the anniversary of the capture of Sevastopol."

Antonescu smiled and politely expressed gratitude. But his smile vanished as he said: "The Crimea Shield is a great honour, Mr Ambassador—but far more important to me is the opportunity of discussing the difficult military situation with Field-Marshal von Manstein. Rumania has her entire military forces mobilized in the field—and I bear the responsibility for this. At Stalingrad I lost eighteen Rumanian divisions. I cannot afford a repetition of such a disaster. I must know what's going to happen next. *Nous sommes alliés*, Mr Ambassador, but there is a tendency in Rastenburg to forget this now and then. I made this observation to the Führer myself at Castle Klessheim three months ago."

The ominous note was not to be missed. Good thing Manstein is coming in person, Killinger thought. But outwardly he betrayed nothing, and received the Rumanian leader's outspoken remarks with equanimity. Besides, the former naval officer from Saxony, subsequently the leader of a Free Corps and of the once greatly feared secret organization "Konsul", was not easily shaken. There was a little more talk about aspects of protocol and organization in connection with Manstein's visit. Then the Ambassador took his leave.

Barely two hours passed and throughout Bucharest the sparrows were shouting it from the roof-tops that Manstein, the C-in-C of the German Army Group South, was expected in Bucharest on 1st July 1943 for several days.

The news pedlars and the gossip gatherers of the secret services of West and East, the small agents and the more important agents, all hurried to their transmitters and passed on the interesting news to their headquarters.

In Moscow too the radio receiver at the Fourth Bureau of the Red Army came to life: Manstein arriving in Bucharest tomorrow! The staff officers of STAVKA, the Soviet High Command, nodded their heads: If the German C-in-C South is off to the Rumanian capital to knock back a few cocktails instead of sitting at his command post in Zaporozhye, surely no major military operation can take place on the Eastern Front. That was what the Soviets were bound to think. It was what they were meant to think.

Twenty-four hours later Manstein was all set to leave for Bucharest. Just then an orderly officer arrived with a signal from Hitler's headquarters: Departure not for Bucharest but for Rastenburg.

"The Führer expects you for a top-secret conference at the Wolfsschanze. Bucharest is being informed that your take-off has been delayed by bad weather."

Thus, instead of flying to Antonescu, Manstein flew to Hitler. This was not a case of bad organization but part of an elaborate deception.

At the Führer's headquarters Manstein was surprised to find a large assembly of generals: Field-Marshal von Kluge, commanding Army

Group Centre; Colonel-General Hoth, commanding the Fourth Panzer Army; Colonel-General Model, commanding the Ninth Army; General of Armoured Troops Kempf; General Nehring, commanding the XXIV Panzer Corps; Colonel-General von Greim, commanding the Sixth Air Fleet; and General Dessloch, representing the Fourth Air Fleet.

East Prussia too was under a high-pressure system bringing fine summer weather. The concrete huts of the Führer's headquarters looked mysterious and dreamlike under their nets of foliage and the grass growing on their roofs.

Hitler welcomed the generals in the tea-room block. He greeted them with great cordiality. He invited them to sit down. Then he opened the conference with a speech.

Its very first sentence revealed the great secret: "I have decided to fix the starting date of Citadel for 5th July."

That meant in four days' time. The generals looked at each other, some with relief, some with annoyance. Model looked serious. Manstein's features were inscrutable. Hoth looked anything but pleased.

This mixed reaction was by no means due to the short schedule of four days. The immediacy of the operation did not alarm any of them. They had all made their preparations. For months the units had been rehearsing the offensive. At the sand table and in practical exercises they had become familiar with the terrain in the Kursk salient. They had practised the blowing up of concrete bunkers with live ammunition, the breaching of wire obstacles, the clearing of mines, and the tackling of tank traps. Never before had a battle been so extensively prepared.

What did worry the generals was the great delay which Hitler had allowed to occur before deciding to strike now. Manstein, Guderian, Kluge, Model, and many others had originally opposed Hitler's plan of resuming the offensive on the Eastern Front so soon after Stalingrad. They had resisted the idea of prematurely employing the reserves, and above all the armoured units built up again by Guderian with the new Tiger and Panther models, in what could well be risky offensive battles.

The Wehrmacht operations staff had added their warning. They had pointed to the threatening developments in the Mediterranean area where Eisenhower was lined up for a landing in Italy. When the landing came those armoured formations from the Eastern Front would be needed in Italy.

But Hitler had pointed to the dangerous situation in the Kursk salient. In this favourable starting position the Russians had assembled enormous offensive strength. Several Tank Armies had been discovered there. In fact, the Soviets had moved 40 per cent of their total field armies, including nearly all their armoured forces, into the Kursk bulge.

That was a dangerous concentration of offensive strength. But it was

also a tempting prize. If this concentration could be annihilated the
Red Army would have been dealt a mortal blow.

This was the thought that fascinated Hitler. And, true enough, the
generals had been unable to deny the force of his argument. Above all,
they favoured the shortening of the front line which would be
achieved by the liquidation of the Kursk salient. This would result in
the freeing of forces and reserves for other fronts, such as Italy.

But they had bound their approval of the offensive to the demand
that the blow must be struck as soon as possible, before the Russians,
who were known to be masters of defence, had protected their striking
forces too thoroughly. And before the element of surprise was lost.

Manstein had demanded that the attack should be launched not
later than the beginning of May. But Hitler had kept hesitating. Once
again he had displayed an inability to take a decision. It was now the
beginning of July—was it not too late? Could there still be any
element of surprise left? That was the crucial question.

Much of Hitler's speech in the tea-room therefore again listed the
reasons for the postponement of the offensive. "We have to succeed
this time! And for this reason we had to wait for the latest heavy and
super-heavy tanks. We are obliged to seize every opportunity to face
the enemy, who is constantly getting stronger, with superior weapons
and formations."

With amazement the generals listened to the Führer making elaborate and verbose excuses. Did he perhaps suspect that the delay would
lead to disaster? And that he alone would be responsible for it because
of his continuous postponement of the date of attack?

Hitler did not seem to be too sure of himself. Colonel-General Hoth
reports that, watching the Führer during his address, he more than
once had the impression that his thoughts were elsewhere.

But when Hitler started discussing operational details his gift as a
spell-binding orator again broke through.

His plan was simple enough—the well-tried recipe of a pincer
operation. This is how it was tersely formulated in his operation order:
"The objective of the attack is to encircle the enemy forces in the
Kursk area by means of a well co-ordinated and rapid thrust of two
attacking armies from the areas of Belgorod and south of Orel and to
annihilate them by a concentric attack." In other words, a battle of encirclement following the well-tried recipe of Minsk, Uman, Kiev, and
Vyazma.

For the northern jaw of the pincers Field-Marshal von Kluge had
chosen the Ninth Army under Colonel-General Model. It would be its

Map 1. Starting position for the great summer battle of 1943. Fourth Panzer
Army and Army Detachment Kempf were to nip off the Kursk salient from the
south, while Ninth Army did so from the north.

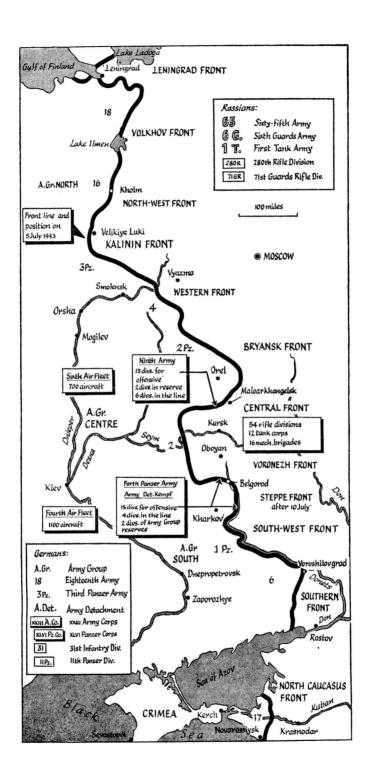

Gulf of Finland
Lake Ladoga
Leningrad   LENINGRAD FRONT

18

VOLKHOV FRONT

Lake Ilmen

A.Gr.NORTH   16   Kholm
NORTH-WEST FRONT

Russians:
65   Sixty-fifth Army
6 G.   Sixth Guards Army
1 T.   First Tank Army
280 R   280th Rifle Division
71 G R   71st Guards Rifle Div.

100 miles

Front line and
position on
5 July 1943

Velikiye Luki
KALININ FRONT

● MOSCOW

3 Pz.

Vyazma
Smolensk   WESTERN FRONT

Orsha   4

Mogilev

2 Pz.   BRYANSK FRONT

Ninth Army
13 divs. for
offensive
2 divs. in reserve
6 divs. in the line

Orel

Maloarkhangelsk
CENTRAL FRONT

Sixth Air Fleet
700 aircraft

A.Gr.
CENTRE

Dnieper

Desna

Seym   Kursk
2   54 rifle divisions
12 tank corps
16 mech. brigades

Oboyan

VORONEZH FRONT

Kiev

Forth Panzer Army
Army Det. Kempf
15 divs. for offensive
4 divs. in the line
2 divs. of Army Group
reserves

Belgorod

STEPPE FRONT
after 10 July

Fourth Air Fleet
1100 aircraft

Kharkov

SOUTH-WEST FRONT

A.Gr
SOUTH   1 Pz.

Dnepropetrovsk   6   Voroshilovgrad

Donets

Zaporozhye

SOUTHERN
FRONT

Germans:
A.Gr.   Army Group
18   Eighteenth Army
3 Pz.   Third Panzer Army
A.Det.   Army Detachment
XXIII A.Co.   XXIII Army Corps
XLVI Pz.Co.   XLVI Panzer Corps
31   31st Infantry Div.
11 Pz.   11th Panzer Div.

Don

Rostov

Sea of Azov

NORTH CAUCASUS
FRONT

Kuban

Black

CRIMEA   Kerch   17

Sevastopol   Novorossiysk   Krasnodar

Sea

task to strike in a south-easterly direction from the area south of Orel towards Kursk, the main effort being borne by three Panzer corps. On the high ground east of Kursk they were to link up with units of Army Group South.

For this link-up Field-Marshal von Manstein had chosen the Fourth Panzer Army under Colonel-General Hoth. With two Panzer corps making the main effort, it was to strike from the area north of Kharkov towards Kursk: its armada of 700 tanks was to burst through the defensive lines of the Soviet Voronezh Front, mainly the positions of the Sixth Guards Army, and after linking up with Ninth Army they were to smash the encircled Soviet forces.

The eastern flank of Fourth Panzer Army was to be covered by the Army Detachment Kempf. Its task was to push in the left wing of the Soviet Voronezh Front by means of offensive operations.

The main-effort divisions of Colonel-General Hoth were to take possession of the commanding high ground in front of their lines as early as 3rd and 4th July in order to gain suitable observation posts for fire control.

Everything had been worked out in great detail. And it was a very considerable force that was being employed there for such a limited operation. Over a width of attack of 30 miles Ninth Army had at its disposal 13 divisions; Army Group South had 15 divisions for 50 miles, with a 16th division due to join it on 9th July.

In no previous battle in the East had there been such a concentration of forces or indeed such painstaking preparation. Manstein's southern group had over 1000 tanks and nearly 400 assault guns. Kluge's northern group was nearly as strong, so that a combined force of 3000 tanks and assault guns was available for the offensive.

One thousand eight hundred aircraft were lined up on the airfields around Kharkov and Orel in order to sweep the skies over Operation Citadel and provide air cover for the tanks.

To get an idea of the scale of these preparations it should be remembered that Hitler started his campaign against Russia on 22nd June 1941 with 3580 armoured fighting vehicles and 1830 aircraft.

Hitler staked everything on the one card. Why?

"This attack is of decisive importance. It must succeed, and it must do so rapidly and convincingly. It must secure for us the initiative for this spring and summer. The victory of Kursk must be a blazing torch to the world."

This is what Hitler said in his operation order of 15th April. And this is what he emphasized at the Wolfsschanze on 1st July. The other point which he kept stressing in his address was this: "It is vital to ensure the element of surprise. To the very last moment the enemy must remain uncertain about the timing of the offensive."

Then he added this warning: "This time we must make absolutely sure that nothing of our intentions is betrayed again either through carelessness or neglect."

If Hitler only knew. This particular hope was not to be fulfilled. The spy was already lurking behind the door.

But let us not anticipate.

Field-Marshal von Manstein, on whose front the main blow was to be mounted, flew off to Bucharest after the conference in the tearoom and presented Antonescu with the Gold Crimea Shield.

And while journalists, diplomats, and agents in the gossipy Rumanian capital were still radioing the news of Manstein's visit to the world's capitals, the Marshal himself had long returned to the Eastern Front.

He had set up his battle headquarters in a train. This train was now standing in a little wood, close behind the German offensive lines.

Barely twenty-five miles farther north, in an oak wood, in a small ravine between Oboyan and Prokhorovka, near the village of Zorinskoye Dvory, sat another general. Here the commander of the Soviet First Tank Army, Lieutenant-General Mikhail Yefremovich Katukov, had his command post in a group of huts. A small herd of half a dozen cows was grazing on the slopes of the ravine in the summer sun. An old woman was tending them. The cows were part of the camouflage —the peaceful scene was intended for the cameras of the German reconnaissance planes which now and again drew their circles in the steel-blue sky above the hills between Oboyan and Prokhorovka.

True, General Shalin, his chief of staff, would curse when at three in the morning he was woken by the shouting of the nearly deaf old woman as she was trying to find a stray cow: "Dochka milaya—my little darling, where have you got to?" But nothing could be done about it. Camouflage was a vital necessity in war.

On 2nd July, scarcely twenty-four hours after Adolf Hitler had let his generals at the Wolfsschanze into the greatest secret of the year, the telephone rattled in Katukov's hut. Nikolay Kirillovich Popel, member of the Military Council of the First Rank Army, was in the room and lifted the receiver.

"Lieutenant-General Popel speaking."

He listened for a long while, then he nodded his head.

"Da, da—yes, yes. Certainly, Nikita Sergeyevich, that's understood."

Popel replaced the receiver and strode quickly across the little verandah to the block-house of the chief of staff, where General Katukov was just then.

While still in the doorway he said: "Mikhail Yefremovich, Nikita Sergeyevich Khrushchev has just been through on the telephone. He'll be here in an hour with General Vatutin, with some special information for us."

Katukov, a tank commander hardened in the difficult battles near Demyansk in 1942, was on his feet at once. The maps of the different front sectors—quick, quick!

Katukov knew that Army General Vatutin, commanding the Voronezh Front, and his member of the Military Council, Khrushchev, were both eager types. If they were coming personally to his command post something was up. Only a fortnight previously Khrushchev had addressed the assembled senior commanders of the Voronezh Front in that same oak-wood ravine on the subject of training the newly enlisted young men born in 1925. That address had caused quite a stir.

"You've really got to look after these young people more efficiently," he had growled at the commanders. "None of that stupid, stale, vague propaganda. The calibres of the new guns, how to handle sticky bombs, the character of the fascist enemy—these are the things they must know. Don't waste time making them learn slogans. But make sure every single one of them knows the vulnerable spots on the new German Tiger tanks—make sure he knows them by heart just as we once knew the Lord's Prayer." That phrase about the Lord's Prayer became the most frequently quoted tag among the instructors.

Just before 1600 hours Khrushchev and Vatutin arrived in the ravine. They went straight to the hut of the chief of staff, where the maps had been pinned to the wall.

And just as at the Wolfsschanze in East Prussia, so here too the secret of the visit was lifted with the very first sentence. "The fascists are attacking between 3rd and 5th July," said Khrushchev. And with a wink he added: "This isn't a guess but a fact. We know it."

Army-General Vatutin nodded. "We had instructions from Supreme Headquarters this morning," he said with particular emphasis, stepping up to the big map. His massive hand smacked down on the Orel region: "Model's Ninth Army will attack our Central Front from the north. The Voronezh Front will be the object of the main thrust of two German armies. Their main effort will be at the centre and on the left wing. Our Sixth Guards Army will have to sustain the first main thrust." Lieutenant-General Popel, the Political Commissar, on whose memoirs this account is based, does not record the feelings betrayed by Vatutin. But there can be little doubt that that sober voice in which he passed on to his army commanders one of the most dramatic and sensational pieces of information of the whole war must have carried a ring of satisfied conviction. For the listeners—Katukov, Popel, and General Shalin, the Army Chief of Staff—did not have the least doubt that his information was reliable.

Naturally, the armies of the Soviet Central and Voronezh Fronts had been preparing themselves for several weeks for the general pattern of the German plan of attack, they had practised their counter-measures, they had strengthened their defences, they had moved their main defensive line to more favourable terrain—but there was a world of difference between merely suspecting one's opponent's intentions and knowing them positively.

Khrushchev concluded the conference with a few curt words: "And now to work! Prepare to welcome the fascists!"

Hitler's great secret, Operation Citadel, was a secret no longer. The battle from which Germany's Führer expected a decisive turn in the fortunes of war had been betrayed. Official Soviet documents, the official history of the war, and the near official memoirs of the Soviet military leaders all confirm it with astonishing frankness.

The traitor was a man in Hitler's most intimate entourage. In Soviet espionage messages he was referred to by the cover name of Werther.

A few hours later the dawn of 3rd July broke over the German front line. Sergeant Fuhrmann and his runner Gabriel were lying behind a bush in a small patch of meadowland near the village of Loknya, watching the high ground beyond the Belgorod–Sumy railway line.

During the night the Panzer Grenadier Division "Grossdeutschland" had moved into its battle stations along the Vorskla, north-west of Tomarovka, where the German 332nd Infantry Division was holding well-established and well-camouflaged positions.

"The Russians are on that high ground up there. They can see every damn thing we're doing, whereas we have no idea of what goes on behind those hills. We don't know what Ivan's up to, or where his batteries are," said Fuhrmann.

"And what's in front of us? Over there, in those sunflower fields, or those meadows, or on those little wooded humps?" asked Gabriel.

"Nothing—according to the 332nd," replied Fuhrmann. "Nothing except cleverly-devised deep minefields. Behind them are Soviet pickets, but they are usually only manned at night."

Fuhrmann, who liked to hear himself called the "chief of staff of 3rd Company", continued his explanation: "Since the beginning of June the Soviets have pulled their main positions five or six miles back from our main line, behind that ridge of high ground, so that we can't overlook their defensive positions or even get at them with our artillery. Anyone wanting to attack them must first of all get through this damned no-man's-land, and of course the Soviet guns are neatly ranged on its principal points and can put down an effective barrage. On the high ground in front are the Soviet OPs, able to direct their artillery against any move we make."

"So we're in the shit, Herr Feldwebel," Gabriel concluded tersely.

"Exactly," Fuhrmann replied.

Sergeant Fuhrmann and Corporal Gabriel had assessed the situation correctly. This was precisely the problem which Colonel-General Hoth had discussed time and again with his chief of staff and with his 1a, his chief of operations, during the many weeks of preparations for the offensive: Unless the offensive was to collapse even in its very jumping-off positions, the enemy's artillery must be systematically silenced by the German artillery and, if not totally smashed, must be at least kept down during the attack.

It was equally vital that at the very beginning of the offensive the enemy's main defensive lines in the focus of the attack should be smashed by intense bombardment.

But how was that to be done if one was 'blind' and unable to over-look the enemy's positions?

From the jumping-off position of Fourth Panzer Army neither the Soviet artillery positions nor their system of defences could be seen. Aerial reconnaissance photographs were of doubtful value because dummy positions and real positions could not be distinguished in them. There was only one solution—that accursed barrier of high ground beyond no-man's-land had to be eliminated. The hills made the Soviets invisible, but the German attack could succeed only if the Soviet lines were seen at once. Consequently, observation posts and artillery positions had to be established on the first line of high ground shortly before the main attack of Citadel.

Sultry and thundery, the night of 3rd July settled on the area be-tween Donets and Desna. At 2150 hours Soviet flares shot up over no-man's-land. A machine-gun stuttered. Strong German patrols were in the dead zone. The 2nd Engineer Company of the "Grossdeutschland" Division had sent out a mine-clearing party of ten men. The engineers were to clear lanes through the minefield and tape them. A dangerous business. Detectors were useless because the ground was so full of steel from the earlier battles that the instruments responded continually. The buried death-traps therefore had to be located by probing with wire rods, then dug out by hand, the detonator removed, and the mine placed aside. And so on to the next.

Rain and darkness. Any false step could mean death or mutilation. Every movement was a brush with eternity.

These engineers were troops outside the limelight—the silent heroes for whom war meant principally sweat, and all too often also blood.

This clearing party of ten men lifted 2700 mines in front of the hills of Butovo during that night of 3rd/4th July. Two thousand seven hundred mines in five hours of total darkness. Or one mine per man per minute. And not one went off.

Dead-beat, the men returned to their position, asleep almost before their heads touched the ground.

Lieutenant Balletshofer meanwhile marked the cleared lanes on the map. A dispatch rider rushed it to Battalion.

Beyond the hills between Belgorod and Rakitnoye were the Rus-sians, waiting for the dawn of 4th July. They had been waiting for the

German attack since the previous day. Everything was at stand-by. Strongpoints and trenches were fully manned. Behind their Maksim machine-guns the Guards gunners were crouching, ammunition belts fed into their weapons. Hand-grenades lay ready within reach. The mortars were aimed, the gun batteries ready to fire, anti-tank gunners were at the ready. The multiple mortars, known to the Russian troops as "Katyusha" and to the Germans as "Stalin's organ-pipes", were loaded and ready to be touched off at an instant's notice. The barrels of heavy AA guns peeped through their camouflage. On the airfields the fighter machines were ready to take off.

The staffs of the Soviet Army Front, down to battalion level, were all at their command posts. Wireless operators were listening intently.

Lieutenant-General Popel describes these hours through the eyes of the Soviet First Tank Army: "The night streets were loud with the noise of engines. Convoys of tanks and guns, covered with dust, were rumbling into the sector where we expected the German onslaught. While German officers were reading out the Führer's Order of the Day, our defences made the final preparations for the reception of the enemy. We thickened our foremost line, moved further guns into position, once more co-ordinated and completed our firing tables and concerted our plans. We moved two artillery regiments of our Army into the strip held by Sixth Guards Army. One armoured brigade strengthened the order of battle of our infantry."

It was a fantastic situation, unique in military history: a kind of frozen alert, down to the last detail.

Nothing had happened on 3rd July. And as the hands of the watches moved towards noon on 4th July, the Soviet staffs heaved a sigh of relief: Nothing more would happen that day. If the Germans attacked it would be at first light in the morning. Tomorrow, perhaps. Perhaps! The Russians had been waiting for forty-eight hours, their rifles loaded. Forty-eight hours was a long time.

Regimental commanders telephoned to divisional staffs: "Are we to continue on full alert? Or can we relax it a little? The troops are beginning to show signs of fatigue."

"No relaxation," came the reply. "Full alert. Full vigilance!"

Between 1225 and 1325 the field kitchens moved up to the Russian front lines to dole out the midday meal. A thundery shower beat down on the scorched land and made fields and woods steam. The soldiers hid under their ground-sheets.

By 1445 the rain had stopped. There was silence between Belgorod, Tomarovka, and Fastov. The Russians were waiting. And on the other side of no-man's-land the Germans were waiting as well. The battalions of XLVIII Panzer Corps and of the SS Panzer Corps were in the foremost trenches. The hum of aircraft could be heard. It grew louder.

The men lifted their heads. Captain Leyk, commanding the 3rd Battalion, Panzer Fusilier Regiment "Grossdeutschland", glanced up at the machines and then down at his watch. "On the dot," he said.

The hand moved to 1450. At the same moment the Stuka squadrons came roaring over the trenches towards the enemy. High above them, covering them, were the fighters. The Stukas banked, then dived with a wail.

On the other side, on the slopes of Gertsovka and Butovo, fountains of smoke rose. This was where the Soviet artillery observers were established. Immediately behind them ran the Russian outpost line.

The next Stuka squadron screamed over the German positions. And a third. A fourth, a fifth.

Over 2500 bombs crashed down on the Soviet side on a strip of ground two miles long and 500 yards deep.

At 1500 hours the last bombs burst. Then the artillery opened up. A roaring, howling inferno.

The foremost line of Leyk's battalion was on the railway embankment. The commander of 15th Company, Lieutenant Dr Metzner, was crouching by his heavy weapons. He glanced at his wrist-watch, then across to the dug-out where the battalion commander was standing, his eyes on his watch.

Ten seconds to go. Five. Now! And into the roar of the gunfire Leyk yelled: "Forward!"

And, like him, battalion commanders on the right and the left, all the way between Fastov and Belgorod, were yelling: "Forward!"

Dr Metzner saw Captain Leyk leap out of the dug-out first and race across the open ground. Everybody knew that the flat piece of ground, totally lacking in cover, was overlooked by the Russians. That was precisely why Leyk had come forward, from his command post, to lead his battalion in its difficult task.

Dr Metzner records that he will never forget that moment.

In exemplary wedge formation, like a flight of migrating birds, the companies and platoons followed the battalion commander, all the way down to sections and individual riflemen. The battalion commander's example seemed to act like a magnet also on Metzner. He jumped out of his heavy-weapons battle HQ, though strictly speaking he should have remained there, and rushed after Captain Leyk, a few yards behind and out to the left.

Under cover of their artillery umbrella, the platoons raced along the lanes cleared through the minefields, the men bent double. Assault guns followed on their heels. Behind them came the Panzerjägers. In between ran the assault engineers, ready to clear any surprise obstacles.

In spite of their stand-by, the covering units of the Soviet Sixth Guards Army were taken by surprise by the impetus of the German

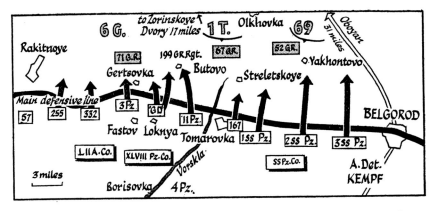

Map 2. Fourth Panzer Army launched its attack earlier than the rest—in the afternoon of 4th July, 1943—in order to gain the range of hills in front of the German lines.

assault, and above all by the intensity of the aerial bombardment.

The German battalions were chasing across no-man's-land. Behind them came armoured OP vehicles and signals vehicles of the artillery, anxious to gain new observation posts on the high ground as quickly as possible.

Presently, however, the garrisons of the still intact Russian strongpoints recovered from their surprise and opened up with everything they had. The Soviet artillery observers, momentarily blinded, began to telephone their reports back to their batteries.

The Soviet artillery now intervened in the action, putting down a murderous barrage. Salvo after salvo crashed into the zone of attack. As the German vehicles began to zig-zag the Soviet mines exploded under them. There was the crash of anti-tank rifles and the whine of mortars. Red fighters screamed down, pouncing like hawks, raking the slopes already reached by German assault parties with their machine-guns and cannon.

In front of Butovo the 3rd Battalion of the Panzer Grenadier Regiment "Grossdeutschland" was lucky. The moment of surprise among the covering lines of the Soviet 199th Guards Rifle Regiment was just too long. The Russian battalion commander evidently failed to realize what the Germans were after and prepared for defence in his main position at which, just then, the attack was not yet directed.

Before the Soviet regimental commander in Butovo realized what was happening the Germans were already established on the ridge west of the village. The Soviet outpost lines were dislodged and their OPs taken by storm. At the same moment the high ground east of the village was seized by men of the 11th Panzer Division.

The time was 1600 hours. By 1645 the German artillery observers

were already on the hill. Their view to the north was now open. For
the first time they could see far into the Soviet defensive system.

On the right wing of the Army too the battalions of the SS Panzer
Corps succeeded in snatching the high ground of Yakhontovo and
Streletskoye from the Russian 52nd Guards Rifle Division. Near
Gertsovka, on the other hand, on the left wing, things were not going
so well. At that point, where the 3rd Battalion of the Panzer Fusilier
Regiment "Grossdeutschland" and the 1st Battalion of the 394th
Panzer Grenadier Regiment of 3rd Panzer Division were in action, the
outpost lines of the Russian 71st Guards Rifle Division were quicker
in appreciating the situation than their neighbouring division. Their
opposition was instantaneous and effective.

Captain Leyk's companies had gained some five hundred yards.
Seven hundred yards. Then mortar salvoes burst among the lines of the
battalion. Leyk was killed. Dr Metzner fell, seriously wounded. One-
third of 15th Company had been killed or wounded. The other companies too were pinned down. Progress now was only yard by yard.
Fewer and fewer men were rising for every successive forward leap.
Many company and platoon commanders dropped out. The new commander of 3rd Battalion, Captain Bolk, was severely wounded; a mine
tore off one of his legs.

By evening the fusiliers of "Grossdeutschland" and the grenadiers of
3rd Panzer Division had at last gained the slopes of the high ground,
but not until nightfall did they succeed in capturing the ridge south-
east of Gertsovka and finally the village itself.

The troops of divisional artillery were pulled forward one by one
and moved into position. Signallers worked feverishly to establish
telephone communications between troops, batteries, and observation
posts, to ensure fire control for the artillery.

The time was 0100 hours on 5th July—D Day. In two hours the
bombardment inaugurating Operation Citadel was due to start.

"Still no contact with Army artillery?" Lieutenant-Colonel Albrecht
asked his regimental signals officer, Captain Maiwald.

"Not yet, Herr Oberstleutnant."

Half an hour later: "Contact yet, Maiwald?"

"Not yet."

Only fifteen minutes to go before the scheduled time for the bombardment. Only ten minutes. Unless the bombardment functioned on
the sector of "Grossdeutschland", at the focal point of the offensive,
where the entire subordinated army artillery was to go into effective
action, the whole success of Citadel would be jeopardized.

At last the load fell from their minds as Maiwald reported: "Contact

established." Now the film strip, rehearsed a thousand times, started unrolling:

Orders. Reports.

Ready to open fire. Ready to open fire. Ready to open fire.

Albrecht stood by the telephone, linked now to all gun positions: "Bombardment to open in one minute. I am counting."

Lieutenant-Colonel Albrecht counted. And 230,000 men of the Southern Group were waiting for the crash of fire and thunder that would signal the opening of Operation Citadel.

One hundred and twenty-five miles farther north, the northern group, Model's Ninth Army, was similarly waiting for the beginning of the offensive. On 4th July not a shot had been fired there along the front south of Orel, between Maloarkhangelsk and Trosna.

It had been a scorching hot day. And as quiet as a Sunday in the country. Yet Colonel-General Model had assembled three Panzer corps and one Army corps in a small space. More than 200,000 men in 15 divisions. Only over the last two nights had the offensive formations been moved into the prepared jumping-off positions.

Army General Rokossovskiy, commanding the Soviet Central Front opposite Model's Ninth Army, had likewise put his troops on full alert since 3rd July. His Supreme Headquarters had informed him—just as it had the Voronezh Front—of the date of the German offensive as early as 2nd July and told him that the German main thrust was to be expected on the right wing of his front, against his Thirteenth and Seventieth Armies.

Rokossovskiy gave orders for the minefields in front of his main defensive line to be closely watched. He was rewarded by the capture of an interesting source of information.

Towards 2200 hours a German mine-clearing party was spotted south of Tagino. The Russians took one of the engineers prisoner—a Corporal Bruno Fermello, according to the Russian records. According to these Soviet sources he belonged to the engineer battalion of the Rhine-Westphalian 6th Infantry Division. But this need not necessarily have been the engineer battalion of 6th Division, since this division had had the engineer battalion of the Bavarian 47th Division, a GHQ unit, additionally assigned to it for the battle of Kursk.

Fermello gave the Soviets very accurate information about the German preparations for the attack and assured them that after a short artillery barrage at 0330 hours the German offensive formations would attack through the cleared lanes in the minefield.

Fighting near Belgorod: vehicles under fire at the anti-tank ditch.
Soviet counter-attack: fire control from the branches of a tree.
German Grenadiers charging.

This information is said to have been so reliable that it was immediately passed on to Rokossovskiy. The C-in-C Central Front reacted promptly by thinking up a nasty surprise for the Germans.

It was a clear, starry night. But over the concealed positions and the camouflaged guns, those cowering messengers of death, lay an oppressive heat.

The German gunners were already by their guns. The armoured units had moved into their jumping-off positions. Grenadiers and tank crews were smoking their last cigarettes before the attack.

At that moment Rokossovskiy pulled off his surprise. It was he who opened the battle.

At 0110 hours, all of a sudden, an infernal roar came from the Soviet side. Artillery of all calibres, heavy mortars, multiple mortars, and other heavy weapons were hurling their shells and rockets at the German assembly positions, their rearward lines, and their approach roads.

A sudden suspicion seized the minds of the staffs of Ninth Army: The Soviets were anticipating them with a major offensive and were about to thrust into the German assembly positions. The Russian bombardment lasted over an hour and caused heavy losses. But the Russians did not come. The German commanders heaved a sigh of relief.

And strictly according to plan, at 0330, the German guns shattered the grey dawn of 5th July. There had never been anything like it on the Eastern Front.

Sergeant Hermann Pingel of the Medical Corps was charging forward together with 9th Company. All medical orderlies and doctors were right in front with the assault parties. It was obvious that the wounded would have to be looked after on the spot; because of the defensive fire to be expected there could be no question of moving them back to base.

9th Company leapt out from their trench as one man. Ahead of them was 200 yards of ground as flat as a table; after that the "Squirrel Ravine" offered cover. That meant running. True, there were mines in the ravine—but what were mines compared with the furious defensive fire of the Russian artillery, the multiple guns, and the much-feared, low-trajectory gun called by the German troops the "crash-boom".

Panting, Pingel flung himself into the scrub at the edge of "Squirrel Ravine". Engineers crawled past him. They were clearing a lane through the minefield. Forward!

At the far end of the ravine were the first Russian trenches: dug into the slope, they had not been hit too heavily by the German bombardment. They were now raking the ravine with machine-gun fire.

"Stretcher, stretcher!" a moan came through the scrub. Pingel rushed over. Corporal Osserowski of the Medical Corps was there already, bandaging an NCO and two riflemen.

Behind a thorn hedge the first dressing station was organized. "You stay here, Ossi," said Pingel. He himself stayed close to the advancing company. The sound of heavy fighting came from ahead.

Corporal Karl Rudenberg of 258th Infantry Division, holder of the Knight's Cross, was the first to reach the Russian position with his machine-gun. Rudenberg, from Stolp in Pomerania, suffered from a stammer and never got a word of command out right—but for steady nerves and courage he had no equal in the 3rd Battalion, 478th Grenadier Regiment.

As Pingel reached the trench all was still confusion. Rudenberg had let himself roll over the edge with his machine-gun. No. 1 Platoon followed him. In hand-to-hand combat the dug-outs of the first Russian position in "Squirrel Ravine" were captured.

Corporal Harms, also a medical orderly, lay on the ground next to three seriously wounded men, wounded himself. But he was bandaging them nevertheless. "Over to the right," he said to Pingel; "Karl's there, he's been hit."

Pingel hurried. There were dead and wounded everywhere. The trenches were deep. At the third cross-trench he recoiled. Cowering against the wall of the trench was Karl Rudenberg. His machine-gun lay by his side. At his feet was a Russian, his arms, chest, and head torn to shreds. Karl's entire right side was torn open.

Pingel laid him down carefully on the trench floor. Suddenly Karl nodded his head towards the Russian, and for the first time in his life Pingel heard him talking freely and fluently, without a trace of his stammer: "He jumped straight at me with a live hand-grenade and held on to it." There was admiration for the Russian's bravery in Karl's voice.

"Looks bad, doesn't it," he then said. Pingel cut open Karl's uniform. The Knight's Cross rolled on to the ground. Pingel pushed swab after swab into the gaping body.

"I'll get a stretcher," Pingel said.

But Karl shook his head and clutched Pingel's shoulder. "Don't go, Hermann," he said, "don't go. It won't take long."

It did not take long, but the ten minutes seemed to Sergeant Hermann Pingel of the Medical Corps to be as long as eternity.

"3rd Battalion is unable to get beyond the second enemy trench on the right-hand slope, Herr Oberst. 1st Battalion is stuck in a minefield in the ravine. It has another 500 yards to go to the enemy positions on the left flank of the ravine in 'Squirrel Wood'. Some companies have lost nearly all their officers and about half their men. The Panzerjäger company has suffered exceedingly heavy losses. The Russian defensive fire is indescribable." The regimental ADC, making this report, had flung himself down next to the commander in the small dug-out. He was panting. His uniform was torn. He had just come back from the front line and had been chased all the way by mortars and the "crash-boom".

Colonel Assman, commanding 478th Grenadier Regiment, nervously tapped his board with his fingertips. The regimental staff were lying in a thick patch of scrub at the entrance to "Squirrel Ravine", screened against aerial spotting.

The new *Hummel* (Bumblebee) and *Hornisse* (Hornet) guns, mounted on armoured chassis and used here for the first time on a major scale, were lined up at the entrance to the ravine and were hurling their heavy shells at the Soviet strongpoints. Three hours later, towards evening, 1st Battalion had managed the remaining 500 yards and was lying right in front of the outpost lines of the Soviet 280th Rifle Division. Assault parties succeeded in breaking into the Soviet trenches. But any attempt to penetrate farther into the deep defensive system failed in the teeth of furious Russian opposition.

The situation of 479th Grenadier Regiment was much the same. The whole of 258th Infantry Division, which, as the right-hand striking force of XLVI Panzer Corps, was to have burst through the Soviet barrier along the Trosna-Kursk road with its first blow, had ground to a complete standstill after a costly assault on the outlying Soviet positions.

Meanwhile, on the left wing of General Zorn's XLVI Panzer Corps, the Bavarian 7th and the Brunswick 31st Infantry Divisions, in co-operation with the Hessian 20th Panzer Division, had launched their assault across fields of rye and thick clover against the positions of two Soviet rifle divisions.

The Bavarians made progress step by step, but soon they too were pinned down by heavy defensive fire. In the rye, where the troops hoped to find cover, fountains of fire spurted up with loud crashes— mines. The fields proved to be gardens of death.

General Hossbach's 31st Infantry Division, whose tactical sign was the Lion of Brunswick, had more luck. The engineer battalion from Höxter, working in completely flat ground without any cover, only a few hundred yards in front of the first Soviet lines, cleared wide lanes through the minefield for the heavy Tiger tanks which were lined up for the attack.

With their 8·8-cm guns the Tigers fired shell after shell into the Russian positions to keep the enemy down. Even so it was a hellish task for the engineers.

The Soviets fired at them from their deep trenches with heavy mortars, safe from the low-trajectory tank guns. It was an unequal duel. And it was the engineers who footed the bill. The commander of 2nd Company and two platoon commanders were killed in the first few minutes. But the engineers nevertheless cleared a road for the Tigers.

The job needed a steady hand and calm nerves. Each anti-tank mine, when the earth had been cleared away around it, had to be lifted carefully just a little way because many of them were additionally secured against lifting by being anchored to a peg by a short length of wire. Yard by yard the parties crept forward—probing, clearing the mines with their hands, lifting them carefully, removing the detonators, and putting the death-traps aside. Down among the engineers crashed the Soviet mortar shells. Over their heads screamed the deafening 8·8 shells of their own Tigers.

At last, after two hours, they were through the minefield. The giant tanks with their 700 horse-power engines and their virtually impregnable 102-mm frontal armour rumbled past them. NCO Willers waved to his party of engineers: "Engineers to close up behind us as far as the first Russian trench."

Willers's engineers threaded themselves into the platoons of grenadiers who, crouched low, were running through the enemy fire behind and alongside the Tigers. They were the assault parties of 3rd Battalion, 17th Grenadier Regiment—the Goslar Jägers.

A few sections of riflemen ran into the tall corn beside the cleared lane. Willers shouted at them to come back. Those fields too were full of mines—small box mines, explosive charges mounted on sticks, and anti-personnel mines.

The Russians had laid these mines the previous spring. Meanwhile they had become invisibly intermingled with the rye. And the fine trip-wire, stretched criss-cross to touch off the mines, was likewise impossible to see.

Even in the clover fields, through which other sections of infantrymen were charging, the treacherous wooden mines were exploding. The thick clover had pushed the small boxes up from the ground. Heaven help the trooper who knocked against one of those deadly "cigar boxes" and touched off the detonator under its lid.

Under cover of fire from the Tigers the grenadiers worked their way forward to the first trench. It was empty. At the beginning of the German bombardment the Soviets had withdrawn its garrison except for observers and anti-tank riflemen.

The trench was deep and narrow, with small ladders against its sides. There were three or four steps up to each machine-gun nest.

"We'll stop here for a moment," said Corporal Ewald Bismann. The Tigers pushed across over the trenches. The Goslar Jägers scurried behind the steel colossi. The armoured wedge continued its advance towards the village of Gnilets.

The time was 0900 hours. The battlefield between the villages of Gnilets and Bobrik shook with the roar of battle. The sun lay heavily over the clouds of smoke. The intelligence officer of the 20th Panzer Division brought a prisoner with him to the commander at his advanced battle headquarters.

"What unit?" Major-General von Kessel asked.

"2nd Battalion, 47th Rifle Regiment of 15th Rifle Division, Herr General," the interpreter replied. "According to this prisoner the Soviet companies suffered heavy losses from our artillery bombardment."

The General reflected for a moment. Then he said to his chief of operations: "Maybe that's their weak point."

To his artillery commander he said: "Let's give the Bobrik area another pounding by all guns."

Then he turned back to his chief of operations: "Get Deichmann's 1st Air Division to make a Stuka attack on the same sector."

And to the commander of the reinforced Panzer reconnaissance battalion of 20th Division he said: "Move your battalion to the right of 1st Battalion for a joint thrust through the enemy positions."

The plan went off. The guns of 103rd Panzer Artillery Regiment roared. A Stuka *Geschwader* pounded the enemy positions. Then the tanks, the Panzerjägers, and the grenadiers of 20th Panzer Division stormed against the Russian lines. The 2nd Battalion of the Soviet 47th Rifle Regiment was dislodged.

The attack moved on. It came up against the second line of defence. This was held by the Soviet 321st Rifle Regiment. The German attack caught some of its battalions off balance. Some of the companies gave way. The regimental front was rolled up. The German tanks and the 1st Battalion, 112th Panzer Grenadier Regiment broke through into the village of Bobrik.

For the first time in this bitter battle the ancient German battlecry of "Hurra, hurra!" was again heard over the noise of battle. The defensive positions of the Soviet 15th Rifle Division had been seized.

The favourable course of events at 20th Panzer Division in turn helped the neighbouring Rhine-Westphalian 6th Infantry Division to make headway; this division had launched its attack at 0620 hours after artillery bombardment and employment of Stukas and bombers.

Outside a storage shed at the Verkhneye Tagino fruit farm Lieutenant-General Horst Grossmann was standing with his chief of operations and from this hill watched developments in the valley of the Oka river. "Tigers forward!" he commanded.

Overhead, the formations of Sixth Air Fleet roared towards the enemy, attacking his positions to both sides of Yasnaya Polyana. The air was filled with the hiss of the *Nebelwerfer* mortar shells and the whine of artillery shells. Assault parties of the grenadier regiments

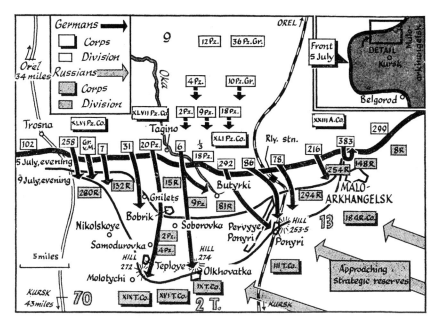

Map 3. In the north of the Kursk salient Model's Ninth Army encountered well-prepared defences. The German XXIII Army Corps, due to cover the left flank of the attack, was pinned down short of Maloarkhangelsk. The Panzer corps secured a foothold on the high ground near Olkhovatka.

leaped forward, assault guns rumbled, anti-tank and infantry guns clattered down into the Oka valley.

"The 58th are crossing the river!" the ADC shouted without taking his glasses from his eyes. "The 18th are already outside Yasnaya Polyana."

At Yasnaya Polyana Lieutenant-Colonel Höke was coolly leading his battalions against the Soviet positions.

"Anti-tank fire from the right; the grenadiers of 58th Infantry Regiment are pinned down," the ADC reported up by the plantation shed. "Russian aircraft attacking."

The time was 0800. Now Grossmann sent his Tigers in.

Major Sauvant's Panzer Battalion 505 thundered through the Oka in their steel fortresses. They reached Yasnaya Polyana and struck at the open flank of the Soviet 676th Rifle Regiment. This attack triggered off a chain reaction among the Russians; the wing regiment of the adjoining Soviet 81st Rifle Division began to waver.

There was now no holding the Tigers. By 1220 they were rumbling into the village of Butyrki, well ahead of the grenadiers.

The Soviet front reports on the situation at noon on the first day of battle in the northern sector reflect a note of grave crisis. The collapse of the Soviet 15th Rifle Division was threatening the entire right wing of the Soviet Seventieth Army. Was the battle about to be decided?

For General Harpe's XLI Panzer Corps the attack likewise progressed successfully. The units involved were the Rhine-Westphalian 86th Infantry Division, the well-tried Mecklenburg-Pomeranian 292nd Infantry Division, and the Saxon 101st Panzer Grenadier Regiment of 18th Panzer Division.

The Soviet 81st Rifle Division, which held the foremost line, offered stubborn resistance. Here too the Russians had evacuated the frontmost trench on the morning of the attack, so that the German barrage had been a blow into thin air.

But Harpe's divisions brought with them a new trump card on which great hopes were being pinned—ninety super-heavy Tiger Ferdinand tanks, belonging to the heavy Panzerjäger Battalions 653 and 654, had been placed under the command of Lieutenant-Colonel von Jungenfeldt to serve as rams for the grenadier divisions.

The Ferdinand was a huge monster of a tank with a combat weight of 72 tons, armed with the well-tried 8·8-cm cannon, with a 21-foot barrel. The armour plating was up to 200 mm thick. Two Maybach engines produced the current for two electric motors, each of them independently driving one of the two caterpillar tracks. In spite of its weight, the vehicle had a top speed of 20 miles per hour. A miracle of engineering. These mobile steel fortresses were built at the Nibelungen Works at St Valentin in Austria.

Its peaceful name of Ferdinand the giant owed to its constructor, Ferdinand Porsche. Hitler expected this raiding tank, which was at the same time a mobile gun emplacement, to bring about a decisive turn in the war. It would make any attack irresistible. For who would withstand that monster? What weapons could defy it? Wherever its shells exploded no grass would grow for a long time. Any T-34 which happened to come into the Ferdinand's sight was as good as finished.

But Ferdinand had an Achilles heel—its drive was too weak and its tracks were too vulnerable. In consequence, many of these giant tanks soon found themselves immobilized with damaged tracks. Another point was that the Ferdinand was completely helpless in close combat against enemy infantry. Apart from its rigidly mounted giant cannon it carried no weapons, not even a machine-gun to deal with enemy tank-busting parties.

Even the ingenuity of the crews of Major Noak's Battalion 654, who carried an MG-42 on board and, when things got really bad, kept up continuous fire with it through the gun barrel, was of little avail. After all, the 8·8-cm gun was not intended as an embrasure for a machine-gun. Thus the Ferdinands drove through the enemy lines like steel monsters, but the grenadiers accompanying them were presently shot up, or at least forced under cover, by the Soviet infantrymen who had remained crouching in their well-camouflaged foxholes. The five or six infantrymen who rode on a plank roughly wired to the stern of each Ferdinand were no adequate force for clearing the terrain of the enemy. Thus the armoured fortresses rolled on without accompanying infantry, on their lonely journey through enemy territory—ramming wedges with nothing to follow them.

Guderian had realized the likely consequences of the Ferdinand's inadequate weaponry and over-complicated construction. But Hitler had not listened to him. As a result, the battle of Kursk was the first and last occasion when these giant tanks with the cosy-sounding name made an appearance as a solid force.

In the late afternoon of 5th July the general situation of the attacking forces continued to be favourable in the sector of XLI Panzer Corps. The regiments of 86th Infantry Division were already in the third Soviet trench position. Colonel Bieber with his 184th Grenadier Regiment was already in action outside the northern part of Ponyri.

Assault guns and half a dozen Ferdinands of Major Steinwachs's Battalion 653, operating on the frontage of 292nd Infantry Division, moved forward at the very first attempt right up to Aleksandrovka, three miles deep into the enemy's defences. Soviet gun positions were knocked out. Assault parties linked up with combat troops of 6th Infantry Division which had captured Butyrki.

But the Soviet infantry refused to panic in the face of the roaring Tiger and Ferdinand tanks. For weeks on end the Russian troops had been trained in anti-tank tactics by Party instructors and experienced tank officers. Everything had been done to inoculate the troops against the notorious "tank panic". The result was unmistakable.

The Russian infantrymen allowed the tanks to rumble past their well-camouflaged foxholes and then came out to deal with the German grenadiers in their wake. Thus the battle continued to rage on sectors which the forward tank commanders believed already won.

Tanks and assault guns had to be brought back to relieve the grenadiers. Then they had to be sent forward again. And pulled back once more. By evening the grenadiers were exhausted and the tanks and assault guns were out of fuel. But the attack had pushed deep into the Soviet defences.

Battalions and regiments reported: "We're getting there! Not easily, and the battle has been bloody and costly. But we are getting there."

And one other thing all commanders reported unanimously: "Nowhere has the enemy been taken by surprise. Nowhere has he been soft. He had clearly been expecting the attack and numerous statements by prisoners-of-war have confirmed this."

That was a nasty surprise. Nevertheless all along the front of XLI Panzer Corps there was a firm belief: "We'll dislodge Ivan."

On Model's left wing, the XXIII Army Corps under General Friessner, the course of operations during the first twenty-four hours was likewise favourable. On this sector, where such experienced and fearless regiments as those of the 78th Infantry Division were employed, and which had meanwhile earned for itself the title of Assault Division, the main features of the battle emerged with almost textbook clarity.

Here too Ferdinand tanks were employed—companies belonging to Major Noak's Battalion 654. They were supplemented by their companion piece—the midget tanks paradoxically named Goliath, only just over 2 feet high, 2 feet 2 inches wide, and 4 feet long. These unmanned midget tanks were remote-controlled by radio or by a wire uncoiling from their stern to a distance of up to 1000 yards. They carried a high-explosive charge of 200 lb. At a speed of 12 miles an hour these midgets rolled straight into enemy positions, anti-tank nests, and gun emplacements. They were touched off by the pressing of a button. Whenever a Goliath reached its target the effect was striking. Mostly, however, they did not reach their targets.

The experienced Württemberg Regiments of 78th and 216th Divisions, reinforced by Jäger battalions, anti-tank guns on self-propelled carriages, assault engineers with mortars and flame-throwers, as well as a battalion of assault guns, hurled themselves against the heavily fortified area around the road junction of Maloarkhangelsk.

In order to blaze a broad trail for the Ferdinands through the thick Soviet minefield, Model employed a further "miracle weapon"—low, tracked vehicles like British ammunition carriers, heavily armoured and weighing four tons, powered by a Borgward six-cylinder engine, known as the B-IV. They carried a high-explosive charge of 1000 lb. which could be jettisoned and touched off by remote control from an assault gun. Panzer Battalion 300 staged a dress rehearsal of these "mine busters" at Maloarkhangelsk; they were edged into the minefield by a driver and thence driven on by remote control. The explosive charge touched off all mines over a radius of forty to fifty yards. Naturally, the carrier vehicle was blown up as well. The driver jumped out after switching on the remote-control device and tried to make his way back. Outside Maloarkhangelsk a wide lane was in fact cleared through the 400-yards-deep minefield by means of eight B-IVs. Four of the drivers succeeded in saving themselves, the other four were killed. The Ferdinands rumbled forward against the Soviet field positions.

Here, on the high ground on the left wing, two rifle divisions of the Soviet XVIII Guards Rifle Corps were defending the important cornerpost of the Russian positions. But the Germans succeeded in breaking in. Towards 1800 hours the 410th Rifle Regiment of 81st Rifle Division was dislodged.

Soviet tanks of the 129th Armoured Brigade were moving up to counter-attack.

By the evening of 5th July the German grenadiers and tankmen, the Panzerjägers and engineers, all knew that in spite of the concentration of all available means, in spite of the successful storming of stubbornly defended and strongly fortified hills, in spite of all the prisoners-of-war who were now trudging past them—that in spite of all these things there could be no question of a decisive penetration having been achieved through the unimaginably strong and deep Soviet defensive zone.

"How deep has Friessner got into the enemy positions?" Model asked his chief of staff, Colonel von Elverfeldt, shortly before midnight on 5th July.

"Barely three miles, Herr Generaloberst; 78th Division is at the railway station of Maloarkhangelsk."

"What news from aerial reconnaissance about movements of enemy reserves?" Model asked his 1c, the intelligence officer.

"Major formations, including armour, are moving up from the east, from the Livny area, against Maloarkhangelsk, Ponyri, and Olkhovatka."

Model bent over his map. He realized what Friessner's divisional commanders had been suspecting for some time: the plan to cover the flank of Model's two Panzer corps, which were bearing the main brunt of the attack at the centre, by a deep thrust of XXIII Corps was not coming off. It would not be possible to intercept the Russian reserves moving in from the east or to prevent them from intervening in the battle.

Lemelsen, Harpe, and Friessner, the corps commanders in Model's Ninth Army, also sat up late into the night, studying the maps with their staff officers. The objectives of the day, their own losses, reports about enemy fighting strength—all these revealed clearly that the breakthrough was not succeeding at lightning speed. It was a case of nibbling one's way forward. This was not a pleasant discovery even though it was not absolutely shattering. Colonel-General Model had taken this possibility into account. More than once he had reminded Hitler of the depth of the Soviet defensive system which had been revealed by German aerial reconnaisance.

That was why Model had based his attack from the outset on the assumption of extremely tough opposition and why he had made a plan which was also in character—he was not going to let loose his entire armour in a wild chase, but he was going to force a breach systematically.

Consequently, his deeply echeloned Ninth Army started its attack with nine infantry divisions, reinforced by armour and assault guns.

Only one Panzer division, the 20th, was employed by Model in the first wave. He kept the bulk of his armoured formations, six Panzer divisions and Panzer Grenadier divisions, as well as several battalions of assault guns, in reserve. "First punch a hole through, and then feed the attack with ever-fresh forces! When a gap has been opened then the tanks can move through and operate freely against the enemy's flank and rear until he is encircled." That was Model's recipe. At daybreak on 6th July he was faced with a difficult decision. Was he to employ his armoured reserves now or should he wait? He decided to employ them, in particular on the sector of XLVII Panzer Corps, commanded by General Lemelsen, in the Butyrki and Bobrik area. It was at the point where the front of the Soviet 15th Rifle Division had been torn open that he hoped to burst through the enemy's defences completely.

Model therefore pulled three of his five Panzer divisions—the 2nd, the 9th, and the 18th—from their assembly areas into the penetration area, and on 6th July moved them into action. The 4th and 12th Panzer Divisions, as well as the 10th Panzer Grenadier Division, he decided to hold in reserve.

Normally such a vigorous follow-up should have resulted in decisive success. After all, the enemy positions between the road and the Orel-Kursk railway had been torn open over a width of twenty miles and to a depth of four to six miles. If strong motorized formations were pushed into such a gap, experience taught that this almost inevitably led to a breakthrough.

But this was not a normal situation. Nothing about this battle could be measured by the usual yardsticks. By no means had the Soviet defensive system been torn open decisively on the evening of 5th July. It remained intact over a further depth of six to ten miles. Never in the history of wars had there been a defensive system echeloned in such depth.

Over a width of fifteen miles at the corner points of the Kursk salient—at the very spot, therefore, where the German attack was made—the soil had been turned over by the Russians in many months of work with trenching tools, and converted into a labyrinth of infantry dug-outs, minefields, and underground bunkers. Every patch of wood, every hill, every collective farm, had been turned into a strongpoint. And all these strongpoints had been linked by the Russians by a system of deep, well-camouflaged trenches. In between were whole strings of anti-tank gun emplacements, buried tanks, gun emplacements echeloned in depth, multiple mortars, flame-throwers, and countless machine-gun posts.

But not only the defences were gigantic. Equally important, if not more important, was the fact that the Soviet High Command had at its disposal exceptionally strong operational reserves. Army General Rokossovskiy had positioned them brilliantly.

According to Colonel Markin, the Soviet chronicler of the battle of Kursk, the operational reserves of the Central Front "received orders, as early as midday on 5th July, to move off, in accordance with the prepared plan, into the jumping-off areas for the counter-attack".

In accordance with the prepared plan! So accurately were the Russians informed about the objectives and the main thrust of Model's breakthrough operation.

On the morning of 6th July the Viennese 2nd Panzer Division appeared on the battlefield with 140 tanks and 50 assault guns. Major von Boxberg's 2nd Battalion 3rd Panzer Regiment mounted its attack on the high ground north of Kashara towards 0900 with 96 Mark IV tanks.

The Tiger Battalion 505 under Major Sauvant, placed under the division, had already taken Soborovka.

Boxberg moved on through the bridgehead south of Soborovka. In a broad wedge the tanks moved through tall fields of grain. Their turret doors were open. The sun burnt down on them.

The enemy's system of trenches on the high ground was rolled up. But the penetration to Kashara did not come off. The Soviet lines of anti-tank guns were too strong and too cunningly placed. No sooner was one overcome than the tanks were facing another.

Above all, the Russians intervened in the fighting with strong armoured forces. Between Ponyri and Soborovka, on a frontage of nine miles, a tank battle began on a scale unprecedented in the history of warfare. It went on for four days.

During the climax of the battle some 1000 to 1200 tanks and assault guns were employed on each side. Numerous air force units and 3000 guns of all calibres completed this terrible duel. The prize was the high ground of Olkhovatka with its key position—Hill 274.

These hills were Model's immediate objective. Here was the crux of his plan of operations, here was the key to the door of Kursk. What was the particular significance of these hills?

The chain of hills of Olkhovatka formed, from a strategic point of view, the middle section of the Central Russian ridge between Orel and Belgorod. On their eastern flanks was the source of the Oka, as well as the sources of numerous lesser streams. From the hills there was a clear view as far as Kursk, situated about 400 feet below Olkhovatka. Whoever commanded this high ground would command the area between Oka and Seym.

Model wanted to seize this ground around Olkhovatka. He wanted to move his reserves into this area, to engage the Soviet troops, above all Rokossovskiy's armoured corps, in a terrain unfavourable to them, defeat them, and then thrust on to Kursk to link up with Hoth.

But Rokossovskiy had seen through Model's plan and had assembled sufficient reserves to protect this Achilles heel of the Soviet defence system.

Sauvant's Tigers drove into a forest of anti-tank guns, into a labyrinth of tank traps, against a wall of artillery. The grenadiers of 2nd Panzer Division found themselves faced by trench after trench. The first wave collapsed. The second wave washed forward a few hundred yards and also came to a stop. When Major von Boxberg's tanks swept forward as the third wave, their push too ground to a halt in the Russian defensive fire. The Austrian 9th Panzer Division under Lieutenant-General Scheller fared no better. The grenadiers of 20th Panzer Division fought a similar furious battle on 8th July near the village of Samodurovka under a scorching sun. Within an hour all the officers of 5th Company, 112th Panzer Grenadier Regiment, had been killed or wounded. Nevertheless the grenadiers swept on through cornfields, capturing trenches, and encountering new ones. The battalions melted away. Companies became mere platoons.

Lieutenant Hänsch rallied his small handful of men: "Let's go, men, one more trench!" The machine-gun rattled. A flame-thrower hissed ahead of them. Two assault guns were giving them fire cover. They succeeded. But the lieutenant lay dead, twenty paces in front of his objective, and around him, dead or wounded, lay half his company.

It was a savage battle. Both parties seemed to surmise something of the importance which history would one day assign to this battle—the decisive battle of the Second World War.

The famous battle of *matériel* of El Alamein, where Montgomery employed 1000 guns to bring about the turning-point in the war in Africa, was a modest operation by comparison. Even Stalingrad, in spite of its more apocalyptic and tragic aura, does not stand comparison in terms of forces employed with the gigantic, open-field battle of Kursk.

On 8th July Model employed the bulk of his 4th Panzer Division under Lieutenant-General von Saucken. From the positions won by 20th Panzer Division, it moved off against the village of Teploye.

Stukas swept over the advancing regiments. Armoured close-support aircraft dived on enemy positions. The tanks of 20th, 4th, and 2nd Panzer Divisions moved among the grenadiers. Massive Tigers, Mark IVs, and assault guns. Their guns barked, shrouding the scene in smoke and fire.

But Rokossovskiy had taken preventive measures. Two rifle divisions, one artillery division, two armoured brigades, and one armoured rifle brigade had been moved in by him the previous day.

The 2nd Battalion, 33rd Panzer Grenadier Regiment, fought its way through this inferno as far as Teploye and ejected the Russians from the village. They withdrew to the last line of hills.

The battalion had already lost 100 men. But the divisional commander did not want to give the Russians time to gather their wits. The 3rd and the 35th Panzer Regiments were lined up on the edge of the village. Armoured troop-carrying vehicles joined them. Dive-bombers shrieked overhead towards the Russian main positions.

"Now!"

On the opposite slope were the well-camouflaged emplacements of the Soviet 3rd Anti-Tank Artillery Brigade. Moreover, T-34s had been dug in. Their flank was covered by a Soviet rifle battalion with anti-tank rifles, simple but highly-effective weapons against tanks at short range. Their handling, just as that of the later German Panzerfaust, required courage and coolness.

The assault on the high ground began. The Russians laid down a curtain of defensive fire.

After a few hundred yards the German grenadiers lay pinned to the ground. It was impossible to get through the Soviet fire of a few hundred guns concentrated on a very narrow sector. Only the tanks moved forward into the wall of fire.

The Soviet artillerymen let them come within five hundred, then four hundred yards. At that range even the Tigers were set on fire by the heavy Russian anti-tank guns.

But then three Mark IVs overran the first Soviet gun positions. The grenadiers followed. They seized the high ground. They were thrown back by an immediate Russian counter-attack.

For three days the battle raged in the field in front of Teploye. The 33rd Panzer Grenadier Regiment stormed the ground. They were dislodged again.

Captain Diesener, the last surviving officer, assembled the remnants of 2nd Battalion and led another assault. He took the high ground. He was forced to fall back again.

The neighbouring 6th Infantry Division similarly only got to the slope of the hotly-contested Hill 274 at Olkhovatka.

In the left sector of the penetration area the village of Ponyri was the focus of the fighting. "We shall never forget that village," is what the men of the Pomeranian 292nd Infantry Division who fought at Ponyri say even to this day.

Ponyri, a strung-out village, and Hill 253·5 were the Stalingrad of the Kursk salient. The most fiercely contested points were the tractor station, the railway-station, the school, and the water-tower. The railway embankment and the northern edge of the settlement had been captured on the first day of the attack. But after that began a savage struggle in which the 18th and 9th Panzer Divisions, as well as the 86th Infantry Division, participated.

On 9th July Hill 239·8 was stormed by 508th Grenadier Regiment. The thing now was to exploit the success and take the decisive Hill

253·5. "Ferdinands forward!" division commanded. Six of these monsters rumbled up and opened their annihilating fire.

"Assault guns to move towards Ponyri!" The guns roared off. Now surely the attack must succeed. With Ponyri in German hands the troops could wheel round towards Olkhovatka.

The 508th Grenadier Regiment thrust another five hundred yards farther to the south. At that point the Russians mounted an immediate counter-attack.

The Soviet commander of the 1st Battalion, 1032nd Rifle Regiment, was driving ahead of his battalion in his jeep. At the schoolhouse he leapt from the vehicle and personally led the foremost line of riflemen into action.

The German spearheads began to give ground. Captain Mundstock, commanding 3rd Battalion, 508th Grenadier Regiment, noticed it. He raced forward in his jeep. At the school he too jumped from his car.

His sub-machine-gun swept the crossroads. The Soviet spearhead of attack halted.

The Russian commander was killed. The next instant, however, Mundstock too collapsed, mortally wounded. A tragic duel of two brave officers.

The Soviets held the crossroads while the Germans held the schoolhouse. During the night of 10th/11th July, Colonel-General Model dipped into his last reserves to throw 10th Panzer Grenadier Division into the inferno. The division moved into the sector of 292nd Infantry Division, which had been bled white. Company after company moved into their jumping-off positions aboard their Renault trucks.

This Bavarian division, whose tactical sign was a key, had a massive gunnery potential—seven artillery battalions, one *Nebelwerfer* regiment, a heavy-mortar battalion, and an assault-gun battalion.

In the face of this fire-power the strong enemy tank attacks against Ponyri railway-station failed on the very first day.

On 12th July the well-conducted artillery fire again caused the collapse of three daylight attacks by the Russians. Heinz Nitzsche of 10th Company, 20th Panzer Grenadier Regiment, watched the forest on the hill in front of their position slowly melt away in the blazing fire of guns and Stukas. He saw the Russian columns moving up, stopping, ebbing away, collapsing. For the first time in his life he saw the roaring rockets of "Stalin's organ-pipes", the Soviet multiple mortars. Was this the sun rising, he wondered. But from the sun flickering trails of fire streaked, screamed closer, crashed, and hit home.

During the following days the Soviets tried time and again to snatch Ponyri back from the Bavarians. In vain. Lieutenant-General August Schmidt and Lieutenant-Colonel in the General Staff de Maizière, his chief of operations, coolly played their trump cards at the key points.

Sergeant Schuller stood by his anti-tank gun, firing shell after shell. Seven Soviet tanks eventually remained in front of his emplacement, burning and smouldering.

On the frontage of Armoured Reconnaissance Battalion 110 the Russians rode a cavalry attack with three squadrons, sabres flashing in the sun.

"Range 800 yards. All weapons continuous fire!"

My God, those horses!

2. The Great Pincers

General Krivoshein waits–Hoth unleashes his tanks– "Herr General, where are the Panthers?"–Chaplain Ruzek comes through hell–All well on the right wing– Breakfast with General Chistyakov.

A ND how, meanwhile, was the situation shaping on the Southern Front?

The nights in July were short. In Central Russia darkness began to retreat shortly after 2 A.M.

General Krivoshein, commanding the III Mechanized Corps, stood at the edge of a forest near Yakovlev. It was a sultry night and there was a smell of pines in the air.

From the Belgorod area came the flashes of gunfire. The distant rumbling from the front, about twenty miles away, was clearly audible: Russian artillery was firing at the German positions.

During that night of 4th/5th July General Krivoshein and his staff, like all the other staffs of the Soviet formations in the Kursk salient, were waiting for the German full-scale attack.

The III Mechanized Corps belonged to the Soviet First Tank Army and was in position immediately behind the Sixth Guards Army whose rifle divisions were holding the southern edge of the Kursk salient, the line between Belgorod and Sumy.

"I wonder where Hoth will make his main effort," Krivoshein asked, addressing the question to himself rather than his staff officers.

His chief of staff replied with great assurance: "Against the highway to Oboyan, of course, Comrade General. That's the shortest way to

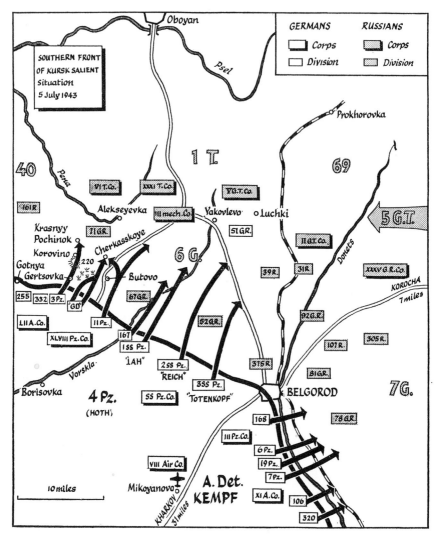

Map 4. On 5th July, Colonel-General Hoth mounted his full-scale offensive, Operation Citadel, by deploying the full strength of his Panzer divisions. Army Detachment Kempf thrust across the Donets to the south of Belgorod.

Kursk. Right in front of our sector he'll try to overrun the positions of 67th and 52nd Guards Rifle Divisions and push straight through to the north. That's why we are in the right place here immediately behind the guards riflemen."

"Yes," said Krivoshein. But there was doubt in his voice. He knew that his chief of staff was expressing the opinion which underlay the defensive plans of the High Command of the Soviet Voronezh Front.

They knew the secrets of the date of the German attack and of their order of battle. And they also believed they had solved the puzzle of Manstein's offensive tactics and concentration of effort. That was why Army General Vatutin had moved Krivoshein's magnificently equipped corps into the Alekseyevka-Yakovlevo area—to cover the Kharkov-Oboyan-Kursk highway and the feeder road from Butovo. That, in Vatutin's opinion, was where Hoth would strike in order to cross the Psel at Oboyan and push on to the north.

But was it so certain that Field-Marshal von Manstein would concentrate his main effort at this point? The southern front, where two German armies with fifteen divisions were ready to attack, was fifty miles wide. Within that fifty miles Manstein might choose one or more narrow frontages for his first penetration of the Soviet defences. And even if one believed reports that Hoth's Fourth Panzer Army was the real striking army and the Army Detachment Kempf merely had the task of covering its flank, it nevertheless remained doubtful whether Hoth would launch his attack in exactly the way envisaged by the Soviet High Command.

General Krivoshein drew at his cigarette. "What STAVKA thinks will happen, and what we think will happen, is of course the most obvious solution. It is what we would do in their place. But Hoth is a cunning fox. Will he really do the obvious? And Hoth is not only a fox but also a methodical man who first studies his operational area, familiarizes himself with the facts of the terrain, the natural obstacles and the favourable features, the water courses, the hills and the valleys, the favourable and unfavourable ground."

His chief of staff listened attentively. He realized that Krivoshein knew the German tank commanders, many of them personally. In September 1939, after the German campaign against Poland, he had held long conversations with Guderian. Krivoshein had then commanded a Soviet armoured brigade which had linked up with Guderian's Panzer corps at Brest-Litovsk.

At a little drinking party in the Voivodship offices after the joint parade, he had created much hilarity among the German officers when, in a toast to German-Russian friendship, he had committed a slip of the tongue and, instead of drinking to "eternal friendship", had drunk to "eternal fiendship". Perhaps the general was just then thinking of that moment almost exactly four years earlier. But maybe he had other worries. He turned to his chief of staff: "Let's go in."

At that moment, twelve miles away, on the high ground of Butovo, Lieutenant-Colonel Albrecht, the artillery commander of the "Grossdeutschland" Panzer Grenadier Division, was engaged in his countdown over the telephone to all gun emplacements: ". . . Two, one—fire!"

And like him the artillery commanders of all German divisions of Fourth Panzer Army between Gertsovka and Belgorod shouted: "Fire!"

A sudden artillery salvo rang out over the hills and valleys of the Central Russian ridge, with a roar of thunder and lightning as if all thunderstorms of the last hundred years were now rolled into one.

It was such a concentration of fire by artillery and heavy weapons as had never before been achieved in this war on such a narrow front. Within fifty minutes more shells were fired off between Belgorod and Gertsovka than in the whole of the campaigns in Poland and France combined.

General Krivoshein glanced at his watch: 0330 hours. The close, expectant night was nearing its end. On the skyline flickered the glow of distant fires. The battle was beginning.

Field-Marshal von Manstein had chosen for the southern front of the Kursk salient a different offensive tactic from that chosen by Model in the north. For him it was not the infantry but the armoured formations which were to achieve a rapid breakthrough.

The reason for his decision was the fact that, in view of the extent of the front, the infantry divisions available to him were insufficient for the traditional tactics of using infantry to achieve a penetration for the armoured formations. Considering that the Soviet defences were echeloned in great depth, the traditional method seemed to Manstein to be too wasteful of time, too costly, and, with his inadequate number of infantry divisions, also too unreliable. Hoth hoped that a forceful punch by his 600 to 700 tanks, concentrated at two points, would break Soviet resistance so quickly that the following engagements with the enemy's strong armoured reserves would take place outside the Soviet system of positions, and for this purpose he employed the entire armoured strength of his army for the first blow. The same recipe was chosen by Army Detachment Kempf. That was Manstein's school. That was his interpretation of the operation order of the OKH, the High Command of Land Forces: by means of a locally overwhelming superiority of all means of attack, a penetration is to be made until the two attacking armies have linked up, and the pocket is then to be closed.

More than 1000 tanks and 300 assault guns moved off against the Russian defences in order to make a breakthrough and then immediately push on into an open area of operations and accomplish the link-up with Model's Ninth Army.

The Soviets realized the German intention: indeed, the placing of their reserves behind Lieutenant-General Chistyakov's Sixth Guards Army was based on it.

But Colonel-General Hoth was similarly informed by German aerial reconnaissance about the assembly areas of the Soviet reserves, especially their armoured reserves. He calculated that, if he observed the OKH instructions "to achieve the link-up with Ninth Army by direct penetration via Oboyan", he would probably just be in front of the Psel crossings at Oboyan when the Soviet armoured corps appeared on the battlefield from the area east of Kursk. They were bound to come across the neck of land at Prokhorovka and would strike at the deep flank of the German offensive wedge at the most unfavourable moment.

Hoth therefore decided to modify his timetable. This is how he put it to his staff: "It would be better to deal first with the enemy to be expected via Prokhorovka before continuing our northward thrust in the direction of Kursk." That meant that, after the breakthrough, all offensive divisions under Hoth would first wheel to the north-east and not strike direct at Oboyan as the Soviets expected.

This was a most important decision.

Hoth's calculation proved correct. His plan of attack upset the Soviet High Command's plan of defence on the southern front of the Kursk salient and might well have brought about a turn in the battle if . . . But let us not anticipate.

From the high ground of Butovo Lieutenant-Colonel Albrecht had his eyes glued to his trench telescope, watching the effect of his artillery bombardment. The bursts were now beyond the enemy trenches, and the wall of fire and smoke was creeping forward into the enemy's hinterland. In the smoke German infantrymen could be made out advancing, like insubstantial shadows.

The orderly officer whispered to the artillery commander: "General Hoernlein is coming over."

A moment later the commander of "Grossdeutschland" Division was standing at the trench telescope next to the lieutenant-colonel: "Morning, Albrecht, how's it going?"

"Everything according to schedule, Herr General."

"Any reports yet from the infantry?"

"Nothing yet."

At that moment Colonel Kassnitz, commanding the Panzer Fusilier Regiment, arrived. He raised his hand to his steel helmet. He was not looking too pleased. "Well, Kassnitz?" Hoernlein asked suspiciously.

"There's a hell of a mess, Herr General. My 3rd Battalion has not gone into action."

"Why not?"

"They were waiting for the tanks, but none came, and so they didn't move off."

Hoernlein and Albrecht were dumbfounded. The tanks not come? That whole armada of Lauchert's Panther Brigade and the 1st Battalion of the "Grossdeutschland" Panzer Regiment under Major Pössel not in action? Surely that was not possible!

Hoernlein was plainly disconcerted by the news. Here, where the main weight of the attack was to be concentrated, all hope hinged on the force of the blow which Count Strachwitz's Panzer group was to have delivered. The High Command had placed the greatest expectations in the 200 new miracle tanks, the Panthers with their 7·5-cm long-barrel cannon, which were to be employed in action here for the first time. Where the devil were they?

As the fusiliers and grenadiers of "Grossdeutschland" Division were scrambling out of their trenches the Panther Brigade Lauchert was also moving forward with its 200 new Panther tanks. They were beasts of prey made of steel—elegantly constructed, weighing 45·5 tons, with a length of 29 feet, a frontal armour of 80 to 110 mm, and a speed of up to 34 miles per hour.

The experts were agreed that this was the tank the men in the field had been waiting for, the tank which would at long last assure genuine German superiority in armour on the Eastern Front.

Only one question worried the technicians and inspectors of the armoured formations—was the Panther really ready for operational use? The trial period at the Grafenwöhr training centre, which had been far too short, had revealed serious troubles. And instead of formation practice, officers and crews had been busy tackling technical problems. Even while the tanks were on the train to the Eastern Front their final drives were still being replaced. Consequently, no proper individual training, let alone formation practice, had been possible. In no sense could the unit be described as ready for action.

Another point was that battalions of 96 Panthers each were too large for operational control by one battalion commander. But all attempts by Lieutenant-Colonel Werner Mildebrath to get an extension of the training period at Grafenwöhr had been in vain. The unit was scheduled to go into action at Kursk.

The front-line troops, who had been hearing stories about the new wonder weapon, had the shock of their lives when they saw how, even as they moved into their starting-off positions, their steel heroes were belching huge flames from their exhaust pipes and some of them actually caught fire.

But the failure in the first attack at Butovo on 5th July was not due to any of these teething troubles. The reason was much more mundane —Lauchert's Panther Brigade had got into an undiscovered minefield in front of the Soviet lines. If a tank kept on moving it struck a mine and had its chains blown off. If it halted it became a huge target for Soviet anti-tank guns, anti-tank rifles, and artillery.

The attempt of the "Grossdeutschland" Fusilier Regiment to advance without tank support resulted in heavy losses. So the familiar cry went up again: "Engineers forward!"

Amidst the inferno of the Soviet defensive fire the 2nd Company of the Panzer Assault Engineer Battalion "Grossdeutschland" cleared a lane through the mines for the Panthers. But this took several hours, vital hours which the Soviets put to good use.

"In the country in front of Cherkasskoye alone 36 tanks remained immobilized in the minefield," Colonel Markin records in his account of the Battle of Kursk. And he adds: "The tanks which had blundered into the minefields withdrew in disorder under the well-aimed fire of Soviet artillery and anti-tank riflemen. The first particularly dangerous assault of the enemy had been repulsed. His attempt to advance simultaneously along the whole breakthrough frontage had thus been foiled." That was entirely correct.

After Colonel Kassnitz's report General Hoernlein realized that the thrust on the left wing of his division had failed owing to the misadventure of the Panther brigade.

But on the right wing of the division things were working out all the better. "How are Lorenz's Panzer Grenadiers doing?" asked Hoernlein. Almost as if the runner had waited for his cue he suddenly appeared in front of the general: "Report from Lieutenant-Colonel Lorenz!"

Hoernlein read: "After meeting stubborn resistance the regiment penetrated into the enemy trenches, cleared them, and is now advancing fast towards the high ground of Cherkasskoye."

On the right wing, therefore, things had gone according to plan. The grenadier battalions of "Grossdeutschland", together with assault guns, tanks of 2nd Battalion of the Panzer Regiment, and Captain Wallroth's Tiger Company had moved off against Cherkasskoye on the dot of 0500. Towards 0915 hours the battalions were already on the hills outside the village, deep in the first Soviet defences.

Count Saurma, commanding the Panther Battalion of "Grossdeutschland", led his tanks with skill and dash. Wherever the situation was most dangerous or confused he would turn up in his command tank. Icy terror, therefore, struck his company headquarters when, towards midday, they heard through their headphones the voice of Saurma's wireless operator: "Panther II-01 hit. Battalion commander seriously wounded."

But the shock lasted only a few seconds. Then they heard a calm voice: "Gottberg to all—battalion will take orders from me." Captain von Gottberg took over command. A few hours later Count Saurma was dead.

As soon as General Hoernlein learned of the success of the grenadiers he immediately switched his plan and transferred the main effort of his thrust from the left wing to the right. The Fusilier Regiment and the Panther Brigade were pulled over to the right.

But there seemed to be a jinx on everything. The rain which had accompanied the thunderstorms of the past few days had turned the Berezovyy bottom into a swamp. One Panther after another ground to a standstill in the quagmire, bogged down to well above the tracks. Several more hours delay for the decisive blow by the armoured fist which was to have accomplished the breakthrough of "Grossdeutschland" Division on the first day! As night settled over the battlefield the village of Cherkasskoye had been captured in spite of all misfortunes, and the anchorage point of the first Soviet line of resistance in front of "Grossdeutschland" had thus been eliminated.

The price was high. The dead and the seriously wounded close to death included Colonel Kassnitz, the commander of the Panzer Fusilier Regiment.

A decisive part in the fighting for Cherkasskoye was played also by 11th Panzer Division which had moved up on the right of "Grossdeutschland" Division. Its Combat Group Count Schimmelmann had broken into the Soviet positions with tanks, grenadiers on board armoured troop-carriers, anti-tank guns, engineers, and assault guns, and parts of it had then wheeled towards Cherkasskoye. With flame-throwing tanks, those terrifying spitfire monsters, the Soviet strong-points in bunkers and fortified houses were reduced.

The flame-throwing tank was a suitable weapon for this kind of fighting. The two flame-throwers mounted in the turret of the Mark III were able to hurl their well-aimed lances of fire into embrasures, windows, and doors over a distance of seventy yards. The hissing jet of fire, lasting three or four seconds, killed and charred everything in a heat of 1000 degrees Centigrade.

Cherkasskoye had fallen. "Grossdeutschland" and 11th Panzer Division were five miles deep in the enemy's main defence zone.

Five miles was a lot. But the Soviet defence zone, echeloned as it was in depth, was by no means pierced. And complete breakthrough had been the real objective of the attack on the first day. For the following day, 6th July, Major-General Mickl, commanding 11th Panzer Division, had already assigned the bridge over the Psel, south of Oboyan, as the objective of the day—thirty miles from the jumping-off positions.

On the eve of the battle Colonel-General Hoth had visited Mickl at his advanced HQ and had reiterated the objective of 6th July for the Schimmelmann Combat Group—the bridge at Oboyan.

This was a timetable on the pattern of the armoured raids of 1941. That was how Manstein had raced with his LVI Panzer Corps against Dvinsk.

Hoth's orders to Mickl were based on the assumption that Lauchert's Panther Brigade would sweep like a tornado over the enemy's main defence zone, followed by the Tigers, the rest of the tanks, the armoured troop-carriers, and the assault guns of the Panzer and Grenadier regiments.

With "Grossdeutschland" Division alone more than 300 medium and heavy tanks were employed—a concentration unprecedented on the sector of a single division in the Russian campaign. Perhaps the German hopes would have come true if the Panther brigade had not been dogged by misfortune on its first day of combat, if it had not suffered irreparable losses. Perhaps!

However, only one day had passed of the battle on the southern front of the Kursk salient. True, this first day had revealed that, here too, the intended strategic surprise had not come off.

The very first detailed reports which Colonel-General Hoth received from his Army Intelligence Officer towards midday contained an interesting and significant statement. In all earlier German offensives the tank wireless operators and those at advanced headquarters had invariably intercepted the excited questions of Soviet commanders to their superiors: "Am under attack. What am I to do?" On 5th July this usually characteristic symptom of confusion and surprise was not heard even once.

The Soviet troops had not been taken by surprise—they were prepared and rehearsed for all eventualities. The tactical surprise, on the other hand—as to the time, place, combination of weapons used, and main weight of attack—had been entirely successful.

In the sector of XLVIII Panzer Corps a broad and deep penetration had thus been achieved into the enemy's main defence zone. For to the left of "Grossdeutschland", on the frontage of 3rd Panzer Division, the first day of battle ended with a successful blow against the Soviet front line.

At 1500 hours on 4th July the Berlin and Brandenburg Regiments, together with the Combat Group Pape, had moved off for an advance attack against the Belgorod-Gotnya railway line and the village of Gertsovka from the strongpoints of 332nd Infantry Division, with a view to seizing suitable terrain for armour. Led by Sergeant Steinführer, the men of 2nd Company, 394th Panzer Grenadier Regiment, captured their day's objective even before nightfall. Division was able to move the 2nd Battalion, 6th Panzer Regiment, forward.

The 3rd Panzer Division was just as successful on 5th July. Punctually at 0500 Lieutenant-General Westhoven's formations moved off against the positions of the Soviet 71st Guards Rifle Division after a brief artillery bombardment and several waves of bombing attacks by VIII Air Corps. The 332nd Infantry Division followed to give cover on the left flank.

Here, too, well-camouflaged anti-tank positions and cleverly dug-in tanks slowed down the advance of the grenadiers. The ground had to be won yard by yard. Ammunition was running low. The companies of 3rd Panzer Grenadier Regiment were exhausted. A scorching hot sun stood in the sky. Lieutenant-Colonel Wellmann, the regimental commander, kept encouraging his battalion commanders. "Only one more hill," he urged them on. That was Hill 220, south of Korovino.

They managed it. They paused. They mopped up the ground and cleared the sporadic Russian snipers who were still sitting in their foxholes, firing away.

Corporal Mogel of 2nd Company led his group at a trot through a maze of trenches. "Halt," he suddenly called, stopping. "Can you hear something?"

They listened. Yes—there were voices. They seemed to be speaking German. They ran forward. Careful now, where the trenches divide. A quick peep round the corner.

Before them cowered a dozen German soldiers, unarmed. A Soviet trick? A trap? The next few seconds brought the solution of the riddle. They were German prisoners-of-war. The Russians had used them for digging defences. When the German attack began they had 'lost' themselves and had hidden in a dug-out abandoned by the Russians.

And because life itself always invents the best stories it may be worth recording a scene which happened on Hill 220 near Korovino amidst the noise of battle. An elderly NCO from among the group of prisoners found himself facing Corporal Mogel: He looked at him and the two flung out their arms as if on command. The nephew had found his uncle.

A small but moving incident on the savage battlefield in the Kursk salient. A moment when humanity broke through the smoke and horror of battle. Just as on the previous day when Chaplain Ruzek from Vienna, the Catholic divisional priest, had walked into an uncleared minefield in order to assist the dying.

The chaplain did not wait for the mine-clearing party. "I can't keep the Lord waiting," he said, and went out. Among the dying were also three seriously wounded men whose life could be saved by prompt medical attention.

One by one, the chaplain carried them on his back out of the inferno of the minefield. Six times he traversed the distance—three times forward and three times back. And many a man was reminded of Jesus Christ walking on the waters of the sea of Genesaret. Step by step the chaplain, carrying his heavy load, walked over the death traps. And not one of them went off.

The dusk of 5th July was beginning to fall as 394th Panzer Grenadier Regiment stormed the village of Korovino. The village had been turned into an anti-tank fortress, since it formed the western anchor of the first Soviet defensive position.

Colonel Pape, the regimental commander, as always in the foremost line, had skilfully mounted the attack and pushed it along with vigour. A short distance outside Korovino he was wounded. Major Peschke assumed command of the regiment and completed the success of the day. The Russians pulled back.

Lieutenant von Veltheim, commanding the light platoon of 2nd Battalion, 6th Panzer Regiment, saw his chance. He followed up the enemy withdrawal and, in the glow of a burning windmill, drove into the last bulwark of the Soviet defence zone in front of the Pena river —the village of Krasnyy Pochinok.

Veltheim was the first to reach the Pena. Thereby 3rd Panzer Division had reached its scheduled objective for the day. It had penetrated the first Soviet defence zone and now stood six miles deep in the Kursk salient.

During the night the Central German 255th Infantry Division also threaded itself into the front to the left of 3rd Panzer Division, next to the Silesian 332nd Infantry Division. Together with 332nd Infantry Division, it was to widen the penetration made by the Panzer Divisions of XLVIII Panzer Corps on the left wing and provide cover for it.

The 6th July dawned slowly. Into the early haze over the low ground the *Nebelwerfers* lobbed their shells. Their whine inaugurated the second day of the attack on the left wing of the southern front; the grey columns of smoke bursting in the enemy positions marked the targets of the Silesian and Central German battalions.

And what was happening on the right wing, at SS Panzer Corps?

Lieutenant-General Chistyakov, C-in-C of the Soviet Sixth Guards Army, had urged his divisional commanders on the evening of 4th July to be particularly careful. "In front of you stand Hitler's Guards formations," Chistyakov had said. "We must expect the main effort of the German offensive on this sector."

It was not a difficult prediction to make. The SS Panzer Corps under General Hausser, with three Panzer Divisions of the Waffen SS, represented a massive force—300 tanks, including numerous Tigers, and roughly 120 assault guns, as well as a whole *Nebelwerfer* brigade. It was an unprecedented concentration of fire-power. Even though the Soviets did not know all these details, they knew enough about the strength of Hausser's Corps, which had snatched Kharkov from them again four months previously.

The Soviet field positions in front of Hausser had been developed into an elaborate, deeply echeloned, and widely ramified fortification system. The 52nd Guards Rifle Division and the 375th Rifle Division, both of them crack formations, occupied the trenches and earth bunkers, reinforced by artillery regiments, anti-tank artillery, battalions of anti-tank riflemen, tank companies, mortar regiments, and other formations. Behind the divisions in the line waited the corps of General Katukov's First Tank Army.

Hausser was watching the attack from the command post of "Deutschland" Panzer Grenadier Regiment.

"It's coming along fine, Obergruppenführer," the regimental commander Hans Harmel reported.

The spearhead was formed by 3rd Battalion. The battalion commander, Günther-Eberhard Wisliceny, ensured that, in spite of the ding-dong fighting, his companies were moving forward steadily. The 10th Company under Captain of SS Helmuth Schreider finally got as far as the first anti-tank ditch, dug in there, and refused to yield an inch in spite of furious Soviet counter-attacks.

The "Führer" Panzer Grenadier Regiment pushed into the gap thus opened. To the right and left of it stormed the battalions of "Totenkopf", "Leibstandarte Adolf Hitler", and of 167th Infantry Division.

The Russians resisted stubbornly. Above all, on the frontage of "Leibstandarte", a Soviet Guards rifle regiment refused to give ground. Georg Karck, commanding 9th Company, 2nd Panzer Grenadier Regiment of "Leibstandarte", eventually forced the decision. With a handful of men he knocked out five enemy bunkers with demolition charges. With his company he then fought his way through the maze of trenches up on the high ground and tore open the enemy positions. The job was done! But no, far from it! For immediately behind the hill a new Soviet system of positions began.

The Tigers rumbled on. Anti-tank rifles cracked. Grenadiers jumped into trenches. Machine-guns ticked. Shells smashed sap trenches and dug-outs. The very first hours of fighting showed that Hausser's divisions were also encountering a well-prepared and well-functioning opposition.

How were the fortifications to be smashed quickly and effectively?

To the right of SS Panzer Corps, south-east of Belgorod, the Army Detachment Kempf meanwhile crossed the Don with two corps and formed small bridgeheads. Three infantry and three Panzer divisions were attacking—the latter being such well-tried formations as 7th, 19th, and 6th Panzer Divisions. They were to undertake the flank cover of the overall operation to the east, and moreover thrust along the Donets via Korocha in order to intercept the rapidly approaching enemy forces before these were able to intervene in the breakthrough battle.

The ground was difficult and enemy opposition strong. Kempf's divisions made only slow progress. This meant a serious threat to Manstein's plan.

At that point a decisive turn came about in the sector of SS Panzer Corps. They had played a trump card which the Soviets, in preparing their defences, had quite clearly underrated. Lieutenant-General Chistyakov, at any rate, had expected the battle to develop quite differently after the first few hours.

Three hours after the start of the German attack Chistyakov was still sitting in the garden of his battle HQ, having a second breakfast under an apple-tree. He was fond of good food. When General Katukov arrived at the HQ with his Military Council member Popel, in order to be a little nearer to the centre of things, Chistyakov pleasantly invited them to join him.

In his memoirs Popel records a little acidly: "On the table were cold mutton, scrambled eggs, a carafe with chilled vodka to judge by the condensation on the glass, and finely sliced white bread—Chistyakov was doing himself well."

But the mutton and scrambled eggs remained uneaten. For suddenly there were shell bursts. Clouds rose above the apple-trees from shrapnel-shell explosions. Artillery! The chief of staff hurried over and reported—as Popel puts it—"hastily and nervously" that strong enemy forces had broken through.

Katukov and Popel ran to their cars and roared off to the battle HQ of their First Tank Army, in order to raise the alarm there. It was high time. The German tanks could already be discerned with the naked eye. They were approaching in several lines, echeloned one behind another. The left wing of the column was steam-rollering its way through a dense little hazel copse. Damn—where had all these Germans sprung from? How had they got through the mile-deep defences?

Chistyakov raced into the house and did not budge from the telephone. What he and his chief of staff learned was far from clear, but it was bad enough. The heaviest blows against the front of Sixth Guards Army had come from the air. With their Stukas and bombers the Germans were flattening out the Soviet defences. Worse still, a novel type of small, high-fragmentation bomb had produced disastrous results, especially among the gun crews.

Worst of all, ground-support aircraft with a fixed 2-cm machine-gun and an anti-tank cannon under the fuselage were smashing up the Soviet armoured counter-attacks and punching a way clear for the offensive forces of the Waffen SS.

In this way Hausser's spearheads succeeded after a few hours of fighting in penetrating the entire first Soviet defensive positions of Sixth Guards Army on the sector of the 52nd Guards Rifle Division. They were now in front of Army battle HQ.

An artillery commander staggered wounded into General Chistyakov's room and reported: "My regiment has been in action for an hour, Comrade General, but one-third of its guns are already eliminated. The German aircraft are dropping vast numbers of small bombs which have colossal high-fragmentation effect. The Stukas are dominating the air space. They are just doing what they like up there. We are helpless."

"And where are our aircraft?" Chistyakov blustered. "Where are the three Air Armies, and the long-range bomber divisions with their two and a half thousand machines which headquarters moved to the Kursk salient? Why was the Luftwaffe not smashed on its field this morning, as planned?"

Why indeed? Chistyakov did not then know what had happened in the sky over Kursk; he did not know that the Soviet air forces had fallen victim to a disastrous error.

Yet the Soviets failed only by a hair's breadth to pull off their surprise blow against the German airfields behind the Kursk front.

3. The Tank Battle of Prokhorovka

*The Russian plan–The German trump card–Air battle
at sunrise–Khrushchev's warning: The next three days
will be terrible–Why isn't Kempf coming?–The hour of
Waterloo–General Rotmistrov's report.*

IN the early morning of 5th July 1943 Major-General Seidemann saw disaster approaching inescapably. He had just finished dressing when his orderly officer burst into the room: "Message from aircraft-reporting service, Herr General."

Seidemann looked up. "Strong enemy air formations approaching on a course for Kharkov."

Seidemann glanced at his wrist-watch. He made a rapid mental calculation. Then he grabbed his cap and pistol holster from a hook. "That could be a disaster," he muttered, and rushed across to the signals bunker.

It was still dark outside. But in 10 to 15 minutes dawn would begin to break. And in exactly 10 minutes the machines of VIII Air Corps would take off from their 16 airfields around Kharkov. It did not bear thinking of.

His staff officers were already assembled in the signals bunker, clutching telephones to their ears. They looked up as the general entered, for at that same moment the first flak guns opened up in the village of Mikoyanovka, where VIII Air Corps had its advanced HQ.

A moment later the general and his officers could hear the mighty stream of Soviet formations droning overhead. They were making for Kharkov, for the crowded German airfields.

On these airfields the German Stukas, bombers, ground-support aircraft, and tank-busting units—roughly 800 machines—were just moving into take-off position to inaugurate the offensive on the southern front with crushing blows from the air and to supply the constant air support for Hoth's Fourth Panzer Army to break through the strong Soviet defences.

This was the plan: The German bomber and ground-support aircraft were first to assemble over the fields, formation by formation, and only then were the 270 fighters to take off to provide cover for the strike aircraft.

This then was the vulnerable spot of VIII Air Corps on the morning of 5th July. These were the minutes during which Seidemann's huge fleet was defenceless—the runways crowded with bombers, and those already in the air not yet protected by fighters. The Soviet High Command had skilfully chosen that precise time for its annihilating blow against the German airpower on the southern front of Citadel. It was cleverly conceived and accurately calculated. It was here that Werther's invaluable information was to yield its sweetest fruit.

Seidemann and his officers instantly realized the disastrous situation as the Russian bomber streams and fighter squadrons were sweeping over Mikoyanovka. The general knew as well as each one of his staff officers that it was too late now to intervene in the course of events on the airfields. Either the German formations about to take off would be smashed on the ground by the bombs of the Soviet squadrons or else they would be shot down in the air by Soviet fighters.

With a deep roar the disaster was approaching at a height of 10,000 feet. Among the Soviet fighter squadrons with their Migs and Yaks there were also American Airacobras.

The Soviet airmen had taken off in darkness from the fields of the Soviet Second and Seventeenth Air Armies in the Kursk and Oboyan area, and even from areas south of Moscow. They were flying in the secure knowledge that their calculation was correct. This time they would repay the feared German Luftwaffe for all its blows during the past years. A few minutes, a few accurately calculated minutes, would ensure victory in the air over the Kursk salient.

And this precisely calculated victory, the Soviets concluded, would deprive Manstein's armies of their air cover; it would rob them of their third dimension and thus doom their offensive on the southern front of Kursk even before the first German grenadier had jumped from his dug-out.

How had the Soviets been able to make this accurate calculation? This was the question which oppressed Seidemann and his officers. On the German side all precautions had been taken and all known tricks used in order to keep the secret. Naturally, it was impossible to hide all preparations from Soviet aerial reconnaissance or from Soviet agents in the hinterland. Airfields, especially dozens of them concentrated in a small area, could not be camouflaged. Nevertheless, the German Luftwaffe High Command had done everything possible to conceal the concentration of 1800 aircraft, about 19,000 heavy and light anti-aircraft guns, and 300 searchlights immediately behind the front line.

This had not been an easy task. After all, the 1st Air Division had to be moved into position for the northern sector in the Orel area, and in the south, in the Kharkov area, VIII Air Corps with its 1185 aircraft and I Flak Corps, reinforced by a flak brigade, had likewise to be brought up.

The 1200 aircraft within Manstein's sphere of command alone required 16 airfields in the Kharkov area. That was a dangerous concentration.

The aircraft were parked in boxes as far apart as possible, and surrounded with makeshift anti-splinter cover. Bombs and fuel were stored in trenches. Camouflage by means of nets and shrubs, checked from the air every day, were to render aerial reconnaissance more difficult.

To render discovery more difficult was one thing—but to hide such a concentration of air power altogether was impossible. Even the fact that the bulk of the machines were not to arrive at the forward fields until the night before the attack was not likely to deceive any reasonably efficient aerial reconnaissance. Besides, what was the use of all these measures if the enemy knew the secrets of the front through well-organized espionage inside the Führer's headquarters?

The Soviets knew the date and the general plan of the German offensive. And they knew only too well that ground operations would be supported by massive blows from the air. Knowledge of the focal points of the offensive, together with the results of aerial reconnaissance, gave them a good idea of the German preparations for their air strike.

At first light on 5th July, as the bomber formations of the Soviet

Khrushchev, Chistyakov, and Ibyanskiy on the Kursk front.
Russian breakthrough in the Orel area.

Seventeenth Air Army roared over General Seidemann's battle head-quarters, everything pointed to the success of the Soviet plan. But their calculation did not come off. Once again it was shown that all military calculations contain some unknown quantity. Over Kursk it had the name of a Nordic deity.

The Luftwaffe's radar instruments, which bore the name of the Goddess Freya, succeeded in locating the approaching enemy formations at a range of over sixty miles, complete with direction and altitude.

These Freya radar installations at the airfields spotted the approaching Soviet formations only just in time. Their reports immediately went to the flak units and to the command posts of the fighter units and groups. It had the effect of a thunderbolt on the fields around Kharkov and the provisional air bases around Belgorod. The commodores and their young commanders realized what was happening. No questions were necessary.

Signals to Corps? Impossible. Radio silence had been ordered. Besides, what was the point of asking? It was one of those moments where responsibility had to be taken without asking questions.

What happened then on all these airfields was an example of soldierly skill: quick telephone conversations between the leaders of the fighter formations and the airfield control officers.

"Enemy attack?"

"Disregard schedule. We take off at once. Scramble!"

And already the pilots were racing to their machines. A moment later the flights moved off, bumping over the temporary runways. The engines screamed. The fighters of Kursk were airborne.

These few minutes decided the battle. Out of the dawn haze the German fighters pounced down on the Soviet bomber squadrons flying at 10,000 feet.

In the rays of the rising sun the spectacle of a vast air battle could be followed from the ground.

For the Soviet fighters the altitude of 6000 to 10,000 feet was particularly unfavourable. At that height the German Messerschmitt fighters were clearly superior to them. In flames, trailing smoke, and exploding, the Soviet aircraft crashed to the ground. Only a few of the bombers reached the German airfields, and those which did dropped their bombs without aim, causing only slight damage.

In the very first moment of the air battle the Russians lost 120 machines. By the end of the day the score was 432, and 24 hours later it had grown by a further 205. Thus Seidemann's VIII Air Corps not only successfully repulsed a dangerous enemy air offensive but also

Retreat: railway lines being blown up.
Defence: the Russians are immediately in front of the German lines.

gained command of the air on the southern sector. Unopposed his bombers and ground-support aircraft started their big blow against the Soviet defensive front. Wave after wave, they blazed a trail for the German attack on the ground.

Among the Stuka formations which were pounding the Soviet switchlines on the Belgorod-Oboyan road ahead of the tanks of SS Panzer Corps was also a pilot whose name was well-known on both sides of the line—Hans-Ulrich Rudel. Wherever he was was the focus of the battle.

The foremost companies of SS Panzer Corps were in the town in front of the well-camouflaged anti-tank and artillery positions of the Soviet 52nd Guards Rifle Division. Rudel saw the dug-in T-34s, he saw the 7·62-cm anti-tank guns, he saw the mortar batteries and the heavy armoured guns on self-propelled carriages with their huge barrels for firing 15·2-cm shells—giant guns employed by the Soviets for the first time at Kursk.

This barrier, this decisive 'centre of resistance' in the Berezov area, had to be breached.

The Stukas dipped. Their bombs crashed on to their targets. Rudel, catching sight of an approaching enemy tank column when he had no bombs left, remembered his old practice Stuka with its anti-tank cannon. And he conceived an idea that was to give the Russians many a headache yet.

Meanwhile the first wave of ground-support aircraft approached at 2500 feet. Into the target area they dropped the new SD-1 and SD-2 bombs—large and small containers shaped like bombs but containing 180 2-kg or 360 1-kg bombs. These containers opened just above the ground, scattering the high-fragmentation mini-bombs among the enemy positions like a rain of death.

The effect was disastrous. The heavily manned Soviet anti-tank positions were largely put out of action by these attacks. The hills and valleys held by the reinforced 151st and 155th Guards Rifle Regiments were one vast sea of flames.

At 1100 hours fifty German tanks broke through at 155th Guards Rifle Regiment, wheeled westward and rolled up the front of 151st Guards Rifle Regiment. The Soviet barrier covering the Belgorod-Kursk highway was burst open. The attack continued at full speed.

At noon on 6th July the "Der Führer" Regiment took the village of Luchki I. This put General Hausser's SS Panzer Corps twenty miles deep into the enemy's defence zone. A huge gap had been torn into General Chistyakov's Sixth Guards Army and the front line lay wide open like a barn door. Through that door Hausser now drove everything he had. The offensive had as much dash as those in the heyday of the blitzkrieg.

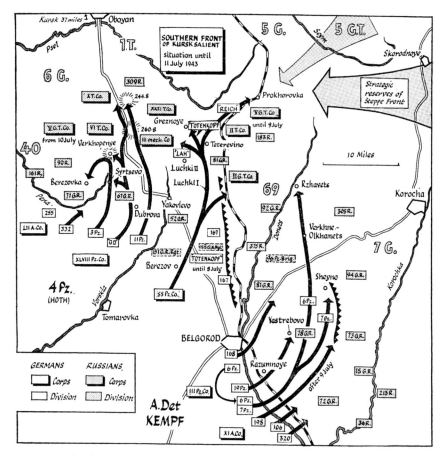

Map 5. The divisions of Fourth Panzer Army were within reach of Oboyan and Prokhorovka, but their speed was not matched by Army Detachment Kempf. Hoth's right flank was in danger.

On 7th July tanks and assault guns crossed the Luchki II-Teterevino road. The battalions fanned out to east and west into the open space. Parts of the "Leibstandarte" and "Totenkopf" Regiments now aimed at the Psel bend and at Greznoye broke into the last Soviet defence lines in front of the river.

Among their foremost tanks was the 6th Company, 1st SS Panzer Regiment. Its commander was Rudolf von Ribbentrop, the son of the German Foreign Minister. Ribbentrop's tank raced ahead of his company and cleared a path through the Soviet area in the direction of Greznoye. Shock troops of the "Deutschland" Regiment and companies of the "Der Führer" Regiment now wheeled east and attacked Prokhorovka. Artillery and mortars supported the thrust against the key positions on the wide neck of land between Psel and Donets.

The Soviet High Command of the Voronezh Front Army Group was horror-struck at this surprise development. There was no other word for it—the front of Sixth Guards Army had been crushed. Only sporadic centres of resistance were still holding out.

The Commander-in-Chief issued one of those categorical commands known to generals of all armies, the kind of command which reveals the highest degree of alarm. Army General Vatutin and his Military Council member Nikita Khrushchev signed the signal. It read: "On no account must the Germans break through to Oboyan."

The signal was received by General Katukov's First Tank Army, among others. Its chief of staff, Major-General Shalin, read it out. And Katukov immediately switched two armoured infantry regiments into the gap in the front of the Sixth Guards Army. "After two hours all that was left of them was their numbers," records Lieutenant-General Popel, the Military Council member of First Tank Army.

In the evening Khrushchev personally turned up at First Tank Army headquarters. "The next two or three days will be terrible," he said. "Either we hold out, or the Germans take Kursk. They are staking everything on this one card. For them it is a matter of life or death. We must see to it that they break their necks!"

At the situation meeting in the evening, Major-General Shalin observed soberly: "We are confronted by an unprecedented concentration of armour. It is the old tactic. But this time the armoured spearheads are led by Tigers, Panthers, and massive assault guns. The cannon of our T-34s cannot pierce the frontal armour of the fascists' giants." Another point made by Shalin on the strength of a dozen written reports was this: the German Luftwaffe was employing new ground-support aircraft fitted with anti-tank cannon. These were employed as a kind of flying anti-tank artillery, pouncing from the sky at the tanks like hawks pouncing on a chicken-yard. Armoured counterattacks were thus shot up by the surprise intervention of these machines. Getman's Soviet tank corps had suffered most. Twelve of its T-34s were knocked out within a very short period by just one of those flying tank-busters.

The account of a Russian artillery observer sounds almost incredible. The attacking aircraft drops from some 2500 feet upon the unsuspecting armoured column. Not until he is within fifteen feet of the last tank does the pilot pull out of his dive. The crack of cannon, a flash, a crash, and through the billowing smoke of the struck T-34 the German pilot climbs away. A moment later he dives in again. Always from behind. Tank after tank is knocked out by his cannon, the target invariably being its most vulnerable spot, the engine compartment, where each hit results in an instant explosion.

General Shalin did not yet know the name of the man who had

achieved this feat. It was Hans-Ulrich Rudel, who had rapidly put into effect the idea which came to him on his return flight from his first mission on 5th July. He had tried these tactics out before, in the Crimea, and his old experimental machine was still in existence. He had ordered it to be flown up to him—his Stuka with an anti-tank gun.

It was here, in the Kursk salient, that Rudel's tank-busting wing was born—Stukas carrying 3·7-cm anti-tank cannon. Together with the new twin-engined Hs-129 armoured ground-support aircraft they intervened in the tank battles with astonishing success.

On the left of Hausser's Waffen SS, at XLVIII Panzer Corps, progress continued to be good on 7th July, the fourth day of the great battle. At dawn the grenadiers of "Grossdeutschland" took Dubrova.

But the misfortunes which had been dogging the Panthers of "Grossdeutschland" Division since the first day of the offensive were not yet at an end. Lauchert's Panther Brigade again blundered into a minefield and suffered very heavy losses.

Captain von Gottberg's 2nd Battalion, Panzer Regiment "Grossdeutschland", saved the situation. It swept the grenadiers of Remer's battalion with it. The attack got moving again. From the ravines on the left wing of the division the battalion of the Panzer Fusilier Regiment also burst forward. In a bold, concerted action the main defensive line of General Krivoshein's mechanized corps was torn open. The crumbling remains of Sixth Guards Army, employed on Krivoshein's front, withdrew in a disorderly fashion, were caught by German artillery, and suffered extremely heavy losses. Krivoshein's brigade and the neighbouring VI Tank Corps were unable to halt the panic and the collapse. They fell back to Syrtsevo on the Pena—the last strongpoint in the last Soviet defences outside Oboyan. Would the river barrier with the fortified country around it halt the German advance on the western flank of the battle? General Krivoshein did not hold out any great hopes, especially as 11th Panzer Division had already fought its way across the Belgorod-Kursk highway and was seizing the patches of woodland to the east of this important road.

In a small dip immediately behind the battle-line General Krivoshein listened to the reports of the runners as they arrived: "The 3rd Company of Kunin's battalion has lost all its officers. Sergeant Nogayev is in command." Or "Headquarters of 30th Brigade has received a direct hit. Most officers killed. Brigade commander seriously wounded."

These were not isolated examples. On other sectors, such as that of 45th Motorized Battalion, things were worse still. Dead. Wounded. Taken prisoner. Overrun.

General Krivoshein tried to halt the German attack by an immediate powerful armoured counter-attack from the fortress of

Syrtsevo. That was on Thursday, 8th July, a scorching hot day. Forty T-34s burst out of the little town. But they ran right across the sights of Count Strachwitz's armoured group and the Tiger company. A fierce duel ensued. The Tigers knocked out ten T-34s.

When the bulk of the Soviet brigade fell back this was like a clarion call for the German troops. The regiments of "Grossdeutschland" moved in to follow up with parts of 3rd Panzer Division, and towards noon penetrated into the heavily fortified little town of Syrtsevo. The Soviets fell back across the river.

Meanwhile, the Armoured Reconnaissance Battalion of "Grossdeutschland", under Major Wätjen, had thrust farther to the north. Strong packs of tanks of the Soviet VI Tank Corps, with ten, twenty, or even forty steel monsters, were approaching from the north-east. Since the Reconnaissance Battalion could not get across the weak bridge quickly enough, division instead placed it in a semi-circle to cover its right flank in front of Verkhopenye. There, Wätjen awaited the enemy's armoured thrusts. Fortunately he had a battalion of assault guns with him.

Major Frantz, an experienced assault-gun commander, hurled himself with his battalion against the rapidly approaching Soviet tank packs. An engagement followed in which tactical skill out-manoeuvred superior numbers and fire-power. Frantz led his assault guns into favourable positions and lured the Soviets into cunningly baited traps.

The wireless operator and loading number in the battalion commander's assault gun was Corporal Eberhard, scarcely more than a boy. Today he is a professor. That was his first action. Twenty-four hours previously he had written in his diary: "We are established in a thick forest. Am reading Hölderlin." The language now was no longer one of poetry. "Hatch covers down!" It was semi-dark inside the gun. The corporal brought the radio code close to his eyes.

"Nail calling Nail 1, please come in."

"Nail 1 receiving, please come in."

And then Corporal Eberhard dictated: "4-18-7-21-4-18-3-9-1 . . ." His left foot was wedged between two armour-piercing nose shells and his right leg rested on some percussion fuses. As usual, the gun commander had loaded up with an extra seven or eight shells.

A change of position to another point on the reverse slope gave them a chance of pushing their heads up through the hatch for a moment and breathing some fresh air. Their eyes took in a gentle, grass-covered slope, a field of sunflowers, and a short stretch of road. But already a cloud of dust rose before them. The commander called out: "Close hatch cover! Inform battalion. Wedge formation of T-34s approaching. Point of attack in front of own position, west of highway."

Eberhard transmitted the message. And Major Frantz laid his traps. "Nail 1, please stand by. Nail 3, come in to speak to Nail."

Signals in rapid succession thus wove the net in which the Russian attack was to be caught. For the young corporal, of course, this was rather like watching an opera with the curtain down. It was his task to translate the major's short, rapid words and orders into numbers from one to twenty-six. And he almost laughed aloud at the ease with which he managed to discharge it. Like rattling off irregular verbs just before the exams, it flashed through his mind.

He called Nail 2 and Nail 3. He used figures to control them. He used figures to warn them. And from these strings of numbers in his earphones and the brief observations exchanged between gun commander, the NCO gun-aimer, and the driver he tried to piece together for himself the picture of the battle.

Together with the T-34s the Russians were also using a few American Mark IIIs. No. 2 Troop had already reported six tanks knocked out. The top scorers were the Section Senkbiel with four. But nothing showed up in front of the commander's gun. The war was more than a mile away. But quite suddenly it was close again. In the shape of T-34 giants.

A pack of T-34s and one Mark III were fast approaching the slope. Sergeant Scheffler had his eyes glued to the driver's visor. The gun-aimer was calmness personified. "Fire!"

Tank after tank was knocked out by the 7·5-cm cannon of the assault guns. The Soviet commanders attacked time and time again. Their wireless traffic showed that they had orders to break open the German line regardless of cost. Seven times the Russians attacked. Seven times they flung themselves obstinately into Major Frantz's traps.

After three hours, thirty-five wrecked tanks littered the battlefield, smouldering. Only five T-34s, all of them badly damaged, limped away from the smoking arena to seek shelter in a small wood.

Proudly the major signalled to division: "Thirty-five enemy tanks knocked out. No losses on our side."

The road to Verkhopenye on the Pena was clear.

Verkhopenye was strung out along several miles on both sides of the Pena river. It was heavily fortified because of the bridge.

General Hoernlein turned his division towards the west. During the evening grenadiers charged past the church under cover of the last Panthers. They seized the eastern part of the town. They reached the river.

On 9th July the western part of the small town with the bridge over the Pena also fell into German hands. The 6th Panzer Regiment and the motor-cyclist riflemen of 3rd Panzer Division drove the enemy from the locality. Duels between anti-tank guns and Mark IVs, between Panthers and T-34s, characterized the fighting.

The bridge over the Pena was damaged, but the 2nd Company and the bridge-building column of Engineer Battalion 39 repaired it during the night in record time, and by mid-morning on the following day built another 16-ton bridge. Now tracked vehicles were able to cross the river.

Now was the hour of decision.

On the morning of 10th July Colonel Schmidt-Ott thrust south from Hill 258·5 with his Neuruppin 6th Panzer Regiment. Simultaneously, Lieutenant-General Westhoven moved his grenadiers, motor-cyclist riflemen, artillery, assault guns, engineers, and anti-tank guns under Lieutenant-Colonel Wellmann over the bridge. The combat group struck at the enemy's rear and took the commanding heights of Berezovka.

After a long time columns of Soviet prisoners-of-war were again seen trudging towards the rear. In the sector of 3rd Panzer Division there were nearly 2000 of them.

East of the road to Oboyan, Count Schimmelmann's Panzer combat group of 11th Panzer Division was in action. Following Stuka intervention, Hill 260·8 was captured. Along the road itself, the Panzer Fusilier Regiment of "Grossdeutschland" probed forward and gained Hill 244·8, directly on the highway.

The highest point on the approaches to Oboyan had thereby been reached and, at the same time, the deepest penetration made into the Russian front. From the high ground one could see far into the valley of the Psel river, the last natural barrier this side of Kursk. With field-glasses the towers of Oboyan could be made out in the fine haze. Oboyan was the objective.

It seemed within arm's reach. Barely twelve miles away. No distance at all, under normal circumstances, for a fast formation. Would XLVIII Panzer Corps make this last leap?

According to Hoth's carefully worked out timetable the following should now have happened: XLVIII Panzer Corps to strike towards Oboyan and seize the crossings over the Psel. Its bulk to wheel eastward and—before thrusting on to Kursk—to defeat, jointly with Hausser's SS Panzer Corps, the enemy's strategic armoured forces approaching across the strip of land of Prokhorovka.

That was Hoth's plan.

In order to cover the eastern flank of his operation and to prevent any further Soviet tank armies reaching the battlefield from the east, from the Soviet Steppe Front, he had intended the Army Detachment Kempf to move into the strip of land east of Prokhorovka, where the Seym and Donets rivers had their sources, at the beginning of the operation.

But here was the error in Hoth's calculations. Where was Kempf? Where was III Panzer Corps, Breith's corps, which was to have reached the neck of land after crossing the Donets and swiftly wheeling north? Where were the experienced Panzer divisions—the Westphalian 6th, the Thuringian 7th, and the Lower Saxon 19th? Wherever they were, they were not where they should have been on 9th July in accordance with Hoth's timetable.

And why were they not in their positions? The war diaries of these experienced units under their outstanding commanders contain a dramatic answer to this crucial question. Stiff enemy resistance had held up the advance of the divisions. The Russians had dug narrow trenches, considerably deeper than a man's height, and against these the German artillery was unable to do much. The terrain, moreover, was infested with mines.

As soon as they had crossed the Donets south of Razumnoye, the regiments were involved in heavy fighting by Soviet armoured forces. The grenadiers of 7th Panzer Division heaved a sigh of relief when the 25th Panzer Regiment from Erlangen at last arrived. Heading the long columns of tanks was Lieutenant-Colonel Adalbert Schulz in his command tank.

Lieutenant-Colonel Adalbert Schulz, generally known as "Panzer-Schulz", spread confidence wherever he went. The grenadiers knew that wherever he was nothing went wrong. They now watched him prepare for action. Fan out. Batten down hatches. Advance in a broad wedge. And already the first tank guns were opening up.

Schulz had got right into a Soviet tank assembly position. The enemy commander clearly lacked combat experience. He led his unit nervously, losing the overall view. As darkness fell on the battlefield thirty-four T-34s, a curious play on numbers, were littering the ground around Razumnoye, in flames or smouldering.

But a strong enemy was well established and brilliantly camouflaged in the thick forests on the ridge of high ground. The division was caught in enfilading artillery fire. The Panzer Regiment was unable to help.

But the corps had to move on, move forward, unless the whole plan was to be upset. Manteuffel regrouped. On 8th July he succeeded by means of concentrated forces in breaking through the Russian barrier on the ridge of high ground behind the Donets.

General Breith immediately exploited this success. Since 6th Panzer Division was clearly encountering difficulties in crossing the Donets bridges at Belgorod to schedule, he did not hesitate long. "The main effort has got to be made wherever the front is moving forward," he said to Colonel Merk, his chief of staff. In consequence, he also moved 6th Panzer Division into the zone of attack of 7th Panzer Division.

The two divisions now burst forward towards the north-east. To their left, 19th Panzer Division was moving forward. Along the

Donets, 168th Infantry Division was punching its own way ahead; its task was to provide cover for the open flank of the Berlin Panzer Corps. Over a broad front the Panzer regiments cleared the way for the grenadiers. Panzer-Schulz on the right, Colonel von Oppeln-Bronikowski with his Paderborn 11th Panzer Regiment on the left. Between them was Count von Kageneck's Tiger Battalion 503. An armada of 240 tanks was sweeping towards the enemy positions.

But east of the Donets too the Russians were established in well-built defensive zones echeloned in depth. Anti-tank gun emplacements, minefields, anti-tank ditches were everywhere. Moreover, there were some tricky swamps.

Breith, an experienced and shrewd commander of armoured forces, realized that in the circumstances he would never be able to thrust sufficiently fast or sufficiently far to the east to keep to the timetable. He therefore made the only correct decision and on 8th July wheeled towards the north.

In a small ravine near Yastrebovo Breith met the commander of 6th Panzer Division. The two command tanks halted alongside.

The maps were spread out on the floors of these mobile armoured signals stations. The corps commander's hand brushed towards the top of the map: "Hünersdorff, you will make a thrust to the north and break through. You will cause the enemy's main defensive zone to collapse!"

And Walter von Hünersdorff, one of the boldest and most experienced tank commanders in the Wehrmacht, moved off. He toppled the Soviet defensive positions. He repulsed an attack by Soviet armoured forces near Melekhovo. Together with 19th Panzer Division he encircled two Soviet rifle divisions.

Forward! Without halting, 6th Panzer Division raced on to the upper Donets. Would it get to Prokhorovka in time?

The Soviet High Command realized the danger threatening from this massive thrust along the flank of the operation. Stalin ordered his strategic reserves from the distant Steppe Front to move towards Prokhorovka in forced marches. Would they arrive in time?

Lieutenant Podgorbunskiy jumped out of the way, saluted, and stared after the general in amazement.

No-one had ever seen the chief of staff in such a state. He was normally a calm, stolid person whom nothing could upset. But now he was running through the little ravine which housed the advanced headquarters of First Tank Army, panting, his face purple, and without his cap. He stormed up the slope towards a little wood. He disappeared in the thick undergrowth.

Up there was an artillery observation post. General Katukov and Nikita Sergeyevich Khrushchev had gone up there an hour previously.

But when Major-General Shalin burst into the command post through its camouflage of branches and foliage, there was only Khrushchev left. Katukov had gone on to the HQ of VI Tank Corps.

"What's up?" Nikita Sergeyevich asked suspiciously on seeing Shalin in a state of utter consternation.

The chief of staff, still trying to recover his breath, wordlessly handed him a piece of paper—a signal on a printed form. It came from General Cherniyenkov's XXXI Tank Corps.

Khrushchev read: "Defences penetrated. Troops in flight and not to be stopped. Usychov." Disaster! Disaster recorded in eleven words.

"Who is that?" Khrushchev asked, his finger excitedly tapping the signature.

"Lieutenant-Colonel Usychov is chief of signals of XXXI Tank Corps," Shalin replied.

"If his report is correct then nothing can stop the Germans from striking across the Psel at the rear of the First Tank Army," Khrushchev muttered. And what he thought, although he did not utter it, was this: If the Germans strike at the rear of First Tank Army, then the Russian defence must collapse along the southern front of Kursk. That would be the end of the battle of Kursk. That would mean victory for the Germans.

Khrushchev sent off General Popel, the War Council member for the First Tank Army. He was to seek out General Cherniyenkov. Khrushchev meanwhile ran down into the ravine to army headquarters with Shalin, to transmit strict and menacing orders to the corps and brigades of First Tank Army, against all retreat, against cowardice and defeatism.

He then alerted General Vatutin, the C-in-C of the Voronezh Front. Vatutin immediately promised to do something against the main danger, which came from Hausser's SS Panzer Corps. And he was as good as his word.

The Soviet II Guards Tank Corps had a combat group deployed near Gostishchevo, in that gap north-east of Belgorod into which General Kempf's divisions had not yet advanced. It had been placed there to stop Kempf's thrust. But now, at this moment of emergency, Vatutin moved it over to the west.

In a small wood east of the village sixty T-34s and several rifle battalions were assembled. About noon the armada moved off. It moved off against the deep flank of Hausser's unsuspecting corps, against the Belgorod-Oboyan highway, against the supply route of SS Panzer Corps.

Only one pair of German eyes spotted the approaching disaster. Captain Bruno Meyer was leading a formation of three tank-buster aircraft on a reconnaissance mission over the wooded region of Gostishchevo in the morning of 8th July. He knew that in this difficult terrain the flank of the SS Panzer Corps had to be guarded from the air unless the ground forces were to run into some unpleasant surprises.

Meyer's eyes swept over clearings and little valleys. Over there! Surely that is . . .

Meyer banked low, hard over the tree-tops. There was no longer any doubt: emerging from the cover of the wood were infantry columns. Behind them rumbled tanks. Ten of them. Twenty. Thirty. More and more of them were coming out of the wood, forming up into a broad wedge and moving off in a westerly direction.

From the conferences he had attended at VIII Air Corps HQ Captain Meyer was acquainted with the situation. He instantly realized the threat of this Soviet advance towards the deep flank of SS Panzer Corps. And Meyer also realized that this was his hour.

He commanded the IV (tank-buster) *Gruppe* of 9th Ground-Support *Geschwader* based near Mikoyanovka. On its fields stood 68 brand-new Henschel Hs-129 armoured ground-support aircraft. Each of these machines was fitted, in addition to its machine-gun, with a 3-cm cannon. They were the flying anti-tank guns of Operation Citadel.

Here now was an opportunity to test the new weapon. By radio Meyer alerted the ground control of his *Gruppe* and ordered take-off by separate *Staffels*—formations of nine machines.

As the first *Staffel* came zooming up, Meyer instructed the pilots by radiotelephony. Then began a historic battle—for the first time in military history a large armoured formation was opposed from the air alone.

The aircraft attacked from low level. Like hawks they pounced on the Russian tanks from behind and from the side. The cannon flashed and barked. Once, twice, three times. Direct hit. Explosion. Fire. In flames the stricken T-34s were careering over the battlefield.

In between the low-level attacks by the Henschel tank-buster aircraft, Major Druschel's Focke-Wulf ground-support *Gruppe* attacked the Russian infantry columns and the hastily positioned flak guns with high-fragmentation bombs.

It was a battle of machines. The Russian tanks were unable to cope with this unaccustomed attacker. They drove across each other's paths, got mixed up with one another, and fell an easy prey to Meyer's flying tank-busters.

After an hour the Soviet brigade was smashed. Fifty tanks littered the battlefield, burnt out or heavily damaged. The deadly threat to Hausser's deep flank was averted even before SS Panzer Corps and Fourth Panzer Army had become aware of it.

But Khrushchev too scored a victory—victory over the panic of XXXI Tank Corps. General Popel, whom he had hurriedly dispatched with two political commissars into the combat zone of Cherniyenkov's corps, very soon encountered Lieutenant-Colonel Konovalov's retreating tank brigade. Popel brought the units to a halt, turned them about and ordered them forward again.

As for the corps commander, Popel found him at an advanced HQ in the foremost line. He had already rallied several regiments.

Although the corps was still somewhat confused, and indeed yielding at many points, the panic was checked. The 29th Anti-Tank Gun Brigade covered the withdrawal and enabled provisional defensive positions to be established. The worst had been averted. But matters were bad enough: Hausser's armoured formations were vigorously pursuing the retreating Russians.

Captain Lex, commanding 3rd Company of "Der Führer" SS Panzer Grenadier Regiment, chased with his men through a gap in the front. Suddenly he found himself before the well-built headquarters of the utterly surprised staff of a Soviet rifle brigade and captured the lot of them—the general, his staff, and the headquarters company.

The "Totenkopf" Division, which had been tied down for several days on the right wing of the corps, resisting Soviet counter-attacks, was relieved by the hurriedly brought up formations of 167th Infantry Division.

The regiments of the Bavarian 167th Infantry Division under Lieutenant-General Trierenberg marched straight across the supply columns to the east and took up defensive positions along the Belgorod-Kursk railway line. On the important high ground north of Luchki I were the observers of six light and heavy troops of 238th Artillery Regiment, directing the concentrated fire of their guns against the Soviet infantry brigades which attacked again and again; on a very narrow frontage of barely 300 yards they were trying to force a breakthrough.

But 167th Infantry Division held out—largely owing to its artillery. Captain Wiede aimed the heavy and effective fire of his horse-drawn 10·5-cm howitzer troop accurately in front of the German trenches and right among the attacking Russians. The gun-aimers worked as if they were on a practice range. The artillery was in command.

Thanks to this defence, General Hausser was able to move his motorized battalions northwards across the Psel along the line of contact between "Leibstandarte" and "Das Reich". The crossing on this important sector was accomplished by Lieutenant-Colonel Kark Ullrich with 3rd Battalion, 6th SS Panzer Grenadier Regiment of "Totenkopf" Division, in the face of murderous Soviet artillery and mortar fire from the higher opposite bank. When the attack seemed to flounder in the heavy fire, Ullrich personally led his men forward and in the late hours of 10th July 1943 stormed the village of Krasnyy Oktyabr, formed a small bridgehead over the river, and held it against exceedingly strong attacks by Soviet infantry and armour.

As a result, "Totenkopf Division" gained a bridgehead over the river between Bogoroditskoye and Veselyy on 11th July. The very thing which the strict orders of the Soviet High Command had said must on no account be allowed to happen had now happened—the last natural obstacle before Kursk had been overcome.

Simultaneously, "Leibstandarte" and "Das Reich" pushed ahead towards Prokhorovka between the railway and the Psel.

General Katukov, the C-in-C of the reinforced Tank Army, was in a spot. Following the collapse of the Soviet Sixth Guards Army he was to have made a counter-attack with all available forces, but at the same time he was expected to bar the German advance towards Oboyan. And now, to top it all, he was being hard pressed himself.

He had no choice but to employ his strategic reserves, which were being supplied to First Tank Army for its intended counter-offensive, one by one, as they arrived.

The result was disastrous. On 11th July not only the Sixth Guards Army was knocked out, but First Tank Army was badly battered, and the hurriedly brought up Fifth Guards Army was frittered away piece-meal.

At Army HQ Lieutenant-General Nikita Khrushchev sat opposite Katukov like a policeman, ordering: "Hold out, hold out, hold out!"

Every hour he rang up Army Group with the impatient query: "When are the reserves of the Steppe Front arriving? Where are the armoured corps of Fifth Guards Tank Army?"

"They are on their way," General Vatutin assured him. And in fact, they were on their way. They were rapidly moving towards the neck of land and towards Prokhorovka.

The moment of decision for the whole of Operation Citadel was approaching inexorably.

On the northern front, on the battlefield of the German Ninth Army, Model on 11th July was similarly on the point of breaking through the last Soviet defences at Teploye. He therefore regrouped his forces, moved all his reserves into the operation area of XLVI Panzer Corps, and fixed 12th July as the date for the decisive breakthrough attack.

The commanders were waiting for H-hour. Between Teploye and the Kursk highway they were to break through with concentrated armoured forces and race ahead to meet Hoth's divisions approaching from the south.

The operation was well planned and accurately co-ordinated. Hoth, too, intended to force the decision on 12th July and to annihilate General Katukov's armoured forces on the neck of land of Prokhorovka before the Soviet Steppe Front Army Group could bring up fresh reserves and intervene in the battle.

Would the plan succeed?

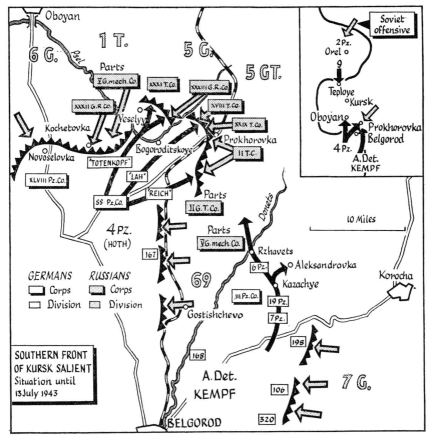

Map 6. The German and Soviet main forces, about equal in strength, clashed at Prokhorovka. The scales were to be tipped by General Kempf's flank attack.

The answer depended on III Panzer Corps of Army Detachment Kempf. It was fighting east of the Donets. Its task, defined by Manstein at the beginning of the operation, was: "To advance rapidly in the general direction of Korocha and attack and destroy the enemy forces expected from the east and north." In other words, Kempf's three Panzer divisions were to intercept the Soviet Fifth Guards Tank Army, prevent it linking up with Katukov's Army, and thereby keep Hoth's flank free.

That was tank strategy in the Manstein manner. Once again, as so often in military history, a fateful decision which was to determine the further course of a whole campaign depended on the clock, on a mere day or a mere hour. The "historic minute of Waterloo" was repeated at Prokhorovka.

In the battle of Waterloo, on 18th June 1815, Marshal Grouchy's flank attack, which was intended to prevent the link-up of the Prussian and the British Armies, would very probably have decided the battle in favour of Napoleon—if only Grouchy had arrived on the battlefield in time.

At Prokhorovka the strategic situation was much the same. In a battle in which roughly equal forces were clashing with each other, the planned flank attack by Kempf's 6th, 7th, and 19th Panzer Divisions, reinforced by brigades of assault guns and the Heavy Tank Battalion 503, was to have tipped the scales.

On 11th July Kempf's leading formations were on the banks of the northern Donets, twelve miles from the fateful locality of Prokhorovka. Difficult combat conditions in the unfavourable river terrain, as well as strong enemy resistance, had slowed down his timetable, but at last the situation seemed to be taking a turn for the better. Colonel Bäke's advanced detachment of 6th Panzer Division was getting ready to cross the upper Donets. The 7th and 19th Panzer Divisions were also coming up. This meant a total of more than 300 tanks and assault guns —a powerful force. If it was thrown in time into the scales of the impending armoured battle it was bound to ensure victory for Hoth.

The race began. In the evening of 11th July General Rotmistrov's Soviet Fifth Guards Army appeared on the neck of land with XVII and XXIX Tank Corps, as well as V Mechanized Guards Corps. Rotmistrov had 850 tanks at his disposal—nearly all of them T-34s—as well as heavy SUs, those self-propelled 12·2 and 15·2-cm guns used as assault guns.

For the moment Hoth only had about 600 tanks of Hausser's Panzer Corps to oppose the Soviet armour, although some of his companies were equipped with heavy Tiger tanks. Together with General Kempf's armoured forces he would have outnumbered the Soviets.

At the Voronezh Front headquarters, General Vatutin, Khrushchev, and their staff officers stood before their situation map. Each one of them knew that the decisive moment of the battle was approaching.

"We've got to strike at Hausser with the Fifth Guards Tank Army, regardless of the situation of our other armies," General Vatutin said. He was one of the most brilliant commanders among the Soviet top military leaders. He realized that time was on Hoth's side.

But there was also a different view held in the Military Council— Wait for First Tank Army and Fifth Guards Army to reform after their

Through mud and along corduroy roads: three miles per day · Field kitchens near Pervomaysk.
Overleaf left: Field-Marshal von Manstein in his command train. With him are Major Eismann, Colonel Busse, Major-General Schulz, and Lieutenant Specht · A Ferdinand tank on the battlefield near Ponyri.
Overleaf right: Tigers moving forward in the Belgorod area.

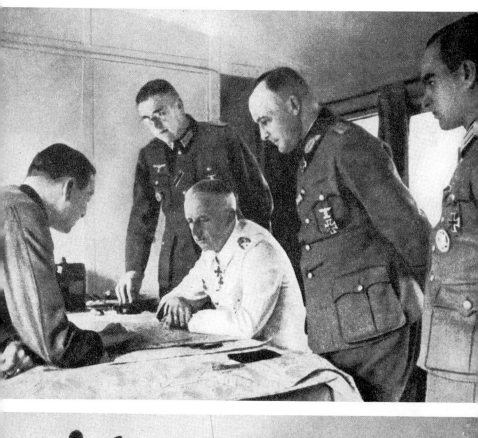

heavy losses of the past few days, and then send it into action together with Fifth Guards Army to counter-attack Hausser's strong forces.

But Vatutin's and Khrushchev's views prevailed. Their argument was as follows: If we wait any longer Kempf will be here. And to fight against Hausser and Kempf simultaneously, in other words both to the front and the rear, would be dangerous.

It was the situation of Waterloo. Then, at noon on 18th June 1815, the French regiments time and again charged the British positions at Belle Alliance. The sodden hillsides were covered with tens of thousands of dead. Both sides were exhausted. The armies were reeling with fatigue. Napoleon and Wellington were anxious. Both knew that victory would go to him who first received reinforcements—Wellington from Blücher, Napoleon from Grouchy. Again and again Napoleon nervously picked up his telescope, again and again he dispatched messengers. If his Marshal arrived in time, the sun of Austerlitz would once more shine over France; if he failed to come, all would be lost.

The situation of Waterloo was repeated at Prokhorovka. On the morning of 12th July 1943 Rotmistrov's tanks were moving in deep echelon against Hausser's Panzer regiments which were at the same time moving into the neck of land. Two huge armoured avalanches, shrouded in dust and smoke, were thundering towards each other in a confined space. There now began an open head-on tank battle such as military history had never seen before. Nor, for that matter, since.

Some 1500 tanks and assault guns were racing, firing, exploding, burning, thundering, and smoking on that minute sea of hills and valleys around Prokhorovka.

An impressive and vivid account of the first few hours of the battle was put on record by Lieutenant-General Rotmistrov. His is one of the best accounts of the battle in modern Soviet military history.

Rotmistrov had a view of the battlefield from a hill near Prokhorovka. "The tanks were moving across the steppe in small packs, under cover of patches of woodland and hedges. The bursts of gunfire merged into one continuous, mighty roar. The Soviet tanks thrust into the German advanced formations at full speed and penetrated the German tank screen. The T-34s were knocking out Tigers at extremely close range, since their powerful guns and massive armour no longer gave them an advantage in close combat. The tanks of both sides were in closest possible contact. There was neither time nor room to disengage from the enemy and reform in battle order, or operate in formation. The shells fired at extremely close range pierced not

Nebelwerfers
The projectiles in their launching frame.
Crew running for cover.
The electrically detonated projectiles scream through the air.

only the side armour but also the frontal armour of the fighting vehicles. At such range there was no protection in armour, and the length of the gun barrels was no longer decisive. Frequently, when a tank was hit, its ammunition and fuel blew up, and torn-off turrets were flung through the air over dozens of yards. At the same time over the battlefield furious aerial combats developed. Soviet as well as German airmen tried to help their ground forces to win the battle. The bombers, ground-support aircraft, and fighters seemed to be permanently suspended in the sky over Prokhorovka. One aerial combat followed another. Soon the whole sky was shrouded by the thick smoke of the burning wrecks. On the black, scorched earth the gutted tanks burnt like torches. It was difficult to establish which side was attacking and which defending. The 2nd Battalion 181st Tank Brigade of XVIII Tank Corps, attacking on the left bank of the Psel, encountered a group of Tigers which opened fire on the Soviet armoured fighting vehicles from a stationary position. The powerful long-range guns of the Tigers are exceedingly dangerous, and the Soviet tanks had to try to close with them as quickly as possible to eliminate this advantage of the enemy. Captain P. A. Skripkin, the battalion commander, ordered: 'Forward, follow me!' The first shell of the commander's tank pierced the side of a Tiger. Instantly another Tiger opened fire on Skripkin's T-34. A shell crashed through its side and a second wounded the battalion commander. The driver and wireless operator pulled their commander from the tank and took him to the cover of a shell crater. As a Tiger was making straight for them, Aleksandr Nikolayev, the driver, leapt back into his damaged and already smouldering tank, started the engine and raced up to meet the enemy tank. Like a flaming ball of fire the T-34 raced over the ground. The Tiger halted. But it was too late. The blazing tank rammed the German Panzer at full speed. The detonation made the ground shake."

On the afternoon of 12th July Rotmistrov's opponent, Colonel-General Hoth, was also well forward on the battlefield. From the headquarters of the "Der Führer" Regiment he watched the fighting. Through a trench telescope he surveyed the battle area which was littered with smouldering wrecks.

Hausser's regiments had been forced on to the defensive, but they held their ground. Time and again Soviet armoured brigades broke into the German main defensive line. But each time they were thrown back, even though the grenadiers were beginning to despair under the ceaseless onslaught of masses of enemy armour.

Heavy fighting developed on the right flank of "Das Reich" Division. There the Soviet II Guards Tank Corps attacked repeatedly from the gap between Hausser's Corps and Breith's divisions which had not yet arrived. That accursed gap!

"The Russian attacks on our flank are tying down half of our effectives and are taking the steam out of our operation against the enemy at Prokhorovka," growled the regimental commander, Sylvester Stadler. Hoth nodded. He asked for a line to Army Headquarters. Major-General Fangohr, chief of staff of Fourth Panzer Army, answered. "Fangohr, have you any news of Kempf? Where is his III Panzer Corps?"

Fangohr had very accurate news because only a minute previously he had been through to Army Group and learnt from Generel Busse, Manstein's chief of staff, that the spearheads of III Panzer Corps were at Rzhavets on the northern Donets.

This was good news. But Fangohr also had some bad news. He had learned from Busse that Model had not mounted his planned breakthrough attack on the northern front of Kursk.

Why not? Because the Soviets were attacking in the rear of Ninth Army, in the Orel salient, and had almost at once achieved a deep penetration at Second Panzer Army.

Orel was threatened, the supply base of the whole of Army Group Centre was in danger, the rear of Ninth Army was in grave peril. Model had to pull some of his forces out of the front in order to switch them against the attacking Russians.

Hoth listened to the news in silence, thanked Busse, and replaced the receiver.

Everything seemed doubly urgent now. It was now vital to force a decision here, on the southern front of the salient. Could he still succeed? He must.

Breith could be relied upon. He was one of the most experienced and most successful tank commanders in the army. Besides, Manstein still had General Nehring's XXIV Panzer Corps in reserve, with two outstanding divisions, the well-tried 17th Panzer Division and the 5th (Viking) SS Panzer Grenadier Division.

The crucial point, however, was that General Breith's III Panzer Corps must get across the Donets.

Rzhavets was 12 miles away from the main battlefield. The roar of the guns of Prokhorovka could be heard from there. The commanders and chiefs of staff of the reinforced 11th Panzer Regiment were sitting beside the command tank of their combat-group leader.

Colonel von Oppeln-Bronikowski was listening to a suggestion by Major Dr Franz Bäke. Kazachye, eight miles short of the river and the objective of the day's attack, had been reached after a daring raid and much hard fighting. Bäke now suggested that the strongly fortified town of Rzhavets should be taken by a surprise coup during the night of 11th/12th July, the Donets crossed, and a bridgehead established.

Oppeln had misgivings. Divisional orders were that the crossing was to be forced on the following day, after artillery bombardment.

Bäke objected that the Russians were there in strength and that a daytime attack was bound to be very costly. A coup under cover of darkness might be easier. Might! But there was no certainty. However, Oppeln was an experienced tank commander and accepted Bäke's reasoning. He agreed. Bäke organized the coup in the traditional manner. With his 2nd Battalion, 11th Panzer Regiment, and the 2nd (armoured infantry carrier) Battalion, 114th Panzer Grenadier Regiment, under Lieutenant Roembke, the small force pushed on towards the river after nightfall. A captured T-34 was placed at the head of the column, to deceive the enemy. True, the German cross had been painted on it—but not very large. And at night all cats were grey. What mattered was the silhouette.

Radio silence. No fire to be opened. No talking. But smoking permitted. In fact, the men were encouraged to ride on top of the tanks, relaxed and smoking, as if this was a normal movement by a unit. "But not a single word in German," the company commanders had impressed on their men.

The ghost column moved on. It was led by Bäke in person, then came a troop of tanks and a few armoured infantry carriers with grenadiers and engineers, then the command tanks. There was only the rumble of the engines and the clank of the chains. Enemy columns passed shoulder to shoulder. The silhouette of the T-34 at the head of the German unit deceived the Russians.

They moved past manned and well-established emplacements of anti-tank guns and multiple mortars. The moon shed a dim light. The Russians did not budge. Sleepily they were leaning in their positions along the road. They were used to such columns. All day long Soviet formations had been rumbling past them. Bäke overtook an enemy infantry column. Fortunately no Soviet soldier thought of hitching a ride on the tanks.

"After about six miles," Dr Bäke records, "our T-34 went on strike. Moved no doubt by national sentiments, it stopped and blocked the road. So our men had to climb out of their tanks and in spite of the Russians standing all round them, watching curiously, they had to haul the T-34 off the road and push it into the ditch in order to clear the way for the rest of the formation. In spite of the order that not a word of German was to be spoken, a few German curses were heard. Never before had I winced so much under a curse as at Rzhavets. But the Russians still did not notice anything. The crew of our T-34 was picked up, and on we moved."

The first houses of Rzhavets appeared in front of them. And the first Soviet tanks. They were T-34s lined up along the road. Their hatches stood open. The crews were lying in the grass. But worse was to come: Lieutenant Huchtmann, riding in the lead tank, excitedly reported by radio telephone: "Russian tanks coming up to meet us. What am I to do?" Bäke replied: "Take a deep breath so I can hear it in my earphones, and start counting them."

Huchtmann counted into his microphone: "One—two—three—four five . . . ten . . . fifteen . . . twenty—twenty-one—twenty-two."

Twenty-two enemy tanks. They moved past the German column, within arm's reach.

Everybody heaved a sigh of relief. But suddenly the Soviet column showed signs of uneasiness. Half a dozen T-34s wheeled out of line and drove back. Had they noticed anything?

Bäke ordered his combat group to move on, in the direction of Rzhavets, and in his command tank III, which carried only a wooden dummy gun, he halted across the road. Seven T-34s moved up, and placed themselves around Bäke's tank in a semi-circle at roughly twenty yards' distance. They levelled their guns. But evidently they were not quite sure what to do. They were foxed by the darkness. Things were looking bad for Bäke. A wooden gun was not much use. But something had to be done to prevent the whole enterprise from being jeopardized at the last moment. It was too late to bring back the combat group. Bäke therefore decided upon a piece of bravado. With his orderly officer, Lieutenant Zumpel, he jumped out of his command tank. Each of them carried an explosive charge, a "sticky bomb", in each hand. They dashed past the armoured infantry carrier of Sergeant-Cadet Dehen who was all set, waiting for permission to open fire.

Five leaps. Demolition charge attached to the first enemy tank. A few Soviet infantrymen were sitting on top of it and turned their heads in alarm. One of them raised his rifle, but Bäke snatched it from his hands. He leapt into the ditch for cover. He found himself chest-deep in water. There were two dull explosions. Lieutenant Zumpel, for his part, had attached his demolition charge to the other tank.

Up again. The next two. Back under cover. But this time there was only one bang. The other charge did not go off.

One of the T-34s menacingly traversed its cannon.

Bäke jumped up on one of his own tanks, which was coming up, ducked behind the turret, and yelled: "Open fire!"

The German gun-aimer was quicker than his Russian opponent. One shot and the Soviet tank was knocked out.

But now hell was let loose. The ghost journey was over. The Russians fired flares. Machine-gun fire rattled wildly from all sides.

Bäke's tanks and armoured infantry carriers raced into the village. Anti-tank gun positions were overrun. Engineers captured a troop of multiple mortars.

From the direction of the river came several dull thuds. "The bridge!" Bäke thought in alarm.

A moment later his tank stood at the bridge over the Donets. The bridge had been blown up. The combat group had missed the turn in the village which led to it. However, engineers and grenadiers managed to reach the far bank by a footbridge. And the surprise among the Russians was such that the Germans succeeded in forming a bridgehead. At daybreak Bäke's vanguard detachment of 6th Panzer Division was firmly established on the northern bank of the Donets. General von Hünersdorff immediately sent across the 1st Battalion, 114th Panzer Grenadier Regiment, under Captain Oekel. By late afternoon on 12th July the Combat Group Horst of 19th Panzer Division had also been brought up. The Panzer Divisions of Breith's corps were able to move across the speedily repaired bridge and extend the narrow bridgehead. Parts of the overrun Soviet formations, which were trying to fall back to the north, were intercepted.

The Russians were so surprised to find German troops at Rzhavets that they made no attempt to resist at all. When a motor-cycle dispatch rider named Gerdsmann of 1st Battalion, 114th Panzer Grenadier Regiment, encountered a horse-drawn Russian gun and raised his carbine the entire gun crew put up their hands, flabbergasted.

However, 6th Panzer Division suffered one blow of misfortune in this bold coup. And this blow, tragically, was struck not by the enemy but by the Luftwaffe. One *Staffel* of He-111s, which had not yet been informed of the successful nocturnal operation, believed the formation on the northern bank of the Donets to be an enemy unit, and attacked. General von Hünersdorff was just holding a conference with his unit commanders alongside his command tank. Several bombs dropped in the immediate vicinity and wounded 14 officers and a considerable number of other ranks. Hünersdorff himself was wounded, but he stayed with his division. Major Bieberstein, commanding 114th Panzer Grenadier Regiment, and Captain Oekel died of their wounds.

That was a bad price to pay for the opening of the door to Prokhorovka. Yet provided the further advance now was rapid, it might well be the price of victory.

But Bäke was unable to exploit his advantage. While he carried out his coup against Rzhavets, the bulk of 6th Panzer Division had been attacking the important high ground of Aleksandrovka, six miles farther east. However, the Soviets vigorously defended this key point of their Donets positions in the flank of the German advance. The battalions of the reinforced 4th Panzer Grenadier Regiment were pinned down by heavy enemy fire outside Aleksandrovka.

Hünersdorff did not hesitate a moment. With Major Bäke's tanks he raced back to the southern bank of the Donets. With half a dozen Panthers he thrust past the stubbornly defended village, took the commanding heights, and thus opened the path into the village itself for the grenadiers.

The enemy defence zone between Donets and Korocha was in consequence pierced on 13th July. The 6th Panzer Division was free to thrust northwards. The tanks of 7th and 19th Panzer Divisions poured through the bridgehead of Rzhavets towards the battlefield of Prokhorovka.

But Hünersdorff was no longer with them. Driving back from Bäke's detachment to his advanced divisional HQ on 14th July he was hit by the bullet of a concealed enemy sniper. The bullet struck his head and splinters of his steel helmet damaged his brain. The unconscious general was flown by a Fieseler Storch aircraft to Kharkov, where Colonel Dr Tönjes, a brain-surgeon who had been specially flown in, operated on him. Three days later, however, Walter von Hünersdorff, aged 45, died of his severe wounds at the army hospital. A nurse watched by his bedside day and night, right to the end—Frau von Hünersdorff, who was in charge of a forward forces convalescent centre of the German Red Cross.

The dashing young tank general, who barely six months previously, in the attempt to relieve Stalingrad, had brought the spearhead of Hoth's Army to within thirty miles of the outposts of Sixth Army, was dead. He died at the moment when the great battle had reached its climax and victory seemed within an arm's reach.

4. The Battle is called off

*Allied landing in Sicily–Soviet breakthrough at Orel–
"I need divisions, Herr Feldmarschall"–Operation Citadel cut in half–Victory given away–The turning-point
of the war.*

WITH lightning speed the overall situation changed. A long way from Prokhorovka decisions were being made which were to wipe out all the successes scored in the Kursk salient. The two most important men of the German Armies in the East, Field-Marshals von Manstein and von Kluge, received top priority calls from the Führer's Headquarters on 13th July, summoning them to the Wolfsschanze in East Prussia.

The Marshals boarded their aircraft and flew over the interminable

Ukrainian and Belorussian fields towards Rastenburg in East Prussia. Once again the small wood there became the setting of a fateful decision.

Hitler received his Marshals in a mood of impatient anger. The "courtiers" of Hitler's Spartan High Command were all running around with long faces. The boss was in a thundery mood.

What a change from twelve days earlier, when Hitler had issued his order for Operation Citadel. The optimism had evaporated. The grand words had died away. The hopes of a tempestuous victory for German arms had vanished.

The spectre that was haunting the huts in the shade of the beeches, the subject which Hitler raised without any preamble, was Italy.

Hitler informed Manstein and Kluge of what, in broad outline, they were already aware. On 10th July 1943, British, American, and Canadian troops had landed in Sicily from North Africa. Italian resistance on the island had rapidly collapsed. The 300,000 men, with the exception of a few units, had simply run away. The Allies were advancing along the coastal roads. The only resistance they were encountering was from German paratroops, Panzer Grenadiers, and anti-tank combat groups.

Hitler did not mince words when speaking of his Italian allies. He was not only angry, but anxious to the point of panic about the future development of the situation in southern Europe.

"Considering the lousy way the Italians are waging the war, the loss of Sicily is as good as certain. For all I know, Eisenhower may land on the Italian mainland or in the Balkans tomorrow. This would be a direct threat to our whole southern flank in Europe. That's what I've got to prevent. And that's why I need divisions for Italy and the Balkans. Now that I've moved 1st Panzer Division from France to the Peloponnese I've nowhere else to draw on, and that's why they have to be pulled out of the Kursk front. I'm therefore obliged to suspend Citadel."

Hitler stopped.

The two Marshals were dumbfounded. Once again they saw Hitler rattled by a crisis, panicking and rushing into decisions. Unexpected or unpleasant events always knocked him off balance. He would then lose his nerve and judge the situation in a totally unrealistic light. This was precisely what was happening again. Although as a rule he underrated the Allies, he now suddenly credited them with reckless plans and dare-devil operations.

In point of fact, as the next few weeks were to show, it was nearly two more months before Eisenhower mounted his attack on the Italian mainland.

But even if he had intended to land in central Italy or in the Balkans immediately after his invasion of Sicily, the German divisions engaged in the battle of Kursk, over 2000 miles away, would have been the last to prevent that kind of development. Pulling them out of Russia would take many weeks. They would arrive in Italy too late, while at Kursk the victory, now within reach, would have been thrown away.

But Hitler seemed mesmerized by the landing in Sicily. He talked fast and loud. It was obvious what irked and annoyed him—the knowledge that it was his fault, his fault entirely, that this confounded situation had arisen.

The Wehrmacht operations staff, who were in charge of operations in all theatres of war except the Eastern Front, had warned Hitler as early as May, and repeatedly since, of the approaching danger in the Mediterranean. Field-Marshal von Manstein and General Zeitzler had urged him not to put off Operation Citadel too long. Guderian had been against it altogether. Model had objected repeatedly. Kluge had voiced his misgivings.

But Hitler had hesitated, wavered, and vacillated. Should he withdraw forces from the Eastern Front and send them to Italy and thus call off Citadel altogether? Should he withdraw mobile formations from France and transfer them to Italy?

In the end Hitler, as usual, wanted the lot: he wanted to fight Citadel and, immediately after winning it, transfer the forces thus released into the countries threatened with invasion—France, Italy, and the Balkans.

That was how the vicious circle had started, that gamble with time. Week by week the Russians were getting stronger in the Kursk salient, and their defences more powerful.

Hitler was therefore compelled also to strengthen the German offensive forces. That in turn took time. Thus, one after another, dates of attack had been fixed and then cancelled. Finally, Hitler expected the new heavy tanks and super-heavy assault guns to ensure German superiority, but these, especially the Panther and the Ferdinand, were still at the testing stage. He ordered the armaments industry to complete them at top speed.

But the manufacture and transport of these giants again took much precious time. And thus the weeks had passed.

Guderian, the Inspector-General of Armoured Forces, was one of those who realized the danger of this bedevilled timetable. He implored Hitler on 4th May to give up Citadel. In a conversation in Munich he said quite clearly, in front of a great many witnesses, that he did not share the excessive hopes placed in the new tanks: "I don't regard the new Panther or the Ferdinand as ripe for active service. They are still suffering from numerous teething troubles, as is perfectly natural with such new types—and we can't possibly clear these up in five or six weeks."

Even Speer, the Armaments Minister, had agreed with him.

That Munich meeting was also the occasion for the grim scene which today seems almost like an extract from an ancient novel and which is described by the only surviving witness, Lieutenant-General (Retired) Wolfgang Thomale, as follows: Guderian and Kluge met again at this Munich conference for the first time since Kluge got Hitler to dismiss Guderian in the winter of 1941. The Field-Marshal wanted a reconciliation and extended his hand to Guderian. But Guderian demonstratively ignored the gesture. Kluge turned purple and addressed Guderian's chief of staff, the then Colonel Thomale, as follows: "Kindly inform Colonel-General Guderian that I request him to follow me to the next room."

There he angrily asked Guderian: "What cause have you for such offensive behaviour?" Guderian too was flushed with anger and controlled himself with difficulty: "Herr Generalfeldmarschall, that's easily answered. Two years ago you made a false report about me to the Führer. You've lost me my Army and ruined my health. I believe that's cause enough. You can hardly expect sympathy from me."

Kluge turned on his heel and left the room without salutation.

A few days later Hitler's Chief ADC, General Schmundt, brought Guderian a written challenge from Kluge to a duel with pistols. Of all people, the Field-Marshal had picked on Hitler as his second. But as Hitler on principle was against duelling he passed on Kluge's challenge to Guderian by way of Schmundt, while at the same time forbidding the duel and ordering Schmundt to inform the protagonists accordingly.

As a result, the history of the Second World War was deprived of the spectacle of an affair of honour between two senior generals, both of them outstanding commanders in the field though very different in character.

Six days after that Munich conference in May Guderian once more tried, this time in Berlin, to persuade Hitler to give up Citadel. The Inspector-General implored him: "My Führer, why do you want to be the attacker on the Eastern Front? Why not let the Russians attack and beat them when they've played their trump card?"

"Beat them when they have played their trump card"—that was Manstein's recipe, the recipe which the Field-Marshal had been advocating ever since the disaster of Stalingrad had dashed all hopes of a speedy victory over the Soviets.

To beat the enemy after he had played his trump card meant not to commit oneself to costly offensive operations, but to let the enemy make all the running and deal him crushing counter-blows at every favourable opportunity. It was a strategy of attrition. And Manstein hoped that, provided it was applied over the entire Eastern Front, the Russian forces would bleed themselves white and Stalin would—perhaps—be ready for peace negotiations some day.

It was one of the great dramatic moments of the war when, on 10th May 1943, Guderian seized Hitler's hand and asked him: "My Führer, why do you want to run the risk of attacking?"

Hitler regarded Guderian and said: "You may be right. The thought of attacking makes me go hot and cold too." Nevertheless, he subsequently ordered Citadel to be launched.

Now, on 13th July, he was again facing his Marshals. History has proved him wrong and his Colonel-Generals and Field-Marshals right. However, he once again took a wrong line. This time he offended against that fundamental principle of warfare formulated by Clausewitz: Once you have taken a decision you should not let any danger or any temptation deflect you from the objective decided upon, but you must remain true to the basic outline of the plan of operations.

Manstein was shocked to find Hitler, just because of the Allied landing in Sicily, prepared to call off Operation Citadel altogether—at a moment when, in his opinion, victory was near. But was victory really still possible in the Kursk salient? It was Kluge who cooled Manstein's ardour. He reported about the situation on Model's northern front. Instead of launching a breakthrough at Teploye on 12th July, the Colonel-General had been compelled to suspend his attacks and to withdraw his mobile formations from the front. Why? Because in Model's rear, on the northern front of the Orel salient, the Russians had made a deep penetration on the sector of Second Panzer Army on that very 12th July, and were now threatening Orel.

Kluge therefore concluded that Model's Ninth Army would not be able to resume the offensive. Not even later. The loss of 20,000 men and the withdrawal of the mobile troops in order to seal off the deep Soviet penetrations north of Orel had, in his opinion, made the suspension of Citadel as a whole inevitable.

Manstein disagreed: "Victory on the southern front of the Kursk salient is within reach. The enemy has thrown in nearly his entire strategic reserves and is badly mauled. Breaking off action now would be throwing away victory!"

That Manstein's assessment of the situation on the southern front of Kursk was correct is clear today from the memoirs of Lieutenant-General Rotmistrov, now Marshal of Armoured Troops, who was then C-in-C of the Soviet Fifth Guards Tank Army. He confirms that the position of the Soviet troops on the upper Donets had "become exceedingly difficult" owing to the approach of Breith's Panzer divisions.

Manstein's proposal therefore made sense: Model's Army should keep strong forces on the northern front in order to tie down the enemy; Hoth and Kempf, on the other hand, were to continue operations and annihilate the enemy forces south of Kursk. In a manner of speaking, half of Operation Citadel would be fought.

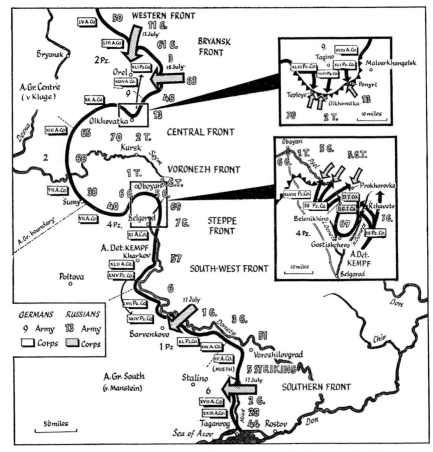

Map 7. Just as a decisive German breakthrough towards Oboyan and Olkhovatka was beginning to take shape, the Soviets went over to the offensive north and south of the Kursk salient. Model's Ninth Army was compelled to pull out strong forces from the Citadel front in order to switch them against the Russian penetration at Orel. Hoth's Fourth Panzer Army was similarly forced to dispatch some of its divisions to stave off the Russian threat on the Donets and Mius. The promising operation in the Kursk salient had to be called off.

But Kluge also rejected this idea. He saw no possibility of leaving Ninth Army in its area of operations and he therefore considered it indispensable to break off the battle and withdraw all formations to their jumping-off positions.

Hitler agreed with him. However, he allowed Manstein to continue the battle on the southern front with his own forces. But that glimmer of hope was to be short-lived.

Hoth resumed his offensive. In co-operation with Army Detachment Kempf he struck a number of successful blows in pouring rain.

Before long the Soviet Sixty-Ninth Army, together with two Soviet tank corps, was trapped in a pocket between Rzhavets, Belenikhino, and Gostishchevo.

But then the whistle sounded also on the southern front. On 17th July Hitler ordered the immediate withdrawal of SS Panzer Corps from the front because he intended to transfer it to Italy. (In fact, the bulk of it was to remain on the Eastern Front for several more months.)

He also ordered that, in view of the critical situation at Orel, two more Panzer divisions were to be transferred to Army Group Centre.

This order meant the end of Manstein's operations at Kursk. With the forces left to him he could not hope to hold the line he had gained. At the beginning of August he had to withdraw to his original jumping-off positions. This withdrawal was accompanied by heavy losses, chiefly of weapons and material. The Soviet armies, until recently hard-pressed, were given a breathing space. They pushed vigorously behind the retreating German divisions. The threatening Russian defeat turned into a victory for the Red Army.

True, Manstein had taken 34,000 prisoners and the Soviets had lost a total of 85,000 men on the southern front of the Kursk salient alone. That was as much as the German Sixth Army had lost at Stalingrad six months earlier, in terms of real losses in battle. But the Russians quickly regained the territory they had yielded.

The last great German offensive in Russia was at an end; it was lost. Worse still, the army reserves built up over many months by laborious and self-denying work, in particular the fast divisions, had melted away in the fiery furnace of Kursk without reaching their appointed objective. The German offensive strength had been broken for a long time to come. From this moment onward the formation of strategic reserves was no longer possible.

Just as Waterloo sealed the fate of Napoleon in 1815, putting an end to his rule and changing the face of Europe, so the Russian victory at Kursk heralded a turning-point in the war and led directly, two years later, to the fall of Hitler and the defeat of Germany, and thus changed the shape of the entire world.

Seen in this light, Operation Citadel was the decisive battle of the Second World War. The official Soviet history of the war is right to call it "The battle of world historic significance".

Yet strangely enough, Citadel, the battle of Kursk, has never gained its proper place in the German mind. If one asks about Stalingrad and then about Kursk the difference is quite striking. Yet it was not Stalingrad but Kursk which was, in every respect, the fateful and decisive battle of the war in the East.

The Soviet Army had survived the disasters of 1941–42; it had overcome the crisis, seized the initiative, and now dictated the order of events. For the first time we find in official Soviet accounts the self-assured statement: "In the operations at Kursk the Soviet troops exceeded those of the enemy in men and material by a factor of two to three."

There was no doubt that the face of the Red Army had fundamentally changed. Its armoured forces had been reorganized and were now able to rely on an enormous output of armour—an output higher than that of the German industry. The battle of Kursk, moreover, saw the emergence of the Soviet SU assault guns, a new type of heavy artillery on self-propelled carriages.

Above all, strategic and tactical handling, especially of mobile formations, had improved out of all recognition. This was shown not only by flexible control in battle but also by the speed with which reserves were switched to the critical points.

Here, of course, the Russians benefited from extensive equipment with American standard army trucks. From the summer of 1942 onwards the U.S.A. supplied to the Soviet Union 434,000 of these heavy vehicles. In this way the U.S.A. had a considerable share in Stalin's victory at Kursk.

But all this material superiority would have been useless had the Soviet Army not also been inspired by a new fighting morale. The slogan of the Fatherland War carried more conviction among the Russian troops than the earlier, outworn slogan of defending world revolution.

However, the German High Command failed to read the signs correctly. The extent to which it clung to its mistaken picture of the Red Army man was shown by its misjudgment and defamation of the political commissar in the Soviet Army. Though the role of the commissar may have been somewhat dubious at the beginning of the war, since the battle of Kursk he revealed himself increasingly as a person respected by the fighting men and their commanders in the field as an ally against short-sighted superiors, stupid bureaucrats, and the danger of cowardly defeatism.

In Germany, the commissars were invariably viewed as whippers-in and brutal fanatics. The disastrous order of the German High Command of 6th June 1941, that captured commissars were not to be treated as servicemen but were to be shot, was one result of this serious mistake. True, most German Army commanders and corps commanders did not comply with the order and even asked for it to be revoked, but even so its consequences were bad enough.

In actual fact the commissars were politically active and reliable men whose general standard of education was above that of the average Soviet officer. To gain a correct understanding of their role one must look at the history of the institution of the political commissar in the Red Army. To a large extent the Soviet officers' corps originally consisted of former Tsarist officers who were, in the eyes of the Bolshevik regime, politically unreliable. There were also the proletarian officers of the Civil War, men without a proper military training and frequently without general education. In this situation the introduction of the commissar was a logical step: in addition to political guidance he was charged with those tasks which in Western armies are the concern of the unit commander—the political instruction of the troops, their education, their intellectual needs, and their welfare. During the first few years following the Revolution the political commissars in many cases had to teach the men to read and write. It is easy to understand that over the years clashes of competence were bound to arise with the officers' corps. The history of the Red Army and that of the last war reveal this clearly.

The commissar presently became the object of extensive further care and further training. In addition to his political education he was put through a very intensive course of military instruction. He had to be in a position to discharge purely military tasks himself; indeed, in the event of the unit commander dropping out he had to be able to step into his shoes—the company Politruk as company commander, and the Military Council member at divisional headquarters as divisional commander. To meet this range of tasks the corps of political commissars naturally had to consist of hard men devoted to the regime, and during the first half of the war these men as a rule formed the mainspring of Soviet resistance and mercilessly saw to it that the troops kept up the fight with all means possible. They may have been merciless, but in most instances they were equally merciless towards themselves.

5. Betrayal at the Führer's Headquarters

No secret is safe at the High Command–Message from "Werther" to "Director"–Rudolf Rössler's signal to Moscow–Red spy centre in Switzerland–Who was "Werther"?

BUT let us return to the battle of Kursk. The thesis is often expounded nowadays that Kursk was a logical, an inescapable Russian victory. But this is a view based on ideology or propaganda.

There is no such thing as a logical victory, or a calculable one, or a just one, or an inescapable one.

The official Soviet *History of the Great Fatherland War* itself furnishes ample evidence. In Volume III we find an exceedingly interesting report which the High Command of the Voronezh Front, in other words Khrushchev and Vatutin, made to Supreme Headquarters after the battle. On 7th July, the report says, success had hung by a thread. It had depended on one single decision—on whether Hoth's divisions would or would not succeed in breaking through to Oboyan. The front of Sixth Guards Army was torn open. All that stood behind it were parts of two Soviet armoured corps. Should they be ordered to make a hopeless counter-attack or should they be kept back for defence? That, according to the report, was the crucial question. What was the right course at this moment of crisis? It was at this point that the mortal enmity between Khrushchev and Marshal Zhukov began.

In order to halt the German armoured thrust, General Vatutin, in agreement with Khrushchev, ordered the remainder of First Tank Army to dig in with their tanks and thus form a wall of anti-tank gunnery.

Marshal Zhukov, on the other hand, who represented Stalin on the southern sector of the Soviet Front, violently objected to this "unnatural use of tanks". He demanded that they should be employed for a counter-attack. When Khrushchev and Vatutin stood their ground, Zhukov got on to Stalin and won him over to his own view. From Soviet Supreme Headquarters therefore came the order: Counter-attack!

The *History of the Great Fatherland War* observes in this connection: "Without being acquainted with the concrete situation, Stalin decided in favour of Marshal Zhukov's view that it was impossible to halt the German armoured attacks from a static position."

But Khrushchev and Vatutin did not give up. They mobilized Marshal Vasilevskiy, and jointly with him they succeeded in getting Stalin to amend his order. The armoured corps of First Tank Army were not employed for a counter-attack but dug their tanks in and formed an armoured wall of fire and steel.

From a military point of view, needless to say, Zhukov was quite right. Tanks are not for digging-in. But in this particular case the solid barrier of tanks and anti-tank guns did in fact stop the German thrust.

The *History of the Great Fatherland War* quotes the report of the Voronezh Front High Command complete with reference number and detailed source, thereby putting it firmly on record for posterity. This report says: "If it had been decided to mount a counter-attack with the armoured formations, we would have quickly spent our strength since there was no coherent front of rifle formations left along the road. The enemy would certainly have broken through to Oboyan and would have begun to extend his success in the direction of Kursk."

"Certainly have broken through to Oboyan"—that would have meant victory for Hoth.

From the German point of view, the battle of Kursk might very easily have taken a different turn. Manstein, for instance, in a conversation with his Army and unit commanders in Kharkov four weeks before the offensive, discussed the question of whether, in view of the known Russian preparations to meet the German north-south attacks, it might not be a better idea to drop this old-style pincer attack and instead strike at the Kursk salient at its weakest point—*i.e.*, frontally— and, having made a penetration, then fan out right and left.

Manstein's senior commanders were enthusiastic about the idea. But evidently it was turned down by the General Staff of Land Forces. Hitler himself, who ever since the campaign in France had a great respect for Manstein's strategic skill, seems to have favoured the idea. This is borne out by the angry remark he made to General Schmundt after the battle: "That's the last time I listen to the General Staff." Schmundt at once reported this remark to Lieutenant-General Balck. It is an interesting testimony. But it does not, of course, alter the fact that Hitler alone was responsible for the defeat at Kursk. It was he who continually put off the date of the offensive.

What emerges most clearly is the extent to which a battle, no matter how carefully planned, still depends on imponderables—the insight of a senior commander, his readiness to take unorthodox decisions, his nerve at the crucial moment, the gallantry of the troops, and finally the commander's courage to act against orders.

Yet high among all these factors ranks one which was decisive for Operation Citadel from the very outset—betrayal. In the battle of Kursk it played an exceptional and dramatic role. The mystery which even today surrounds this betrayal of a vital secret remains one of the most disturbing riddles awaiting solution.

Ever since the spring of 1942 German counter-intelligence had been discovering more and more evidence that the Soviet High Command was being currently supplied with excellent information—information about the most closely guarded secrets concerning the German conduct of the war.

German armament production, strength and composition of the armies in the East, new weapons, and above all the plans and intentions of the German High Command became known to the Soviets. Part of this espionage was clearly due to partisans and agents in the rear areas behind the German front. In addition, deserters who were political opponents of the Nazi regime, or officers and other ranks who had been taken prisoner, were deliberate or unwitting sources of information for Soviet intelligence. To this must be added an efficient aerial reconnaissance. Moreover, tapped German telephone lines in the field and intercepted radio signals, transmitted by staffs and fighting units *en clair* either from pressure of time or carelessness, represented important and rapid sources of information in the tactical sphere. But all that was not enough to explain the detailed knowledge which the Soviet leaders had of the strategic intentions, plans, and preparations of the German High Command—a knowledge which Colonel-General Franz Halder, Chief of the General Staff of Land Forces until the autumn of 1942, described in the following words in 1955, when he testified as a witness at a court trial: "Nearly all German offensive operations became known to the enemy as soon as they had been planned at the Wehrmacht High Command, even before they reached my own desk; this was due to treason by a member of the OKW. Throughout the war we were unable to stop this leak."

The amount of information which even a small spy-ring can collect is best illustrated by the following example.

In the summer of 1942 a transmitter operated by enemy agents was pin-pointed after a long search and pounced upon at Otwock, a suburb of Warsaw. Two former Polish officers, Captain Arzyszewski and Lieutenant Meyer, and a number of their principal helpers, were arrested. The two Polish officers had been dropped by parachute south of Warsaw by a Soviet aircraft in the summer of 1941. They had been equipped with a transmitter and 2500 dollars. Their task had been to build up an espionage ring for the collection of military information and its transmission by radio to Moscow.

The captain had been continually travelling about the country, collecting information, while the lieutenant had been working the transmitter. German counter-intelligence found the code and nearly five hundred copies of the coded signals sent to Moscow. When these had been decoded the German security officials were speechless. The amount of secret military information which the two agents had collected behind the German lines over the space of a year defied description. The signals provided a complete picture of the German order of battle for the summer offensive of 1942. But not only the order of battle—detailed objectives, units to be employed, transport of corps and divisions had all been recorded accurately and correctly. The Soviet General Staff could have had no difficulty in deducing the key points of the German spring offensive merely from the information supplied by the two Polish agents. A real bargain at 2500 dollars.

What action did the German High Command take after this alarming discovery? Surely the Otwock incident should have opened the eyes of the German military leaders to the dangers of agents with transmitters—that new type of spy which emerged in the Second

World War? Surely they realized that the Warsaw spy-ring was not an isolated case? Did the experts take their discoveries straight to the Führer's headquarters in order to report to Hitler and the High Command? No.

Adolf Hitler himself never saw the comprehensive report from German radio security about the breaking of the Warsaw spy-ring. General Erich Fellgiebel, Chief of Wehrmacht Signals Communications at the Führer's headquarters, returned the report to radio security on the grounds that it was too long to be shown to the Führer. When an abridged version was submitted it was described as "too alarming": the Führer, it was said, would only be upset if he saw it.

The numerous agents whom Moscow had placed behind the German lines, not only in Germany itself but in nearly every country of Europe, long before the outbreak of the war, continued to work assiduously, cunningly, and with astonishing boldness. Rings of agents with radio transmitters in direct contact with Moscow, with the General Staff of the Red Army, were everywhere—in Paris, Marseilles, Bordeaux, Brussels, The Hague, Berlin, Berne, Geneva, Lausanne, Copenhagen, Oslo, Hammerfest, Bucharest, Belgrade, Sofia, Athens, Istanbul, and Cairo.

A number of such transmitters were discovered in Brussels in the winter of 1941, and in Berlin and Paris in the summer of 1942. When decoded, the copies of the signals transmitted revealed a staggering picture—the Soviets were informed about practically all vital secrets and all military plans of every campaign.

Over the next few years German radio security succeeded in discovering and intercepting the radio traffic between Soviet agents in Switzerland and Moscow. But the signals were so brilliantly enciphered that many of them were not decoded until 1944.

A brief analysis of the signals found or intercepted reveals that in all phases of the war in Russia the Soviet General Staff was served magnificently by its agents. Some of the information could have come only from the highest German military quarters—indeed they must have been dictated from the High Command and the Führer's headquarters straight into the transmitter key of the Soviet agents in Geneva and Lausanne.

On 9th November 1942, when the divisions of the German Sixth Army held nine-tenths of Stalingrad and the Soviet High Command was preparing its counter-blow on the Don, German radio security intercepted coded signals which, decoded subsequently, ran as follows: "For Dora. Where are the rearward defensive positions of the Germans on the line south-west of Stalingrad and along the Don? Director."

A few hours later came the supplementary question: "For Dora. Where are now 11th and 18th Panzer Divisions and 25th Motorized

Division which were formerly employed on Bryansk sector? Director."

The sender of these signals, the "Director", was the chief of military intelligence in Moscow. The addressee was the chief of the Soviet espionage network in Switzerland, known by the cover name of "Dora".

On 26th November, when Soviet armoured corps had already forged a ring of iron around Stalingrad and Sixth Army, "Director" signalled to "Dora": "Send information about concrete measures planned by OKW in connection with advance of Red Army at Stalingrad."

This signal is particularly interesting. Evidently the Soviet Command was not quite sure of its fantastic success in having encircled an entire German Army. Were they afraid, by any chance, of having run into a German trap? Did they need confirmation?

On 2nd December, "Director" in Moscow instructed his branch office in Switzerland: "Top priority task in the near future is the most accurate determination of all German reserves in the rear of the Eastern Front."

On Christmas Day 1942, he demanded: "Werther is to state clearly how many replacement divisions in all are being formed from recruits by 1st January. Reply urgent."

This message for the first time contains the most mysterious name of Soviet espionage in Germany—"Werther". On 16th January 1943, "Werther" was again mentioned in a signal: "For Dora. Lucie's and Werther's information about Caucasian front and all top priority information about Eastern Front, as well as on dispatch of new divisions to Eastern Front, to be sent to us without delay with precedence over all other information. Last information from Werther was most valuable. Director."

At the time these signals were decoded by German experts little or nothing was known about the names mentioned in them. Today we know nearly everything.

"Dora" was the cover name of the chief of the Soviet espionage network in Switzerland—Alexander Rado, a Soviet agent of Hungarian origin. His group included fanatical communists, superbly trained professional agents. Among them was Rudolf Rössler, a German refugee, whose cover name was "Lucie". Rössler was a real ace of Soviet military espionage against Germany, comparable to the Soviet star spy Dr Sorge, who held a post in the German Embassy in Tokyo until the winter of 1941 and kept Stalin supplied with vital information. Rössler was born at Kaufbeuren in 1897. From 1930 he worked in Berlin as the manager of a publishing firm and co-operated with clerical, liberal, and communist organizations. He had close contacts with Left-wing intellectual circles, including Schulze-Boysen, then still a communist student leader and subsequently chief of the "Red

Choir" centre in Berlin. He was also on friendly terms with national-Bolshevik groups, and men from Ernst Niekisch's circle were among the authors on his list.

One of Rössler's friends was a Swiss student who—as was later discovered—was even then working for Swiss intelligence. His name was Xaver Schnieper—a name we shall encounter again.

In 1934 Rössler emigrated to Switzerland. In Lucerne he founded the Vita Nova publishing firm which brought out humanitarian, theological, and philosophical books. Until the outbreak of the war Rössler was not active as an intelligence agent. Clearly he was deliberately keeping back. His moment arrived when the war started. He now set his carefully prepared apparatus in motion. In Germany he tapped the sources he had long prepared. His best source was right inside the OKW. His chief supplier was "Werther".

Who was the man who took cover under the name of Goethe's tragic figure, the man who was specially commended in a signal from Moscow on 16th January 1943? "Werther" was the great mystery-man of Soviet military espionage in the German leadership. "Werther" was the supplier of the top secrets which all came direct from the High Command of the Wehrmacht and from the Führer's headquarters—secrets known only to the initiated.

Whenever Moscow wanted to know something of particular importance, some particular secret of the top leadership, its signals called for "Werther". "Werther" must do this, "Werther" must do that. Always "Werther".

On 16th February 1943 "Director" instructed "Dora": "Find out at once from Werther through Lucie whether Vyazma and Rzhev are being evacuated." And on 22nd February: "Immediately get from Werther OKW plans about objectives of Kluge's Army Group."

And what was the answer? "Werther" supplied the information required. But who was "Werther"?

At the beginning of March, Army Group Centre began its strategic concentration for the offensive against the Kursk salient. Ten divisions were transferred to Second Panzer Army in the Orel area. This transfer, together with others needed for the offensive, faced the German High Command with serious transport problems. Altogether 320 railway transports had to be brought to their destinations in eighteen days. The whole plan hinged on the smooth running of the transport. It was the Achilles heel of Operation Citadel. And the Soviets promptly learnt all the details.

Colonel in the General Staff Hermann Teske, then General of Transport, Centre, the best-informed man on this point, states in an essay: "The Russians must have been informed about the German strategic concentration plans at a very early stage, because both deployment lines were the targets of heavy nuisance raids ever since the middle of March. Since the enemy invariably used the most effective forces for these operations, it must be assumed that their employment was controlled from the highest strategic command."

In other words, the Soviet High Command possessed such accurate, reliable, and detailed information about the German preparatory deployment for Citadel that it was able to direct its counter-moves on a strategic scale. Only the exceptional gift for improvisation displayed by the German railway engineers prevented the deployment being dangerously disorganized. Even so, things were quite bad enough.

On 15th April 1943 Hitler signed Operation Order No. 6 for Citadel and in it laid down 3rd May as the earliest date for the offensive. Five days later, on 20th April, "Dora" reported to "Director": "Date of offensive against Kursk, originally envisaged for first week of May, has been postponed." And on 29th April "Dora" added: "New D-day for German offensive is 12th June."

This information was accurate. It contained one of the best guarded secrets of the German Wehrmacht, a secret known only to a dozen men. On 7th May 1943 "Director" instructed "Dora": "Discover from Werther through Lucie all details about the plans and intentions of OKW and report to us urgently." The reply from "Dora" came promptly on 9th May in a long signal of more than 120 coded groups: "Dora to Director. From Werther . . . OKW is convinced that . . ." And then came a flood of information about the ideas held in the High Command of Land Forces, their ideas about a Kuban bridgehead, about the defence of Novorossiysk, and a great many other top secret German intentions.

On 13th May Moscow received the following warning: "Dora to Director. From Werther: German reconnaissance has identified Soviet concentrations near Kursk, Vyazma, Velikiye Luki."

On 30th May Moscow demanded precise information about the German offensive plans: "Director to Dora. Urgently instruct Lucie and Werther to discover: (1) At precisely what point of the southern sector of the Eastern Front is the German offensive to open? (2) With what forces and in which direction is the thrust to be made? (3) Apart from southern sector, where and when is a German offensive planned on the Eastern Front?"

Five days later, on 4th June, four weeks before the opening of the German offensive in the Kursk salient, a signal to "Dora" instructed all collaborators to concentrate their whole attention on timely information about the date, plans, and objectives of the German offensive at Kursk.

On 10th June promptly a reply from "Dora" contained detailed information about Manstein's orders of 28th May to the motorized formations of Fourth Panzer Army.

On 12th June, before a single German soldier had seen the new miracle tank in which Hitler was placing so much hope for the outcome of Citadel, "Director" was already informed about the existence of the Panther: "Director to Dora. Instruct Lucie and collaborators to establish all data about heavy tank named Panther. Important points: construction of this tank and technical characteristics, strength of armour. Is it equipped for flame-throwers and for smokescreen laying? Location of factories manufacturing this tank. Monthly output figures?"

The boldness of the questions alone is staggering. They embrace the alpha and omega of a top military secret. "Dora's" reply was not intercepted but there is no doubt that it was comprehensive and exhaustive.

If one looks today at the decoded signals which went out over the frequencies of the secret Swiss transmitter during the weeks preceding Citadel one still feels stunned by the magnitude of the operation. Yet German radio security intercepted no more than a fraction of the signals exchanged. But they are sufficient to show that "Director" in Moscow was being served superbly well.

He was told about the composition of the German offensive formations on both points of thrust of the Citadel front. He was told the precise number of German Panzer Divisions and their equipment. He was told the plan, the points of main effort, and the first operational objectives, which the messages correctly list as Oboyan and Maloarkhangelsk. Surely it was no coincidence that these two objectives proved to be so strongly fortified that they successfully resisted capture by the German troops.

"Director" in Moscow was informed about conversations made among the top leaders of OKW, in Hitler's closest circle, and in the OKH General Staff.

The signal transmitting the final date of the Citadel offensive is not among the documents in German possession. The message about the secret conference at the Führer's headquarters on 1st July is likewise missing. However, Soviet sources testify that both these pieces of information were received in Moscow.

Who was the man who supplied this information? For more than twenty years the hunt has been on for "Werther". But nobody has so far succeeded in catching him.

Today all the great agents of the Second World War are known— Dr Sorge, who worked for Stalin in Tokyo and was posthumously made a "Hero of the Soviet Union" on 7th November 1964, the twentieth anniversary of his execution. "Cicero", Himmler's man in Ankara who photographed the top-secret documents, which Sir Hughe Knatchbull-Hugessen, the British Ambassador, kept in his safe, and then sold them to Himmler's plenipotentiary. "Coro", who was

Lieutenant Schulze-Boysen who worked for Moscow in Berlin. The French woman agent known as "The Cat". "Kent" and "Gilbert", Moscow's top agents in Paris and Brussels. "Dora", "Sissie", "Lucie", "Pakbo", and "Jim", the pillars of the "Red Choir" in Switzerland. Only "Werther's" identity has remained undiscovered to this day. And yet he was undoubtedly one of the most important agents, one whose information helped decide the outcome of the war.

Sorge won the battle of Moscow, as the Soviets themselves now admit. "Werther" vitally influenced the turn taken by the battle of Kursk, the battle which itself marked the turning-point of the war.

What kind of man was he who conducted his desperately dangerous business right in the lion's den, in the Führer's headquarters, and for this business adopted the name of a tragic hero in German literature? Werther as a literary figure was a symbolic character for Goethe's own experiences in Wetzlar, his hopeless love for Charlotte Buff, the fiancée of Christian Kestner. The story of his more recent namesake, who played his dramatic role 150 years later on the stage of the Führer's headquarters, on the other hand, has not yet been written.

As in the case of many other spies, the start of "Werther's" activity cannot be determined with complete accuracy. It is not even quite certain when the name first appeared as a source in the signals transmitted from Switzerland to Moscow. What is certain is that "Werther" began to operate in the summer of 1942.

That was roughly the time when German counter-intelligence in Berlin had rounded up the "Red Choir", a Soviet espionage network. "Coro", who was the Luftwaffe Lieutenant Harro Schulze-Boysen, had been trapped by radio security. His magnificent organization with contacts in several ministries and military departments was smashed. Moscow lost one of its best, most reliable, and most fanatical agents.

A few weeks later, however, the gap had been closed. "Werther" replaced "Coro". And "Werther's" information was even better, and arrived even more promptly than "Coro's". Alexander Rado passed them on to Moscow as priority signals. Rachele Dübendorfer in Geneva, known as "Sissie", operated the secret transmitter. The contact between the Swiss centre and "Werther", however, was Rudolf Rössler, alias "Lucie", the German refugee and publisher of humanitarian pamphlets in Lucerne.

Let us take a closer look at this contact of "Werther's". After many years of unmolested activity Rado's secret transmitter was seized by the Swiss police in October 1943. Rado escaped. He hid out among Swiss communists, in a place held ready for that very contingency.

Rado's deputy, Alexander Foote, a British subject, continued the work but was himself caught red-handed at his transmitter a few weeks later. Before long Rachele Dübendorfer and finally, about the middle of May 1944, Rudolf Rössler, were rounded up by the police.

But Moscow's agents did not remain long under Swiss detention. One by one they were released. Not till after the war were they tried by a Swiss military court for "espionage in favour of a foreign state". Rado, his wife, and Foote, were sentenced *in absentia* to prison terms ranging from twelve months to three years. The couriers and radio operators got away with short terms of imprisonment and fines.

But one name did not figure among the sentences at all—Rudolf Rössler. The Swiss General Staff submitted an affidavit testifying that during the war Rössler had worked for Swiss intelligence and done valuable service. The military court thereupon declared that he had no case to answer.

This verdict by the Swiss divisional court, dated 23rd October 1945, establishes therefore that Rudolf Rössler was a double agent. The man who controlled "Werther" was working simultaneously for the Swiss secret service and the Soviets.

This fact is attested also in yet another Swiss document—in the indictment at a trial in 1953 when the spy Rössler was again the principal figure. Just as a leopard does not change his spots, so Rössler clearly could not stop spying. After the war he again worked for the Eastern bloc, this time for the Czechoslovak secret service. He supplied excellent information about military secrets from the Federal German Republic, about the envisaged structure of the future German Army, about the weapons of U.S. formations stationed in Western Germany, about the results of manoeuvres, about types of jet bombers, and about military bases in Jutland. In short, military secrets of the kind he used to collect from German military sources during the war. Over the six years from 1947 to 1953 Rössler produced 160 reports, each of them of roughly 20 pages. For these he received a fee of 48,000 Swiss francs, plus expenses.

He was tripped up in 1953 because something went wrong with his Düsseldorf cover address. He would send his reports to "Josef Rudolf, Linienstrasse 106": one package, which for some reason could not be delivered, was returned to its fictitious sender, "Josef Schwarz, Zurich". The Swiss postal authorities were unable to find Josef Schwarz and opened the package. In a tin of honey they found microfilms full of alarming military information.

This time Rössler's work for the Swiss secret service during the war was no help to him. He was tried for espionage in favour of a foreign power and sentenced to twelve months' imprisonment. He served his sentence. He lived for a few more years and died in 1958. He is buried in the village cemetery of Kriens in the Canton of Lucerne.

The official indictment drawn up by the Swiss Public Prosecutor against Rössler and his friend Xaver Schnieper on 14th July 1953 contains the following concise account of Rössler's career as a spy: "In the spring of 1939 Schnieper made the acquaintance of an officer of Swiss intelligence, Major Hausamann. In the autumn of the same year Schnieper persuaded Rössler to collect information for him. By way of an intermediary, Rössler subsequently supplied Major Hausamann with information of very great value to Swiss intelligence until 1944. From the autumn of 1942 onwards, Rössler passed a considerable part of his reports, which were of special interest to the Allies, to a friend in Geneva who, in turn, passed them on to Rachele Dübendorfer, of Geneva, for Russian intelligence. The Russian intelligence network then operating in Western Europe with a large number of transmitters has since become known by the name of 'Red Choir'. In this organization Rössler bore the cover name of 'Lucie'. In the winter of 1943–44 the Russian transmitters located in Geneva and Lausanne were seized by the police. Criminal proceedings before a military court were instituted against the persons engaged in the organization, on charges of supplying information detrimental to foreign states: these persons included Rössler, who was under detention from 9th May until 6th September 1944. On 23rd October 1945 the Divisional Court 2B found him guilty of systematic intelligence work directed against foreign states, but, on the grounds of Article 20 of the Criminal Code, declared him not culpable. It has never been possible to establish from whom Rössler received his information at the time, or the method by which it was passed on. But as a supplier of information he was certainly outstanding."

This assessment by the Swiss Public Prosecutor is undoubtedly correct. But two points are underplayed in this report: Rössler had entered Switzerland not as a harmless refugee but as a well-trained Soviet agent who had built up in Germany an important network of agents for D-Day—i.e., for the event of war. In order to have as little trouble as possible with Swiss counter-intelligence organizations, he established contact with Swiss intelligence after the outbreak of the war. He thereby became a double agent, but his main work was for Soviet intelligence. His skill is proved by the fact that he was not only an informer of Swiss intelligence but that he also had closest access to the information evaluating departments of the Swiss secret service, the departments where all secret information about Germany was collected and analysed for the Swiss General Staff.

In this way Rössler not only possessed the information which came to him from his own network in Germany, but he also had access to the secret material which arrived from Germany through Swiss secret channels at the Büro Ha of Section V of the Swiss General Staff. The Soviets in consequence got excellent value. The Soviet spy network in Switzerland cost 30,000 dollars per month. But for this 30,000 dollars "Director" in Moscow received not only the material produced by his own communist network, but thanks to Rössler the sum included a kind of subscription to all important pieces of information which the Swiss secret service was getting about Germany on its own account and by way of its own excellent agents. A truly unique achievement in the history of espionage.

There are two documents which prove beyond doubt that Rössler did in fact supply material from Swiss sources for Moscow. On 17th April 1943 Alexander Rado sent a signal to Moscow with detailed data about the manpower of the German Armies in the East. The most important passages of this message were as follows: "From Dora to Director. Results of total mobilization on Wehrmacht manpower since 1st January 1943: increase in numbers of men fit for active service due to new call-up 286,000. In addition . . . (a few words garbled) 290,000. Additions due to transfers from other parts of Wehrmacht and volunteer recruits over 95,000 men. Deferred for the time being a further 57,000 juvenile volunteers. From the training army, some local defence and construction battalions fit for garrison duty or fit for labour duties only have been transferred to the Luftwaffe and to the Todt Organization. Normal increase in troops fit for active service, servicemen discharged from hospital, etc., only 190,000 men."

A happy coincidence enables us to prove that this important information of Rado's came from the Swiss secret service. On 14th April 1943—three days before Rado's signal—Major Hausamann passed on to the Swiss General Staff the following secret memorandum under No. 623: "Effects of total mobilization on manpower of German Wehrmacht since 1st January 1943. (1) Army: Increase in troops fit for active service by new call-ups: 286,000 men. A further approximately 290,000 men, who were to have been called up between April and June, have been deferred for the moment. Increase in men fit for active service by way of special enlistment: 108,000. Increase in men fit for garrison duty and fit for labour duty only by way of special enlistment: 62,000. Increase by way of transfer from other Wehrmacht branches and from voluntary recruitment (wartime volunteers and juveniles): over 95,000, a further 57,000 (wartime volunteers) have been deferred for the time being. Troops fit for garrison duty or for labour duty only have been and are being largely posted from the training army to formations not belonging to the Army proper, such as local defence and constructions units of the Luftwaffe and the Todt Organization. Normal intake fit for active service, servicemen discharged from hospitals, etc., was only 190,000 during the first three months of this year. . . ."

This report is one of roughly 25,000 which the Büro Hausamann (cover name: Büro Ha) passed on to the Swiss High Command during the war. Since 1963 it has been deposited in the German Military Archives in Koblenz as a "confidential document". The code book, which would reveal the agents, is not available.

These documents show the extent to which the leadership of the Third Reich was infiltrated with foreign agents. The German military authorities and Ministries were swarming with spies. While the Gestapo and the SD, the Security Service, were shadowing the broad masses, hunting political malcontents, grousers, and defeatists, and while Freisler's People's Court was mass-producing its death sentences for second-rate and third-rate offences, the really dangerous and fatal information gatherers in top military and political posts remained unnoticed and undiscovered.

Who were they? What made them work for Swiss intelligence and for Moscow?

Long before the war Major Hausamann had built up a secret organization in Germany in order to supply the Swiss General Staff with information about military events and about the intentions and objectives of the National Socialist leadership. An extremely well-camouflaged network of informers was set up in the military commands by way of recruitment of collaborators.

When the war broke out this organization supplied exceedingly valuable material. The information was partly taken to Switzerland by couriers from Berlin, Cologne, and Munich—for the most part people crossing the frontier illegally—but also by way of diplomatic bags. Moreover, travelling businessmen frequently, for a variety of reasons, placed themselves at the disposal of agents.

Thanks to an ingenious trick, particularly important information went to Switzerland, to the Büro Hausamann, direct from the Führer's headquarters, or from its Berlin relay transmitter. In this way, for instance, the secret date of the German attack on Norway and Denmark, accurate to the day and hour, reached the Swiss High Command during the last week of March 1940.

The Swiss General Staff and the Swiss Federal Council decided to pass the information on to Winston Churchill, then First Lord of the Admiralty. He received it on 30th March and on 3rd April submitted it to the War Cabinet in London. There the sensational news was assessed in conjunction with other reports from Sweden and found to be lacking in substance. Prime Minister Chamberlain pushed it aside as implausible. A hundred hours later Denmark and Norway were occupied by German troops.

This is a classical example of how the best reports from the agents in the field can be in vain if they are wrongly assessed by headquarters. For this reason the recipient of any intelligence report is always anxious to know the source from which it comes, in order to assess its reliability or otherwise.

The entire espionage material of the Hausamann secret intelligence bureau is now kept locked away in the Koblenz Military Archives in the form of 771 35-mm films of 36 frames each. Herr Hausamann made this valuable material available to the archives for the purpose of military research, but he insisted on a contract stipulating that no part of it may be published without his permission.

The documents represent an unbroken succession of daily reports by Hausamann to the Swiss General Staff, from 31st August 1939 until 30th April 1945. I have myself inspected the films, and there is not the slightest doubt left that Major Hausamann's informers were established in Germany's top military commands and that he had contacts even among Hitler's closest entourage.

Of particular interest are the reports which Hausamann received from departments of OKW and of the Commander-in-Chief Training Army. He received current reports about military operations in France and in Italy, operations of the Luftwaffe, and economic news. Troop transfers, the situation in German training units, details of special training courses and training areas—all these were his daily bread. Lists of men killed in action and casualty totals were passed on to the Swiss High Command by Hausamann almost daily in great detail.

Hausamann moreover received information from the closest entourage of the Reichsführer-SS. Another of his informers must have occupied a key position in the German Foreign Office, because extracts and even photographs of original documents of the secret memoranda submitted to Hitler for information or decision by Ambassador Hewel, the Foreign Ministry liaison official at the Führer's headquarters, are included in the Hausamann files.

Important directives of the German Foreign Office were supplied to Hausamann from the German Embassies in Berne and Stockholm.

The Swiss General Staff and Federal Council were thus exceedingly well informed about top-secret military and economic conditions in Germany. In view of Switzerland's neutrality this would not have been such a disaster—had not Rudolf Rössler passed on these intelligence gems to the "Director" in Moscow.

Needless to say, German counter-intelligence, in particular the Reich Central Security Office, did all they could to track down the mysterious suppliers of news once the first decoded signals from Alexander Rado, mentioning "Werther" as the source, had landed on the desks of the German radio security experts.

The first question which the German spy-catchers asked themselves was: How does the information get to Switzerland?

Towards the end of March 1942 the Foreign Counter-Intelligence Department was tipped off that the Swiss Consul in Cologne was making rather a lot of journeys to Switzerland. And not only a lot of them, but also very sudden ones. He would often cancel appointments, invitations, and conferences because a few hours later he had to catch the Cologne-Basle train. The diplomat travelled in a courier compartment and his luggage as a rule consisted of a black briefcase.

On 29th March an attempt was made to get an illegal glimpse of the contents of this case. It did not, however, come off because the traveller was exceedingly alert. The security men merely succeeded in photographing the case from the outside.

Thereupon an accurate copy was made of the case. On the consul's next trip an attempt was to be made to switch the cases. As the consul passed the platform barrier he found himself wedged in among five "travellers" in a great hurry. One of them brushed so close past him that he made him drop the case.

Another "traveller" was already standing by, ready to pass him the substitute with a polite bow. But the plan again misfired because the consul, in the manner of British diplomats, had his briefcase secured to his wrist by a thin chain.

It may be a coincidence—but it would be an exciting coincidence—that on 31st March 1942—*i.e.*, only two days after the first German counter-espionage attempt against the diplomatic briefcase—Major Hausamann sent his general a report about the latest directives from the Führer's headquarters on the subject of the planned summer offensive of 1942. It begins with the words: "Directives have been issued by the German Führer's Headquarters . . ." Then follows an accurate account of the directions for transfers of German Army reserves.

Hausamann's report continues: "The German leadership has now decided to move the bulk of its army formations available in central Russia into action against the enemy even before the strategic concentration in the Ukraine is completed. There are weighty reasons for this German decision and for its implementation, the weightiest being that the German advanced positions from Novgorod to Kursk must be consolidated . . . when the German armies mount their thrust beyond Kharkov and in the Donets bend. Simultaneously with this operation, regarded as decisive by the German OKW, the German leadership intends . . . to tie down the largest possible number of Russian land and air forces in the big arc west of Moscow (from Kalinin to Kaluga)—see also other reports on this subject."

This was the essence of the operation plan for the German summer offensive in 1942, a plan still being worked out. In order to realize the significance of this report one must remember that, according to the OKW diary, the strategic concentration plans for the summer offensive were discussed for the first time a mere three days before, on 28th March 1942, at a secret conference at the Führer's headquarters. How secret this conference was emerges from a report by General Warlimont, the Deputy Chief of the Wehrmacht Operations Staff. He writes: "At a special conference at Headquarters on the afternoon of 28th March, to which, for reasons of security, only a very small circle

of officers from the highest Wehrmacht, Army, and Luftwaffe staffs
had been invited, the Chief of the Army General Staff made a detailed
report of the intended strategic concentrations for the summer campaign, as they emerged from instructions given to him verbally."

Warlimont concludes as follows: "Moscow, for the time being, was
dropped altogether as the objective of the offensive—contrary to the
entry in Goebbels's diary." This allusion is to an entry made in his
diary by Goebbels on 20th March. This named Moscow as the objective
of the summer offensive. Hitler's political confidant was therefore far
less well informed than the Swiss General Staff, and, thanks to Rössler,
the Soviet High Command.

So staggering is this story that one would refuse to believe it
were it not attested by unquestionably genuine documents. On 28th
March, in the afternoon, a top-secret conference was held at Hitler's
headquarters. Three days later, an abstract of the conversation lies
on General Guisan's desk in Berne. And another twenty-four hours
later, on 1st April, Rachele Dübendorfer taps it out over her secret
transmitter in Geneva: "Dora to Director: First directives for German
summer offensive. . . ."

It is interesting that this message was not attributed to "Werther"
as a source, but was marked "From Teddy". And "Teddy" was the
cover name for the Swiss informer in the German High Command of
Land Forces, the OKH. This suggests therefore that the reports from
the Swiss source in the Führer's headquarters were not identical with
"Werther's" information. In other words, Hitler's heavily guarded
Wolfsschanze must have harboured more than one spy.

German radio security experts had their first suspicions of this early
in 1944. More than 1000 intercepted signals exchanged between
"Director" and his agents had been decoded. The identity of "Director" was known. "Kent" and "Gilbert", his intelligence chiefs in
France and Belgium, had been rounded up. The identities of "Dora"
and "Lucie" were known, as were also the names of their radio
operators and contacts.

But nothing had yet been discovered about the informers who must
be inside Hitler's headquarters, at OKW and OKH.

Close-range tracking parties, from a special radio police unit of the
Wehrmacht which was normally engaged in monitoring radio communications behind the front, was employed in the greatest secrecy
on the terrain of the Führer's headquarters and the OKH in the Mauerwald forest near Rastenburg. But it failed to discover even a trace of
illegal radio traffic.

Special short-wave interception units had the Führer's headquarters
under radio surveillance for weeks on end. Nothing. No suspicious
radio traffic.

Yet the discovered telegrams proved that at least some of the information got to Geneva from East Prussia within a matter of hours. That was possible only by radio because the telephone lines had long been most carefully watched.

It simply had to be the radio. But there was no illegal radio traffic. Was not the conclusion inescapable that the leak was in the legitimate radio traffic? Supposing the information went on quite legitimately over the regular transmitters of the Führer's headquarters, the transmitters which put out the directives to the Army Groups and Armies? Either from Rastenburg itself, or from the Berlin relay transmitter.

The operators there would receive their coded texts and instructions concerning the frequency. What they tapped out, and where it went—that they did not know. Suppose one let an operator send out a coded message on a frequency which Rössler or Hausamann were monitoring in Switzerland? But the suspicion was dismissed as absurd. True, it would be simple enough, but it seemed unthinkable. It presupposed, for instance, that a very senior officer in OKW signals communications was involved, that Rössler knew the code, and that a senior staff officer at an Army or Army Group HQ was also involved. The point was that the transmitted signals were all logged and needed a recipient; in the event of a check a senior officer, either an Army Chief of Operations or some other officer of similar standing would have to be there to acknowledge receipt. It seemed preposterous.

Really preposterous? But there is no other explanation.

Only thus, in this most simple and yet most cunning way, could Rössler, alias "Lucie", have received his urgent information by radio from the Führer's headquarters and the OKH.

It was simple enough. A certain frequency would be watched in Switzerland at certain times; the times at which transmissions went out from headquarters or from Berlin. If the message contained the call sign WRTR they would know that it was intended for Swiss ears and record it.

But surely the code was changed from time to time? Certainly—but code can be transmitted by courier. Everything was possible—provided that the Chief of Wehrmacht Signals Communications at the OKW or one of his top officers belonged to "Werther's" crew.

And "Werther" himself? Was he perhaps not a human being at all? Was his name only the nameplate for a generals' plot at the Führer's headquarters, a conspiracy which for reasons of political opposition was supplying Hitler's military secrets to the Swiss agent Rössler? In that case "Werther's" organization would not have been a Soviet agent at all but a Swiss intelligence source which possibly was not even aware that its reports were passed on to Stalin. This view has been mooted repeatedly in recent years. It was an explanation which the German public seemed to accept quite happily.

But there is a very revealing test that can be applied. If "Werther's" information transmitted by "Lucie" to "Director" was identical with the Swiss material received from the German top leadership then Major Hausamann must have had the same detailed and accurate information about the battle of Kursk as that transmitted by "Lucie" to the Kremlin.

Was that the case? On 25th June Hausamann, in secret report No. 1027, reported on the strategic concentration of Fourth Panzer Army on the southern front of the Kursk salient. But this report is strangely imprecise. It contains neither the date of the offensive nor its objective. Instead, Hitler's dummy orders concerning General Jodl are reported in full in Hausamann's memorandum. As late as 8th July Hausamann's report No. 1105 still expressed the view that the fighting in the Kursk salient was not a German offensive at all but the consequence of a Soviet attack.

Rössler's reports to "Director" could certainly not originate from this information; his reports were so accurate that Nikita Khrushchev, then member of the Military Council with the rank of Lieutenant-General, together with Army General Vatutin arrived in person at the headquarters of the Voronezh Front Armies on 2nd July 1943, to inform them of the date of the German offensive. The conclusion is unavoidable that at least this supremely important message from "Werther" was not a duplicate. It was an original—exclusively for Moscow!

Is it unreasonable to conclude that "Werther" was an informer for the Soviets, and for the Soviets alone? So exclusively, in fact, that not even Rössler dared to make his reports available to the Swiss. This, incidentally, would have been a logical step because the Soviet intelligence services were careful not to pass on the reports from their agents even to their own allies.

"Werther", the Russian agent, must have been a man who enjoyed Moscow's confidence. A man perhaps like the Swede Wennerström, who was a major in the Swedish armed forces but for fifteen years worked for the Soviet secret service and secretly held the rank of a Russian general. It was only by chance that he was trapped on 20th June 1963, just before he had hoped to slip out of the country.

"Werther", on the other hand, has not been unmasked to this day. Is he still enjoying the fruits of his treason in some part of the world? Is he waiting for new employment? Or is he perhaps still active?

The cover names of Soviet intelligence agents are never accidental or meaningless. They always bear some relation to the agent himself. "Dora" was Rado changed about. "Pakbo", the cover name of Rado's source on the subject of political opposition to Hitler and Mussolini, was compounded from the names of the Swiss journalist Otto Pünder and his Italian contacts. "Taylor", who figured in Rado's reports as a source of economic information, was the English transliteration of the name of the German agent Schneider. "Lucie", Rössler's cover name, was derived from his place of residence, Lucerne. "Sissie" had been the pet name of Rachele Dübendorfer when young.

What, then, about "Werther"? Was it some allusion to the literary interests of the man concerned or to any scholarly work done by him in the field of Goethean research? Or was it a kind of phonetic rendering of the Russian word *vertep*, which means a den of robbers and, according to one theory, meant the Führer's headquarters?

Or must one accept the theory, now most commonly held, that "Werther" was a collective name for many informers, whose separate reports were put together by Rössler and sent out with the attribution to "Werther"? This explanation is tempting in many ways. The form and content of many a "Werther" dispatch would seem to support it. The comprehensive coverage of so many different spheres from which the secrets came, the prompt supply of detailed information—was it feasible that a single person could manage all that? A person, moreover, who in addition to his role of traitor must have held an important post, a post he had to fill efficiently unless he was to lose it. There are also a few interesting mistakes and errors of the kind which might have arisen from teamwork.

On the other hand, it is against all Soviet intelligence practice to send instructions to a phantom, to command a phantom, or to grant it special rewards. If the Russians relied on the report of an agent one can be sure that they knew him well. After all, acquaintance with the source of a piece of information is vital for its correct assessment.

It is not the purpose of this book to play detective. All that we wanted to do was to assign to this mysterious spy and the information he supplied to the Russians a proper place in the overall picture of Operation Citadel. There, with his identity still masked, "Werther" stands on the margin of a decisive battle in history.

We say: on the margin—because to explain the course and outcome of Operation Citadel in terms of "Werther" alone would mean to oversimplify the huge forces involved, the bold decisions taken, and the achievements and mistakes of both warring parties. Kursk, that gigantic battle, was the culmination point of the war in the East, the turning point of the campaign in Russia. And this historic turn was brought about by a good deal more than the work of just one enemy agent.

The question why the battle of Kursk, opened so hopefully, was eventually lost, and why the last great German offensive ended in fiasco in spite of massive numbers of armour and men, can only be answered by looking back beyond it, to the last weeks of 1942 and the beginning of 1943.

PART TWO: *Manstein*

1. Stalin wanted more than Stalingrad

*"General Badanov, keep moving, this is our moment"–
Journey's end at Tatsinskaya–Tanks in front of Manstein's command post–Rostov, escape-hatch for a million
troops–First Panzer Army falls back–Farewell Ishcherskaya–Twenty-six miles on blank ice–Descent from the
mountain passes–Krasnodar, the turntable on the Kuban–
Jackpot of 400,000 men.*

THE time was Christmas 1942. The headquarters of Field-Marshal
von Manstein, C-in-C Army Group Don, was at Novocherkassk,
twelve miles behind the Lower Don. The Marshal and his staff officers
looked weary. They were all depressed by the fate of Sixth Army.

But behind their anxiety about the situation at Stalingrad there
was an even graver one. The Soviet High Command was patently out
to exploit the fortunes of war, or rather Hitler's mistakes in making
Sixth Army rush ahead too far without adequate cover for its weak
flanks, to achieve a far greater prize than the mere annihilation of one
army.

Behind the operations of three Soviet army groups, which had been
ceaselessly attacking between Volga and Don ever since 19th November 1942, which had encircled Stalingrad and torn open the Italian-
Rumanian front for some sixty miles—behind that operation was more
than just the liberation of Stalingrad and the encirclement of Paulus's
Army. Behind it was a far greater, a breath-taking plan of the Soviet
High Command. Carefully prepared over a long time, dearly bought
with great sacrifices, with lost armies, lost territory, and very nearly a
lost war, the great counterblow was at last to be struck—here, from the
Volga, from the womb of old Mother Russia, from Stalingrad, the holy
place of the Bolshevik revolution. All past omissions were now to be
redeemed, the great operation against Hitler was now to be mounted
—the giant blow as against Napoleon, the annihilation of the Germans
in the vast, open spaces of Russia. Stalin intended no more and no less
than the shattering of the entire southern wing of the German armies

in the East. A super-Stalingrad for a million German troops—that was his objective. By means of a gigantic operation of eight armies altogether, striking towards Rostov and the Lower Dnieper from the middle Don and the Kalmyk Steppe, he wanted to cut off and annihilate the German southern wing—three groups with altogether seven armies.

There is no parallel in military history for an operation plan of similar gigantic scale. Moreover, it seemed like success. Hour by hour more alarming reports arrived at Manstein's map table. How and with what was he to stem the Red flood? How was he to seal the huge gap between Don and Donets? The German High Command was facing a danger such as it had not faced before.

"Quiet," grunted the Soviet general. His reproachful glance fell on his orderly officer who was talking to a runner. Alarmed the major fell silent. The only sound now was the crackling of the fire in the stove of the peasant hut which served the Soviet XXIV Tank Corps as its command post during the night of 23rd–24th December 1942.

The general was pressing a telephone to his ear. "Da—yes, yes." He chuckled. Then he gave his name again.

"Everything according to plan," the general reported. "The Italians seem to have been blown away. They have no resistance left in the area behind their Eighth Army either. My formations are advancing unimpeded. We are already deep in the enemy hinterland and are covering some thirty miles a day. Our spearheads are at Tatsinskaya." Major-General V. M. Badanov, commanding the Soviet XXIV Tank Corps, was clearly proud of the telephone report he was making to the C-in-C of the First Guards Army. And General Kuznetsov sounded pleased too: "Excellent, Comrade Badanov. I shall report your successes to headquarters. But keep moving, always keep moving—this is our moment!"

It was indeed Badanov's moment. His XXIV Tank Corps, assigned to First Guards Army, was racing far ahead of the Soviet offensive wedges which were advancing through the shattered front of the Italian Eighth Army, on towards the Donets. Badanov encountered hardly any appreciable opposition. Blocking units employed in the depth of the Italian front, in the catchment area of the Chir, soon scattered under the impact of the Soviet attacks. Guns and motor vehicles were abandoned. Many officers removed their badges of rank and tried to make good their escape. So why should the other ranks be more heroic? They threw their weapons away and fled also.

All Badanov's corps had to do was to keep moving. By the evening of 23rd December 1942 their spearheads had reached Tatsinskaya, the important forward airfield and supply centre for Stalingrad, 150 miles behind the shattered Italian front. The corps had covered this distance in five days—blitzkrieg in the best German tradition! A distance

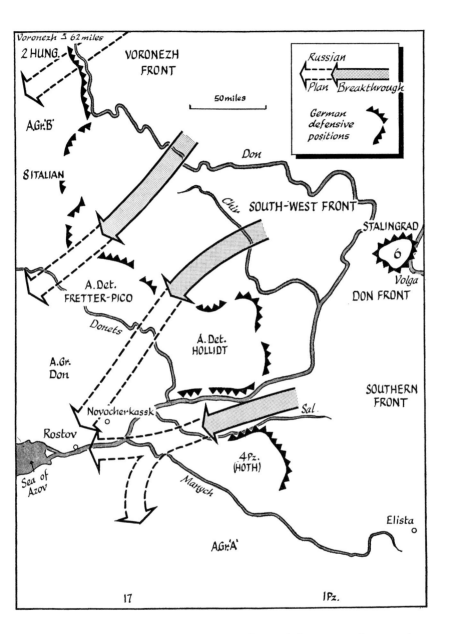

Map 8. At the end of 1942, following the collapse of the German front on the middle Don, Stalin saw his chance of a decisive victory. He intended to seize Rostov by a huge pincer movement and thus close the gateway to the Caucasus. By means of an even bigger operation he intended to envelop the German Army Groups 'B' and Don.

of 150 miles in five days—that was nearly the distance and the speed of Manstein's famous Panzer raid to Dvinsk in the first week of the war. Then, eighteen months earlier, his LVI Panzer Corps had covered the distance from the area east of Tilsit to Dvinsk, a distance of 170 miles, in four days. The Russians had learnt a lot since then.

As General Badanov replaced the receiver of his field telephone he turned to his chief of staff: "What d'you think, Comrade Colonel, do we attack the German base and the airfield tonight or do we wait till tomorrow?"

The Colonel slowly shook his head. "Tomorrow the Germans celebrate Christmas—that's the most sentimental of their feasts. They make up little presents, they stick candles on fir trees and prepare for their Holy Night. That'll make them careless. We might take them by surprise."

Badanov nodded. Then he made out his orders for his unit commanders.

The plan succeeded. In thick fog during the small hours of 24th December Badanov's tanks moved off. They rolled straight down the runways of the airfield of Tatsinskaya.

Of course, VIII Air Corps realized the threatening danger, but Fourth Air Fleet was not allowed to order the evacuation of the important supply base and its huge stores. Orders said: Hold on. But how was one to hold on, far behind the main German defensive line on the Chir, when faced with a Soviet armoured corps? A mere 120 men, one 8·8-cm gun and six 2-cm flak guns—that was all the Germans had to oppose the Soviets with at Tatsinskaya.

General Badanov records in his memoirs that the Soviet armoured spearheads found the German gun positions and strongpoints unmanned. The aircrews too were in their bunkers. "Everybody was sleeping peacefully," the general records.

According to his account the signal for the attack was given by a mortar battery. A few hours later the vital supply base for the encircled city of Stalingrad fell to the Russians without appreciable resistance. Badanov states that 350 aircraft and enormous quantities of *matériel*, food supplies, and ammunition, including complete train transports, were captured.

The poor defence of the important base of Tatsinskaya was certainly a serious blunder. But one thing is certain: Badanov's figure of captured aircraft cannot be correct. Only 180 machines were on the field. Most of these took off under enemy fire, in spite of the fog. And 124 arrived safely at other airfields.

Nevertheless it was a terrible blow. Tatsinskaya was not only the supply centre for Stalingrad but also a communications centre—the railhead of the important lines from Rostov and the Donets area. The development was particularly serious for Army Detachment Hollidt.

This formation was still a long way to the east of Tatsinskaya, on the Chir, and now found itself threatened from the rear. Once more the price had to be paid for Hitler's disastrous strategy of holding on at all costs. Nothing was ever to be surrendered. Hold on, hold on, hold on—whatever the price.

Admittedly, the position held by Hollidt on the Chir was of very considerable importance. It was from there that XLVIII Panzer Corps was to support Hoth's relief attack towards Stalingrad. For that reason, favourable salients in the front line seemed useful to OKH. But wish and reality were incompatible. The danger grew from day to day, and the prospect of success became less. Hitler, however, refused to see the danger. When Manstein asked for reinforcements Hitler's reply was: "I haven't got any." When he proposed strategically unavoidable withdrawals, Hitler lamented: "Without the Caucasian oil and the mineral wealth of the Donets area the war can no longer be won."

Manstein was in a difficult position. He had to battle not only against the Russians but also against the Führer's headquarters. Any other man would have caved in. But Manstein found a way. He resorted to an ingenious system of strategic make-shift arrangements.

In this he had the help of three experienced commanders in the field, men on whom he could rely—Colonel-General Hoth, whose Fourth Panzer Army was still fighting south-east of the Don; General Hollidt, whose mixed Army Detachment in the big Don bend was holding the main defensive line of the Gnilaya and the Chir; General Fretter-Pico, whose newly organized Army Detachment was trying to set up a blocking position in the area between Millerovo and the Kalitva river.

The main danger now was Badanov, the spearheads of the Soviet First Guards Army. For it was a mere eighty miles from Tatsinskaya to Rostov. Manstein knew that, in the present conditions, a fearless tank commander could cover the distance in three days. And Badanov certainly was fearless. If he struck at Rostov things would be really critical. If the Soviets succeeded in slamming the only door, the only overland link with the armies of Army Group A in the Caucasus, then 800,000 men would be trapped. And Fourth Panzer Army as well. Field-Marshal Manstein realized this. And General Badanov realized it too.

The Field-Marshal sat at Novocherkassk and together with his chief of staff, Major-General Schulz, and his chief of operations, Colonel Busse, coolly evaluated the situation. This was the moment for bold, daring, but also fateful decisions. It was one of those moments when a general must decide how much he can expect from his officers and men. Manstein knew the capacity of his formations but he also knew the limits to which they could be stretched. That too was part of his genius as a general.

Manstein asked Hoth, whose army on the southern front of Army

Group Don was still engaged in the relief attack towards Stalingrad, to let him have one division in order to save Tatsinskaya. On his own responsibility, because he realized the disastrous situation, Hoth transferred to him his most powerful Panzer Division, the 6th Panzer Division under General Raus. Colonel von Hünersdorff, Manstein's chief of staff during the offensive operations of the previous year, now commanded the Paderborn 11th Panzer Regiment in that division.

In an icy night march the division was transferred to the north, to Army Detachment Hollidt, where Colonel Wenck, its indefatigable chief of staff and a brilliant improviser, had built up a first weak line of defence from a motley array of formations.

It was a difficult and a fateful decision which Manstein and Hoth had taken upon themselves. For with the loss of his 6th Panzer Division Hoth also lost his last feeble hope of being able to hold on in his hard-pressed position thirty miles from Stalingrad, and thus of ever being able to resume the relief attack.

But then this relief attack, though begun with such high hopes, had in any case virtually failed. Even without a successful blow against Badanov, Hoth's situation would soon have become untenable because he too would be threatened with encirclement. The only choice he had was between a greater and a lesser disaster.

And the greater disaster could be averted—if at all—only by means of Manstein's plan. And this plan was based on the following considerations. The only real armoured formation which Hollidt still possessed on the Chir was General Balck's well-tried Silesian 11th Panzer Division. It had been engaged in skirmishes with penetrating enemy tanks on the left wing of Hoth's group ever since mid-December. Colonel Count Schimmelmann commanded its 15th Panzer Regiment. True, he only had twenty-five armoured fighting vehicles left, but General Balck had nevertheless been able, with this force of tanks, reinforced by Panzer grenadiers, engineers, and flak, and with 336th Infantry Division under General Lucht, to annihilate two strong enemy striking forces in a kind of running battle and in knocking out sixty-five tanks without losing a single one himself.

The outstanding part played in this fighting by the infantry is also shown by the fact that 336th Infantry Division knocked out ninety-two enemy tanks in five days.

This success enabled Manstein to move 11th Panzer Division against Badanov's corps after a tiring night march on 23rd December in a temperature of minus 20 degrees Centigrade. Jointly with 6th Panzer Division, which was coming up in forced marches, it was to halt General Badanov's daring and dangerous raid.

In the flat, snow-covered steppe between Kalitva and Chir the German Panzer regiments again demonstrated the meaning of modern tank tactics. While the Grenadier battalions of 306th Infantry Division

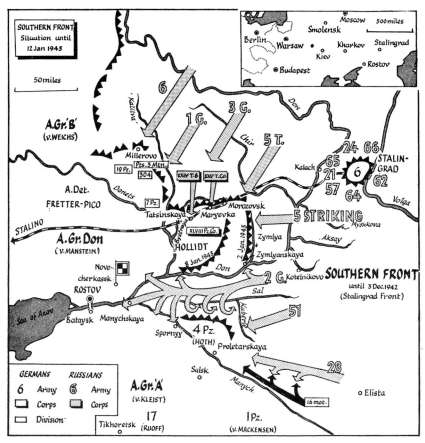

Map 9. Nine Soviet armies were racing towards Rostov. The deepest penetration was accomplished by the Second Guards Army, whose movements appear on the situation map as a nine-headed hydra.

sealed off the important supply centre from the east and then sent in assault parties of 579th Grenadier Regiment to recapture parts of the airfield, the German counter-attacks were mounted. As early as 24th December an armoured advanced detachment of 6th Panzer Division, supported by assault guns, captured the area north of Tatsinskaya. By 27th December General Balck's formations had laid an iron ring around the Russian corps at Tatsinskaya. The 6th Panzer Division now blocked the retreat of the Soviet formations, cut them off from their supplies, and screened off the front along the Bystraya against any attempts from the north for their relief.

Then began the battle for Tatsinskaya. Badanov's armour was trapped. The corps had been taken by surprise. Badanov sent one SOS after another to his Army Group. General Vatutin replied with reassuring signals. He urged him to hold on. He employed what forces he had—two motorized corps and two rifle divisions—to relieve Badanov. He was determined to save Badanov and get his corps moving again. Too much was at stake for the Soviet Command: they wanted to get to Rostov. But the Russians too were at the end of their strength that winter.

General Raus with his 6th Panzer Division resisted all attacks. And Balck's 11th Panzer Division, together with 4th Panzer Grenadier Regiment, commanded by the fearless Colonel Unrein, and with the grenadiers of 306th Infantry Division, turned the battle into a costly defeat for Badanov's regiments at Tatsinskaya.

The Soviet XXIV Tank Corps was wiped out in heavy night fighting in a cutting cold. Badanov's units resisted desperately. Many groups fought to their last round. The burning grain silos and storage depots of Tatsinskaya lit up a ghostly battle scene—rammed tanks, crushed anti-tank guns, overturned supply columns, wounded men frozen to death.

By 28th December it was all over. Isolated Soviet troops broke through the German encirclement in the north of the town and made good their escape across the Bystraya stream. Badanov's corps, which so hopefully launched its offensive towards Rostov just before Christmas, had ceased to exist.

The Soviet High Command and the Supreme Soviet bestowed on Badanov's regiments the halo of heroes. Their gallant stand to the last, and above all their unparalleled armoured raid deep into the rear of the German lines were to be a shining example to the rest of the Red Army. The newly raised corps was therefore granted the title of "II Tatsinskaya Tank Corps". And Badanov himself was the first officer of the Red Army to be decorated with the Order of Suvorov.

German blitzkrieg methods with large armoured formations had clearly become the model for Soviet operations. For the moment, however, these new tactics did not bring them success. The German tank commanders were still superior in skill. This was again demonstrated four days later. Late on New Year's Eve, just before the beginning of 1943, the Soviet XXV Tank Corps ran into a trap in an attempt to imitate Badanov's method. An error and recklessness led it into disaster.

Misled by the very slight resistance they had encountered when breaking through the southern wing of the Italian Eighth Army, the Corps omitted to send reconnaissance units out. It was thought that there was no serious adversary left. The Russian armoured brigades emerged from their patches of woodland north of the Bystraya stream with their headlights full on and made for the ford near Maryevka. They intended to cross the river in a southerly direction in order to strike at the rear of the German Army Detachment Hollidt.

But the battle outposts of 6th Panzer Division on the Bystraya noticed the Soviet advance towards the ford. General Raus swiftly made his plan for a night engagement. He ordered his 7·5-cm anti-tank troops forward in order to delay the Soviet tanks. The 11th Panzer Regiment was alerted and kept in readiness. The bulk of the Soviet XXV Corps was allowed to cross the ford into Maryevka with most of its tanks. Then the crossing point was sealed off with the anti-tank troops held in readiness and with heavy armoured scout cars.

And now General Raus opened the nocturnal tank battle between Maryevka and Romanov. The enemy, held up frontally, was attacked from both flanks and in the rear. The Russians were taken by surprise and reacted confusedly and nervously. Raus, on the other hand, calmly conducted the battle like a game of chess.

Blazing T-34s lit up the scene. Using separate packs of tanks, the Soviets again and again tried to force a breach. Who was a friend and who an enemy? This question could be answered only at closest range. Furiously the Soviet tank commanders tried to exploit the robust construction of their T-34s and to eliminate the German Panzers by ramming them. But the mobility of the Panzer IV and the experience of the German tank commanders paid off—especially in the break-through attempt of a Soviet armoured group at Novomaryevka, where Major Dr Bäke held a covering position with his 2nd Battalion, 11th Panzer Regiment.

Bäke had ten Panzer IVs available, and only a handful of infantry-men. Soviet T-34s attacked towards 0300 hours and broke into the village. Battles of tank against tank developed between the houses. The straw-thatched huts were soon ablaze. The flickering flames produced bizarre shadows.

Standing about in the village were a few damaged, unmanned German tanks, awaiting repair. These provided an unexpected support for Bäke's small fighting force. In the uncertain light of the blazing village the Russians regarded the wrecks as intact tanks and time and again concentrated their fire on these tempting stationary targets. This gave Bäke's tanks the time and opportunity to move into good firing positions themselves. Eventually he withdrew his little armada from among the damaged tanks and houses of the village.

In the course of this disengagement Bäke's command tank—which, like all other command tanks, merely carried a wooden dummy gun because of the space inside being needed for the bulky radio equip-ment and the map table—happened to cross the bow of a T-34. The Russian immediately traversed his gun to open fire. "Ram him!" Bäke ordered. But the manoeuvre would hardly have saved him. Salvation came from the tank of the commander of 7th Company, Captain Gericke. His Panzer IV was lying in ambush at a street corner, its gun ready for action. He saw the Russian tank just in time: "Fire!" It was a direct hit.

When he rallied outside the village, Bäke found that he was left with six tanks and twenty-five men. Once it got light and the Russians realized their superiority things might look ugly. For that reason the night had to be exploited for the counter-attack. At night deception was possible. Night favoured the weaker side. Under cover of darkness one might, by means of lights and noise, make six tanks look like a whole battalion.

Major Bäke posted his six tanks all round the village. On the pre-arranged flare signal they all attacked. The twenty-five infantrymen, strung out between the tanks, yelled "Hurra" as loud as they could and fired as many rounds as possible from their small arms. The tanks also made as much noise as possible and fired tracer ammunition. The bluff succeeded.

Bäke quickly reached the centre of the village. The Russians, suspecting a large-scale attack, fell back towards the Bystraya. But there they were caught by the German anti-tank guns which were waiting for them.

The Russians had crossed the Bystraya with ninety tanks. When day broke, ninety wrecked T-34s littered the wintery battlefield. Thus XXV Tank Corps, the second offensive wedge of the Soviet Guards Army, was wiped out.

The losses of 6th Panzer Division amounted to twenty-three armoured fighting vehicles. And since it remained in possession of the battlefield, most of these were made battle-worthy again by the workshop companies.

With the smashing of the two Soviet armoured groups on the northern front of Army Group Don the immediate danger threatening Rostov from the north-east was averted.

The equally dangerous Soviet thrust by the Soviet Sixth and First Guards Armies from the northern edge of the breach in the direction of the Donets via Millerovo was successfully halted by the weak formations of Army Detachment Fretter-Pico.

Army Detachment was rather a grand name for the forces available to General Fretter-Pico for sealing a gap of nearly 120 miles. At Millerovo parts of 3rd Mountain Division resolutely and successfully resisted superior enemy armoured forces. Field-training regiments and draft-conducting battalions, together with von der Lancken's battered Panzer group, had to face the assault of enemy armoured divisions.

Eventually the 304th Infantry Division was transferred to Russia from France. From coastal-defence duties along the peaceful Atlantic Wall, its regiments, after a mere twelve hours' fighting in the East, found themselves at breaking point. The fact that Fretter-Pico and the division's experienced commander, Major-General Sieler, nevertheless succeeded in nursing the riflemen and gunners through the initial shock of being faced with powerful enemy armour and in turning them, within a few weeks, into tough fighters, was an amazing achievement. Luckily, Fretter-Pico had two experienced and battle-tested Panzer Divisions at his disposal—the Thuringian 7th and the Lower Saxon 19th, whose indefatigable counter-attacks made the defensive fighting easier for the infantry and also protected the northern flank of the threatened front. Thus the Army Detachment Fretter-Pico, though in fact a weak corps, became a successful breakwater between Don and Donets and by its elastic method of operation prevented a strategic breakthrough by an enemy more than twenty times its numerical superior. Fretter-Pico rightly observed: "It was a victory for the infantryman's fighting morale."

The successful German defensive operations between Don and Donets held the door open for the German armies still in the Caucasus against the northern jaw of the Soviet pincers.

But the absence of the forces employed to avert this danger was now acutely felt by Manstein on the right wing of his front, at Hoth's Fourth Panzer Army, between Don and Manych. And now disaster threatened there.

Every morning at daybreak during those last few days of December, Colonel-General Hoth set out in his armoured command car on a tour of his shrunken divisions and visited their commanders at their headquarters. Many a regiment was reduced to the strength of a weak battalion. Battalions were down to company strength. Fourth Panzer Army was left with a mere fifty to seventy battle-worthy tanks, normally the equipment of a single weak battalion.

At nightfall the tough and energetic army commander returned to his headquarters, completely exhausted. Colonel Fangohr, his chief of staff, was waiting for him with the situation map, the signals from Manstein, and the log of telephone conversations. It was a hopeless struggle. Fourth Panzer Army was spending itself in costly defensive fighting.

In the evenings there was only one subject: How, having given away its 6th Panzer Division, could the army hold the front with the small forces it had left? Hitler persisted in refusing to release 16th Panzer Grenadier Division which was still holding positions at Elista. The 5th (Viking) SS Panzer Grenadier Division, promised by Army Group A from the Caucasus, was still somewhere in transit.

Day after day Fangohr reported how he had been on to Army Group. And day after day he received the same reply from Manstein's chief of operations, Colonel Busse: We keep asking Hitler to release First Panzer Army and put it under our command—but in vain. OKH cannot make up its mind about anything.

Step by step, Hoth moved his troops back from switchline to switch-line, towards the south-west. From the Myshkova sector to the Aksay. From the Aksay to the Sal. Then to the Kuberle. By sudden sharp counter-attacks he kept harassing the enemy who was pressing hard on his heels. Toughness, ingenuity, fresh ideas, indefatigable drive, and fearlessness—these were the qualities which enabled the colonel-general to stand up with his weakened LVII Panzer Corps to a superior Soviet force of three armies. And all the time he was conscious of his responsibility for the further course of the fighting—he must prevent a Russian advance to Rostov from the east and south-east, just as Hollidt and Fretter-Pico had averted it from the north, and he must cover the rear of the German armies still in the Caucasus.

At long last, at the end of December, Hitler authorized the evacuation of the Caucasus. But the rearguards of First Panzer Army were still on the Terek, 400 miles from Rostov.

The situation map of the southern front of the German armies in the East looked terrible. Everywhere there were red arrows, indicating Soviet thrusts, and the thin blue lines of the German positions were submerged in this red sea. There was no longer any secure contact between Hollidt's and Hoth's formations, since, about mid-January, Fourth Panzer Army had been forced towards the south-east, behind the Manych. Between Don and Sal was a new, dangerous gap of twenty-five miles. Into that gap two Soviet armies of Yeremenko's Army Group were now advancing—the Second Guards Army and the Fifty-First Army.

They kept moving forward. They covered their flanks to right and left, but the bulk of both armies was inexorably moving towards Rostov. Its movements, entered on the situation map, looked like a huge, nine-headed hydra—a hydra whose tentacles were threatening both Hoth and Hollidt. But the first part of this advancing hydra had already reached the Don to the north-east of Rostov. This was the Soviet III Guards Tank Corps under General Rotmistrov, the crack formation which earned its Guards title in the fighting for Stalingrad.

A chill ran down the spines of the staff officers of the German Army Group Don at Novocherkassk whenever they glanced at their situation map. The world's eyes were still riveted on Stalingrad, but down here, at Rostov, at the bridges of Bataysk, the real decisions were made. Here a disaster was threatening which was three times the magnitude of Stalingrad. Could the race against time and against the Soviets be won? Would Field-Marshal von Kleist's Army Group A get to Rostov in time to slip through the narrow door?

On 7th January 1943, an icy-cold Thursday, Captain Annus, the orderly officer, burst into Manstein's room: "Herr Feldmarschall, Soviet tanks have crossed the Don only twelve miles from here and are making straight for us. They are evidently trying to mop us up. Our Cossack[1] covering parties have been overrun. We've nothing left."

Manstein calmly regarded his orderly officer. All he said was: "That so?"

It was one of those moments when the Field-Marshal showed that he was not only a strategist of genius but also a man of imperturbable temperament. He hated alarms and excitement.

"We've got all sorts of things left, Annus," he said to the captain with a smile. "Scrape together whatever you can find. That tank repair shop next door—surely there are bound to be a few more or less operational tanks there. Collect whatever can be used, and go and knock out the Soviets. Get the staff organized for defence. We're staying put. I'll leave you to cope with this little disturbance!" Annus, staggered by the Field-Marshal's stolid calm, rushed out. The tank repair shop! Why didn't he think of it himself?

Half an hour later the captain led a small, motley handful of armour from Novocherkassk against the Don, intercepted the forward Soviet reconnaissance units, and threw the enemy armoured spearheads back across the river. The day was vibrant with excitement and with frost.

This episode is typical of the drama of the situation. One Soviet tank regiment with a go-getting commander might well have decided the war at this point. For the capture of Rostov would have decided the war; it would have meant the undoubted encirclement of three or four German armies with roughly a million men.

Why did Yeremenko, the Soviet Supreme Commander of the Southern Front, not assign this task to such a go-getter? Did he over-rate the German defensive forces? Or had the example of Badanov's XXIV Tank Corps had a sobering effect?

With a dark scowl General Malinovskiy listened to the reports about the unsuccessful Soviet armoured thrust against Novocherkassk. "Even the best troops can't do the impossible," his chief of staff said apologetically.

The general nodded. He did not need to be told. As the experienced commander-in-chief of the Second Guards Army, Malinovskiy knew that even a crack formation such as his III Guards Tank Corps was now exhausted. It was dangling at the end of an extremely tenuous supply

[1] Cossack units from Russian and Ukrainian steppes, as well as units of Caucasian and other non-Russian tribes in the German-held parts of the U.S.S.R., had either defected to the Germans or been raised by them from the civilian population. They were traditionally anti-Russian rather than specifically anti-Soviet, and served as "auxiliary units", usually mounted, on the German side. After the war Stalin took savage reprisals against some of these tribes, often deporting the entire population to Siberia and abolishing such limited local autonomy as they had enjoyed. After Stalin's death and Khrushchev's denunciation of Stalin's crimes some of the tribes were brought back from east of the Urals and allowed to re-settle in their old homes. (Translator's note.)

thread. Its fighting power was melting away, that once so dramatic fighting power with which General Rotmistrov had stopped the German relief attack towards Stalingrad.

Malinovskiy was aware of all that and so was Yeremenko, the C-in-C of Army Group Southern Front. Even Nikita Sergeyevich Khrushchev, the powerful Military Council member for the Army Group, realized the difficulties. But Moscow headquarters refused to see them.

Khrushchev and Yeremenko had to justify the orders of head-quarters. And these orders were now on Malinovskiy's map table: "Second Guards Army will reach the Donets by the evening of 7th January. The III Guards Tank Corps will cross over to the western bank of the Don and take firm possession of the river crossings. The 98th Rifle Division will widen the penetration. The II Guards Mech-anized Corps will .... The V Guards Mechanized Corps will ...."

"Will, will, will!" Malinovskiy exploded, his hand slamming down on the map table at each word. "And what about the Germans who are still there? Not Rumanians or Italians, but Germans! That's something headquarters seem to have forgotten!"

But what was the use of arguing? "Bataysk must fall—Rostov must be taken!" These were the daily orders from Khrushchev and Yere-menko. Orders in writing. Orders by telephone. Verbal orders. Urgent directives.

The armies passed on the orders to the corps. And the corps passed them on to the regiments. And the regiments to the battalions.

But orders were not yet battles won. Progress was slow. Much too slow.

Not until 20th January did the spearheads of Yeremenko's slowly advancing forces cross the Manych at Manychskaya and thrust towards the west in the direction of Bataysk. Colonel Yegorov commanded the advanced detachment. Eight T-34s, three T-70s, nine armoured in-fantry carriers, five armoured scout cars and 200 infantry riding on the vehicles were charging towards the great objective—the objective they hoped to take by a surprise coup. The bulk of III Guards Tank Corps was waiting for its cue to follow up. Everything had been carefully planned. Farther south, Fifty-First Army moved its III Guards Mech-anized Corps towards Bataysk with a strong armoured combat group. The door was to be slammed shut. Already the railway line to Rostov had been cut and the Lenin collective farm reached.

In the Manychskaya bridgehead Malinovskiy was standing ready to follow up with two corps. The danger threatening the southern wing of the German Eastern Front was tremendous. Three German armies were in danger of being cut off. The gap was now only nineteen miles wide.

Rearward base in the Vitebsk area.
By sleigh to the dressing station.

A mere nineteen miles stood between roughly 900,000 German troops and the fate of Stalingrad. Nineteen miles—no distance at all. It was one of those rare moments when history was visibly and breathtakingly concentrated within a few square miles, waiting to be given a crucial push one way or another.

"How can we push in this dangerous bridgehead of Manychskaya?" Field-Marshal von Manstein asked his chief of operations, Colonel Theodor Busse.

"Hoth can't possibly do it on his own," Busse replied.

"No, he obviously can't. But what have we left?"

Manstein stepped up to the map. It showed clearly what had happened during the past week. The Field-Marshal had at last wrung from Hitler permission for the Army Detachments Hollidt and Fretter-Pico to fall back to the Donets. This now made it possible for forces to be pulled out to support Hoth and to defend Rostov.

"We'll take Balck's 11th Panzer Division from Hollidt, pull it through Rostov to the southern bank of the Don, and give it to Hoth for his counter-attack against Malinovskiy's bridgehead," Manstein was thinking aloud.

"But the 11th on its own won't be a match for the strong Russian armoured corps at Manychskaya," Busse objected.

Manstein nodded. "But Hoth still has the intact 16th Motorized Infantry Division which managed to disengage itself from Elista. Count Schwerin successfully piloted it through the Soviet Twenty-Eighth Army. With its Panzer Battalion 116 and a company of Tiger Battalion 503 it is just what's needed to strike against Manychskaya."

Manstein was referring to the superb achievements of Count Schwerin's 16th Panzer Grenadier Division during the past few weeks. Everyone still called it the 16th Motorized Infantry Division, for it was under that name that it had gained fame originally. The "Greyhound Division" had accomplished one of the most unusual, the most adventurous, and downright fantastic tasks of the whole Russian campaign—it had formed the easternmost outpost of the German armed forces in the Kalmyk Steppe and had secured the area around Elista as far as the Caspian Sea and the southern estuary of the Volga. Long-range reconnaissance parties of its Motorcycle Battalion 165 had got within sight of the Caspian, blown up oil trains from Baku, and by a ruse even telephoned the station-master of Astrakhan.

For months the division had covered the 200-mile gap between First Panzer Army and Fourth Panzer Army against the Soviet Twenty-Eighth Army, thus protecting the two Panzer armies against being encircled from the Kalmyk Steppe. All alone in the boundless steppe,

T-34s attacking.
A heavy anti-tank gun scoring a direct hit on an enemy tank.

reduced entirely to their own devices, the men from the Rhineland, Westphalia, and Thuringia discharged their task brilliantly. When the overall situation called for it, Count Schwerin, against Hitler's orders to the contrary, withdrew his formations at the right moment and established new switchlines along the Manych. Eventually, in mid-January 1943, the 16th Motorized Infantry Division foiled a particularly dangerous operation of the Soviets between Manych and Don.

At that moment General Kirchner's LVII Panzer Corps had fallen back to the Manych in furious fighting. There, Hoth's Panzer Army was desperately trying to hold the Manych line. To hold that line was vital if the Don crossing near Rostov and Bataysk was to be kept open.

Until 12th January Kirchner was able to hold a bridgehead over the Manych east of Proletarskaya with 23rd Panzer Division, 5th (Viking) SS Panzer Grenadier Division, and 17th Panzer Division, as well as the Tiger Battalion 503. Then the 16th Motorized Infantry Division was overtaken by fast Soviet formations. Strong units of armour and infantry of the Soviet Twenty-Eighth Army were thrusting towards Proletarskaya in order to force a crossing of the Manych there. Simultaneously a mechanized corps of Fifty-First Army attacked between Proletarskaya and Salsk. And a further corps of the Second Guards Army was wheeling towards Spornyy from the north. From there it was to move on towards Tikhoretsk in order to link up with units of the Soviet Transcaucasian Front.

The objective of this boldly conceived Soviet operation was to split up the German Army Group A, to prevent First Panzer Army from getting to Rostov, and at the same time to cut off and surround the Seventeenth Army.

It was an exceedingly dangerous operation at the worst possible moment: the retreating transport columns of First Panzer Army were jammed up at Bataysk. Numerous hospital trains and supply columns were bogged down outside the town. The few poor roads from south to north were clogged for miles on end. A Russian thrust into these immobilized columns would have meant chaos.

Frederick the Great once said: "A general must not only have courage; he must also have *la fortune.*" Major-General Gerhard Count Schwerin had a lot of courage and he also had *la fortune.* Two days before the Russian thrust at Manych from the north, Captain Tebbe's Panzer Battalion 116 captured a Soviet General Staff officer in the course of a counter-attack. The officer's dispatch case contained maps and orders. They were the Soviet plans and directives for their operation against Spornyy.

Count Schwerin did not hesitate. With all the forces at his disposal he chased towards Spornyy.

The Russians had already crossed the dam as well as a temporary bridge which had been built over the damaged parts, and were now moving fast towards the west, towards the retreat roads of First Panzer Army. Their objective was Bataysk.

It was a well thought-out plan. But General Gerasimenko, the C-in-C of the Soviet Twenty-Eighth Army, had made his calculations without Schwerin.

The morning of 15th January was clear and frosty. Captain Gerhard Tebbe's Panzer companies, with riflemen of the Münster 60th Motorized Infantry Regiment riding on the tanks, were moving against the Russian strongpoints from the north-east. They took no notice of what was happening on their right or left. They just drove on. They radioed signals. They fired their guns. They punched their way through. They seized the high ground in the rear of the Russians who had already crossed the river. They about-turned and with three assault parties attacked the enemy-held village.

A T-34 and four 7·62-cm anti-tank guns, positioned to cover the village, were knocked out. Two T-34s came to their aid. One of them was hit at once, the other turned back.

On the left wing of the armoured combat group was a troop of Lieutenant Kühne's 3rd Company. The troop commander was Sergeant Hans Bunzel, a Thuringian with quite a reputation for dealing with bridges and fortified hills. He was one of those resilient and resourceful men who are the backbone of any tank regiment.

He demonstrated this again on 15th January 1943. His tanks pushed as far as the Spornyy dam over the Manych. Bunzel in his Panzer III was driving furiously towards the bridge. His 5-cm tank cannon was pounding the Soviet anti-tank guns covering the bridge.

The sergeant was thinking back to that July day in 1942, when, with four tanks of his troop, he had tried to take the Manych dam, the frontier between Europe and Asia, at that very spot—only in the opposite direction. But on that occasion the dam was blown up right in front of his eyes.

Would he succeed this time? Yes—this time he was luckier. All went well. On the southern slope the Russian anti-aircraft guns captured a year ago were still in position, even though somewhat rusty.

As soon as Hans Bunzel had snatched the Spornyy bridge from the Soviets, Lieutenant Klappich with the 3rd Battalion, 60th Motorized Infantry Regiment, drove up along the southern bank of the Manych in a dense blizzard and cautiously approached Samodurovka.

Here too the Russians had already established a strongly protected bridgehead with units of their 2nd Mechanized Rifle Brigade—another dangerous base for the Soviet thrust against Bataysk. Klappich attacked. In fierce fighting he pushed on to the western edge of the village. The chief of staff of the Soviet brigade was taken prisoner.

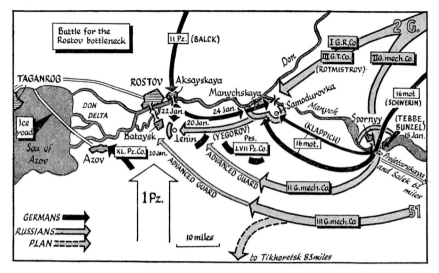

Map 10. Lieutenant Klappich's battalion held on to Samodurovka, preventing the Second Guards Army from pushing into the Rostov bottleneck. The German divisions gained time to attack the Soviet bridgehead at Manychskaya and wiped it out. In this way Rostov was kept open for the withdrawal of First Panzer Army.

His interrogation and the documents found on him revealed the full extent of the danger threatening the bottle-neck from the enemy forces deployed at Manychskaya. Rotmistrov had strict orders to open the final attack against Bataysk on 23rd January. His reinforced corps was to launch the assault against the town at 0630 hours. The 55th Tank Regiment and newly brought up motor-sleigh battalions were intended as an advanced detachment for taking the Bataysk bridges by a surprise coup. The commander of the army's armoured forces had personally taken command.

Lieutenant Klappich realized that this was no time to ask questions. He made the only correct decision—to hold Samodurovka. To hold it at any cost. To hang firmly to the village and thereby continue to threaten the flank of the main Soviet bridgehead at Manychskaya.

Klappich's battalion was a thorn in the flesh of the Soviet forces which were already operating in the approaches to Bataysk. Like a lance, German-held Samodurovka was pointing dangerously at Rotmistrov's bridgehead at Manychskaya. Rotmistrov could not risk pushing past the village to help his advanced detachments close the door of Bataysk. General Rotmistrov was forced to engage Klappich.

Klappich did not yield an inch. He tied down Rotmistrov's formations and stopped them from moving into the bottleneck. One first lieutenant between victory and defeat. One Grenadier battalion upset Stalin's plan. For this decisive action Klappich was awarded the

Oak Leaves to the Knight's Cross. Thanks to his action, Manstein's combined counter-attack with 11th Panzer Division and 16th Motorized Infantry Division against the strong Soviet offensive forces in the Manychskaya area and bridgehead on 22nd January was still in time.

On 22nd January 1943 General Balck's 11th Panzer Division was pulled over the Don at Rostov.

Rotmistrov's advanced detachments under Colonel Yegorov had organized themselves for all-round defence near the Lenin collective farm.

Balck's spearheads attacked. Yegorov lost five of his eight T-34s and two of his three T-70s. He had to fall back. The Soviet spearhead at Bataysk was smashed.

On 23rd January 11th Panzer Division, together with parts of 16th Motorized Infantry Division, burst through the Soviet positions covering Manychskaya in a dashing assault. The village was of particular importance. There the Manych flowed into the Don. There the great highway crossed the wide river. While the village and the bridge remained in Russian hands the Soviets would be in a position to renew their thrust towards Rostov from the south whenever they felt like it.

Attack! Count Schwerin moved off from the south-east with his Panzer Battalion 116 and 156th Motorized Infantry Regiment. The 11th Panzer Division made a frontal attack against the village. It was strongly held. Numerous tanks had been buried between the houses, forming steel bunkers. They were barely identifiable and very difficult to silence.

Worse still was a cunning obstacle on the south-eastern edge of the village, an obstacle which had not been spotted by reconnaissance. "Watch out! Deep anti-tank ditch!" the commanders of Captain Tebbe's Panzer Battalion suddenly heard in their earphones.

But already they were caught in front of the ditch in the furious fire of anti-tank rifles and anti-tank guns. The ditch was almost invisible under the snow. One Panzer IV, whose crew had mistaken the soft snow for firm ground, had already crashed into it.

Captain Tebbe and Lieutenant Gittermann, his ADC, drove along the ditch. At one spot it had been levelled out by shell bursts. Get through! And the two tanks moved into the village.

But two Panzer IVs against a dozen dug-in T-34s—that was hardly an equal battle. Tebbe was hit first. Then Gittermann. The crews were able to "abandon ship". They dodged, crawled, and rolled to the snow-covered anti-tank ditch. Bleeding, half-frozen, and totally exhausted they reached the foremost outposts of their battalion,

Clearly they could not succeed that way. The fire-power of the T-34s buried in the village had to be eliminated. But how?

Balck resorted to a ruse. On the morning of 25th January he concentrated the fire of the entire available artillery on the northern part of the village. He ordered smoke shells to be fired. Armoured scout cars and armoured infantry carriers moved forward cautiously and fired tracer in all directions.

Balck was feigning a full-scale attack on the north-eastern part of Manychskaya. The Soviet brigade commander fell for the bluff. The unsuccessful German attack of the day before confirmed him in the belief that the Germans would now try their luck from the north-east. In order to meet this presumed attack with massive defensive forces he ordered the dug-in T-34s to be made mobile again and switched them to the north-eastern edge of the village.

That was precisely what Balck had been waiting for. With his chief of operations, Lieutenant-Colonel Kinitz, he sat in a good observation post on a hill south of Manychskaya. As soon as he saw the Soviets regroup he immediately got his divisional artillery to switch its fire to the southern part of the village. Only one troop, firing smoke-shells, continued the sham attack in the north.

Then came the order: "Panzers forward!"

The German attack came almost under the bursts of their own shells. The 3rd Battalion, 15th Panzer Regiment, under Captain Schmidt rolled up the village from south to north. Count Schimmelmann meanwhile with his regiment attacked the Russian tanks in the north-eastern part of the village from the rear and annihilated them. The enemy infantry fled, was caught up among the tanks, and suffered heavy losses.

Captain von Hauser sent out his Motorcycle Battalion 61 to pursue the fleeing Russians. Past the still-raging tank battle in the north-eastern part of the village the wild chase continued, completing the Soviet disaster.

It was a strange and a memorable battle. German losses, thanks to the successful ruse, were astonishingly low: one man killed and fourteen wounded. The Soviets, on the other hand, lost twenty tanks and over six hundred dead in Manychskaya alone.

On the following day, Rotmistrov, the general commanding the defeated corps—later to emerge as the "lion of Prokhorovka" and the master of the great tank battle in the Kursk salient—sent the following sober and unmistakable message to General Malinovskiy, C-in-C of the Second Guards Army: "In view of the situation and their heavy losses the troops can no longer engage in any active operations at the moment."

Clearly, twenty tanks, or two-thirds of a tank battalion, were an appreciable loss even for the Russians in January 1943. Not only the Germans had had to cover the great distance from Brest-Litovsk to Stalingrad; the Soviets had also had to cover those 1200 miles, and mostly in flight. They too were at the end of their strength.

General Rotmistrov's report on the situation of the armoured and motorized formations of Second Guards Army on 26th January contains clear proof: The V Guards Mechanized Corps was down to 2200 men, seven tanks, and seven anti-tank guns. All brigade commanders had been killed. The 3rd Guards Armoured Brigade and the 2nd Motorized Guards Rifle Brigade were down to six tanks and two anti-tank guns. The 18th Guards Armoured Brigade was down to eight tanks, two anti-tank guns, and a combat strength of fifty men; the II Guards Mechanized Corps had only eight tanks left.

Thus the entire Second Guards Army was left with a mere twenty-nine tanks and eleven anti-tank guns on 26th January. That was the harsh reality on the Soviet side during those early weeks of 1943. It is not surprising therefore that in his memoirs Marshal Yeremenko writes: "All further attempts to take Rostov and Bataysk in January 1943 remained unsuccessful."

The Rostov door to the Caucasus remained open. The First Panzer Army succeeded in slipping through. In never-ending columns its formations were pulled out through the narrow bottleneck.

Four days later, on 1st February, Lieutenant Renatus Weber from Hamburg, orderly officer on the staff of XL Panzer Corps, was sitting in the icy drawing-room of an old patrician house in Taganrog, pouring out all the excitement of the past twenty-four hours in a letter home.

The young lieutenant described to his mother an exciting adventure from the great retreat from the Caucasus. The staff and the light units of XL Panzer Corps had slipped out of the trap across the ice of the Sea of Azov.

"This crossing of the ice marks the end of our expedition to the Caucasus. We were incredibly lucky to get out of the Rostov bottleneck alive," the lieutenant wrote to Hamburg.

No-one who lived through this march over the sea will ever forget it. It was an adventure which is not only recorded in the corps' history but indelibly engraved on the memories of officers and men.

XL Panzer Corps had evacuated its sector far away on the Terek, at the foot of the Higher Caucasus, during New Year's Eve, during the very last hours of 1942. Good-bye, Ishcherskaya, scene of much bloody fighting; good-bye, northern Caucasus and Caspian Sea. But there was no nostalgia in the parting—only hope that one would still be in time to escape from the great trap. Once again Hitler had been unable to take an important decision. He had only permitted First Panzer Army to withdraw partially and at certain points, and from his distant headquarters at Rastenburg he decided what sector had to be held and how long.

The great retreat from the Terek to the Don took thirty days. During the day it meant holding out and fighting, during the night it meant marching. Thus they withdrew from one sector to the next.

Marching at night, they pulled out of the promised land of Caucasian oil—the regiments of the Terek divisions who had fought their way to the very gates of Groznyy and had got within an arm's reach of Baku. They were the Berlin 3rd Panzer Division, parts of the 5th (Viking) SS Panzer Grenadier Division, the Brandenburg, Lower Saxon, Saxon, Silesian, Anhalt, and Austrian Regiments of 13th Panzer Division, of 111th, 370th, and 50th Infantry Divisions, and of 5th Luftwaffe Field Division. In addition there were Cossack squadrons, volunteer battalions of Caucasian mountain tribes, and the formations of the Rumanian 2nd Mountain Division.

Corporal Alsleben of the Panzerjäger Company, 117th Infantry Regiment, jotted down a few sentences, a few key words, in his diary each day. The whole long march of 11th Infantry Division thus unrolls before our eyes like a film strip—a film typical also of the retreat of all the other regiments involved. During the day, fighting. Then, towards 2000 hours, departure. Sometimes not until 2200 hours, or even 0400 hours.

Alsleben reports: "Panzerjägers are covering our withdrawal road. Endless columns are flowing back along them. Rain. Muddy roads. The Russians are pressing on our heels. The rearguard is suffering heavy losses. Abandoned trucks are blown up. Damaged vehicles are left behind."

His entry of 6th January first mentions the name which is remembered by all who went through this retreat: "Soldato-Aleksandrovskoye. Our division is temporarily holding the Kuma sector."

The Kuma sector! The Kuma was the first natural river barrier once the Terek had been abandoned. The divisions and corps had to cross the river to get back. It was vital to secure the bridges until all straggling formations had crossed it—all the supply columns and damaged vehicles—and to blow it up afterwards to slow down the dangerous Russian pursuit and allow the infantry and supply columns to gain a little time.

Soldato-Aleksandrovskoye was particularly important because the railway running along the northern bank of the Kuma had to be kept open as long as possible to allow for the evacuation of supply dumps. Those dumps were vitally needed—food supplies, spares, motor fuel, ammunition.

Major Musculus, commanding the Panzerjäger Battalion 111, established a barrier in front of these important bridges with his companies, together with grenadiers and engineers of 50th Infantry Regiment, and for three days resolutely blocked the approaches to all Soviet attacks from the south and east. The Russians were anxious to seal off the Kuma bridges before the German formations crossed them.

Between the Kuma and its eastern tributary the Zolka, a deep and ice-cold mountain torrent, the Soviets charged against Soldato-Aleksandrovskoye from Georgiyevsk. Between the villages of Letrovskiy and the Kuma Lieutenant Piedmont with his 2nd Company of the Panzerjäger Battalion and one troop of 117th Artillery Regiment had set up a switchline right in the middle of a treacherous swamp, directly on the only road leading to Soldato-Aleksandrovskoye. This was the road by which the Russians hoped to reach the bridge.

What happened is described by Lieutenant Piedmont in a very revealing account. His unit was on undulating ground with a view of no more than three hundred yards. Shortly before nightfall a sentry reported enemy cavalry, a few hundred horsemen attacking. Piedmont brought two machine guns into position alongside a solitary house. He alerted the anti-tank guns. He was about to send out his reconnaissance parties—but the Russians were already on them. They came galloping up in a broad front in roughly squadron strength—a hundred and fifty horsemen, their sub-machine-guns at continuous fire.

But now the two German machine-guns suddenly opened up. The two guns, under Hain and Klabus, were firing high-explosive shells into the cavalcade. Nearly half the attackers collapsed in the first burst of fire from the Panzerjägers; only loose horses raced on. The rest wheeled to the right and left. Piedmont's men were just about to cheer when the second wave appeared. A bigger wave than the first.

"Fire!" The Russian sub-machine-gun bullets rattled against the protective shields of the anti-tank gun. One of the German MGs had a stoppage. But the Soviet attack was shot up fifty yards in front of Piedmont's lines.

Now came the third attack. Only one machine-gun was left in action. The anti-tank guns were out of ammunition. Their sub-machine-guns chattering and with shouts of "Urra" the Soviets charged again. The bulk of them collapsed in the German fire. But thirty or forty horsemen rode down Piedmont's position. They also rode down the artillery emplacements behind it. But they were too few. They were picked off one by one, or got into the impenetrable swamp. They wheeled eastwards, back towards the Zolka, and splashed back through the water to the eastern bank.

Fortunately there was no fourth attack. That would have been dangerous. Piedmont had no ammunition left. The road through the swamp was jammed with abandoned vehicles whose drivers had first got under cover themselves. Not until night was it possible to clear the road again.

Lieutenant Piedmont's report states factually and undramatically: "This cavalry attack left a strange impression on all of us. To begin with, we did not take the attack seriously; it was too much like a joke. But before long we were unpleasantly surprised by the effect it had on

our morale. The rapid succession of the attacking waves was un-
nerving, and the bravery of the Russians was uncanny. Only the protective shields of the guns saved us from the bullets of the sub-machine-
guns which the horsemen fired from the saddle at full gallop. Later,
when our men moved into new positions, their knees were still shaking.
About two hundred Russians were littering the ground, dead or
wounded. Our casualties were two men slightly wounded."

Meanwhile, on the far side of the Zolka, Major Musculus with his 1st
Company was holding the village of Mikhaylovskiy, hard-pressed by
the Soviets who were striking towards the river from the east.

The combat group of 111th Infantry Division was surrounded. In
hand-to-hand fighting it fought its way out. It crossed to the far bank,
through the icy water of the deep stream, the non-swimmers being
passed on from one soldier to the next.

Step by step the Panzerjägers were falling back to the Kuma
bridges at Soldato-Aleksandrovskoye. Machine-gun parties which had
already penetrated into the villages were dislodged again with hand-
grenades and sub-machine-guns.

Musculus's Panzerjägers thus gained two days' time for the regiments
of 111th Infantry Division and 3rd Panzer Division.

Things were pretty hot also at the neighbouring 50th Infantry
Division. General Friedrich Schmidt found himself exposed to extremely heavy tank attacks. His 122nd Grenadier Regiment lost its
entire 3rd Battalion in a mass attack by a Soviet armoured brigade.

The front was reeling. A two-mile gap was yawning between 50th
Infantry Division and 111th Infantry Division. Suppose the Russians
struck now? They did strike.

But Schmidt threw his 150th Artillery Regiment into the threatened
gap. Together with assault guns from 13th Panzer Division they succeeded in smashing the enemy tank attackers before they reached
their line. The enemy infantry suffered heavy losses from the grenadiers' machine-gun fire. The Soviet regiment ebbed back.

In this fighting the 3rd Battalion, 123rd Grenadier Regiment,
especially distinguished itself. It launched a massive counter-attack
and threw back the enemy who had penetrated into their positions.
The attack by a Soviet punitive battalion, which was driven ruthlessly
against the German lines and penetrated right to the battalion command post, was wiped out by mortars and in man-to-man fighting.
The commander of 3rd Battalion, 123rd Grenadier Regiment, was a
Captain Erich Bärenfänger, holder of the Knight's Cross. No one suspected that twenty-seven months later this young officer would be the
youngest general of the German Wehrmacht in its final tragic battle for
Germany, the battle of Berlin.

At very first light on 9th January Lieutenant Klümpel of the
Panzerjäger Battalion 111 moved off with an anti-tank troop of his 1st

Company to secure the bridge over the Kuma north of the town. The river at that time was deep and the banks steep. It was a good tank obstacle—providing the bridge was blown up in time. But it had to remain intact until the last German forces had gained the northern bank. That was always a risk, always a gamble.

The approach to the bridge led over a high dam. Klümpel had a plan: he positioned one 3·7-cm anti-tank gun at the southern end of the bridge and two more by the dam on the northern bank. The rearguard was just crossing the bridge when another truck approached. They waited tensely.

It was not an enemy truck, but Sergeant Reinecke's vehicle. There were two men in the cab. They raced over the bridge. Then the driver pulled up, heaving a sigh of relief. Only then did he notice that his platoon commander Reinecke next to him was dead.

A Russian T-34 came into sight. About three hundred yards south of the bridge it went into position—out of the effective range of the 3·7 guns. Fortunately it contented itself with firing its cannon—instead of charging the bridge and attempting a coup.

The moment of the gamble had arrived. Should they wait any longer? Perhaps some stragglers were still on the far bank? But the risk was too great. It was high time to blow up the bridge.

Lieutenant Buchholz ordered Sergeant Paul Ebel, a section commander in the engineer platoon of 50th Grenadier Regiment: Blow it up now! Paul Ebel, an agricultural worker in civilian life, nodded. The Panzerjägers and Grenadiers gave him covering fire with everything they had—HE shells, machine-guns, sub-machine-guns, and carbines. All their fire was aimed at the T-34. Ebel sprinted over the dam to the bridge. He succeeded in lighting the fuse. A big flash. A roar like thunder. But when the smoke dispersed everyone's heart missed a beat—only part of the bridge had been blown up. One of the cables had failed. The bridge was still usable.

On the far side the Russians ran up to the half-destroyed ramp. The T-34 followed them slowly. They were hoping to get across.

Under cover of the smoke Ebel had made his way back over the dam and was now standing crestfallen at the failure of his mission. "Ebel!" Buchholz called over to him. "Ebel, there's nothing for it—you've got to have another go at it!"

The sergeant cursed under his breath. Again covering fire was opened from all barrels. The Russians again took cover. The machine-gun bullets again rattled against the T-34. Ebel once more reached the bridge unscathed. He was fiddling with the fuses. The minutes seemed to drag eternally. Now he retreated a few steps. He flung himself down against the slope. And now the big detonation shook the ground. With a roar and a rumble the high bridge went up. Under cover of the dense smoke Sergeant Ebel made his way back over the dam to the north bank. For his feat he was awarded the Knight's Cross.

Not until 10th January did the Russians succeed in advancing cautiously over the river. The rearguard had won three days for the bulk of the troops. Three whole days.

This kind of fighting lasted for four weeks altogether. On 31st January Corporal Rolf Alsleben from Hildesheim noted in his diary: "We are almost out of the wood now. We've marched over three hundred miles since Mozdok. A whole month of retreat."

Yes, they were almost out of the wood. They were close to Bataysk, near the last bridges, near the last loophole out of the big trap.

At the same time, Lieutenant Renatus Weber of the staff of XL Panzer Corps wrote in his diary: "We are in the Belyy area, south of Rostov, with parts of 3rd Panzer Division, some corps troops subordinated to it, and some squadrons of cossacks. New operation orders have come for our corps. We are to be employed in the Donets area. Assembly in the Taganrog area, beyond the Sea of Azov. Some of the way we are to march over the frozen sea!!" The two exclamation marks are a reflection of Renatus Weber's feelings at the prospect.

The operations staff and a Cossack squadron set out from the village of Ilinka in the early morning of 31st January 1943. The light units of the corps and the Cossack squadron were to take the road over the frozen Sea of Azov. The tanks and heavy vehicles were routed over the bridge of Bataysk and through the Rostov bottleneck because the ice would not bear their weight.

The 31st January 1943 was a hazy winter's day. At first the trek made good progress along the road from Tikhoretsk to Rostov, the K1. Then came the fishing village of Azov. Large signposts now diverted the columns: Turn here for the ice route. Over the sea, forward march!

Engineers had built a ramp down to the frozen surface of the sea and accurately marked out the first few hundred yards of the ice road.

But the distance across to Taganrog was twenty-six miles. At first the track ran across the Don delta, through frozen marshes and dunes and over an island. Then came the deep sea.

At first the ice was milky white and bumpy. But over the deep water it became smooth and clear as glass. The route was only thinly marked; a few empty petrol cans at long intervals. But one could hardly go wrong because the creaking, brittle road was littered with spectral signposts. Buses, trucks, and heavy staff cars which had broken through the ice, with often only their roofs showing. Signposts and warning signals at the same time.

The ice cover was treacherous. There were holes and there were thin patches. The haze compelled the drivers to move slowly. In long-drawn-out columns, infantry and horse-drawn transport moved forward. The Cossacks were trotting towards Taganrog in extended formation.

For the first time the men of 3rd Panzer Division had a new kind of companion—a kind unknown to the advancing troops but henceforward to become a regular feature of their retreat. Civilians were trekking along right and left. Cossack families following their menfolk who had joined German volunteer units or enlisted as auxiliary police, and who now feared the return of the Soviets. A motley transport—peasant carts piled high, cattle and horses on long ropes, and children.

Towards midday the haze lifted a little. And almost at once the Soviet ground-attack aircraft arrived. At barely a hundred and fifty feet the IL-2s swept over the ice. They dropped bombs. They fired their guns. There was no ditch, no shrub, no house—nothing to provide cover. As far as the eye could see there was nothing but the frozen sea, as flat as a pancake.

The columns scattered. The Cossack squadron chased off in all directions, the horsemen galloping over the ice as if the devil were at their heels.

The bombs raised gushing fountains of ice. Splinters tinkled over the frozen sea. One could only pray or fire. Many were praying. But many also flung themselves down on their backs and with their rifles or machine-guns let fly furiously at the Soviet aircraft. Fortunately the sky soon clouded over again. It even began to snow. Under the white veil the trek continued across the sea, winding along slowly like some giant snake.

General Siegfried Henrici, commanding the XL Panzer Corps, and Colonel Carl Wagener, his chief of staff, did not leave their command post until late in the morning. A thick blizzard reduced visibility to virtually nil. As the small column stopped at a point where the tracks on the ice divided, a peasant cart overtook them at a fair speed and without any hesitation took the left fork.

Colonel Wagener signalled the muffled driver to stop. He assumed him to be a local auxiliary and in his best Russian asked him the shortest way to Taganrog. Horrified the man stared at the Russian-speaking colonel. Wagener understood: he was being taken for a Russian. He therefore repeated his question in German. The terrified soldier burst out laughing with relief. In broadest Saxon he replied: "Very sorry, Herr Oberst, but I'm a stranger here myself." And with a sly smile he added: "But my instinct tells me: Arthur, keep to the left!"

The instinct of Arthur, the Saxon, was quite correct. At least where the Sea of Azov was concerned.

About three miles east of Taganrog the ice road terminated in another ramp built by the engineers and rejoined the coast road from Rostov to Taganrog. The columns of XL Panzer Corps were again on firm ground. But now all the transport difficulties associated with Russia's roads were with them again—jammed-up trucks, guns stuck in the mud, impassable swampy stretches. Only now did the infantry-men realize what a fast and smooth journey they had had over the sea.

The heavy formations of First and Fourth Panzer Armies were mov-ing westwards with difficulty along the congested road. Mixed up with them were the ground formations of the Luftwaffe and various rear-ward services. And among them also were the treks of the Caucasian mountain tribes. Vehicle after vehicle—trucks, staff cars, armoured scout cars, guns, light tanks. An interminable queue.

Harassed field police were desperately trying to unravel the bunched-up traffic at bridges and crossroads.

The spearheads of XL Panzer Corps reached Taganrog on the evening of 31st January. As he was warming himself by a hurriedly lit fire, Major Kandutsch, the Corps Intelligence Officer, thoughtfully asked his Baltic interpreter: "What do you suppose we shall remember most about our march across the Sea of Azov?"

The answer came promptly: "The fear, Herr Major, the fear!"

Indeed, fear had marched with them all the way over the ice. But they had escaped the trap. And the day's other news reminded them of the fate which, thanks to Manstein's skill, they had been spared. It was the 31st January 1943, the day when the German Sixth Army died at Stalingrad.

Lieutenant Renatus Weber also thought of Stalingrad at this hour of salvation. In his letter to his mother, written from Taganrog, he said: "In the last analysis we owe our escape to the resistance of Sixth Army at Stalingrad, who cut the railway and tied down strong Russian con-tingents."

What the young lieutenant wrote then remains true to this day. It has, moreover, been since confirmed by historical fact. The salvation of First Panzer Army, and indeed of the whole of Army Group A and of parts of Army Group Don, was due not only to Manstein's generalship and the gallantry of the troops, but very largely also to Sixth Army which had been holding out in Stalingrad throughout January.

In its death struggle, Sixth Army had not only tied down half a dozen Soviet armies and kept them on the Volga, thereby preventing them from intervening in the decisive battle of Rostov, but—and this was possibly of even greater importance—the fighting on the Volga meant the blocking of the three principal railway lines from Stalingrad to the west and hence vastly increased supply difficulties for the Soviet armies operating against Rostov.

Indeed, these supply problems were the real reason why Stalin's gigantic pincers could not snap shut around the German armies in the Caucasus and on the Don and thus trap the entire southern wing of the German forces.

Soviet records support this statement. In the *History of the Great Fatherland War*, volume three, page 98, we read: "The Soviet southern front, in particular the Second Guards Army, which was due to take Rostov at the beginning of January, was low in all kinds of supplies, notably fuel and ammunition, because the battle of Stalingrad was paralysing supplies and in particular rail traffic."

Thus, on 31st January, just as the resistance of Sixth Army in Stalingrad was collapsing, the rearguards of Fourth Panzer Army crossed the bridges of Rostov. The Soviets were unable to slam the door shut.

On 5th February, the Panzerjägers of General Recknagel's 111th Infantry Division had arrived on the spot and, with the support of some 8·8-cm guns, kept the Russian tank packs at a healthy distance from the escape hole.

On 6th February at 2200 hours the last units of Recknagel's Lower Saxon regiments crossed the bridges of Bataysk and moved through Rostov—by then a dead city. Behind them rumbled the thunder of demolitions—the Bataysk bridges were being dynamited. And not before time, for already Soviet reconnaissance parties were crawling over the ice of the Don to the bridge piers in order to disconnect the demolition charges. Did they succeed? Or was the desperate haste of the retreating Germans to blame for the fact that demolition was only partially successful?

Two days later, during the night of 7th–8th February, in the fitful light of tracer ammunition, Panzer No. 300 crossed the Don bridge at Aksayskaya. Lieutenant Klaus Kühne of the 16th Motorized Infantry Division was the last man to cross this miracle of German army engineering skill. In ten days of ceaseless day and night work Lieutenant Kirchenbauer's bridge-building unit 21 had built that bridge over the ice-covered Don. It was strong enough to withstand storm and drifting ice, and to carry loads in excess of sixty tons—in other words, suitable for all armoured vehicles and the heaviest artillery.

A few minutes later, Sergeant Wagner of the demolition squad of Engineer Battalion 675 blew up the massive pontoon bridge. It took one and a half tons of high explosives.

The job was done. The long journey of First Panzer Army from the Terek to the Don was successfully concluded—a distance of 375 miles. The Fourth Panzer Army had been successfully wheeled from the approaches of Stalingrad over the Manych to the northern shores of the Sea of Azov.

But meanwhile, what had happened to the divisions of Seventeenth Army which had penetrated far into the forests and mountain ranges of the Caucasus? To the snow-covered passes of Mount Elbrus, Klukhor, and Sanchar? And down to the coastal road on the Black Sea? And to the oilfields of Maykop?

The disaster of Stalingrad and the Russian push to the Don meant that their positions on the eastern edge of the Black Sea, up on the mountain passes and down by the drilling rigs of the oilfields, had become untenable. They had to be pulled back. The army was already on the move. By the time the demolition of the pontoon bridge of Aksayskaya rang out over the snow-covered Don Cossack steppe like a salute in honour of the salvation of half a million men of First and Fourth Panzer Armies, the corps of Seventeenth Army in the western Caucasus had also, in a manner of speaking, turned the corner. The worst part of the retreat had been successfully completed. Colonel-General Ruoff's formations had been obliged to hold on to their positions even after the departure of First Panzer Army from the Terek at the beginning of January, in order that the flank of Kleist's Army Group A should not be pushed in by the Russians. On 10th January, at long last, XLIX Mountain Corps evacuated its old positions in the high part of the Caucasus and began to move back to the Maykop area.

The plan of the withdrawal envisaged Seventeenth Army disengaging itself sector by sector towards the north-west, via the "Cable-car Line" and the "Gothic Line", into a bridgehead in the lower reaches of the Kuban. It was Hitler's idea to establish there a kind of springboard into Asia, where 400,000 men would be held ready to be moved forward again in the summer of 1943 against the Caucasus and its oilfields. The base for this bridgehead was to be the Crimea.

This plan was typical of Hitler's strategy of illusions. It was unbelievable. Was this the man who in 1940 and 1941 had stunned the world by well-thought-out operations and bold improvisation? At that time he tended to be over-cautious in critical situations. Since Stalingrad, however, he had been conducting the war with an almost pathological obduracy, simply refusing to accept clear and unmistakable facts.

Yet these facts were only too obvious even to the most junior staff officer. At Stalingrad 250,000 men were encircled. Between Chir and Don the situation was disastrous. Yet 200 miles from Rostov, on the Kuban, 400,000 men with more than 2000 guns were to be immobilized —just as though they were encircled.

Hitler had originally even intended to move First Panzer Army into the Kuban bridgehead as well. Only the most determined representations by the commanders in the field persuaded him to give up this absurd idea and to transfer the bulk of First Panzer Army to Manstein, switching only its LII corps and 13th Panzer Division into the Kuban bridgehead. And that was quite foolish enough.

What the bridges over the Don at Rostov meant to First and Fourth Panzer Armies, the Kuban bridges at Krasnodar and Ust-Labinskaya meant to the infantry, rifle, and mountain corps of Seventeenth Army. They were vital pivoting points and equally vital supply centres for the retreating corps.

Here too, therefore, a nerve-racking race began against time. And against the enemy.

These were no longer mobile troops, indeed hardly motorized units, but only greatly weakened small armoured formations of 13th Panzer Division—mostly infantry, rifle units, mountain troops, and horse-drawn artillery who covered this distance of 250 miles in four weeks, without motor vehicles, with only pack animals, and with horses pulling the guns and supply carts. Much of the way they were engaged in fighting. From the icy slopes of Mount Elbrus, Klukhor, and Sanchar, and from the marshes of the Gunayka valley, they moved down into the Kuban plain, and then north-west into the "Gothic Line", the last bastion before the Kuban bridgehead.

This retreat too was an achievement almost without parallel in military history. A chapter in the war, marked by gallantry, dedication, and readiness for sacrifice on the part of officers and men, and not with weapons only but equally so with spades, alongside horses and mules.

Here more than anywhere else did the German Wehrmacht reap the benefits of its progressive, modern structure, its lack of social barriers and class prejudice. The German Army was the only army in the world in which officers and men shared the same food. The officer was not only the leader in battle but also the "foreman", a "trooper with epaulettes", whose unhesitating participation in carrying loads or freeing stuck vehicles set an example which conquered fatigue. In no other way could the adventure of this great retreat have succeeded.

Retreat is invariably a depressing chapter for the troops. Since November 1942 General de Angelis's XLIV Jäger Corps and General Konrad's XLIX Mountain Corps had been defending their positions in the western Caucasus, on the road to Tuapse and along the famous Military Highways of the Central Caucasus, with an incredible amount of enthusiasm and readiness for sacrifice. And all the time they were in sight, within a few miles, of their ultimate objective—the Black Sea and the Turkish frontier. They could not make it.

In mid-November 1942 the great rains came. The Caucasian mountains, valleys, and forests were swept by cloud-bursts and gales. The rivers broke their banks. Brooks turned into raging torrents. Bridges were carried away, telephone wires were ripped from their poles. The mud was knee-deep. Movement was impossible even with peasant carts and beasts of burden. Horses and mules broke into the morass up to their bellies. Vehicles and guns were immobilized. Horse-drawn field kitchens were caught on the fords by the torrential streams and men and horses were swept away like toys and drowned. Foxholes and command posts were flooded. Grenadiers and riflemen died in their trenches of cold and exhaustion. Horses and mules disappeared in the quagmires or developed mange and died.

The gunners dragged their ammunition into dry caves in the rock.

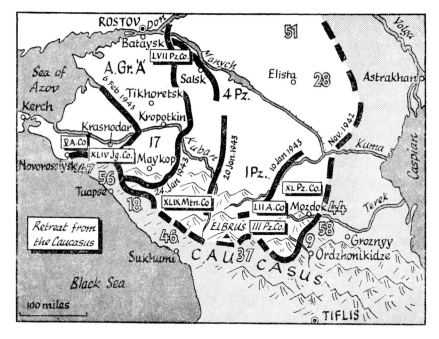

Map 11. In a difficult withdrawal operation First Panzer Army pulled back towards the north, while Seventeenth Army, using a succession of improvised interception lines, pulled out of the Caucasus into the Kuban bridgehead in a mere four weeks.

But what was the use of it all? It was easy enough to fire a shell but it was impossible to score a hit: because of the strong cross-wind the deviations were incalculable and targets were invariably missed.

The work done by the medical orderlies in collecting the wounded and transporting them back was beyond description. Each day of this atrocious war was filled with heroic deeds of humanity. And in the end the war itself died in this mountain world of howling storms and eerie lightning. It was drowned in the raging torrents. It froze to death among the glaciers. It was suffocated in the mud and the rubble of inundated valleys. There was no time left for killing. No aircraft took off any more, neither bombers nor reconnaissance planes.

Artillery, flak, and assault guns were withdrawn. The positions high up in the mountains were evacuated. The blood-drenched Zemasho, 3400 feet high, south of Krasnodar was abandoned—the last mountain before the coast, the mountain from which they had seen the sea and the road to Tuapse, their longed-for objective.

Here Major von Hirschfeld and Major Dr Lawall had fought and bled with the riflemen of 98th Regiment. Now, so near their objective, they had to abandon their positions. Just like the men of First

Panzer Army had done on the blood-soaked battlefield on the Terek.

On 10th January the withdrawal operation known as "Cable Car", the retreat towards the Goryachiy Klyuch to Maykop line, began for all formations of Seventeenth Army. The group of Colonel von Le Suire, which had held the high mountain passes with units of 1st Mountain Division, had disengaged itself from the enemy on 4th January and made its way back, to the Maykop area, in twenty-three days of fighting.

The Württemberg 125th Infantry Division fell back to the area south of Krasnodar. This was a vital line, as Krasnodar was to be the turntable for the withdrawal of the whole of Seventeenth Army.

For Colonel Alfred Reinhardt, at that time commanding the 125th Infantry Division, that meant that the town with its river crossings had to be held at all costs. Krasnodar must not be surrendered. Not only because of its importance as a traffic junction but also because it was a huge supply centre. It contained enormous stores of all kinds of goods. And since the heavy ice in the Strait of Kerch ruled out, for the time being, all other approaches to the Kuban area, the 400,000 men of the Seventeenth Army were utterly dependent on the stores in Krasnodar—at least until the Strait of Kerch was clear of ice. And that would not be for another seven weeks at least.

Reinhardt's task therefore was not unlike that performed by Hoth's divisions at Rostov. The 125th Infantry Division had to prevent the Russians from emerging from the northern slopes of the Caucasus. It must stop them at all costs from getting near the only two usable roads of retreat from Goryachiy Klyuch to Krasnodar and to Krimskaya and Novorossiysk. Reinhardt's division had to defend Krasnodar. It had to secure the roads. And it had to keep in check the partisans in the forests. That was quite a job.

Under cover from 125th Infantry Division the XLIV Rifle Corps was successfully pulled out of the swamp via Krasnodar with all its heavy weapons. A magnificent achievement.

Meanwhile, XLIX Mountain Corps under General Konrad had to disengage from the enemy in the snow-covered passes of the Higher Caucasus. Here the companies of the Franconian-Sudeten 46th Infantry Division under General Haccius acted as the rearguard covering the difficult withdrawal. It worked out all right. The worst part of it was the recovery of the heavy weapons from the by then quite impassable valley of the Gunayka and the Pshish.

One has to read the account of Colonel Winkler, the artillery commander, to get an insight into the difficulties involved in the withdrawal of the heavy guns. During the dry season they had been moved into the roadless valleys, and now they were standing axle-deep in mud on the valley floor. In this chaotic situation Colonel Winkler worked wonders with a mere dozen tractors.

It really was a case of doing the impossible. Three tractors hitched to a gun. Heave! And again! Yard by yard the guns were pulled out of the sticky mud. Then they were taken apart. Piece by piece the troops manhandled them down the steep slopes. Then they loaded them on sledges. And then on pack animals. And finally on vehicles.

Not even the Russians, who were masters of improvisation, achieved anything like it. They were defeated by the difficult terrain and only managed to follow the retreating Germans at a considerable distance. Only hard work, sweat, ingenuity, and unshakeable courage saved the corps of Seventeenth Army.

When the Soviets had reformed, their main attacks were aimed at the German withdrawal road from Saratovskaya to Krasnodar. This, the only highway to the north, was known as the "Stalin Highway", and was negotiable in all weathers even by heavy vehicles. The Russians tried desperately to get at this road. The large forests offered them favourable jumping-off positions. For months combat squads and partisan formations had seeped into the area south of Krasnodar. The German line was so thin that this was unavoidable. Thus a dangerous partisan area had gradually developed. Now and then a group or a leader of these formations was caught behind the German lines.

The engagement reports of 97th Rifle Division record an episode typical of the savagery of this type of partisan warfare. A unit of Turkmen volunteers who had fought bravely at Tuapse alongside 97th Rifle Division used a small abandoned village near Severskaya for their sleeping quarters during the winter nights. Occasionally the unit commanders would forget to post sentries.

One morning the Turkmens did not turn up for duty. A German patrol cautiously approached the village, which seemed suspiciously quiet. The patrol leader was the first to enter a house, pistol in hand. His men heard him yell an angry oath. And then they were able to see for themselves. The same picture in every hut: the Turkmens were lying in their beds with their heads cut off. Chalked on the walls was the slogan "Traitors will not escape revenge!"

This gruesome scene was part of the psychological warfare conducted by the Soviets against the much-feared co-operation of various non-Russian, anti-Bolshevik nationalities with the German Wehrmacht. A good part of the Soviet intelligence effort behind the German lines was concerned with watching and foiling these collaborators. It worked extremely well. Officers and commissars of this secret front recruited suitable inhabitants behind the German lines by means of regular call-up orders. Moscow's emissaries in this dangerous struggle were real dare-devils.

Lieutenant Alex Buchner of 13th Mountain Jäger Regiment describes how one day his Karachay militia, while out on patrol in the spurs of the Caucasus, captured a tall Soviet officer. Under interrogation he

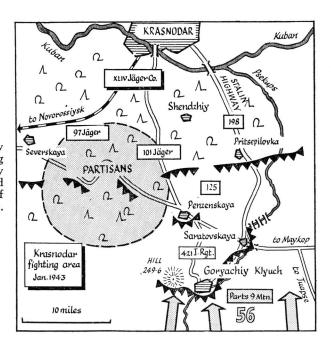

Map 12. In heavy defensive fighting 125th Infantry Division covered the withdrawal of XLIV Jäger Corps.

Inside map labels:
KRASNODAR
Kuban
Kuban
XLIV Jäger Co.
to Novorossiysk
Shendzhiy
STALIN HIGHWAY
Psekups
198
97 Jäger
Pritsepilovka
Severskaya
101 Jäger
PARTISANS
125
Penzenskaya
Krasnodar fighting area Jan. 1943
Saratovskaya
to Maykop
HILL .249·6
421 I. Rgt.
Goryachiy Klyuch
to Tuapse
Parts 9 Mtn.
56
10 miles

refused to disclose how he had got behind the lines. He merely rolled his eyes and remained silent.

When the Karachay had stripped him of his uniform for a closer examination, the prisoner began to betray clear signs of nervousness as Buchner picked up his fine peaked cap to cut off the big enamelled Soviet star from it as a souvenir.

A few knife cuts into the top of the cap revealed everything: out of the lining came maps printed on tissue paper, orders and authorities from Moscow, and identity documents. The patrol had caught the man who was to have built up a secret front in the Kuban area.

But partisan units also engaged in merciless open combat in the wooded region of Severskaya. The 8th Troop, 125th Artillery Regiment, was overrun there by strong forces. The 7th Troop escaped the same fate only thanks to the vigilance of an infantry platoon providing cover for it.

Interrogation of a captured sergeant confirmed 125th Infantry Division in the view that the Russians were extremely anxious to block the German route of retreat. "Our commanders," the sergeant said, "have read out to all units an order from headquarters. It said that the German retreat route must be cut, at no matter what sacrifice."

This was not surprising. The prize, if the attempt succeeded, was the bagging of the whole of XLIV Jäger Corps.

The most savage fighting on the right wing was for the crucial hill

249·6. This was held by 3rd Battalion, 421st Grenadier Regiment, under Captain Winzen. Unshaven and haggard with sleeplessness, the captain sat in his stone hut. Outside the machine-guns were barking.

A runner came galloping up to the command post: "They're coming again, Herr Hauptmann!"

They were coming. Just as yesterday and the day before. Only one in every four had a uniform, and one in every three, at best, carried a rifle. They had no heavy weapons at all. They yelled "Urra!" and charged. Right in front were young officers, some still cadets from officer training centres. Behind them came boys of thirteen or fourteen, as well as old men and invalids.

It was the scraping of the barrel. The German machine-guns mowed down the first wave. Those behind it picked up the rifles of the wounded and killed, and charged on. To judge by their features, all Caucasian tribes were represented.

Soon mountains of dead and wounded piled up a mere fifty yards in front of the positions of 3rd Battalion. It was impossible to identify the units of the killed as the men did not carry any documents.

We know now that they were hurriedly levied special formations of the Soviet Fifty-Sixth Army and came under the newly raised Soviet 9th Mountain Division.

This inferno continued for four days. They came again and again. They used the mountains of their own dead for cover. Behind these gruesome parapets they reformed and with a spine-chilling yell of "Urra!" they would charge again, over their own dead.

"Hand-grenade throwers forward!" the German platoon commanders called whenever a pause intervened in the fighting. Only with hand-grenades could the Soviet assembly positions behind the mountains of corpses be reached.

But what was the use of it? Like shifting dunes the mountains of dead crept closer and closer. Fifty yards became twenty-five. Then ten. "Urra!" And then already they were in the command post.

Captain Winzen rounded up every man he had. Immediate counterattack. Quick! Every man knew why they had to be quick. They had had some grim experience of these fanatical militias. Like lightning the German assault party was back in their old battalion command post. But the scene before them was frightful. The boys had avenged their dead. The men of 3rd Battalion had another grim reminder that they were fighting in Asia.

The only man found still alive and not massacred in the recaptured battalion command post was a seriously wounded Russian lieutenant. When Captain Winzen interrogated him amidst that scene of carnage and demanded an explanation for the atrocities, the Russian merely shrugged his shoulders and said, "You Germans know how to fight; we are still learning."

They learnt all right. But for the moment they were still making bad mistakes and costly ones. Thus the commanders of these Red "Home Guard" and partisan units at Krasnodar led their men in a strange manner. They put out their tactical orders to their subordinate officers over the radio *en clair*, together with frightful threats: "Unless you attain the objective I'll have you shot!" or, "If you retreat I'll order fire to be opened on your units!"

The forward monitoring service of 125th Infantry Division listened in to all this, and Reinhardt and his staff therefore always knew in advance where to expect an enemy attack. His tactical reserves were always on the spot before the Soviet attacker.

"At times I conducted operations entirely on the strength of the Russian commands by radio," General Reinhardt recalls. Wherever the "Urra!" of the charging regiments shattered the grey dawn, the combat squads of the Baden-Württemberg battalions were already behind their machine-guns, their carbines ready on the parapets of their dug-outs, and hand-grenades within easy reach. Then the attack came.

A hundred times death swept over the plain, into the undergrowth and against the flat flanks of the river valleys.

The "Regimentsgruppe Ortlieb", a combat group of roughly regiment strength, was holding the village of Penzenskaya. It was situated at the important road fork where the old highway to Krasnodar crossed the east–west road from Maykop to Novorossiysk.

The Russians were stubbornly trying to take the village. Major Ortlieb had to organize his men for all-round defence. Supplies for his force had to come through by heavily armed convoy. Every such convoy was an adventure. The Russians were lying in wait like Red Indians, their snipers picking off the German drivers. Their engineers mined the roads and buried in it remote-controlled high-explosive charges. It was a small-scale war, but exhausting.

Ortlieb was holding the western approaches to Krasnodar.

The other important strongpoint covering the approach to the vital centre of Krasnodar was Saratovskaya, immediately on the "Stalin Highway" which ran from the Maykop oilfields through the mountains to Krasnodar. This road was negotiable by heavy trucks and in all weathers. But it had a few dangerously vulnerable points—the bridges over the deep cut valley north of the town.

The commander of 125th Infantry Division needed every single man at the focal points of his defensive front; thus the bridges had to be covered by Ukrainian volunteer units. They were commanded by reliable German NCO's—but it was not the same thing.

During the night of 27th–28th January, at 0200, Reinhardt was woken by his orderly officer, Lieutenant Roser. "Herr Oberst, the Russians have got to the bridges!"

"All three of them?" Reinhardt asked, flabbergasted.

"All three of them, Herr Oberst."

For a moment Reinhardt was heard muttering Swabian curses. Then he ordered: "Get Lieutenant Sauter!"

The commander of the 14th Panzerjäger Company, 421st Grenadier Regiment, was sent off to the bridges with a machine-gun platoon and a 7·5-cm anti-tank gun. A company of 420th Grenadier Regiment was

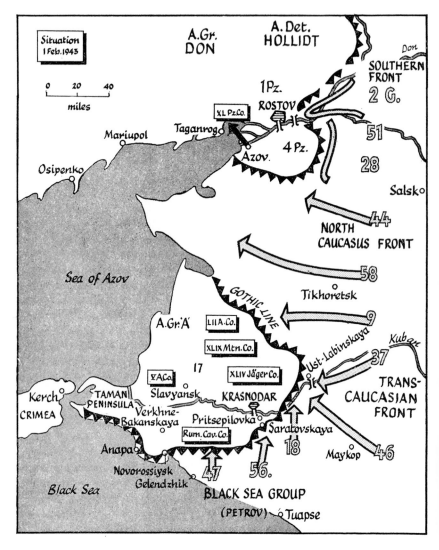

Map 13. Five German corps were assembled behind the Gothic Line. Stalin employed six armies in his attempts to reduce the German defences.

loaded on trucks. Reinhardt himself went along with this company.

They came to the first bridge.

"Patrol forward!"

"Bridge not held by friend or enemy!" the report came back.

Reinhardt's eyes flashed angrily.

Off to the next bridge.

All by himself, a German NCO was crouching behind his machine-gun by the ramp. He gestured over to the third bridge, not lit up by fires. "As soon as the first few bangs came from over there, together with a handful of fleeing Ukrainians, my Ukrainian lot also took to their heels. An enemy assault party made an attack but were stopped by my fire and have evidently withdrawn now."

Sauter cautiously approached the third bridge with his assault party. A Slovak fighting vehicle was burning on its ramp. In the light of the fire a few Russian infantrymen could be seen digging in. A Russian sentry by the approach to the bridge was just searching a supply vehicle for booty.

"Just what I want," muttered Sergeant Maier of 14th Company. He crept up to the truck. Softly he hissed: "Psst!" The Russian straightened up. Maier struck with his rifle butt. The Russian keeled over noiselessly.

That was what Sauter was waiting for. With his combat squad he moved up to the most convenient range. Then he raked the surprised Russians with HE shells and machine-gun fire.

The company of 420th Grenadier Regiment, which followed Sauter, crushed the last resistance. The bridge was clear again.

That was most fortunate. For on the following day the last battalions of 198th Infantry Division, the Slovak Fast Division, as well as the Special Service Battalion 500 and the Cyclist Battalion of 101st Jäger Division, passed through Saratovskaya and continued in the direction of Krasnodar. They would have been lost if Reinhardt's Swabians had not kept the road open. One more instance of a major turn in the situation depending on the resolution of a single commander or indeed the gallantry of one man behind a machine-gun guarding a bridge.

At last Reinhardt was able to order his combat groups still holding covering positions to the east and south of Krasnodar to fight their way back.

The Russians immediately followed up. They tried desperately to overtake the German rearguards and break through to Krasnodar. These were very different formations from the wild hordes of the last few weeks. These were all young people, well trained, in new khaki uniforms and short greatcoats. None of their equipment was of Russian origin—uniform, underwear, socks, and boots all bore the American stamp GI. Not till you came to their skins were they Russian.

Their light weapons too came from the U.S.A., and in their pockets the Soviet soldiers had Camel cigarettes. Roosevelt's inexhaustible war production was now also being employed against the German armies on the borders of Europe and Asia.

But even these crack troops with their American equipment did not succeed in breaking through to Krasnodar. On 30th January the 125th Infantry Division had taken up new defensive positions to both sides of Pritsepilovka. On the same day, on the left wing of the army, the last units of XLIX Mountain Corps crossed the Kuban by the army bridges of Ust-Labinskaya which had been kept open by formations of 13th Panzer Division and 46th Infantry Division. Twelve hours later these bridges were blown up by the rearguards of the Franconian-Sudeten 46th Infantry Division. But the Seventeenth Army was not out of the wood yet.

2. Alert on the Black Sea

Secret session in the Kremlin–Stalin wants to trap the Seventeenth Army–Adventure in Ozereyka Bay–One artillery battalion–Major Kunikov's coup at Novorossiysk–Fighting in the "Little Land"–Political Commissar Brezhnev.

ON 24th January 1943 a secret meeting took place at the Kremlin. On that day Stalin put forward a plan for one of the most unusual operations of the whole war in Russia.

With the aid of documents, military essays, and the memoirs of Soviet army leaders this dramatic conference in the Kremlin's underground bunker can now be reconstructed fairly accurately.

Under conditions of greatest secrecy Stalin had summoned the Commanders-in-Chief of the Caucasian Front and of the Black Sea Fleet to the war room of the Soviet High Command. On the wall of the conference room hung a huge situation map of the Black Sea area with the Caucasus, the Kuban Steppe, and the coastal strip. The generals had this map before their eyes as Stalin embarked on his great speech. It started gently enough, vibrant with exultation over the great victory of Stalingrad which was beginning to take shape. But as he continued, Stalin became increasingly angry—angry about the failure of his generals to turn the success of Stalingrad into a huge victory.

True, the German Sixth Army was in a deadly stranglehold. But all the other great opportunities which Stalin had expected to spring from the loss of twenty German divisions between the Don and Volga had melted away like snow under the sun.

"The troops of the Black Sea Group have failed to accomplish the tasks assigned to them and have been unable to reach Tikhoretsk," Stalin complained. He stepped up to the map and swept a pointer across mountains and steppes, right through the blue and red lines indicating the positions and movements of friend and foe. "The troops of the Northern Group have similarly failed to reach their objective," he continued. His pointer tapped Salsk and Rostov.

There was embarrassed silence. The generals knew that Stalin had read their reports, with all their explanations of why the great plan for the encirclement of the German Army Group A had not come off. But they also knew that he refused to believe their reports.

Like Hitler, the dictator in the Kremlin also mistrusted his generals. And like Hitler he believed that, provided only the military people were "kept on their toes", given strict orders, and perhaps an occasional idea, all must work out according to plan.

"What are the fascists trying to do?" asked Stalin, like a schoolmaster. "The answer is obvious," he answered his own question. "Hitler is withdrawing only part of his Army Group A from the Caucasus across the Don. As for the other part, his Seventeenth Army, he clearly intends to concentrate it on the mainland of Asia, in a bridgehead on the Taman Peninsula."

Map 14. Stalin planned to cut off the German Seventeenth Army by way of a combined land and seaborne operation.

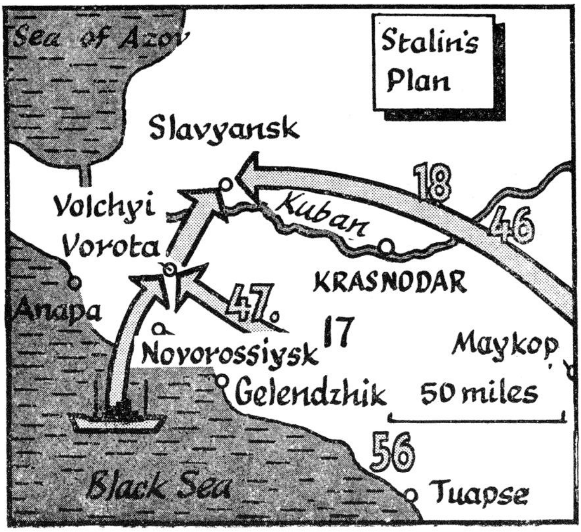

General Antonov, the Deputy Chief of General Staff, demonstratively nodded. And just as if this were an agreed signal Stalin now turned to him. "What is our information, General Antonov?"

The deputy chief of staff stood up and walked over to the map: "According to information from our secret intelligence service, the German High Command intends to resume its offensive against the oilfields next summer. For that purpose, Seventeenth Army and parts of First Panzer Army are to remain on the mainland of Asia."

"Just so," Stalin added. "Their Seventeenth Army is withdrawing only slowly, fighting all the way, in order to save all its heavy material and hang on to as much ground as possible. In doing so, Hitler offers us another chance to annihilate the fascists after all—provided we act quickly. We've got to cut off their retreat to the Taman Peninsula."

Stalin was obviously mesmerized by his plan. And his generals realized that he was backing it with the whole of his personal authority. Anyone opposing it would be the butt of his anger. "General Petrov," Stalin continued, looking across at the Commander-in-Chief of the Black Sea Group, "General Petrov will thrust into the Krasnodar area with his Forty-Sixth and Eighteenth Armies!" The pointer moved on the map from Maykop to the Kuban. "He will seize the Kuban crossings and follow the river to the west towards the Taman Peninsula."

He raised his voice: "Simultaneously, Novorossiysk will be taken by a double encirclement!" The stick smacked imperiously against the map. "Forty-Seventh Army will mount a frontal attack against the Novorossiysk front and break through."

General Petrov shook his head doubtfully. Stalin saw it and turned to him: "I know what you're going to say. I haven't read your reports for nothing. Forty-Seventh Army, you'll say, has too few assault formations, too few tanks, and too few guns for such an operation into the depth of the enemy area."

Stalin made a dismissive gesture. "I've heard all that before!"

And just as if he had planned this rhetoric effect, he continued slowly and emphatically: "We will take Novorossiysk by a combined land and sea operation. A strong landing force of special army and navy troops will be landed by the Black Sea Fleet in the enemy's rear in a surprise coup at night. This force will smash the German coastal defences at a favourable point and establish a beach-head. Armoured brigades and airborne regiments will follow up and enlarge the breakthrough towards Volchyi Vorota. They will then join up with the units of Forty-Seventh Army which will have broken through north of Novorossiysk. After their link-up the two columns will advance together to meet the armies coming down from the Kuban and join up with them."

With his pointer Stalin indicated this pincer movement on the map.

And, just as if it had all been accomplished already, he said: "Thus the German Seventeenth Army is cut off from the Taman Peninsula."

The generals were dumbfounded. An amphibious operation! A type of warfare of which the Soviet Army had no experience whatever! Surely even the Western allies, who possessed special amphibious troops, had suffered a disastrous defeat at Dieppe five months ago?

But the generals and admirals knew that Stalin was not to be talked out of his plan. The idea had sprung from his own imagination. And he was obsessed by the desire to trap Colonel-General Ruoff's retreating forces after all.

The plan was worth a high stake. After all, the prize of Stalin's combined land and sea operation, if it came off, would be about 400,000 German troops with 110,000 horses, 31,000 horse-drawn and 26,500 motor vehicles, as well as 2085 guns. In other words, a force twice as big as the German Sixth Army in the bag at Stalingrad.

The inspired touch about the plan was the sea-borne landing. The Germans' landward front was manned with their own and Rumanian formations, and the events of recent weeks had shown that they were putting up an effective resistance. But along the coast the Germans clearly did not envisage any great danger. The coast was therefore only lightly held, and on many sectors predominantly by Rumanian units. Provided the surprise came off, the plan had some prospect of success.

Major Dr Lahmeyer, commanding Army Coastal Artillery Battalion 789 at Glebovka, had gone to bed late on 3rd February. The evening report had kept him busy longer than usual: the front was creeping closer. His battalion's positions, with their 10·5-cm long-barrel guns and 10·5-cm howitzers, were now gaining increased importance as the corner point of the "Gothic Line" and the Kuban bridgehead. There was something in the air. During the past few days there had been a lot of activity out at sea. Soviet patrol vessels had been moving about off Ozereyka Bay. German aerial reconnaissance reported great activity in the ports of Gelendzhik and Tuapse.

Over the past week there had been a great deal of radio traffic. But two days previously, on 1st February, the ether had abruptly fallen silent. It was an ominous silence. Was anything up? Was the Soviet Black Sea Fleet concentrating and was it keeping radio silence in order not to give itself away? These were the questions asked by the staff officers of coastal defence.

Lahmeyer had been on the telephone to Army Command in Slav-yansk towards 2000 hours. There too the radio silence had been noted with interest. There was much speculation and discussion. Colonel-General Ruoff ordered a "Grade 1 alert" for the Crimean coast. If the Russians were really preparing an attack by their Black Sea Fleet then

Map 15. The Russians attempted a landing in Ozereyka Bay on 4th February, 1943. They were repulsed by German artillery.

surely—at least that was the conclusion reached in Slavyansk—it could only be against the Crimea or perhaps the Kerch Straits.

However, an operation against the Taman Peninsula was not entirely ruled out among Ruoff's staff, and for that reason a "Grade I alert" was also ordered for the coastal defences of Anapa. A naval action in the Novorossiysk area, on the other hand, was considered improbable by Army Staff. Therefore no alert was ordered there. Neither for Novorossiysk nor for the coast south of Anapa.

General von Bünau, commanding the 73rd Infantry Division, and Colonel Peslmüller, his artillery commander, did not share this view. For days they had been pointing to the possibility of a landing in Ozereyka Bay. Aerial reconnaissance had shown considerable concentrations of landing craft in the Gelendzhik–Tuapse area. Intercepted and decoded signals from Soviet commands suggested a landing operation not too far from Gelendzhik. In view of this situation the artillery commander had held an exercise in Ozereyka Bay lasting for several days. The result had not been encouraging: available forces and ammunition were not sufficient to deal with a major landing operation.

The only tactics with any prospect of success, therefore, would be not to open artillery fire until the landing forces were so close that their own naval gunnery could no longer give them cover; in other words, fire not to be opened until the enemy was within about two hundred yards of the coast. These then were the orders given to the coastal guns.

Major Lahmeyer had gone to bed in his peasant hut at Glebovka towards midnight. At 0100 he was rudely awakened. Bombs!

At the same moment Lieutenant Erhard, the orderly officer, burst into his room: "The Russians are on the move, Herr Major! They're bombing the whole countryside. A report has just come through from the observation post in the Ozereyka valley that our dummy position in the bay is being shelled by heavy naval guns."

The dummy position? "That's good," laughed Lahmeyer. "What about the gun emplacements?"

"Everything seems all right there, Herr Major."

"Better still." Lahmeyer was pleased. He hurriedly got into his uniform and went to the field telephone in the next room. The observation post of 3rd Troop and the Howitzer Troop directly on the coast came through.

"Muzzle flashes of heavy naval guns out at sea," reported the observer, Lieutenant Kreipe.

"Can you make out the ships?" asked Lahmeyer.

"No, Herr Major, it's pitch dark; all we can see are the muzzle flashes, and I don't want to switch on our searchlights yet."

"Good!"

Lahmeyer made sure his other troops were all right. The 3rd under Lieutenant Holschermann had moved into a carefully camouflaged position in the undergrowth on the eastern flank of the Ozereyka valley a few days earlier. The bay and the sea lay in front of their guns as if on a plate, while they themselves were well hidden.

Immediately behind the beach, opposite 3rd Troop, Lahmeyer had posted two 10·5-cm howitzers in a patch of shrub. The gun commander there was Sergeant Will Wagner.

The 2nd Troop under Lieutenant Mönnich was dug in on a slight hill near Glebovka. It commanded the valley, the bay, and also the road leading up from the beach.

The 1st Troop under Lieutenant Kerler was rather less than a mile farther back, on high ground on the Abrau Lake, with a clear field of fire to the bay and to the sea. On the slopes to the right and left a few Rumanian light field howitzers were in position, belonging to the Rumanian 38th Infantry Regiment.

Officers and men were already at their guns. None of them had yet been hit by bombs. Nor had there been any hits by naval gunnery. In accordance with the plan not a shell was yet being fired from the German side.

It was a black night—the new moon. The next day a solar eclipse was due. Would the Russians really attempt a landing operation in this pitch darkness?

Lahmeyer telephoned General von Bünau, commanding 73rd Infantry Division: "The fireworks do seem to suggest a landing, Herr General."

Bünau shared Lahmeyer's anxiety. He telephoned corps. But corps was sceptical. "A landing at that point? Anapa perhaps, or the Crimea. But there?"

Lahmeyer got through to Captain Dabija Nicolai, commanding the 5th Company of the Rumanian 38th Infantry Regiment. The Rumanians were in charge of coastal defence on the beaches in front of Lahmeyer's sector.

"Coastal defence" was rather a grand term for the field positions with machine-guns and infantry foxholes behind the mined barbed-wire fence along the sandy beach.

Until shortly after 0100 Captain Nicolai was still in telephone communication with most of the strongpoints. But some of them presently failed to reply. Either the wires had been cut or the positions had been hit by Russian shells.

According to the observers the fire of heavy naval guns was falling on the beach, shattering the barbed wire and covering the far end of the bay where the machine-gun posts were. The Russian shells dropped as far as Glebovka.

Major Lahmeyer stepped outside his hut. Like a night storm the thunder and lightning came over from the sea. Bombers were droning overhead. They were dropping brilliant white flares as well as bombs.

What Lahmeyer and his troop commanders could not see were the Soviet naval units and landing craft at station behind and between the ceaselessly firing destroyers and cruisers.

It was here, in the sector of Army Coastal Artillery Battalion 789, on the bay formed by the Ozereyka estuary into the Black Sea, that the Russians had planned their main landing. It was an ideal spot. A semi-circular bay, about a mile and a half wide, with rubble and sporadic shrubs. In front of it a flat, sandy beach. To the right and left steep, wooded slopes which would speedily offer shelter and cover.

At 0200 hours Vice-Admiral Oktyabrskiy, aboard the heavy destroyer *Kharkov*, glanced at his watch and signalled to the gunnery officer. "Lift fire!"

The new firing data were given to the guns.

"Will it work, Comrade Admiral?" the commander of the destroyer asked his C-in-C of the Fleet.

The admiral shrugged. The captain knew what he was thinking. The Navy was not happy about the timing of the landing. The Admiralty had insisted, time and again, that an operation such as this required a full moon. A full moon was necessary for the landing forces to make an accurate landfall, to make use of cover, and to see what progress one's neighbouring unit was making.

And the naval forces too would have required a certain minimum of

Battle among the Caucasian peaks.
Mules being loaded in the Laba valley.
Supplies by donkey: a village in the Crimea.

light to ensure co-operation between the naval units and the landing-craft. How could one possibly co-ordinate the separate movements in pitch-darkness?

These had been the arguments of the Navy. But the Army, and Stalin with it, had disagreed. Darkness was important, the generals had declared. The Russian soldiers, they argued, had experience of night fighting whereas the Germans lacked such experience.

"While it is still dark, at 0200 hours, the assault detachments of the first wave will land with 1500 marine troops and armoured forces, and establish a beach-head. Gun emplacements identified by aerial reconnaissance will first be neutralized by naval covering forces, and wire obstacles on the beach, minefields, and machine-gun posts will be smashed." These were the orders for "Phase One" of the plan.

"Phase Two" stipulated: Before daybreak the second wave will make its landing with heavy weapons. By daybreak it will be in the bay, in order that the naval units can steam away from the proximity of the coast still under cover of darkness.

That was what the order said, and that was how things were done.

For an hour, from 0100 to 0200, Russian heavy naval guns pounded the bay with their shells. They fired them generously and produced an infernal concert. A thunderous fireworks display. The exploding mines on the beach were like the echoes of the booms of the guns. The barbed-wire obstacles were ripped to shreds.

The time now was 0200. The wall of explosions was moved up the beach, inland.

First wave! Officers shouted. Lamp signals were exchanged between the destroyers. Landing-craft with marines chugged towards the beach, between the destroyer flotilla. Among them were two large, flat-bottomed craft with American Grant, Stuart, and Lee tanks. Naval guns were putting up an umbrella of shellfire to protect the landing-craft and the beach-head. Like a huge line of fountains the splashes of the shell-bursts rose up at the far end of the bay—a sizzling curtain of fire and smoke.

Lieutenant I. P. Bogdanov was standing on the roof of the wheel-house of the landing-craft carrying his platoon, watching the spectacle through his night glasses. "It's got to work out right," he muttered.

But in a decisive point it did not work out right. True, barbed-wire obstacles were ripped to pieces. The mine belts were blown up. The Rumanian pickets were smashed. But the position which the Soviet Black Sea Fleet had been pounding for sixty minutes in the belief that it was smashing a German shore battery was only the dummy position of 3rd Troop. Hits among the other troops were not serious.

Panzer grenadiers with adhesive high-explosive charges.
Artillery observers with walkie-talkies advancing with the infantry.

A Rumanian light howitzer position had received a direct hit and the crew had run away. Nicolai's infantrymen, on the other hand, held out behind their machine-guns in the undergrowth of the steep flanks of the bay.

As the enemy fire was lifted from the beach towards the hinterland every man on shore knew that the crucial moment had arrived—the moment when the Russians would make their landing.

Lieutenant Kreipe ordered his heavy searchlight to be briefly switched on from the most easterly of the hills immediately on the coast. Its beam groped across the beach and leapt out to the sea. The scene was as bright as day. The searchlight revealed an armada of small, grey shadows.

Now they were close enough. "Fire!" Holschermann's guns barked. "Fire!"

The 10·5-cm shells of the howitzers thundered into the surf. Wagner had practised this operation so often that his men were used to the terrifying crashes of the shells exploding so close.

Shell after shell was lobbed out. They just could not miss their targets.

Sergeant Wagner had plugged his ears with cotton-wool. He was crouching behind some shrubs on the beach, scanning the sea through his night binoculars. The searchlight of 3rd Troop flashed up again and again. Even though its position had suffered a couple of hits, one of them damaging the equipment, and although it was now being systematically shelled by the Russians it kept coming on briefly to light up the targets for the gunners to fire at point-blank range.

Now and again came the flash of an explosion—a landing-craft blowing up on being hit. Tall spouts of water shot up wherever the shells lashed the sea.

Wagner watched the Soviet landing-craft approach the sandy beach through the inferno. "Now they're on the beach!" He doubled over to the first gun. "Shorten range by fifty yards!"

The gun-aimer nodded.

Wagner also ran over to the second howitzer. And now shells were crashing down on the beach itself. Lieutenant Holschermann's troops on the opposite eastern slope continued to fire at the approaching Russian boats.

Nevertheless, the first wave of Soviet marines reached the beach. At once they were caught in enfilading machine-gun fire from the Rumanian pickets.

"Where the devil are those tanks?" Lieutenant Bogdanov grumbled. Surely the flat-bottomed craft with the tanks had been alongside his cutter? And he had himself watched the first tanks move down the nose-ramp into the water.

Cautiously Bogdanov raised his head. There—a Stuart tank was creeping up the beach a few yards from him. Its engine was spluttering. Then it stopped.

Bogdanov ran over. He climbed on its stern. He yelled at the commander in the turret: "Don't just stand here—keep moving! And where are the others?"

The tankman waved his arms despairingly and cursed. "It's the water!" And then he added, "The water was too deep. It got into the engine through the exhaust!"

That was why the tanks did not come. In the darkness and the general confusion they had been dropped too far out. Incredibly, the Soviet Command had not allowed for this possibility. Simple upward extensions of their exhaust tubes would have saved those tanks.

But the landing-craft too were only arriving in a trickle. Some of them turned back under the effective German fire. Others lost their direction in the dark and made their landfall too far to the east, where the beach was only a narrow strip with an unscalable cliff behind it.

Sergeant Leonid Sedonin worked his way forward with his squad to the eastern corner of the bay. There he came upon a position with three light infantry guns, abandoned by its Rumanian crew after a direct hit. But two of the guns were still intact. Sedonin, who was an artillery man, immediately seized his opportunity and with the two captured guns opened fire at Sergeant Wagner's howitzer position.

Fortunately for Wagner, Captain Radiu, the commander of the Rumanian engineer company immediately behind the bay, heard about the Soviet coup from a runner. He did not hesitate long. With a platoon of engineers he crept up to the position. Hand-grenades. A leap over the stone parapet. A burst of sub-machine-gun fire.

Sergeant Sedonin was killed. And Captain Radiu also lay dead by the recaptured emplacement.

The Russian assault parties meanwhile were forming up on the beach. They worked their way up to the slopes surrounding the bay. They dug in their mortars. They crouched behind their machine-guns.

The tanks which had got ashore moved on into the undergrowth. They silenced the Rumanian machine-gun posts. They moved on inland, in the direction of Glebovka.

Wagner's howitzer position was under heavy mortar fire. Half his crew were killed. The other half were wounded. The Russians charged. Wagner and the few survivors made their escape into the adjoining forest.

The sergeant dragged himself over to Lieutenant Holschermann. "The Soviets have got our position. We didn't have time to blow up our guns. You smash them up for us!"

Holschermann opened up at the position with a 10·5-cm long-barrel gun and smashed the howitzers together with their Soviet captors.

The time was 0330. The flanks of the narrow Ozereyka Bay re-echoed the din of battle. The Soviets had suffered heavy losses. But their officers again and again rallied their units. They worked their way up to the edge of the forest in the bay. They probed along the banks of the Ozereyka stream. They dug in.

The command post of the Soviet officer in charge of signals for the whole landing operation was by a small clump of trees, near the mouth of the Ozereyka. Runners crawled up to the post to make their report. Time went by.

But out at sea the bulk of the force was still waiting. At last the signals commander decided to give the fleet the arranged radio and lamp signal: "Beach-head established!" And he added the code sign for "Urgently require reinforcements."

The staff officers aboard the flagship of the Russian covering naval forces had been anxiously awaiting this signal for the past sixty minutes. Their anxiety was twofold; not only was the signal from the bay late, but the transport fleet with the bulk of the landing forces had not yet arrived. The naval command was taking its time. Why?

The mystery has since been solved by Soviet publications. The delay was not due to bungling, but was deliberate. The Admiralty wanted to get its own way, over the Army Command, and carry out the landing at first light. Consequently another half-hour passed after the call for help from the bay before the landing fleet with the bulk of the invasion troops was on the spot.

It was an impressive armada that approached the bay. Over a hundred transports—steamers and cutters, ancient craft on their last legs and the most up-to-date motor vessels.

The landing units slowly sailed through the lines of the covering warships. Three brigades of marines, as well as an airborne regiment, altogether some six thousand to eight thousand men, were wedged together in those ships. Tanks, guns, and assault guns were well stowed away on board special craft. The sea was calm. The sight of the war-ships raised the morale of the troops. The heavy destroyer *Kharkov*, the flagship of the covering naval force, glided slowly over the sea. Immediately next to it were the silhouettes of two cruisers and five destroyers. Farther to the right were three gunboats. In between were motor torpedo-boats, minesweepers, anti-submarine craft, and coastal defence units. All of them crowded together in a narrow space.

What the troops did not realize as their transports carried them towards the beach was the astonishing fact that the naval units were sailing past them out to sea. The Admiral was adhering strictly to his timetable. And that timetable demanded: at 0415, shortly before dawn, all naval units will withdraw from the proximity of the coast.

Only a few minor units were eventually kept near the coast by contrary orders.

As the transport fleet arrived at the coast dawn was just breaking. On land, dozens of pairs of eyes were glued to night binoculars and trench telescopes, scanning the sea.

German and Rumanian observers were amazed to see the vast Soviet armada. Telephone communications had ceased to exist. Runners were hurriedly sent off.

The troop commanders in Major Lahmeyer's troops had similarly lost contact with battalion. They were on their own. The observers reported: "Enemy landing craft in square . . . "

And then followed the fire data: "Target-point Caesar—second charge—percussion fuses—the whole troop direction 20 plus—range 4950—Fire!"

The third salvo of 2nd Troop straddled the deck of a large transport, turning it into a pile of rubble and triggering-off a chain reaction of explosions. Immediately afterwards, the foremost landing craft with artillery and assault guns received such a heavy hit that it capsized.

Holschermann's troop was firing at will. Already a blazing transport was drifting out to sea. Two others capsized just off shore. A flat-bottomed craft with tanks keeled over. A smouldering cutter rammed a motor vessel. Landing craft capsized. Assault craft raced up the beach and ran into a wall of fire and smoke.

The warships which should have intervened in the fighting at that moment, to support the landing operation—the Guards cruisers *Krasnyy Kavkaz* and *Krasnyy Krim* with their 18-cm guns and 10-cm anti-aircraft guns, and the heavy destroyer *Kharkov* with her four modern 13-cm SK guns and her large number of 7·6-cm anti-aircraft guns—these warships had long disappeared below the horizon and were now steaming towards their home ports. Strictly according to schedule.

What was the bulk of the Soviet landing fleet to do in this grotesque situation? There was no-one present who was either willing or able to see the plan through. Thus the fleet with its three brigades of landing troops again steamed out to sea and stood by, undecided.

After an hour of hectic exchange of signals with the most diverse commands, the Admiral commanding the fleet eventually ordered it to return to base. An incident without parallel in military history.

The companies which had landed in Ozereyka Bay knew nothing of all that. They fought bravely. On the morning of 4th February a Russian assault party with three tanks had reached Glebovka and charged the position of a Rumanian mortar battalion in an old vineyard manor. As soon as the Rumanians caught sight of the tanks they abandoned both wine-cellars and mortars.

If the commander of the Russian assault party had then had a company with him Glebovka would have fallen to him immediately.

But all he had was a platoon.

When Lahmeyer received news of the situation he at once employed the men of his 2nd Troop in a counter-attack, taking with them all the battalion's machine-guns. But nothing came of it. The Russians had already established themselves in the position and were pasting the counter-attacking German gunners with their captured mortars.

Lahmeyer thereupon got Lieutenant Kerler's 1st Troop west of Glebovka to bombard the manor and the vineyard. The Rumanian captain Dabija Nicolai with his 5th Company then charged and dislodged the Russians.

By evening the main danger had passed. Guns of Reserve Flak Battalion 164 and Panzerjäger Battalion 173 under Captain Gutschera knocked out six Soviet tanks which had broken through. The reinforced 13th Company, 229th Jäger Regiment, under Lieutenant Wieczorek, together with Rumanian assault parties, thrust from Glebovka down to the shore. The beach was a ghastly graveyard.

Capsized and sunken transport craft lay in the shallow water. Between them stood the water-logged and wrecked tanks. The surf was pounding against their tracks. It was lapping over the dead whom the sea had spewed out on to the beach.

The clearing parties counted 620 killed. Thirty-one American tanks were destroyed. By the morning of 6th February 594 prisoners had been taken. The rest of the 1500 Soviet troops who landed with the first wave must have been drowned. Isolated groups probably escaped into the hinterland, others tried to fight their way through to the Russian land front at Novorossiysk. But only a few succeeded.

That was how Stalin's grand operation failed in Ozereyka Bay. It failed not only through a number of serious mistakes, but also through the vigilance and gallantry of a German coastal artillery battalion and that of Rumanian units.

The validity of this conclusion, for both parties, was confirmed during those same days of January 1943 only a few miles away from Ozereyka Bay. There it was a Russian officer who impressed his personality on the operation. It was the episode of Stanichka. It heralded in a special chapter of the war in Russia.

During the same night that Stalin's main landing operation was staged at Ozereyka, a commando detachment of a few hundred men was landed near Stanichka, a suburb of Novorossiysk, as a diversion and deception for the Germans. Major Z. L. Kunikov an officer in the marines, an engineer by profession, was in command.

Kunikov had picked his men from the most varied units of the Black Sea Fleet. They were all dare-devils and had been specially trained for close combat and sabotage.

On 4th February, two hours before dawn, Kunikov's men embarked at Gelendzhik on units of the 4th Coastal Defence Flotilla under

Lieutenant N. Y. Zipyadon. When the ships were nearing Cape Myshkako, with another fifteen to twenty minutes' sailing time before them, Soviet artillery on the eastern side of the bay opened fire on the German coastal defences and coastal batteries.

Under cover of this barrage Zipyadon's small fleet raced towards the beach near Stanichka. When the water was about chest high Kunikov's men jumped overboard and waded on land.

Within a quarter of an hour the first two hundred and fifty marines were on the beach. They were at the very gates of Novorossiysk and already held the first few houses of the suburb of Stanichka.

The naval fortress of Novorossiysk was relatively strongly held by 73rd Infantry Division. In the town were infantry, engineer, and Panzerjäger units, as well as the staff of 186th Grenadier Regiment. There were also two senior commands with their staffs—the Harbour Commands 16 and 18.

On the western mole was a troop of 10·5-cm howitzers. The nucleus of the defence of the bay and the harbour was a flak combat detachment of Reserve Flak Battalion 164 with two 8·8-cm guns. The coastal defence proper, down on the beach, was in the hands of units of the Rumanian 10th Division.

And under the eyes of these forces, Major Kunikov made a landing at Stanichka! In the first light of dawn his small force had sailed into Tsemes Bay. Past the naval guns. Past the threatening 8·8-cm guns emplaced on a bare hill a thousand feet above the harbour mouth. Not a shot had been fired from the German side.

"I saw the ships all right. But there hadn't been an alert and I couldn't tell whether they were German or enemy units," the lieutenant

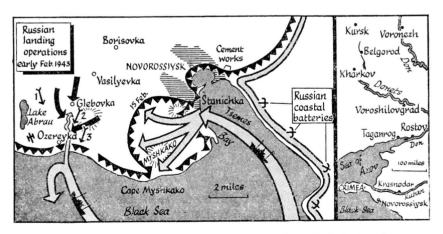

Map 16. Soviet landing troops succeeded in gaining a foothold in the bay of Novorossiysk. The fighting for the "Little Land" developed into a seven-month battle.

commanding the flak combat detachment with the two 8·8-cm guns subsequently stated at a court martial.

Eventually when the Russian artillery opened up and the lieutenant realized what was happening, it was too late for action. Kunikov's beach-head was on dead ground below the German guns.

The second 8·8 gun position, according to the evidence of Sergeant Ebers, never saw the landing-craft at all. Its telephone connection to troop had been cut immediately the barrage started. Moreover, the gun very soon received several hits and went out of action.

The beach covering parties of the Rumanian 10th Infantry Division were totally demoralized by the heavy Russian shelling. And as soon as the first Soviet soldier appeared in front of their shattered beach defences the Rumanians fled without firing a shot.

Half an hour later one of Kunikov's assault parties was in front of the position of the still intact 8·8 gun. As these were permanently emplaced guns without tractors the German lieutenant ordered his gun to be dynamited and fell back with his men. He was later tried by court martial but acquitted.

The second gun, the damaged one, was blown up by its crew when all attempts to re-establish contact with troop proved unavailing.

With that kind of defence it was not surprising that Major Kunikov's first wave not only suffered no losses but rapidly gained ground and was able to secure and extend a beach-head for the rest of their force. The six hundred men of the Russian commando force which followed the first wave thus found a well-established position.

On the German side, however, everything went wrong. The commands in Novorossiysk reacted nervously. The fact that coastal defence was in Rumanian hands made matters more difficult. Far too late, in the small hours of 4th February, some hurriedly collected units were launched against the Soviet beach-head.

But all was confusion. Nobody knew what had happened. The Rumanian commands, who would have had the necessary information, had fled into the mountains. Kunikov's men had dug in singly or in small groups and were firing wildly all over the countryside, suggesting to the uninformed that a whole division had landed. This total ignorance of the situation made the German command unsure.

Soviet sources enable us to reconstruct very accurately the course of operations during the decisive first few hours of the Stanichka landing. Lieutenant Romanov, with the first group of the advance party, seized a Rumanian bunker immediately on the beach at his first attempt. The Rumanians left their machine-gun and 3·7-cm gun intact. Romanov only had to post his men behind them and await the German counter-attack. In the end, when a platoon of 14th Company, 170th Grenadier Regiment, charged, the German troops were mown down by the fire from the bunker.

Kunikov's second group had penetrated into Stanichka and established themselves in the buildings of a school, in order to cover the flank of the beach-head against Novorossiysk. Engineers and grenadiers of 73rd Infantry Division tried to dislodge the Russians. Eventually the Germans drove Kunikov's men from the schoolhouse and encircled the combat group.

It was a dangerous crisis for the Russians. If the flank cover of the beach-head were to be wiped out, the whole operation would be in jeopardy. The Germans would be able to roll up the beach-head from Stanichka and prevent the bulk of the Soviet marines from reaching their vital objective—the commanding heights behind Stanichka with Mount Myshkako, whose slopes, with their thick undergrowth, provided good cover for the attackers.

The operation hung in balance. This was the crucial minute of the battle of Novorossiysk, a battle which lasted altogether seven months, or 302,400 minutes.

The hero of that minute was the Soviet rating Kornitskiy. He decided that first engagement. When he realized the hopeless position of his combat group he tied fifteen hand-grenades round his waist, pulled the pins, leapt up on the wall of the school yard, and flung himself right among the assembly area of a German infantry platoon. A human land-mine, he blew up himself and the Germans.

The ring was burst open. Kornitskiy's example lent the Russians furious strength. The two combat groups succeeded in linking up and establishing a defensive front. The road to the high ground of Stanichka and to the 1400-foot-high Mount Myshkako was secure. Kunikov succeeded in occupying the commanding heights. The rating Kornitskiy, who was posthumously made a Hero of the Soviet Union, had averted the dangerous crisis of the first hour and paved the way for the most important blow. Battles are won by men.

In the morning of 4th February both German and Soviet staff found themselves confronted by an extremely surprising situation. The Soviet Commander-in-Chief Black Sea Group, General Petrov, until quite recently disconcerted by the failure of the main landing in Ozereyka Bay, realized that, against all expectation, a handful of his soldiers had captured a beach-head immediately in front of Novorossiysk and had moreover captured a strategic key position on the Novorossiysk front. What had been intended as a diversion turned out to be a major success.

General von Bünau, commanding 73rd Infantry Division at Novorossiysk, and General Wetzel, commanding V Corps, acknowledged with surprise the successful Russian coup. But they also realized that only small Russian forces had in fact landed. Both sides, therefore, were looking at the same facts. But the conclusions they drew from them were totally different. And that was where the great disaster began.

Anybody acquainted with Soviet fighting methods and with Russian soldiers should have realized that whenever a local penetration was achieved something had to be done about it immediately. Once the Russians were allowed to dig in and establish their defences it was exceedingly difficult to dislodge them.

An immediate counter-attack should have been made with whatever forces were available. Naval staff, personnel, and harbour command officials should have been drawn upon as well as all available units, such as 73rd Infantry Division, the Rumanians, and the Convict Battalion 10. Everything should have been thrown into the battle there and then. Including the cooks and the clerks, the cobblers and the bakers, and the countless administrative officials. Everything. And at once.

But division and corps wanted to play it safe. They set a well-prepared attack in motion. Companies and battalions were moved up from the most varied sectors of the corps' front, and the counter-attack was fixed for 7th February.

But 7th February was three times twenty-four hours away. General Petrov, on the other hand, waited only twelve hours. Then he moved.

Under cover of the superbly accurate Soviet shore guns, emplaced on the eastern side of Tsemes Bay, only about a mile away, he moved a whole airborne regiment into the beach-head on cutters and small coastal craft during the night of 4th–5th February. The Russian soldiers jumped overboard near the coast and swam ashore through the icy water.

During the next two nights Petrov resolutely switched into the beach-head all those formations which had originally been envisaged for the main landing in Ozereyka Bay—three brigades of marines and special troops. In all more than eight thousand men. They included crack formations such as the 225th and 83rd Red Banner Marine Brigade. Then there was the 165th Rifle Brigade which was equipped with armour-piercing weapons. Thus the beach-head two and a half miles wide and two miles deep was packed to bursting point with troops and weapons. Under the pressure of this force it was extended to twelve square miles—*i.e.*, to three miles by four.

The man who, as the political commissar of the Soviet Eighteenth Army, was boosting the morale of the troops in the beach-head, the man who provided the political and propaganda drive which sustained the adventure—this man was Leonid Brezhnev, then a political officer with the rank of colonel.

It was Brezhnev, today the top man in the Russian Communist Party, who gave the beach-head its name, a name which became a stirring slogan—"Little Land, the land of the boldest and bravest".

If one did not know that Leonid Brezhnev's parents named their

son after Saint Leonidas, one might be tempted to draw a parallel with
Leonidas, King of the Spartans, who in 480 B.C. held the narrow pass
of the Thermopylae, the only road between Central and Northern
Greece, against a superior Persian army and there died with every one
of his small force, the hero in whose honour the Spartans erected a
memorial with the immortal lines: "Go, tell the Spartans, thou that
passest by, That here, obedient to their laws, we lie". Here
was the oldest recorded instance of an order to hold out until death.
But, as we have said, Leonid Brezhnev, the son of working people, was
christened upon his birth in 1906 after a saint of the Orthodox Church
and not after the hero of Sparta. But in spirit he was his peer.

On 7th February the German counter-action designed to liquidate
the beach-head began "according to plan". What might have been
possible three days earlier now proved an insoluble task for the German forces.

The Russians had dug themselves in superbly. In deep, one-man
foxholes they were positioned on the flanks and in the undergrowth
of Mount Myshkako and refused to budge. Each one of these one-man
fortresses had to be taken in close combat. Improvised anti-tank barriers and extremely well-camouflaged "crash-boom" guns represented
further obstacles. But worst of all were the Soviet shore batteries firing
on the attackers from the hills on the eastern side. Their fire was
directed by radio from the high ground behind Stanichka by observers
from whose eyes nothing remained hidden.

The runner Heinz Steinbauer had an illustration, in the very first
hour of his active engagement, of what the companies of the Franconian 213th Infantry Regiment were in for at Stanichka. The 1st
Battalion had been moved over from Anapa. The 1st Platoon, 2nd
Company, lost its entire No. 2 section as a result of a direct shell-hit
while still moving up towards Ulitsa Anapskaya. The next twenty-four
hours were taken up by fierce house-to-house and street fighting.
Friend and foe were separated only by the width of a street. Ulitsa
Anapskaya could just not be crossed.

The conquest of two blocks of houses in an area two hundred yards
square cost twenty-one killed and seventy wounded. The commander
of 73rd Infantry Division was horrified: his battalions had only just
been brought up to strength again.

The reports of 198th Infantry Division, brought up shortly after the
Soviet landing, and which sent its 305th Grenadier Regiment into
action at Stanichka, likewise provide an impressive picture of the
type and the savagery of the fighting. The 305th Grenadier Regiment
also experienced the effects of the Russians' superior gunnery during
the very first hours of their employment. While still moving up to the
line they lost entire sections through direct hits by heavy coastal guns.

When, after fierce house-to-house fighting, the battalions tried to thrust forward beyond the edge of the town they encountered an impenetrable artillery barrage. It was impossible to get through. The Russians were established on the pathless, wooded hills and could not be spotted. But they were able to observe every step of the attacking formations.

Moreover, the German battalions were quite inadequately equipped with heavy weapons. The few assault guns of Assault Gun Battalion 191, which had been assigned to them, were unable to get through the Russian lines of anti-tank guns. By the evening of 8th February the regiment, having suffered heavy losses, was back in its jumping-off position.

The next day was the same. Again they were short of artillery. Their combat strength melted away. The 2nd and 3rd Battalions lost their commanders.

On 9th February, Hitler at the Wolfsschanze lost his patience. He issued a categoric order that "the Russians must be thrown into the sea". That same evening 125th Infantry Division was pulled out of its positions near Krasnodar, moved through the blazing and still contested city, and brought into action against the Russians in the "Little Land". But the Swabian infantrymen did not achieve anything either. The fatal mistake of the first few days was still exacting its toll. Once again it was a case of too little and too late.

Eventually, the regiments of six of the most experienced and battle-hardened German divisions were moved up and these launched furious attacks against the "Little Land". Bavarians, Swabians, and Austrians of the 4th Mountain Division were locked in exceedingly costly fighting on Mount Myshkako. The 125th, 73rd, and 198th Infantry Divisions and several Rumanian regiments suffered extremely heavy losses in the "Little Land".

The battles for the "Little Land" raged for seven months. In the end the Russians had 78,500 men and 600 guns in the three by four miles of beach-head: everything brought in by sea and supplied by sea. But they did not succeed in breaking out of their beach-head and striking at the rear of the German lines. After the failure of their principal landing operation at Ozereyka, the fighting in the "Little Land" became for the Soviet High Command a matter of propaganda, of morale, and no doubt also of politics. After all, it was Stalin's landing, and therefore must not be abandoned.

And so Leonid Brezhnev sailed across to the beach-head again and again. He made speeches. He distributed decorations. And he issued Party cards to the newly enrolled members of the Bolshevik Party. An entry in a serviceman's pay-book "Fought in the Little Land" was sufficient for immediate acceptance into the Party of Lenin and Stalin. They fought there, they were commended, and they died.

Major Kunikov was killed in action. In his honour the former suburb of Stanichka today bears the name of Kunikovka.

Lieutenant Romanov was killed in action.

The marines of the first wave were nearly all buried under the soil of Mount Myshkako.

Leonid Brezhnev himself escaped death by a hair's breadth. His fishing cutter struck a mine. Brezhnev was flung overboard. He was rescued, unconscious, by sailors. When he regained consciousness later on land Brezhnev is reported to have said: "You can kill a Soviet man, but you can never defeat him!" That, at least, is what the official *History of the Great Fatherland War* says in Volume III on page 114.

3. The Third Battle of Kharkov

The Waffen-SS evacuates the city–An order from the Führer is not the Eleventh Commandment–Stalin draws a wrong conclusion–Order to Vatutin: "Get that left wing moving!"–Popov walks into the trap–Kharkov falls for the third time–Stalin fears disaster–The miracle of the Marne repeated on the Donets.

IT is time we returned to those sectors of the front where about the middle of February 1943 the real strategic decisions were in the balance.

While the first heavy fighting was still raging on Mount Myshkako and the Soviet command was still hoping to achieve a break-out from the "Little Land", it became increasingly obvious that the Soviet Forty-Seventh Army was not succeeding, as envisaged in Stalin's plan, in piercing the defensive line of the German Seventeenth Army north of Novorossiysk and in linking up with the seaborne landing. Colonel-General Ruoff was still in control of the situation and was falling back, step by step, towards his prepared "Gothic Line".

On 12th February Ruoff abandoned Krasnodar. Two days later Manstein abandoned the hotly contested pivot of Rostov farther north. Colonel-General Malinovskiy, meanwhile appointed Commander-in-Chief of the Southern Front, and Khrushchev, his Military Council member, entered the city with the Russian advanced detachments.

Map 17. Stalin's bold plan for the annihilation of the German southern wing in February 1943.

Solemnly, Nikita Sergeyevich Khrushchev reported to headquarters in Moscow: "Over Rostov, the citadel of the quiet Don, the victorious Red Soviet Banner is once again proudly flying."

There was a mood of victory in the Kremlin. At Stalingrad Hitler's Sixth Army was lying under the snow, dead. Krasnodar and Rostov had been liberated.

Between Voroshilovgrad[1] and Belgorod, where the armies of Germany's allies, the Rumanians, the Italians, and the Hungarians, had disintegrated, a two-hundred-mile gap was yawning. And into this gap Stalin had been driving strong mobile forces ever since the end of January. They had crossed the Donets and were now reaching out towards Kharkov, the metropolis of the Ukraine's heavy industry. In spite of all reverses of recent weeks the hour now seemed at hand for breaking the back of the German Southern Front. If the Soviet armies crossed the Donets in force, if they thrust on boldly through the gaping German lines, and if they reached the Dnieper, then von Manstein's Army Group would be cut off from its rearward communications and von Kleist's Army Group on the Kuban and in the Crimea would once more be in mortal danger. The great hours of final and decisive victory —had it arrived once again?

The Soviet Army Group commanders thought so. Stalin thought so. "This is our moment," he kept reminding his generals. He conceived a new grand operation—he would engage and defeat Hitler east of the Dnieper. Boldly and almost heedlessly he drove his armies towards

[1] Now Lugansk.

what he thought would be the decisive victory on the banks of this huge Russian river. His objective was to overtake the Germans before they got to the river, to encircle them and annihilate them.

Those were days of terrible suspense. From morning till nightfall the shadow of mortal danger hung over the German armies on the southern wing.

In this situation, which called urgently for a decisive shortening of the line in order to release forces, Hitler at his headquarters once again stubbornly insisted that not an inch of ground must be surrendered. In long conversations he would argue with his generals that he could not continue the war if the Donets basin, "the Ruhr of the Soviet Union", was lost.

But one man was nevertheless determined to oppose this strategy, the strategy which had led to Stalingrad and which was bound now— unless the wheel was wrenched round at the last minute—to lead to a super-Stalingrad. That man was the C-in-C Army Group Don, Field-Marshal von Manstein.

This methodical strategist was sitting at Stalino, watching developments with anxiety but without the slightest trace of panic. He was waiting for his moment. On 6th February he flew off to the Wolfs-schanze. In a four-hour talk he eventually got Hitler to accept Frederick the Great's thesis: "He that would defend everything will defend nothing."

It was one of those rare moments in the war when Hitler authorized a strategic withdrawal on a major scale. He agreed to the surrender of the eastern Donets region as far as the Mius. Manstein heaved a sigh of relief.

Now at least there was a chance. The race against time, against the weather, and against the Russians could start.

The Army Detachment Hollidt pulled back from the Donets to the much shortened Mius position, fighting all the way. Everything now depended on whether it could maintain a solid line there.

The formations of First Panzer Army, under the command of General of Cavalry Eberhard von Mackensen, were switched to the threatened northern wing of the Army Group on the middle Donets.

Hoth's Fourth Panzer Army worked its way north from the Lower Don, through snow and slush, to the area between the Donets and the Dnieper bend on the western wing of Army Group Don.

The roads were covered with deep snow. The drivers were overtired. There were endless traffic jams. There were accidents. The columns were strung out over great distances. The engineers got no sleep at all. Time and again the divisional commanders toured their regiments, urging them on, reminding them of the dangers, imploring them: forward, forward!

It was a gigantic race. The Soviets had an eight-fold superiority in numbers and weapons.

Manstein, his attention constantly focused on the enemy's intentions and strength, had nothing but his strategic skill to set against the menace of greater power, the only strategy available to the commander of a numerically inferior force—the "second strike", the counter-attack when the enemy had dealt his blow, what Clausewitz called "the flashing sword of retribution".

Field-Marshal von Manstein had moved his command post from Stalino to Zaporozhye. From there he closely followed the developments on the north-western wing of his Army Group. It was, however, no longer called Army Group Don, for on 14th February, as part of an operational reorganization, it had been renamed Army Group South.

Nor could one really speak of a front. There were individual combat groups scattered about the countryside, setting up centres of resistance at a few vital points. A platoon here, an anti-tank gun there, or a machine-gun section; a whole company somewhere else. The term "company" sounded reassuring, but the companies of First Panzer Army were down to an effective strength of between twenty and sixty men at the most. And with that handful of men they were expected to hold sectors up to a mile and a half wide—if the company was lucky. If it was unlucky it would be bypassed during those endless dark nights by Soviet ski-squads and would find itself surrounded in the morning. The following day the battalion would then have one company less, and the so-called front line would have one gap more.

All staffs up to division level were therefore employed in the main defence zone, forming centres of resistance. Even the Army command of First Panzer Army had formed a reinforced company from its headquarters personnel, and this unit had been in action for several days.

Things were not much better with the neighbouring units on their left. The Army Detachment Lanz—later to become the Army Detachment Kempf—which, together with the remnants of German reserve formations, the Corps Cramer, the Italian Alpini Corps, and a few other reserves, had taken over the sector of the Italian Eighth and the Hungarian Second Armies, found itself engaged in savage defensive fighting east and south-east of Kharkov.

Manstein was anxiously watching this sector too. For if the Russians succeeded in overrunning the formations of Army Detachment Lanz and in crossing the Dnieper at Kremenchug—as Stalin in fact intended—then the way would be clear to them as far as the approaches to the Crimea. If they succeeded in blocking those routes, then Seventeenth Army would be trapped. Then Stalin's dream would come true—the annihilation of Hitler's entire southern wing along six hundred miles, the annihilation of three armies and two army detachments. The result would be a chain reaction: Army Group Centre with its five armies would then find itself suspended in mid-air and unable to hold out; it would certainly collapse. If there was a quick way to victory over the German armies in the east, this was it.

"This is what Stalin is aiming at," Manstein kept saying to his chief of staff, Major-General Friedrich Schulz. "He is going for the big prize and he's not afraid of risks. We've got to lure him into taking extreme risks. That's our only chance!"

Manstein's grasp of the Soviet operations was as accurate as if he had been privy to the plans and intentions of Stalin's Supreme Council, the STAVKA. He suspected then what has since been confirmed—that Stalin, his general staff, and the top Soviet Army leaders were convinced that no general in the world and no god of war could now possibly avert the German catastrophe between Donets and Dnieper.

This is how Stalin formulated it: "The armies of the General Army Group South have been smashed and can only try to withdraw behind the Dnieper." Any German resistance east of the Dnieper, according to Stalin, was unthinkable. A solid front on the Mius? Impossible, Stalin decided.

When one's mind is made up about something it is easy enough to find support for one's view. About mid-February, the chief of staff of the Soviet Army Group South-West Front, Lieutenant-General S. P. Ivanov, submitted to the Soviet High Command a report which contains the following sentence: "All reconnaissance data indicate that the enemy is evacuating the Donets area and pulling his troops back behind the Dnieper."

General Vatutin, the C-in-C South-West Front, unreservedly endorsed this view. And not only the able strategist Vatutin—the C-in-C Voronezh Front, Colonel-General Golikov, also believed that Manstein's armies were in full retreat. The fact that the Army Detachment Hollidt had just disengaged itself from the Donets was evaluated as visible proof.

The idea that General Hollidt might halt his divisions on the Mius and there establish a defensive line seemed to Golikov not worth considering. It was just not possible.

The thought of a general German retreat was in fact so tempting that, in the General Staff in Moscow and for Stalin personally, the assumption rapidly became an article of faith: the Germans are in general retreat from the Donets basin and are trying to get behind the Dnieper! When the chief of staff of the Southern Front still expressed some slight doubt, Stalin himself sent his personal reassurance to him: "The enemy is in retreat and his massed columns are withdrawing behind the Dnieper."

It was an astonishing error. An error due in part to certain secret-service failures which will be touched upon presently.

Whatever the reason, the Army Group headquarters along the Soviet line, and indeed the Soviet High Command itself, were intoxicated by the idea of a defeated German southern front in full flight. What, therefore, could be more natural than to try to cut off the retreat of Manstein's withdrawing armies and to inflict upon them a crushing defeat?

The Soviet Army Groups Voronezh Front, South-West Front, and Southern Front received orders "regardless of supplies or enemy rearguards to thrust through the retreating enemy, reach the Dnieper before the onset of the spring mud, and thus cut off Manstein's retreat to the river".

A STAVKA order to the South-West Front, dated 11th February 1943, demanded: "You are to prevent the enemy's withdrawal to Dnepropetrovsk and Zaporozhye, to throw back the enemy forces into the Crimea, block the approaches to the Crimea, and thus cut off the German southern group."

This then was the great gamble. The gamble which Stalin decided to take, the gamble which Manstein had been hoping for.

One particular occurrence, more than anything else, confirmed the Soviet High Command in its error—a dramatic occurrence, the disobedience of a German general. In retrospect it looked a superb ruse, but in fact it was nothing of the sort.

The Army Detachment Lanz—which then still belonged to Army Group B and was not yet subordinated to Manstein—on 11th February received a strict order from Hitler that Kharkov must be held, even though the city was already strategically outmanoeuvred by two Soviet armies and was about to be encircled.

The hopeless task of defending Kharkov fell to the lot of the newly-raised SS Panzer Corps, under General of Waffen-SS Paul Hausser. The corps had only just arrived from France and included the two crack divisions "Das Reich" and "Leibstandarte Adolf Hitler".

The order to hold Kharkov was foolish and motivated entirely by considerations of prestige. Manstein tried to talk Hitler out of it. Far more important than hanging on to the city at that moment was to intercept the enemy who was racing ahead south of Kharkov, to defeat him, and to halt his headlong advance at long last, in order to relieve the left flank of Army Group South and prevent a Soviet breakthrough to and across the Dnieper.

But Hitler was unwilling to surrender the industrial and political metropolis of the Ukraine. In spite of his unfortunate experience, Kharkov, like Stalingrad a short while before, was beginning to be a matter of prestige. And for the sake of prestige he was prepared to drive first-rate fighting formations, such as "Leibstandarte" and "Das Reich", into the fate of Stalingrad.

Two days later, on 13th February, Hitler repeated his strict order that Kharkov must be held, if necessary by all-round defence. Lanz transmitted the order to Hausser. Now at last Hitler was reassured: he relied on the absolute obedience of the Waffen-SS Corps and over-looked the fact that the corps commander, General Paul Hausser, was a man of common sense, strategic skill, and with the courage to stand up to his superiors.

Thus something happened which tended to give the lie to the legend so often pinned on the Waffen-SS and its leaders—the legend that they were a party formation serving the Führer with blind obedience.

On 14th February the encirclement of the city was almost complete. Soviet tank packs pierced the northern, north-western, and south-eastern defences and penetrated to the very edge of the city. The supply route from Poltava to Kharkov was under Soviet artillery fire. Hausser requested General Lanz to authorize a break-out. His sober appreciation of the situation is laid down in the corps diary under entry 138/43 of 14th February 1943. It reads:

"Enemy facing Kharkov's eastern and north-eastern front greatly strengthened on 14.2. Attacks along Chuguyev and Volchansk roads repulsed by last reserves. Enemy penetration eight miles deep near southern airfield as far as Osnova. Mopping up now in progress but with inadequate forces. No forces available for sealing off enemy penetration north-west of Kharkov, at "Grossdeutschland" Division. All offensive troops tied down in the south for the moment. 320th Infantry Division not yet absorbed into main defensive line. Its condition, according to general-staff reports, precludes offensive employment for next few days.

"Inside Kharkov mob firing at troops and vehicles. No forces available for mopping up since everything in front line. City, including railway, stores, and ammunition dumps, effectively dynamited at Army orders. City burning. Systematic withdrawal increasingly improbable each day. Assumptions underlying Kharkov's strategic importance no longer valid. Request renewed Führer decision whether Kharkov to be defended to the last man."

General Lanz sympathized with Hausser's appeal. But he refused to re-examine the hold-on order in view of the clear instructions he had received from Hitler only a few hours earlier as his final word. His decision was made easier for him by the fact that 320th Infantry Division, which had been fighting its way back from the area of the shattered Hungarian Second Army, had still not arrived.

Paul Hausser, an experienced general-staff officer of the old imperial army, retired with the rank of lieutenant-general in the Reichswehr in 1932, and later enlisted in the Waffen-SS, did not give in. For him, orders—even Führer's orders—were not sacred commandments. He telephoned Lanz and implored him. But the general persisted in turning down his request. Once more Hausser signalled to Army Detachment Lanz:

"Decision on disengagement required by twelve noon. Signed Hausser."

Lanz refused.

Thereupon, in the afternoon, the SS Panzer Corps reported:

". . . . At 1645 hours on 14.2 issued orders to evacuate Kharkov and perform evasive movement behind Udy sector during night 14–15.2., orders simultaneously also to Raus's corps. Appreciation of situation to follow by letter."

General Lanz was in an exceedingly difficult situation in view of Hitler's express orders. Although he and his staff privately sympathized with Hausser he nevertheless ordered him, by signal No. 624 at 1725 hours:

"Panzer Corps will hold to the last man its present position on the east front of Kharkov in accordance with Führer's order."

On the evening of 14th February General Lanz even ordered the corps' offensive formations, which had been engaged in defensive fighting in the south of the city, to hand over some units for the defence of Kharkov and simultaneously dislodge the enemy from Olshany in the rear of the hotly contested city. The signal from Army Detachment Lanz ran:

"Führer's decision:

(1) The eastern front of Kharkov must be held.

(2) The considerable SS formations now arriving must be employed in freeing Kharkov's communications and in defeating the enemy forces pressing against Kharkov from the north-west."

It was an unrealizable order.

In the city centre the partisans were already taking up arms. Hausser, after a further consultation with Ostendorff, his chief of staff, and Lieutenant-Colonel Müller, his chief of operations, once more telephoned Lanz in the evening. But the commander of the Army Detachment again referred to Hitler's explicit order and refused Hausser's request to authorize the evacuation of Kharkov. It was Stalingrad all over again.

During the night of 14th–15th February the Russians broke into the north-western and south-eastern parts of the city. Once more they were repulsed in an immediate counter-attack by a detachment of tanks of the "Das Reich" SS Panzer Grenadier Division.

At noon on 15th February the Russians attacked again. There was now only a minute gap in the ring round the city, to the south-east. Once that was sealed off Hausser's corps, as well as the "Grossdeutschland" Panzer Grenadier Division in the northern part of the city, would be lost.

It was in this situation that Hausser, in agreement with his neighbouring corps under which the "Grossdeutschland" Division came, ordered his divisions to do at long last what the logic of warfare, his responsibility as a commander in the field, and indeed the bravery of the troops had long been demanding—to evacuate their positions and fight their way back. Hausser was not having another Stalingrad.

Towards 1300 hours Hausser reported this decision to Army Detachment in the following signal:

"To avoid troops being encircled and to save *matériel*, orders will be given at 1300 to fight way through behind Udy sector on edge of city. Fighting through enemy lines in progress, also street-fighting in south-west and west of the city."

The signal was sent. A Führer's order was being disobeyed. What would happen?

At 1530 hours Hausser's signal-station received a strict order from General Lanz: "Kharkov will be defended under all circumstances!"

But Hausser took no notice of it and did not reply to it. He mounted his break-out to the south-west. Tanks cleared the way for the grenadiers. Artillery, flak, and engineers covered their flanks, intercepted the pursuing enemy, and then about-turned at the Udy sector.

Twenty-four hours later the rear parties of "Das Reich" Division punched their way through the blazing city.

At the crossroads, in the flickering light of blazing houses, stood the huge assault guns of "Grossdeutschland" Division. They were waiting for the rearguard of their division, because General Hoernlein's "Grossdeutschland" Division had abandoned its positions north-west of Kharkov following Hausser's break-out, and was now fighting its way back through the city. The battle was following the logic of the front line—not some unrealistic order from Rastenburg.

The well-tried "Grossdeutschland" Panzer Grenadier Division also had some exceedingly heavy fighting behind it.

During the early hours of the morning the last dispatch-riders and armoured infantry carriers of Remer's battalion roared through the deserted streets. Infiltrated Russians were already sniping at them from windows and ruins. In the Red Square partisans hoisted a huge red flag.

And what was happening at the Wolfsschanze? White with fury, Hitler received the report of the disobedience of his SS Panzer Corps. But before he could make up his mind what to do about Hausser, the correctness of Hausser's decision was becoming obvious. He had saved two quite indispensable, fully operational, and experienced Panzer Divisions, as well as the "Grossdeutschland" Panzer Grenadier Division, for the decisive phase of the defensive battle.

Moreover, the resistance of the defenders of **Kharkov** and their counter-attack had enabled 320th Infantry Division under Major-General Postel to link up again with Army Detachment Lanz. Thus the temporary surrender of the biggest Ukrainian city was, contrary to all fears, yielding nothing but strategic advantages.

But what no-one on the German side could have suspected was the psychological effect which the evacuation of Kharkov had on Stalin and his General Staff. This is now attested by Soviet sources. The liberation of Kharkov, the fourth largest city in the Soviet Union, not only resulted in a further heightening of the Soviets' intoxication with victory, but also confirmed Stalin in his reading of German intentions. He knew Hitler, and he thought it inconceivable that Hitler's own Praetorian Guard would abandon Kharkov except as part of a general order to retreat.

A perfectly logical conclusion—only it happened to be wrong. Stalin had made no allowance for a man's courage in disobeying orders from above.

In consequence the dictator in the Kremlin whipped his offensive forces forward with even greater recklessness. This applied particularly to the South-Western Front. Major-General Kharitonov's Soviet Sixth Army was to cross the Dnieper on the right wing between Dnepropetrovsk and Zaporozhye. Kharitonov had two rifle corps, two tank corps, and a cavalry corps. The spearhead of his Army was formed by

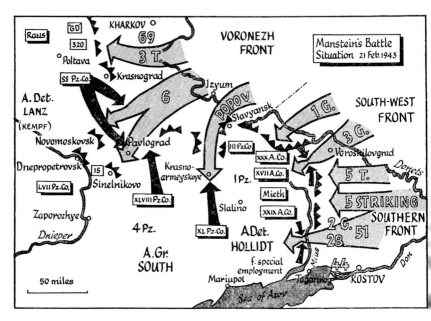

Map 18. Manstein's improvised blow against the Soviet breakthrough: the Soviet spearheads were halted everywhere and caught between pincers.

a hundred and fifty tanks. On the left wing Popov's armoured group, with four tank corps and two independent armoured brigades, a ski brigade, and three rifle divisions, was pushing towards the rear of Army Detachment Hollidt via Slavyansk in the direction of the Sea of Azov.

Manstein at Zaporozhye was watching Stalin's game on the situation map tensely, but with iron calm. As the Kremlin's reckless timetable took clearer shape, and it became obvious that the Soviet High Command was aiming at an operation on the vastest scale, Manstein's staff officers overheard the Field-Marshal saying: "And the best of luck to you!"

The best of luck! The moment had almost come when Stalin would have to pay dearly for his mistake, the moment when Manstein would move.

On 17th February Hitler arrived at Manstein's headquarters, excited and nervous. He sensed that it was not he who was weaving the pattern, but that outstanding strategic brain which, as long ago as 1940, as chief of staff of Army Group A, had worked out the formula for victory in the French campaign. Then Manstein had conceived the idea of making his unexpected thrust to the Channel by way of the roadless Eifel and the forests of the Ardennes, allegedly impassable for tanks. And now he had another plan. Once again he proved his gift for reading the thoughts and intentions of his opponent and reacting to them accordingly.

Manstein reported to Hitler on the situation: Army Detachment Hollidt had established itself on the Mius and was resisting strong attacks by three Soviet Armies. The eastern flank of the German Army Groups A and South was just about covered, even though enemy cavalry units were still roaming beyond the northern wing of the front.

A penetration made by the Soviet IV Guards Mechanized Corps in the centre of the Mius front had been crushed in a rapid counter-attack by 16th Motorized Infantry Division and units of 23rd Panzer Division. The Soviet corps was surrounded south of Matveyev Kurgan and very nearly wiped out; its entire staff had been taken prisoner. The defensive flak on the Mius was holding out.

General von Mackensen's First Panzer Army, adjoining Army Detachment Hollidt on the left, together with General Henrici's XL Panzer Corps and 5th SS (Viking) Panzer Grenadier Division, had succeeded in intercepting attacks by units of the Soviet First Guards Army at several points, and sealing them off, but a wide gap continued to exist between First Panzer Army and Army Detachment Lanz (Kempf). And the most powerful Soviet thrust was now directed into this huge gap.

The spearhead of this thrust was formed by Lieutenant-General

Popov's strong Armoured Group, which had already penetrated to
Krasnoarmeyskoye and was now aiming at Stalino¹ and Mariupol on
the Sea of Azov. For his first engagement Popov had 145 T-34s and a
further 267 tanks were being held in readiness for him by the South-
West Front—held in readiness for the intended final blow.

This then was the situation. And how was it being met?

Manstein continued his report: Mackensen was facing Popov's
armada with General Sigfrid Henrici's XL Panzer Corps. With this
corps' well-tried units, the 7th and 11th Panzer Divisions, the 5th SS
(Viking) Panzer Grenadier Division, and parts of 333rd Infantry
Division newly arrived from France, Henrici was to fight a decisive
engagement in the spring battle on the southern front.

Here then was some hope—supported by a Panzer corps.

But farther to the west there was only hope—unsupported. The
Soviet Sixth Army was advancing almost irresistibly towards the
Dnieper. For that reason Manstein intended to employ there all his
available forces, especially the SS Panzer Corps released from
Kharkov. But Hitler objected. "No," he said. "Why such a concentration of forces against an imaginary enemy?" Hitler wanted Kharkov
recaptured first. Kharkov! He just could not swallow the fact that
Hausser had abandoned this metropolis, this great administrative
centre of Ukrainian heavy industry, against his express orders. Stubbornly and blindly he refused to let Manstein use the SS Panzer Corps
for a mobile flanking attack against the Soviet Sixth Army and demanded, first of all, a locally limited counter-attack against Kharkov.
Not until that was accomplished was Manstein to proceed against
Kharitonov's Sixth Army.

Manstein was dismayed. The timetable proposed by Hitler was
desperately dangerous—a timetable based on prestige and short-
sightedness. Manstein had no intention of complying with Hitler's
demand. He knew what was bound to happen very shortly, and with
a good deal of diplomacy persuaded Hitler to postpone the decision
until the following day.

Twenty-four hours later Hitler received a very salutary demonstration of how right Manstein had been and how wrongly he himself had
assessed the situation. Right into the midday conference of 18th
February burst the news that the Soviets had penetrated in force into
the gap between First Panzer Army and Army Detachment Lanz
(Kempf), and had advanced to within forty miles of the Dnieper—a
mere sixty miles from Zaporozhye.

Hitler glanced suspiciously at Colonel Busse, the chief of operations
of Army Group South. Was he being bluffed? "I'd like to know more
about that," he grunted.

¹ Now Donetsk.

And as if he had only been waiting for this cue, Busse began to reel off the details. "The Soviet 267th Rifle Division is here, south of Krasnograd," he said, pointing to the map. His finger then came down on Pavlograd: "A tank battalion of 35th Guards Rifle Division has taken Pavlograd. The Italian division which was to have defended Pavlograd has taken to its heels."

His lips pressed together, Hitler looked at the map. To admit that he had been wrong was not in his nature. But the next report brought in by Major Eismann, the intelligence officer, left him no choice. The third division of SS Panzer Corps, the "Totenkopf" Division, which Hitler had ordered to be moved hurriedly up to the front to participate in the recapture of Kharkov and which had detrained at Kiev, was stuck in the mud near Poltava. Now Hitler had to give in. He gave Manstein the green light to launch his pincer operation against the Soviet Sixth Army and Popov's Armoured Group.

As Manstein was sketching out his plan on the map, explaining possibilities and justifying his decisions, Hitler had a lesson in truly bold strategy and inspired but calculated risks. Nothing about this plan was half-hearted; there was no shying away from risks, but each was carefully weighed against the alternative of certain disaster.

Manstein explained that he would pull out all the Panzer divisions— and he meant all of them—from the hard-pressed Mius line in order to employ them against the enemy on the north-western wing of Army Group. He would do that regardless of the fact that on the Mius six Soviet Armies were charging against Hollidt's five corps. The danger of the enemy breaking through, of his shattering that thin line and his capturing the Donets region from the east, was indeed considerable.

But Manstein icily explained to Hitler: "There's no other way. We have no choice. We've got to face that danger. The enemy thrust towards the Dnieper is the more dangerous of the two. It is this thrust that must be smashed. It is the only way to avert the danger to the eastern wing."

Hitler became jittery. The man with the much-vaunted iron nerves got into a panic at this sober calculation of his marshal. He lamented, he demanded first one thing and then another, and he was on the point of watering down Manstein's plan and turning his bold operation into one of those half-measures which had marked his strategy ever since that disastrous summer of 1942.

A Soviet combat-group commander put an end to Hitler's ill-conceived interference. It was he who saved Manstein and the German southern front. What happened was this. On 19th February the spearhead of the Soviet XXV Tank Corps thrust from Pavlograd to the railway-station of Sinelnikovo and thereby closed the railway junction through which ran the only two direct lines by which Army Detachment Hollidt could be supplied.

More significantly still, this raid brought the Soviets to within forty miles of Zaporozhye. Between the Führer of the Greater German Reich and the spearheads of the Soviet Sixth Army there was not a single major German unit left. Urged by his entourage, Hitler thereupon decided to make a hasty departure by air from Manstein's increasingly inhospitable headquarters. As his FW-200 took off from the forward airfield of Zaporozhye, escorted by two Me-109 fighters, the most forward Soviet tanks were a mere six miles away.

The Field-Marshal heaved a sigh of relief when his distinguished visitor disappeared in the grey, wintery sky towards Vinnitsa. Now at last he had a free hand.

"What can we use against that enemy formation at Sinelnikovo?" Manstein asked at his situation conference. "The 15th Infantry Division, Herr Feldmarschall," the chief of staff replied.

The 15th Infantry Division! General Buschenhagen's Main-Franconian Regiment had only left La Rochelle on the Atlantic coast nine days before, aboard seventy railway trains. Well equipped with weapons, winter clothing, skis and sledges, cross-country vehicles, and an outstanding Panzerjäger Battalion. A real godsend, the advanced party had arrived in Dnepropetrovsk the previous day, on 18th February. The first operational battalions were to follow on 19th February. But where were they now? Where and how could they be got hold of in a hurry in order to direct them straight against the enemy?

Radio-telegrams, teleprinter messages, telephone calls: "Where is the commander of 15th Infantry Division?"

He was soon found: General Buschenhagen was stuck at Vinnitsa. Fog and blizzards were delaying his take-off.

But his chief of operations, the energetic Lieutenant-Colonel Willemer, was found at Nizhnedneprovsk Uzel, a little railway-station north-east of Dnepropetrovsk.

Willemer decided on his own responsibility to let the forward companies travel straight on to Sinelnikovo. He rang through to Dnepropetrovsk station: "All incoming transports of 15th Infantry Division to continue journey at once!"

Towards midnight on 19th February the first train arrived at Nizhnedneprovsk Uzel station. It carried three companies of 88th Grenadier Regiment.

A hurried conversation took place between the divisional chief of operations and Captain Berckel, the battalion commander. The wagons with the horses and vehicles were uncoupled. Company and platoon commanders were briefed. A whistle of the engine—and off they went.

Rifles and machine-guns aimed outwards now, the train steamed on through the winter night, towards Sinelnikovo.

Tense, the men lay behind windows and carriage doors, their weapons at the ready. An icy winter wind whistled through the carriages. A distance of fifteen miles had to be covered—and the fireworks might start at any moment.

Berckel glanced at the luminous dial of his watch: "Nearly there." It had been a strange train journey, from the Atlantic direct to the battlefield on the Dnieper.

With a noisy puff the train pulled up. Out! Before the Soviets in their warm, cosy sheds realized what was happening the Franconian grenadiers were right among them, taking them prisoner and mopping up the railway sidings.

The second train arrived without opposition. It carried the battalion headquarters staff, three more rifle companies, one machine-gun

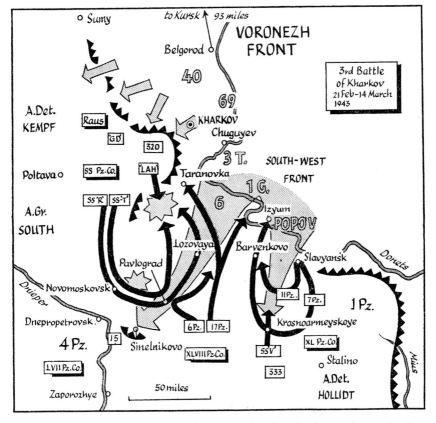

Map 19. Too late did the Soviet High Command realize the danger threatening its Sixth and Popov's armoured group. They were smashed in daring mobile operations. Manstein's corps pushed through to the Donets and formed up for attack on Kharkov.

company, and three 7·5-cm anti-tank guns on self-propelled carriages.

The surprise came off. In heavy night fighting the 88th Grenadier Regiment took the village and held it against strong attacks by enemy armour.

The Soviets now cut the railway line east of Nizhnedneprovsk Uzel, but Major-General Buschenhagen, who presently arrived by Fieseler Storch, made his units detrain on the open track. The companies of 88th, 81st, and 106th Grenadier Regiments, as well as the Engineer Battalion 15 took up switch lines between Sinelnikovo and Novo-moskovsk—a last obstacle before the great Dnieper bend.

It was a dramatic moment. Only in retrospect does one realize how much hung in the balance just then.

At Krasnoarmeyskoye, seventy-seven miles east of Sinelnikovo, the spearheads of Popov's Armoured Group had already cut the railway from Dnepropetrovsk to Stalino and were threatening the industrial heart of the Donets basin.

General Felix Steiner's 5th SS (Viking) Panzer Grenadier Division tried to dislodge the Russians from Krasnoarmeyskoye. While still on the move they had received a signal from Manstein: "Strong enemy—Popov's Armoured Group—advancing across Donets at Izyum in southerly direction towards Krasnoarmeyskoye. 'Viking' will wheel to west immediately. Objective: tie down Popov's Armoured Group."

But at first this did not quite come off. The Scandinavian and Dutch volunteers of the "Nordland", "Germania", and "Westland" SS Panzer Grenadier Regiments succeeded for the moment in halting Popov's spearheads and pressing them together—but the division had too few tanks and was altogether too worn out by the heavy fighting in the Caucasus, on the Don, and on the Mius.

It was the skilful and flexible gunnery of the "Viking" Division's artillery regiment which saved the situation. Steiner's artillery commander, General Gille, by a masterly tactical manoeuvre south of Krasnoarmeyskoye, succeeded in creating the impression that a considerable concentration of German forces was present there. By continuous searching and sweeping fire the batteries unnerved Popov's staffs who believed themselves faced by a superior force. Popov became less resolute in his push towards the south-west.

Now everything was going Manstein's way.

Popov's armoured corps pushed past Slavyansk, which was being held by General von Funck's 7th Panzer Division. General Balck's 11th Panzer Division and the bulk of the Brandenberg 333rd Infantry Division were now able to manoeuvre between Popov's assault formations and cut off their supplies.

Now began the first act of the great drama between Donets and Dnieper.

Lieutenant Bogdan Shvakuk of the Soviet 663rd Anti-Aircraft

Artillery Regiment did not have time to send off his report from Krasnoarmeyskoye to his brigade at Andreyevka. He still carried it in his dispatch-case when a burial party of the German 333rd Infantry Division found him dead and stiff in his shattered gun emplacement.

But the report showed how on the Soviet side, from the general down to the lieutenant, a mistaken assessment of the situation had taken root: they were all blinded by the certainty of a victory already won.

The report found on the dead lieutenant was dated 11th February 1943. It began with the words: "I convey greetings from the liberated town of Krasnoarmeyskoye where a few scattered fascist groups remain to be captured. Private Butusov today captured three fascists who crawled into our command post. They were taken to headquarters and shot. I myself intercepted a Red Army soldier who was walking about with two horses. I immediately suspected him of being a German. I handed him over to Private Gvozdik to be taken to headquarters of IV Guards Tank Corps. He was shot while trying to escape. This evening a group of eleven fascist soldiers was killed, so that a total of fifteen German soldiers, including one officer, were wiped out today."

At the end of his message the lieutenant urged the brigade political commissar to stir up Comrade Kitayev, in command of supplies for 633rd AA Artillery Regiment. "Supplies are badly organized. Neither ammunition nor food, nor even a drop of vodka arrive in the forward lines. And vodka is the very thing the men want for their victorious chase after the Germans."

Just as Lieutenant Shvakuk put his name under the above report the victorious chase of Popov's Armoured Group was coming to an end at this particular point, near Krasnoarmeyskoye.

The regiments of the "Viking" Division struck at Krasnoarmeyskoye from the east and south-east and intercepted the thrust of the Soviet IV Guards Tank Corps. Now came the moment for General Henrici's XL Panzer Corps. Counter-attack! Since their memorable march across the Sea of Azov, the bulk of the divisions had been employed in the line near Slavyansk. Now the time had come to change over to mobile operation against Popov's group. The C-in-C First Panzer Army, General von Mackensen, gave Henrici the green light.

Everything now went with clockwork precision. The 7th Panzer Division, which had been holding Slavyansk, was permitted to evacuate the town and was moved into the Krasnoarmeyskoye area. The Russians did not notice anything.

Over roads made soft by the thaw, General von Funck's Thuringian units were working their way forward against the eastern flank of the Soviets.

Meanwhile in the Slavyansk area General Breith's III Panzer Corps had also taken over the sector hitherto held by XL Panzer Corps. In this way, further armoured forces were freed for action against Popov's Armoured Group.

Balck's Silesian 11th Panzer Division was engaged north-east of Krasnoarmeyskoye in a thrust into the rear of the Soviet Armoured Group. The Silesians cut off Popov's supplies. The trap was set.

On 18th February the forward monitoring platoon of XL Panzer Corps decoded a signal sent from Popov's Group to South-West Front. It begins with the words "All wheels are standing still" and reports a disastrous supply situation as a result of the supply-line south of Slavyansk being cut.

"Interesting," said Colonel Carl Wagener, Henrici's chief of staff, when the message was put on his desk.

Interesting.

These intercepted Soviet signals had become a source of re-assurance for the German staffs.

Since 6th February, Lieutenant Fassbender, the commander of the monitoring platoon of the Panzer Corps' signal battalion, had been intercepting the ultra-short frequency on which the Soviet Armoured Group talked to its Army Group HQ. Since the code was rather primitive, Fassbender's men had cracked it within a week.

On 12th February Major Kandutsch had presented the chief of staff with his first decoded messages. From that day onward these secret enemy signals had been the daily bread of Corps, Army, and Army Group: they were now privy to Popov's and Vatutin's thoughts and they knew, even before the Russian regimental commanders did, where their battalions were going to attack. And so they were always ready at the right spot at the right time.

"All wheels are standing still." Surely this alarming report of 18th February should have at last opened the eyes of General Vatutin, the C-in-C of the Soviet South-West Front, as to the true situation?

From the outset Popov had mistrusted the optimism of his commander-in-chief. And perhaps it was not fortuitous that his signal began with a quotation whose allusion must have been clear to the recipient: "All wheels are standing still at your mighty sinew's will" was one of the best known proletarian battle slogans.

But Vatutin was no more ready to abandon his illusions than was Stalin. The operations of the German XL Panzer Corps were seen by both of them as evidence that the Germans were trying, by means of desperate rearguard actions, to screen the withdrawal of Manstein's Army Group.

Reality was quite different. Popov's brigades, their supplies paralysed, were rapidly facing disaster. With 11th Panzer Division on the right, 7th Panzer Division on the left, and the SS (Viking) Panzer Grenadier Division in the middle, the German XL Panzer Corps thrust northwards as soon as the returning frost had made the roads firm again.

The points where Popov's immobilized armoured brigades and motorized rifle battalions were offering desperate resistance were simply bypassed and left to be dealt with by the regiments of the Brandenburg 333rd Infantry Division which was following the German armour.

"Don't waste time fighting against villages and towns. Keep moving!"—that was General Henrici's principle, a basic tenet of modern flexible warfare. Popov's proud Armoured Group was cut up like a cake.

During the night of 20th–21st February Lieutenant-General Popov implored Army General Vatutin to authorize the withdrawal of his Group.

But Vatutin replied with a categorical No. "Attack the enemy," he urged him. And he added confidently: "The enemy is retreating. He must not escape across the Dnieper!"

Soviet headquarters were just as blind—indeed, that was probably where the grotesque misjudgment of the situation originated. Thus, also on 21st February, Lieutenant-General A. N. Bogolyubov, the deputy chief of the operations section of the Great General Staff and one of Stalin's intimates, telephoned the chief of staff of Southern Front and informed him: "The enemy, moving in solid groups, is retreating. Vatutin's forces are making excellent headway. Their right wing is now beyond Pavlograd. The reason why Popov's Armoured Group is still hanging back is simply that it is not attacking with sufficient vigour."

At the very hour when Bogolyubov passed on to the Southern Front Stalin's disastrously false appreciation of the situation, Colonel-General Hoth, C-in-C of the German Fourth Panzer Army, now engaged in defensive fighting in the wide gap on the Dnieper, received new orders. What he now received was Manstein's decisive instructions, the move for which the Field-Marshal had been carefully paving the way over the past fortnight, the move over which he had argued with Hitler and for the sake of which he had daringly denuded the front on the Mius and before Kharkov. Now the moment had come.

The order addressed to Hoth was impressively brief. It ran: "The Soviet Sixth Army, now racing towards Dnepropetrovsk through the gap between First Panzer Army and Army Detachment Kempf, is to be defeated."

For this purpose Hoth was given three corps, two of which he instantly launched for a pincer movement against General Kharitonov's

Sixth Army which had rushed forward in a criminally foolhardy way—General Hausser's SS Panzer Corps from the north-west and General von Knobelsdorff's XLVIII Panzer Corps from the south-east. Rendezvous at Pavlograd.

General Kirchner's LVII Panzer Corps was still being assembled in the Dnieper bend.

This opening, to use a chess term, revealed Manstein's strategic skill. It held the secret of what presently became a successful operation by an inferior force against a numerically vastly superior opponent.

The battle began. The date was 19th February 1943. Hausser's 2nd SS (Das Reich) Panzer Grenadier Division thrust deep into the flank of the Soviet Sixth Army. Stukas of Fourth Air Fleet, under Field-Marshal von Richthofen, cleared the way for it. Kharitonov's IV Guards Rifle Corps was dislodged. The XV Rifle Corps was torn apart. After heavy fighting the railway centre of Pavlograd on the Samara river fell to the Germans.

The southern jaw of the pincers, General von Knobelsdorff's XLVIII Panzer Corps, attacking northwards with 17th and 6th Panzer Divisions, gained the area around Pavlograd on 23rd February. Thus the spearhead of the most dangerous Soviet thrust towards the Dnieper crossings had been chopped off: the superbly equipped Soviet XXV Tank Corps was cut off.

This corps now sent panicky radio signals to the Soviet Sixth Army, requesting new orders. The answer it received showed that the Soviet command had still not understood what was happening. General Kharitonov sent a signal in reply: "Stick to your orders and thrust towards Zaporozhye!"

One may now shake one's head at so much obstinacy—but why should Kharitonov be better informed than General Ivanov, the chief of staff of the South-West Front? Ivanov, in his situation report made to headquarters on 20th February and passed on to Sixth Army on 21st February, stated: "Movements of enemy forces discovered by aerial reconnaissance between Stalino and Prokovskoye confirm our view that the enemy is continuing his withdrawal towards Zaporozhye."

What incredible blindness! General Ivanov was disastrously wrong. The German forces which he thought were withdrawing were in fact the divisions of XL and XLVIII Panzer Corps which Manstein was deploying for attack.

When Kharitonov's decoded order to his XXV Tank Corps was placed on Colonel-General Hoth's desk, Hoth merely nodded and passed it over to Major General Fangohr, his chief of staff, with the remark: "Suits us!"

Panzers and grenadiers attacking in hard frost. "Scorched earth": near Oposhnya, 20th September, 1943.

As in a game of chess Manstein now moved his pieces. What had until then been separate offensive actions against Popov and against the Soviet Sixth Army were now pulled together and turned into a co-ordinated offensive. Direction of the thrust—north-east. First objective —the Donets.

On 23rd February Henrici's divisions broke the last resistance in the Krasnoarmeyskoye area and along a broad front, bypassing Barvenkovo, thrust through to the north and west.

Popov's corps tried to escape to the north and to cover its retreat. The General radioed to Vatutin, imploring his help. All that remained to him was a handful of tanks, and they were out of fuel. He had no artillery left, next to no ammunition, and no food supplies.

At that moment, when Popov's Armoured Group was already doomed, Stalin rang through to General Vatutin. The dictator was feverish with suspense. He could not wait to be told that his armies had reached the Dnieper in order, as he believed, to deny the crossings to the fleeing Germans and to inflict upon Manstein's Army Group a defeat four times the magnitude of Stalingrad.

Vatutin, however, had been getting increasingly nervous as a result of Popov's reports and tried to raise objections. But Stalin angrily reproved him: "Get that left wing of yours moving!"

And so, at 1730 hours on 23rd February, Vatutin signalled to Popov: "I wish to remind you emphatically that you are to use all means available to you in order to halt and annihilate the enemy in the Barvenkovo area. I am holding you personally responsible."

Poor Vatutin!

In the late evening of 24th February he at last realized the full extent of the error which had bedevilled him and headquarters for the past fortnight. He realized that Popov's Armoured Group was clearly smashed and that Sixth Army was in dire straits with large parts of it cut off and surrounded.

Precipitately Vatutin now ordered all offensive operations throughout his Army Group to be suspended and defensive operations to be started. To relieve his armies he asked headquarters to intensify offensive operations by his neighbouring Army Groups in the area of Kharkov and on the Mius.

It was too late. Already the German XL Panzer Corps was thrusting past Barvenkovo, where Popov with the rest of his Armoured Group and with parts of First Guards Army was heroically trying to intercept and seal off Henrici's attack. While 333rd Infantry Division took Krasnoarmeyskoye on 27th February, assault groups of the Berlin 3rd Panzer Division gained the Izyum-Slavyansk highway and cut it.

Fording an arm of the Kuban.
Light flak on the Kuban.

On 28th February the 7th Panzer Division reached the Donets south of Izyum. Popov's Armoured Group was annihilated.

In the evening of 28th February XL Panzer Corps was again on the Donets over a broad front, in the positions which had had to be abandoned in January, during the Russian winter offensive.

In a twenty-one-day battle Popov's Armoured Group, the powerful spearhead of Vatutin's Army Group, had been smashed. It left behind 251 tanks, 125 anti-tank guns, 73 heavy guns, 217 machine-guns, 425 trucks, countless mortars and anti-tank rifles, as well as 3000 dead on the battlefield between Krasnoarmeyskoye and Izyum.

The Soviet Sixth Army, which strangely enough bore the same number as the German Army sacrificed on the Volga by Hitler's obstinacy, suffered the same fate through Stalin's overweening pride.

In vain did the Soviet High Command try to help the threatened Army by making its neighbour on the right, the Third Tank Army, launch an attack. But German Stuka and ground-support aircraft of Fourth Air Fleet smashed the Tank Army's assembly positions.

In a headlong offensive Hoth's Panzer Corps now drove the retreating Russian formations before them. They encircled them. And they smashed them before they got to the Donets.

Six tank corps, ten rifle divisions, and half a dozen independent brigades had been wiped out or badly mauled. A total of 615 tanks, 400 guns, and 600 anti-tank guns had been destroyed; 23,000 Soviet dead littered the battlefield. The ratio of dead to wounded is normally put at one to five. That would mean an effective loss of 100,000 Russian troops. Only 9000 were taken prisoner—a comparatively low figure. But this is easily explained: the German formations lacked the forces to seal up the big pocket in the difficult terrain really closely. Moreover, the cold weather forced the troops to spend the nights in the villages, under cover and near a stove. In consequence, there were bound to be gaps, and through these a considerable number of enemy troops managed to slip and make good their escape across the frozen Donets, but without weapons, without vehicles, and without any equipment whatever.

It was a fantastic victory which Manstein's formations had won. The greatest danger which had threatened the German eastern front since the beginning of the campaign in 1941, the danger of its total annihilation, was averted. The consequences of the defeat of Stalingrad were eliminated. And it had all been done with a minimum of forces, but with a degree of strategic skill that would be remembered long after the German war in the East. Bold manoeuvring, calm and sang-froid, and above all a skilful flexible handling of operations—in fact the very reverse of Hitler's rigid hold-on strategy—had ensured victory.

It was a demonstration by Field-Marshal von Manstein of what

German strategy on the eastern front would have to be like in the future if the Red Army was to be defeated.

There was something like a deep sigh of relief along the entire front. Since November 1942, when the disaster of Stalingrad began between Volga and Don, there had been nothing but defeats and retreats. Now a breath of victory was again blowing over the icy battlefields of the east. Officers and men once more determined to make the most of this turn in the fortunes of war and to accomplish whatever could be accomplished.

The most tempting strategic objective for the moment, however, was Kharkov. Could it be recaptured?

As February draws to its close between Don and Donets a sudden break in the weather must always be expected. The advent of spring. But more than anything, the advent of mud. And once that brown or black sticky mass lies knee-deep on roads and paths, all traffic must come to a standstill and the war itself grind to a halt.

As late as mid-February the German Command would have given anything for "General Mud" to arrive in the Ukraine in order to stop the tempestuous advance of the Soviets between Donets and Dnieper. Stalin's generals, on the other hand, had placed all their hopes in a late spring: they hoped to be west of the Dnieper before the onset of the muddy season, in order to catch Manstein's armies. Now, at the beginning of March, the hopes of the two sides had changed very considerably. Now the Germans were praying for winter to continue, because the initiative was in their hands. The Soviet Army leaders, on the other hand, scowled at their barometers every morning, studying weather reports and wanting only one thing—a thaw, and mud.

Mud was the only thing that could stop Manstein's mobile divisions with their regained offensive vigour, now that the annihilation of Sixth Army and Popov's Armoured Group had left a hundred-and-twenty-mile gap in the Soviet front, a gap in which no Russian troops were left. The Russians' only salvation could come from "General Mud". But the weather god this time sided with the Germans. The winter continued. And Manstein reached out towards Kharkov.

The Soviet High Command had no other choice than, in a bold, improvised move, to switch two tank corps and three rifle divisions from the Soviet Third Tank Army, which came under Army Group Voronezh Front; these units were moved quickly to the south, into the path of Hausser's SS Panzer Corps, in order to protect Kharkov.

But Hausser again coped with a very difficult situation. True, his battalion had to shovel their way through chest-high snow, but the Russians made the mistake of moving precisely between the defensive lines of the 1st SS (Leibstandarte) Panzer Grenadier Division and the two attacking divisions of the SS Panzer Corps. Hausser thereupon wheeled the wing of the 3rd SS (Totenkopf) Panzer Grenadier Division and on 3rd March had encircled the Soviet force west of Bereka in a pocket formed by "Totenkopf", "Das Reich", and "Leibstandarte".

Ground-attack aircraft broke up all Russian attempts to form up for action. General Rybalko's tank corps and rifle divisions were wiped out. It was a savage battle. Stalin's Guards regiments were fighting Hitler's crack divisions. The general commanding the Soviet XV Guards Tank Corps was killed in close combat, only a hundred yards from Hausser's command post.

Then a dramatic turn occurred in the situation—warmer weather arrived. The temperature at night was no longer low enough to keep the soil frozen. The thaw was on its way, and with it the mud.

The Russians tried everything to gain a few hours or days. Twenty-five miles south of Kharkov, near Taranovka, Zmiyev, and Merefa, where von Knobelsdorff's XLVIII Panzer Corps was pushing across the railway line from Lozovaya northwards towards Kharkov, Major-General Shafarenko with his 25th Guards Rifle Division flung himself against the German Panzer divisions. For five days he held that important position and covered Kharkov against capture from the south.

But disaster came from the west and the north. For now the SS Panzer Corps was in action again. With the crushing of the combat group of the Soviet Third Tank Army, the SS Panzer Corps had a clear road. On Colonel-General Hoth's order it struck at the city from the left—*i.e.*, by means of a westerly enveloping movement—and by 8th March again stood on the western edge of the Ukrainian metropolis. The final act of the third battle of Kharkov had begun.

Hausser won that battle in six days. The man who, almost exactly four weeks previously, had abandoned the city in defiance of Hitler's strict order, now reconquered it. And there was no doubt that this general's insubordination, which had saved the SS Panzer Corps, the "Grossdeutschland" Division, as well as the gallant 320th Infantry Division, was a vital rung in the ladder leading to the German victory between Donets and Dnieper.

But Hausser's victory was marred by a reproach which is still occasionally levelled at him by military historians. It is suggested that for reasons of prestige, he penetrated into the city from the west too soon and allowed himself to be engaged in costly street fighting instead of letting Kharkov fall to him through encirclement, an extensive encirclement which would moreover have contained the enemy forces within the city and prevented them from escaping along its southern front. Is this criticism justified? What precisely was the course of events leading to the recapture of Kharkov? The general is entitled to an objective examination of this question.

According to the diary of SS Panzer Corps, Hausser on 9th March

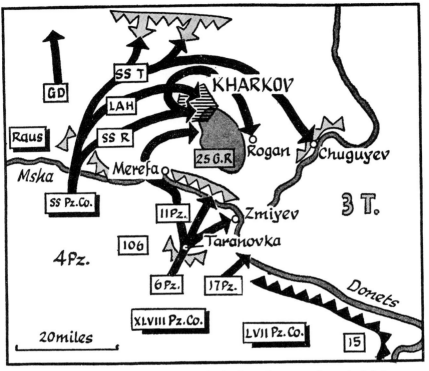

Map 20. Waffen SS divisions recaptured Kharkov after some dramatic fighting on 15th March, 1943.

1943 at 0920 hours received from Fourth Panzer Army the following order by radio: "SS Panzer Corps will seal off Kharkov tightly from west to north. Conditions inside the city are to be reconnoitred. Opportunities to seize the city by a coup are to be utilized. Signed Hoth."

Hausser acted accordingly. He sealed off the city. He reconnoitred the situation inside. He saw a chance of taking it by a coup. And, according to his report to Fourth Panzer Army, he deployed his assault detachments for the attack. On 10th March "Leibstandarte" and "Totenkopf" thrust past Kharkov in the north.

In the evening of 10th March, at 2000 hours, Fourth Panzer Army teleprinted the following order to corps: "SS Panzer Corps will take Kharkov. Its eastern wing will cut the Kharkov–Chuguyev road. Strong forces will thrust into the city from the north-east. In the west the city is only to be sealed off."

In accordance with orders, "Leibstandarte" penetrated into the city on the morning of 11th March. The 3rd Battalion, 2nd SS Panzer Grenadier Regiment, under Max Hansen pushed right through to the

Red Square in tough street fighting and so opened the access routes to the city centre.

While the companies of Sepp Dietrich's 1st SS (Leibstandarte) Panzer Grenadier Division were already engaged with the Soviet 19th Rifle Division and the 179th Armoured Brigade in the south-eastern part of Kharkov, some thirty miles south of the city, on the Msha stream, General Shafarenko with his reinforced 25th Guards Rifle Division was still pinning down the German XLVIII Panzer Corps.

Colonel-General Hoth, a master of mobile operations, made a virtue of necessity. The last thing he wanted to do was to get himself pinned down along the front. That applied equally to XLVIII Panzer Corps and to Hausser. For that reason Hoth employed the Waffen-SS formations in a sweeping encircling attack round Kharkov, regardless of the fighting in the city itself.

At 1450 hours on 11th March the following order from Army arrived for Hausser by teleprinter: "Fourth Panzer Army will prevent enemy's escape eastwards from front of XLVIII Panzer Corps. For that purpose SS Panzer Corps will detach SS 'Reich' Division from western edge of Kharkov, leaving only weak pickets, and lead the division round north of Kharkov over to eastern wing of corps. It will be corps' task with this division to launch a thrust east of Kharkov, in a southerly direction towards Zmiyev, into the rear of the enemy facing XLVIII Panzer Corps and prevent enemy from escaping towards Chuguyev. . . . Hoth, Colonel-General."

When this order arrived the "Das Reich" Division had just got to a sixteen-foot-wide anti-tank ditch on the western edge of Kharkov. The Russians were dug in on the far side, and from secure positions subjected the Germans to effective defensive fire. Fall back or cross the ditch—that was the question. The 16th Company of SS (Der Führer) Panzer Grenadier Regiment did not hesitate. It took the seven-foot-deep ditch. With their trenching tools the men hacked small steps into the stone-hard sides of the ditch and thus burst out of it and towards the first row of houses.

They managed it. Thus the way into the city had been opened also from the west.

Hausser saw his opportunity of pushing straight through the southern part of Kharkov and thus striking at the enemy's rear on the Msha along the shortest and, moreover, a well-surfaced road. Quicker in fact than if he had pulled "Das Reich" out of the operation and led it all the way round the city along those terrible muddy and time-wasting roads.

By noon on 12th March the combat detachments of "Das Reich" Division were already at the central railway-station. But Colonel-General Hoth, remembering the bitter experiences of Stalingrad, the Manych, and Rostov, was reluctant to believe that one could push

one's way through a big city that quickly. He therefore firmly reminded Hausser, in a radioed order transmitted at 1150 hours on 12th
March, that he should stick to his orders, which demanded that "Das
Reich" should disengage from street fighting and be brought over to
the eastern wing round Kharkov.

Hausser obeyed. He still believed that the "Leibstandarte" and
"Das Reich" Divisions would have been able, jointly, to break Soviet
resistance in the city in a very short time and thereafter wheel round
to the south. Nevertheless he obeyed Hoth's order.

The Combat Detachment Harmel was set in motion and, together
with units of "Totenkopf" Division, worked its way round the city.
At Rogan, Harmel dislodged the battalions of the Soviet 1288th Rifle
Regiment. The road to Chuguyev was clear.

On 15th March the pocket was sealed up. The same day the last
Soviet resistance collapsed at the Kharkov tractor plant.

Which way to Chuguyev would have been the better, or led more
quickly to the desired result, cannot be examined in this book. But one
thing emerges with complete certainty from the evidence available
today: the general commanding the SS Panzer Corps, then the most
battle-worthy of all major formations on the German southern front,
was guided solely by military considerations in his battle for Kharkov.
Nevertheless, Adolf Hitler for a long time refused to forgive him his
action. Whereas Generals Hoernlein and Postel, the commanders of
"Grossdeutschland" Panzer Grenadier Division and 320th Infantry
Division, were awarded the Oak Leaves, Paul Hausser did not receive
this decoration until four months later, after his SS Panzer Corps had
again been engaged in heavy and costly fighting.

A nocturnal telephone conversation concluded the Soviet defeat of
Kharkov. Vatutin ordered General Rybalko to fight his way out of the
Kharkov pocket with the remnants of Third Tank Army. At that
moment the spectre of an immeasurable catastrophe hovered over the
situation map of the Soviet South-West Front.

Frightful disasters had befallen the Soviet command during those
past four weeks.

The Soviet Sixth Army? Smashed.

Popov's Armoured Group? Annihilated.

The divisions of Third Tank Army? Numbers on a sheet of paper.

Sixty-Ninth Army? Truncated.

It was a terrible balance sheet: three Soviet Armies and parts of a
fourth, as well as an entire Armoured Group, had been smashed. A
dozen corps and brigades were in flight. Fifty-two divisions and
brigades, including twenty-five armoured brigades, had vanished from
the situation map at Soviet headquarters.

If the Germans succeeded in exploiting the situation and in following up from Kharkov in a northerly direction, then the consequences were unforeseeable. Belgorod would be lost. Kursk would become impossible to defend. But if Kursk fell then the rear of the far-advanced Soviet Army Group Central Front would be unprotected and its five Armies would be left in mid-air. They would scarcely be able in this position to stand up to a pincer attack from Kursk and Orel.

That then was the situation which kept the telephones of all Soviet commands buzzing. Signals were pushed out into the ether: Reserves! But where were there any reserves left? General Katukov's First Guards Army and the Twenty-First Army, the last strategic reserves of the Soviet High Command, were switched to the front line.

The defeat of Kharkov was wiping out the victory of Stalingrad. The alarm bells of Kharkov were heard ringing as far as the city on the Volga. Stalin ordered General Shumilov's badly mauled Sixty-Fourth Army to be rushed westwards to help at Kharkov. A distance of six hundred miles! Veterans of the battle of Stalingrad were now to save the situation at Kharkov.

Again the outcome of a great and decisive battle hung in the balance.

"What's the present effective strength of 340th Rifle Division?"

"It has two hundred and seventy-five men left, Comrade General."

Only two hundred and seventy-five men out of an original twelve thousand.

"And the Army's Armoured brigade?"

"Not a single operational tank left, Comrade General."

To spare General F. I. Golikov, the Commander-in-Chief of the Soviet Voronezh Front, any further questions, Major-General Kryuchenkin, commanding Sixty-Ninth Army, said, "I have no operational unit left. Not a single tank. My artillery has shrunk to a hundred barrels. The divisions are just skeleton units; not one of them has more than a thousand men."

This then was the situation of the Soviet Sixty-Ninth Army on 17th March 1943. And this was the Army which, after the fall of Kharkov, was expected to halt the German SS Panzer Corps as well as Raus's corps in their attack on the important transport centre of Belgorod.

It was a dramatic change. Only quite recently the Red Army had celebrated a string of major successes on its southern front and had found itself advancing along a highroad of impressive victories. Soviet armoured spearheads had stood on the Dnieper. Victory had beckoned to them across that great river, that river of destiny of the Russian Empire, that river flowing through its wealthiest provinces. And now these armies were in retreat again. And that was not all. The next few weeks looked gloomy. The spectre menacing the Russians is described in the *History of the Great Fatherland War* as follows:

"The German thrust towards Belgorod threatened the rear area of the whole of our Central Front. A thrust towards Kursk, together with an attack from the salient south of Orel, might lead to the encirclement of strong Red Army forces. The situation remained exceedingly serious so long as no fresh forces were available. The enemy made good use of his success: the 'Grossdeutschland' Division took Borosovka and the SS Panzer Corps mounted its attack against Belgorod on the morning of 17th March. Sixty-Ninth Army was unable to offer organized resistance and, in order to evade encirclement, fell back behind the northern Donets. On 18th March the enemy penetrated into the town and occupied it."

A glance at the map will reveal what had happened. Strong German armoured forces were deep in the flank of the Soviet Central Front which formed an echeloned bulge towards the west. This was Manstein's chance. He had seen it during the first few days of March and had then proposed to Hitler that he mount a pincer attack from the south and the north against the Kursk bulge containing half-a-dozen Soviet armies.

Conditions for such a move were particularly favourable, since counter-attacks by the German Second Army and the stubborn resistance of the German Second Panzer Army north of Kursk had cleared up the situation also on the southern wing of Army Group Centre. The threat was like a nightmare to Stalin's headquarters. He had no forces left to counter such an operation.

But help came to the Russians from two sources. Field-Marshal von Kluge categorically refused to make available any formations from the Armies of his Army Group Centre, insisting that they were in need of rest after the fighting they had just been through. He did not realize what today we know from the records—that in view of the Soviet disposition of forces such an operation simply could not have gone wrong.

To complete Stalin's luck, his powerful ally, "General Mud", at last arrived on the battlefield. Thus the culmination of the battle by way of a thrust of Fourth Panzer Army and Army Detachment Kempf, although it could have been launched after some quick regrouping, did not come about.

Manstein's headlong victorious advance from the Dnieper to the Donets, incredible though it may now seem, was not exploited for a final strike. The German High Command believed it could put off until tomorrow what might just—and only just—have been possible that day. A great opportunity was missed. The seed was planted for a disaster which was to decide the war—the Kursk salient was left in existence. The Soviet command was now relieved of its worst worry —one which had been haunting it ever since the battles of annihilation of 1942. Stalin's Central Front had been saved by a miracle comparable to the miracle of the Marne. And time at Kursk was now beginning to work for Stalin, and against Hitler.

No-one suspected then that this was probably the most fateful decision since Stalingrad. One hundred and eleven days later Operation Citadel was launched against the Kursk salient. These one hundred and eleven days of vacillation lost Germany the war. For what might well have succeeded in March, in spite of all misgivings—namely a fundamental change of the situation through a German victory in the Kursk salient—ended disastrously, as we know, the following July. But this disaster, in March 1943, was still hidden in the womb of the future.

When on 23rd March 1943 Field-Marshal von Manstein issued his Order of the Day on the occasion of his victory between Dnieper and Donets, he had every reason to commend his troops and their commanders in the field. Their successful actions had saved the German eastern front from the most dangerous threat since the beginning of the war. The severed connection with Army Group Centre had been restored and the coal of the Donets basin saved for the German war industry. The forces of the German southern front were again in their old positions—the position they had held throughout the winter of 1941–42 and from which in 1942 they had launched their spring offensive towards the Caucasus and the Volga.

One cannot conclude this decisive chapter without asking what caused Stalin and his High Command to make such disastrously wrong decisions in the midst of a string of victories as the decisions taken by STAVKA between 7th and 25th February.

No doubt Stalin and his top commanders were led into error through a variety of causes, but the directives sent to Southern Front from 21st February onwards, as well as the appreciation of the situation made by South-West Front on 20th February, strongly suggest that they had been misled by secret-service information which they thought reliable.

This may be deduced both from the *History of the Great Fatherland War* and from a number of memoirs. Stalin had great faith in the information from his secret service, especially as it confirmed him in his hopes. There is reason to believe that the source of that information was "Werther".

Secret reports of the Swiss General Staff, originating from Hausamann and undoubtedly passed on to Moscow by Rössler, stated from 11th February onward that the German troops in the Donets area were in retreat. Only strong rear parties would be left behind and, if need be, sacrificed.

Thus Report No. 284 of 16th February, marked SECRET, says:

"In the Donets area the penetration of a Russian Tank Corps to the railway and road from Gorlovka to Dnepropetrovsk has rendered impossible any gradual withdrawal of major German formations as envisaged by the German Command. All German counter-attacks have

failed at and west of Krasnoarmeysk.... On the German side everything is in a state of dissolution, flooding back, largely without artillery
and ammunition. The German plan for a gradual concentric retreat by
the bulk of the German troops in the direction of Stalino is no longer
possible because of the confusion produced by the Russian penetration
at Shakhty. As a result, the Germans are being overtaken by a new
disaster. Losses to be expected on the German side will greatly exceed
their losses at Stalingrad. Since 12th February the removal of stores
by rail via Gorlovka or via Stalino has no longer been possible; lines
and stations are congested and in chaotic condition."

This report is entirely in line with the directives which Stalin issued
to his commanders-in-chief and to his Army Group Southern Front at
the time.

But there is more to come. Report No. 291 of 17th February—a
report which no doubt was likewise passed on to Moscow—states:
"The objective of German resistance following the Russian breakthrough at and west of Krasnoarmeysk [meaning Popov's break-
through] is now confined to covering the German withdrawal from
the Donets bend, first of all to a line from the Dnieper bend to the Sea
of Azov, in the second leap to the line Dnieper bend–Berdyansk, in
the third leap to the Lower Dnieper."

Was that not Stalin's theory?

Report No. 307 of 21st February states: "The consequences of the
fall of Kharkov and the collapse of the improvised German Donets
front are assessed as disasters at OKW. Since 17th February the formations and the remnants of more than forty German divisions have
been in danger of being cut off, of being smashed in hopeless defensive
fighting, of being mauled in fruitless counter-attacks, or of being overtaken and annihilated by the pursuing Russian masses. These formations include nearly half of all German armoured troops and tanks
still left to the German Army and Waffen-SS."

Again Stalin's theory.

The concluding paragraph of the report states: "Indifference and
fatalistic despair are now rapidly and very noticeably diminishing the
fighting morale of the German troops all over the southern parts of
the eastern front, even among the German reserves which have not
yet been in action at all but can see the disaster from their improvised
position behind the lines."

Are not these dramatic reports from inside the German High
Command the explanation of the otherwise almost inexplicable orders
issued by Stalin and his commanders-in-chief, including such gifted
men as Vatutin? Are they not the explanation behind that reckless
gambling in the face of all warning signs from the front? Only the
information received from "Lucie" can explain the Soviet course of
action.

But why should "Werther" have transmitted such misleading information? The agent who always supplied such excellent information straight from the Wolfsschanze, the Mauerwald, or the Reich Chancellery to his chief, "Director" in Moscow?

The answer is simple. During the spring battle between Donets and the Dnieper not only the tactical but also the strategic decisions were largely taken at Manstein's headquarters and not at the Führer's headquarters. Manstein brooked no interference and acted in accordance with the demands of the moment, and not the intentions from the Wolfsschanze. Hitler, moreover, was not at Rastenburg during the decisive days, but in Vinnitsa with only a small staff. Most of the staff of the German High Command and of the Führer's headquarters had remained behind in East Prussia—including "Werther" and his informers.

Hence Manstein's intentions and the potentialities of the situation were not grasped there, and opinions were based on the pessimistic interpretation of the situation in which the senior staff officers in East Prussia, far from the battlefield and far from the Führer, indulged.

These circumstances explain why a usually so well-informed contact of "Director" in Moscow and of the Swiss General Staff—the contact at the Führer's headquarters—was for once wrongly informed and supplied this incorrect assessment to his clients.

The incident illustrates the drawbacks of treason by a single individual. Even the best spy can make a mistake. And if that mistake happens to confirm the recipient of the information in a dangerous piece of wishful thinking, then that information may give rise to disaster.

One hundred and eleven days later, however, "Werther" made good his error.

PART THREE:
Battles on the Northern Wing

1. Leningrad: Tragedy of a City

*A twentieth-century siege–Two slices of bread a day–
Famine–Total war–Zhdanov and the Komsomol–A secret
OKW order and its background–A whole city was to have
been blown up.*

SEVEN months of struggle on the southern front had ended in
January 1943. That struggle, though spread over a front of over
six hundred miles, will always be remembered by one name—Stalingrad,
the city of destiny on the Volga. Similarly, the operation which
was to follow that of Stalingrad would be remembered by the name of
another city—Kursk. This labelling of military events with the names
of great urban centres is no accident, no arbitrary decision, but
symbolical.

The war in the vast Soviet empire was concentrated at the great
focal points of the country's political, economic, and spiritual life. It
was therefore no coincidence that, at the very time when Stalingrad,
the metropolis on the Volga, was dominating events on the southern
front, another metropolis became the pivot of an important campaign
on the most northern wing of the German front in Russia—Leningrad.
The most powerful naval fortress on the Baltic, the home of the Red
Fleet, the cultural jewel of Russia, with its 3,000,000 inhabitants the
second largest city in the Soviet Union—Leningrad became the focal
point of military operations on the northern wing of the eastern front.

Anything that happened between the Polar Sea and Lake Ilmen
after September 1941 concerned Leningrad, the white city on the
Neva. The fierceness and savagery of the fighting here, as in the case
of Stalingrad, was largely nurtured by political mythology: Leningrad
bore the name of the father of the Bolshevik world revolution, just as
earlier, as St Petersburg, it had borne the name of Russia's greatest
Tsar. Here the revolution was born, the revolution which made Leningrad
the "Jerusalem of Communism", the birthplace of the Red
century.

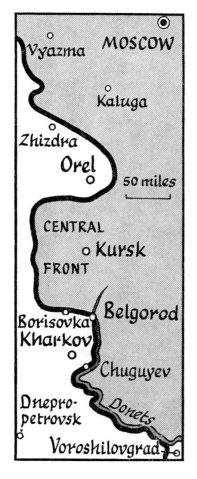

Map 21. The front line between Vyazma and Voroshilovgrad in March 1943.

Leningrad's role in the Second World War began with a fateful mistake on the part of Hitler.

Instead of taking Leningrad—as envisaged in the plan for Operation Barbarossa—by concentrated armoured assault as the first objective of Army Group North, even before the attack on Moscow, Hitler about the middle of September suddenly suspended the attack in the suburbs of the metropolis and ordered Field-Marshal von Leeb to confine himself to encircling the city.

It was an incomprehensible decision. Leningrad's last defensive positions had already been pierced. The suburb of Uritsk with the terminus of the Leningrad tramway had been taken. The last fortifications on the Duderhof Hills had been stormed by 36th Motorized Infantry Division and 1st Panzer Division; Schlüsselburg[1] had been

[1] Now Petrokrepost.

captured by Harry Hoppe's Combat Group and the Hamburg 76th Infantry Regiment. The city was in the grip of panic. At that moment Hitler called off the operation and withdrew the armoured forces to switch them to the offensive on Moscow. He wanted to conquer Leningrad by starving it out. The decision left the officers of 1st Panzer Division flabbergasted. "Did we fight our way from East Prussia right to the very gates of Leningrad just to walk away again as if the whole thing had been a mistake?" they grumbled.

Hitler, who learnt about this unrest, gave his officers an explanation. In a "Most Secret" document of 7th October 1941 he informed all his commanders in the field as follows:

The Führer has again decided that a capitulation of Leningrad, or later Moscow, must not be accepted even if offered by the enemy.

Our moral justification for this measure is patent to the whole world. In Kiev very heavy risks were run by the German troops as a result of demolition charges touched off by time fuses, and the same has to be expected, on an even larger scale, in Moscow and Leningrad. The fact that Leningrad has been mined and would be defended to the last man has been announced by the Soviet radio itself. There would also be a serious risk of epidemics.

No German soldier must therefore enter these cities. Anybody attempting to leave the city in the direction of our lines is to be repulsed by force. Lesser gaps, not entirely closed, which would enable the population to stream out towards the interior of Russia are therefore to be welcomed. The same applies to all other cities: before capture they are to be worn out by artillery bombardment and aerial attacks, and the flight of the population is to be encouraged. . . . All commanding officers are to be informed that this is the Führer's will.

Hitler's justification for his order not to occupy Leningrad and instead starve it out may not reflect the true reason for his decision. Nevertheless, the argument is very likely to have made it easier for him to put his siege strategy into action. Above all, it enabled him to win over his generals who of course would have preferred to seize the city. His argument was difficult to refute. It was true enough that after the occupation of Kiev in September 1941 the German troops had suffered appreciable losses as a result of time-fused mines left behind by the Russians. Entire blocks of buildings had been dynamited by the Russians by remote control. The main thoroughfare had been totally gutted as a result. The reports of these events had greatly upset Hitler. Those kind of unusual, adventurous, and "fanatical" operations invariably made a deep impression on him and he rather tended to overrate them.

After the occupation of Kharkov at the end of October 1941, Sixth Army also captured plans for the mining of the city. If the Russians had had time to put these plans into effect the occupation troops would have been buried under mountains of rubble. Quite a lot of damage was done as it was. General Georg Braun, commanding the 68th Infantry Division, was blown up in his house on 14th November 1941. It was the building which had served Khrushchev for his quarters as the Military Council member before the evacuation of the city. The mine with the time fuse had been installed with his permission while he still occupied the building.

Hitler frequently talked about these operations and compared them, not without some admiration, with the fire of Moscow which had triggered off Napoleon's disaster in Russia.

It was not unreasonable to assume that Zhdanov, the energetic ruler of Leningrad, would have done no less than had been done at Kiev. But Hitler, moreover, had accurate information about the situation in Leningrad from his secret service. Finnish intelligence was particularly helpful in this respect. This information about Soviet preparations for the blowing up of their city had long been regarded as suspect by the experts until the sensational Soviet publications in 1964 and 1965 fully confirmed it.

In an essay entitled "That Was a Secret", Colonel Starikov in *Voyennoistoricheskiy Zhurnal* describes plans for the mining of cities and the installation of demolition barrages in threatened major centres. Among other things, Starikov reports that General Braun's house in Kharkov was blown up on 14th November at 0420 hours by means of a radio signal. Only a shortage of electrical detonators and high explosives prevented the envisaged mining of all major squares, bridges, thoroughfares, and transport installations.

Even more dramatic than Starikov's essay is a report by Admiral Panteleyev, entitled "The Naval Front" and published in Moscow in 1965. Panteleyev was chief of staff of the Baltic Fleet which in August 1941 was assigned to the Leningrad Front.

The admiral reports that after 12th September 1941 special units were set up in Leningrad under the command of the Party, charged with preparing the total demolition of the city. The tactical and strategic command was with a special unit at the Chief Directorate for Partisan Affairs in the Red Army. The motto was: "If the enemy penetrates into our city he must be buried under its ruins." The plan provided for detailed destruction schedules for all major buildings, bridges, subways, railway-stations, parks, and so on. It is full of phrases like "to be blown up", "to be burnt down", "to be destroyed", "already mined with time fuse". It was a destruction programme of breathtaking cold-bloodedness. It is doubtful whether all these plans could in fact have been carried out. But if so, the German occupiers of Leningrad would have had to leave the city in a great hurry—just as Napoleon left the blazing city of Moscow.

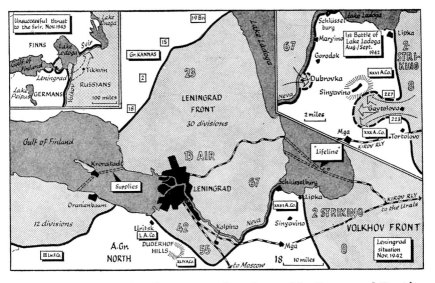

Map 22. For nine hundred days Leningrad was besieged by German and Finnish troops. In November 1941 an attempt was made to close the ring round the city by linking up with the Finns on the Svir (inset top left). Fierce fighting raged along the nine-mile-wide corridor south of Lake Ladoga in the summer of 1942 (inset top right).

Four weeks after his secret order, on 8th November 1941, Hitler also gave an explanation to the restive German public and to the world at large which had been astonished to see the campaign against Leningrad halted. This was somewhat different from the "Most Secret" document intended for his commanders in the field, but it was imbued with the same spirit. In his traditional speech at the Munich Bürgerbräu beer cellar he said:

"Anyone who has surged from the East Prussian frontier to within six miles of Leningrad can also manage that last six miles into the city. But this is not necessary. The city is encircled. No-one is going to liberate it and it will drop into our lap."

He was to be proved wrong. And this mistake marked the beginning of a disastrous chain of events at Army Group North, events which undoubtedly contributed to the outcome of the war.

Hitler pinned down an entire German Army on sentry duty to a single city. He allowed the enemy to hold on to an important centre of his war industry and to the naval base of the Red Baltic Fleet. He did not even clip off the Oranienbaum[1] pocket, that extensive Soviet bridge-head on the southern edge of the Gulf of Finland, immediately to the west of Leningrad. He continued, as the Finnish Field-Marshal

[1] Now Lomonsov.

Mannerheim so well put it, to "drag this heavy rucksack along on his back right through the war".

Even more incomprehensible was the fact that, instead of capturing Leningrad, and thereby establishing a direct land link with his Finnish allies, Hitler blocked his own path and moreover saved the Soviets the loss of roughly forty-two divisions which were trapped in Leningrad and in the Oranienbaum pocket.

When Hitler called off the attack on 24th September 1941 the capture of the city would have been a matter of just a few days. The suspension of the offensive and the withdrawal of Fourth Panzer Group with the fast divisions of XLI Panzer Corps at that very moment were errors of equally far-reaching effect as Hitler's halt order short of Dunkirk. There, as a result of his misjudgment of the enemy situation, Hitler omitted trapping the British Army, and thereby rendering Britain defenceless. Likewise he now missed the decisive move at Leningrad on the northern wing of the eastern front. Instead of accomplishing a final victory with 200,000 to 300,000 prisoners and the immeasurable booty of an industrial city, he recklessly set in train a strength-consuming battle of nine hundred days which ultimately ended in defeat.

What caused Hitler to make this mistake? Why did he not listen to his commanders in the field? Why did he count on Leningrad's rapid collapse? He underestimated the resilience and toughness of the Communist Party in that city.

Leningrad was ruled by Zhdanov. This Ukrainian, born in Mariupol in 1892, was an exceptional man. His toughness, resolution, and personal courage inspired the resistance of the whole city. Zhdanov gave the world its first demonstration in modern history of what merciless total war meant in a constricted area.

Hitler's dislike of anything to do with water or the sea contrasts curiously with his interest in matters of land warfare. Just as at Dunkirk, his water-shyness again misled him at Leningrad. He believed the city to be encircled, but he overlooked the fact that although Leningrad was cut off by land from the Soviet lines in summer, it was by no means totally encircled. The hinterland of Leningrad reached to the western bank of Lake Ladoga which, at that point, is only twenty miles wide. No wider than the English Channel between Dover and Calais. And along the lake's eastern bank ran the main Soviet front.

During the day, admittedly, shipping on the lake was at the mercy of the Luftwaffe. But not so at night. Thus Lake Ladoga provided an escape route for Leningrad from the first day of its encirclement. The German attempt, in October and November 1941, to move around the lake with fast formations of XXXIX Panzer Corps in order to link up with the Finns on the Svir and thus to make the blockade complete, had been a failure.

Thus, following the surrender of Tikhvin, the German Eighteenth Army only held a nine-mile coastal strip on the southern bank of Lake Ladoga with Schlüsselburg and Lipka as its corner stones. Access to this coastal strip was by way of a dangerously narrow corridor: to the right was the Volkhov front, where the Soviets were continually exerting pressure, and on the left the Neva, behind which the Russians of the Leningrad Front had dug themselves in with their Sixty-Seventh, Fifty-Fifth, and Forty-Second Armies. At the middle of the corridor the dreary, swampy landscape was commanded by the hills of Sinyavino. The southern end of the bottleneck was formed by the Kirov railway which linked Leningrad with the Urals by way of Volkhovstroy.

Shortly before the city was surrounded, Zhdanov had moved out of the city some 650,000 key workers of the armament industry, and 40,000 railway trucks with machinery, machine tools, and raw materials into the Russian hinterland. This shows clearly that in the summer of 1941 the Soviet Command expected to lose Leningrad. And it also explains why the city was not equipped for a prolonged siege.

Stocks of raw materials and foodstuffs were soon exhausted. The civilian population and the 200,000 troops had to be supplied by air since the nocturnal traffic by small ships over Lake Ladoga hardly counted. But the Soviet Air Force was not equipped for a task of such magnitude. Between 14th and 28th November it flew in a mere 1200 tons of foodstuffs, or eighty-six tons a day.

That was almost exactly the amount flown into Stalingrad a year later by the German Luftwaffe—and that amount was not enough for the 250,000 men there. Yet in Leningrad there were still over two million people in the winter of 1941. For the 250,000 men of Sixth Army in the Stalingrad pocket the experts had calculated 306 tons of food per day as the minimum to keep them alive. In Leningrad ten times that number of people had to make do with less than one-third of that quantity.

During the West Berlin airlift in 1948–49 the quantities flown in for the 2,500,000 inhabitants were, to begin with, 4500 tons a day, and subsequently 10,000 tons a day. Leningrad received less than 100th of this amount. The result was famine—famine without parallel. The daily bread ration for a worker was 250 grammes—about five thin slices. Leading employees and their families received 125 grammes per head. The troops too had to tighten their belts. Men in the front line received 50 per cent of the normal food ration, the rearward services and headquarters personnel only 33 per cent.

At the end of November a slight improvement occurred, due to another fact which Hitler had overlooked—Lake Ladoga froze up. The ice cover was five feet thick. Leningrad had regained a solid link with the Soviet land front on the eastern bank of the lake.

Across the ice a road was marked out—the "Leningrad lifeline". At night trucks rumbled across the lake. But most of their cargo was ammunition, spares, and raw materials for the war industries. Food-stuffs came at the bottom of the list. On their return journey the trucks evacuated wounded, children, and old people from the city, as well as women incapable of labour duties. Some 800,000 people were evacuated in this way.

But trucks used up fuel and motor fuel was in short supply along the whole Soviet front. For that reason Zhdanov got his labour force to lay a rail track over the ice which was linked up to the Volkhovtsroy–Moscow railway line on the far side of the lake. Now 4000 to 5000 tons of cargo could be brought into the city in this fashion during the winter. But even this was neither here nor there, since 80 per cent of all transported cargo was raw material for the armaments factories which, even in this starving city, were still turning out mortars, sub-machine-guns, and above all tanks for the entire front.

In the summer of 1942 Zhdanov's labour columns accomplished a particularly remarkable feat: they laid an electric cable and a fuel pipeline on the bottom of Lake Ladoga. The electricity which kept the armaments factories going came from the Volkhov power-station on the Svir. When the lake froze over again a high-voltage line was set up on the ice.

Hunger was a terrible incentive. It forced all inhabitants into the labour force or into the fighting battalions. Anyone who did not work or fight simply received no rations and died. There are no reliable statistics about the sacrifices of Leningrad. Soviet sources put the losses at 600,000 to 700,000 dead. What Zhdanov and the Party accomplished by way of mobilizing the civilian population for labour and defence tasks is downright incredible: 32,000 women and girls were employed as nurses with the forces; 90 per cent of all Leningrad Komsomol members were on active service at the front; 600,000 children and juveniles were constantly employed in developing the city's defences. They dug 440 miles of anti-tank ditches—with nothing but spades and pickaxes. They erected 200 miles of tree-trunk barriers and built 5000 earth bunkers. The official figure of 600,000 juveniles employed compels one to conclude that this labour force included the nine-year-olds and probably even eight-year-olds.

Never before and nowhere else on earth has such a mobilization of civilians ever been achieved. Certainly not in the defence of Berlin. When the Battle Commandant of the Reich capital demanded from the Gauleiter a daily supply of 100,000 civilians for the building of defences the Gauleiter rejected the demand as unrealizable. The Reich Defence Commissar of Berlin, Dr Goebbels, did not succeed in raising more than 30,000 civilians for the building of defences on any single day.

But not only in Leningrad did the Communist youth of Russia represent a decisive fighting force. Of a total of 11,000 Heroes of the Soviet Union—an honour corresponding to the German Knight's Cross —7000 came from the Komsomol. No comparative figures are available to show how many of the 7200 bearers of the German Knight's Cross came from the Hitler Youth.

Starving and shivering, in temperatures of minus 40 degrees Centigrade, these children threw up fortifications. Starving and shivering, workers toiled in their bomb-damaged, unheated factories. Shifts of twelve or fourteen hours. Then they dragged themselves home. At home there was no light and no water; once the furniture and the books had been burnt there was no fire in the stoves. On the following day they would reel back to their work place. Anyone who did not turn up received no rations. And woe to the defeatist!

They did not freeze during the summer. But then there was also less food. And working time was fifteen hours. Added to this were voluntary shifts. At night the women trudged out to the front line and strongpoints in long columns with handcarts or sleighs, bringing ammunition to the troops and collecting the wounded and those too feeble to fight.

The most horrible sight of all were the ghastly transports of the dead. Death, which is almost invisible in our modern cities, had become such an everyday and public occurrence that people were dulled by familiarity with it. A man, a woman, or frequently a child would drag a cart or a primitive sledge—sometimes only a few planks—on which a dead body, wrapped in old rags or old paper, was pulled to the mass grave at the cemetery.

Behind this gruesome façade Zhdanov and the Party kept the machinery of survival going. And not only of survival. Time and again he called on the generals: "We must attack! We must cut through the bottleneck of Schlüsselburg and regain our connection with the Volkhov front!"

Indefatigably he made his plans and passed them on to headquarters. They were all based on the same simple recipe: a break-out by the Soviet Sixty-Seventh Army on the Neva, in an easterly direction, with a simultaneous attack by the Second Striking Army from the other side, from the Volkhov Front, to meet the units from Leningrad. The distance was less than nine miles at the narrowest point. And for nine hundred days these nine miles were the focal point of the battle of Leningrad.

The worst thing about military mistakes is that they invariably carry with them a string of further mistakes. When, in the spring of 1942, Hitler realized the mistake he had made at Leningrad in the autumn of 1941, he decided to correct it. "Leningrad must fall," he said in Directive No. 41, the operation plan for 1942.

When Manstein had reduced Sevastopol, the world's strongest fortress, Hitler decided to switch the Field-Marshal with his Eleventh Army and his powerful, super-heavy artillery against Leningrad.

But what would have been correct a year before was now wrong. For in the summer of 1942 the strategic centre of gravity of the German front was in the south, where an offensive towards the Volga and the Caucasus was being mounted. There, at that decisive point, all available forces should have been concentrated. Including Eleventh Army. The price for its absence was soon to be paid at Stalingrad.

But Hitler by then was beyond listening to criticism. Leningrad must fall. Manstein's plan was simple and cunning at the same time: he intended to break through the Soviet positions with three corps from the south. He proposed to penetrate to the edge of the city. Then he would halt. Two of his corps would wheel eastwards. They would cross the Neva. And they would then crush the city.

It was a good plan. And nothing that Manstein had planned had so far gone wrong. But Leningrad was to confirm the well-known quotation about the "tide in the affairs of men, which, taken at the flood, leads on to fortune; omitted, all the voyage of their life is bound in shallows and in miseries".

2. South of Lake Ladoga

Dance of death on the Neva–Gorodok: power-station and hospital–Red Banner sailors charging over the ice– Hand-to-hand fighting in the trenches–Tigers to the front–Soviet breakthrough–Colonel Andoy's Panzerjägers halt the Russians.

AT the beginning of August 1942, even before Manstein knew that Leningrad was his new assignment, Moscow already knew Hitler's intention. The "Red Choir" espionage ring radioed the plan to Moscow. And Stalin at once prepared his counter-blow.

In feverish haste new formations were raised for the Volkhov Front. Hurriedly trained recruits from all parts of the Soviet empire, with often only three weeks' training, as well as punitive regiments, Siberians, and Turkmens were moved up. Sixteen rifle divisions, nine brigades, and five armoured brigades with three hundred tanks were raised by the C-in-C, Volkhov Front.

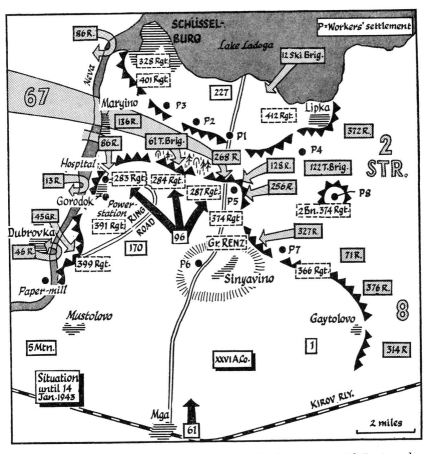

Map 23. The Soviets tried to establish a direct overland connection with Leningrad. They attacked the German corridor from east and west.

And on 27th August Manstein was deploying his forces for his offensive along the southern front of the Leningrad pocket, the Russians launched their attack, striking from the Volkhov Front against the German bottleneck in order to link up with the positions at Leningrad. The eastern front of the German Eighteenth Army was pierced near Gaytolovo.

On either side of the penetration area units of the Saxon 223rd and Westphalian 227th Infantry Division were standing firm. Colonel Wengler with his Westphalians of 366th Grenadier Regiment offered such stubborn opposition that even the Soviet *History of the Great Fatherland War* cannot avoid mentioning him. Wengler prevented the penetration being widened towards the north. Though encircled by the Russians he held his position on the edge of a small forest for several days, preventing all penetration. Wengler's Westphalians held like a dam in the Russian flood.

The Russians pushed eight miles to the west. They got to just outside Mga, the junction of the Kirov railway—their great objective. The bottleneck was constricted to less than half its width.

In view of the situation Manstein had no other choice but to use his ready-deployed offensive forces for defence and counter-attack. In heavy fighting his formations, together with units of General Lindemann's Eighteenth Army, achieved a complete defensive success: 12,000 prisoners were taken and 244 tanks destroyed. The first of three Lake Ladoga battles was over.

But there could be no question now of mounting the planned attack against Leningrad. The ammunition was spent and the weakened formations had first to be replenished. September passed. October passed. Things remained quiet around Leningrad. With the approach of November the disaster of Stalingrad was approaching. For the time being all plans of attacking Leningrad had to be shelved.

Manstein disappeared from the stage of the battle between Neva and Volkhov. He moved south again in order to write one of the most exciting chapters in the history of this war—the battle between Volga, Donets, and Dnieper.

December passed at Leningrad. Positions froze rigid in the Arctic cold. On the Neva and on the Volkhov the troops sat in subterranean towns dug deep into the soil. And so came January. The twelfth of January.

Lieutenant Winacker of the engineers was an early riser. By 0700 he had already drunk his morning coffee and was now walking down the communication trench outside the Gorodok hospital to the foremost machine-gun.

An icy wind was blowing up from the Sinyavino bog across the sector of 170th Infantry Division. It cut through fur and to the marrow. The thermometer was down to minus 28 degrees Centigrade.

"Morning, Lührsen," Winacker said to the man behind the machine-gun.

"Morning, Herr Oberleutnant."

"Cold."

"Damned cold."

"Anything happening?"

"Nothing, Herr Oberleutnant. But somehow I don't like the look of it. Have a look yourself. Not a single Ivan in sight. Not a living soul about. Normally they scuttle around at this time, dragging their soup and bread into their positions."

Winacker glanced at his wrist-watch: not quite 0730. He raised his glasses to his eyes. He put them down again and wiped the eyepieces which were misted over from the cold. Then he looked across the wide, frozen river to the west. The landscape was suspiciously quiet.

The Neva had been frozen over since 7th January. It was between 650 and 900 yards wide at that point near Gorodok. The ice was nearly three feet thick in places—strong enough to bear tanks. One could not be too careful.

Lieutenant Winacker had set up the command post of his 2nd Company, Engineer Battalion 240, in what used to be the hospital of Gorodok. Every day, and frequently also at night, in spite of the frost, the engineers laid anti-tank and infantry mines along the river-bank. They had driven steel girders into the steep slope dropping down to the river and moreover laid anti-tank mines in the pine forest on both sides of the hospital. The triangular patch of forest on the right flank was virtually paved with mines.

The lieutenant carried his mine plan accurately in his head. That was why he was now staring hard into the strangely silent, grey, dawn landscape. From the high bank of the Neva, almost forty feet above the river, he could sweep with his binoculars the whole sector of his company. He could also see deep into the Soviet positions on the far bank. Of course, they had carefully camouflaged their trenches, but from the higher, eastern bank it was nevertheless possible to catch a glimpse of what was happening among the bushes and the shell-torn pine woods.

"Really, I've never known the place as dead as this," the fair-haired man from Düsseldorf muttered to himself. Yet during the past few days there had been a good deal of activity among the snow-covered bunkers.

A cold breath came up from the river valley. The world between Schlüsselburg and Gorodok lay frost-bound and silent. Suddenly Winacker became agitated. He called across to the machine-gunner: "Look at it, Lührsen—all those footsteps in the snow on the Neva! They were over on our bank during the night!" Winacker planted his elbows in the snow of the parapet, aimed his glasses at the slope below, and searched the river-bank with its wire obstacles and shell craters yard by yard. "They were lifting mines! Hell! Didn't anyone—"

The lieutenant did not finish his sentence. Instinctively he ducked against the side of the trench. Lührsen also flopped down into the trench. A sudden salvo of gunfire made the earth tremble. There was a roar of thunder. To the right and left of the trench the bursts tore up the hard, frozen ground. The shell splinters clattered against the wall of the trench.

Winacker and Lührsen were lying on the trench floor. They were waiting. Was this merely a sudden strike? Or was there more to come?

The minutes dragged. The hurricane of fire grew in intensity. Now Winacker had no doubt. "Lührsen, they're coming today!" he yelled into the corporal's ear, and hurried over, bent double, to his command post in the hospital.

The shell bursts seemed to be chasing him. Nevertheless his subconscious mind recorded: multiple mortars! With a whine and a hiss the rockets swept low over the steep bank. Now came a new note of rumbling thunder: heavy naval guns. "That's the Red Fleet in Leningrad harbour," it flashed through Winacker's head.

But the worst sounds accompanying him as he ran to the hospital were the bursts of the "crash-boom", the flat-trajectory missiles of that superb Russian all-purpose gun of 7·62-cm calibre.

As Winacker reached the garage of the hospital the company was already taking up battle stations. The buildings themselves were under heaviest bombardment. All telephone lines to Battalion, to Division, and to the observation posts were severed.

Between Schlüsselburg, Lipka, and Sinyavino there was only smoke and fire. The swamps and the thick forest on the Neva and on the Volkhov Front were once again ploughed up. From 4500 barrels the Russians unleashed a hurricane of fire over the German positions, a bombardment of an intensity hitherto not experienced at this northern end of the eastern front.

A total of 4500 barrels! From Leningrad and from the Volkhov Front they were firing at the two German sectors of only nine miles each. That meant one gun for every twenty feet. For two hours and twenty minutes the hurricane of steel howled, flashed, and crashed down on the Neva Front, and for an hour and forty-five minutes it swept the eastern side of the bottleneck.

"They aren't joking this time," the men said in their dug-outs, their strongpoints, their foxholes, and their trenches. Many of them were in solid bunkers deep below ground. Veritable subterranean towns had been built on the Leningrad and Volkhov fronts during the long wait. The strongpoints were linked by a cunning system of trenches.

The Russians were aware of this. That was why they were pounding these positions with such concentrated fire. That was why they were pounding the machine-gun posts, the gun emplacements, the command posts, the approach roads, the lateral communications, and the camps in the woods. They smashed bridges, buildings, trenches, and all telephone wires. And then they attacked. Immediately behind the slowly lifting artillery barrage, the Soviets charged against the German lines. With them came ground-support aircraft.

From the east, from the Volkhov, Lieutenant-General V. S. Romanovskiy's Second Striking Army attacked. Its sector of attack extended from Lipka on Lake Ladoga to Gaytolovo and was eight miles wide. Seven divisions and an armoured brigade were carrying the attack. The sector was defended by one reinforced German division, General von Scotti's Westphalian 227th Infantry Division.

From the west, from the direction of Leningrad, the divisions of General Dukhanov's Sixty-Seventh Army were attacking the German lines, their focal point being in the sector between Maryino and Gorodok. The Russians used five divisions and one armoured brigade. They were opposed, at first, by General Sander's North-German 170th Infantry Division alone. Only later was the Silesian 28th Jäger Division under General Sinnhuber moved alongside it.

The objective of the two-pronged Russian offensive was to crush the narrow German bottleneck running through the Russian land connection to Leningrad along its entire width and then to thrust through to the Kirov railway at the southern end of the bottleneck.

How did things go at Gorodok, that key point of the German defences on the Neva? Corporal Lührsen survived the artillery barrage unscathed in his narrow trench. As the creeping barrage moved on towards the hinterland he rose and shook off the dirt and snow which had half buried him. Then he scrambled out of the trench.

And then he saw them coming—the regiments of the Soviet 13th and 268th Rifle Division. In close line abreast they were charging across the perfectly flat, snow-covered ice of the Neva. There was less than a yard between each man and his neighbour. Veritable giants in front—sailors of the Red Banner Baltic Fleet. They were employed particularly at Gorodok and Maryino. With them came mine-clearing parties with their detectors, working their way forward in leaps and bounds.

The men of 2nd Battalion, 401st Grenadier Regiment in the trenches outside Maryino saw the same picture. "They've gone mad," they said. The riflemen of Cyclist Squadron 240, holding a position on the bank to the right of the Gorodok hospital, called out to each other, "They think we're all dead!"

They gripped their machine-guns more firmly. "Load—prepare for continuous fire!"

"Wait for it," their sergeants reminded them. "Let them get nice and close," muttered Grenadier Pleyer, the machine-gun commander. His number two nodded. Their machine-gun was well protected under the concrete roof of the power-station.

That was how they waited south of Schlüsselburg, at Maryino, and at the power-station. That was how they waited opposite the paper-mill factory and outside the hospital. And that was how they waited in the trenches of Dubrovka, where the assault started ten minutes later; over there the Soviet 45th Guards Rifle Division had been entrenched on the near bank since the fighting in the summer. For that reason the Soviet High Command had allowed the other offensive divisions a ten-minute lead in its tactical timetable.

The creeping barrage of the Russian artillery had moved on far into the hinterland. The advanced observers of the German artillery were meanwhile crouching by their walkie-talkies, calling their batteries and regiments, passing through the new targets. Time and again they would ask: "Curtain fire on square . . . "

A moment later the shells of the field howitzers and guns would roar over the German positions and crash down on the ice of the Neva. Huge holes were torn into the ice cover. A curtain of fire and steel was laid in front of the German strongpoints. The German gunners then sought out the Soviet assembly positions for the second and third wave of the attack on the far bank of the river.

Captain Irle, commanding Reconnaissance Unit 240, had gone forward with his cyclist squadron. What he saw approaching across the ice of the Neva through the German artillery barrage and towards the strongpoints of his hundred and twenty men and the neighbouring sector held by barely three hundred men of 2nd Battalion, 401st Grenadier Regiment, made his throat go dry.

What he saw was the bulk of two divisions. Altogether ten battalions, as is now attested by Soviet sources. In other words, at least four thousand men. The charging Russians had no cover—not a tree, not a shrub. They knew that they could be seen like deer being driven down a clearing by beaters right in front of the guns. But they were relying on the effects of their massive preliminary artillery barrage.

The spectacle lasted seven minutes. Now the first wave of the attack was half-way across the river, within four hundred yards.

Then three hundred yards. Two hundred. "Fire!"

The German machine-guns started rattling. The mortars thudded, rifles cracked. As if mown down by a scythe, the attackers fell down on the ice. Many of them rose again. They ran on. "Urra!" But only a few reached the icy river-bank. There they were caught in the aimed fire of the German infantrymen. They made for cover. Or they died.

The second wave swept over the ice. A third, a fourth, and a fifth.

In front of the hospital and the power-station the dead and wounded were lying on the ice of the Neva in thick black piles. Wave after wave broke—most of them even before they reached the shattered steel girders in the steep river-bank.

The front had also come to life at Dubrovka. Here Major-General A. A. Krasnov's 45th Guards Rifle Division was trying to burst out of the labyrinth of trenches of its bridge-head and into the positions of Colonel Griesbach's 399th Grenadier Regiment. The German and Russian positions merged into each other. Frequently an immobilized tank, a few coils of barbed wire, a few mines or girders across a length of trench, was all that divided one side from the other. Just as during those long years of positional warfare in the First World War.

In the first battle of Lake Ladoga, in the summer of 1942, the Russians had captured the bridge-head at Dubrovka. In November, except for a few hundred yards, they had been dislodged again by a German counter-attack. Every yard testified to battle and death.

There was that gruesome corner of a trench where the frozen limbs of dead Russians were sticking out of the ground. First they had been buried by shellfire. Then they were exposed by shellfire. Now they were signposts for runners and patrols: "To the right of the dead man's hand," "To the left of the dead man's hand."

Knocked-out tanks leant over the dug-outs like mortally wounded animals. Minefields had been laid next to each other and on top of each other, until no engineer was able to render them safe. It was a nightmarish landscape of war.

General Krasnov's three Guards regiments reached the first shattered German trenches. But that was as far as they got. In the deep and cunningly-planned trenches of the main defence zone the Russians were thrown back in hand-to-hand fighting with grenades, trenching tools, and sub-machine-guns.

The report of 399th Grenadier Regiment states that during the night following the first day of fighting the trenches had to be cleared of dead Russians to ensure a clear field of fire for the German machine-guns.

One of the centres of the attack, needless to say, was Schlüsselburg. There the Soviet 86th Rifle Division tried to charge across the frozen Neva south of the town in order to roll up the town from the flank.

This sector was held by 1st Battalion, 401st Grenadier Regiment, men from Hamburg and Lower Saxony belonging to 170th Infantry Division, together with units of 328th Grenadier Regiment which belonged to the Westphalian 227th Infantry Division. The Russian crack regiments were unable to gain a foothold on the eastern bank of the Neva. Their attacks collapsed on the ice under the German defensive fire. General Krasnov had to call off the attack.

At Maryino, however, at the junction between Captain Irle's Reconnaissance Battalion 240 and the 2nd Battalion, 401st Grenadier Regiment, the Russians succeeded with their fifth wave and at the enormous cost of 3000 dead and wounded, in breaking into the German position and in gaining a foothold near the *dacha* north of Gorodok.

Russian engineers quickly established crossing facilities for their heavy armament over the treacherous ice of the Neva. Tanks rumbled across the river, ripped open the last German centres of resistance, and widened the penetration.

In vain did Lieutenant-Colonel Dr Kleinhenz, commanding 401st Grenadier Regiment, try to reorganize resistance in the foremost line. He was seriously wounded, as was his ADC. The Russians came charging up the steep bank.

Major-General Dukhanov, the C-in-C of the Soviet Sixty-Seventh Army, perceived his opportunity and instantly threw everything he had into the penetration area. He withdrew the remnants of 86th Rifle Division from Schlüsselburg and employed them at Maryino. There he concentrated the bulk of three divisions, and with hurriedly brought-up tank battalions he fanned out to the north, south, and east.

Parts of the German 401st Grenadier Regiment were forced back towards Schlüsselburg. Two platoons of Lieutenant Winacker's engineers were caught in the vortex. With the rest of his reconnaissance battalion and some straggler grenadiers, Captain Irle hurriedly established a thin, intercepting line so that the Russians should not burst unopposed into the rear areas, to the artillery positions, or to the south, into the rear of Gorodok. For if General Dukhanov were now to succeed in smashing the positions of 170th Infantry Division at Gorodok and Dubrovka by means of flanking attack, the road across the bog and over the Sinyavino hills to the Kirov railway would be clear. The battle on the Neva had reached its climax.

The hospital in the forest at Gorodok had been knocked about a good deal in two and a half hours of bombardment. Half the roofs of the buildings had been stripped, the windows had lost their glass, and the walls were pitted with shell bursts. But the basements still offered secure cover for the men who, propped up against the walls, were snatching one or two hours' sleep before they went forward again to relieve their comrades in the trenches where hell was let loose.

Corporal Lührsen lay seriously wounded in the cellar of the main building, amid many of his comrades. More and more wounded were being brought in. Fewer and fewer men were left to relieve the ones in the line.

The Neva was covered with dead Russians. Not one of them had reached the steep bank across the river. Yet in the afternoon the Russians had got there nevertheless: having broken through at Maryino, a few Soviet attacking formations had wheeled south. They were now trying to crack that important, stone-built bulwark on the bank of the Neva.

The situation looked bad. Lieutenant Winacker's engineer company was reduced to one platoon. Apart from them there was just one platoon of the Cyclist Squadron 240 and some straggler grenadiers from Carsten's combat group who had fought their way through to the hospital.

Towards midday Major Schulz, commanding the Engineer Battalion 240, whose battle headquarters were in the power-station, arrived at the hospital. Winacker, dare-devil that he was, had just gone out with a few men to reconnoitre the situation to the right of the hospital where the Russians had broken through.

Captain Irle was holding out there at what they called the "ring road" with the remains of his reconnaissance battalion. They were the

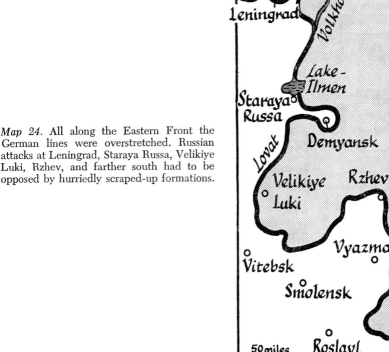

Map 24. All along the Eastern Front the German lines were overstretched. Russian attacks at Leningrad, Staraya Russa, Velikiye Luki, Rzhev, and farther south had to be opposed by hurriedly scraped-up formations.

only German forces standing between the Russians and the rearward battle zone with the artillery positions of 170th Infantry Division.

"Hardly enough to hold out with, Herr Major," Winacker said after his return to Schulz. Until reinforcements arrived everything would depend on that engineer battalion.

The engineers, the artisans of battle, were accustomed to such tasks. Though properly the builders of bridges, the operators of river ferries, the layers and clearers of mines, familiar with high explosives and detonators, with hammer and pliers, compasses and slide-rule, throughout the Second World War they were frequently drawn upon for infantry fighting at moments of great crisis. That was precisely the situation on the Neva in January 1943.

Major Schulz moved the 3rd Company of his engineer battalion into the sector to both sides of the hospital. Its commander, Lieutenant Brendel, took over command. By evening Russian tanks and infantry had moved into the small triangular wood some six hundred yards to the side. Heavy mortar shells were tearing into the masonry. The first fires had broken out among the roof joists.

But Brendel turned the smouldering block of buildings into a spit-fire fortress. Behind each window his engineers established a machine-gun post, in each dormer window they set up a sniper's nest or an observation post.

Down in the triangular wood the Russians were assembling for a charge. Platoon by platoon they scuttled from the small copse at the penetration point on the river-bank across the flat ground into the shell-torn patch of woodland.

The artillery observer in the hospital was still in radio contact with his battery whose positions were about three miles farther back. He kept the battery commander currently informed. Thus, at the right moment, a concentrated burst of fire from Bauer's battery of 240th Artillery Regiment would crash into the triangular wood, smashing the Russian assembly positions. Two T-34s, which were to lead the charge, ran into one of the well-camouflaged mine barriers and remained immobilized, their tracks blown off. There was jubilation behind the embrasures in the hospital.

Bauer's field howitzers continued to pound the little wood. Eventually the Russians decided to evacuate their dangerous offensive position; as they scuttled back to the bank of the Neva they were caught in heavy machine-gun fire from the windows of the hospital.

"Relief parties out!" The call rang out through the basement. The weary men picked up their rifles and stumbled up the stairs. They relieved their comrades who, in 26 degrees below zero Centigrade, reeled out of their trenches half frozen, towards that most wonderful thing on earth, the hot stove in the hospital basement.

Colonel-General Lindemann had no illusions about the critical situation in the bottleneck following the Russian breakthrough. He was a realist who knew his job. In the light of reports from the front the presumable objective of the Russians was beginning to take shape on the situation map at Eighteenth Army headquarters. General Govorov was throwing all his available forces into the gap he had punched open at Maryino. Using roughly four divisions and one armoured brigade he quite evidently intended to cut through the bottleneck before German reinforcements arrived, unite with the equally strong Soviet striking formation attacking from the east, and then wheel southwards to roll up the German defensive positions on the Neva and along the eastern side.

This plan inevitably entailed several centres of gravity. One of these

Russian assault parties landing near Novorossiysk.
Ozereyka Bay after the unsuccessful Soviet landing attempt in February 1943.

was Workers' Settlement No. 5, in Russian *Poselok* 5, or P5 for short. The only usable road through the bog, both northwards to the lake shore and southwards via Sinyavino to Mga on the Kirov railway, ran through this settlement.

The second centre was Gorodok with the hospital and the power-station. Here the Russians were denied direct access to the Sinyavino hills. Gorodok, moreover, was the corner-post of the German lines south of the Soviet penetration area.

If Lindemann had had a fully equipped division in reserve, with a battery of assault guns, a tank battalion, and some heavy artillery, things would only have been half as bad. But Eighteenth Army Command had no such division available. Nor could it get one from any of its neighbours.

The time was mid-January 1943. The disaster of Stalingrad was also hanging over the ice of the Neva. The situation was just as difficult on the sectors held by the immediate neighbours of Eighteenth Army. At Rzhev, at Velikiye Luki, and at Demyansk the survival of entire armies was at stake. The front was over-stretched everywhere. And everywhere the Russians were attacking. And as everywhere else at this decisive hour the northern wing of the Eastern Front lacked that famous last battalion to tip the balance.

Colonel-General Lindemann therefore had no other choice than to practise that disastrous strategy of cunning makeshift operations which had been typical of the Eastern Front ever since the winter of 1942–43. Regiments and battalions had to be scraped together to master crises instead of facing the enemy with concentrated large-scale formations, with divisions and brigades, and defeating him by superior general-ship.

The only instantly available reserves which Lindemann could throw into battle were five Grenadier battalions of the well-tried 96th Infantry Division. The 96th was a fine division, raised in Hanover and including soldiers from the whole of northern and western Germany. If 96th Division had been available in its entirety on 12th January— who knows how things might have turned out? But on the very first day of battle the 96th had been ordered to give up its units right and left. Thus it was only half a division with which General Noeldechen in the evening of 12th January undertook the difficult task of mounting a counter-offensive from the Sinyavino area in a north-westerly direc-tion in order to throw the enemy back across the Neva.

Five battalions against five Soviet divisions.

A small compensation for the missing divisional troops was supplied by a battery of 8·8-cm guns from 36th Flak Regiment, a heavy-artillery

The third battle of Kharkov: Waffen SS Panzers advancing through the northern suburbs.

battery with 15-cm howitzers, and above all a company of Tiger tanks —the 1st Company, Tank Battalion 502, under Lieutenant von Gerdtell. The four Tigers with their 8·8-cm long-barrel guns and the eight Mark IIIs, intended as escorts, were to prove decisive against the enemy's tank battalions.

Bodo von Gerdtell, however, lost his life in the very first action. He was buried at the cemetery in the Sinyavino bog.

Through chest-high snow, covering the inhospitable bog, and through shell-torn forests the battalions of the 283rd, 284th, and 287th Grenadier Regiments made their way northwards on 13th January. Gorodok, "Scheidiswald", "ring road"—these were the savage names of the next few days.

"Ring road"! During the very first assault four Tigers made their debut. Colonel Pohlmann's Grenadier battalions had repulsed the Russian infantry in twenty-eight degrees below zero Centigrade. But then two dozen Soviet T-34s attacked. Two of them were knocked out by Lieutenant Eichstädt and Corporal Gudehus. Two out of twenty-four. The remaining twenty-two steel monsters forced the grenadiers into a dangerous situation. Three company commanders were killed in rapid succession.

Then the Tigers appeared. It was a historic engagement. After some not very successful actions by 1st Company, Tiger Battalion 502, employed at Leningrad as an experimental company since August 1942, the powerful steel monsters now showed their paces. The hard bark of their 8·8-cm long-barrel guns meant the knell of the T-34s. Twelve Soviet tanks were soon blazing in the bog. The rest fled in confusion. The Soviet counter-attack towards the south had been halted.

At dusk the Russians once more attempted a local tank thrust at the "Scheidiswald" forest through which the "ring road" ran. Once more the Tiger Company was alerted: "Enemy armour approaching! Form up at once!"

Sergeant Hans Bölter set off with two Tigers and his Mark III as an escort. Bölter, seven times wounded and fifteen times knocked out in his tank, was to rise from sergeant to captain over the next eighteen months. He was one of the most successful tank commanders of the war.

The two Tigers were pushing through the snow. In the twilight the contours of the massive monsters with their white paint blended into the winter landscape. A Soviet anti-tank gun was overrun. Bölter ordered the second Tiger to give him cover by taking up station a little behind him to the left, in echelon. Just then the first spurts of snow rose besides Bölter's Tiger—the bursts of enemy anti-tank shells.

A quick glance round. Over there! Bölter swivelled the turret. The gun-aimer got a T-34 in his sights. The driver stopped. "Fire!" The shell swished from the barrel. A miss. Again. The second round was a direct hit. The T-34 burst into flames at once. The 8·8-cm shell had torn it open, just like the paw of a tiger.

Everything went as smoothly as on the tank training ground near Fallingbostel. Bölter's Tiger knocked out two more T-34s. Their blazing wrecks cast a ghostly light over the bog.

But then Bölter got hemmed in by three Russian tanks. They tried to out-manoeuvre him. They were a daring lot, those Soviet tankmen of 61st Tank Brigade.

Bölter's gun-aimer moved like clockwork. "First the one on the right," the sergeant calmly commanded. Fire! And again. Fire! A hit.

The two other T-34s now tried to escape into the bog. They wanted to get out of the pool of light. But Bölter's Tiger devoured those two T-34s as well. "About turn! Back."

"What's happened to our escort tank?" Sergeant Bölter asked.

"Radio's shot up," the operator replied. "No contact."

Two minutes later came a fearful crash. "Hit in the engine," the driver called out. And another crash.

The blazing Russian wrecks on the snow-covered bog were providing an excellent illumination for a well-concealed Soviet anti-tank gun. Bölter's Tiger lay on this floodlit stage like a stationary target. An easy prey to the Soviet anti-tank gun.

Bölter's Tiger was in flames. There was danger of the ammunition exploding. The sergeant had no choice but to order his men out. The crew leapt down into the snow.

Soviet infantrymen appeared. A short exchange of pistol and sub-machine-gun fire. Then Bölter and his men raced to a nearby clump of bushes.

At last the second Tiger approached. "Has he seen us?" Bölter wondered. "Suppose he takes us for Russians?" Better be careful. But how was he to attract attention? He yelled. But the noise of battle drowned his voice.

Resolutely he leapt up on the right-hand trackguard of the Tiger and edged forward to the wireless operator's slit.

Just as he got there he heard the operator inside call out: "Russians on our tank!"

What now? Bölter shouted for all he was worth. But would they hear him inside with all that din of battle?

"All I need now is for the commander to raise the turret door and pot me with his pistol," he thought. He kept a sharp eye on the turret. Just then the hatch was raised a couple of inches.

The sergeant yelled the commander's name. Fortunately the commander understood instantly. The turret door was flung open. Three words of command. And off they went to search the ground for the remaining men of Bölter's crew. One after the other they picked them up. Only then did Bölter realize that he had three shell splinters lodged in his back.

Luck and misfortune are often closely associated in war. While Colonel Pohlmann, the commander of 284th Grenadier Regiment, was conducting the operation in the "Scheidiswald" and the action of his Tigers in the front line, a heavy Soviet air raid was made on his regimental command post on the "ring road". Twenty-three officers and men of the cycle platoon and the regimental staff were killed. It was a heavy blow.

Meanwhile, the neighbouring regiment, the 283rd Grenadier Regiment under Colonel Andoy, had moved off in the direction of the power-station and the hospital, where the Germans were holding out against fierce Soviet attacks. Andoy's battalions arrived at the very moment when the Russians were mounting their full-scale attack with strong forces of their 61st Tank Brigade and the rifle regiment of their 136th Rifle Division.

At the power-station Andoy's troops dislodged the Soviets with their first assault and linked up with the men inside. At the hospital the fighting was tougher. The block of buildings was already totally surrounded. The Russians tried to keep their ring closed at all costs, in order to move step by step into the sealed-off compound.

But the 283rd forced a breach and burst through to the hospital. They were enthusiastically welcomed by the engineers under Lieutenant Brendel who, with his 3rd Company, Engineer Battalion 240, had turned the blazing hospital into a veritable fortress. That night a battalion of 96th Infantry Division took over the flank cover. The wounded were taken away out of the fighting line.

The following morning the Russians attacked again. At all the windows the engineers lay behind their sand-bags and from there had to watch the scene below them in the trenches: twenty-six tanks were overrunning the 9th Company, 283rd Grenadier Regiment. They just drove over the trenches. They ran their broad tracks over machine-gun posts and infantry firing pits to crush the grenadiers inside. Brendel's men felt dry in their throats.

But the Russian winter on the 60th parallel proved their saviour. The temperature was 22 degrees below zero Centigrade and the soil was rock-hard. Equally hard were the edges of the infantry dug-outs. The tank tracks were unable to do much damage. The grenadiers just crouched in their foxholes. Very uncomfortable no doubt, but not fatal.

When the tanks had overrun the positions and moved up to the hospital, firing wildly to keep down the defenders, the Soviet infantry charged. They scarcely expected any German resistance.

But from the overrun trenches and infantry foxholes of 9th Company rose the grenadiers. And the charging Russians were suddenly, totally unexpectedly, faced with murderous infantry fire. Their charge collapsed.

The Soviet tanks meanwhile got within range of the 2nd Battalion, 36th Flak Regiment, and of the heavy artillery. Colonel Andoy's Panzer-jägers moved in. Chunks of earth, frozen rock-hard, sailed through the air. It was a battle of tanks against artillery.

In the end artillery, flak, and the Panzerjägers of 283rd Grenadier Regiment came out on top. Twenty-four Soviet tanks lay smouldering or blazing on the edge of the Sinyavino peat-bog at the end of this winter duel. Thus the worst danger had been averted on the sector of 170th Infantry Division on the bank of the Neva.

3. Between Volkhov and Schlüsselburg

Wengler's barrier–Assault by 122nd Tank Brigade–Ziegler's battalion moved through the enemy–The inhospitable hills of Sinyavino–Struggle for Poselok 5–A troop of artillery in the "Scheidiswald"–The Blue Division at Krasnyy Bor–Graves in the bog.

IN the meantime the situation at the centre of the bottleneck, near Poselok 5, had come to a head. Events had also taken a dangerous turn on the eastern front of the German corridor to Lake Ladoga. Since the early morning of 12th January the seven divisions of the Soviet Second Striking Army had been attacking the German lines between Lipka on Lake Ladoga and Gaytolovo north of the Kirov railway.

Lipka, the northern corner-post of the German positions, was held by the 2nd Battalion, 287th Grenadier Regiment, despite furious attacks by the Soviet 128th Rifle Division. Farther south, however, near Poselok 4, the Soviet 372nd Rifle Division succeeded in making a penetration. The 1st Battalion of the East Pomeranian 374th Grenadier Regiment was overrun. But the 2nd Battalion held its positions at Poselok 8 and yielded no ground whatever.

As dusk fell on 12th January, towards 1600 hours, Major Ziegler's men at Poselok 8 had repelled five heavy Russian attacks. The Soviet 372nd Rifle Division was determined to achieve a breakthrough there at

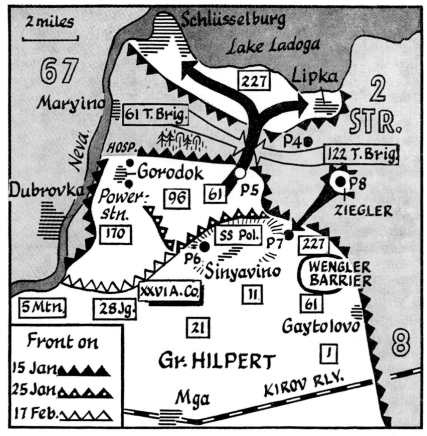

Map 25. The Soviet armies linked up north of Poselok 5. Cut-off German forces succeeded in breaking out to the south.

all costs. They were Siberian regiments and tough Asian units, attacking ruthlessly. But Ziegler's Pomeranians stood as firmly as the trees of the Volkhov forest.

Since the beginning of the year the reinforced 374th Grenadier Regiment, the counter-attack unit of the 207th Mopping-up Division, had been placed under 227th Infantry Division for the defence of the eastern side of the bottleneck. The 2nd Battalion had dug in exceedingly well around Poselok 8. The Russians charged. They shelled the positions heavily. They charged again.

By 13th January Ziegler's positions had been levelled; but the men hung on, supported by 196th Artillery Regiment whose advanced observers were in the foremost lines. The assault regiments of the Soviet 372nd Rifle Division bled to death in the ancient, shell-torn forest and in the frozen bog.

South of Poselok 8 the situation developed less favourably for the defenders. There the Soviets had formed a second concentration. Colonel Polyakov had trained his 327th Rifle Division for this attack over a long period. He had got them to build exact replicas of the carefully reconnoitred German positions of the 3rd Battalion, 374th Grenadier Regiment, as well as the defences of Colonel Wengler's 366th Grenadier Regiment. They were accurate down to the last detail—the palisade fence, the communication trenches, the machine-gun posts, and the bunkers.

Colonel Polyakov applied pressure at the junction between the two German formations. There, at the "round copse", the Soviet 327th Rifle Division was to avenge the serious reverse suffered by the Fifty-Fourth Army in the first battle of Lake Ladoga, during the late summer of 1942.

Then Wengler, with his men from the Rhineland and Westphalia, had prevented a strategic widening of the Soviet penetration. This time Polyakov intended to burst through the German barrier at all costs. His assault regiments pierced the foremost German positions. They broke through south of P8. They tried to roll up the main defensive line to the north and south. If they could succeed in doing that the front of 227th Infantry Division would collapse and Polyakov's men would have a clear road to the commanding high ground of Sinyavino.

But the Soviet plan did not come off. Again Wengler's men held the southern corner-post of the penetration area. The Jägers of 28th Jäger Division, together with the 1st Battalion, 83rd Jäger Regiment, fought their way through right up to Wengler's command post and there reinforced his defensive barrier. Right at the centre, like a rock in the surf, stood Poselok 8 with Major Ziegler's battalion. Five hundred German soldiers here upset the plan of the Soviet Command: although entirely surrounded, the Pomeranians defended their hedgehog position against all attacks. They held out on 12th January, on 13th January, and on 14th January. No supplies were reaching them, and no ammunition. They had no contact with Division or with their regiment.

Alone, depending entirely on their own resources, Ziegler's battalion discharged a vital task. Instead of being able to push on westwards, the Russians had to deal with Poselok 8. Considerable forces of the Russian 327th Rifle Division, as well as of the 18th Rifle Division which were brought up subsequently by the Soviet High Command, were pinned down at this hotly contested spot.

On 15th January, after four days of battle, the German defenders were running out of ammunition. In the morning the Russians once more charged after a heavy artillery bombardment. With shouts of "Urra" they approached, but they were halted by the machine-gun fire of the Pomeranians. Russian tanks of the 122nd Tank Brigade, which had made a few penetrations, were knocked out by mines and high-explosive charges. By then the defenders were nearly out of ammunition. They would hardly be able to repulse another attack. Ziegler was faced with the alternative of being overrun and annihilated or breaking out and saving at least the men.

The major summoned his officers and put the question to them. Should they hold out? Should they surrender? Or should they make a last effort and break out?

Surrender was out of the question. To allow oneself to be killed did not seem to make much sense. That left a break-out. But it would be a break-out into uncertainty. No-one knew where the German lines were. Attempts to restore the broken radio contact remained unsuccessful.

There is a point where courage loses its meaning. To let oneself be killed pointlessly is no military virtue. Against hundredfold superiority, against a hail of bombs and shells, neither willpower, nor courage, nor yet obedience or dedication are any use. True, courage and bravery have frequently triumphed on the battlefield over a greatly superior enemy. But in the battles of *matériel* of a modern war there is a certain point where the outcome is dictated by mass—the mass of men and weapons.

Ziegler's decision to break out was therefore entirely correct and, in the best meaning of the word, courageous.

The secret break-out from Poselok 8 began at 2300 hours. The major himself was at the head. Next to him was Oskar Schwemm, a man from Lodz, who spoke Russian fluently. He had put on the uniform of a dead Soviet lieutenant over his Wehrmacht uniform. Behind them came a strong assault party, then a combat group with fixed bayonets and rifles ready for action. They were followed by the wounded who were drawn on *akjas*, those small, boat-shaped, Lapland sleighs, each of them pulled by two men. Flank cover was provided by men with sub-machine-guns. The rearguard was formed by the bulk of the battalion. No firing except by express order of the major. No smoking. No talking.

As the last rearguards in the abandoned positions put up a wild fireworks display, the ghost column was trudging through the knee-deep snow in the pale light of the moon at a temperature of 25 degrees below zero Centigrade. Their pointer was the constellation of Orion, because their route lay to the south. "*Stoy*," Schwemm suddenly said, his voice deliberately raised. The men at the head of the column halted at once. In front of them were the silhouettes of several T-34s. That was the Russian armoured ring round Poselok 8. Schwemm trudged over to them. He talked to the Russian troop commander. The others watched them lighting cigarettes and gesticulating. Lieutenant Becker, the battalion adjutant, believed he could hear the heartbeats of every one of his men like thunder-claps echoing over the frozen bog. At last Schwemm returned. He shouted a few Russian words of command which no-one understood and cursed noisily. But to Ziegler he said softly, "I've got the password. It's *Pobeda*. It means 'Victory'. Maybe it's a good omen."

Just as important as the password was the rest of Schwemm's information. He knew the location of a major gap in the Soviet armoured ring. Through that gap they now moved out. Thanks to the password they also got through a second Russian picket line without a shot being fired. "*Pobeda!*" Schwemm called out to a sentry, and then the column wheeled to the left.

But there was still no sign of the German lines. No noise of battle, no fires in the sky, no Very lights.

And then, quite suddenly, they were in front of a Russian mortar position. Schwemm called out the password, but the Russian officer was suspicious. He approached closer. The man from Lodz quickly took a few steps towards him. He told him his unit was on the way to the front, on a special assignment against the German lines.

Lieutenant Becker stood less than two paces from the two. His hand was in his greatcoat pocket, gripping his pistol with the safety catch off.

The Russian did not seem quite to believe Schwemm's story. But the man from Lodz dispelled all suspicion. At last they were able to move on. But they were uneasy. All those mortars just behind them! Supposing the Russians noticed something was wrong?

In a whisper Ziegler had a command passed on to the rearguard: "We must overwhelm the mortar position!" And so the battalion brought with it a genuine Russian lieutenant and forty-one prisoners. They even got them through the most advanced Russian infantry strongpoints, although here they had to fight their way through.

After three-quarters of an hour, in the grey light of dawn, the ghost column reached the advanced German battle outposts. There was considerable celebrating at the regimental command post of 274th Grenadier Regiment as Ziegler reported. Not only because the combat group which had already been written off had arrived safely, but also because Colonel von Below urgently needed every fit man at Poselok 5 which had in the meantime become the focal point of the battle in the bottleneck.

On the Neva the Russians had not yet succeeded, any more than on the eastern side of the bottleneck, in breaking through the German defences over a broad front. Only two narrow wedges, penetrating from Maryino in the west and past P8 in the east, were slowly pushing through the upper part of the German corridor. But it was on the high ground of Poselok 5 that the Soviet assault formations intended to link up. If they succeeded, a narrow overland link would have been established with Leningrad and the German forces of 96th and 227th Infantry Divisions, which were still holding out at Schlüsselburg, Lipka, and Lake Ladoga, would be cut off.

That was what Colonel-General Lindemann wanted to prevent at all costs. But XXVI Army Corps' two divisions in the bottleneck were insufficient for clearing up the Russian penetrations. The frontages held by 170th and 227th Infantry Divisions were much too wide as it was —something like fifteen miles each.

After the costly fighting of the first few days there were no reserves left for attack, for halting the broken-in Russian wedges or for preventing their link-up.

On 14th January, Eighteenth Army had brought up two regimental groups of the East Prussian 61st Infantry Division from the Pogostye pocket—a combat area on the Kirov railway, twenty miles south-east of Mga—and on 15th January moved them into the bottleneck. Two regimental groups instead of the whole division. One regiment had to be left behind at the Kirov railway. Once again it was a case of driblets instead of a massive operation.

Lieutenant-General Hühner, commanding the 61st Infantry Division, led the group himself. He thrust past Sinyavino and Poselok 5, and re-established the link with 227th and 96th Infantry Divisions surrounded at Lipka and Schlüsselburg. But Hühner's forces were too weak to hold open the land link from Poselok 5 to Lake Ladoga, Schlüsselburg, and Lipka against the Soviets attacking from east and west.

The main fighting was for the miserable workers' settlement with its few hutments and a small peat-processing plant. A mere point on the map—P5. But a very bloody point. The Soviets used two divisions and two armoured brigades to attack this small bastion in the bog. P5 was a kind of road junction; through it led the only north-south road. The German forces in the northern part of the bottleneck were supplied by that road. If the Russians succeeded in occupying P5 the northern part of the German corridor would be cut off from its rearward communications.

Throughout four days and nights Hühner's group held out along the low railway embankments of the peat-works' sidings and the large, rectangular basins where the peat was cut, in a cruel cold of 25 to 30 degrees below zero Centigrade. They were holding open the southward escape road through P5.

What was needed now to prevent a link-up of the Russians was a few dozen tanks, a battery of assault guns, an artillery regiment, and a few battalions of infantry with armour-piercing weapons. But since the Germans lacked even these modest forces the Russians succeeded, on 18th January, in taking Poselok 5 after savage fighting and in cutting off Hühner's combat group.

The Russian account in the *History of the Great Fatherland War* conveys a picture of the fierceness of the German opposition. In Volume 3 we read:

Parts of the Soviet 136th Rifle Division twice broke into Poselok 5 but were unable to gain a foothold. Three times during the night of 16th January the regiments of 18th Rifle Division charged the settlement from the east without being able to take it. A few units of the division got within fifteen or twenty yards of the fortified positions but had to fall back time and again. The Germans were fighting with the courage of desperation. By the evening of the following day parts of the division, supported by 61st Tank Brigade, reached the eastern edge of the settlement and began to fight for each single house. On the morning of 18th January the fighting flared up again with renewed violence. From the west parts of 136th Rifle Division and 61st Tank Brigade burst into the settlement.

Through German eyes the dramatic hours of 17th and 18th January looked like this. In front of the high brick wall of the peat plant in P5 was a bunker. This was General Hühner's battle headquarters. By the flickering light of a candle in the evening of 17th January the general was studying the map. Three hours previously Army had given permission for all German formations still in the northern part of the bottleneck to rally and break through to the south, via P5, to establish a new main defensive line along the high ground of Sinyavino. Dispatch-riders had been sent out and were now chasing over the snow-covered bog. Radio signals were going out to Schlüsselburg, Lipka, and the field positions along the lake: Break out! Break out at nightfall, in the direction of P5.

This meant that Poselok 5 had to be held open at all costs, in the face of massive enemy pressure, in order to allow the formations breaking out to pass through.

The field telephone whirred. Telephone communications with Corps and Eighteenth Army were still intact. Hühner picked up the receiver. At the other end was the commander of XXVI Corps, General von Leyser. "What's the situation, Hühner?"

"To say we are in the shit would be putting it optimistically, Herr General! My last reserves consist of one NCO and twelve men. Just now they're outside, on a counter-attack to seal off a small penetration quite close to this bunker."

At that moment there was a crack in the line. "Hello," called Hühner. "Hello!"

Not a sound. The general looked up at his ADC. "Finished. The line's dead."

"Never mind, Herr General; at least no-one can tell us now what to do," the lieutenant replied resignedly.

Hühner nodded and ran his pencil over the map. Apart from his

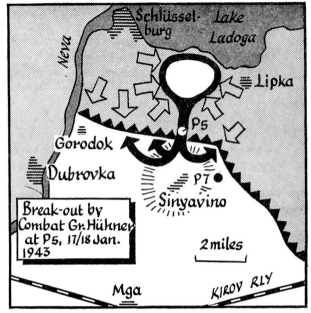

Map 26. General Hühner held Poselok 5 until all the German formations stationed to the north of it had passed through to the south.

own forces—the 151st and 162nd Grenadier Regiments—there was the group of 328th Regiment from Schlüsselburg, a battalion and the Fast Detachment of 96th Infantry Division from Lipka, as well as the gunners, Panzerjägers, mountain Jägers, and grenadiers of 227th Infantry Division from the strongpoints on Lake Ladoga—all these had to be let out of the trap.

Would they get out? The Russians were applying considerable pressure. Naturally they knew what was up. They were therefore trying to take Poselok 5 as fast as possible.

The small bunker shook with the bursts of the Soviet artillery. A runner arrived from Colonel von Below: "Soviet tanks approaching across the railway embankment." Hühner had only a single Mark III with a long-barrel gun left. It was standing in the factory grounds, well camouflaged. Action!

The lieutenant in the tank allowed the Russians to come quite close. Then, firing from his concealed position at about eighty yards' range, he scored a direct hit on the gun mantlet of the third in the file of Soviet tanks. It instantly burst into flames. The next shell knocked out the lead tank. The second one, caught thus between its neighbours, was an easy prey.

The two hundred wounded from the hutments and the factory were quickly put on *akjas*. Under the supervision of the medical officer, a young lieutenant, small parties of medical orderlies and walking casualties manoeuvred the *akjas* down the highway to P6.

They were not a minute too soon. Under the cover of their artillery the Russians had worked right up to the factory ground and were lying close by the bunker.

The adjutant mounted an immediate counter-attack with signallers, clerks, and runners, and dislodged the Russians from the factory compound.

In the early hours of the morning, while it was still dark, a runner burst into the bunker by the brick wall. The 151st Grenadier Regiment, the spearhead of the forces breaking out, had arrived. The decisive moment of the break-out had come. With hand-grenades and cold steel the East Prussians fought their way out. It was a costly move. Across the snow of the bog, with no cover, right through the assembly positions of two Russian divisions and two armoured brigades, the combat groups fought their way through to the new German main defensive line which ran from Gorodok over the hills of Sinyavino. That line was being held by engineers of 96th Infantry Division, Jägers of the 5th Mountain Jäger Division and the 28th Jäger Division, as well as by riflemen of the 4th SS Police Division.

The focal point of the fighting was at Poselok 5. There lurked the enemy. Machine-gun parties lay behind stacks of peat. Riflemen were concealed in the thick undergrowth. From the flank Russian companies were charging, trying to deny the road to the German troops. The Russians were spraying the bog with both artillery and multiple mortars.

At 0600 hours the 151st Grenadier Regiment encountered the last enemy group just south of P5. Forward! Pistol, bayonet, hand-grenade, trenching tool—these were their weapons.

Major Krudzki, the regimental commander, was killed in the lead group, by the side of Lieutenant Kopp, the commander of 6th Company and a bearer of the Knight's Cross. But the East Prussians not only fought their way through but they left not a single one of their wounded or dead behind.

Behind them the Russians again penetrated into the escape corridor. Thus each successive combat group had to clear its way anew. It was always the same picture: they took their wounded with them in the middle of their columns. The snow was nearly three feet deep. Medical orderlies pulled the *akjas*. Now and again a horse was used to pull a piece of fencing on which, wrapped in tattered blankets, would lie four seriously wounded. Forward! Altogether six thousand troops and two thousand wounded were ferried through the escape gap in the bog.

At daybreak General Hühner finally ordered his combat group at P5 to disengage. The heavy losses which the Soviets had suffered during the night, in the continuous hand-to-hand fighting, reduced his risk. The withdrawal was less dangerous than the general had feared. The German flank cover held out. Even the Russian tanks only followed up hesitantly.

In the early light of day the massive barrier of the Sinyavino hills lay like a magnet before the men's eyes. That was their objective. There lay salvation. That was their destination as they were moving across the bog, in very open formation, their weapons at the ready.

They trudged through the deep snow. They flung themselves into any dip in the ground as soon as the Russian machine-guns started barking from their hiding places in the thick scrub or from behind a wall of snow.

Then, under fire cover from their comrades, the men would cautiously crawl forward, a yard at a time. Hand-grenade out. Throw! A flash and a crash. Screams and groans. Forward!

Among the shell craters, just before they reached the high ground of Sinyavino, they wiped out a Soviet combat group. And then they were at their destination. On 20th January Hühner's men reeled into the intercepting line. The companies of his 151st and 162nd Regiments now numbered thirty to forty men each. The 1st Company, 162nd Grenadier Regiment, which had gone into battle with one hundred and twenty-eight men on 15th January, was by now reduced to a mere forty-four.

Lieutenant Dressel, wounded and supporting himself on a home-made crutch, trudged past the first German pickets ahead of his men. The pickets were engineers from 96th Infantry Division who were already busy mining the ground in front of the new main defensive line on the northern flank of the Sinyavino hills. They welcomed Dressel and the men of 5th Company, 287th Grenadier Regiment, who were coming from Lipka.

But after their first questions the engineers fell silent, moved aside, or turned back to their work. They could see that many of the company's men were missing. And they could also see that most of those who had got through were wearing bloody bandages and were scarcely able to stand up on their feet.

When Dressel reported at the temporary battalion headquarters he found only Captain Albrecht, the regimental adjutant, there. The battalion commander? Missing. The battalion adjutant? Killed. Most of the company commanders were killed, missing, or wounded. The battalion was down to eighty men.

"It's no use, Dressel—anyone still able to hold a rifle must go straight into the new line," Albrecht said. "The line from Gorodok on the Neva across the bottleneck over the Sinyavino hills down to Wengler's barrier on the eastern side must be held at all costs."

Dressel nodded. And like him the rest of his company, all those who had only just fought their way back to the German main defensive line, immediately took up positions again.

These were the coldest days of the winter, 35 to 40 degrees below zero Centigrade. During the day the Soviets sprayed the positions with artillery and multiple mortars. And during the icy nights the Russian infantry would charge again and again against the newly-established and still rather thin German front. The Russians wanted at all costs to take the commanding high ground of Sinyavino. But the new positions were held. This had been made possible by the successful break-out of the German formations in the northern part of the bottleneck; otherwise there would have been no forces available to defend these strategically important hills south of the Neva.

Thus the evacuation of the strip of shore along Lake Ladoga, the northernmost point of the narrow German corridor near Leningrad, was in every respect a superb tactical achievement. Some 800,000 men were saved, including nearly 2000 wounded. The heavy equipment which had to be left behind had previously been destroyed. The Soviets took virtually no booty, and, more important still, they took no prisoners. The complete success of the German evacuation is indirectly confirmed in Soviet military history by the fact that the announcement of their victory makes no mention—contrary to their usual practice—of prisoners or casualties.

Nevertheless, the German evacuation of the southern shore of Lake Ladoga with Lipka and Schlüsselburg was a great psychological success for the Russians: the blockade of Leningrad had been burst open. True enough, the Soviet High Command, after a gigantic employment of men and material, had gained only a five- to seven-mile-wide

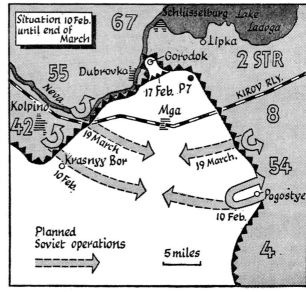

Map 27.
The Russians did not achieve the strategic objective of the second battle of Lake Ladoga: the Kirov railway with Mga remained in German hands.

corridor from the Volkhov Front to Schlüsselburg, a narrow strip of peat-bog through which ran only minor tracks to the Neva. Nevertheless, a land link had been established with Leningrad for the coming summer, however narrow, a link which would remain usable once the "lifeline", the Russian road across the ice of Lake Ladoga, had again turned to water.

Hitler's plan to strangle and starve the city into submission, the plan upon which his entire strategy on the northern wing depended, had failed. Naturally, this was realized by the Finns, Germany's allies on the northern wing of the Eastern Front, whose military operations depended on the course of the German ones. Finnish confidence in their German allies was shaken. Their military plans collapsed. Finland's Field-Marshal Carl Gustav Baron von Mannerheim had intended, as soon as the beleaguered city fell, to switch his corps, which were bogged down along the Karelian encirclement front, over to an attack against the Murmansk railway. In this way the Soviet Union's vital northern communications were to be cut, the route by which the huge American supplies were arriving. The loss of this American aid would have put Russia in a difficult economic situation and deprived the Soviet High Command of much of its offensive momentum.

This shows how important the capture of Leningrad would have been, and how important, on the other hand, was the insignificant but politically weighty Russian victory on the shore of Lake Ladoga. True, the Soviet Command failed to reach the great strategic objective of its second battle of Lake Ladoga. It had originally hoped to crush the entire bottleneck on a broad front, at least as far as the Kirov railway, including Mga. That would have ensured a safe overland communication with the encircled city and its final relief.

This objective was not reached by the Russians. The Soviet offensive collapsed against the Sinyavino hills, where shell crater lay next to shell crater. Lieutenant-General A. A. Zhdanov, member of the War Council, the defender of Leningrad, had gained—figuratively speaking —a superior farm track instead of a wide highway. All he had gained was a thin supply-line, which was moreover controlled by German guns. From the high ground of Sinyavino the advanced artillery observers were able to overlook the entire area as far as Lake Ladoga.

In material terms, therefore, the Soviet High Command had scored

Opposite, top: A leader who went forward with his tanks: General Paul Hausser, commanding the SS Panzer Corps, on an armoured infantry carrier. *Bottom:* Soviet artillery moving into position.
Overleaf, top: Leningrad: Supplies being brought to the city at night, along the "Road of Life", the city's vital lifeline across the frozen Lake Ladoga. *Bottom:* By contrast, the "road of death": this is how the dead were taken to the cemetery when there were no coffins left in the city.

only a moderate success. And the price it had paid for it was exceptionally high: the two Soviet Armies employed there, the Second Striking
Army and the Sixty-Seventh Army, lost 225 tanks alone. That was
more than seven tank battalions. Their casualties are difficult to
estimate.

The psychological effect among their own people and among their
allies, however, more than offset the enormous losses suffered by the
Soviets. Belief in victory and confidence in the top leadership received
a tremendous boost. And Zhdanov succeeded brilliantly in making
the breach of Leningrad's blockade into a celebration for the whole
of the Soviet Union.

When, late at night on 18th January 1943, Leningrad radio asked its
listeners to stand by for a special announcement, the rumour that the
blockade ring had been burst open was already sweeping through the
mortally wounded city. No-one went to bed. The first flags were hung
out. Gramophone music came from the windows of the drab houses,
windows scantily boarded up against the cold. There was hope
again—hope of an early end to the city's sufferings.

Certainty came about midnight. Until then the authorities hesitated
—presumably to make quite sure. The announcement on Leningrad
radio began with the words: "The ring has been burst open. We have
long waited for this day, but we knew that it must come. As we laid
our dear ones to rest in the frozen ground of the mass graves, without
ceremony, we swore an oath to them by way of a farewell: 'The ring
will be burst open!' "

Admittedly the Russians had failed to reach the Kirov railway. But
this failure was soon made good: within twenty-five days Soviet railway pioneers had built a temporary twenty-two-mile line across the
bog, along the shore of Lake Ladoga, from Polgami to Schlüsselburg,
and on from there, over a temporary bridge, until it linked up with
the line to Leningrad. The line, of course, was liable to be cut any
day by a German attack. But that was known only to the experts.

On 6th February this field railway was put into operation. At once
the bread ration in Leningrad was increased from 250 to 600 grammes
(9 ounces to 1 pound 5 ounces) for workers, and from 125 to 400
grammes (4½ ounces to 14 ounces) for the rest of the population. These
figures show more clearly than anything else that Leningrad continued to be a city encircled and besieged. The narrow corridor, no
more than five to seven miles wide, with its makeshift railway, did not
ensure regular supplies for the fortress city.

Previous page, top: The Russians tried to cross Lake Ilmen by motor sleigh: the
attack was smashed by German artillery. *Bottom:* Heavy army artillery south of
Lake Ladoga.
Opposite: Rest for man and beast.

It was this situation that compelled Soviet command to continue its efforts on the blood-drenched battlefield south of Lake Ladoga, in order to achieve its strategic objective—the Kirov railway with the traffic centre of Mga. The battle thus continued. Without pause the second and third phases of this second battle of Lake Ladoga began.

The two old corner-posts of the German defence continued to play their former part—the strongpoint of Gorodok with its hospital and power-station on the Neva and, at the other end, the fortified positions of 366th Grenadier Regiment at Poselok 7, known as the "Wengler barrier" after the regimental commander. It was these two corner-stones and the barrier on the high ground of Sinyavino which decided the fate of the new battle.

The hospital of Gorodok was now only a ruin. The main wings were gutted. But Lieutenant Brendel's engineers of 3rd Company, Engineer Battalion 240, held the shattered masonry against all Soviet attacks. Of particular assistance, chiefly against Soviet tank attacks, was the 1st Battalion, 240th Artillery Regiment, under Major Bauer.

The guns were on the southern edge of the "Scheidiswald" wood. Lieutenant Volkmann had been at the hospital since the beginning of the fighting, as the advanced observer directing the fire. Again and again he relieved the grenadiers and engineers by timely defensive fire or concentrated bombardment of the focal points of the attack. In the late afternoon of 17th January the battery, on the strength of Volkmann's precise data, had smashed a Soviet assembly position in the triangular wood. Then suddenly contact was lost. Not a single shell came over from the guns any longer. What had happened?

Volkmann's radio operators again and again called the gun position of the battery. No reply. No contact with Regiment either.

"I'm going to get some sleep," the lieutenant said, and lay down on a bunk in the basement. The smoke of the smouldering wreckage on the first floor was wafted down into the shelter over the draughty passages and staircases. There was a stench. Eyes watered. But Volkmann was dead tired and fell asleep at once. But half an hour later he was woken. "Herr Leutnant, Herr Leutnant, we've got contact with Regiment!"

Volkmann sat up. "And what happened at the battery?"

The NCO hesitated. Then he said, "The battery was overrun by Soviet tanks. It seems everyone was killed. There's only the wireless operator left in some hideout and from time to time he's in contact with Colonel Hertz."

Lieutenant Volkmann leapt up from his bunk. Overrun? All killed? "And the guns, what happened to the guns?" The NCO shrugged.

It was about a mile and a quarter to the gun position. A mile and a quarter—first through the ring encircling the hospital, then across ground exposed to the enemy. But Volkmann did not hesitate long. "I've got to know what's happened. Maybe they need help. I'm going!"

Volkmann pushed five hand-grenades under his belt and tucked his sub-machine-gun under his arm. Thus he walked out into the night, alone. He worked his way forward from tree to tree. From one thicket to another. He took cover in shell craters or in the snow-filled peat cuttings.

He reached the rails of the peat railway. Behind it must be the corduroy road which led from the power-station to the divisional command post at Rangun. He kept the road over to his right. Careful now. He must be almost there. Then he recognized the gun position of No. 1 Troop. Behind their parapets the guns stood silent in the moonlight.

Volkmann vaulted over the parapet. He bent down. The gun-position officer—dead. Around the guns lay the gunners. Torn to pieces by shells. Riddled with sub-machine-gun bullets. Suddenly Volkmann jerked up. He held his breath, listening. There it was again—moaning. Cautiously he crept over to No. 4 gun. He knelt down. Under the gun carriage was the gun-aimer. Seriously wounded by a burst of sub-machine-gun fire, but alive.

Volkmann spoke to the wounded man in a whisper. Yes, he was conscious. As the Soviet tanks had overrun the position, the gun-aimer had flung himself under the carriage. The infantry following up had then mown everyone down. Major Bauer, the battery commander, happened to be at the position. He must be lying quite close. Volkmann looked for him. He found him. Dead, like all the rest.

Strangely enough, the Russians had not destroyed the guns. They probably intended to haul them away. Obviously they thought they were safe and had plenty of time.

Time, thought Volkmann. But first he hurried over to the first-aid bunker. It was empty. The medical officer and his orderly were lying by No. 2 gun, dead. At the entrance Volkmann found an *akja*, one of those boat-shaped Lapland sleighs, complete with towing harness and blanket. He put on the harness. He placed the gun-aimer on the *akja*. Thus he set out on his return trip. The wounded man groaned whenever the sleigh jerked. Volkmann was sweating in spite of 20 degrees below zero Centigrade. Soviet patrols were crossing his path. Time and again he flung himself down. He held his breath and pressed his palm over the wounded man's mouth.

Soviet artillery was spraying the bog and the forest with shellfire. Volkmann had to take evasive action. He lost his sense of direction. Now he had to be doubly careful so that he should not be shot by some German outpost.

At last the lieutenant heard faint voices. Talking German. He shouted. A few minutes later he was at the command post of his neighbouring division, the 96th Infantry Division.

Major-General Noeldechen listened to the lieutenant's story with amazement. The guns still intact? Perhaps there were some seriously injured there? Lieutenant-Colonel Deegener, the chief of operations, immediately raised a strong assault troop of engineers and grenadiers. Under Lieutenant Volkmann's direction they fought their way through to the gun position of the overrun battery.

This time they did not get there without a fight. The Russians too were on the move. They wanted to haul in the German guns. But Volkmann's assault party took them by surprise and occupied the gun position. Another assault party arrived at the gun position from 240th Artillery Regiment, dispatched by Colonel Hertz.

By dawn all the dead had been brought in, the gun positions of the battery had been remanned, and their defences restored. The fire power of an entire battery had been saved for the defenders.

In the half-destroyed bunker of the battery commander, crouched behind his radio set and wounded, they found the hero of the engagement—Corporal Signaller Palaska. Throughout the fighting at the gun position he had held out at his set, the only survivor in the command post. Outside the bunker stood a KV-1 which was firing continually. Now and again Palaska established contact with Regiment and was able to direct the fire of the other gun positions against the Soviet tanks. His fire control was so excellent that the Soviet tanks had to vacate the gun positions again.

Colonel-General Lindemann, C-in-C Eighteenth Army, was told about the bloody intermezzo on the southern edge of "Scheidiswald" in his morning reports. He was studying the map at his battle headquarters. "Will that new defensive line of ours hold in the bottleneck, Speth?"

But before Major-General Speth, his chief of staff, was able to reply, Lindemann continued: "We've got to hold the Sinyavino hills! They're the only point from where we can prevent, or harass, or even watch traffic in the Russian corridor between Lipka and Schlüsselburg. And that's not all—if we lose the hills we shan't be able to hold on to Mga. And once the Russians have got Mga they've got the Kirov railway, and the whole siege of Leningrad, our strategic objective, would become pointless."

Colonel-General Lindemann was right. Marshal Voroshilov, the co-ordinator of Soviet operations on Lake Ladoga, was making every possible effort and accepting enormous sacrifices in order to capture those commanding hills between Volkhov and Neva, together with their corner-posts. He wanted to burst open the ring around Leningrad once and for all.

Ceaselessly, Russian divisions carried out frontal attacks against the high ground. They charged the corner-posts at Poselok 7 and Gorodok. They pounded them with every kind of artillery. They threw in their tank regiments. They called up their ground-attack aircraft to bomb the positions, wave after wave. It was all in vain. General Hilpert, who had been commanding all German troops in the corridor since 24th January, under the designation of "Corps Group Hilpert", had abandoned the "Scheidiswald" wood and the peat-bog south of Poselok 5. The new main defensive line ran from Gorodok direct over the Sinyavino hills to Poselok 7 and the "Wengler barrier".

At times there were as many as a dozen German divisions in action in the corridor. Apart from the old East Prussian divisions from the southern zone of the Army, there was the 5th Mountain Division from the south-eastern part of the Leningrad ring and the 28th Jäger Division from the Volkhov.

The Combat Group Hühner was holding the most exposed north-eastern edge of the Sinyavino hills. Their engineers and the Fast Detachment of 61st Infantry Division were subjected to particularly fierce attacks but never yielded to the Soviets for a minute. On their right and left the two other East Prussian infantry divisions, the 1st and the 11th, together with the Jägers of the Silesian 28th Jäger Division, fought with the same tenacity. The savage hand-to-hand fighting around the ruined church of Sinyavino was among the fiercest of the war.

Against this "East Prussian phalanx" all Russian attempts to force a breakthrough to Mga via Sinyavino came to grief. In icy cold, in snowstorms, and under the roaring thunder of the Soviet artillery the shrunken companies held out in their trenches, strongpoints, and half buried shell craters. After eight days of ceaseless attacks the Soviet High Command realized that they were not getting very far. The peat-bog of Sinyavino was covered with corpses.

The Military Council members and the Commanders in Chief of the two Soviet Armies intervened with their High Command. "It's no use. We are being bled white and we still can't take those hills. In fact, they cannot be taken by frontal attack. The Germans have powerfully reinforced their positions. They have moved everything they've got to the Sinyavino barrier, at the price of denuding their deep flanks. But those flanks on the Volkhov, in the Pogostye area and at the south-eastern corner of the ring round Leningrad, at Kolpino, are now dangerously weak. That's where we should strike!"

It was a logical idea and a tempting plan—a pincer attack aiming at a double encirclement of all German forces north and east of Mga. If it came off, not only would the Kirov railway have been reached but a dozen German divisions would also be in the bag. Stalin and the High Command were enthusiastic about the plan of their commanders in the field. They set about putting it into effect. But Stalin, just as Hitler, invariably made the mistake of underrating his opponent. Once again he wanted to achieve too much with too few forces.

On 10th February the Soviets mounted their pincer attack south of the Pogostye pocket in the east, and from the area of Kolpino and Krasnyy Bor in the west. (See map, p. 239.)

On the eastern side the offensive of the Soviet Fifty-Fourth Army encountered the German 96th Infantry Division which had been pulled out of the Sinyavino front to be rested and replenished at Pogostye. Instead of enjoying their well-deserved respite, General Noeldechen's decimated regiments had to face up to some savage forest fighting. In co-operation with formations of the 61st and 132nd Infantry Division the Russian attack was repulsed. After a slight gain of territory it ground to a halt. The Soviets dug in but were eventually pushed back step by step. On the western side the front of 4th SS Police Division and the Spanish Blue Division (250th Infantry Division) stood up to the onslaught of seven Soviet rifle divisions, five brigades, and three armoured brigades.

The Spanish battalions of 262nd, 263rd, and 269th Grenadier Regiments under the command of General Esteban-Infantes bore the brunt of the Soviet thrust at Krasnyy Bor. There the enemy attacked with three rifle divisions and two tank battalions, altogether 33,000 men, supported by about 60 T-34s, several formations of anti-tank guns, and 187 batteries of artillery with altogether 1000 guns. Against this vast power the Spaniards on their twenty-mile sector only had a reinforced infantry regiment of 2500 men, as well as three battalions with roughly 2000 men. Added to this there were a few special units and artillery amounting to twenty-four guns, but no tanks.

Between them and their left-hand neighbours was a gap of about four miles, guarded only by patrols. Owing to his shortage of men General Esteban-Infantes had not been able to form a second line, but he had kept back two cycle squadrons, two companies of engineers, and two troops of artillery as a reserve. And that was not much.

After fierce hand-to-hand fighting the Russians succeeded in gaining two miles of ground and in taking Krasnyy Bor. But this success cost them 11,000 men killed, and moreover they got stuck on the Izhora. The Spaniards resisted stubbornly with daggers, trenching tools, and hand-grenades. Their extraordinary gallantry deserves to be recorded.

Thus, to quote but one example, Grenadier Antonio Ponte succeeded in knocking out several penetrated Soviet tanks with hand-grenades and mines. After he had destroyed the last T-34 Ponte was reported missing. He must have died somewhere in that icy land, on the Neva, crushed by tank-tracks or torn to pieces by a hand-grenade. He was awarded the highest Spanish decoration for gallantry, the Laureada San Fernando.

The Blue Division lost 3200 men; its Fusilier Battalion lost nearly

90 per cent of its strength. But the Spaniards held on to their strong-points and thus protected the deep flank of Hilpert's group. A counter-attack with parts of the hurriedly brought up Bavarian 212th Infantry Division under Major-General Reymann dislodged some Soviet forward groups. This dashed their hopes of achieving a pene-tration.

The right-hand neighbours of the Spaniards, the 4th SS Police Division, reinforced by parts of the 2nd SS Motorized Infantry Brigade and the Flanders Legion, had likewise halted Soviet attacks across the frozen Neva after fierce hand-to-hand fighting.

Exhausted and dispirited, the Soviet regiments withdrew to their jumping-off positions. But after a four weeks' breathing space, the Soviet High Command made one more attempt on 19th March, this time a little farther to the north, to apply a small pincer movement. On the Neva, in the Krasnyy Bor area, where four weeks earlier the Spanish volunteers had stood up to the Soviet assault, volunteers of the Flanders Legion, within the framework of the SS Police Division, now faced the attacking divisions of the Soviet Fifty-Fifth Army.

When the Russians had broken into the German positions the Flemings in battalion strength, under their commander, Captain Schellong, mounted their counter-attack. In bitter hand-to-hand fight-ing, supported by 8·8 flak combat parties and a few Tigers of 1st Company, Heavy Tank Battalion 502, they captured the old main defensive line of the Blue Division and held it against all Soviet attacks. They held it for eight days.

Then some lorries of the divisional supply commander arrived be-hind the hotly-contested lines with a battalion of 5th Mountain Division in order to relieve the Flemish company. The Mountain Jägers jumped into the trenches and infantry foxholes of the Flemings. But in most of them they found dead men. Only forty-five men of the Flanders Legion climbed into the waiting trucks. Forty-five out of five hundred.

Losses on the Russian side were even more frightful. The second battle of Lake Ladoga was a blood-bath. The peat-bog of Sinyavino, the woods of Kolpino and Krasnyy Bor, were one ghastly battlefield. Russian losses were estimated by the German Army Group North at 270,000.

The hospital and power-station of Gorodok were likewise wrecked by shellfire, devastated and abandoned. On 17th February the engineers of 170th Infantry Division eventually gave up this old corner-post of the front. About three miles farther south, on the so-called Burma Road, ran the new shortened line from the Neva via Sinyavino to the "Wengler barrier", held by North German and East Prussian grenadiers and by Silesian Jägers. The staying power of the German infantry, engineers, Panzerjägers, and artillerymen, and their perseverance under the worst possible weather and fighting conditions, once more prevented the enemy at Leningrad from reaching his objective.

This was a different fighting technique from that applied about the same time some nine hundred miles farther south by Field-Marshal von Manstein in smashing the Soviet offensives between Don and Donets. The C-in-C Army Group South achieved his success by daring and highly mobile operations of his fast troops and by the bold manoeuvring of his tank commanders. In the corridor south of Lake Ladoga, on the other hand, the decision lay in the hands of infantry-men, individual fighters, supported by engineers, Panzerjägers, and artillery.

Both methods show that, in spite of all crises, in spite of their dangerous reverses and heavy losses, the German armies in the East were still able to offset the numerical superiority of the Russians by flinging into the scales the morale and perseverance of the troops and the skill of their commanders.

All Soviet successes during the winter of 1942–43 were due to the fact that at the decisive focal points of their offensives the Germans were always short of a minimum of mobile reserves—of forces, in other words, which might be rapidly switched to any crisis point.

At Stalingrad, on the Manych and on the Mius, on the Don and on the Donets, it had always been the same problem. The decisive two or three experienced mobile divisions were lacking. The German Supreme Command was faced with a difficult and crucial task, on the solution of which depended not only the fate of the German front in the East but victory or defeat generally. The problem was how to raise strategic reserves to halt the Soviet mass attacks on all sectors of the front from the Arctic to the Black Sea.

4. Demyansk

The pocket in the Valday hills–One hundred thousand men on outpost duty–Pivot of Soviet strategy–Major von Rosenthal outwits Timoshenko–Retreat down the "Kurfürstendamm"–Evacuation within ten days–Twelve divisions saved–Timoshenko is censured.

SOME hundred and fifty miles south of Leningrad, between Lake Ilmen and Lake Seliger, the mushroom-shaped German front at the beginning of 1943 still projected deep into the Soviet hinterland.

That was the area of operations of the German II Army Corps around Demyansk. The mushroom contained twelve divisions with roughly 100,000 men. The stalk of the mushroom was only six miles across.

The story of these men is one of the most exciting of the War.

How did this "peninsula" of Demyansk come into being? Let us cast our minds back to the year 1941 when, during the German offensives of that year, the II Army Corps under Count Brockdorff-Ahlefeldt reached the strategically important Valday hills and cut the railway link between Moscow and Leningrad. But there the divisions got stuck. There, throughout the winter, they held on to their far-advanced bastion. It was an important bastion if the offensive against Moscow was ever to be resumed. The salient of Demyansk would then be an ideal jumping-off line for new offensives.

The Soviet General Staff was only too conscious of this. For that reason it applied the northern lever of its great winter offensive of 1941–42 just at the Valday hills. The Russians made every effort to burst through the German barrier between Lake Ilmen and Lake Seliger so as to make the German front at Leningrad and Rzhev collapse by a blow at the rear of Army Groups North and Centre.

The divisions of II Corps stood fast. On 8th February, 1942, however, they were encircled and thereafter had to be supplied by air. In 14,500 missions the transport units of the Luftwaffe with their JU-52s established the first successful airlift in history.

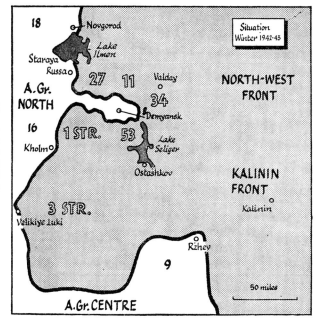

Map 28. The Demyansk "mushroom" projected deep into enemy territory. Hitler wanted to hold this position as a springboard for an offensive against Rzhev.

At the end of April 1942 a relief attack from outside and a counter-attack from within the pocket re-established the connection with the main German line on the Lovat river. It was near the ruined village of Ramushevo that, on 21st April at 1830 hours, the men who had thrust westward from inside the pocket were able to wave to the spearheads of General von Seydlitz-Kurzbach's relief forces across the thousand feet of turbulent water in the swollen Lovat.

"They're here! They're here!" shouted Captain Georg Bochmann's Panzerjägers of the "Totenkopf" SS Division. From the far side waved Captain Petter and a corporal of the engineer battalion of 8th Jäger Division.

Only the Lovat in spate divided them. As soon as the bridges were built a corridor existed again between the main German front of Sixteenth Army from Staraya Russa to Kholm and the divisions in the Demyansk area. Admittedly this corridor, or pipe, leading to the Demyansk combat zone was alarmingly narrow. But II Army Corps held on. It barred to the Soviets the way across the land bridge between Lake Ilmen and Lake Seliger. It tied down five Soviet armies. But throughout 1942 there was a permanent danger that the Russians might cut off the Demyansk mushroom at its stalk. For many months 100,000 German troops were on the brink of disaster.

The Soviet High Command realized its opportunity and made its Demyansk front one of the starting points of its great winter offensive of 1942, an offensive which was intended by Stalin to lead to the smashing of the German front in the East. Demyansk was an important factor in Stalin's calculations.

Just as Stalingrad was to be the decisive breach which would bring down the German southern front, so the Soviet offensive against Demyansk represented an attempt to roll up the front of Army Group North. On the Volga the Soviets succeeded in making the decisive penetration and annihilating the Sixth Army. On the Valday hills, on the other hand, the Russian calculation went badly wrong.

Stalin had chosen Marshal Timoshenko to annihilate the 100,000 men of the German II Corps. The marshal employed three armies. The Eleventh and Twenty-Seventh Armies were to attack the northern front of the narrow strip of land from Lake Ilmen, while the First Striking Army would thrust against the corridor from the south.

Timoshenko was confident of victory. His northern group comprised thirteen rifle divisions, nine rifle brigades, and armoured formations with altogether 400 tanks. Facing this massive might were three German divisions—the 8th Jäger Division, and the 81st and 290th Infantry Divisions. Timoshenko's southern group consisted of seven rifle divisions, four rifle brigades, and armoured formations comprising 150 tanks. Facing them was a single German division—the Rhineland-Westphalian 126th Infantry Division.

With these forces Timoshenko wanted to break through the six miles in the stalk of the mushroom of Demyansk. A mere three miles for each of the offensive groups. A small push, and II Corps with its 100,000 men would be in the bag.

The attack began on 28th November, 1942, with a massive bombardment by Soviet artillery. This was followed by carpet bombing. Low-level aircraft made continuous sorties over the German positions. The Soviets had complete control of the air. There was no appreciable Luftwaffe support for the German forces in the Demyansk combat area. Nor was there a single major armoured formation. After the departure of 8th Panzer Division for Vitebsk, Sixteenth Army was left only with assault guns and a few tank companies belonging to 203rd Panzer Regiment raised in France in 1941. These forces, fighting as part of "Group Saur" at Staraya Russa, were commanded by Lieutenant-Colonel Freiherr von Massenbach. This was the only operational reserve of the Army. All that separated the infantrymen at Demyansk from Timoshenko's waves of tanks were ditches, barbed wire, and mines.

Amidst smoke and dust, fire and lightning, the T–34s approached. Alongside them charged the rifle battalions, shouting "Urra!"

"Charge the German lines! Once you've got across the first few trenches you'll have done the job," the Political Commissar had assured the Russian companies. That had encouraged them. During the first few hours of the battle the Russians achieved a few penetrations on the northern front of the corridor. Timoshenko moved his reserves into the breaches.

Lieutenant-General Höhne, who commanded the formations inside the corridor, threw his engineers, signallers, gunners, and drivers into the penetration points. By companies and troops, Massenbach's 203rd Panzer Regiment was switched from Staraya Russa to the critical points. Captain Semisch cleared up several dangerous local penetrations with the bulk of 1st Battalion. But they were short now of infantry.

The II Corps in the Demyansk area proper—now, because of Brockdorff-Ahlefeldt's sickness, under the command of Lieutenant-General Laux—similarly scraped together its last reserves. Company offices were emptied, workshops and supply companies denuded of all staff, and every available man switched to the threatened fronts of the corridor. But none of this had any effect.

An SOS was sent to the neighbouring X Corps. But that Corps' formations had their hands full themselves at Staraya Russa.

An SOS was sent to Sixteenth Army. Its C-in-C, Colonel-General Busch, thereupon personally telephoned General Laux and expressed his regrets: "Laux, I can't spare a single battalion from the Army front."

And Army Group? Army Group had no reserves left either. Manstein's Eleventh Army, which a short while previously had helped to cope with the crisis of the first battle of Lake Ladoga, was no longer in the area. Developments at Stalingrad had compelled OKH to switch the Field-Marshal with his Army Command, his Army troops, and several other parts of his Army from the northern front to the southern front. Strong formations were held up at Velizh and Vitebsk and involved in heavy fighting. The fact was that the front was ablaze along its entire length.

Thus Höhne's divisions on the Valday hills were reduced to their own resources. The small combat groups defended themselves against a vastly superior force. Discipline, battle experience, and comradeship proved decisive factors. But where there is no centre of resistance left because the artillery has smashed everything up, where no anti-tank guns are left standing and not a single machine-gunner can fire any longer—there no amount of valour and discipline is of any avail. There a resolute enemy can break through and steamroll the remaining defenders. And steamroll was just what Timoshenko did. Two hundred or five hundred yards a day, at some points as much as a thousand. Any moment his decisive breakthrough into the rearward area of Sixteenth Army might take place.

In this dangerous situation, when it was clear that General Höhne's divisions would not be able to hold out much longer, Army Group North decided to take a gamble. At the beginning of December Field-Marshal von Küchler withdrew three divisions of his Eighteenth Army from the very thinly held lines along Lake Ladoga, from the ring surrounding the Oranienbaum pocket and from the Volkhov, and switched them into the Demyansk mushroom. He kept back the 28th Jäger Division which was to be sent to Finland to join Twentieth Mountain Army.

In December 1942 the two North German Infantry divisions, the 58th and 225th, as well as the Rhineland-Westphalian 254th Infantry Division, were about to face their most severe fighting yet.

To switch these divisions of Eighteenth Army into the threatened Demyansk corridor was a correct and a necessary decision. At the same time, their withdrawal from the northern sectors of the front meant that five weeks later, when the Soviets opened the second battle of Lake Ladoga, the German forces in the bottleneck between Leningrad and Volkhov were too weak to stop the Russians from breaking open the blockade of Leningrad.

It was the same pattern again: too few forces. Always and everywhere it was a case of too few forces. Since the autumn of 1942 it had been a case of "too little and too late" on all fronts.

However, Hitler was not to be diverted from his strategy of defending every inch of territory once conquered. He stuck to his theory

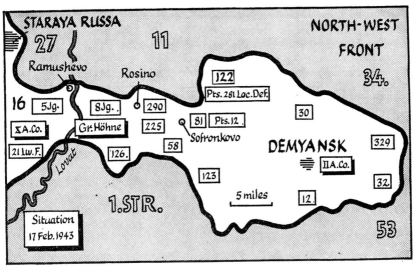

Map 29. From 28th November, 1942, until mid-February 1943, Marshal Timoshenko tried to nip off the six-mile-wide corridor to Demyansk.

that far advanced and exposed strongpoints must be held in order to keep favourable jumping-off positions for future offensives. Thus disaster ran its inexorable course.

The individual regiments and battalions of the three divisions hurrying down from the north were, immediately upon their arrival in the Staraya Russa area, rushed into the mushroom on trucks or on foot and at once sent into action.

A particularly threatened sector of the northern front of "Group Höhne" was defended by parts of the 8th Jäger Division and Major-General Schopper's Silesian 81st Infantry Division. This division was at the focal point of the Russian attack. Its combat groups were encircled. They fought their way free. They were encircled again. And again they burst the ring open in savage hand-to-hand fighting. On 17th December the two grenadier regiments of 81st Infantry Division, the 161st and 174th Grenadier Regiments, totalled 310 men. But in front of the divisions' sector lay 170 knocked-out Soviet tanks. These figures speak for themselves.

The Silesians were relieved by 225th Infantry Division on 17th December. During their first twenty-four hours in the line the Panzer-jägers of 376th Grenadier Regiment under Colonel Lorenz added a further eighteen T-34s to the tank graveyard in front of their main defensive line.

On the southern barrier of the mushroom were the units of Major-General Hoppe, the conqueror of Schlüsselburg. Fifteen months earlier the "fox of the peat-bog" had cracked the workers' settlements to the east of Leningrad, one by one, with a single reinforced regiment, and then, in co-operation with the Hamburg 20th Motorized Infantry Division, taken Schlüsselburg by a swift coup. Meanwhile Hoppe had been made Commander of the Rhineland-Westphalian 126th Infantry Division. His regiments were involved in extremely severe defensive fighting. Nevertheless the Soviets did not succeed in penetrating into the German main line. Luckily, they hesitated too long.

Hoppe collected his battalions, pulled them back to a shortened line, and established a new defensive front. Thus the mortally dangerous Russian breakthrough to the north was once more prevented at the last minute. On 4th December reinforcements arrived—the 209th Grenadier Regiment and the reconnaissance battalion of the Northwest German 58th Infantry Division.

A Soviet tank attack happened to come directly in front of the guns of the Panzerjägers and attached flak combat troops of 2nd Battalion, 209th Grenadier Regiment, and was completely shot up. Together with 58th Division, General Hoppe's 126th Infantry Division cleared up the situation on the southern front of the corridor and established a new defensive line against which all further Russian attacks came to grief.

The next combat formation of 58th Infantry Division, the 154th Grenadier Regiment, had been switched to the northern front of the corridor immediately upon arrival and was fighting as part of 290th Infantry Division.

The danger was greatest at Rosino. There the Russians were thrusting southwards with strong tank support. The battle was at its height. But in savage fighting the defenders succeeded there too in sealing off the penetration and establishing a new line. Timoshenko was halted. Furiously his troops tried to force another breach with tanks and flamethrowers. But they did not succeed. It was a miracle. How was it possible that Timoshenko, with his vast numerical superiority and strong concentration of effort at a few points, was prevented from achieving a strategic penetration of the overstretched German front?

The explanation cannot simply be found in the gallantry of the defenders. There were a number of other decisive factors. During the long period of "siege warfare" the German defensive positions had been most carefully fortified. Co-operation of flak, Panzerjägers, artillery, and assault guns with the infantry was excellent. Officers, NCOs, and men of the divisions employed were attuned to each other. And the two corps commanders, Generals Laux and Höhne, were outstanding officers, not only skilled commanders in the field, but also great improvisers.

In the fighting near Rosino two German assault guns of the Assault Gun Battalion 184 particularly distinguished themselves. Their actions in the battle zone of 377th Grenadier Regiment of 225th Infantry

Division are typical illustrations of why Timoshenko's armoured thrusts against the German lines on both sides of the Demyansk mushroom collapsed time and again. The reports of the two assault gun commanders, which are on record, are an impressive testimony of how these weapons intervened effectively at the focal points of the battle.

One of these assault guns, a Mark III with a short barrel, was commanded by Sergeant Horst Naumann, a twenty-one-year-old Berliner. His orders were to move up east of Sofronkovo on the left of the road, ready to engage targets to the north. Sergeant Riss with his long-barrel assault gun was standing to the right of the road, ready to engage targets to the east. The distance between the two was about a hundred yards. Between them was a small hill, the most advanced point of the German switchline. Here were the positions of Captain Widmayer's 3rd Battalion, 75th Jäger Regiment, which at Christmas had been switched from the sector of 5th Jäger Division on the left wing to this critical point and placed under 225th Infantry Division.

The time was 0930. Now and then there was enemy mortar fire. Otherwise things were quiet. As a rule the Russians attacked punctually at 1000 hours. So they probably would not have to wait long. It was just as they thought. A few minutes later hell was let loose—multiple mortars, artillery, trench mortars firing fragmentation and phosphorus shells.

"Close hatches," Sergeant Naumann ordered. Simultaneously the turret door was slammed shut at Sergeant Riss's long-barrel gun.

For an hour the assault gun crews sat in their steel boxes. All round them shells were pounding the ground. Splinters and chunks of rock rattled against the steel walls. Whenever a burst occurred quite close the men inside held their breath, waiting for the next. Would it be closer still? Or farther away? It was farther away. They heaved a sigh of relief. Suddenly everything fell silent. Naumann opened the turret door. He peered out. There was nothing to be seen. Everything was hidden by thick smoke. But the experienced gun commander knew that the distance to the edge of the wood was four hundred yards. That was where the enemy must be hiding. That was where he must come from.

They waited like hunters. This was nothing new to Naumann. He had already accounted for fifteen Soviet tanks. Would he come out on top again? Or was his number up today?

The smoke was dispersing. Naumann did not take his eyes off the slight hill eighty yards to the right of his gun. And there it was—a tank turret appearing over the skyline. Followed by the body of a T-34. It was approaching fast.

"Target to the right! Tank!" Naumann called. The sergeant gun-aimer already had the T-34 in his sights. He was turning the handles of the aiming mechanism. The first shell left the short barrel. A hard crash from the other side. "Direct hit!" said the commander. Gun-aimer and gun-loader were working like men possessed. The gun spewed out shell after shell.

The crew of the first T-34 was trying to abandon the tank. The hatches were flung open. Only fifteen feet from the immobilized Soviet tank, on the reverse slope, the German infantry were dug in. Hand-grenades and machine-gun fire knocked the Soviet tank crew to the ground.

The second T-34 appeared. Four times the short barrel barked. "He's burning!" Two more Russian sixteen-ton tanks appeared over the brow of the hill, firing. Their shells fell short. Naumann's gun-aimer needed two shells for each of them. Then these two Soviet tanks were in flames as well.

The sweat was pouring down the face of the gun-aimer. The engagement had only lasted a minute but four enemy tanks were already blazing in front of the assault gun.

"We'll move up that hill," Naumann commanded. The driver opened his throttle. The gun rattled forward. Before it had reached the top Sergeant Naumann, watching through his scissors telescope, spotted another T-34 approaching at about two hundred yards. "There's another! Fire!"

The Soviet tank received several hits. Then its turret door was flung open and flames were seen leaping out. Its ammunition was exploding in successive bursts of flame. Shells were now screaming down on the hill with the German assault gun.

"Enemy artillery is trying to find our range," Naumann said calmly over the intercom.

"Call it a day, Horst?" asked the driver. Naumann was about to agree when he noticed a sixth Soviet tank moving up towards the knocked-out ones.

"There's one more coming! Fire!" Speed decided the duel. The assault gun was quicker, and a sixth enemy tank was now smouldering, mortally hit, a mere forty yards away.

Horst Naumann, only just 21, was the first NCO in assault guns to receive the Knight's Cross. His battery was cited three times in the German High Command communiqué for its actions in the operations at Demyansk, and Naumann was subsequently made an officer for repeated bravery in the face of the enemy.

For another fortnight Timoshenko tried to force a breakthrough on the northern front by repeated attacks with his divisions and armoured brigades. Then their strength failed. More than two hundred Soviet tanks lay in front of the German positions, gutted or shot to pieces.

On the southern front of the Demyansk mushroom Timoshenko's First Striking Army mounted one more full-scale attack on 2nd January.

Once more it was the bled-white regiments of 126th Infantry Division and the battalions and combat groups of 58th and 225th Infantry Divisions which bore the brunt of the fighting. Timoshenko kept shifting the battle farther to the east, towards the lines of 123rd Infantry Division and parts of 12th Infantry Division. But the Marshal found no weak spot there either.

Then he gave it up. During the forty-six days from 28th November to 12th January his three armies had lost over 10,000 killed, as well as 423 tanks.

German casualties were not much smaller. The fierceness of the fighting is attested by the fact that the casualty list of the German divisions in the Demyansk corridor and combat area showed 17,767 officers, NCOs, and other ranks as killed in action, wounded, or missing. Seventeen thousand, seven hundred and sixty-seven men in fifty-seven days, between 28th November and 23rd January! A terrible blood-letting, a huge price paid by the outposts on the Valday hills.

But there was no doubt that the Russians would attack again. There was no doubt either that the price paid would go on increasing and that sooner or later the entire garrison would be killed. Another Stalingrad.

Was this risk justifiable any longer in view of the general situation with overstretched lines and insufficient forces? The answer of the commanders in the field was No.

No was also the answer of Colonel-General Zeitzler, Chief of the Army General Staff at the Führer's Headquarters. He tried to persuade Hitler to authorize a withdrawal from the bastion in the Valday hills. But Hitler at first was deaf to argument. "Hold on", was his thesis. The advanced "fortresses" of the front would, as he saw it, provide the jumping-off positions for future offensives. Hitler was still clinging to the strategy of conquering the Soviet Union by occupying its wide-open spaces and economically important territories. The gruesome warning of the ruins of Stalingrad had shaken him a little, but he was still reluctant to revise his opinion.

When it became obvious during the second half of January 1943 that the Sixth Army in Stalingrad was lost because it had not been ordered in time to withdraw from the Volga to the Don, Colonel-General Zeitzler again urged Hitler to spare the 100,000 men in the semi-pocket of Demyansk the fate of the Sixth Army and to save these indispensable twelve divisions for OKH.

Hitler no longer flatly rejected the request; he was now vacillating between common sense and obstinacy.

The war diarist of the German High Command, Helmuth Greiner, recorded on 30th January, 1943: "Yesterday the Führer asked for a report about supplies in the Demyansk area to enable him to come to a decision about the evacuation of the pocket. In this connection the Führer incidentally mentioned that he found it difficult to decide in favour of evacuation since, for the time being, he still intended to launch an operation towards Ostashkov to close the gap in the front, even though he regarded the elimination of Leningrad as more important."

An astonishing idea—an attack from Demyansk towards the Rzhev area! There was this huge gap of eighty miles between Army Groups North and Centre, and Hitler wanted to close it by an offensive from the threatened Demyansk pocket! Even though he "regarded the elimination of Leningrad as more important".

The elimination of Leningrad! Exactly twelve days previously the Russians had burst open the German ring round the city. And Hilpert's Corps group was just then desperately repulsing the furious attacks of vastly superior Soviet armies on the Sinyavino hills.

Once again it was clear that Hitler's once so cool and realistic assessment of strategic questions had given way to a pathological, unreal kind of wishful thinking. Nevertheless, the cup of Sixth Army once more passed by the II Corps at Demyansk. The 100,000 men in the Valday hills were saved by two factors—the grim and spectacular fall of Stalingrad, and a major in the Army General Staff by the name of von Rosenthal.

On 31st January, 1943, Hitler, convinced at last by the disastrous news from the Volga, yielded to Zeitzler's insistence. On the following day, 1st February, Zeitzler in a signal to Sixteenth Army gave II Corps the green light for the evacuation. The withdrawal in the almost roadless territory was to be carried out step by step and not a single item of *matériel* was to be left behind.

"Evacuation within seventy days," said the order of the High Command. Seventy days! The officers in the divisional staffs smiled. A lot could happen in seventy days! Certainly the withdrawal must not take anything like two and a half months. And fortunately, as we shall see, it took nothing like it. It was accomplished in one-seventh of the time allowed because General Laux and his staff off their own bats had been preparing the evacuation long before the order had arrived from the High Command.

Since mid-January Laux, in tacit agreement with Sixteenth Army, had been making the necessary preparations. The chief of operations of 225th Infantry Division, Major von Rosenthal, headed a planning staff in charge of all questions connected with evacuation. Naturally, the word evacuation could not appear in official service communications, and the term "operation rubbish clearing" was therefore used as a code name. All those not in the know were allowed to believe that the preparations being made were for an imminent offensive.

Clearance and labour columns were formed. Tracks were laid. Corduroy roads were built. A system of routes was brought into being, running radially from the head of the mushroom to the corridor, providing the opportunity for several columns to withdraw simultaneously. The men toiled hard. Prisoners of war were employed as well. Mechanized snow-ploughs chugged through the combat area. Thus emerged "Highway One", "Corduroy Avenue", "Kurfürstendamm", and "Silesian Promenade".

Anything unnecessary in the rearward depots, supernumerary vehicles, and equipment belonging to supply columns was brought to the narrow-gauge railway which began shortly behind the Pola and ran through the corridor to the Staraya Russa area. There the evacuated *matériel* accumulated at a number of collection points. Only mechanized and horse-drawn sleighs were kept back to be used for the secretly planned withdrawal through deep snow.

Major von Rosenthal and his planning staff worked day and night. Their "underground organization" worked with admirable precision and not a shadow of suspicion was aroused at High Command.

When the official evacuation order at last arrived on 1st February, 1943, most of the preparations had been completed. The evacuation of the heavy equipment could be started at once. By mid-February, at a date roughly when, without Rosenthal's preparations, the evacuation would just about have begun, some 8000 tons of equipment, 5000 horse-drawn and 1500 motor vehicles had already been evacuated. Corps informed the Chief of the Army General Staff that it was now possible to reduce the evacuation period to forty days. Even that was not the last word.

Since early February 1943 howling blizzards had been sweeping the Valday hills. They piled up the snow into drifts many feet deep, and they buried the tracks and roads which had been laid through the forest. Mechanized snow-ploughs had to be brought in to clear them again. All means of camouflage were employed to deceive the enemy and his sources of information among the civilians in the combat area.

An icy wind from Lake Seliger swept over the high ground in front of the main defensive line of 32nd Infantry Division. It whipped up the snow and quickly blotted out the tracks of the German patrol on reconnaissance in the difficult terrain in front of the lines of 94th Grenadier Regiment. But in the lee of a huge snowdrift the men again discovered what Sergeant Kretschmer had spotted once or twice before—a solitary ski trail.

The sergeant pointed to it with his ski stick. "That one's barely half an hour old—someone must have crossed over just before we got here."

Kretschmer's companions nodded. Corporal Behrens said, "No wonder Ivan's always so well informed about everything that's happening on our side. Once he discovers we are planning to retreat he's sure to pounce on us."

On their skis the men trudged back to their battalion command post. Sergeant Kretschmer made his report: "Solitary ski track in the direction of the Russian lines." And, being an experienced leader of assault parties and patrols, he added: "Either some Soviet civilian from the combat zone who's working as a contact, or a Soviet agent, disguised as a local inhabitant and probably living in one of those caves used by the local civilians for shelter."

All headquarters personnel were familiar with this danger. With a line held so thinly it was impossible to prevent a shuttle service of enemy agents. One had to make the best of it. The best, in this case, meant feeding false information to those travelling between the lines. They had to be fooled, they had to be fed red herrings and sold pups.

All along the line, therefore, at the beginning of February, special-duty detachments appeared from strange units and attracted a good deal of attention. Among the Schleswig-Holstein 30th Infantry Division, for instance, "handing-over parties" of a Luftwaffe field division were being held. On the sector of 26th Fusilier Regiment a handing-over party of a Luftwaffe field regiment was very much in evidence on 12th February, busily preparing the "take-over".

The deception was also kept up in the ether. Loosely coded signals asking for reinforcements were sent to Army Headquarters. Army replied with prearranged orders concerning the construction of accommodation for new units, heavy artillery, and mortars. Ghost units which did not exist at all set up radio transmitters at very clearly discernible staff quarters.

The secret skiers between the fronts, the partisans, and the agents reported it all to the Soviet Command. But the Russians were suspicious. What their agents were reporting from the combat zone, what scouts were discovering and aerial reconnaissance photographing, did indeed suggest reinforcements for the German front at Demyansk. But was not a withdrawal more logical?

Take that report about the horses. The infantry divisions had been bringing them up again into the combat zone from the rearward areas. Was not that a measure which clearly suggested withdrawal? And the German troops were talking about withdrawal. And what they talked about soon reached the native huts.

Suspicion or not, deception or not—the Soviet High Command decided to launch a new, instant offensive against the narrow corridor leading to the Demyansk combat area.

The *History of the Great Fatherland War* reports the considerations which then engaged the Soviet High Command in connection with these operations. We read in Volume 3: "The broadly based offensives of the Red Army in the south, on the central sector of the front and at Leningrad were tying down the enemy's forces and compelling him to expend his reserves. Thus favourable conditions had also been created for the elimination of the Demyansk bridgehead in which there were altogether 12 divisions representing the main forces of the German Sixteenth Army." A correct and logical analysis.

The German Eighteenth Army, the neighbour of Sixteenth Army on the left, was fully occupied at Leningrad. South of Demyansk, at Vitebsk, the German LIX Corps was engaged in heavy fighting at the junction between Army Groups Centre and North. At Rzhev the Ninth Army had been tied down in a heavy defensive battle for more than two months. And farther south Field-Marshal von Manstein needed every single battalion in order to cope with Popov's Armoured Group and with Vatutin's thrust across the Donets to the Dnieper.

It was fairly obvious therefore that Sixteenth Army could not count on effective help from its neighbours if things should get dangerous again around Demyansk. As for any reserves of its own, Sixteenth Army had none left at all. Its very last armoured detachment, the 203rd Army Panzer Regiment, known as the Army's fire brigade, had been sent to France by order of OKW at the beginning of the year.

The Soviets knew all that. And knowledge of this situation gave them confidence. Once again it was Marshal Timoshenko who received from the Soviet High Command the task of capturing the 100,000 German troops in the Demyansk area. It was clear that the Marshal's career would be in jeopardy if he failed again this time. The "Fox from the Don" therefore employed all the forces at his disposal for a pincer attack against the narrowest point of the corridor.

On Monday, 15th February, at 0600 the German troops were rudely awakened in their dug-outs in the Demyansk mushroom by a sudden barrage of Soviet artillery. "Hell!" they said. "They're going to get us after all, at the last minute!"

As we can read in the *History of the Great Fatherland War,* the Soviet operations had been carefully co-ordinated. Three days previously, on 12th February, the new Russian offensive had opened on the Leningrad front, south of Lake Ladoga, against the Kirov railway. Thus the German Eighteenth Army was tied down. Army group North would not be able to get any reserves this time from that source.

At the Rzhev salient and in the penetration area of Velikiye Luki the Soviets were likewise attacking. Hence no help was to be expected from the neighbouring Army Group, especially as its northern wing had been tied down in heavy fighting for a number of weeks. Thus the divisions of Sixteenth Army on the Valday hills had to cope with this new mortal threat unaided.

Since 0700 hours Timoshenko had been attacking the northern front of the Demyansk corridor with six rifle divisions and three tank regiments; his blow was against the positions of three German divisions—the 290th, the 58th, and the 254th Infantry Divisions.

On the southern front of the corridor the attack of the Soviet First Striking Army with its six rifle divisions and three rifle brigades struck at the regiments of General Hoppe's 126th Infantry Division. Six against one! And the first wave of the Russian attack moreover included fifty heavy T-34s.

There were dangerous penetrations, especially on the southern sector of 126th Infantry Division. But nowhere did Timoshenko succeed in achieving a breakthrough. The German Command in the battle area realized that this was only the prelude. So far the Soviets had employed only two armies, but there were altogether five of them ranged round the Demyansk mushroom. Five armies against 12 divisions! The full-scale Soviet attack from all sides could begin at any minute. In view of this situation, and above all in view of the critical position on the southern front of the corridor, there was not a minute to be lost. The front had to be shortened. General Höhne needed reserves for the dangerously threatened walls of the corridor. And then—get out of the trap!

General Laux spoke to Sixteenth Army over the directional radio link and put his anxieties to the Commander-in-Chief. This useful and secure wireless link had been set up by 1st Luftwaffe Signals Regiment in May 1942. It was an excellent link and, above all, saved the many

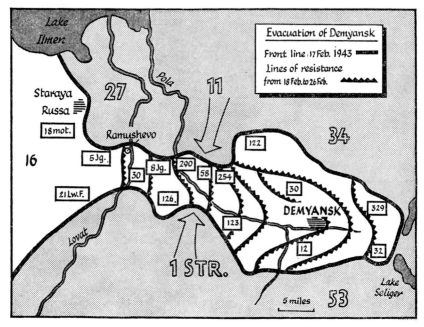

Map 30. Operation Ziethen, the evacuation of the Demyansk pocket. In ten days, twelve divisions pulled back step by step.

casualties which used to be incurred time and again in repairing the long-distance cables. Before this directional radio link was set up the 3rd Company, 1st Luftwaffe Signals Regiment, had lost fifty men killed and a hundred wounded in the course of a few weeks merely from repairing and servicing cable lines—that was half the company. All this was now a thing of the past. And the new link, moreover, was free from interference.

"What's your suggestion?" Field-Marshal Busch, a reasonable man, asked the corps commander.

Laux replied: "The evacuation must start at once, Herr Generalfeldmarschall."

"Is that possible?" Busch asked anxiously.

"It is possible," replied Laux. And it was possible.

The preparations made by von Rosenthal's special staff had progressed so far that Laux could now undertake to accomplish the withdrawal in twenty days. Twenty days instead of the originally envisaged seventy. In view of the dangerous situation the Führer's Headquarters agreed. At once the signal for Ziethen, the code name for the evacuation, was sent out. The date was the 17th February, 1943.

In the late afternoon, in the thickening dusk, the divisions farthest to the east and north wheeled back to the first line of resistance. The Schleswig-Holstein 30th and the Mecklenburg 12th Infantry Divisions, forming as they did the corner-posts, remained in their positions for another twenty-four hours. The most daring and most dangerous withdrawal in the history of war had begun.

The war diary of the Schleswig-Holstein 30th Infantry Division provides an impressive picture of the precision which marked the evacuation, of the organizational skill of headquarters staffs and of the rigid discipline of the troops. It had all been accurately planned.

Traffic control and movement supervision ensured the smooth passage of columns at crossroads, bridges, and bottlenecks. All movement was calm and unhurried. There were no lights. There was complete silence. Whenever vehicles broke down they pulled out of the column to perform the necessary repairs on a quickly cleared patch of ground alongside the route, and subsequently filed in again. A continuous reminder of the threatening danger was the distant gunfire from the corridor. If the walls of the corridor gave, the troops would be faced with disaster.

But the troops showed no nervousness. They had full confidence in the regiments which by then had been holding the lines along the barely six-mile-wide corridor for several months. They would also manage the next twenty days. From hour to hour the front along the bottleneck was reinforced with reserves drawn from the retreating divisions.

But a lot might still go wrong. Every battle is a mathematical problem with more than one unknown factor. One of them is the enemy: who knows what he is planning and what he is doing? Another unknown quantity is the weather. And now the weather began to intervene. Violent blizzards set in. Within a few hours all roads and tracks were buried under the snow. Men and horses toiled through the deep, powdery snow. Mechanized vehicles sank to their axles in the soft, white mass. There were congestions. There were hold-ups. There was a danger of the timetable collapsing, even though everything so far had worked like clockwork. The enemy, too, intervened. By the morning of 19th February the Soviet Command realized that the positions on the eastern edge of the combat zone had been abandoned. The Soviets took up the pursuit with cavalry and ski troops. The weather favoured them. The fast ski battalions chased through the snowstorm, burst through the German rearguards, and tried to gain the roads to block the withdrawal of the German divisions. The Eutin 1st Battalion, 6th Infantry Regiment, under Major Vogel was marching through gently-falling snow. Suddenly the Russians were upon them. In hand-to-hand fighting, with hand-grenades and cold steel, Vogel's men had to fight their way through. Through fields deep in snow, past enemy-held villages, the companies eventually regained contact with the withdrawal road.

But there was one thing which cheered the troops. For the first time in many months they enjoyed lavish German artillery fire. Now there was no longer any need to save ammunition. The huge stacks of shells in the ammunition dumps, hitherto jealously guarded by the calculating pencils of superintendents, now seemed inexhaustible. And they had to be used up. Hence all guns were firing to capacity.

During the stormy night of 19th–20th February the third interception line was taken up accurately on schedule—the front line ran in a wide arc around the town of Demyansk. In this way the highway and the bridges over the Yavon and Pola rivers were held open for the withdrawing formations. The well-established positions were held by regiments of the 12th, 30th, and 122nd Infantry Divisions. Under cover from them the mechanized and horse-drawn units of the heavy and light artillery, the flak, and the Panzerjägers, as well as signal troops and ambulances moved through the town. The marching columns of grenadier regiments were taken along a route by-passing Demyansk.

In the raging blizzard every man had to watch out not to lose contact with the man in front of him, not to get parted from his column, not to drift from the trodden path. Patrols on skis provided cover between the moving columns. Their job was to prevent the Russians from infiltrating into the withdrawing formations. Corps and divisions had issued strict orders not to light open fires at resting points so as not to provide signposts for the enemy.

But it happened all the same. One column came across a fairly well-stocked supply dump on the fringe of Demyansk. The quartermaster in charge generously distributed the stores to the passing troops. The stocks included a few casks of French cognac. There was a good deal of drinking and the troops filled their hip flasks. The cold night tempted them into indulging rather too freely.

With drunkenness came recklessness. Soon a small wooden house just off the main street of Demyansk was in flames. It had a sobering effect, but it was too late. The howling gale drove a fierce shower of sparks through the streets and alleys of the town. The sparks flew through the cracks of the scantily boarded-up windows and found their way through the rotten roofs into attics. Everywhere fires sprang up. The raging flames steeped the horse-drawn carts and the hurrying columns in a ghostly light.

Transit through the town was badly disorganized. Telephone wires from rearguard headquarters to Corps melted in the fierce heat of the burning houses. It was too late to save anything. Demyansk burnt down to the ground—with the exception of a single building, the field hospital with fifty seriously wounded Soviet troops. It was saved from the blaze by engineers and remained intact. The wounded were left behind in the care of their Russian doctor and nursing staff.

The Soviets were now vigorously pressing upon the retreating German formations. Rearguards were involved in heavy fighting. Particularly dangerous situations arose at the bridges over the Pola and the Yavon. Yet nowhere did Timoshenko's fast troops succeed in overtaking or enveloping the German divisions. The fifth and sixth interception lines were taken up according to plan.

By 27th February, ten days after the beginning of the withdrawal, the battle area of Demyansk and the corridor had been evacuated. Ten days had seen the completion of a task scheduled for twenty, and originally envisaged to take seventy days. A fantastic achievement.

Even the Soviet history of the war cannot deny the German achievement and, in consequence, Timoshenko's failure. "Mistakes in the command of our troops in the field are to be blamed," we read in the *History of the Great Fatherland War*, as published during the Khrushchev era.

Marshal Timoshenko was held responsible for the German success. True, some 1200 square miles of ground were abandoned to the Soviets. But not a single gun was left behind. Not a single vehicle in working order fell into Timoshenko's hands, and not a single serviceable weapon. Several hundred tons of ammunition were blown up; 1500 damaged vehicles and 700 tons of food supplies which could no longer be removed were rendered useless. All that was left behind were 10,000 carefully tended graves—silent witnesses to fourteen months of savage fighting around Demyansk.

Twelve divisions—*i.e.*, 100,000 men with all their weapons—had been saved. These were appreciable reserves for the Army Group's threatened northern front. They enabled Field-Marshal Busch to repulse all further Soviet thrusts across the Lovat into the rear of Army Group North. In the Staraya Russa area alone Timoshenko's armies were to suffer costly defeats in five major battles during the next few weeks.

5. Operation Buffalo

Rzhev, a breakwater in the Russian flood–Four summer battles and four winter battles–The front is 200 miles too long–Retreat for 250,000 men–"Your officers are packing their bags!"–The engineers' "infernal gardens"–A bridge blown by telephone–A fantastic retreat–Twenty-two divisions are freed.

O F all the countless Russian towns and villages which during the Second World War were at the centre or near the centre of decisive battles, such as that fought at Demyansk, about half a dozen have gone down as chapter headings in military history. Tens of thousands of soldiers remember those focal points of the war in Russia and will never forget them. Names like Stalingrad. Or Sevastopol. Or Rostov. Certainly Leningrad and Moscow. And last but not least Rzhev, a town on the upper Volga. At the beginning of the war it had 54,000 inhabitants and a varied, thousand-year-old history.

From October 1941 until March 1943 this town was a corner-post and a crucial point of the Eastern Front. Because of its favoured situation in the upper reaches of the Volga, where timber had been rafted downstream through the centuries, Rzhev had always been a highly coveted prize and a bone of contention of the princes and grand dukes of Lithuania, Tver, Kalinin, and Moscow. It had been much wooed and much fought over. Since time immemorial it had been the object of economic and military rivalries between the Baltic and the upper Volga. Its strategic position also determined its fate in the Second World War. In October 1941, grenadier battalions of the East Prussian 206th Infantry Division and the reconnaissance battalion of the Rhineland-Westphalian 26th Infantry Division had taken Rzhev in the course of their offensive against Moscow and, as a result, had been the first German units to get to the Volga. Europe's biggest river, the national river of Russia, had been reached.

In vain did the Soviets try to dislodge the Germans. During their first big winter offensive they concentrated their efforts on this point. They succeeded in recapturing the town of Kalinin, also on the Volga. The German command was compelled to abandon this easternmost position of its drive against Moscow. But Rzhev held out and became the decisive bulwark of Army Group Centre in the strategic approaches to Moscow.

In January and February 1942 Colonel-General Yeremenko had personally been ordered by Stalin to dislodge the divisions of the German Ninth Army with his Striking Army. He first mounted an unsuccessful frontal attack on Rzhev and next tried to envelop it. In savage and costly fighting the regiments of Ninth Army held their ground. Yeremenko and his guardsmen swept south across the frozen string of lakes from the direction of Ostashkov. There was a serious threat that Army Group Centre might be made to collapse by this thrust from the north.

But Rzhev, like Demyansk, stood unshaken, a huge breakwater in Yeremenko's flood, a flood which was halted at Velizh and Velikiye Luki. It was in the Rzhev area that Ninth Army under Colonel-General Model accomplished the turning-point in the first Russian winter battle on the Central Front.

Through four more summer and winter battles Rzhev held out like a rock. Officers and men of Ninth Army surpassed all standards of military achievement. And Colonel-General Model revealed himself in those operations as one of the major defensive strategists of the last War.

Soviet specialized publications on the history of the War testify to the anxiety caused to the Soviet command by the fact that Rzhev remained firmly in German hands. Model's army was aimed at Moscow like a fist—the Kremlin was a mere 112 miles away. As long as this force was within 112 miles of Moscow the threat to the Soviet capital persisted. And so long as Hitler had a chance of resuming the offensive against the heart of the U.S.S.R. there was some military sense in holding on to Rzhev.

The disaster of Stalingrad, however, finally put an end to all hopes of a new large-scale offensive against Moscow. Following the loss of Sixth Army with a quarter of a million men, the German Command lacked the manpower for such a vast offensive operation.

But Hitler continued to put off the decision—just as he did at Demyansk—to abandon this exposed and strength-consuming salient 330 miles in length. He stubbornly defended his view against OKH, against Army Group Centre, and against the commanders in the field.

Today, with the benefit of hindsight, it is easy to criticize Hitler's hesitation. But at the time it was a genuinely difficult decision. After the reverses of the first Russian winter the salient of Rzhev was the only projecting bastion left to the Germans on the way to the Kremlin. It was the last remaining piece of ground on the Volga. There, in the Rzhev area, was Vyazma, the town which had gone down in history, the spot where, in 1941, in the decisive double battle of Vyazma and Bryansk, the last Soviet resistance in the approaches to Moscow had been swept aside and where 630,000 prisoners had been taken.

Then the approach of winter had nipped the fruit of victory on this historic battlefield. Supposing one were to try again . . .? Supposing one were to take another chance . . .? What military leader could close his eyes to such speculations? What general would readily surrender such a position?

To evacuate Rzhev would mean not just abandoning a line or a position; it would mean abandoning all hopes of victory. Hitler knew that once his forces abandoned the town they were not likely to return.

But the disaster of Stalingrad and the subsequent crisis on all parts of the front, from Leningrad through Kharkov to the Caucasus, compelled Hitler to yield to the persistent advice of his Chief of the General Staff. On 6th February, 1943 he authorized Ninth Army and parts of Fourth Army to withdraw from the Rzhev salient and take up a switch-line that was two hundred miles shorter and formed the chord to the arc of the former bulge.

The code name for this great withdrawal was Operation Buffalo. The OKH staff had allowed Ninth Army four weeks to prepare this huge exodus. Four weeks! This would ensure that the troops were ready for defence in their new positions before the onset of the muddy period.

Colonel-General Model was sitting in the map room of his advanced battle HQ near Sychevka with his closest collaborators and assigned each man his task. The chief of staff, Colonel Freiherr von Elverfelt, the chief of operations, and the transport officers were squatting over stacks of maps and paper. The senior engineer officer of the army was also present.

What was to be done? First of all the new defensive position had to be reconnoitred. Then the separate lines of resistance had to be laid down for the disengagement.

And then came the evacuation proper of the operations area, which was over sixty miles deep. About 125 miles of roads had to be built for motor vehicles. Nearly 400 miles of tracks had to be laid for sleighs and horse-drawn transport. And all that in the depth of winter. All weapons and other supplies were to be evacuated. So were all other economic assets, such as livestock, grain stores, and agricultural machinery. For this purpose 200 railway trains and motor convoys with a capacity of 10,000 tons were available. Loading schedules had to be worked out for each wagon and each vehicle. Even the saddle-bags of motor-cyclists and horsemen were included in the calculations.

Nothing was left to chance. A particularly important task was the evacuation of 60,000 civilians, the families of men and women who had collaborated with the Germans. They could not be left behind and abandoned to Soviet reprisals. Finally, when all rail transport had been completed, some 600 miles of rails and 800 miles of wire were to be dismantled and salvaged.

The vital basis of this huge withdrawal operation was the movement schedule for twenty-nine divisions as well as Army and OKH troops—in all 250,000 men with all their weapons and equipment. All this in the face of a strong enemy. Transport and combat readiness, withdrawal and fighting had to be co-ordinated. It was a gigantic enterprise.

Security was a major problem. Everything had to be camouflaged as far as possible, even from one's own troops. Once again, however, it turned out that all secrecy was, in the final analysis, useless. About mid-February, when the German troops were still largely in the dark about the secret Operation Buffalo, the Russian loudspeakers in the line were already inciting the German rank and file: "Your officers are packing their bags. Make sure they don't leave you behind!" Soviet espionage was again exceedingly well informed. "Werther" was serving "Director" extremely well.

In fact, the German officers had other things to worry about than their bags. One problem that gave them a great many headaches was whether to base the withdrawal on sleighs or wheeled vehicles. At the time, in mid-February, the snow still lay deep. But what would conditions be like in early March? There was only one way out—prepare for all weathers.

The thaw came on 1st March. The roads were under water. At 1900 hours the withdrawal was due to start. So it must be wheeled vehicles. Like a gigantic, creaking caterpillar the army moved into action. Telephone wires were taken up, mines were primed. But with nightfall the temperature suddenly dropped again. Ice on all roads. So it was sleighs after all. Feverishly everything was transferred. At 1900 hours punctually the most advanced formations began their withdrawal. Only rear parties remained in contact with the enemy.

The battalions of the Munster 6th Infantry Division moved out of their positions on the Volga near Rzhev. They marched through the night. They were weighed down by weapons, trenching tools, field packs, and hand-grenades. After the long period of positional warfare the troops were no longer used to marching. In silence they trudged alongside sleighs and carts. The columns grew longer and longer. At

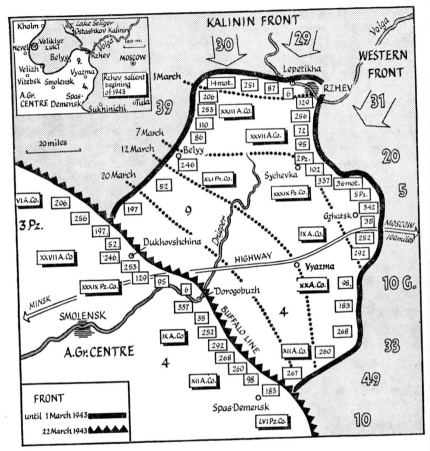

Map 31. Twenty-nine divisions were needed to hold the salient of Rzhev. Operation Buffalo in the spring of 1943 resulted in a shortening of the front and the saving of twenty-two divisions. A massive reserve was established in this way.

last, at break of day, the companies reached the first prepared fortified positions in the snow. They had covered twenty miles.

In the positions on the Volga, meanwhile, only the rear parties were left—one-third of the original complements. Where nine groups had been established the previous day there were now only three. The men scuttled to and fro, from one gun position to another, loosing bursts of fire from rifles and machine-guns in order to convey the impression of a fully manned position.

But the Russians were suspicious and decided to investigate for themselves. As darkness gave way to the first grey light of day shadowy figures appeared before the trenches of 9th Company, 58th Grenadier

Regiment. They were immediately on top of the defenders. Now they were in the trenches. Lieutenant Hötzel, commanding the rear party of the regiment, just then happened to be in the sector. He was well known for his sangfroid. He first ordered one of the machine-guns to keep raking the forefield to prevent any further Russians from getting near the trenches. Then, with a party of men he rolled up the occupied length of trench from both ends.

Half an hour later it was all over. The Russians who got away, who escaped from the trench back into no-man's-land, had been unable to take a single prisoner back with them. And just that had been their objective. The Soviet Command remained in the dark.

On the left-hand sector of the old position on the Volga, however, the situation developed more dangerously. There, in a projecting salient at Lepetikha, the Russians prefaced their attack with a murderous mortar bombardment. Then two hundred Red Army men burst from a ravine on the far side of the Volga and charged across the ice.

The Soviet mortaring had fortunately caused only few casualties among the thinly-held German lines. As the Russians came charging across the river Hötzel's men were already behind their light infantry guns and machine-guns. The Soviets had the river to cross, followed by a patch of open ground. As they were halfway across the river Hötzel commanded: "Open fire!"

Guns and machine-guns hurled their salvoes and burst right among the attacking infantry. Only a few men got through to the German trenches. There, overpowered, they surrendered.

Thus a handful of bold grenadiers, armed only with infantry weapons, covered the rear of the withdrawing formations. Twenty-four hours after the bulk of the forces had withdrawn the rearguards abandoned their positions and took up a new defensive line about four miles farther back.

Things were getting serious. By now the Soviets must have spotted the withdrawal. And they would surely follow up vigorously with strong formations in order to overtake the departing German divisions, cut off their retreat, encircle as many as possible, and wipe them out.

That had to be prevented at all costs. Rearguards, as a rule, are not fitted for that kind of task for long. How then was the Russian pursuit to be slowed down effectively?

The demolition of all roads, tracks, railways, bridges, and buildings, as so thoroughly practised by the Soviets during the German advance and as ordered by the Führer's Headquarters for the armies on the southern front ever since the disaster of Stalingrad, was not a really effective means of holding up an enemy for long. Moreover, it had been shown time and again that rearguards usually lacked both the time and the manpower for a really effective demolition of all vital installations.

There was, however, another possibility. In both World Wars one of the most efficient ways of delaying an enemy pursuit was the use of mines; these could be employed in a great many different ways. First of all, there was the tank mine which went off as soon as something heavy, such as an armoured fighting vehicle, a lorry, or a gun, pressed on it. Then there was the anti-personnel mine whose detonator responded to the slightest touch and which either exploded instantaneously or first bounced up into the air to about three feet and then exploded, in which case the fragments would strike a man's head and body.

With these infernal eggs the evacuated German positions, trenches and dug-outs, river and stream crossings, sunken roads, and bottlenecks were virtually paved. Linked high explosive charges were cunningly placed at artificial road blocks.

But this kind of conventional mining was nothing new to the Soviets. During their own retreats in the first two years of the War they had gained a lot of experience in this field and become past masters in the art of mine warfare. As a result, they knew where to expect mines and how to render them harmless. Conventional mining, therefore, was no longer an efficient means of seriously delaying the Soviet advance in wide open spaces. Something more effective had to be done.

The senior engineer officers of Ninth Army and its Corps knew their business. They had experience of the First World War, and some of them also of Africa, where Rommel had shown consummate skill in using mines for protecting and blocking the dangerously exposed desert areas.

These "infernal gardens", as Rommel used to call the sophisticated minefields, were perfect death traps combining both psychological and weaponry refinement in the lay-out of mines and explosive charges. An enemy formation blundering into such an "infernal garden" immediately lost its offensive momentum. For if the man in front was torn to pieces, or one's neighbour killed or severely wounded, when vehicles were blown to smithereens and even tanks were immobilized, then obviously no-one dared to take another step until the ground had been probed inch by inch. When the mine-clearing parties arrived their electrical detectors, responding to all metal, frequently only discovered dummies—empty food tins or shell fragments deliberately dug in. And as soon as a wanderer in the "infernal garden" became careless again he would step on a genuine mine and be killed. Or if he discovered the danger in time and dug up the mine, and the one next to it, and yet another, he might still be blown sky-high because frequently a second layer of hidden mines was laid below the ones which had just been cleared.

Rommel's African "infernal gardens" were planted at Rzhev in a novel manner.

The experienced engineers of Ninth Army invented ever new ways of concealing their mines. They fixed the charges to the front doors of houses. If the door was pushed open death would strike on the threshold with fire and splinters. The detonators of hidden tank mines were connected to windows by means of thin wire. If the window was opened death would strike again. Death would lurk even behind harmless ladders, hand-carts, shovels, and spades. As soon as a tool was lifted off the wall a booby-trap would be touched off by a hidden wire. Insidious infernal machines were hidden under the treads of stairs. They lurked in stoves, wired to the stove door. Booby-traps were connected to the lids of alluring half-open boxes with "documents"—always objects of particular interest to the Russians. Engineers specially trained for this type of mine warfare frequently set their traps under the fire of the charging enemy. The effect of this mine warfare was staggering. What the most powerful rearguards could not have achieved the mines and booby-traps accomplished in a most spectacular manner. During the first twenty-four hours of their vigorous follow-up the Russians suffered such heavy losses in the "infernal gardens" of Rzhev that something like panic broke out. The air was humming with Russian signals containing warnings, blood-curdling accounts, and urgent instructions to be extremely careful. Fear of hidden German mines haunted the Russian troops like a spectre, slowing down their advance.

The radio-monitoring service of the withdrawing divisions was able to follow the devastating effects of the German mines owing to the fact that the Soviet signals were usually transmitted *en clair*. Thus 206th Infantry Division intercepted the following message from a Russian commander to his division: "I stable my horse and enter the house—and there is a big bang. Stable and horse are gone. Those damned Fritzes plant their mines anywhere except where we suspect them." Another signal prohibited the troops to enter any buildings, use any wells, or pick up any valuables until mine-clearing parties had gone over the ground. A mine psychosis arose, corroding the courage, the nerves, and the spirit of the pursuers. Just that had been Model's objective.

In a mere twenty-one days he evacuated the salient of Rzhev. In twenty-one days the divisions of Ninth and Fourth Armies withdrew roughly 100 miles, fighting all the way. They abandoned a front line of 330 miles and, 100 miles farther back, occupied a new line forming the chord of the old arc, a frontage of only 125 miles. A saving of over 200 miles. And of virtually an entire Army. An Army HQ staff had been freed, four Corps HQ staffs, and twenty-two divisions, including three Panzer divisions. It was a decisive strategic move. For Army Group Centre it meant the end of the terrible period without reserves which had followed the heavy losses of the winter of Stalingrad.

Official Soviet military history, however, refuses to acknowledge Model's achievement. It refuses to admit that, faced with two Soviet Army Groups, whose divisions were continually attacking the German salient, one and a half German Armies succeeded in withdrawing without serious danger. The Soviet Armies accomplished not a single penetration into the German withdrawal, not a single serious thrust into the German flank, let alone any envelopment.

This circumstance amounts to a serious criticism of the tactical skill of the Soviet leaders at the time. That is why Soviet war historians react so irritably to all examinations of this operation.

It is simply not in keeping with historical truth if the Soviet *History of the Great Fatherland War*, Volume III, states: "By means of vigorous following up, the Kalinin Front and the Western Front interfered with the planned progress of the German withdrawal. The German troops left behind part of their equipment and suffered heavy losses in men and technical material."

It then continues: "Since the War a number of West German military historians have attempted to represent the retreat of the German troops as a model of a successful planned withdrawal. However, the losses suffered by the enemy during his retreat testify to the questionable nature of all such claims. His forces, compelled by the Red Army's blows to withdraw precipitately from Rzhev, were not given the time to evacuate the town systematically."

In support of this thesis the Soviet publication quotes the writings of General of Infantry Grossmann, commanding the Munster 6th Infantry Division. But Grossmann, the chronicler of the operations around Rzhev, proves the exact opposite in his account of the engagement of his old division, employed there to the very end, as well as in his account of the battle as a whole.

The war diaries of the 78th Assault Division and the 98th Infantry Division, which are preserved in their entirety, provide further evidence. The allegation that Rzhev had to be evacuated by Model precipitately is disproved by an interesting and probably unique episode in military history. Hitler, made suspicious by many an unhappy experience and disaster due to bridges not having been blown up in time, had decided to convince himself personally that the big bridge over the Volga in Rzhev had in fact been demolished after the withdrawal of the German troops.

Needless to say, Hitler had no intention of driving to Rzhev in person. Instead he conceived the quaint idea of supervising the demolition of the bridge by telephone. Thus a direct telephonic connection was established between Hitler's situation hut at "Werewolf", the Führer's Headquarters at Vinnitsa, and the demolition squad at the Rzhev bridge. Receiver pressed to his ear, the Führer and Supreme Commander of the German Armed Forces thus personally supervised the blowing up of the bridge astride the river. He could hear the crash of the detonation as the massive piers were blown sky-high. Only this acoustic demonstration convinced him that his orders had in fact been obeyed. It was several hours after this demolition and after the last German rearguards had left the town that the first Soviet scouts began to probe across the Volga.

Strictly according to plan, Model's divisions and the left wing of General Henrici's Fourth Army took up the newly established and well-fortified line from Spas-Demensk via Dorogobuzh to Dukhov-shchina, the new Buffalo line, before the onset of the muddy period. Within a period of seven weeks the position had been established by 29,000 engineers and construction troops protected by wire obstacles and minefields, and reinforced with strongpoints and bunkers. The bulk of the forces arrived, about-turned, and stood fast.

The German front held. The dramatic winter battle of 1942–43 was over. With the successful evacuation of the Rzhev salient all critical spots at Army Groups North and Centre had been eliminated. In the south the entire industrial region of the Donets basin was again in German hands.

6. Velikiye Luki

Fortress in the swamp–Three divisions against one regi-ment–Aleksandr Matrosov of the Guards Rifles–Unsuc-cessful relief attempt–Fifteen tanks rumble into Citadel's courtyard–Diphtheria in the "Budapest" strongpoint–One slice of bread and eight rounds in the pistol–"I've come from Velikiye Luki"–One man of each rank is hanged.

NO consideration of the winter fighting would be complete without some mention of the battle of Velikiye Luki, the ancient fortress in the vast swampy region north of Vitebsk between Lovat and Western Dvina. A beautiful old town, with 30,000 inhabitants at the beginning of the War, Velikiye Luki used to attract Intourist parties with its folklore.

Velikiye Luki began to play an important part during the German offensive battles of 1941 and continued to do so during the first Soviet counter-offensive from the Moscow region. The Lower Saxon 19th Panzer Division, parts of the Hessian 20th Panzer Division, and the infantrymen of 253rd Infantry Division had taken the town by storm in August 1941 after heavy fighting.

Four and a half months later the first Soviet offensive was launched against the fortress in the swamp. On 9th January, 1942, Colonel-General Yeremenko and General Purkayev drove their striking armies across the chain of lakes from Ostashkov against Vitebsk, with a view to gaining the vast area to the west of Moscow by means of an enveloping attack and to annihilating the German Army Group Centre which stood poised for its leap to Moscow. But the Soviet thrust was halted by the German infantry in desperate fighting. It spent its force against the breakwaters of Kholm, Velizh, and Velikiye Luki.

Parts of the 83rd Infantry Division, hurriedly switched from France to Russia, were defending the "city in the swamp", the fortress astride the vital routes from Leningrad, Kiev, and Moscow to Belorussia and the Baltic.

Throughout the summer of 1942 the Soviet Third Striking Army again and again tried to break the defenders of Velikiye Luki with sudden and heavy artillery bombardment. However, the German 277th Grenadier Regiment under Colonel von Rappard fortified its positions. Supplies were difficult as there was no such thing as a continuous front along either side of Velikiye Luki. On the northern side, especially towards Kholm and the Lovat, there were only weak pickets. Only just south of Kholm did a continuous line start again, held by 8th Panzer Division. But the division staff had to watch in amazement how, immediately south of them where the front abruptly ended, the Russians were recruiting young men in the hinterland with complete impunity, driving away all livestock and collecting any useful material. In this situation a vital part was played by the German armoured trains—the armoured train No. 3 from Munich and the auxiliary armoured train No. 28. Without them it would have been impossible to get supplies through to Velikiye Luki.

On 19th November, 1942, the second great Soviet winter offensive began on the southern front, with the main weight at Stalingrad and on the Don. On the northern front, meanwhile, Soviet large-scale attacks were designed to tie down the German forces and sweep away those irritating German breakwaters in the Vitebsk area. The Soviet Third Striking Army was to get into Vitebsk at long last. But in order to take Vitebsk it would first have to capture Velikiye Luki.

General Purkayev attacked the town with three divisions. Three divisions against one regiment. The Soviets thrust past Velikiye Luki in the north and south, through the chain of strongpoints of 83rd Infantry Division, and encircled the town. Inside the fortress were

7500 German troops under Lieutenant-Colonel von Sass, defending a
front line of thirteen miles. They were grenadiers, gunners, engineers,
baggage and medical units of 83rd Infantry Division. They were reinforced, or had simply been joined by the following units who found
themselves inside the "fortress" after their retreat: railway engineers
and construction units, *Nebelwerfer* units of the 3rd Mortar Regiment,
and Light Observation Battalion 17, a German local defence battalion,
and a battalion of Estonian volunteers, composed of Estonians who,
in the course of the fighting, had come over in bulk from the Red
Army. There were, moreover, three troops of Army Flak Battalion 286
and a troop of light flak, as well as the heavy mortars of 2nd Troop,
Army Artillery Battalion 736, the 3rd Battalion, 183rd Artillery Regiment, and parts of the 70th Motorized Artillery Regiment. A miniature
Stalingrad.

General Purkayev naturally wanted to take the town by storm. But
the attempt miscarried. He thereupon started to batter it systematically
by artillery and aerial bombardment. Day after day this pounding
continued. Building after building, bunker after bunker, street after
street were reduced to rubble. Fire gutted the ruins.

The German defenders of Velikiye Luki received their meagre supplies of food and ammunition from the air. Because too many of the
dropped supplies were coming down among the enemy lines outside
the small combat area of only seven square miles, Stukas were used to
deliver the supplies for the first time in the War. For that purpose the
Sixth Air Fleet had organized a mixed operational formation. It was
led by Heinz-Joachim Schmidt, the Commodore of 4th Bomber
Geschwader. He was based, together with his operations staff, at the
Great Ivan Lake in order to be as near as possible to the threatened
town. In spite of the great superiority which the Russians had in the
air and in spite of their anti-aircraft defences all round the fortress in
the swamp, the flying formations did everything in their power to drop
their "supply bombs" accurately into the progressively shrinking
dropping area. Food and ammunition containers as a rule hit the target
accurately. Nevertheless, supplies soon had to be curtailed by 25 per
cent and later had to be cut down by half.

On 13th December, after a heavy barrage, four rifle divisions and an
armoured brigade under General Purkayev mounted their general
attack on the western part of the city. There was savage fighting for
the bridge over the Lovat. This was held by Lieutenant Albrecht with
his column of engineers against a tenfold Russian superiority. Time
and again the Russian companies penetrated into the small German
bridge-head. Each time they were dislodged in hand-to-hand fighting
with trenching tools, bayonets, and hand-grenades. Lieutenant Albrecht was seriously wounded. Shot through the throat he lay at his
post but continued to direct the defensive fighting of his engineers.

On the second day of Christmas, 26th December, 1942, the Soviets attacked with strong armoured forces from the south and south-west. In fierce house-to-house fighting they forced their way right across the town on a narrow front. The defenders' heavy infantry weapons and anti-tank guns were eliminated one by one. In this way the German strongpoints were rendered almost helpless in the face of the enemy tanks.

The Soviet rifle battalions fought with outstanding gallantry. In particular the Komsomols, fanatical young communists, distinguished themselves by their devotion to duty throughout the next few weeks. Private Aleksandr Matrosov of the 254th Guards Rifle Regiment earned the title of Hero of the Soviet Union by sacrificing his life.

Matrosov put an end to his company's heavy losses outside a German bunker whose machine-gun had been pinning the Russians down and exacting a heavy toll from them. Matrosov crept up to the bunker's firing slit, covered it with his body, and thus blocked the view of the bunker's crew. Matrosov held on to the machine-gun barrel, and his fingers were still gripping it tight when he had long since died. His company used the pause in the fire to storm the bunker.

At the beginning of 1943 there were only two strongpoints left in the frozen swamp—the Citadel and the railway-station. The Citadel was held by Captain Darnedde, commanding the Field Depot Battalion of 83rd Infantry Division. With 427 men he defended an area of no more than 100 by 250 yards.

At the railway-station, in the eastern part of the city, Lieutenant-Colonel von Sass with 1000 men was holding the wrecked railway installations and the barracks. The troops were hoping to be relieved. It was that hope that kept them going—in spite of biting cold and a gnawing hunger. Out of forty-five supply containers dropped over their positions only seven had reached their target. The three hundred horses originally in the city had long been eaten. There was only one loaf of bread for every ten men per day. Twenty men had to share one tin of meat.

It is scarcely imaginable for us today what these men went through. Without sleep, without the least bodily care, full of lice, filthy and starving, they yet fought on. Some 3000 shells crashed down on them each day. They had no time to move their dead out of the way. The wounded lay among the wreckage, only scantily looked after. Drinking water had to be brought in, under danger of death, from a pond outside the ramparts. And in that pond lay a knocked-out Soviet tank with its dead crew.

But where was the main German line? Was nothing done to relieve the encircled city? The attempt was made all right. But once again it was a case of inadequate forces.

The first on the spot was General Brandenberger's 8th Panzer

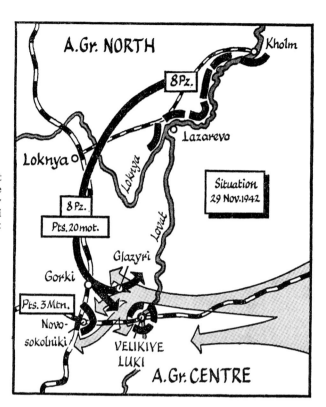

Map 32. The first attempt to relieve the encircled city of Velikiye Luki from the north-west was a failure.

Division. The regiments of this Berlin-Brandenburg division—which had always been employed in the East, and which had its own peculiar character owing to its many Baltic officers—had just abandoned its positions south of Kholm. It was to have been taken to the Stalingrad area by train. However, this laudable intention had to be cancelled in view of developments on the division's own doorstep.

On the evening of 21st November 8th Panzer Grenadier Regiment received an order by telephone: "The regiment will mount an immediate attack against the enemy advancing west of Velikiye Luki who has already crossed the Leningrad-Odessa railway. The regiment will thus save Novosokolniki."

"Save" was the actual word. Novosokolniki, a rear base and centre of field hospitals, was already being attacked by Soviet tank battalions and a motorized brigade. It was being defended by supply units of 3rd Mountain Division under Colonel Jobsky.

On the following morning the regiment made contact at Gorki with unsuspecting enemy forces and succeeded in dislodging them. On the following day the division's two Panzer Grenadier Regiments fought their way to the east: 28th Regiment under its commander

Lieutenant-Colonel Baron von Wolff, stormed the high ground east of Gorki, and 8th Regiment attacked in the direction of Velikiye Luki.

Captain Bernd von Mitzlaff's 2nd Battalion, 8th Panzer Grenadier Regiment, reinforced by a dozen captured tanks, dislodged the Soviets and took the village of Glazyri. Things had now begun to move.

Major Schmidt was containing the enemy with what few armoured fighting vehicles 10th Panzer Regiment possessed. Mitzlaff's battalion stormed the high ground east of the village. In the distance they could see the spires of Velikiye Luki. Once again the moment had come where that decisive battalion was lacking which might have tipped the balance. Schmidt's tanks were out of ammunition. The 1st Battalion was still hanging back. The 2nd Battalion had to regroup for defence. Soon the enemy had rallied again. The Soviet regiments mounted their counter-attack.

Once more Colonel von Skotti's well-tried 80th Artillery Regiment came to the rescue. Skotti again proved himself a past master in directing and concentrating his regiment's entire fire-power. The gunners bore the brunt of the fighting since at that time 8th Panzer Division possessed anything but adequate armour. It was equipped with captured Russian tanks, some Czech Skoda-38 fighting vehicles, and a few German Mark IVs. The battalions were halted. Even the intervention of Combat Group Jaschke with parts of the Hamburg 20th Motorized Infantry Division and the 291st Infantry Division could not change the situation. The first attempt to reach the encircled city of Velikiye Luki in one smooth move from the north-west had failed.

There was only one kind of help which Colonel von Skotti was able to give the beleaguered city—he ordered his long-barrel troops to move up to the front lines and pounded General Purkayev's regiments of the Third Striking Army as they were pressing against the city.

Preparations for a relief attack from the south-west were meanwhile under way. While General Kurt von der Chevallerie with the divisions of his LIX Corps was holding a cover line around Vitebsk, General Wöhler, the former Eleventh Army Chief of Staff, formed a relief group which got to within six miles of Velikiye Luki by 24th December.

Combat groups of 291st and 331st Infantry Divisions, parts of the reinforced 76th Panzer Grenadier Regiment, of 10th Panzer Regiment, and of Assault Gun Battalion 237 pushed this relief wedge via Novosokolniki to within sight of the encircled city. But there the troops and vehicles, having suffered exceedingly heavy losses, got stuck in the deep snow. Yet Wöhler did not give up.

The Austrian 331st Infantry Division under Lieutenant-General Dr Franz Beyer eventually got to within two and a half miles of the western edge of Velikiye Luki. But they did not get beyond that point.

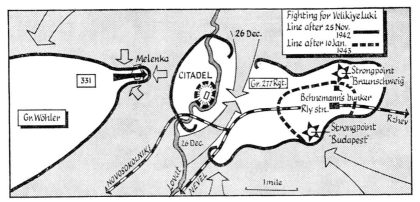

Map 33. The second attempt to relieve Velikiye Luki also ground to a halt a few miles from the city. Resistance inside the fortress collapsed.

A mere two and a half miles! No distance at all—but the distance between heaven and hell.

One last attempt was made on 9th January. A combat group under Major Tribukait, the commander of the Jäger Battalion 5, mounted an attack against the fortress with tanks, assault guns, and armoured infantry carriers. The few infantry carriers belonged to 8th Panzer Division, the tanks were from 1st Battalion, 15th Panzer Regiment, and the assault guns from the reinforced Panzer Battalion 118.

"Keep moving and firing!" had been their order. Don't stop. The crews of knocked-out vehicles were to climb on to the outside of others without halting. With this method of "keeping going and firing" Tribukait did in fact succeed in piercing the strong enemy ring. A number of tanks and infantry carriers were lost, but the group got through.

It was exactly 1506 hours when Darnedde's half-starved men saw the tanks from the ramparts of the Citadel. They wept with joy and fell into each other's arms. "They've done it!" they kept shouting, "They've done it!"

Fifteen armoured fighting vehicles clanked into the courtyard of the Citadel; they included the last three tanks of 1st Battalion, 15th Panzer Regiment, under Lieutenant Koske. But the fortunes of war had turned against Darnedde's battalion. As soon as the overrun Russians realized the Germans had broken through they concentrated their artillery and furiously pounded the area of the Citadel.

Tribukait immediately ordered his tanks to get out of the confined yard among the ruins, to which there was only one approach. But everything seemed to conspire against him. Just as one of the fifteen tanks was passing through the entrance in the ramparts it received four direct hits and remained lying motionless, its tracks shot to pieces.

Tribukait's small force was now in a trap and became the target of furious Russian shelling by guns of all calibres. One tank after another fell victim to the Soviet bombardment. It was an unprecedented disaster. Tribukait's surviving Jägers and tankmen joined the defenders in the role of infantry.

On 15th January a parachute battalion made an attempt to get into the Citadel. But that attempt failed too.

Disaster came to the eastern part of Velikiye Luki on 16th January. There was diphtheria inside the "Budapest" strongpoint. The building containing the command post of 2nd Battalion, 277th Infantry Regiment, and the dressing station with three hundred wounded was blazing. Russian tanks were outside. At that point Major Schwabe gave up. Lieutenant-Colonel von Sass likewise surrendered in his wrecked command post.

When General Wöhler received the signal informing about the situation he decided to put an end to the tragedy inside the Citadel. He radioed to Major Tribukait who, as the senior officer, had been in command since 9th January: "The defenders will fight their way out westwards to their own lines."

The defenders will fight their way out—all well and good. But what about the wounded? Tribukait consulted with Darnedde. They concluded that the wounded would have to be left behind. To avoid panic the break-out was kept secret from them. Only the medical officer and four medical orderlies who were to stay behind with the wounded and share their gloomy fate were let into the secret. Captain Dr Wehrheim, the medical officer, was handed a sealed letter only to be opened two hours after the break-out.

At 0200 at night the defenders assembled. There were only 180 men left. They all knew what was at stake. And they moved off with the kind of determination shown only by men doomed to death. They broke through three Soviet lines. They knocked-out an anti-tank gun and two machine-gun posts. They overran the crew of a Russian strongpoint and at 0530 hours eventually arrived at the German main defensive line with seven prisoners.

The wounded in the Citadel, of course, had discovered what was up. Eyes wild with fear they had listened to every noise. They had heard the words of command. And as the silence of terminated battle crept through the basements a ghostly operation began: thirty casualties who believed they could just about keep on their feet set out under the leadership of a lieutenant and a sergeant. Eighteen of them reached the German lines after a frightful journey.

Subsequently a third group also made its way back to the German positions.

Altogether eight men made their escape from the eastern part of Velikiye Luki and, after the most incredible adventures, fought their way through to the German lines. Eight out of a thousand. One of them was Lieutenant Behnemann, commanding 9th Troop, 183rd Artillery Regiment. The story of his journey through the enemy lines is one of those dramatic odysseys from the chronicle of escapes which constitute a special chapter of the war in Russia. It is worth recording here.

The date was the 13th January and the time 1900 hours. A few centres of resistance were still holding out among the railway sidings. Lieutenant Behnemann counted the men in his bunker. There were forty-one left. Twenty of them were seriously wounded and were lying on the floor and on bunks.

The men were a sorry sight. For nights on end they had stood in the trenches, a little cold coffee substitute in their flasks and one-seventh of a loaf of bread in their knapsacks—their daily ration.

At 2200 contact was lost with the observation post. The sentry who had just been relieved at the blockhouse next to the bunker came in and reported:

"OP and Battalion HQ are being shot up by a Soviet tank. They're both blazing."

Clearly, the end had come for Major Hennigs, the artillery commander of Velikiye Luki. Less than twelve hours previously he had rung through to the bunker: "You hold the bunker, Behnemann! I'm hanging on to the OP."

The men were dozing. The air was thick enough to cut. The wounded were moaning. The medical orderly had no morphia left for them and no dressings.

At daybreak, towards 0700, Behnemann went across to the small blockhouse to have a look for himself. Things were getting critical. The house was more or less destroyed. In its floor a shell had torn a deep hole. It was possible to get through that hole, under the floor, and watch events outside through the wrecked external wall.

Behnemann could see clearly that the OP was in Russian hands. Obviously they were about to storm the bunker.

A T-34 was already slowly moving up alongside the trench. Behnemann was watching it. And thus he missed what was happening behind him. Suddenly there was a noise. Orders shouted in Russian. Shots. The Soviets had reached the blockhouse and the bunker from the other side.

Behnemann rolled under the floorboards. Less than two feet away from him, along the outer wall, were Russian soldiers. They were tossing hand-grenades at the door and firing their sub-machine-guns through the firing slits of the bunker.

A German voice shouted from the bunker entrance: "Don't shoot— we surrender. We're all wounded!"

A Russian replied in German: "Come out!" The bunker door opened. Behnemann's men reeled out, their hands up.

"Where guns?" the Soviet NCO asked the first German. He nodded his head towards the bunker.

"Get them, quick, quick," the Russian shouted. The men about-turned and brought out their weapons and ammunition.

By then an interpreter arrived on the spot. He ordered the prisoners to get into the blockhouse with raised hands.

Behnemann crept even farther away from the hole in the floor and pressed himself into a corner. Overhead the interrogation began.

"Officer?" was the first question, as always. Then: "Occupation?" Whenever the answer was "worker" the interpreter said: "Good."

"Peasant? Good."

One of them replied: "Office worker." And the interpreter said: "Also good."

One question asked repeatedly was: "Photo?" What was meant was a camera. But only one German NCO possessed this coveted article.

After the interrogation the prisoners were made to jump down into the trench. "Quick, quick!" Then they were marched across to the "Red House".

The wounded had flung woollen blankets over their shoulders and were staggering along the trench. There was no ill-treatment. But there was that ceaseless shouting: "Davay, davay—quick, quick!" Accompanied by a nervous and menacing clicking of rifle bolts.

All day long Behnemann lay under the floor of the blockhouse. In the early afternoon a long column of prisoners was marched through the old firing pit. Something like 500 or 600 men. They were a sorry sight. A few officers were reeling through the snow in stockinged feet. Their felt boots had been taken away.

"Anything rather than that," Behnemann thought. "Anything." At that moment the man from Visselhövede in Lower Saxony made up his mind. Captivity was not for him. He had no map—only a pocket compass. And in his pockets he had a pistol with eight rounds. And his daily ration—one-seventh of a loaf of bread. That was his whole equipment. Would it be enough to cross the vast swamp and reach the German lines?

The time was 1930 hours. The first night of Behnemann's escape was beginning. He crawled out of his hiding place. He swung himself out of the window. He boldly walked upright down the trench and then let himself roll down the slope to the right.

The ruined scenery was steeped in an eerie light by the brilliant moon. The frozen snow crunched and cracked under his felt boots. Careful now. Behnemann had reached the spot where the Russians had cut through the barbed-wire fence to lead their prisoners through.

That was where Behnemann wanted to slip through too. "Stoy," a voice called. Behnemann continued running. Another shout: "Stoy!"

Damn. He flung himself into the snow. For half an hour he acted a dead man. Then he crawled on, working his way through the wire.

Suddenly there was activity all round him. Russian soldiers were rounding up loose horses and driving them in the direction of Maksimovo. That was a piece of luck. A single man moving along the edge of the herd of horses would not attract attention.

Behnemann hurried on. Suddenly he started: surely there was something crouching in the snow. Motionless. Cautiously he approached it —a dead German soldier. Fifty yards on—another. Frightful markers along the road. Every thirty or fifty yards was another lifeless soldier. Sagged over forward. Or wrapped in a blanket. Or fully extended in the snow. All of them clearly wounded men who had wanted to take a moment's rest on their march into captivity and in doing so had frozen to death.

Not until a good way farther down did the terrible signposts come to an end. Behnemann was walking briskly. The night was bright and silent. He glanced at his compass. Four days earlier he had taken a bearing on the triangulation point two and a half miles north-west of the city. That was where he was now making for.

Sleigh tracks crossed the swamp in all directions. Behnemann had to dodge into the scrub whenever a Soviet sleigh column approached.

After two and a half miles he reached the triangulation point. He scuttled across the first big supply route from east to west. He was to cross another six or eight such compacted snow roads in the course of that night. Alongside the road or on the ridges of clear snow ran Russian field telephone cables. During that first night Behnemann cut many of them with his pocket knife. After that he no longer bothered.

There was not much traffic. He encountered only about twenty vehicles, all of them driving confidently with unmasked headlights. They, of course, had nothing to fear from partisans. By 2400 hours Behnemann had reached the frozen Lovat river. He had to cross it. On the far side, parallel with the river, ran the road from Nevel to Staraya Russa. He kept on to the north.

Around 0500 he crossed the Nesva. And then the last east-west highway near the village of Molodi. Behnemann knew it from observation through his trench telescope: it was the only village which stood out from the swamp forest.

Day was breaking. And daytime was the enemy of wild beasts and men on the run. He had to find a hideout. He found it a hundred yards beyond the road—a willow thicket over six feet high. A day is a long time. And at twenty degrees below zero Centigrade, when one had to stay put in the same spot, it was positively unending. The lieutenant counted the trees around him. He estimated distances and every half-hour he performed ten knee-bends. Then, for a change he would "mark time at the double", or else beat his arms round his body.

Dusk fell at long last. It was twenty-four hours since he had set out.

He had only slept standing up and had sucked snow to assuage his thirst. To cope with his hunger he had eaten small pieces of bread. He never broke off more than a minute piece and then took a long time chewing it. The bread pulp went all sweet in his mouth if he chewed it long enough. Above all, he must not be in a hurry to swallow it.

Progress during the second night was particularly laborious. First his route lay through a thick forest deep in snow. Then across a flat swamp with tall tufts of reed and thick patches of willow. Wearily Behnemann moved on, and for the second time came upon the Nesva river. And then it happened. He slipped, rolled down the steep bank, and struck the ground with his head. He got to his feet in a daze. He caught his breath. Immediately opposite, on the far bank of the frozen stream, was a Soviet sentry eyeing him curiously. The Russian worked his rifle-bolt to get a round in the breach. But he did nothing else.

Behnemann stood rooted to the ground. One minute passed. Two minutes. A second Russian appeared on the far bank. The two exchanged a few words. The new man ran down the far bank and shouted: "Parol!" That meant the password.

Behnemann cut and ran. The bullets sang past him. He scrambled up the bank. He raced, panting, towards a ditch. He flung himself into it. He pressed himself firmly to the ground. There were voices around him everywhere.

"They'll find you, they'll find you," he kept saying to himself. But they did not find him. The moon set. Now it was dark. That was what saved Behnemann. When the noise had died away, he moved on, now to the west. He had set his compass to 40—the direction of a conspicuous star. He kept to this course.

He was enveloped by a dark, thick forest. The zig-zagging trails of animals in the deep snow were the only sign of life. Behnemann followed the trails. Here there was no need to be afraid of encountering a human being. He therefore continued to push on even after daybreak. At 0800 he was at the edge of the forest. He was surrounded by tall reeds. Slowly he moved forward, step by step.

Suddenly there were voices. Cautiously, he peered through the reeds. He caught his breath. He was right in the middle of a line of Soviet sentries, established in front of the thick reeds. Every two hundred yards a machine-gun. In front and in between them were sentries with rifles.

He crawled and rolled into a snowy hollow. From there he observed. He chewed his last piece of crust and swallowed several handfuls of snow.

Hours passed. The cold tingled through his skin, and crept over his body like icy fingers. It lay heavily on his brain and on his heart. His breath was slow. Behnemann counted his pulse beat. It was forty-five. Near the danger-point of freezing to death.

At 1700 hours the Russian sentries on the edge of the reeds were relieved. Here was his opportunity. Ducking low, Behnemann pushed ahead between the sentries. But in the bright moonlight there could be no hope of slipping through the front line. At the same time he lacked the strength to crawl back.

Regardless, he walked back upright. He turned north. From somewhere on his right came a shout: "Parol!" He paid no attention. There was a crack of carbine fire. And three short bursts from a machine-gun.

He crossed the open ground, avoiding the thickets where the sentries were posted. He had walked for a little over a mile when he suddenly found himself in the middle of the Russian main defensive line. All round on the high ground he was able to make out the course of the front. Machine-gun fire towards the west enabled him to discern the positions. Bent double, he ducked and slipped through the lines. He lost his gloves. He tore his cap in two and wrapped the bits of cloth round his hands so they should not get frost-bitten with all that flinging of himself down in the snow.

His strength was now failing fast. He was talking to himself, semi-audibly. "I can't go any farther," he said and collapsed. But a moment later he picked himself up again: "I can manage a little way yet!"

This was repeated every half hour. Always he remained in the snow just to that danger-point where indifference may mean death. But each time he forced himself up again. He followed the tracks of the hares, running straight towards the moon, towards the west. From 0200 onwards the planet Venus fixed his direction for him. At 0400, at the end of the third night and the beginning of the third day, he suddenly found himself in front of a barn. There was hay inside. He flung himself down. Sleep!

But hunger, thirst, and the fear of freezing to death stopped him from getting more than two hours' feverish dozing. Then he pulled himself up again. He could not die here in this hay. He had to get out. He stepped outside. The grey dawn was all round him. He reeled on. He saw some farmhouses.

"Parole!" someone shouted. Let them shout. He moved on, unconcerned. Ten paces. Twenty. Then something flashed in his brain: What did that voice say? Parole? That final "e"—surely that was not part of the Russian word? Could it be . . .?

But thinking was too difficult. He could only manage it in slow motion. His brain seemed frozen stiff.

He had staggered on another five hundred yards across open ground. But the nagging in his mind continued. Parole! Could it have been a German who had challenged him?

Day was breaking. In the brighter light now he could make out a railway track. A railway! Suddenly he was the trained artillery officer again. That must be the line to Loknya, part of the Odessa–Leningrad main line. And that sector between Loknya and Novosokolniki, immediately west of Velikiye Luki, was in German hands. He knew that for certain. The last battle reports he had listened into at his OP had reported that this sector of railway had been crossed and secured in a relief attack by a combat group of 8th Panzer Division.

No point in hesitating. He was finished one way or another. So he turned about and reeled back to the farmhouses, to human habitations. He reached an isolated peasant hut. He drew his pistol. He knocked. An old man opened the door. He stared at him. Behnemann pointed outside: "Germanski soldier or Ruski soldier?"

The old man shook his head: "Germanski." And he pointed across to a stone-built house. Behnemann staggered out of the door. He dragged himself across. His lips trembled as he spelt out for himself the tactical sign on the door: 5th Troop, 80th Panzer Artillery Regiment. "The 8th from Cottbus," he muttered. He knew the famous 3rd Light Division which in 1940 had been transformed into 8th Panzer Division and had proved its value as an armoured formation on the northern and central fronts.

He reeled through the door, into the big room which housed the command post. The troops looked up startled as they caught sight of the spectre in the door—an emaciated figure, one hand wrapped into the hood of his camouflage cape, the bearded face disfigured with frost boils. They sat as if turned to stone.

The ghost-like visitor stared fascinated at the iron stove. And at the white enamelled German Army can in which coffee substitute was being heated. He picked it up. He raised it to his lips and drank. He kept on drinking. Then he put it down. And only then did he utter his first words: "I've come from Velikiye Luki."

Then the others leapt up and pushed a chair under him. He dropped into it and laughed and laughed. His tears were streaming down his frozen white face. He had been on the go for sixty hours. In the icy cold he had walked twenty-five miles. And they had not caught him. He had escaped from the hell of Velikiye Luki—he, Lieutenant Behnemann of 9th Troop, 183rd Artillery Regiment.

Thus Behnemann escaped captivity and the revenge which a fanatical Soviet leadership was later to take for the defeats of Velikiye Luki. After the War they picked out from their P.O.W. camps the German troops who had fought at Velikiye Luki; took them back to the fortress and there tried them by court martial. One man of each rank was sentenced to death by hanging—one general, one colonel, one

Army surgeons at work by night: a dressing station near Olenino. Serious casualties being loaded into a Junkers aircraft in the steppe between Don and Donets. Three men stayed behind.

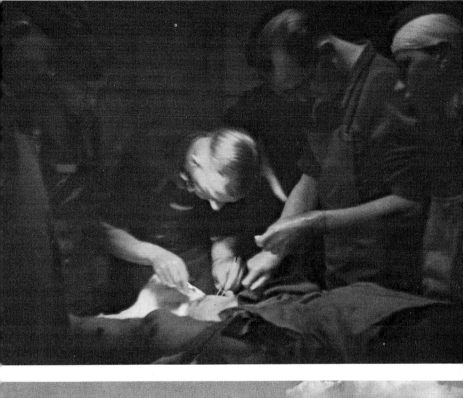

lieutenant-colonel, one major, one captain, one lieutenant, one top sergeant, one sergeant, one senior corporal, one corporal, and one private.

On 29th January, 1946 the men were publicly hanged in Lenin Square in Velikiye Luki. Among them were the commander of 277th Infantry Regiment and the former town commandant, company commanders, railway officials, junior commanders, and rankers. All others who could be rounded up were sentenced to twenty or twenty-five years' imprisonment. Only eleven of them survived to return to Germany between 1953 and 1955.

That was Velikiye Luki, one of the focal points of the winter battle of 1942–43. The end of this critical operation was brought about by a general more powerful than any other on either side—mud.

The Demyansk pocket: Attack.
A captured strongpoint.

PART FOUR: *Last Chance*

1. What Next?

11,200,000 men mobilized–Defensive or offensive–Strike the enemy when he is spent–The wrong decision.

NO-ONE who has not experienced Russian mud can know what mud is. With the onset of the thaw at the end of March 1943 the war on the ground came to an end. Every boot, every vehicle, every military movement got stuck in the deep morass. The front was immobilized. It ran from Leningrad via Staraya Russa, along the salients of Orel and Kursk to Belgorod, then along Donets and Mius down to the Sea of Azov. In the Kuban bridge-head the Seventeenth Army was holding out, guarding the approaches to the Crimea and so covering the southern wing of the German armies in the east. This front line, ossified in the mud, put an end to the period of crises. The great landslide triggered off by the disaster of Stalingrad had been halted, the main danger to the German front in the East had been averted, the situation had been stabilized.

But the mud would dry out, and the thaw would be followed by spring and summer. And what would happen then? That was the strategic problem. How was the war in the East to be continued against the background of the war as a whole? Two campaigns had failed to bring the Soviet Union to its knees.

How, in the face of these reverses and crises, was the third campaign in the East to be conducted? What was there that the German Command could put its hopes in? Was there any hope left?

One thing was certain. The spring mud provided the German Command with a valuable breathing space at the beginning of 1943. With the straightening of men-consuming salients reserves had been gained for the first time in months. Time, reserves, and armaments— those were the three elements of war.

When Adolf Hitler first conceived Operation Citadel he was thinking not merely of a military operation. His secret directive dated April 1943, for the rounding-up throughout the conquered territories of prisoners of war and of all civilians capable of work, shows how clearly he realized the bottlenecks in the German economy. There was a shortage not only of troops but also of workers. And the more men were called up for military service in Germany, in order to meet the demands for more troops, the wider became the gaps in the armament works, the mines, transport, and food production.

In January 1943 the High Command of the Armed Forces demanded 800,000 men—but even the most ruthless call-up was able to produce only 400,000. These men were lost to the war economy and their places therefore had to be taken by foreign workers, above all by labour from the East.

Small wonder, therefore, that in his "Directives for the Securing of Prisoners of War, Labour Forces and Booty", Hitler laid it down that an important aim of all military operations, apart from destroying enemy formations, was the rounding-up of prisoners and civilian labour for vital war employment. The war had reverted to its most primitive form—its aim was booty and slaves.

These efforts were not unsuccessful. In May 1942 there were 9·4 million men in the forces; in spring 1943 the figure had risen to 11·2 million. Nevertheless, at that time, in the spring of 1943, there were 36·6 million civilian workers, compared with 35·5 million in May 1942. In other words, Germany had two million more soldiers and one million more civilian workers.

There was also a very marked increase in production—in spite of aerial bombardment and anxiety about food supplies. Albert Speer, the new boss of the armaments economy, organized the mass production of vital war material. Whereas at the beginning of 1942 only 350 tanks and 50 assault guns were produced each month, the figure for tanks had doubled by the beginning of 1943 and that for assault guns had quadrupled.

Thus, the skill of engineers and the hands of millions of men and women workers in the armament industry conjured up—there is no other term for it—new weapons from bombed factories. They were, above all, the heavy tanks of the Tiger I and IA type, the new medium tank known as the Panther, the huge assault guns of the Ferdinand type, and heavy anti-tank and flak guns on self-propelled carriages. These were the engineering triumphs which it was hoped would bring about a turn on the battlefields.

Only in one field was there a strange and incomprehensible in-activity—Germany's military leaders failed to hear the approaching footsteps of the atomic age. German physicists kept writing memo-randa and raising the subject at conferences. They pointed to the possibility of developing an entirely novel type of explosive based on the phenomenon of nuclear fission discovered by German scientists. But the Army's Weapons Development Office declined to take up the proposal because it had been "decided as a matter of principle" that

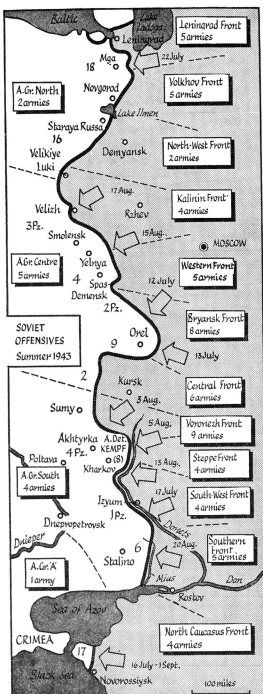

Map 34. Sixty-one Soviet armies were lined up against the Germans after the battle of Kursk. What would happen next?

Baltic

Lake Ladoga

Leningrad Front
5 armies

Leningrad

22 July

Mga
18

Novgorod

A.Gr. North
2 armies

Volkhov Front
5 armies

Lake Ilmen

Staraya Russa
16

Demyansk

North-West Front
2 armies

Velikiye Luki

17 Aug.

Velizh

Rzhev

Kalinin Front
4 armies

3 Pz.

Smolensk

15 Aug.

MOSCOW

A.Gr. Centre
5 armies

Yelnya

4

Western Front
5 armies

Spas-Demensk

12 July

2 Pz.

Orel

Bryansk Front
8 armies

9

13 July

SOVIET
OFFENSIVES
Summer 1943

2

Kursk

Central Front
6 armies

3 Aug.

Sumy

5 Aug.

Voronezh Front
9 armies

Akhtyrka
4 Pz.

A.Det.
KEMPF
(8)

Steppe Front
4 armies

Poltava

Kharkov

13 Aug.

A.Gr. South
4 armies

Izyum
1 Pz.

17 July

South-West Front
4 armies

Dnepropetrovsk

Donets

Dnieper

6

20 Aug.

Southern
Front
5 armies

A.Gr.'A'
1 army

Stalino

Mius

Don

Sea of Azov

Rostov

CRIMEA

North Caucasus Front
4 armies

17

Black Sea

16 July - 1 Sept.

Novorossiysk

100 miles

no weapons would be developed whose completion would take more than nine months.

It is easy, with the benefit of hindsight, to argue that in 1943 the war could no longer be won anyway. That it could no longer be concluded victoriously was realized by the German military leaders even then. The question they had to face up to was: "How can it be prevented from ending in disaster?"

The answer did not necessarily point to political revolution, rebellion, tyrannicide, or resistance, but revealed a good few other and less revolutionary alternatives.

A sober assessment of the military and economic situation shows that, with the military successes of the spring of 1943 and the new economic mobilization, the German Command had one more chance of working out a new strategy for the war in Russia. A strategy no longer based on the illusion of conquering the vast Soviet Union—that disastrous illusion—but on the hard fact that Germany's strength was, at best, adequate to weakening the Red Army and shaking Stalin's power to such an extent that the Kremlin might be prepared to negotiate. Not victory, but a draw. That was the logical conclusion from past experience. Would Hitler understand the urgent need of the moment and pull the rudders round in time?

Field-Marshal von Manstein, the man who had proved himself one of the most important generals on any front, was the principal spokesman for the concept that the war in the East should be so conducted that, at least, it would not lead to military disaster. Admittedly, such a conduct of the war would not conceal the failure of the campaign but indeed make it more conspicuous.

Yet the truth could no longer be concealed. The plan behind Operation Barbarossa, the plan to defeat the Soviet Union in a rapid blitzkrieg, seize its economic wealth, and outmanoeuvre the positions of the British Empire in Africa, the Middle East, and Persia by way of a gigantic pincer movement through the Caucasus and Egypt—that plan had collapsed once and for all with the German retreat from El Alamein and the Caucasus. That was why the German Command now had to be content with much less and attempt a negotiated settlement in the East.

The moment of decision had come. A whole epoch had arrived at the crossroads. There was still time to avert the threatening catastrophe, to correct the mistake of 22nd June, 1941. History stood menacingly on the battlefield from the Baltic to the Black Sea. Rarely can a decision have hung in the balance to quite that extent. At the same time—was there really any chance of a draw?

The road from Stalingrad to the Donets had been a costly one also for the Russians. Stalin had not achieved his objective of encircling the German southern wing. The Red Army too was badly mauled.

What then were the prospects? This is what Field-Marshal von Manstein thought: "The kind of offensive with far-reaching objectives, as conducted by us during the preceding years, was beyond our strength. Our obvious choice now seemed to be the defensive."

The defensive! But what kind of defensive? There are two kinds of defensive operations—rigid defence, holding on to all the ground that had been won, and a flexible, elastic defensive, combining yielding and counter-attack. A rigid defence was not practicable. The German forces were not adequate for it. The front from the Black Sea to the Arctic Ocean was too long to be reinforced as a rigid defensive line. Army Group South, for example, had only forty-one operational and three local defence divisions for a front line of 470 miles. According to the rules of defensive strategy this was twenty to thirty divisions too few. A rigid defence would have run the risk of the Russians, with their vast numbers of men, their powerful concentrations of artillery, their packs of tanks, and their increasingly massive air formations, attacking with crushing superiority at several points simultaneously and breaking through the German front.

Indeed, the Soviet High Command had developed this pattern to a fine art during the winter of 1942 and 1943. As soon as a sector of the German front had crumbled the Russians swiftly aimed an attack with strong striking formations against another.

In this way the German Command was compelled to keep switching its strategic reserves and its few mobile formations, without these forces ever getting to the right place in time. The result was Soviet penetrations, encirclement of isolated sectors of the front, and eventual retreat entailing serious losses of men and *matériel*. The great battle between Caucasus, Volga, and Donets was a good illustration.

Clearly, clinging to rigid lines held out no hope of success in 1943. What then was the basis of Manstein's belief in a strategy of a draw? Manstein said: "We had to exploit those factors which still represented a German superiority. Even though, in the larger view, we were now on the defensive, we had to try to deal painful blows to the enemy, causing him considerable casualties, the loss of large numbers of prisoners, and generally predispose him to come to terms. We had to make sure that, even within the framework of a defensive strategy, we should be able to conduct those flexible operations which constituted our main strength."

In other words, the idea was not to go over to the offensive in a big way, but to let the Russians do the attacking and then, at the right moment, strike a blow just when the momentum of his attack was spent. In fact, the strategy was demonstrated by Manstein in the spring of 1943, in the great defensive battle between Donets and Dnieper. If the war was to be continued at all—and the demand for "unconditional surrender" made meanwhile by the Allies at Casablanca left Germany no alternative—then Manstein's strategy held out the only hope of escaping certain military defeat.

But anyone who thought that Adolf Hitler could be made to acknowledge the facts of the situation and abandon his extravagant plans found himself bitterly disillusioned. No sooner had the retreats and front shortenings of the spring of 1943 provided him with a few tactical and strategic reserves than he again began to indulge in feverish illusions. Hitler's overweening pride was stronger than his sense of judgment. He allowed himself to be tempted once more into taking the offensive. The Kursk salient, that projecting balcony between Orel and Belgorod, lured him into mounting his great pincer operation known as Citadel.

To this end he staked all his reserves, in particular his armoured forces which had only just been reorganized by Guderian. He wanted to annihilate the bulk of the Soviet armoured forces concentrated in the Kursk salient and immediately behind it, and in doing so wipe out the entire central Soviet reserves of 1943. He believed that, by means of a decisive battle, he would regain the initiative in the East. Indeed, he even dreamt of following up this operation by an offensive against Moscow.

Guderian, Manstein, Model, and many other generals implored him to abandon the idea. They pointed to the dangers inherent in such an operation, and certainly in a further postponement of the opening of a summer offensive. The Wehrmacht Operations Staff urgently advised against it: in view of the overstretched front and the threat of invasion in the West and in Italy such reserves as were available would be needed elsewhere. There were days when Hitler heeded their warnings, when he vacillated and shied away from his great gamble. But in the end he staked everything he had and flung it on the blood-drenched battlefield of Kursk.

We already know what happened. Operation Citadel, betrayed by agents, misfired. The strategic reserves which had only just been painfully reconstituted and replenished were used up; the new armoured forces with their first Panther battalions and Tiger companies were whittled away in attacks on the gigantic Soviet defences in the Kursk salient.

And then came disaster. The Soviet Command did precisely what Manstein had been advising Hitler to do—strike when the opponents' thrust had spent itself. Just when the battle of Kursk was at its zenith the Soviets launched a full-scale attack against the rear of Model's Army which was attacking from north to south. In the north of the Kursk front they thus forced the Germans to call off their offensive and exploited the confusion to achieve a penetration into the lines of Second Panzer Army in the Orel area.

There, from 12th July, 1943, onwards, the Soviet diversionary attack north of Kursk developed into a savage defensive battle in which considerable parts of the offensive wing of Ninth Army were involved. Even though a catastrophic penetration into the deep left flank of the southern wing of Army Group Centre was once more prevented, the Soviets nevertheless achieved the suspension of Operation Citadel at the very last moment, just before Manstein and Model were able to bring it to a successful conclusion.

As a result, the situation for the German High Command was now worse than before the stabilization of the front in the spring of 1943. Nearly all its reserves had been spent. The main motorized forces on the Eastern Front had been either smashed or badly mauled. The line was stretched to breaking point. That was the moment for which the Soviet High Command had been waiting for twelve months, the moment of which Stalin had been dreaming since the summer of 1942. Hitler had gambled away not only victory but also all hope of a draw.

2. The Legacy of Kursk

Soviet attacks everywhere–Belgorod and Orel are lost– The drama of Akhtyrka–"Is your general still in the wood?"

CONSIDERING the exceedingly difficult situation in mid-1943 the German armies in the East still managed to achieve some remarkable successes. The Second Panzer Army and Ninth Army under the command of Colonel-General Model scored exceptional defensive successes in the Orel bulge. Once again the battle-weary divisions prevented a Soviet breakthrough to Bryansk and the Dnieper.

But the Red Army did not let up. On 17th July strong forces of two Army Groups on both sides of Izyum attacked the positions of the German First Panzer Army on the middle Donets. Colonel-General von Mackensen managed once more with his weakened corps to seal off the attack and somehow to contain it. Along the front of General Hollidt's Sixth Army on the Mius, however—the river near the Sea of Azov contested so fiercely ever since December 1941—the Russians succeeded in making a penetration east of Stalino, near Kuybyshevo on the eastern bank of the Mius, and in following up as far as Marinovka in the sector of the Saxon 294th Infantry Division. The 513th Grenadier Regiment had to abandon the small town but the division managed to seal off the dangerous penetration.

Manstein threw in the SS Panzer Corps from the north and the experienced 16th Motorized Infantry Division from the south, and subsequently also the 23rd Panzer Division. These fast formations succeeded in preventing the worst disaster by once more halting the Soviet thrust against the heart of the Donets region. However, available forces were no longer adequate to eliminate the danger. The disastrous pattern of "too little and too late" was repeating itself.

Almost as soon as it had accomplished its counter-attack and, by 3rd August, regained the old main defensive line along Sixth Army's front, the SS Panzer Corps had to be pulled out again and switched to the north.

True enough, the long-overdue evacuation of the Kuban bridge-head was now put in hand and 13th Panzer Division and other formations moved north from the Crimea. But while stop-gap arrangements succeeded on the Mius and on the middle Donets in checking the dangerous situation, in early August a serious new threat was taking shape in the Belgorod area, on the northern wing of Army Group South. Strong Russian forces were spotted by German aerial reconnaissance in the area to the east of Belgorod. A large-scale attack by the Soviet Voronezh Front via Kharkov to the Dnieper seemed imminent.

Stalin intended to repeat his abortive attempt of the spring of 1942: he wanted to cut off the German Army Group South from its rearward communications and inflict on it, as well as on Army Group "A", an inescapable defeat. Army General Vatutin, whose political adviser was Nikita Khrushchev, mounted his full-scale offensive to both sides of Belgorod on 3rd August, 1943, following a massive artillery barrage; for this offensive he used five Armies.

According to Soviet records Vatutin had a six-fold superiority in artillery and armour over the German forces. Along the breakthrough frontage he had 370 guns and mortars to each mile of front line. Behind the rifle divisions stood the corps of two further élite tank armies, the First and the Fifth Guards Tank Armies. Their armour had been concentrated to provide gigantic local striking power—112 tanks to each mile of front line.

Furious fighting broke out along the sector of Second Panzer Army in the Orel area. But farther south the situation was even worse. While Sixth Army managed for the time being to hold its regained main defensive line in the face of renewed Soviet attacks, the catastrophe of the German southern front was now rapidly approaching both sides of Belgorod, where the German front had been seriously weakened by the transfer of some of its mobile formations to Sixth Army and to the southern wing of Army Group Centre at Orel.

After three hours of battle the Soviet rifle divisions of the Fifth and Sixth Guards Armies had penetrated deep into the German defences. Vatutin sent in his two tank armies. They ripped open the German front along the junction of Hoth's Fourth Panzer Army and its neighbour in the south, the Army Detachment Kempf, and pushed through deep into the German defensive zone. They by-passed Kharkov and made for Poltava. Field-Marshal von Manstein immediately rushed up tactical reserves from all parts of his front. But Belgorod could no longer be saved.

To complete the disaster, Model had been getting into even greater trouble in the Orel salient farther north. The Second Panzer Army was eventually compelled to evacuate Orel to avoid the risk of a dangerous encirclement.

Belgorod fallen! Orel fallen! Kharkov in a hopeless position! Was total collapse inevitable this time?

The Kremlin certainly hoped so. For on the evening of 5th August Stalin, for the first time since the beginning of the war, ordered a thunderous artillery salvo to be fired in Moscow. Proudly the special announcements reported: Belgorod and Orel have been retaken. Two historical, strategic, and transport centres of the Ukraine and central Russia had been recaptured. Celebrations and commentaries made it clear that the Kremlin no longer feared any future change of ownership. The Russians realized that they were on the way to victory. And the salvoes in Moscow inspired the Soviet commanders in the Belgorod area to race towards the great objective which Marshal Stalin had outlined to them nine months previously—to force the German Army Group South away from the Dnieper, towards the Sea of Azov, and there to annihilate it.

Was Manstein's fate sealed? Between Hoth's Fourth Panzer Army and the Army Detachment Kempf was a dangerous gap of thirty-four miles. The road to the Dnieper was wide open to the Russians. Moreover, Hitler made things even easier for Stalin by ordering General Raus's XI Corps, which was falling back towards Kharkov along the highway, to move into the city. Once again he commanded: "Kharkov must be held at all costs."

Colonel-General Hoth pulled his Fourth Panzer Army back towards the south-west, in order to build up a new defensive line north of Kharkov. The question was whether this could still be done. The Lower Saxon 19th Panzer Division had fought with XLVIII and III Panzer Corps in the heavy battles at the Soviet penetration points and was now fighting its way back westward through the Russian lines.

On the afternoon of 6th August Lieutenant-General Gustav Schmidt, commanding 19th Panzer Division, was at the battle HQ of XLVIII

Panzer Corps. The Corps commander General von Knobelsdorff, showed him on the map where he intended to establish the interception line of Fourth Panzer Army in the Grayvoron-Akhtyrka area. "The main thing is to get our forces there as quickly as possible, Schmidt. Advanced units of the 'Grossdeutschland' Division have already taken up an interception line. We've got to halt the Russians, otherwise the whole Army Group is heading for total disaster!"

Schmidt nodded and said confidently, "We'll manage, Herr General!" He moved his regiments off in the direction of Akhtyrka. But he did not know that his division had already been overtaken by the Russians. Soviet armoured formations were already deep in his rear and on the morning of 7th August had cut the highway at Grayvoron, through which the corps' new switchline was to run.

No-one noticed the impending disaster. Only a few hours previously the transport units of 19th Panzer Division had driven down the road unmolested. Unsuspectingly the division staff drove off towards Akhtyrka in order to get the new lines ready for action.

General Schmidt was driving at the head of the column in his command tank. His radio operator was twiddling the knobs and remarking to Lieutenant Köhne, the ADC, "An unusual amount of Russian radio traffic. They're jabbering as excitedly as if they were in the middle of a battle."

Köhne had no time to reply. Like lightning from a clear sky, hell was suddenly let loose. The crash and flames of anti-tank shells. They were coming from the woods along both sides of the highway. They straddled the column neatly. The vehicles were smashed. They burst open. Sheets of flame. The smell of burning. Smoke.

A burst immediately before the bows of the divisional commander's tank caused it to get stuck in the shell crater. "Get out!" the general shouted. They scuttled into the roadside ditch.

T-34s now appeared on the road and within a few minutes had shot up the column. Lieutenant Köhne saw Lieutenant-Colonel von Unger, the chief of operations, killed by a machine-gun burst. One T-34 was making straight for them. One by one they raced into the wood. Russians were swarming about everywhere. Behind a massive tree-trunk the general, Lieutenant Köhne, Corporal Schütte, their driver, and the radio operator got under what cover there was. Their entire fire-power was two carbines and two pistols.

A group of Russian infantrymen had now spotted them and was trying to winkle them out. They were soon out of carbine ammunition.

The general whispered something to Köhne. Then he said aloud to Schütte and the radio operator, "We haven't a hope. You two try to get through. Lieutenant Köhne and I will try to divert the Russians and give you fire cover."

Schütte looked at his general in surprise. Divert the Russians? Fire cover? When they had just established that the general and Köhne each had only four rounds left in their pistols?

Lieutenant-General Gustav Schmidt, from Carstorf-on-Unstrut, born in 1894 and decorated with the Oak Leaves, guessed the thoughts of his driver, his companion of many years, smiled, and repeated with feigned severity: "Off you go; that's an order!" And he added to Schütte: "If you make it—go and see my wife, give her my love and tell her everything."

The two raced off. First the radio operator. Then the driver. They did not get far. They got right among the Russians and were taken prisoner. They were marched to an old toolshed, where a corpulent major-general had his command post. While they were being interrogated in the general's presence a lieutenant came in and reported something.

The Russian asked Schütte through the interpreter, "Is your general still in the wood?"

Schütte replied cautiously, "We don't know where the general is."

Thereupon the Soviet General sent them off with the Russian lieutenant, five men, and a hand-cart. The dead bodies of General Schmidt and Lieutenant Köhne lay by the tree-trunk.

As the party with its two dead returned to the Russian brigade headquarters Schütte and the radio operator came to attention in front of the Russian general and Schütte said, "Herr General, we request permission to bury our general and the lieutenant."

The interpreter translated. The Soviet general nodded and said to his lieutenant, "Show them a good spot!"

They buried their dead at the edge of the village of Berezovka. The date was 7th August, 1943, and the time 1500 hours. Five years and three months later Corporal Schütte returned home from Soviet captivity.

PART FIVE: *To the Dnieper*

1. The Fourth Battle of Kharkov

XI Corps in a hopeless position–Panic among 282nd Infantry Division–Soviet tanks roll into the city–6th Panzer Division saves the day–Rotmistrov's T-34s run into an ambush–Drama on the edge of the sea of sunflowers–Hitler: "Kharkov must be held"–Manstein: "I would rather lose a city than an Army"–"Mein Führer, I request freedom of movement."

COLONEL Sörgel, the commander of 73rd Panzer Grenadier Regiment, assumed command of the Lower Saxon-Westphalian 19th Panzer Division after General Schmidt's death. The Soviets were pressing ahead vigorously and the bulk of the division in consequence found itself in a pocket at Grayvoron, a pocket which already contained 255th Infantry Division and parts of 57th and 332nd Infantry Divisions, as well as the Silesian 11th Panzer Division. The command over the forces in the pocket was assumed by General Poppe.

Four Soviet Armies were charging the combat groups in their hedgehog positions. But the Russians did not succeed in pushing in the walls of the pocket. On the contrary—11th and 19th Panzer Divisions concentrated all their assault guns and tanks to force open a corridor and in a dramatic break-out the encircled regiments of the infantry division managed to get out towards Akhtyrka, where the advanced parts of the "Grossdeutschland" Division had already prepared positions for them. They about-turned and held the new front.

In this way the XLVIII Panzer Corps under General von Knobelsdorff, in co-operation with other fast divisions of Fourth Panzer Army, succeeded once more in checking the Soviet advance to the Dnieper between Sumy and Akhtyrka. However, lack of mobile reserves made it impossible to seal the front which had been torn open at a great many places. The danger of a Soviet breakthrough persisted. This anxiety weighed heavily on the hard-tried Army Group South. If the enemy launched a breakthrough attack north-west of Kharkov or in the south, on the Mius front, then there would be nothing to stop him until he had reached the Dnieper.

That was the writing on the wall, or rather on the situation maps, which worried all staff officers. If the Russians were now to succeed in crossing the Dnieper, the Army Group would be lost. To prevent this happening, at least a minimum of reserves had to be made available. But with a strategy based on holding on to everything and abandoning nothing where could they come from? Kharkov was the latest illustration of that strategy. Hitler ordered the city to be defended. But if his order was obeyed, would not the eventual loss of Kharkov also mean the loss of the whole of XI Corps with its six divisions? Six whole divisions! Just the forces which, provided Kharkov was abandoned, might avert the disaster threatening on the Mius and on the northern wing of the Army Group. But Hitler ordered: "Kharkov will be defended."

The man who had to implement this order was General of Armoured Troops Erhard Raus, an Austrian, an experienced and much-decorated tank commander who has been mentioned in this book before—during that icy New Year's night of 1942-43, on the battlefield of Tatsinskaya, when the fate of Stalingrad was still in the balance. Now he and his XI Corps on the Donets had once more been given the task of halting a major Soviet offensive at a crucial point.

General Vatutin's armies, having broken through the northern wing of Hoth's Fourth Panzer Army, were already spilling into the Poltava basin. If General Konev's armies of the Steppe Front now succeeded in thrusting speedily via Kharkov to the Dnieper then Manstein's Army Group would be finished and von Kleist's Army Group in the Crimea would be cut off.

This was the anxiety which gave the Field-Marshals sleepless nights. It was vital that General Raus should prevent a breakthrough by Konev and that he should tie down Konev's forces long enough for Colonel-General Hoth to halt Vatutin's tank armies.

With his own four divisions—the 168th, 198th, 106th, and 320th Infantry Divisions—as well as with two formations of Fourth Panzer Army which had been pushed over towards XI Corps following the Russian breakthrough—the 167th Infantry Division and the 6th Panzer Division—Raus slowly fell back to the outer defensive belt of Kharkov in eight days of delaying resistance.

They were scorching autumn days. Over the roads hung thick clouds of dust.

"Kharkov must be held!"

Six months earlier even the crack regiments of the "Grossdeutschland" Panzer Grenadier Division and the two SS Panzer Divisions "Das Reich" and "Leibstandarte" had been unable to hold the city. And six badly mauled divisions were to hold it now? On 11th August Hitler ordered the experienced Berlin 3rd Panzer Division to Kharkov, to cover General Raus's open left flank.

General Westhoven's regiments moved up from the Mius, that river of sturgeons, rumbled past Stalino, and across the battlefield where, towards the end of July, the battalions of the Soviet Fifth Striking Army and Second Guards Army had been dislodged in heavy counter-attacks.

Riding in the armoured infantry carrier of the commander of 2nd Company, 3rd Panzer Grenadier Regiment, Corporal Otto Tenning saw once more the terrible battlefield where only a few days earlier a counter-attack by his division had smashed a Soviet bridge-head.

Thousands of Russians were lying dead on the vast sun-scorched plain. Most of them still grasped their mounted bayonets in their rigid hands or even in death clutched their short-handled anti-tank hand-grenades.

A sickly smell of death hung over the fields. The men in the infantry carriers pressed handkerchiefs to their noses. With a shudder Tenning said to himself: "That's our handiwork."

The swirling dust settled on the vehicles of 3rd Panzer Grenadier Regiment and covered the scene with a veil. It settled on hands, helmets, and faces, and also on the half-ripe tomatoes which Tenning had placed on the armour-plate above the driver's seat next to the machine-gun, so they should ripen more quickly in the sun. They were driving towards the battle of Kharkov. They were about to reach a village which none of them had heard of as yet. A village whose name would be engraved on their memories as a place of carnage—the village of Polevoye.

The 3rd Panzer Division was employed on the left open flank of XI Corps outside Kharkov. To the left of it there was nothing. Only the gap in the front which separated Hoth's Fourth Panzer Army from Army Detachment Kempf, the gap through which General Vatutin's armies were pouring. Some of these had already wheeled round to envelop the city.

The huge supply dumps which had been set up in the Kharkov area on Hitler's orders and which contained three months' supplies of any-thing that two armies might need, were doomed. All the things which were in such short supply in Germany—here they were about to fall into enemy hands in unimaginable quantities.

One of these stores of Army Group South was at the Feski collective farm about fifteen miles north-west of Kharkov. In large warehouses and underground cellars, served by sidings connecting with the main line, was stored a whole year's output of the French spirits industry, as well as millions of cigarettes, cigars, and tins of food. Enough for a medium-sized town to live on comfortably for six months.

The quartermaster of III Panzer Corps was heartbroken at the thought that this dump too would before very long fall into Russian hands. He therefore sent word to all the divisions he could get hold

of: Send whatever transport you can spare and collect as much of the
stuff as you can.

He was not over-hopeful. For a long time all units had been com-
plaining of a shortage of vehicles whenever a transport task had to be
tackled. But in any war, whenever it is a matter of food or drink, the
soldiers of no matter what nationality invariably overcome all difficulties. To his amazement the quartermaster found a large fleet of
vehicles arriving at his dump.

Here was proof again, if any was needed, of how inflated, in spite
of all assurances to the contrary, the transport and baggage sections
of many formations had become. A great deal of stuff was being carried around which merely served the comforts of supply service and
which frequently, during withdrawals, congested the main roads and
prevented the fighting forces from moving freely.

But for once, in the case of Feski, this bad practice proved useful.
Within two days the transport of about a dozen divisions had taken on
board the major part of the valuable stores and carried them to the
troops of Army Detachment Kempf. This unit had just been renamed
Eighth Army and was now under the command of General Wöhler,
Manstein's former chief of staff. The only thing the troops showed no
interest in were the huge carboys filled with vodka. They were left
behind—after all, the choice between French cognac, Spanish port,
and Italian chianti was difficult enough. Who needed vodka?

No-one, of course, suspected that this despised Russian vodka would
turn into an effective secret weapon. But this was precisely what happened. No sooner had the Russians reached the dump than the
fighting spirit of the regiments evaporated for the time being. It took
them about three days to empty all those carboys of vodka. And that
was a very remarkable achievement.

Otto Tenning wrote in his diary: "While the comrades on the other
side were sleeping off their vodka hangovers and forgetting all about
this accursed war, the newly brought up SS 'Viking' Panzer Division
used the time for digging in undisturbed on the high ground behind
Feski." Thus an outflanking of Raus's group from the north was prevented. Kharkov was safe for another forty-eight hours. And that, in
Manstein's difficult calculations, was a lot.

But the fortunes of war are capricious. Only rarely is one side
favoured consistently. War is not a mathematical problem. Every
battle is largely affected by imponderables—the fortitude of a soldier,
the resolution of a commander, but equally the faint-heartedness of
a commander, the fear and, at worst, the panic which may grip a unit.

This was shown again at Kharkov. The new 282nd Infantry Division,
raised in France in 1942, with some of its officers and men lacking
active experience in the East, was employed at the junction between
XI and XLII Corps. It still used horse-drawn transport, the MG-34

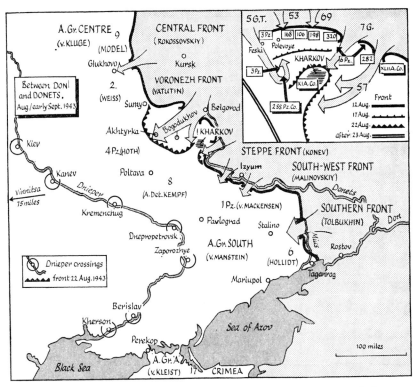

Map 35. The fourth battle of Kharkov. The city was holding out. Nevertheless, on 22nd August, 1943, Manstein ordered XI Army Corps to evacuate the city. He needed the corps to prevent a Soviet breakthrough to the Dnieper.

machine-gun, and for anti-tank defence it only had the 3·7-cm gun. In the course of the disengagement its regiments had to wheel back from their well-built positions on the Donets. And, suddenly, on 10th August, the regiment on the left wing, 848th Grenadier Regiment, was attacked by a strong Soviet armoured formation.

To find oneself in the midst of a tank attack while engaged in withdrawal is a highly dangerous business even for an experienced and hard-boiled unit. For 848th Grenadier Regiment it was too much. It suffered heavy casualties. And suddenly panic broke out. The regiment was scattered. Its remnants fled into Kharkov.

The incident touched off a chain reaction in the weak German front. The whole division was in confusion. Soviet armoured formations thrust unimpeded through the retreating German units. Lieutenant-Colonel von Löffelholz, the chief of operations, tried desperately to halt the fleeing formations. He did not succeed. In despair over the tragedy for which he was in no way responsible but which might well lead to the loss of Kharkov he faced the Soviet T-34s alone, with just his pistol. The Russian tanks rolled on, over him, towards Kharkov. They rolled into the eastern part of the city. They thrust into the tractor plant. They drove through the gates of the factories where the furnaces were working, where pneumatic forging presses were thundering, where tens of thousands of hands were manufacturing spares for the German armoured forces. Was this the end of German resistance in Kharkov? Would the defensive strength of the German divisions collapse in panic and chaos?

Aghast, Army Group headquarters registered the collapse of fighting morale. For the first time in the war the frightening thought emerged that draconian courts martial might be necessary to stop the rot. On 12th August there was serious discussion of whether that ultimate deterrent of any army should be resorted to—whether every tenth man of 282nd Infantry Division should be shot. The idea was not applied in practice. The troops, overstressed as they were, rallied. The experienced Rhineland-Westphalian 6th Panzer Division under Colonel Crisolli saved the situation. It stormed the tractor plant, dislodged the Soviets from the city, and sealed the dangerous penetration of Kharkov.

The Russians next tried their luck in the west. Except for a narrow corridor the city was now encircled. The famous Soviet Fifth Guards Tank Army, coming from the north-west, hurled itself against the hotly-contested metropolis of the Donets basin.

The regiments of 3rd Panzer Division were engaged in heavy fighting at the village of Polevoye, the centre of the Soviet attack. The guns of 75th Panzer Artillery Regiment fired till the barrels were red-hot. Soviet aircraft dropped leaflets: "Comrades of 3rd Panzer Division," they said, "we know that you are brave soldiers. Every other man in your division has the Iron Cross. But every other man on our side has a mortar. Surrender!" The men of 3rd and 394th Panzer Grenadier Regiments looked grave. But they pushed the leaflets away contemptuously with their feet. Men with their records were not persuaded into surrender.

The vast fields of sunflowers lay under the scorching sun. Behind the fields General Raus had posted his anti-tank guns, assault guns, and 8·8 flak battle groups in a chequer-board pattern. Eighty batteries of artillery completed this cover along the northern edge of the corridor into Kharkov. The SS "Das Reich" Panzer Division was now also arriving; its Panthers, Tigers, and assault guns were concealed in positions of readiness and two Panzer Grenadier regiments took up well-camouflaged switchlines along the Kharkov-Bugodukhov railway line.

On the Russian side General Rotmistrov's Fifth Guards Tank Army was deploying for attack. Stalin had commanded: "The city must fall quickly."

His impatience was due to a curious circumstance. Because of a mistake in a situation report he had already informed the Allied military attachés in Moscow that Kharkov had fallen. And he did not feel like issuing a denial. His order was motivated by prestige. But prestige usually is a bad counsellor. German aerial reconnaissance of Fourth Air Fleet spotted the preparations for the frontal attack on the corridor. Stukas of General Seidemann's VIII Air Corps dived on the Russian positions. The formation only had 1800-kg bombs available—giant bombs originally intended against warships. These heavy bombs now crashed down on villages and forests where Rotmistrov's tanks were concentrated. Enormous fountains of earth spouted up and the explosions, running through the ground like earth tremors, were felt a long way off. The Soviet attack was delayed by twenty-four hours. But Rotmistrov was tough.

By the morning of 19th August, in spite of the defensive barrage of the German artillery, Rotmistrov's tanks had pushed forward in three wedges through dips in the ground and fields of sunflowers, right up to the main road from Akhtyrka to Kharkov. They attacked. They got into the defensive chequer-board of anti-tank and flak guns. What had happened to the German Panzer regiments and assault-gun battalions in the Kursk battle a few weeks earlier was now experienced by the Soviet tank battalions outside Kharkov: they were broken up by a well-planned anti-tank defence system and knocked out in huge numbers. The last packs which forced their way through were attacked by lurking Panthers, Tigers, and assault guns, smashed up or driven back. One hundred and eighty-four knocked-out T-34s littered the battlefield. But Stalin wanted Kharkov.

The next day General Rotmistrov changed his tactics. With a huge armoured wedge—two hundred tanks, all of them T-34s—he attacked along the railway line. The armoured armada disappeared in five hundred acres of sunflowers. As if cut by an invisible reaper, the sunflowers, taller than a man, sank down under the tracks of the tanks. The steel fleet was approaching. But on the edge of the sea of sunflowers the hunters were lying in wait—a phalanx of Panthers, Tigers, and assault guns of the Ferdinand type. Drawn up between them the irresistible 8·8s.

Rotmistrov's tanks were emerging from the cover of the field. "Fire!" A roar of thunder, flashes of lightning and sheets of flame. The sound as of church bells bursting. One hundred and fifty Russian tanks were wrecked on the edge of the field of sunflowers.

But Rotmistrov had another hundred and sixty tanks in reserve. And Stalin wanted Kharkov.

Behind the curtain of smoke the sky was blood-red. The noise of battle abated. Night fell dark and sultry. Shortly before midnight came the renewed clank of tracks and the roar of engines from the fields of sunflowers. There was a new moon and it was so dark a man could not see his own hand. This time General Rotmistrov wanted to make darkness his ally. Flares hissed through the night.

"Action stations! Enemy tanks attacking." Firing orders: "One o'clock; armour piercing—one hundred—open fire!" A T-34 received a direct hit and was soon blazing like a torch. In its light the men could see the low enemy tanks rolling along the road. Soon the German tanks had made contact.

Panthers and T-34s were ramming one another. They were firing at each other at point-blank range. Boldly and vigorously the Russians thrust through the German anti-tank zone. But by now the bulk of the German tanks had joined battle.

The plateau where this nocturnal engagement was taking place was lit up by the faint glow of battle. Visibility was about one hundred yards. It was a gigantic nocturnal duel between two armoured armadas. Blazing tanks, knocked out by assault guns and anti-tank gun crews, served as markers for the T-34s in their breakthrough attempt.

After three hours the battle fell silent. No-one knew what the situation was. But at daybreak the facts were revealed: General Raus, an experienced commander in many tank-battles, had won the duel. More than eighty gutted T-34s lay on the battlefield. Of the enemy tanks which had made a nine-mile-deep penetration only three reached the western edge of Kharkov. There they encountered the headquarter personnel of 106th Infantry Division whose anti-tank squad knocked out two of them and captured the third.

But the divisions of XI Corps also suffered heavy losses. The 394th Panzer Grenadier Regiment of 3rd Panzer Division was down to the strength of two rifle companies. Numerous officers of all units had been killed in action. Captain Deichen's reconnaissance battalion consisted of only eighty men, and the 331st Grenadier Regiment of 167th Infantry Division, brought up as a reserve, arrived with a mere two hundred men.

Things were much the same with the other units of XI Corps. The 6th Panzer Division had fifteen tanks left, the Tiger Battalion 503 was down to nine tanks, and the three assault-gun battalions had altogether twenty-four assault guns left. But Kharkov was still in German hands. And the Soviet Fifth Guards Tank Army had been defeated.

At Army Group South headquarters General Busse recorded the incoming reports. Kharkov was holding out. But Field-Marshal von Manstein was in no mood for spectacular victories. Sooner or later Kharkov would be encircled. And that would not only mean half a dozen divisions trapped but the Russians would be able to push past the city to the Dnieper, into the rear of Eighth Army. Bending over his map, Manstein said to Busse, "I'd rather lose a city than an army."

Manstein did not know the orders of the Soviet High Command, but he made a shrewd guess, and history has proved him right. On 10th August the Soviet High Command had given orders for all major routes from Kharkov to the Dnieper to be cut, together with all rearward communications of Manstein's Eighth Army and First Panzer Army. Those were the stakes. Not just Kharkov.

Manstein drew Hitler's attention to this possibility. But Hitler categorically demanded that Kharkov should be held. "The fall of the city could have serious political repercussions," he implored the Field-Marshal. "The attitude of the Turks depends on it. And Bulgaria's attitude. If we abandon Kharkov we'll lose face in Ankara and Sofia."

But Manstein remained firm. "I am not prepared to sacrifice six divisions for some questionable political consideration," he said to Busse.

He remembered Stalingrad. On 22nd August he therefore ordered Kharkov to be evacuated. The savage fighting for the important Soviet metropolis of the Donets region, the city which had changed hands four times in twenty-two months, was over.

Reluctantly Hitler agreed. He accepted Manstein's decision because he was not yet able to do without his strategic skill in the south of the Eastern Front. But from then on the venom of suspicion against his best man worked in his heart. Manstein, the finest general on the Eastern Front, continued to stave off disaster with his ingenious system of stop-gap expedients. It was a dangerous game of switching his reserves from one place to another. In order to avert the danger of an enemy breakthrough on his northern wing in the Kharkov area, Manstein was compelled to withdraw forces from his southern wing and switch them to the north. But no sooner was the threat there contained than a crisis arose in the south, where the Russians were now striking at a greatly weakened front.

While Kharkov was still being evacuated, armies of the Soviet Army Group Southern Front under Colonel-General Tolbukhin charged across the Mius and burst through Hollidt's Sixth Army. Less than three weeks before, the SS Panzer Corps and the divisions of XXIX Army Corps, including the 23rd and 3rd Panzer Divisions and the 16th Panzer Grenadier Division, had managed to stabilize Hollidt's front. But now his SS Panzer Corps and 3rd Panzer Division were on the northern wing. And Tolbukhin had a clear road. He could strike deep into the heart of the Donets basin, above all at Zaporozhye on the Dnieper. If he succeeded, the Crimea and the German Seventeenth Army in the Kuban bridge-head would be cut off.

But how was this to be prevented? One did not have to be a staff officer to see what needed doing. And Manstein did not mince words when he explained the situation to his supreme Commander, Adolf

Hitler: If OKH stands by its directive to defend the Donets region, then forces amounting to at least half a dozen Panzer divisions must be made available! If OKH lacks those forces, then the exposed salient on the Mius cannot be held. In that case the front must be pulled back so that the enemy can at last be halted along a shortened and more favourable defensive line. "In that case I request freedom of movement," Manstein wrote to Hitler in East Prussia.

No words sounded more alarming to Hitler than "freedom of movement". In his eyes a general demanding freedom of movement was on the verge of mutiny. Hitler's reply, sent from the Wolfsschanze by telephone and reflecting the flap at the Führer's Headquarters following Manstein's request, was: "Don't do anything. I am coming myself."

2. Fighting on the Mius

Conference at Vinnitsa–The Donets region is at stake –Soviet breakthrough at Kuybyshevo–Hollidt's Sixth Army can no longer hold out–XXIX Corps is encircled– "Fix bayonets!"–Safety behind the Tortoise Line– Soviet attack on a broad front–Manstein and Kluge demand a Commander-in-Chief, East–The whole southern wing is in danger–Urgent message to Manstein–Withdrawal behind the Dnieper authorized at last.

THE woods around Vinnitsa are hot and close in summer. There is no cool shade and there is no refreshing breeze. The heat of the Ukrainian summer lies heavily over the tops of the conifers. It is a bad spot for people affected by the weather.

The Führer's Headquarters known as "Werewolf", from where Hitler directed the summer campaign of 1942, had therefore been a bad choice. Hitler, sensitive to the weather, did not feel well in this climate. He was nearly always bad-tempered, aggressive, and mistrustful of everybody.

He was happy when he left his forward headquarters again in late October 1942. Since then the block-houses had been standing empty. Only the arsenals, the communications centre, and the security huts had been occupied by rearward services of Army Group South. "Werewolf" was only a command post for Hitler's occasional visits, his base during his very rare inspection tours to the central sector of the Eastern Front. Only reluctantly did he move to the airless woods behind the Dnieper. He disliked them. He had never been happy there. He had neither a lucky hand nor a clear head under the heavy heat of the pine-woods.

He was disgruntled therefore when on 27th August he had to leave his beloved East Prussian Wolfsschanze for the Ukraine. Only a small staff accompanied him in the stately, four-engined Condor machine. The advance party had left the day before in several of Commodore Bauer's fast Heinkel machines in order to get everything ready at Vinnitsa.

"Werewolf" looked as secret and silent as in the summer of 1942. Except that then the German armies were racing ahead towards Stalingrad and into the Caucasus, whereas now, in the summer of 1943, they were pulling back. Vinnitsa lay in the path of the full-scale Soviet offensive.

Hitler had summoned Manstein and his army commanders to a conference at Vinnitsa. On his own initiative the Field-Marshal had moreover brought along the commander of his XI Corps, General Raus, the defender of Kharkov, who came straight from a major battle. He was also accompanied by the commander of 23rd Panzer Division, General von Vormann, whose regiments, together with 16th Panzer Grenadier Division and combat groups of 17th Panzer Division, had been standing up to the assault of nine Soviet divisions and nine tank brigades in the Izyum area on the middle Donets for the past two weeks. The C-in-C Army Group South thus had with him two important witnesses whose integrity, in view of their personal performance and the exemplary bearing of the troops under their command, could not be questioned by Hitler. Their evidence about the dangerous over-stretching of the front was bound to carry weight.

Manstein quoted two figures to demonstrate the trouble. Army Group South had lost a total of 133,000 men in the heavy fighting of the past few months; yet it had only received 33,000 men to replace them. That was a deficit of 100,000 men. But the Field-Marshal was able to go into even greater detail. Hollidt's Sixth Army had lost 23,830 men between 17th July and 21st August, 1943; these had been replaced by 3312 men. Deficit: 20,000 men. Colonel-General von Mackensen's First Panzer Army had lost 27,291 men over the same period; its replacements had been 6174 men. Deficit: 21,000 men.

These were the figures which Manstein presented to Hitler, figures which spoke for themselves. He continued: "This then is the position on our side, my Führer. And here"—he drew out the written situation report of Sixth Army of the night before—"here is the information about the enemy, my Führer." He turned to the C-in-C Sixth Army: "General Hollidt, will you please give the Führer a comparative picture of the enemy's and our own strength?"

General of Infantry Hollidt, an experienced army commander at crucial points of the Eastern Front ever since November 1942, needed no pieces of paper. He carried the impressive figures of his Sixth Army in his head: "My XXIX Corps has 8706 men left. Facing it are 69,000 Russians. My XVII Corps has 9284 men; facing it are 49,500 Russians. My IV Corps is relatively best off—it has 13,143 men, faced by 18,000 Russians. Altogether 31,133 Germans against 136,500 Russians. The relative strength in tanks is similar: Tolbukhin yesterday had 165 tanks in operation; we had 7 tanks and 38 assault guns."

Hollidt stopped. Manstein immediately took up the thread. Calmly he argued: "The enemy is stepping up his pressure. With our available forces the Donets region cannot be defended, my Führer. Things are no better at First Panzer Army. Nor will Eighth Army and Fourth Panzer Army be in a position to prevent a Russian breakthrough to the Dnieper in the long run. Moreover, to the best of our knowledge the situation on the southern wing of Army Group Centre, at the Second Army, is also exceedingly dangerous. Either you let us have fresh forces, and that means twelve divisions, or the Donets region must be abandoned in order to free the necessary forces within the Army Group itself. I see no other solution."

Hitler tried to avoid a decision. He acknowledged the difficult situation. He was aware of the heavy losses, especially among commanding officers. He thanked the commanders-in-chief for the performance of their troops. But then he demanded brusquely that every inch of ground must continue to be contested until the enemy was convinced of the fruitlessness of his attacks. Yet Manstein did not yield. Reinforcements or retreat, he insisted. "Where am I to find reinforcements?" Hitler argued.

Manstein replied: "Get Army Groups Centre and North to make available any formations they can possibly spare, my Führer, so that we may employ them here, at the focal point of the Soviet offensive."

"I need to think about it," Hitler said evasively. But Manstein did not let up. Now, he argued, was the moment of decision.

And Hitler made his decision. Since he regarded a voluntary evacuation of the economically vital Donets region as unacceptable, he promised Manstein immediate reinforcements of several divisions, which he would take from Army Group Centre. Moreover, the battle-weary formations of his Army Group were to be replaced by others from quieter sectors of the front.

Manstein and his generals returned to their headquarters greatly relieved. They began to work out plans for the new situation. But their plans were in vain.

Just as if they had been present at the conference-table in Vinnitsa, the Russians attacked the two wings of Kluge's Army Group Centre the very next day and achieved local penetrations on the fronts of both Second Army and Fourth Army. In the circumstances there could now be no thought of the envisaged—and indeed already ordered—transfer of troops to help Manstein. Field-Marshal von Kluge personally saw Hitler at once, on 28th August, and explained to him that he could not spare a single division. Army Group North, which had so far succeeded in holding its extensive line, refused to give up any of its formations. Manstein received nothing. And, as he had expected, the situation began to turn critical, especially on the Mius.

During the night of 27th–28th August two fast Soviet Corps burst through the weak lines of Sixth Army, wheeled south towards Mariupol, and through three undefended Yelanchik valleys pushed on into the rear of XXIX Corps. Any delay would be extremely dangerous. The battle-weary formation of Hollidt's Sixth Army fought on a front of a hundred and twenty miles, without any strategic reserves. For the past ten days the divisions of XXIX, IV, and XVII Corps had been trying to halt the full-scale attack with all possible stop-gaps. But Hollidt, a circumspect commander, lacked men more than weapons.

The headquarters staff of the SS Panzer Corps, its Corps troops, and

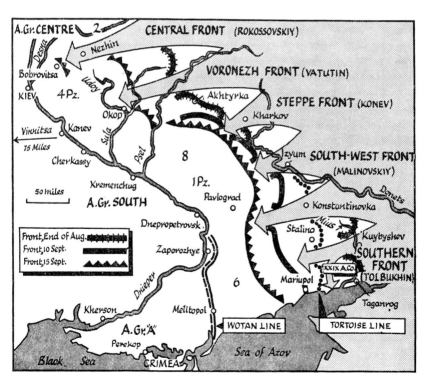

Map 36. Army Group South battling to hold the Donets region. On 14th September, 1943, Soviet divisions broke through the northern wing of the Army Group.

the "Leibstandarte" had been moved by Hitler to Italy; the "Toten-kopf" Division was fighting at Kharkov; the 16th Panzer Grenadier Division, and the 17th and 23rd Panzer Divisions had been working as the fire brigade of First Panzer Army in the Izyum area since early August. Thus, Sixth Army was left with three weakened Corps. Each mile of front line was held, on an average, by a hundred and thirty to a hundred and sixty men. How could they stop the onslaught of the Soviet masses?

Ten days earlier, on 18th August, on the sector of XVII Corps between Kalinovka and Hill 175·5, the 294th Infantry Division had been overrun by the Soviet Second Guards Army and Fifth Striking Army. The Soviet command was now pushing one Corps after another through the narrow gap near Kuybyshevo. That gap, originally, was a mere two miles wide. A mere two miles. What an opportunity for Hollidt—if only he had possessed the most modest tactical reserves.

But the Soviets appeared to be exceedingly well informed about the situation on the German side. With total unconcern Tolbukhin drove his divisions through the dangerously narrow channel. And Hollidt lacked the strength to nip off that reckless Soviet thrust which was only two miles wide.

In vain did Picker's Combat Group of 3rd Mountain Division and advanced parts of 13th Panzer Division, brought up from the Crimea, hurl themselves against the flanks of the corridor which had meanwhile been widened by the Soviets to eight miles. In vain did the assault guns of Assault Gun Brigade 259, together with the Armoured Combat Group of 13th Panzer Division, launch an immediate counterattack from the south-west towards the north. They gained half a mile, then another half, and finally got four miles into the penetration area. But they lacked the strength for the final push.

Everything now happened as it was bound to happen. Sixth Army was no longer able to halt the Soviet breakthrough. On 28th August the enemy corps swept forward to the south and on 29th reached the coast at Taganrog.

XXIX Army Corps, along the Sea of Azov, was surrounded. Desperately the Lower Saxon 111th and the Franconian 17th Infantry Divisions, together with the Central German 13th Panzer Division, tried to stave off annihilation. Remnants of the 15th Luftwaffe Field Division and the Bielefeld 336th Infantry Division, both of which had been smashed, fought their way through to the bulk of the forces in the pocket. On 30th August, 1943, thanks to vigorous support from Rudel's Stuka *Geschwader*, 13th Panzer Division and Assault Gun Brigade 259 eventually succeeded in prising open the Soviet ring at Fedorovka. Into this breach now stormed the infantry divisions which had been ordered by General Brandenberger to break out on 31st August. At the very centre were General Zimmer's 17th Infantry

Division from Nuremberg. Colonel Preus's 21st Grenadier Regiment burst through the Soviet ring across the hills of Toropilovskiy.

Farther south, the 111th and 336th Infantry Divisions broke out from the northern shore of the Sea of Azov in the direction of Mariupol and Melitopol. This concentrated combat group was commanded by Lieutenant-General Recknagel. "Fix bayonets! We're off!" Every man, down to the last driver, knew what was at stake. As in the far-off days of the great German offensives the traditional battle cry of "Urra!" again thundered over the battlefield between Mius and the Sea of Azov. Flak and assault guns formed the spearhead.

They succeeded. At the cost of great sacrifices the formations linked up again with the main front. The chief of operations of 111th Infantry Division, Lieutenant-Colonel Franz, carried in his pocket an intercepted *en clair* signal from the C-in-C of the Soviet Fifty-First Army to the general commanding his XIX Tank Corps, dated 30th August. "By 12 noon the German General Recknagel will stand as a prisoner before me in Taganrog market-place." But that was a service which the XIX Tank Corps was unable to render to its Army Commander.

The fate of XXIX Corps showed what a reckless gamble the fighting on the Mius had become. Field-Marshal von Manstein was not inclined to continue with it. In very blunt telephone conversations he demanded Hitler's agreement to pull Sixth Army back by some forty miles. The name of the new line was "Tortoise". Army engineers and enlisted building workers of the Todt Organization had built it in feverish haste as a barrier protecting the important industrial centre of Stalino. Would it stand up? How long could it stand up? That was the crucial question for the fate of the entire Donets region, whose possession—as Hitler kept telling his generals—was an indispensable prerequisite for the continuation of the war.

Stalin knew Hitler's worries and therefore gave him no respite whatever on his southern wing, on the front of Manstein's Army Group. In the Izyum area Malinovskiy attacked the First Panzer Army and the northern wing of Sixth Army during the first days of September; General Vatutin simultaneously got ready for a large-scale attack against the front of Hoth's Fourth Panzer Army in the Akhtyrka area. General Konev's Steppe Front charged the positions of Eighth Army, striking from the Kharkov area, from the north and east, and eventually forced General Wöhler to pull back his front again. Crises everywhere. Nothing but crises.

Manstein telephoned Kluge. The two marshals commanding the focal points of the Eastern Front arranged to fly to East Prussia together and to compel Hitler to take certain fundamental decisions. He must send them reinforcements. And, equally important, they

wanted to get Hitler to give up the unhealthy and unprofitable concentration of power vested in him in his capacities of Head of State,
Supreme Commander of the Wehrmacht, and Commander-in-Chief
of Land Forces.

The marshals demanded an integrated Supreme Command for all
theatres of war under a single, fully responsible Chief of a Grand
General Staff. Hitler, moreover, was to give up the personal direction
of operations in the East. He was to appoint a military Commander-
in-Chief for the whole of the Eastern Front, a Commander-in-Chief,
East, who would have complete and independent control of operations
in Russia. They wanted to put an end to Hitler's disastrous direct interference in the conduct of the war in Russia.

This move represented a legitimate attack by the most senior commanders in the field upon the dangerous concentration of power in
the supreme leadership of the Reich—a move of historic importance
but still insufficiently known and appreciated.

The conference at the Führer's Headquarters in East Prussia took
place on 3rd September. But the man at the Wolfsschanze was not
prepared to bow to his marshals. True, Kluge succeeded in wresting
from him his agreement to the withdrawal of the southern wing of
Army Group Centre behind the Desna; Hitler also agreed to abandon
the Kuban bridge-head and move the Seventeenth Army over to the
Crimea; he finally let Manstein pull back Sixth Army from the Mius
to the Tortoise Line if there was no other way out. But that was all.

Again Hitler could not get himself to take the big decision. He
stuck to his terrible delusions, refused to acknowledge the strength of
the enemy, and just would not see that it was no longer a question of
winning victories but of averting a threatening defeat. So he took half-
measures, opted for short-term solutions, and resorted to expedients.
Give up the Donets basin? Certainly not. Withdraw forces from other
theatres of war and switch them to the Eastern Front? Certainly not.
Most brusquely of all he rejected the idea of a Commander-in-Chief,
East.

Having achieved nothing, the two Field-Marshals returned to their
hard-pressed fronts. That was the evening when Allied troops landed
on the southern tip of Italy.

Three days later the price had to be paid for the reckless unconcern
of the Führer's Headquarters. A concentrated, vigorous thrust directed
by Colonel-General Malinovskiy's South-West Front with its Third
Guards Army against the junction between the German First Panzer
Army and Sixth Army tore open the newly established Tortoise Line
on both sides of Konstantinovka. Two fast Russian Corps raced past
the remaining corner-posts of 62nd and 33rd Infantry Divisions,
through a gap nearly thirty miles wide, aiming at Pavlograd. Somehow General Fretter-Pico with 23rd Panzer Division and the Combat

Group of 16th Panzer Grenadier Division managed to intercept the enemy. General von Vormann even succeeded, on 11th and 12th September, in co-operation with 9th Panzer Division, in closing the gap between Sixth Army and First Panzer Army. In a dashing armoured raid the reinforced Panther Battalion of 23rd Panzer Division under Captain Fritz Fechner even reached the supply route of the Soviet XXIII Tank Corps. But what was the use of it all? The exhausted infantrymen were finished.

Once more Soviet tanks forced a breakthrough to the west. Their advanced detachments were racing towards the Dnieper crossings at Dnepropetrovsk. Simultaneously the armies of the Soviet Central Front, under Army General Rokossovskiy, struck at the junction between Army Group Centre and Army Group South, and with strong forces cut right through the front of Second Army.

The northern wing of Manstein's Fourth Panzer Army was outflanked and had to be pulled back. A dangerous new gap had been torn in the front. The Russians now had a clear run to the middle Dnieper, and Kiev was threatened. Manstein was not prepared to let matters drift.

On 7th September he sent an urgent teleprinter signal to Hitler: "Fifty-five Soviet divisions and two tank corps are now facing the Army Group. Further forces from other Soviet fronts are being brought up. The Russians have concentrated their main effort here, on the southern front. I need reinforcements or a free hand for a further withdrawal to shortened, more favourable, sectors."

The tone of the signal was curt, firm, and uncompromising. Hitler realized that Manstein was in earnest. Once more, on 8th September, he got into his four-engined Condor and flew out to Zaporozhye, Manstein's headquarters. He was in a gloomy mood. At the Führer's Headquarters the unconditional surrender of Germany's Italian allies was being expected at any moment. The European southern flank, in consequence, was uncovered. The enemy was in Germany's rear. Standing in front of his large situation map in Zaporozhye, Manstein, in the presence of Field-Marshal von Kleist and the newly appointed Commander of Seventeenth Army, General of Engineer Troops Jaenecke, gave the Führer a detailed picture of the fighting of the past few days. Urgently he pointed to the danger threatening his northern wing, where the Russians had made all preparations for enveloping the Army Group. "If that comes off, then two armies will be lost, my Führer—and nothing can ever bring them back again."

Manstein's hand swept down over the map to the front of Sixth Army. "And things are no better here. Mariupol is in danger. The gap here is thirty miles wide. I've no forces left to close it and to hold the Tortoise Line. Whether we like it or not, we've got to move back."

Hitler was listening very intently. "What do you propose?" he asked.

Manstein had his answer ready: "First of all I propose to pull Army Group Centre back to the Dnieper at once. That will shorten its front by a third. With the forces thus saved the Dnieper line, including the approaches to the Crimea on the lower Dnieper, can be strengthened and held along a line stretching from Zaporozhye to Melitopol, the Wotan Line."

Hitler shook his head. No. Pull back Army Group Centre to the Dnieper? Out of the question. That would mean losing too much material. And it would take much too long.

Hitler's objection to a withdrawal to the Dnieper showed that he had no understanding for the kind of fast, large-scale movements that Manstein had repeatedly performed during the past few months. Only Manstein's skill in this field had so far averted the catastrophe which had been threatening the southern wing for months. But Hitler refused to see this.

At least he understood one thing when he saw the situation map in Zaporozhye—Army Group South urgently needed reinforcements if it was to hold out. He promised Manstein a corps with four divisions from Army Group Centre. It was to be made available at once, at the junction between the two Army Groups, in order to prevent the envelopment of Manstein's northern wing. Hitler moreover promised him four further divisions, so that the most important crossings of the Dnieper could at last be made secure. So far no preparations had been made at the Dnieper for a really effective defence of the river and the bridges in the event of a Soviet breakthrough.

Admittedly, in early August 1943 OKH had completed a study on the construction of the "Eastern Wall"—*i.e.*, the fortification of the Dnieper line—and had submitted the report to Hitler. On 12th August he had ordered work to be started immediately. But apart from local security measures nothing had been done. This omission was soon to prove disastrous.

Finally, in order to persuade Manstein to hold out well in front of the Dnieper, Hitler promised him parts of Seventeenth Army which, since 4th September, had been in the process of being pulled out from the now useless Kuban bridge-head back into the Crimea.

Manstein, let down so often before, suggested that all these orders should be issued straight away, from Zaporozhye. But Hitler angrily scotched this suggestion. Nevertheless, as he was climbing aboard his Condor to fly back to his Headquarters, he once more turned to

A Russian field position is taken in the Demyansk area.
Prisoners.

Manstein and said to him placatingly: "You'll get your divisions for the Dnieper bridges; the order is going out this very evening."

The order went out all right. Army Group Centre was ordered to detach 4th and 8th Panzer Divisions as well as two infantry divisions. But it was not obeyed. Field-Marshal von Kluge found himself unable to hand over the divisions. And so everything remained as it was.

Twenty-four hours later Manstein furiously telephoned the Chief of the General Staff of Land Forces, Colonel-General Zeitzler: "Kindly inform the Führer," he opened the conversation, "kindly inform the Führer that he may expect the beginning of a disastrous Soviet breakthrough to the Dnieper at any moment." In his teleprinter report he added a final sentence which records for history who, with his piecemeal measures and half-way decisions, bore the blame for the grave developments of the past few weeks: "If some foresight had been shown and if the reinforcements, now made indispensable by the situation, had been made available in good time, the present crisis, which may well lead to the final decision in the East and hence of the war generally, would have been avoided."

Until that day no general had so clearly pinned the blame for the catastrophe in the East upon Adolf Hitler. And his reaction? No reply from the Führer's Headquarters. But Hitler was mistaken if he thought he could bind Manstein to his orders by just keeping silent.

The Soviet High Command had no consideration for Hitler's wishful thinking. Stalin did not wait. He did not waste time by resting his formations, as the Führer's Headquarters had hoped, but urged on his weary armies to keep up their attacks on Manstein's northern wing. "Smash Army Group South—that's the key to victory," was Stalin's slogan. In the reconquered areas behind the front, throughout towns and villages, he mobilized anybody able to carry a rifle. Young boys and old men were enlisted into depot battalions. They were clothed and trained on the way to the front. They drew a rifle, a tunic or uniform trousers, a pair of boots, and perhaps a steel helmet. They were taught to load and to fire. No more. And then they attacked. In this way the Soviet Southern Front recruited 80,000 men in the regions along the Sea of Azov within a mere three weeks. This was total war.

On 14th September there happened what Stalin had hoped for and Manstein had foreseen—Soviet divisions of the Voronezh Front broke through on the northern wing of the Army Group, tore open the German front, and thrust through to the south-west, in the direction of the Dnieper. The Soviets reached Okop between the Sula and Uday rivers, and were thus a mere seventy-five miles from Cherkassy. Farther north, in the Nezhin–Bobrovitsa area, the spearheads of Rokossovskiy's Central Front were within forty-six miles of Kiev, the

Street fighting in Velikiye Luki: Russians charging.

Map 37. Mid-September 1943 saw the start of the boldest withdrawal in military history. About a million German troops were pulled out of a 600-mile front, over six Dnieper bridges, and again fanned out to hold a 400-mile line on the near bank.

Ukrainian capital. There was a real danger now that the Russians might seize the vital Dnieper crossings in the rear of the German lines.

By now every chance had been missed to halt the enemy in front of the Dnieper by bringing up reserves. It had been missed through Hitler's fatal indecision. Manstein curtly reported to the Führer's Headquarters: "Enemy breakthrough to Kremenchug and Kiev within the realm of possibility. Tomorrow morning I shall order Fourth Panzer Army to withdraw to the Dnieper on both sides of Kiev in order to prevent the Army being encircled in small groups and smashed in front of the river." But Manstein also announced his immediate withdrawal of Eighth Army and First Panzer Army to the

Dnieper. And he added this warning: "Whether we shall succeed in crossing the river without the arrival of covering forces is doubtful."

There was dismay in the Operations Department of OKH: even Field-Marshal von Kluge, normally a supporter of Hitler's hold-on strategy, had sent a signal that day which could not be more serious. "The withdrawal of the bulk of my forces to the 'Eastern Wall' [the Dnieper line] is becoming unavoidable," he reported. Hitler nevertheless had an urgent signal sent to Manstein: "Order must not be given. Führer expects you for report at Wolfsschanze tomorrow."

The fourth conference between Hitler and the Marshal opened in an atmosphere of electric tension. "What is at stake now is no longer the holding of the Dnieper line or of the economically important regions of the Donbas, my Führer, but the fate of the Eastern Front." That was how Manstein opened the talks.

His courageous words and the hard facts behind them at last made Hitler see reason. He agreed to the withdrawal of the main front behind the Dnieper and the Desna. Only on the southern wing was Sixth Army to hold the Wotan Line east of the Dnieper, from Melitopol to the Dnieper bend at Zaporozhye. On 15th September Manstein issued the relevant orders. An important decision had been made. But had it been made in time? Or was it already too late? Would the troops reach the river crossings and cross the bridges before the Russians overtook them?

A breathtaking chapter in the history of the war was opening.

3. The "Eastern Wall"

The Dnieper, a river of destiny–Protective wall to guard industrial wealth–The Zaporozhye dam–An order of ninety lines–Evacuation along six hundred miles of front– Endless trek–Scorched earth.

THE Dnieper—what a river! After the Volga and the Danube, the third biggest river in Europe, the second biggest in European Russia. It has its source in the Valday hills, flows 1419 miles to the south, into the Black Sea, and is the lifeline of the fertile Ukraine. On its banks stood the cradle of the Russian State. An impressive river. Up to forty feet deep and up to two miles wide. As is the case with nearly all Russian rivers, its western bank is a steep cliff and hence an ideal defensive position.

It was easy to see why, in the summer of 1943, this river represented the silent hopes of the German General Staff and the troops in the field. Here, behind this natural barrier, a strong defensive zone could be established—that "Eastern Wall" of which OKH had been dreaming ever since the defeat of Kursk. Here the Red Army could be awaited, here it could be brought to a halt.

Hitler had known his generals' views for a number of months. But since his strategic creed consisted of "holding on at all costs" and retreat, even as a strategic delaying action, was a mortal sin in his eyes, he had for a long time forbidden the construction of fortifications, bunkers, and trenches on the western bank of the Dnieper. "The knowledge that there is a well-established fortified line behind them merely induces my generals and troops to take to their heels," Hitler argued. Not until mid-August, when the Soviet assault was already sweeping towards the Dnieper, did he grudgingly and half-heartedly authorize the beginning of work on an "Eastern Wall" along the Dnieper and Desna. He authorized it—but he did not make any manpower available for it.

Now, in mid-September, the sins of omission of many months were to be made good within a few days or hours.

The situation had become really dangerous. For if the approaching Russians were not halted at the Dnieper barrier—what then? The Crimea would be lost. The Ukraine would be lost. The Rumanian frontier would be within easy reach of the Russians. It was clear enough: the fate of the war in the East really hung on the Dnieper.

For Stalin, the Dnieper represented the most tempting strategic, economic, and political prize. The vast river was not only a military line; it was also the last great barrier in front of the vital raw materials of the Ukraine and Rumania. So long as the Wehrmacht controlled the granary of Russia, the fertile regions west of the Dnieper, there would be bread and milk, eggs and meat. More important still—behind the Dnieper were not only fertile fields. Below the black earth of those fields lay the most highly coveted treasures of the industrial century. At Krivoy Rog the Ukrainian iron ore was mined. At Zaporozhye and Nikopol were the precious manganese ores and non-ferrous metals—copper and nickel—which were so vital for armaments manufacture. More than 30 per cent of Germany's requirements were covered from these sources.

Finally, behind the two-mile-wide anti-tank ditch represented by the Dnieper lay the oilfields of Rumania, at that time, in 1943, the most important in Europe after the Russian fields.

One-half of Germany's total mineral oil requirements were met from Rumanian wells. Without that oil large-scale operations by mobile troops and massive air forces were impossible and the war would be lost. So long as Germany controlled Rumania's oil she need have no anxiety about fuel for tanks and aircraft. The Dnieper had become the river of destiny of the war. Provided the German forces could hold it, the leadership of the Reich would remain militarily and economically operational.

This is not just a theory based on German over-optimism, but a view fully supported by the Official Soviet *History of the Great Fatherland War*, Volume 3. It seems incredible that, even in the summer of 1943, the man at the Wolfsschanze continued to close his eyes to the facts. On 21st June, 1943, when Manstein had put the question to OKH: Was the Donets region to be held or was it more important to make the Russians bleed themselves to death on the Dnieper that summer, OKH had replied: "The Führer wants both!"

The Führer wanted both. But both was not to be had.

Stalin had long realized the importance of the Dnieper barrier for the future course of the war. And he assumed that his opposite number in East Prussia was assessing the situation equally coolly and would attempt to withdraw in good time behind that vital defensive barrier. Such a withdrawal was just what Stalin was worried about. He regarded a timely German withdrawal behind a fortified Dnieper line as the greatest threat to his own chances of victory. That was why, ever since the spring of 1943, he had been urging his marshals: You must stop a German defence being organized behind the Dnieper; you must stop it at all costs. We must get to the Dnieper! That was the wish, the hope, and the overriding idea in the Soviet General Staff.

The Soviet plan for the summer and autumn of 1943 was logically based on this idea. The Soviet High Command intended to smash the southern wing of the German armies in the East by its summer offensive and, in following up these movements, cross the Dnieper. To achieve this objective Stalin employed all the forces he had. According to the *Journal for Soviet Military History* the Soviet High Command concentrated on its southern wing 40 per cent of all its rifle formations and 84 per cent of all armoured formations.

Stalin in this way achieved a tremendous concentration of power. Both in men and *matériel* he had a six-fold superiority over his German opponents. What he was preparing was the most powerful Soviet operation of the Second World War. Everything was staked on this card—armies, weapons, partisans, espionage, and propaganda. The troops' morale was raised to a high pitch. The Dnieper was proclaimed a sacred objective whose recapture would mean the dawn of victory.

Stalin appealed not only to the honour and patriotism of his generals, commanders, and soldiers, but also to their vanity. On 9th September, in a directive to all fronts and armies, Stalin promised his officers and other ranks the highest decorations if they distinguished themselves in overcoming the Dnieper and Desna.

An interesting point is that in doing so the Soviet Command did not apply the German principle that any soldier—no matter whether private or general—could earn any distinction for bravery. Stalin's directive revealed a class structure reminiscent of the old Imperial German Army. Army commanders were promised the Order of Suvorov, First Class. Division and brigade commanders were promised the Order of Suvorov, Second Class, and regimental and battalion commanders the Order of Suvorov, Third Class, for successful operations against the Dnieper. Other ranks contributing by a decisive feat of heroism to the overcoming of the great river would be recommended for the title of Hero of the Soviet Union.

Wednesday, 15th September, in Zaporozhye, the town on the Dnieper bend, was a typical Russian late summer day. From the river came a cool breeze. The massive, elegant dam, then the biggest in Europe, provided an ideal bathing spot for the troops. The dam astride the river was a huge and impressive structure—2500 feet long, with a railway track and a dual-carriageway road running along its top. With the water backed up by the dam the turbines of the power-station generated 550,000 kilowatts. The power-station supplied electric current to the whole West Ukrainian industrial region. The plant was a showpiece of the Bolshevik regime, a symbol of the communist aim of electrifying and industrializing the whole country. For that reason the power-station bore the name of Lenin, the man who in 1920 coined the slogan: "Communism means Soviet power plus electrification of the whole country."

During their retreat in 1941 the Soviets, on Stalin's express order, had destroyed their technical miracle on the Dnieper. It was not to fall undamaged into German hands. The dam was blown up and the shipping lock rendered useless. But either there had been no time for further destruction, or else what had been done was thought sufficient— the fact was that the power-station remained intact. However, an unlucky shell caused a serious fire and water burst into the machinery. As a result, the power-station was out of action for some time. However, after the first difficult repairs to the dam, generation of power was soon resumed. Even so it took yet another three years of laborious work before, early in 1943, power output was back to the old figure.

Since then Major-General Kittel, the military commandant of the Zaporozhye dam, had been solicitously guarding this industrial jewel. Two flak regiments protected the dam and the power-station against attack from the air. Booms and torpedo nets of the navy screened it against surprise raids by Soviet naval commandos and against drifting mines and aerial torpedoes. As the front got closer, Kittel strengthened the forces protecting the installations by way of "private recruitment". Whatever stragglers turned up in Zaporozhye he intercepted and formed into a combat group. It was a somewhat motley crowd, and half a dozen different divisions were represented in the formations raised by the general for the defence of the city and the dam.

The headquarters of Army Group South were in an administrative building in the western part of the busy and neat industrial city. Manstein's closest collaborator, General Busse, was sitting in the map room on 15th September, 1943. He was putting the final touches to the withdrawing order. The Field-Marshal came in late at night, after his return from the Führer's Headquarters, together with Colonel Schulze-Büttger, the chief of operations. Once more they went over the order. Soberly it began with the sentences: "Army Group will pull back to the Wotan Line on the Dnieper. The speed of the withdrawal will be determined solely by the maintenance of the fighting capacity of the troops."

Maintenance of fighting capacity. That was Manstein's great anxiety. Every man on his staff knew how great that anxiety was. Busse, who as his chief of staff was responsible for the co-ordination of all strategic measures, put it into words: "All they need now, over there, is one or two generals who have more or less grasped and mastered our principles of tank warfare—and we'll be in trouble. They will thrust through the gaps which are bound to arise owing to the contraction of our forces towards the bridges, and they'll get to the Dnieper bridges before us. They only need one Guderian—and God help us!"

"We must hope that they haven't learnt the lesson yet," Manstein said. "The last few weeks incline me to believe that they haven't."

Manstein was alluding to the development of the critical situation at Akhtyrka and Stalino. There the Russians had missed a unique opportunity of pushing through to the Dnieper with a ruthless tank thrust from the north to the south-west, of pressing Army Group South back against the Sea of Azov and annihilating it well east of the few Dnieper crossings.

Although the Soviet generals had penetrated deep into the German front they had failed to exploit their breakthrough. They had not yet produced a Guderian, a Rommel, a Hoth, and least of all a Manstein. Not yet.

Manstein's withdrawal order, on which the life or death of four armies depended, was a mere ninety typewritten lines long. A mere ninety lines. They represented a plan of battle of crucial importance. The last two points, numbers 7 and 8, demonstrated Manstein's style of leadership. They ran: "(7) All decisions to be taken and orders to be given on the strength of the above directives must be based on the realization that any difficulty is mastered by an intact force, whereas no operation, least of all a retreat, can be accomplished with troops which have lost their fighting capacity or morale. Armies will not simply pass on downward the further objectives listed in the present directive, but will exercise strict day-to-day leadership. (8) The armies will report their intentions without delay. . . . Army Group will thereupon co-ordinate the movements."

It was Manstein's most difficult and most dangerous operation of the whole war. His forces were engaged in a savage defensive battle. The 600-mile-long front was torn open at many points. The battle-weary formations as well as the "fire brigade" units were hard-pressed by a superior and confident enemy. In this situation a force of four armies consisting of fifteen corps HQs and sixty-three and a half divisions and everything that went with that kind of machinery—roughly a million troops and civilian Wehrmacht employees—were to pull back several hundred miles, step by step and fighting all the way, without losing cohesion and without panic. A million men had to be detached from a front of about 600 miles; three of its four armies, with their fifty-four and a half divisions, had to be pulled back towards six bridges in order to withdraw, platoon by platoon, across one of the greatest rivers of Europe.

But that was only half the task. On the far side of the river First Panzer Army, Eighth Army, and Fourth Panzer Army, as well as their northern neighbours of Army Group Centre, would have to fan out again as quickly as possible into a front of 450 miles before the hotly pursuing enemy could reach the western bank himself. A glance at the map illustrates this boldest and most daring disengagement manoeuvre in military history. If it came off the great crisis would be overcome; if it did not come off the German armies in the East would be facing defeat and a possible loss of a million men. The fate of the war itself would be in jeopardy.

As if the purely military aspect of the withdrawal was not difficult enough, there was a string of additional tasks to add to Army Group's worries. Some 200,000 wounded, complete with the hospitals and staffs of the German, Hungarian, Rumanian, Slovak, and Ukrainian Red Cross, had to be moved back. A large part of the Russian civilian population was likewise to be evacuated. Experience during recent withdrawals had shown that in all regained territories the Red Army immediately mobilized all able-bodied men between sixteen and sixty and incorporated them in the fighting units. The *History of the Great Fatherland War* reports that a single Soviet army, the Thirteenth Army, had enlisted 30,000 men in the recaptured areas of its front at the beginning of September and thus swelled its fighting formations. These men were given weapons as they joined the forces, often during battle—the weapons of men wounded or killed.

But there were twenty-five Soviet armies on the Southern Front. And all of them did their recruiting in this manner. General Nehring, then commanding XXIV Panzer Corps, in a commentary on this practice, observed: "These men were not 100 per cent soldiers, but they ran along with the rest, they burst into the gaps in the line and flooded us." That, in fact, was the significance of this mass recruitment. To prevent such a dangerous strengthening of the Red Army, men of military age and the workers of the principal industrial and food production enterprises were therefore evacuated with the German forces. In the sector of Army Group South these civilians totalled roughly 200,000. Since their families were allowed to join them the real number of people following the German retreat was about twice as much.

In consequence, the German regiments, the Ukraine police units and auxiliary units, the volunteer Cossack squadrons of the Caucasian tribes, the Turkmen legions, and the columns of workers were followed by huge, motley treks of civilians. They were allowed to take with them their possessions and domestic animals. Endless processions were moving along roads and tracks towards the Dnieper. The whole population was on the move. A lieutenant from Hamburg wrote to his mother: "This trek is exciting and unreal, curious and grim at the same time. A country and an army are on the move, and everything is making for the great river which we hope will give us a safe defensive line again."

But the Red Army was to be denied more than mere manpower. A special order by Reich Marshal Göring, issued as Commissioner for the Four-Year Plan on Hitler's behalf on 7th September, instructed army commanders to carry off all stocks of foodstuffs and raw materials, all the livestock of collective and State farms, and the industrial and agricultural machines of armaments works. Grain and oleaginous fruit, horses, cattle, sheep, and pigs, threshing machines and tractors, lathes and machine tools, as well as vehicles of every kind—all these were to be taken along to behind the Dnieper. And, finally, also the rolling-stock of the railways by means of which this gigantic exodus was to be accomplished. Nothing but an empty countryside was to be left behind.

And not even that. In order to delay the Russian advance as much as possible in its final stage east of the Dnieper, so that the pursuit could not immediately be followed by a leap across the river, a zone of twelve to twenty-five miles east of the Dnieper was to be turned into a desert. Whatever could not be removed was to be totally destroyed—blown up, burnt down, devastated—every house, every bridge, every road, every path, every tree, and every barn. The enemy was to enter a wilderness, where he would find no place to lay down his head for a rest, nothing to eat or drink, nothing to give him shelter, and nothing to help him on. Scorched earth. For the first time this method was to be incorporated in the German strategic plan on a

major scale; for the first time the frightful scourge of fire and devastation was to be applied. The method which Stalin had repeatedly
practised in 1941 and 1942, though with varying success.

Thus the German forces from the Donets region and the eastern
Ukraine moved off to the west. With them went 200,000 head of cattle.
And vast numbers of horses—153,000 altogether. Pressed close together, their bodies steaming, they moved across the black earth of
the Ukraine like huge columns of prisoners, under billowing clouds
of dust. Some 270,000 sheep were driven to the west; some 40,000
peasant carts were jolted towards the Dnieper. And as the sun disappeared behind the thick clouds of dust raised by the endless trek,
3000 trains were rolling down the lines between Stalino and Kiev,
carrying grain, oleaginous crops, humans, tractors, threshing machines,
machine tools, and damaged tanks.

Exciting as these figures are, the German Command was wrong in
believing that a country could be swept in the course of a hurried
retreat or that a wide belt of it could be turned into an impenetrable
desert.

A few hundred thousand cattle, horses, and sheep do not win a
war. Wrecked factories and mines do not paralyse the production of a
determined nation for ever. Measures of this kind are not a guarantee
of victory, but are apt to damage a nation's reputation for a long time.

The troops realized this instinctively. Manstein himself gave orders
that these measures should be limited to what was absolutely necessary from the military point of view. An Army Group directive
stipulated therefore that the population remaining behind must be left
enough grain and livestock to tide them over until the next harvest.

In the area of Sixth Army one-fifth of the grain stocks were left
behind. The Army's war diary, however, complains that this measure,
motivated by humanitarian considerations, resulted in a military dis-
advantage since the Red Army immediately confiscated this grain
upon its arrival. This is in fact confirmed by the *History of the Great
Fatherland War*, even though it is interpreted differently: The population, it is claimed, had hidden the grain from the Germans in order
to hand it over to the Red Army after it had liberated them.

Very soon it became obvious that the order to leave behind nothing
but "scorched earth" could only be implemented to a limited extent.
In most cases the military operations and the belatedly started
retreat left the troops no time for elaborate demolition. This is confirmed by entries in the war diaries of many divisions. A typical
account is that of 23rd Panzer Division: "Operation 'Scorched Earth'
was practised by the division, as also by its neighbours for quite a
short time only since it proved impracticable." Similar statements can
be found in the official account of the "Grossdeutschland" Panzer
Corps and many other divisions.

General Nehring, whose Panzer Corps was employed at the focal points of Manstein's Army Group and, at the time in question, was in action south-east of Kiev, reports: "In the area of my XXIV Panzer Corps 'scorched earth' was not practised, if only for lack of time. Large numbers of livestock were left behind. Likewise the harvest. Here and there a barn was burnt down. But the villages remained unscathed." General Busse, Manstein's chief of staff, reports: " 'Scorched earth' was practised only on a narrow strip of land on the enemy bank. More than that was impracticable. But the measure undoubtedly contributed to the difficulties which the Russians encountered in preparing their attack across the river."

Nevertheless, the German Wehrmacht is being severely blamed to this day for its evacuation and destruction measures in the Donets region. Generals, officers, and other ranks received heavy sentences in the Soviet Union after the War, some of them being condemned to death. Even Field-Marshal von Manstein was sentenced by a British military court in Hamburg in 1949. Admittedly, on seventeen points of the "scorched earth" indictment Manstein was acquitted because the court acknowledged the military necessity of the measures. There was only one point which the British court did not accept as a military necessity—the abduction of some of the civilian population. On that count, among others, Manstein was found guilty. The sentence of the British military court was subsequently reduced, but it nevertheless helped to confirm the view, in Germany and abroad, that "scorched earth" had been an unpardonable German invention. That is not so. No-one wishes to gloss over what happened in Russia—but history should be separated from propaganda.

"Scorched earth"—that grim picture of blazing villages, smouldering towns, black mushrooms of smoke rising over dynamited factories —it is a frightful picture, but not exclusive to the campaign in Russia. "Scorched earth" was not invented between Donets and Dnieper. The strategy of devastation is as old as war itself. And in the Second World War it was Stalin who first proclaimed it and made it an essential part of his own operations.

On 3rd July, 1941, ten days after the German attack, he declared in his first broadcast speech to the population, the troops, and the partisans: "We must organize a merciless fight. The enemy must not lay hands on a single means of transport, on a single loaf of bread, on a single litre of fuel. Collective farmers must drive their livestock away and remove their grain. What cannot be moved must be destroyed. Bridges and roads must be dynamited. Forests and depots must be burnt down. Intolerable conditions must be created for the enemy."

Does this not sound just like the speech which, in Heinrich von Kleist's play *Die Hermannschlacht*—i.e. "The Battle of Arminius"—

Hermann or Arminius, the leader of the Germanic tribes resisting the Roman legions, addressed to his princes in the year A.D. 9: "If you will round up your wives and children and get them to the right bank of the Weser ... if you will devastate your fields and kill your herds, if you will burn down your homesteads—then I am your man."

They burnt their homes. They killed their cattle. Just as Caesar's retreating legions after their first crossing of the Rhine in 55 B.C. had burnt down farmsteads and villages, driven off the livestock, and cut down the crops.

In 1689 the French Minister of War Louvois ordered the German Palatinate to be devastated because he wanted to create a protective belt of waste land along France's eastern frontier. "Brûlez bien le Palatinat," he urged the French generals. Over a strip of land a hundred miles long and fifty miles deep, from Heidelberg to the Moselle, in a densely populated and cultivated territory, fire and sword created a "scorched earth".

Fifteen years after Louvois, during the wars of the Spanish succession, British troops under John Churchill, the famous first Duke of Marlborough, practised "scorched earth" tactics in the Ingolstadt-Augsburg-Munich area in order to deny all shelter to the French and Bavarian troops.

At about the same time the Swedes under Charles XII produced a "scorched earth" zone in Russia, east of the Vorskla, in order to protect their winter quarters from the Tsar's troops. The Swedish King had in fact imitated the tactics of Peter the Great who, the previous year, had laid waste the region of Smolensk and thus prevented the Swedes from marching on Moscow.

The Russians were certainly good at this job. They had practised it most successfully against the Swedes a few years previously, on the Neva. General Sherementyev then wrote to the Tsar: "I would inform you that Almighty God and the most Holy Mother of God have granted your desire: we have sacked and devastated everything so that in this land there is nothing left now to destroy."

A little over a hundred years later another letter from Russia spoke of "scorched earth". It was from a simple peasant's son from the Hohenlohe district, a musketeer in Napoleon's Grand Army, who sent a field post letter to his parents from the Berezina: "The Russians have destroyed their stores, driven away their livestock, set fire to their houses and mills, and wrecked their wells." The peasants back home in the Tauber valley read the report with horror.

The great founder and teacher of European military science, the Prussian General Carl von Clausewitz, adds further touches to this picture: ". . . they also destroyed the bridges and hacked off the numbers from the verst poles, whereby a good means of orientation was lost."

Even in the western hemisphere, in America, the cradle of modern civilization, we meet with the strategy of devastation. Abraham Lincoln, the liberator of the slaves and America's most popular President, in 1865 employed "scorched earth" as a decisive form of fighting in the Civil War. And his generals "scorched" in a big way. Professor Williams, an American contemporary, wrote about General Grant, Lincoln's commander-in-chief, whom he called "the first great man of our age": "He understands that the destruction of the enemy's economic resources is an equally effective and legitimate form of warfare as the destruction of his army."

And Grant's subordinate, General Sherman, acted accordingly. He burnt down Atlanta, he burnt the State of Georgia, he devastated one of the richest tracts of land in the American South. Not through barbarity, but by applying the inescapable logic of war. When the Mayor of Atlanta protested, Sherman replied: "War is cruelty and cannot be refined."

War is cruelty. Everywhere. And it will remain so, more than ever, in view of our modern means of warfare. Anyone who ever waged war also practised "scorched earth". Frenchmen and Swedes, Americans and British, Russians and Germans, Japanese and Chinese.

Who first coined the term "scorched earth", and where, cannot be established. But the earth was scorched. In all centuries and in all latitudes of our globe—on the Rhine and on the Neckar, on the Oder and on the Vistula, on the Danube, on the Vaal in Boer country, and on the Chattahoochee in America. But the scorched earth on the Dnieper weighs most heavily on our consciences: those cinders are still hot.

4. Race to the River

Through rain and mud–Who will be faster?–The Chapayev partisan group sends a signal to Vatutin–Alarm at Kanev–Three times the call of a bittern–Boats on the nocturnal river–Soviet crossing at Grigorovka–And in the "wet triangle" on the Pripet–The bridge at Kanev.

THE rain was pelting down. The rich, black earth of the Ukraine was drinking its fill after the hot summer. All the dust was turned to mud, and the mud turned the country into a morass. Before long all tracks became impassable, knee-deep swamps. Trucks got stuck, horse-drawn transports moved only with difficulty. Only the heavy tractors and the tracked vehicles were able to cope. Divisions, regiments, and battalions were immobilized. And this was only mid-September. The worrying question was: Was this the onset of the autumn mud? Had it come so early this year? If so, the German armies were facing disaster on their retreat to the coveted "Panther Line", a short way east of the Dnieper. No-one had expected the mud just yet.

Army Group South had passed down to its armies Manstein's directive of 18th September, to get back to the river and across it as quickly as possible and, once on the western bank, to deploy mobile forces in order to secure all threatened points between the bridges. For the time being the forces along the river consisted only of supply units, repair services, training units, and field railway commands, as well as a few emergency and transport units. It was a race in the mud.

Mackensen's First Panzer Army fought its way back to the bridge-heads of Zaporozhye and Dnepropetrovsk. On 19th September, a fine autumn Sunday, the operations group of General Henrici's XL Panzer Corps crossed the river by ferry near Antonovka, south of Dnepropetrovsk, following fierce defensive fighting. Twenty-four hours later it recrossed the river from the western bank, over the Zaporozhye dam, to enter the semi-circular bridge-head which, on the eastern bank, covered the city and dam. XVII Corps with its infantry divisions stood in this bulge projecting twelve miles to the east. The Russians, fortunately, had so far confined themselves to patrol activity and the bulk of Lieutenant-General Lelyushenko's Third Guards Army had not yet arrived. The wide Dnieper valley presented a peaceful picture. Only the transport and the supply units hurrying westward suggested the impending events. The river crossings at Kremenchug and Cherkassy were the objectives of Wöhler's Eighth Army.

The situation was critical on the sector of Fourth Panzer Army. With two Corps, the VII and the XIII, it was fighting its way towards the German bridge-head of Kiev, hard pressed all the time by the Russians. Its XXIV Panzer Corps, which had become separated from it, was to cross the river at Kanev, seventy-five miles south of Kiev, and had now been put under Eighth Army. The Corps was commanded by General Nehring. His was a heavy responsibility. The Soviet Third Guards Tank Army under General Rybalko, forming the spearhead of the Soviet Dnieper offensive, was trying to overtake the Germans and cross the river ahead of Nehring. XXIV Panzer Corps once again found itself at the focal point of battle—as it had been so often in the fighting between Donets and Dnieper.

Painfully the vehicles and marching columns of the divisions were making their way from the Orshitsa to the Dnieper—the Lower Bavarian 10th Panzer Grenadier Division, the 57th, 34th, and 112th Infantry Divisions. Their regiments came from Upper Bavaria and

Rhine-Hesse, the Moselle, the Rhineland, and Westphalia, and the Palatinate. Would they get across the river ahead of the Soviets?

"Fortunately the mud's worrying the Russians too," Colonel Hesse, the chief of staff, was consoling Captain Dr Köhne, the Corps intelligence officer. Köhne was in despair because none of his officers had so far returned from their reconnaissance trips. "Lieutenant Weber yesterday took twelve hours to cover six miles, Herr Oberst," Köhne lamented.

"Don't cry," the chief of staff said to him. "The truck with Bonin's operation files is stuck too. The divisions are all stuck in the mud, and their commanders think we are crazy to ask them to withdraw. They can see no reason for withdrawal since there are no Russians chasing them. But they don't know the position of the Army; they don't know that we've got to fall back if we don't want to be outflanked. That's why we've got to hurry and get back to that bridge quickly."

Hesse had unfolded the map on his knees and was studying the latest entries. "The Russians are pushing into the wide gaps which have necessarily resulted from our armies contracting towards the few bridges," he was thinking aloud. "They're trying to get to the river, and if possible across the river, before us." The map very clearly reflected this intention: the Corps withdrawal area, marked in blue, lay isolated between the fat, red arrows of the Soviets. Neither on their right nor on their left was there contact with other German units.

Just then Second Lieutenant Greiner, the Corps HQ interpreter, burst in. He was totally covered in mud after a long and complicated drive back from the HQ of 10th Panzer Grenadier Division. His report was not encouraging: "The men are struggling through the mud. They haven't had any sleep for days, there's not a dry stitch on their bodies. They've been in action for weeks. But they're holding out. The Dnieper is attracting them like a mirage. Lieutenant-Colonel de Maizière, the chief of operations, said to me: 'The men are looking forward to a well-built defensive line. They're looking forward to bunkers and troop quarters where at long last they will be able to hang on, where they'll find a dry bunk and the end of this retreat. The end of perpetual fear of being ambushed, outflanked or cut off!'"

Hesse was listening with a stony expression. Bunkers! Defensive line! Rest and safety! Should he tell the lieutenant that he did not believe in any of these things? Should he tell him that in their future sector beyond the Dnieper probably nothing was waiting for them except a few trenches and emergency units? Perhaps not even these —but the Russians. He did not confide his anxieties to the lieutenant. Instead he asked him, in a deliberately official voice: "What are the Russians doing on the sector of 10th Division?"

Greiner took the hint. After all he belonged to the intelligence section which had to process the enemy reports. So he replied: "The

Russians are already shunting troops to the west, towards the Dnieper, by the Poltava–Kiev railway."

"You aren't serious, Greiner?"

"Indeed I am, Herr Oberst. General Schmidt and his intelligence officer, Captain Prince Castell, expressly instructed me to inform you. According to reliable reconnaissance the Soviets have repaired the wrecked railway with astonishing speed, using a labour force beyond our imagination, and are now using the line. Naturally, signalling equipment has not yet been repaired, so they are running their train transports to the west by sight. The transports are already moving beyond Grebenka."

"That makes the situation even more dangerous," Colonel Hesse observed.

On 21st September, towards 1600 hours, a sheaf of intercepted signals was put on the desk of General Wöhler, the C-in-C Eighth Army, at his advanced battle headquarters at Smela. They were monitored signals of partisan transmitters, transmitted *en clair*. They were signed: "Chapayev group" and, evidently in reply to a query, reported that there were no German forces on the western bank of the Dnieper in the loop north of Kanev.

The reports were substantially correct. Apart from a German punitive company there was nothing at all on the western bank of the Dnieper loop between the villages of Grigorovka and Rzhishchev. Wöhler was uneasy. Aerial reconnaissance reported the Russian spearheads to be close to the river in that area. Was Vatutin planning a surprise coup in the Dnieper loop north of Kanev? Wöhler would not put it past him. The Soviet Colonel-General had proved himself a brilliant tactician and daring commander during the past few months.

Wöhler at once drafted an alarm order to Nehring. The signal arrived at XXIV Panzer Corps at 2045 hours: Nehring was to switch fast forces via Kanev to the southern bank of the threatened Dnieper loop at once.

But Wöhler realized that even fast forces of XXIV Panzer Corps could not fly. If the Russians were going to cross the river on 22nd September no unit of Nehring's could get there in time. What was to be done?

Major-General Dr Speidel, the Eighth Army chief of staff, had an idea. At Cherkassy, south of Kanev, was a weaponry training centre of Army Group South. They would have to cope. At 2230 hours the commandant of the centre was ordered by telephone to organize the members of the course into an emergency unit at once, switch them to Kanev, and deploy them on the western bank north of Kanev. Two hours later the men had climbed into trucks and rumbled off into the night. The rain had stopped. Wind and warm weather had quickly dried out the roads. But the night was still chilly. Over the

Dnieper a raw mist was swirling. It veiled the far bank. It veiled what Wöhler and Nehring were afraid of.

Guards Private I. D. Semenov cautiously parted the reeds and peered out towards the river. He listened. Nothing. By his side the partisan was crouching. "Where is that skiff?" Semenov asked.

"Five steps from here, under the bank. It's covered with reeds."

"Let's go." Three times Semenov imitated the call of a bittern. The reeds rustled. Three other Guards soldiers came crawling up—V. N. Ivanov, N. Y. Petukhov, and V. A. Sysolyatin. They slipped alongside Semenov and the partisan. They did not know that at that moment the eyes of history were turned on them. They did not know that their names would go down in the records. They did not even know whether they would pull it off—whether they would get safely across the big river, as the first men of Third Guards Tank Army, or indeed of the whole Red Army which was now racing towards the Dnieper. The youngest of them was Petukhov, a boy of eighteen. None of the others was more than twenty-two. All four of them were members of the Komsomol. What were they up to?

As General Wöhler had correctly surmised, the signals from the Chapayev partisan group, informing Colonel-General Vatutin about the unprotected western bank at Grigorovka, were to prove of considerable importance. The shrewd Soviet C-in-C had instantly seized his opportunity. The Dnieper loop, projecting towards the north-east, seemed a suitable place for a river crossing for tactical reasons alone; now the favourable report from the partisans tipped the balance. Vatutin telephoned General Rybalko. Rybalko was enthusiastic. He had himself put through to his 51st Guards Tank Brigade.

"Comrade commander, are your advanced detachments on the river?"

"Da, da, tovarishch general."

"Are you in touch with the Chapayev partisan detachment?"

"Da, da, tovarishch general."

There was only an imperceptible pause. Then came the fateful order. "Cross the river, then!"

Four words, but the great battle for the Dnieper hinged on them. "Engineers and crossing equipment?"

Rybalko's voice turned icy. "You can't wait for them. Make yourselves rafts or swim across. Understood?"

"Da, da, tovarishch general."

And 51st Guards Tank Brigade crossed the river on rafts or by swimming.

Lieutenant Sinashkin, commanding the brigade's sub-machine-gun company, had been ordered to cross the Dnieper between the villages of Grigorovka and Zarubentsy. His company was to be the advanced detachment. Privates Semenov, Ivanov, Petukhov, and Sysolyatin were volunteers from his company. It was past midnight. The mist was rising more thickly from the river. It reduced visibility to sixty or seventy yards. Almost noiselessly Semenov and his comrades crawled to the bank. There! They removed the reeds. They pushed the skiff out. Semenov held on to it.

Softly now. The partisan folded two old sacks round the oars. The guardsmen had already wrapped their sub-machine-guns in pieces of cloth to prevent any tell-tale noise. They climbed into the boat. Carefully, so it should not capsize. Semenov rolled over the gunwale and pushed off with one foot. They were caught up by the current. But the powerful Sysolyatin was already dipping the oars into the water and pulling vigorously. The partisan sat in the stern, steering with the small rudder. Silently the skiff drifted in the current. "Row harder, or we'll drift too far," the partisan hissed. "Harder still." Sysolyatin rowed hard. Like a black shadow the steep western bank emerged from the night.

"A few more strokes."

"That's enough—let her drift now."

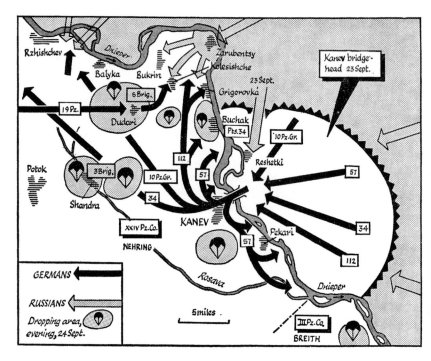

Map 38. The Soviets made an all-out attempt to force the Dnieper at Bukrin. The battle was to be decided by the first large-scale parachute drop. But General Nehring's XXIV Panzer Corps inflicted a heavy defeat on the Russians.

"Jump." Semenov went overboard. The water was up to his waist but the river-bed was firm. He pulled the skiff to the bank.

They listened. The night was breathing peacefully. The partisan, a fisherman from Grigorovka, had landed the guardsmen at the exact spot—two hundred yards north of the village. Here they were to engage the German sentries in an exchange of fire and feign an attempted landing. The German pickets were to be drawn here. And meanwhile Lieutenant Sinashkin with the bulk of the company and 120 partisans would cross the river a thousand yards farther to the north, immediately below Zarubentsy, and form the first small bridge-head there for the brigade which was to follow. Immediately upon landing the company was to mount an attack on Grigorovka. Towards 0200 the shots of the four guardsmen rang out in front of the German double guard on the edge of Grigorovka.

"Fall in at the double," the German NCOs yelled into the troop quarters in the village. A platoon of a punitive company was stationed there. One platoon! Men whose prison sentences had been converted to service on the Eastern Front. They were all there was on the Dnieper at Grigorovka. Semenov with his four men dodged in and out of the peasant huts. Again and again they loosed bursts of sub-machine-gun fire. One moment they were in one spot and the next they were somewhere else. They created the impression that a whole battalion had crossed the Dnieper at Grigorovka.

Sinashkin's company, meanwhile, was crossing the river above and below Zarubentsy, silently and without a single shot. How did they do it? Did they have engineers to help them? Pontoons? Ferries? Inflatable dinghies? Sinashkin had none of these. His men had nailed together some planks and beams. They had lashed barrels to them. Those were their rafts—some smaller, some bigger. Each carrying four men and a gun. Strong swimmers hung on to them and helped guide the rafts. At dawn Sinashkin's company mounted its attack and dislodged the German pickets from Zarubentsy and Grigorovka.

Thus, in the morning of 22nd September, the Russians had crossed the Dnieper north of Kanev. They had established a bridge-head while XXIV Panzer Corps, which was supposed to occupy and defend this sector, was still east of Kanev on the far bank of the river. The Russians had a clear run. From Kanev all the way down to south-east of Kiev, along the whole sixty miles of river-front assigned to the Corps, there was not a single real fighting unit.

Disaster was in the air. To make matters worse, the Soviet Thirteenth Army at about the same hour on 22nd September crossed the river 120 miles farther north, at Chernigov, exactly on the junction between Army Groups South and Centre. It was the spot where a crossing had been expected least of all because here, where the Pripet ran into the Dnieper, was a vast, swampy area.

However, since mid-September partisans had secretly been laying well-concealed corduroy roads through the swamp and thus provided the Soviet formations with rapid and concealed approaches through the swamp to the river. In consequence, on 26th September the Soviets succeeded in forming a small bridge-head which was pointed menacingly like a finger towards the Polish frontier.

True, weak combat groups of 2nd, 8th, and 12th Panzer Divisions as well as of 20th Panzer Grenadier Division succeeded in containing the bridge-head in the Dnieper–Pripet triangle, and infantry divisions brought up from other sectors of the front managed to seal off the most dangerous penetrations for the time being. Nevertheless, the gap torn into the front between Army Groups Centre and South would obviously become the scene of dangerous developments.

But not yet. True, some clear-sighted men in the German General Staff, in the "Foreign Armies, East" Department, kept uttering warnings about the dangerous Pripet estuary. But in September that danger was overshadowed by a more imminent one—the danger threatening the German defenders on the Dnieper from Lieutenant Sinashkin's bridge-head at Grigorovka. Soviet military writers have called it the "Bukrin bridge-head".

On the morning of 22nd September, 1943, there was not a staff officer in the zone of Army Group South whose attention was not focused on that fishing village. At 1100 hours the telephone rang in the room of the commandant of the weaponry training centre in Cherkassy. General Wöhler, the C-in-C of Eighth Army, was on the line in person. He asked: "How many men did you send to Kanev yesterday?"

"One hundred and twenty NCO cadets, Herr General."

"One hundred and twenty?" There was silence for a moment. "Rush those hundred and twenty men to Grigorovka at once by truck. They are to counter-attack the enemy forces which have crossed the river and seal them off."

One hundred and twenty NCO cadets of the weaponry training centre were all the forces which the C-in-C Eighth Army had available at 1100 hours on 22nd September to oppose the Soviet bridge-head of Bukrin. It was obvious that this could be nothing but an inadequate piece of improvisation. But there were simply no other forces available. Nehring's divisions had to hold the Kanev bridge-head against fierce enemy attacks. Nehring's first fast formations could not be expected across the river before the evening of 22nd September. And a lot might happen at Grigorovka in twelve hours.

At last all the feverish telephoning produced a ray of hope. At Kiev parts of 19th Panzer Division had already crossed the Dnieper on 21st September and were stationed close to the city. The armoured reconnaissance battalion of the division was called out as they were

eating their midday meal. "Everybody aboard!"—and off they raced
to what was at that moment the most threatened point on the entire
Eastern Front. The Hanoverian 73rd Panzer Grenadier Regiment
under Major von Mentz followed. And behind them came the main
body of the division.

From Kiev to Grigorovka was just under sixty miles. By a good road.
Two and a half hours for a reconnaissance battalion provided they
really stepped on it. They were an anxious two and a half hours for
Eighth Army. Would the Russian general realize his unique opportunity, burst out of his bridge-head as far as the Rossava, and drive
a wedge between Eighth Army and Fourth Panzer Army?

At 1928 hours on 22nd September a signal from Wöhler arrived at
General Nehring's command post at Prokhorovka on the eastern bank:
Available forces to be switched to the western bank as quickly as
possible in order to reinforce the Reconnaissance Battalion of 19th
Panzer Division engaged in heavy fighting in the Dnieper loop. As
quickly as possible! Nehring hoped to accomplish it by the following
morning. But General Rybalko also knew his job.

The morning of 23rd September began with a nasty surprise for
Nehring. "Enemy tanks attacking!" a shout went up. Ten, twenty,
thirty—forty-four T-34s were rumbling along the eastern bank of
the Dnieper, coming from the north, against the outpost lines of 253rd
Grenadier Regiment belonging to the Moselle 34th Infantry Division.
Soviet infantry were riding on top of the tanks. The Russians' intention was obvious—they wanted the bridge. Nehring's Corps was to be
prevented from crossing the river. General Rybalko wanted his own
tanks to move over and block the crossing on the far side. A bold and
logical plan. And it seemed to be succeeding.

After the heavy fighting of the preceding days Colonel Hippel's
253rd Grenadier Regiment was down to a few hundred men. The
Russians drove through the main defensive line and raced towards the
bridge. A few miles in front of it, at Reshetki, was the command post
of 14th Company. Captain Augustin had a 7·5-cm anti-tank gun, two
self-propelled gun carriages with crews, belonging to 3rd Company,
Panzerjäger Battalion 34, and two dozen men. He saw disaster
approaching, barricaded himself in a few houses of Reshetki, and
stood his ground. With his tiny force Augustin knocked out 16 T-34s.
The enemy infantry were forced off their tanks and took cover. A
dozen T-34s turned back and scattered in the open ground. But eleven
broke through. They rambled on towards the bridge. All that was left
there was a weak covering party with anti-tank and flak guns.

One of those moments had come when an entire campaign can
depend on the courage and sacrifice of a few men. And these men
rose to the occasion. Back at Corps HQ Colonel Hesse had in the
meantime scraped together all available armour-piercing weapons

from his divisions, rushed them to the approaches of the bridge, and put them under the command of Colonel Ferdinand Hippel, commanding 253rd Infantry Regiment.

The Colonel received the Soviet tanks with everything he had. With anti-tank and infantry guns, with mines and sticky explosive charges, the T-34s were repulsed. By 1000 hours the danger was averted. But half an hour later, at 1030 hours, Eighth Army passed on to Nehring a signal from Fourth Panzer Army: The units of 19th Panzer Division in action at Grigorovka are in greatest difficulties. They need help urgently.

The time was 1400 hours. Nehring now had his command post at Keleberda on the eastern bank of the Dnieper. The field telephone rang. Wöhler was on the line: Things were looking bad in the Dnieper loop. Zarubentsy was in enemy hands. Grigorovka was being contested. The enemy was thrusting to the west and south-west. The enemy was ferrying guns and vehicles across the river.

Luckily, Nehring had moved his transport units and rearward services across the Dnieper a few days previously. He could therefore risk quickly pulling his fighting formations over the bridge, regardless of the severe and dangerous enemy pressure. He moved his advanced command post directly to the ramp of the bridge on the eastern side. General August Schmidt, commanding 10th Panzer Grenadier Division, was put in charge of the bridge-head. His chief of operations was an experienced staff officer, Lieutenant-Colonel de Maizière. It was this division from Lower Bavaria which was now responsible for the Corps's safe crossing of the river.

That reliable chronicler on the staff of XXIV Panzer Corps, Lieutenant Renatus Weber, records his impressions in a letter home: "As we were forcing our way across the Dnieper on 23rd September, against the opposition of Russian tanks, I was reminded of the tragedy of Charles XII of Sweden who was compelled to surrender to the Russians with the remnants of his army at Perevolochnaya in 1709 because he had no chance of crossing the river. We, luckily, had our railway bridge." Luckily indeed.

That was the bridge of Kanev. Engineers of XXIV Panzer Corps had given it a second tier—high above the rail track they had built a road bridge in such a way that rail traffic continued throughout the construction work and simultaneously a bridge was made available for the troops and their vehicles.

Since 1500 hours the regiments had been moving across that strangely high bridge, that two-tiered masterpiece of army engineers. At Corps headquarters, on the eastern ramp, the situation was tense. Who would win the race? When would the Russian aircraft appear and attack the bridge? It was odd they had not done so already. But they did not come.

By 2115 the Bavarian regiments of 57th Infantry Division, commanded by Colonel Trowitz, were across. They immediately fanned out and occupied the bank to both sides of the bridge. Lieutenant-General Lieb's Hessian-Westphalian 112th Infantry Division was crossing now. It had been brought up in forced marches, frequently covering forty miles without a halt, to make sure it regained contact with the bulk of the Corps.

Shortly after midnight 258th Grenadier Regiment was clattering over the planks. Its 7th Company was led by Lieutenant Isselhorst. In the first platoon, in the left file, was Corporal Hellmold from Düsseldorf—tired, exhausted, shivering. The regiment was immediately moved northwards along the river, into the Dnieper loop, against the Soviets who had landed at Grigorovka.

The Moselle 34th Infantry Division under Lieutenant-General Hochbaum likewise got across the bridge under cover of darkness and also moved off at once, towards the left wing of the Corps sector. The last division to cross the bridge was to be 10th Panzer Grenadier Division. Its combat groups were still defending the progressively shrinking bridge-heads on the eastern bank. At 0330 hours on 24th September its Lower Bavarian regiments at last crossed the Dnieper bridge to the west. Dawn was breaking.

General Nehring was standing by the bridge, looking up at the sky and searching the grey horizon. Would the Russian air force come? But it did not come. Very odd. Not a single air raid on the bridge. It was incomprehensible. Did Army General Vatutin have no air force?

Vatutin had an air force all right. The whole Second Air Army had been assigned to his Army Group. But it was fully employed in protecting the troops crossing in the Dnieper loop against attacks by the Luftwaffe. Lieutenant-General Krasovskiy had no aircraft to spare for an attack on the Kanev bridge. Whatever machines he had he needed for another big operation, a unique operation in the war, an operation which Stalin believed would lead to decisive victory on the Dnieper. On the German side, meanwhile, no-one had an inkling of that great surprise.

Nehring was watching the marching columns. "How much longer do we need?" he asked Lieutenant Weber who was standing next to him. "Just under an hour, Herr General." Weber's estimate proved correct. By 0430 hours XXIV Panzer Corps had crossed to the other bank with all its formations. In thirteen and a half hours. A tremendous achievement. But it also showed how small the divisions had become.

Nehring was the last man to cross the river. All that was left on the eastern bank now were small covering parties and small rear parties which would hold the ramp until the bridge was blown up. They had inflatable dinghies and assault boats down on the bank—they would no longer get across by the bridge. Theirs was the most difficult task of the war—to act as the rearguard, to delay the enemy as long as possible. When could one pull out? How long dared one stay? A rearguard commander has no-one to give him orders at the crucial moment. He alone bears the responsibility. With no-one to advise him he must tread the narrow path of duty. It is a difficult post.

At 0500 exactly General August Schmidt, the commander of 10th Panzer Grenadier Division, stood with Captain Bopst, commanding Engineer Battalion 10, in a small ravine on the western bank. In front of them an NCO knelt by an electric switch-box.

"Everything ready?"

"Everything ready, Herr General!"

Thank God, the two officers were thinking. A mere twenty-four hours earlier they had not been at all sure that "everything" would be "ready" at the right moment to dynamite the Kanev bridge.

The Corps commander, the chief of staff, and the engineer commander of the Corps had been anxious whether the charges could be fixed to the bridge before the Russians got there. It had been a test of everyone's nerves. But now everything was ready. General Schmidt once more climbed to a spot from where he could see the bridge and looked at it through his binoculars. It stood quiet and deserted. He returned. "Now!"

The engineer NCO pushed down the plunger. Everybody flung himself down. A crash as of thunder. Flashes of lightning. Debris whirled through the air. Smoke and dust. When the smoke had cleared, all that was left of the huge bridge was a few shattered piers. Beams and planks were bobbing downstream on the Dnieper.

Only now did everyone reflect on how strange it was that the Soviet High Command had not made a single serious attempt to gain possession of this Dnieper bridge. Either by airborne troops, by parachutists, or by a boldly conceived tank attack. Or indeed by way of the partisans of whom there were swarms in all the forests. What was the reason for this failure? Did the Soviets doubt their ability to pull off the kind of successful operation against vital river crossings that the German had repeatedly performed during the early stages of the war? Like Manstein's armoured thrust to Dvinsk.[1] Or Guderian's coup against the Desna bridge at Novgorod Severskiy. Or Reinhardt's seizure of the Volga bridges at Kalinin. Or that model of a bold strike during a withdrawal which 16th Motorized Infantry Division accomplished against the bridge over the Manych in January 1943. The Russians attempted nothing of the kind on the Dnieper. They relied on their improvising skill and were confident that they could manage without solid bridges. And it looked as if they were going to be proved right.

They crossed the great river at many points, quickly and without

[1] Latvian: Daugavpils.

losses, using only improvised means. And not only in the Dnieper loop at Pereyaslav or upstream at Chernigov. During the few remaining days of September the Soviets achieved twenty-three river crossings along the 440 miles from Loyev to Zaporozhye.

But the Soviets nevertheless made one mistake in their calculations. True enough, they got their companies, battalions, and even regiments across the river quickly and established bridge-heads on the other side; but they found it difficult to enlarge these bridge-heads on a scale which would have allowed a major offensive to be launched from them. They had enormous difficulties in ferrying tanks, heavy equipment, and ammunition across the river. For that they would have needed solid bridges, but these could not be built from their minute bridge-heads.

When the Soviet Command realized its mistake it tried to right it quickly by a radical solution. It mounted an operation such as the Russians had carried out on that scale only once in the course of the whole war.

5. The Bukrin Bridge-head

The Russians are across the river–Bad news from every-where–The Kolesishche windmill–"Action stations—para-chutists!"–Three Soviet brigades jump into disaster.

CORPORAL Hellmold had not had such a good breakfast for months as the one on 24th September. All night his company had been on the move. Marching and marching. But at the end of it, at daybreak, the men were cheerful. At last they were out of that mouse-trap in front of the Kanev bridge. Now they would get some rest. But first of all, breakfast. The cookhouse orderly had issued jam, sardines, corned beef, and real coffee. After breakfast they flung themselves in the straw. Sleep. The time was 0800. But they were not to get their well-earned rest. "Company commanders to see the regimental com-mander!" a shout went through the barn.

Lieutenant Isselhorst scrambled to his feet. These sudden sum-monses were always a bad sign. True enough, ten minutes later the hated order came: "Fall in at the double! Get ready to depart!" The usual chaos ensued: "Where the hell is my . . ." "You haven't . . .?" Every other sentence began with a soldier's oath. Outside the trucks pulled up. At least they would not have to march. But when infantry were given rides on trucks it usually meant that the situation was critical.

Lieutenant Isselhorst briefly put 7th Company in the picture when the men had fallen in. The Russians had crossed the Dnieper farther to the north, at Grigorovka. They had to be held until stronger German forces arrived.

"Same old story," the men grunted. Second Lieutenant Kirberg got his No. 1 Platoon aboard the trucks. They moved off.

The news from the Russian crossing-points in the Dnieper loop was bad. At the same time, considering that General Rybalko's Third Guards Tank Army had established itself on the right bank forty-eight hours previously, it was surprising the situation was not a great deal worse still.

On 24th September the Russian bridge-head between Grigorovka and Bukrin was about three miles deep and four miles wide. With half a dozen tanks and two battalions the Russians in the late afternoon of 24th September pressed against Major Guderian's Armoured Recon-naissance Battalion 19 which had been rushed up to seal off the bridge-head. The Russian pressure was from the Dnieper loop to the south-west. Nine miles upstream, near the village of Balyka, a Soviet brigade with roughly a thousand men of Lieutenant-General Moskalenko's Fortieth Army had meanwhile also crossed the river and was push-ing south-east against weak advanced detachments of 19th Panzer Division which were the only German forces at that point. It was clear that the two Soviet groups intended to link up.

The Armoured Reconnaissance Battalion 19 went in to oppose the Russians both at Balyka and at Bukrin. Major Guderian, the youngest son of the Colonel-General, proved himself a master of improvisation. Repair and transport parties were fighting in the line. The Russians were held. But it was not possible to dislodge them from their posi-tions in the narrow ravines which intersected the high western bank of the river.

Nehring switched the reinforced Armoured Reconnaissance Bat-talion of 10th Panzer Grenadier Division under Major Waldemar Mayer towards Balyka. But no sooner had he ordered them off than another piece of bad news arrived. A small Soviet combat group of fifty men had crossed the river on the morning of 24th September near the village of Stayki, a further nine miles upstream, and established itself among the ravines of the bank. Part of 34th Infantry Division, motor-ized on a makeshift basis, was dispatched to deal with this new danger. "Clear up the bridge-head and destroy the forces this side of the river," was their order.

But even this minute bridge-head could not be eliminated. It was the same old story: once the Russians had gained a foothold it was difficult to dislodge them. They were past masters at stubborn defence. They would crouch in their firing pit or behind their parapet, firing; they hardly ever gave up until they were looking down the barrel of a German rifle or feeling the point of a bayonet in their back. At Stayki, moreover, the terrain particularly favoured the Russians. The ravines and clefts in the rock of the steep bank offered ideal cover. The flat ground in front of their positions was easily raked with machine-gun fire, causing any attack to collapse.

The German combat groups sealed off the Russians. They bombarded them with mortars. With artillery and infantry guns they cut off their supplies. Intercepted enemy signals revealed heavy losses. And after three days also hunger.

But the Russians did not give up. And even though the bridge-head was small it nevertheless required continuous watching and sealing off. Otherwise it might suddenly turn dangerous. And this kind of danger was threatening all along the front. Nehring continued switching ever new combat groups from Kanev to the enemy crossing-points, above all to Balyka and the Bukrin-Grigorovka area.

Major Hertel's battalion of 258th Infantry Regiment was digging in outside Grigorovka in the gathering dusk of 24th September. The 7th Company was at the Kolesishche windmill. Everybody was busy digging when the call went up: "Enemy aircraft!"

Russian aircraft came roaring overhead. Everybody jumped into trenches and firing pits. Some of the Soviet machines seemed to be flying unusually low. Behind them, with parade ground precision, always two abreast, came a strong formation of large machines —at least forty-five of them. Over to the left was a similar stream. They were heavy transport machines. They were flying at 2000 to 2400 feet. Fast fighters and interceptors were out on the flanks and above the formations. "I've never seen that many Russians in the sky before," Sergeant Schomburg remarked.

They were not dropping any bombs. They were not firing their cannon or machine-guns. They came sweeping up from the Dnieper and flying over the German lines, totally unconcerned. Clearly they had no inkling that there were Germans below them in the trenches and strongpoints.

Dusk fell early on the Dnieper. This was the end of September, and darkness began to settle towards 1700 hours. But why did the Russian aircraft have their internal lights on? And now some of the low-flying machines even probed the scrub-covered ground with powerful searchlights. "What the hell are they up to?" Hellmold muttered. The NCO by his side was pressing his binoculars to his eyes. "They're up to some monkey business," he grunted. The next moment his suspicions were confirmed. "They're jumping," he yelled. "Parachutists!" He snatched up his Very-pistol. He fired a white flare. In its blinding light the billowing parachutes were clearly visible.

What followed was one of the most dramatic, extraordinary, and fascinating chapters in the history of the war. The documents available to the present author from the German side include the personal records and recollections of General Nehring, as well as the war diaries of the German units involved and recollections of numerous eye-witnesses. From the Soviet side, the essays and memoirs published since 1962 have been used, in particular an account by G. P. Sofronov.

It was a breathtaking affair. Corporal Hellmold and the company were still stunned. A large-scale operation by parachutists? That was something even the oldest hands of the Russian campaign had never experienced. Some of them knew from hearsay that back in February 1942 the transport units of the Württemberg-Baden 260th Infantry Division had some encounter with Soviet airborne brigades in the rear of XIII Army Corps. Apart from that, the Russians were only known to have gone in for commando-type drops of from five to eighty men, mainly for sabotage purposes or for supplying special equipment and leaders to partisan groups.

Hellmold and his comrades were watching the spectacle in amazement. But they were brought down to earth by a sharp order from Lieutenant Isselhorst: "Open fire on enemy parachutists!" At once the fireworks started. The crack of rifle fire. Bursts of machine-gun fire rattling skyward. The bullets tore through the parachutes. They ripped them open and made them flutter like flags. The men beneath them plummeted down like stones. Where the parachutes remained intact the parachutists themselves were helpless as they came slowly sailing down—an easy target for hundreds of rifles.

Over on the windmill hill, on the left wing of the battalion, a 2-cm flak gun started barking. It was pumping its shells into the massed formations of aircraft overhead. One of them was hit. Its fuselage was ripped open. Out of the fire and smoke dropped the parachutists. Most of their parachutes did not open. And the few men who succeeded in opening theirs died nevertheless, swept down to the ground by the wreckage of the machine.

More and more transports were droning westwards above the Kolesishche windmill. It was dark by now. Tracers and signal flares plunged the sky into a bright light and made the snow-white silk parachutes phosphoresce. Containers with weapons, ammunition, and food supplies were sailing slowly down. A short way off, in a patch of wood, the parachutes got entangled in the trees. Some of these were decorated like bizarre Christmas trees.

Major Hertel came running up: "Section Pfeifer and Section Zorn

—follow me." The men raced off with their battalion commander. Half an hour later they brought back the first prisoners. The Russians, it soon appeared, belonged to the 5th Guards Parachute Brigade whose bulk was being dropped farther west, at Dudari. The descent at Kolesishche in the operations area of 112th Infantry Division was by groups which had lost touch with the main body.

Search parties were organized. Reporting centres were improvised. Wherever parachutes were found on the ground the Russian paratroops could not be far away. They were rounded up one by one in the ravines before they had a chance of orientating themselves or joining up to form groups. "Ruki verkh!" And anyone not putting his hands up quickly was felled by hand-grenade or sub-machine-gun. At the break of day the Grenadiers saw the sails of the Kolesishche windmill turning in the morning breeze from the Dnieper. From one of the sails dangled a torn parachute, red with the blood of the dead man who was still hanging from the ropes, mangled.

Farther west, in the Dudari area, where the main body of the brigade was dropped, the same disaster occurred. Here the Soviets dropped straight into a column of 10th Panzer Grenadier Division moving towards Balyka. And immediately, at the village of Dudari, the Russians got into the deployment area of the Armoured Troop Carrier Battalion of 73rd Panzer Grenadier Regiment. This formed the spearhead of the Lower Saxon 19th Panzer Division which was moving up from Kiev under the command of Colonel Källner, to relieve its hard-pressed reconnaissance battalion.

No parachute unit could have been dropped more unluckily or more disastrously. The Russians jumped into an area bristling with German weapons. They came down like a vast blizzard. It was a blizzard of death.

Lieutenant-Colonel Binder, at that time chief of operations of 19th Panzer Division, gives the following dramatic account: "The first drop was at 1730. While still in the air the Russians were caught in the fire of machine-guns and a multiple 2-cm flak gun. The Soviet formation was very open—the big machines arrived singly, or two at a time at the most, at intervals of half a minute, and so dropped their parachutists. This made our opposition even more effective. Some of their machines evidently realized the disaster and wheeled back to the north. Our devastating defensive fire and the brilliant white flares which were zooming up everywhere clearly unnerved the Soviets. They were now dropping their men haphazardly, all over the place. Split up into small and very small groups, they were doomed. They tried to take cover in the narrow ravines, but were soon winkled out and taken prisoner or killed."

Only the brigade commander succeeded in rallying 150 men around him and gaining a foothold in a patch of woodland east of Grushevo.

There he resisted furiously. The 3rd Company, 73rd Panzer Grenadier Regiment, under Second Lieutenant Goldmann had a foretaste of what might have happened if the Russians had made their drop under more favourable conditions and had had time to dig in for defence. They certainly had marksmen with steady nerves among them. Goldmann's company suffered heavy losses—most of them shot through the head. Only after savage fighting were the 150 men overpowered. Their commander was taken prisoner. A few groups fought their way through to the partisans operating in the vast forests west of Cherkassy.

What was the object of this costly Soviet adventure? Three brigades with roughly 7000 men were dropped—the 5th Brigade close to the Dnieper loop in the Dudari area; the 3rd Brigade farther to the rear, along the swampy Rossava stream; and parts of the 1st Brigade immediately behind the Kanev bridge. A few groups of this brigade landed rather far to the south, in the operation area of the German III Panzer Corps, Nehring's neighbour on the right.

Captured orders and maps revealed two objectives. On the one hand, the Soviet High Command wanted to cover the tactical Bukrin bridge-head against German counter-attacks. The 5th Parachute Brigade was to prevent the move of German reserves from the south or south-east in the direction of the Dnieper, and was therefore to establish a barrier in the area west of Kanev against the approaching German units. The 3rd Brigade was to hold the Shandra-Lipovyy area until the arrival of the Soviet Fortieth Army and to pin down German tactical reserves.

It was a good plan. But it was executed too late. The German formations were already in the exact locations to which the parachute brigades were to have denied them access.

But in addition to this tactical objective the airborne operation by the three brigades pursued a much bigger and strategic objective. This emerges clearly from a glance at the map of the dropping area: the 1st and 3rd Brigades and the western group of the 5th Brigade had the task of establishing themselves along the swampy banks of the Rossava stream. Together with the forces which had crossed the Dnieper at Balyka, Rzhishchev, and south of Kanev they were to form an extensive bridge-head and thus establish a second screen around the Bukrin river crossing. In this way a large deployment area would have been secured, allowing for the envisaged assembly of two Soviet Armies.

According to the evidence of the captured commander of the 5th Brigade the first drop was to be followed, on 26th or 27th September, by another large-scale air landing operation south-east of the Kanev bridge. Freight-carrying gliders were to arrive with heavy equipment and tanks. The small formations dropped on 24th September in the operation area of III Panzer Corps were only advanced detachments and covering forces for this operation. The total failure of the first phase evidently led to the cancellation of the airborne landing.

Everything, in fact, was cleverly planned but wrongly realized. The result was a military disaster. In the dropping area between Dudari and the Rossava 1500 parachutes were found during the first twenty-four hours, 692 dead counted, and 209 men taken prisoner. Among the prisoners were also the band-leader and the librarian of 5th Brigade. What on earth were they sent into action for? "Orders," the two said under interrogation. "Orders" was also what the captured brigade commander said. "I was instructed to take every man I had." And so he took every man he had, even though only half of them had been trained in jumping, with an average of seven to ten trial jumps each. The other half had never jumped before and were a mixed lot from seven regiments. The medical personnel consisted exclusively of women.

Their clothing and equipment was as chequered as their composition —some wore flying overalls, others leather jackets, yet others tunics. By contrast, the women doctors and medical orderlies were strikingly well equipped.

But the most incomprehensible aspect of the whole operation was the drop in the evening, with night approaching, when the normal thing would have been a daytime drop. True, the Russians were fond of the night and usually found their way about at night far better than the Germans. But even so a drop at dusk was a serious and fatal mistake. Parachute troops are not very mobile immediately after landing, since they lack means of transport. The dark, moreover, makes it more difficult for scattered men to rally. Added to this was the fact that, for reasons of security, the units and their officers had not been briefed about the operation until an hour and a half before take-off. In consequence there had been no chance for officers, let alone rank and file, to study the target area on the map. They dropped on to totally unfamiliar ground.

In vain did the officers try to pinpoint their position with the aid of sketch-maps hurriedly made during the approach flight. In the dark they were unable to find the landmarks entered on them. Many of the prisoners admitted sadly: "It was a disaster!"

Another disaster was the incompetence of many pilots. They got mixed up with each other, lost their place in the formation, or dropped their men at the wrong spot. When they encountered flak they climbed to over 3000 feet, which resulted in an even greater scatter of parachutists and freight containers. Many of the parachute troops, moreover, were unprepared to find themselves in action; they had expected a kind of exercise drop over territory clear of the enemy and had not reckoned with any kind of resistance. When, after jumping, they found themselves under murderous fire this came to them not only as a surprise but as a severe shock. Those who reached the ground unhurt and fit for action were nevertheless demoralized. General Nehring summed up his judgment as follows: "The Soviet Command simply lacked an appreciation for the timing, the target area, and the possibilities of this operation. It was amateurish. The strategic idea was correct, but its execution was bungled. Clearly there was no expert behind it. The units were much too scattered to be rallied quickly for systematic, co-ordinated action.

"Of course it was a lucky accident for us and a disastrous one for the Soviets that three German divisions happened to be moving through the dropping area. But even without this accident the operation would not have succeeded because its timing was wrong. Had the drop been executed before XXIV Panzer Corps had crossed the river—i.e., in its rear on the far bank—with the simultaneous seizure or destruction of our improvised bridge at Kanev—that would have meant a really critical situation for our Corps. And not only for the Corps but for the whole Army.

"At first light on 23rd September, when those forty Soviet tanks charged from the woods near Kanev and got to within a few miles of the eastern approach to the bridge, and were only halted at the last moment, the full extent of our dangerous situation became obvious. That would have been the great moment for the Russian Command. At that moment a combined operation by their ground and air forces could have achieved their strategic objective of unhinging our front on the Dnieper.

"Indeed, even in the early afternoon of 23rd September the sudden seizure of the bridge by a coup from the air might have been decisive."

But twenty-four hours later, on 24th September, when Nehring's XXIV Panzer Corps had already crossed the river, the Soviet Command had missed its great opportunity. It employed its parachute brigades too late and to no purpose. But then the history of war is the history of missed opportunities.

The disaster of the Bukrin bridge-head must have been a heavy blow to the Soviet airborne forces. They never recovered from it until the end of the war. They mounted no more operations of any significance.

For a long time Soviet military historians maintained complete silence about this unsuccessful operation by three parachute brigades. The *History of the Great Fatherland War* and many standard works by Soviet historians make no mention whatever of the Kanev airborne operation. Only a minute symbol in map No. 56 in the *History of the*

A barn is on fire, the ploughs are abandoned.
Blazing stooks in the fields.

Great Fatherland War hints at the operation: under the name of the village of Bukrin there is a neat little red parachute. But in the text there is not a word of commentary, no explanation, no reference. Only this minute symbol records for the initiated what happened in the skies over the great Dnieper loop between Kiev and Kanev on 24th September, 1943.

Only quite recently have the Russian military periodicals begun to discuss the operation. Their accounts confirm the German picture, and indeed reveal even more clearly the insufficient execution of the operation. Here is an example.

The 5th Airborne Brigade missed its dropping area by more than twenty miles. In order to deceive the Germans a number of absurd precautions were taken: not till after the drop were the front-line troops in the appropriate area informed of the employment of airborne troops. The commander of 5th Airborne Brigade did not pass on the order for the operation to his units until 1600 hours on 24th September—*i.e.*, an hour and a half before they emplaned. Where then was the time to be found to explain the operation and the objective to the men?

And the plan itself. It had been drafted bureaucratically and without regard for the actual situation on the front. The transport of the brigades to their take-off fields was to be accomplished between 17th and 21st September; because of the heavy demand on railway transport it was not in fact concluded until 24th September—*i.e.*, the day of the operation.

But there was worse to come. Because of bad weather many transport aircraft arrived late, or not at all, at their operational fields. Besides, far fewer aircraft arrived than had been demanded. And finally, owing to "poor condition", none of the machines was able to take on board the envisaged twenty parachutists. In consequence, there were only fifteen or at the most eighteen men to each aircraft. Thus all plans were upset.

Things were no better with 3rd Airborne Brigade. It landed 4575 men, but without their 45-mm guns. Thirteen machines did not find the dropping areas and returned to base with their complements. Two aircraft missed their targets and dropped the parachutists far in the rear areas. Another let its men jump directly over the Dnieper; they were all drowned. Another so completely missed its target area that the parachutists landed deep in the Soviet rear.

For the 5th Airborne Brigade only forty-eight transport aircraft turned up instead of sixty-five. Take-off was delayed by an hour and a half because of fuelling trouble. Moreover, there was not enough

Mine clearing.
House-to-house fighting south of Orel.

fuel at the fields. Aircraft took off singly, without schedule. Nevertheless, 5th Brigade succeeded in dropping two battalions with over 1000 men. Further drops were cancelled because of fuel shortage.

And what happened to those who dropped? According to Soviet reports, forty-three groups with altogether 2300 men under the command of officers of 3rd and 5th Brigades regrouped as partisans in the German rearward areas, principally in the forests between Kanev and Cherkassy, where large partisan encampments had previously been set up.

A mere 2300 out of some 7000. Radio equipment was another sad chapter. The commander of 3rd Airborne Brigade and his chief of staff had no radio transmitter. Because of the great scatter during landing and the loss of many instruments most commanders were without radio contact. In order to restore such contact, three airborne groups with transmitters were dropped during the night of 27th–28th September; they missed their target. Thereupon, on 28th September, a PO-2 aircraft took off with radio equipment; it was shot down. Not until the end of September did the Fortieth Army succeed in making its first radio contact with 600 parachutists in the forests of Kanev.

It is also astonishing that the partisan formations in the forests near Kanev had not been included by the Soviet High Command in the operation plan for the airborne landing, although seven partisan detachments are said to have been operating in those wooded regions. Did the idea not occur to STAVKA and the generals? Or was the fighting power of the partisans at that time not as great as is being made out today? At any rate, the disastrous airborne operation west of Kanev revealed that in the summer of 1943 the Soviets were not yet very impressive in this sector of warfare.

Marshal of Artillery Voronov is quite right when he regretfully observes in his memoirs: "It is very sad to have to admit that we, who were pioneers of air landing operations, had no practicable plans for the employment of these troops." Voronov is right in every respect: the Red Army really was the pioneer of airborne operations. Parachutists were used in manoeuvres in the Caucasus as early as 1932.

In the posthumously published papers of General Köstring, for many years German Military Attaché in Moscow, we read: "During those exercises in the Caucasian mountains I saw for the first time the entirely novel employment of parachute troops. The experience remained unforgettable for me if only for the reason that years later, at the German Air Ministry, I was told that the pictures which I sent back to Berlin of this and later parachute descents had induced Göring to set up a parachute force himself."

The disciples subsequently outstripped their masters. It would seem that the technical, *matériel,* and personnel problems of a parachute force proved insoluble for the Red Army.

PART SIX:
Between Kiev and Melitopol

1. A Village named Lyutezh

*Corporal Nefedov and twenty-two men–A fateful stretch
of the Dnieper bank–Kravchenko's tanks ford the Desna–
STAVKA changes its plan–Regrouping at night.*

O N the evening of 25th September, 1943, General Rybalko had
no more than a vague suspicion of the disaster which had befallen the first large-scale Soviet airborne operation. He was still
hoping that his parachutists might have achieved a tactical success
at least at some points. And he tried, by means of thrusts from his
small bridge-heads at Bukrin and Balyka, to make contact with them
and help them.

But the silence in the radio receivers was not due to technical
trouble. What scattered groups were still hiding out near Dudari,
Shandra, and Buchak were rounded up by German search-parties during the next few days.

The German Command was alarmed by the operation. It could not
believe that the Russians would stop at this first attempt. The Führer's
Headquarters, Army Group, and Army feared further landings. They
feared that the Soviets would try at all costs to gain a strategic bridge-
head in order to deploy strong armoured forces on the right bank. Because of these fears the German 20th Panzer Grenadier Division and
the 7th Panzer Division were brought up before the end of the month.

An order of Army Group South proves that Field-Marshal von
Manstein had no doubts about Vatutin's objective. Manstein radioed
to Wöhler: Eighth Army must deal with enemy forces brought across
the river and dropped from the air as quickly as possible, to prevent
bridging operations aimed at bringing up the enemy's tank army.

The enemy's tank army referred to in Manstein's order was Rybalko's
Third Guards Tank Army. Manstein had good reason to regard it as
a nightmare. But its great surprise move was not here at Bukrin, but

somewhere quite different. The surprise began with the adventurous enterprise of a sergeant.

Forty-eight hours after the unsuccessful air drop at Bukrin another coup was mounted seventy-eight miles farther north, at the very gates of the Ukrainian capital—a coup which led to the turning point on the middle Dnieper. The story of that coup proves once again that even in modern war the course of events is determined by courageous individuals.

While General Nehring's combat groups were still busy winkling out the last Soviet parachutists at Bukrin, the most advanced parts of the Soviet Thirty-Eighth Army—*i.e.*, the 240th Rifle Division—reached the river near the village of Svaromye, above Kiev. On the opposite side, on the German-held bank, was the village of Lyutezh. The sector was defended by General Hauffe's XIII Corps, and the 100-feet-high steep bank was held by the Hessian 88th and the Brandenburg 208th Infantry Divisions. The Dnieper at that point was 650 to 750 yards wide and between 6 and 20 feet deep. Below Kiev it was considerably wider.

In accordance with Stalin's order of 9th September, Thirty-Eighth Army was being got ready at once for the crossing of the river. But just as in the Bukrin loop seventy-two hours earlier no engineers or bridging equipment had yet arrived. Trees were therefore hurriedly felled in the near-by woods and joined together for rafts. As darkness fell over the river on 26th September combat groups of 931st Rifle Regiment pushed off from the eastern bank on rafts and small fishing boats. They had almost reached the western bank when a rifle shot rent the night: a German sentry had spotted the small flotilla. Flares hissed up into the dark sky and plunged the river in brilliant light. Boats and rafts were shown up like targets on a rifle range. German machine-gun fire raked the water. Tracer ammunition showed which way the bursts went. The first boat was riddled. So was the second. On the low rafts the Red Army men flung themselves flat down on the tree-trunks and let themselves drift with the current. The bullets passed over them or smacked into the water. But then came the bark of German light infantry guns. Direct hits were scored on one raft after another. The attempted landing by 931st Rifle Regiment ended in disaster.

A few miles farther south a similar attempt was made by battalions of 836th and 842nd Rifle Regiments. But they too were caught in the German defensive fire while still half-way across the river. The battalion of 836th Rifle Division was completely shot up. Not a single man reached the bank. The bulk of 2nd Battalion, 842nd Rifle Regiment, did not fare much better. But towards 0400 hours one platoon, No. 2 Platoon of 5th Company under Sergeant Nefedov, succeeded in reaching the German bank with twenty-two men aboard four small fishing boats. They dug in on the steep bank some two hundred yards from the river. Their armament consisted of eight sub-machine-guns, five carbines, and one light and one heavy machine-gun. German counter-attacks in platoon and company strength on the morning of 27th September were repulsed by Nefedov and his men from their favourable positions.

It was the same old story—a resolute leader with a handful of determined Soviet soldiers. Every single man would have to be forced out of his firing pit separately.

By the evening of 27th September Nefedov had only ten men left. He radioed his regiment. He transmitted the exact position of his group. And during the night of 27th–28th September the Russians managed to get seventy-five men across to him in fifteen fishing boats. In the grey dawn, moreover, Captains Sava and Vanin, each with a combat group, paddled across the river to Nefedov on small rafts.

By 30th September, 240th Rifle Division had in this manner transferred two regiments with field artillery and parts of a heavy mortar regiment. The bridge-head now had a front of two miles and a depth of one mile. No-one on the German or the Russian side suspected that this short stretch of steep bank represented the bridge-head from which the Dnieper battle would presently be decided. For several days the village of Lyutezh was fiercely contested. If it fell the Russians would have the beginnings of a strategic bridge-head. It did fall. The question now was whether General Hauffe's XIII Corps

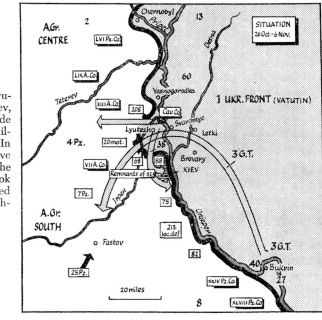

Map 39. At Lyutezh, north of Kiev, the Soviets made up for their failure at Bukrin. In a surprise move Vatutin forced the Dnieper, took Kiev, and raced on to the south-west.

would have the strength to recapture Lyutezh and, at the very least, seal off the enemy bridge-head.

Late in the evening of 3rd October the field telephone rang at Brovary at the command post of Lieutenant-General Kravchenko, commanding the Soviet V Guards Tank Corps: the general was to go at once to Voronezh Front headquarters; Army General Vatutin wished to see him urgently. "It's most urgent," the orderly officer repeated. Kravchenko flung himself into his staff car and was driven away at speed. The next hour was of greatest interest to the history of the war.

This is how Kravchenko describes the scene: "Vatutin and his Military Council member Khrushchev informed me about the successful crossing of 240th Rifle Division. But Khrushchev poured cold water on the success: 'The units which have crossed over have suffered heavy losses and are engaged in hard defensive fighting. It is doubtful whether they will succeed in hanging on to that patch of ground on the right bank unless we support them with tanks.' At that point Vatutin interposed: 'Unfortunately, the Desna runs between your tank corps and the Dnieper, and the Desna is three hundred and thirty yards wide. To build a bridge in the present circumstances would take at least eight or ten days. But eight days from now will probably be too late; we must give them tank support at once. Your corps is the nearest. We've no other choice—you must drive your tanks through the Desna. You've got to find a ford.'"

Kravchenko was an energetic man and grasped the situation. All he said was: "I'll see to it, comrade Commander-in-Chief." He at once drove back to his corps, which was deployed in the forest north-west of Brovary, a few miles from the Desna.

Kravchenko's account continues: "Desna fishermen and tank personnel of 20th Brigade knew of a shallow spot near the village of Letki. Komsomol members tested the river bottom by diving. It consisted of sand and was therefore negotiable. But the river was still some seven feet deep. That was more than the wading depth of our T-34s. We therefore had to turn our tanks into makeshift submarines. All slits, hatches, and covers on the tank hulls and the turrets were made watertight with tow and putty or pitch, and moreover covered with oiled canvas. The air entered the engine by way of the hatch covers and the exhaust gases were let out through a vertical extension to the exhaust tube. The ford was marked out by two rows of posts. The tanks then drove off in bottom gear through the strange corridor, the drivers steering blind to the orders of their commanders who sat in the turrets."

The *History of the Great Fatherland War* commends this splendid achievement with full justification. But when it says: "Never before had armoured troops overcome a similar river obstacle by crossing it underwater", then this statement is true only for the Red Army. For two years previously, on 22nd June, 1941, the German 18th Panzer Regiment of General Nehring's 18th Panzer Division drove across the Bug north of Brest-Litovsk, where the river was over twelve feet deep. Admittedly, these "diving tanks" had been specially prepared and tested for the operation. But they drove completely blind because even the closed turrets were submerged in the water.

But to return to Kravchenko's report. The general states: "Once across the Desna, the corps quickly reached the Dnieper. But this river was too deep to be forded. The ninety T-34s which we had ready for action had to be got across the river by improvised means since we had no pontoons. The operation was accomplished with two large barges which the retreating Germans had left behind, only slightly damaged, in the shallow water by the bank. Each of the barges held three tanks. Ten crossings were made during the night of 5th–6th October and sixty tanks ferried across. They moved into action just as they arrived. Twenty-four hours later the bridge-head had been extended to a depth of four miles and a width of six miles."

From that moment onward Kravchenko's Tank Corps was the key unit of the Soviet defence in the bridge-head on the western bank of the Dnieper. The T-34s prevented General Hauffe's infantry division from pushing in the Russian defensive positions. The Lyutezh bridge-head stood firm. As a result, the Soviet High Command found itself faced with a totally new situation. The STAVKA operation plan had not envisaged the main thrust across the Dnieper to be mounted from Lyutezh. The decisive attack was to have been made from the Dnieper loop at Bukrin. There, Vatutin had assembled three strong armies, with General Rybalko's experienced and well-equipped Third Guards Tank Army as the spearhead.

According to STAVKA directives of 29th September, Rybalko's instructions were to smash the German defences in the Kiev area by means of a pincer movement mounted from the Bukrin bridge-head, to take the Ukrainian capital from the south, and then to wheel towards the south-west in order to envelop the entire German southern wing. This plan once more reflected Stalin's old dream of finally annihilating Manstein's Army Group.

But again Stalin's calculations were over-optimistic. Nehring's XXIV Panzer Corps and General von Knobelsdorff's XLVIII Panzer Corps, which had been moved into the sector, foiled Stalin's plan. True enough, a renewed attempt by 7th Panzer Division at the beginning of October to break through to Grigorovka from the north-west and smash the Soviet bridge-head again failed. But at least the bridge-head was now sufficiently well sealed off and was being contained. A counter-attack by 112th Infantry Division, with the 2nd

Battalion, 258th Grenadier Regiment, had even led to the recapture of the high ground along the Dnieper south of Grigorovka, thanks to a bold thrust by Isselhorst's company. A solid and insuperable German defensive line thus barred Vatutin's way to the west. He was bottled up in his bridge-head. All attempts to burst open the German front came to nothing. Twice in the course of October the Russians mounted major offensives. On both occasions they failed.

The *History of the Great Fatherland War* sums up the defeat in the Bukrin bridge-head as follows: "The course of the fighting made it clear that no rapid success was to be expected at this point." It was a fine defensive achievement of the German corps.

In view of this situation the Soviet High Command changed its plan. The dramatic circumstances in which this was done are described by Marshal Grechko, at that time Vatutin's second-in-command, in a brilliantly written essay published in 1963. It reveals most instructively the secret of the Russian victory on the Dnieper.

On 18th October, Grechko reports, the Military Council of Army Group reported to the Soviet High Command that Thirty-Eighth Army had broken the enemy's resistance in the Lyutezh bridge-head, north of Kiev. There was now an opportunity for exploiting this success, but Army Group did not have the necessary forces at its disposal. The Soviet High Command failed to react to this important communication.

"A few days later," Grechko continues, "the Military Council member of Army Group again wrote to the High Command. There was now an opportunity, he reminded them, of scoring a decisive success from the Lyutezh bridge-head, but this would require a tank army to be switched to this sector."

Vatutin's idea clearly was to get away from Bukrin, where the Soviet forces were stuck, and to switch the focal point of the offensive to Lyutezh. But it was difficult to get Stalin to abandon his Bukrin plan. The situation was the same as on the German side: the generals in the field had a difficult time with their master.

It is impossible to decide whether Stalin eventually gave way to the arguments of the Voronezh Front—which, incidentally, was renamed the First Ukrainian Front on 20th October—or whether Vatutin, Khrushchev, and Grechko acted on their own responsibility. Grechko records: "The Military Council of Army Group decided to switch the focal point of the attack from Bukrin to Lyutezh. This meant that the entire Third Guards Tank Army, several rifle corps, and the bulk of the artillery had to be pulled out of the Bukrin bridge-head and transferred to the Lyutezh area, a distance of about a hundred and twenty miles. It was a difficult operation, involving two crossings of the Dnieper and one of the Desna. And everything under the very nose of the enemy who must not notice anything, as the success of the operation depended on strategic surprise."

This decision, revealed in Grechko's essay, reflects an entirely new element in the conduct of operations. For the first time the Russians were abandoning their peculiarity of sticking to a decision once it was taken and carrying it through regardless of losses. Here Vatutin and Grechko chose the Manstein tactics of what chess players call castling and thereby took their first step towards a modern strategy. This included, moreover, the art of concealing one's deployment and deceiving one's opponent. In these fields too, Vatutin and Grechko displayed masterly skill.

Grechko reports: "Regrouping began during the night of 25th–26th October. The formations of Third Guards Tank Army of VII Artillery Corps, of XIII Rifle Corps, as well as other troops left the bridge-head. Pouring rain reduced visibility and muffled the noise. The troops rallied on the far side of the river; they rested during the day and marched at night. There were four march routes, all of them parallel to the front line. They made it in seven nights. Elaborate security measures were taken. There was a complete ban on radio traffic for the formations on the march. On the other hand, all communications of Third Guards Tank Army were left behind in the Bukrin bridge-head and they kept up a busy radio traffic. In the old positions the withdrawn tanks and vehicles were replaced by dummies. They looked so genuine that twice towards the end of October the German Luftwaffe bombed them. Feigned attacks from the bridge-head suggested to the German Command preparations for a non-existent offensive. Their purpose was to stop the Germans from withdrawing troops, and indeed to induce them to pump further reserves into the make-believe focal point. Dummy bridges were built over the Dnieper to suggest the bringing up of new forces and confirm the enemy in his belief that the full-scale offensive would be launched here, in the Bukrin area. This camouflage and deception succeeded completely. Not only did Manstein not withdraw any troops at Bukrin but he actually reinforced them."

Thus the ruse of Bukrin ranks with the great and decisive deceptions of the last War. Field-Marshal Montgomery, a past master in deception, twice resorted to this means on a large scale—once in North Africa, in the decisive battle of El Alamein, when he misled Rommel about his intended attack in the north by elaborate dummy installations in the south. The second time, on an even larger scale, was in the summer of 1944 when his dummy installations in the British Isles persuaded Hitler that a second landing in France was imminent and thereby stopped him from switching all available forces to Normandy in time.

Of course, the Soviet regrouping did not, as Grechko suggests, remain entirely unnoticed by the German Command. Fourth Panzer Army headquarters, according to Hoth's war diary, were well aware that strong Soviet armoured forces had crossed the Desna and were moving towards the north-west. Fortunately for the Russians, bad weather prevented extensive German aerial reconnaissance, so that the diary records: "Impossible to establish their whereabouts."

Hoth's reconnaissance also established a concentration of motorized formations in the Lyutezh area. Hoth even decided to break up these enemy preparations by an armoured thrust. But Hitler forbade this attack.

Thus Lyutezh, now bristling with arms, became the gate through which the Russians were to mount their big sally. Vatutin's preparations went ahead undisturbed. By the beginning of November he had assembled three armies and one tank corps, as well as a cavalry corps east of the river. He had massed artillery on a fantastic scale. Grechko writes: "Two thousand guns and mortars as well as five hundred rocket-launchers were ready for action in the bridge-head. Thus, along the offensive frontage of Thirty-Eighth Army, a sector of four miles, an artillery density of over ninety barrels per thousand feet was achieved. That means one gun or mortar for roughly every ten feet. No previous offensive in the East had been supported by such a massive concentration of artillery. Altogether the Soviet forces in the breakthrough sector of Lyutezh were far superior to the Germans— the infantry by a factor of three, the artillery by a factor of four and a half, and armour by a factor of nine."

The Russian plan was worth this effort.

What was that plan? Broadly speaking, the capture of Kiev, this time from the north; the annihilation of the German Fourth Panzer Army; the seizure of communication centres west of the Dnieper including Zhitomir, Berdichev, and Vinnitsa, far in the rear of the German front; finally a wheeling towards the south with the object of enveloping and annihilating the entire German southern wing. A bold stroke.

Would it succeed? Would Stalin at last achieve what he had tried to accomplish ever since Stalingrad?

2. The Objective was Kiev

*In the basement of the Petrovtsy schoolhouse–Charge
by the Guards–Men from the North Sea and Brandenburg into the breach–Tanks with howling sirens and
blinding searchlights–Kiev cannot be saved–Extinction
of 88th Infantry Division–The tragedy of 25th Panzer
Division–Unsuccessful German counter-attack–Hoth is
fired.*

THE village of Novo-Petrovtsy was in the Lyutezh bridge-head
immediately behind the Soviet lines. In the basement of the
wrecked schoolhouse was Army General Vatutin's command post.
Barely fifty yards away were the battle headquarters of Third Guards
Tank Army and Thirty-Eighth Army. Their two commanders-in-chief,
General Rybalko and General Moskalenko, were at their forward
command posts, together with their Military Council members. The
corps commanders and division commanders also had their HQs
quite close. There is probably no other instance in military history
of so many senior commands, all the way up to an Army Group command, being crammed together in such a small space, immediately
behind the main defensive line, in the middle of a bridge-head filled
to bursting with troops.

This accumulation of generals in the front line was by no means
a mistake—it was part of the plan. Among other things, the troops
were to be made to realize the exceptional importance of an action
requiring a special effort from the Commander-in-Chief all the way
down to the last rifleman. Meetings were held for the Russian troops,
at which political instructors, Military Council members, meritorious
communists, and much-decorated soldiers made speeches. An atmosphere of euphoria and confidence in victory was created.

Outstanding soldiers were solemnly accepted into the Communist
Party as members or probationers; in October alone this Army Group
enrolled 13,000 men. Publicity was given to pledges that the men
would not spare their lives to ensure victory, and that Kiev would be
taken by the twenty-sixth anniversary of the Revolution. The pledge
of Sergeant Valentin Kommissarov received widespread publicity: "I
will fight while there is blood in my veins, while my eyes can see and
my hands can hold a rifle."

In the basement of the schoolhouse Nikita Sergeyevich Khrushchev
on 1st November outlined the plan of the operation to the Military
Council members in the presence of Vatutin. "Whatever the cost,

Kiev must be taken on the anniversary of the October Revolution," he declared.

Whatever the cost.

Vatutin did not count the cost. He let loose hell.

At the break of day on 3rd November two thousand guns and five hundred multiple mortars bombarded the German position at Lyutezh. For forty minutes the shells crashed through the morning mist. The fiery muzzle flashes rent the twilight and the haze. As soon as the mist began to lift, aircraft of the Soviet Second Air Army appeared and dropped their bombs over the German front. Thereupon the rifle regiment of Thirty-Eighth Army, supported by Kravchenko's V Guards Tank Corps, charged. "Urra!"

The blow fell on three German divisions—the 88th, the 68th, and the 208th Infantry Division, units from Franconia, Hesse, and Brandenburg. The blow was so devastating that the Soviet rifle formations encountered virtually no resistance along the first few hundred yards. Only later in the day did the German opposition stiffen. Nevertheless, General Moskalenko's divisions succeeded in ripping open the German front over a width of six miles and in penetrating some four to six miles deep into the German defensive zone.

Colonel-General Hoth rushed his Hamburg 20th Panzer Grenadier Division under General Jauer, as well as parts of the Brandenburg 8th Panzer Division, to oppose the Soviet formations which had broken through. In vain. The offensive momentum of six rifle divisions and one tank corps could not be halted.

By the time the men from Hamburg reached their assigned interception line the infantry battle was already in full swing there. The Russians had reached the spot before them. Furiously and grimly the Grenadier regiments resisted. They mounted counter-attacks. They made evasive moves. They charged again. They attacked jointly with combat groups of the Thuringian 7th Panzer Division. They even gained some ground.

Just then Vatutin opened the second act of his offensive. In the evening of 4th November he set in motion the armoured brigades of General Rybalko's Third Guards Tank Army. They thrust through the breach opened up by Thirty-Eighth Army. They overtook their own infantry and kept driving on.

Darkness fell. And then something happened which the Germans, who had meanwhile re-formed for defence, had never experienced before. The battlefield was lit up as bright as day and an infernal noise filled the air: Rybalko's tanks were driving up against the German positions with headlights full on and with sirens howling. Without stopping they fired shell after shell from their cannon. On top of their tanks sat the infantrymen of two rifle divisions, the 167th and

136th. On this steamroller of fire they were riding deep into the German front. Rybalko hoped that the searchlights would create panic. He had also remembered the effects of the "Jericho device" which the German Stukas had used against Soviet infantrymen: the howling sirens as the Stukas dived down had invariably created something very near panic among the Russian infantry. Rybalko hoped to produce the same effect with his screaming, ghostly, armoured armada. And he succeeded in doing so at many points along the thinly-held front of XIII and VII Corps.

More effective, of course, was the fire-power of the massed brigades of T-34s. In spite of a counter-attack by its armoured group, General von Manteuffel's 7th Panzer Division was unable to prevent the Russians from crossing the Irpen five miles west of Kiev and advancing along the Zhitomir road towards Fastov, the most important communications centre south-west of Kiev. A counter-attack by the main body of 7th Panzer Division and the regiments of 20th Panzer Grenadier Division, though initially successful, was unable to achieve anything decisive against the threat from both flanks. The Thuringians and Franconians had to give ground. The 90th Grenadier Regiment from Bergedorf was pushed into the northern part of the town; on 5th November, after nightfall, it forced its way out of the town and through the Russian front under the command of Captain Otto, evacuating all its wounded.

The 88th Infantry Division fell back to the western part of Kiev. The Division's commander, Major-General Roth, tried to restore order among his formations. But he was later killed in action against the spearheads of the Russian infantry.

At the command post of Colonel-General Hoth's Fourth Panzer Army a glance at the situation map revealed the Russian intention. General Rybalko's Tank Army was aiming past Kiev towards the great strategic supply lines and lateral communications of Manstein's Army Group. General Moskalenko's Thirty-Eighth Army, on the other hand, was striking straight at the Ukrainian capital.

A drizzle was veiling the battlefield of Kiev in a cold grey light. Nature may have been grey, but Colonel-General Hoth's strategic situation was black. Again, as throughout the past few months, there were no adequate German reserves available to operate with. Hitler continued to keep the few available Panzer divisions on the lower Dnieper because he did not on any account want to lose the Nikopol region with its deposits of manganese ore. He was also anxious about the approaches to the Crimea.

For that reason the Thuringian-Hessian 1st Panzer Division was brought up from Greece at the end of October 1943 and assembled in the Kirovograd area. This replenished and refurbished division was to explore the possibilities of a counter-attack in the area north of

Krivoy Rog, but for the time being was still busy exchanging its tropical kit for the necessary winter equipment. Hitler's one big reserve, Seventeenth Army, he kept stationed in the Crimea because he did not want this "aircraft carrier" off the Rumanian oilfields to fall into Russian hands. All attempts by Manstein to get some formations of Seventeenth Army for the Dnieper battle failed in the face of Hitler's refusal. He adduced political and economic arguments. An evacuation of the Crimea, Hitler argued, would produce unfavourable reactions among the neighbouring Turks, Rumanians, and Bulgarians. It was the same old problem which had always led to clashes between Manstein and Hitler: was the northern wing of Manstein's Army Group to be reinforced to stave off its threatening strategic envelopment or were economic and political interests to be given priority? There were not enough forces to do both these things. Hitler himself realized the dilemma. "But," he lectured Manstein, "that's a risk that has got to be taken, and I am prepared to take it upon myself."

Colonel-General Hoth was sitting at his command post at Markarov, on the Kiev–Zhitomir highway, bending over his maps. His chief of staff, Major-General Fangohr, was making his report: "Kiev can no longer be saved. The 7th Panzer Division, the 20th Motorized Division, and the Combat Group of the SS "Das Reich" Panzer Division have been forced away from Kiev. Inside the city the 88th Infantry Division can no longer halt the unfavourable developments. What matters now is the timely interception of the dangerous thrust which fast Soviet troops are aiming at our rearward communications in the Fastov-Berdichev-Zhitomir area. If we lose the marshalling yards of Fastov and Kazatin the lifeline of the entire Army Group will be in danger."

Hoth nodded. The field telephone rang. It was VII Corps, asking for help. But where was Hoth to find any help? Events were moving inexorably. The Soviet Thirty-Eighth Army stormed Kiev. The bulk of the German 88th Infantry Division was wiped out in the blazing city. Only remnants without heavy arms or equipment fought their way through to the south and west.

At midnight on 6th November, as the Soviet revolution anniversary dawned, the armoured spearheads of General Kravchenko's V Guards Tank Corps were rumbling down Kreshchatik, the main boulevard of Kiev, in the city centre. Infantry with sub-machine-guns belonging to the independent 4th Reconnaissance Company entered the ruins of the Party headquarters building and hoisted the Red flag. Three days after the opening of the attack the Ukrainian metropolis was again in Russian hands.

Hardly anything had functioned correctly among the German

defenders in the area north of Kiev. The armoured formations had largely been moved into action in ignorance of the actual situation; the main part of 19th Panzer Division had even been switched to Bukrin. The one thing that had worked admirably well was the organization of the German railwaymen. Not a single railway-engine was left behind in Kiev. When the last station was abandoned, the Reich railway personnel and field railway commandos had altogether moved out 24,911 wagons loaded with salvaged equipment.

The hero of the day was Nikita Sergeyevich Khrushchev. The Party Chief of the Ukraine entered Kiev in general's uniform and was hailed as its liberator. It was his great day.

General Rybalko, the real victor, did not care for celebrations. With the brigades of his Third Guards Tank Army he raced past the city towards the south. Although he was repulsed there by 10th Panzer Grenadier Division he quickly regrouped and thrust into the wide gaps in the front of VII Corps south-west of Kiev. He overran the Irpen sector. He cut the rearward communications of the German formations still holding out at Kiev. He blocked the great highways running into Kiev. And on 7th November he took Fastov, the communications centre thirty miles south-west of Kiev, the town through which ran all the supply lines of the northern wing of Manstein's Army Group. The two local defence rifle battalions, an emergency battalion raised from men on leave, and the few flak personnel belonging to combat and searchlight troops, ordered to defend the town, were swept away by Rybalko's armoured forces. The small headquarters staff of the commander of 7th Panzer Division, rushed to the spot on 5th November, was unable to avert the disaster and had to fight its way back to Division on foot.

This time events happened too fast even for the German railwaymen who had, in the first instance, pulled their evacuation transport back to Fastov. The entire rolling stock stood on the sidings of the vast marshalling yards. It included forty-five engines. It proved impossible to save anything of the railway stock—and in the East this was more valuable than anywhere else. It was a disaster. Even worse was the fact that Rybalko was already in the rear of Army Group South.

When the alarming news about the fall of Fastov reached Manstein he took off at once for Rastenburg to see Hitler. He wanted to persuade him to release three Panzer divisions, earmarked for the defensive battle on the lower Dnieper, and let him have them for defence and counter-attack in the Fastov area.

But Hitler again refused. His fear of losing the ore deposits and the Crimea was greater than his concern for Manstein's northern wing. Manstein was in despair. "If things go wrong, my Führer,

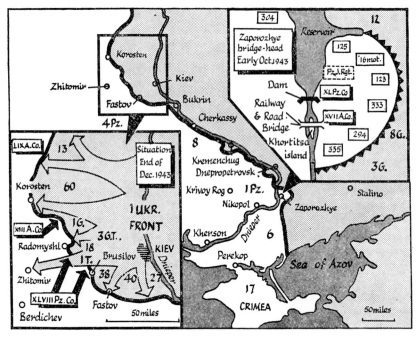

Map 40. Bypassing Kiev, Rybalko's tank army was aiming at the supply lines of Manstein's Army Group. A crisis also developed in the Zaporozhye bridge-head. During the night of 14th–15th October General Henrici had to give orders for the hydro-electric power-station and the dam to be blown up.

then the whole of Army Group South is doomed," the Field-Marshal warned him. This warning at least produced a small concession— Hitler authorized the employment of two Panzer divisions, the 1st Panzer Division and the SS "Leibstandarte Adolf Hitler" Panzer Division, not on the lower Dnieper but at Kiev. But both formations were still in transit and not readily available.

Thus only one decision was left, and that was to prove disastrous— to use 25th Panzer Division. It was to be employed at Fastov straight from the trains which brought it from France.

The division had only been raised during the summer. It had been stiffened by the replenished 9th Panzer Regiment, transferred from Norway to France and there put through its first operational exercises. Now it was in transit to Fourth Panzer Army. Its commander was General von Schell, a competent soldier. But what use was the commander? The division was not welded together, it had never yet been in action as a division, and moreover lacked experience of the Eastern Front. But Colonel-General Hoth had no other choice. Regardless of all misgivings he had to employ the division at Fastov in order to keep the communications centre in German hands at all costs.

Hoth's decision was, moreover, justified by one further consideration. General von Schell had received from Guderian not only a Panzer regiment, but also the complete Tiger Battalion 509. That meant 45 Tigers. As well as the 90 Mark IV tanks of 9th Panzer Regiment. And 135 battle-worthy tanks held out real hope. Rybalko, at a rough estimate, did not have many more—and his were the inferior T-34s.

But once again we come up against the fact that battles and entire campaigns are not infrequently decided by mistakes, muddle, or wrong orders. The Tiger Battalion and the main part of the Panzer regiment of 25th Panzer Division, which might have averted the fate of Fastov, missed the battlefield altogether. While the wheeled units of the division were being unloaded at Berdichev, in order to move on Fastov, the armoured formations were not there. Twenty-four hours earlier they had been sent on by rail to the south-east and were just then arriving at the station of Kirovograd, 120 miles away from Berdichev. Kirovograd, of course, had been the division's original destination. The armoured formations had simply not been redirected by Army in time.

As a result, the Panzer grenadiers, artillerymen, and engineers had to face Rybalko's tank brigades with virtually no tanks and without the assault guns of the Panzerjäger Battalion. The 146th Panzer Grenadier Regiment almost at once encountered strong packs of T-34s belonging to 55th Guards Tank Brigade south of Fastov. The Russian patrols had spotted the German columns in good time and the brigade commander had coolly prepared a surprise attack for them. The German 9th Company was shot up. The 6th Company walked straight into an inferno. The company commander, nearly all subordinate commanders, and 160 men were killed by the fire of the T-34s. Panic broke out and swept through the whole of 2nd Battalion.

In spite of these heavy losses General von Schell personally led his battalions forward again. But their striking power was gone. When the advanced parts of 9th Panzer Regiment at last turned up from Kirovograd two days later the greatly reduced battalions again mounted an attack on Fastov under the leadership of their division commander. They dislodged the Russians. They penetrated right to the edge of the town. One assault party even seized the railway sidings. After fierce fighting they were dislodged again. But they broke in once more. Again they had to pull out. In the end the attack got stuck on the high ground a mile and a half outside the town. A decisive thrust into the deep flank of the Soviets was no longer possible. The German losses were too great. When Corporal Fitschen arrived at 6th Company with a group of stragglers he found only two men and one NCO out of the group's 12 men. The company was down to 75 men fit for action. A mere 75. Ten days previously 240 men had climbed aboard the train in France.

Nevertheless the unlucky 25th Panzer Division achieved one important thing—it halted Rybalko's sweep to the south and together with a combat group of the SS "Das Reich" Division, the 10th Panzer Grenadier Division, and the newly-brought-up 198th Infantry Division, sealed off the Soviet breakthrough. This gave Manstein enough time to move up fresh forces for a massive counter-attack.

Stalin's chance of annihilating the German southern wing was once more lost. Admittedly, the Soviets succeeded in making an appreciable leap to the west and in taking Zhitomir with the large supply dumps and foodstuff depots of Fourth Panzer Army. The Army Group's XIII Corps under General Mattenklott managed for the time being to seal off the penetration with 8th Panzer Division and 20th Panzer Grenadier Division. Farther north the LIX Corps with 291st Infantry Division and Corps Detachment "C" prevented a Soviet breakthrough along the juncture of the Army Groups to both sides of Korosten. The worst danger to Manstein had passed. His XLVIII Panzer Corps represented a powerful force of no less than six Panzer divisions and a few Grenadier divisions; these were now assembled south of a line from Fastov to Zhitomir, ready to strike at the flank of the Russian westward thrust.

For once Manstein had really wrested from Hitler an appreciable fighting force. The divisions had been brought up from all parts of Europe—from Norway, Greece, and northern Italy. They included outstanding, experienced, and in part newly equipped formations with extensive experience of the Eastern Front, such as the 1st SS "Leibstandarte" Panzer Division, and the 1st and 19th Panzer Divisions of the Army. The Corps was placed under the command of General Hermann Balck, one of the Wehrmacht's best commanders in the field. But to inflict a decisive defeat on four Russian armies plus two independent corps which were already assembled in the bridgehead of Kiev, and to throw them back across the Dnieper—for that the six divisions of XLVIII Panzer Corps were not strong enough.

Guderian realized this. On 9th November he had asked Hitler for stronger forces. "Bring up all available divisions of Army Group South and Army Group A, even at the cost of great risks," he had suggested. But Hitler decided in favour of a counter-attack which, as usual, he mounted with inadequate forces. And the mistake had to be paid for. True, LIX Army Corps succeeded in stabilizing the situation at Korosten. The XLVIII Panzer Corps recaptured the area around Zhitomir-Radomyshl-Brusilov-Fastov, and with this successful counter-attack once more demonstrated what German armoured forces, led by experienced tank commanders, could still accomplish in the fifth winter of the war. A greatly superior army had been out-manoeuvred, its offensive strength had been checked, an entire corps had been smashed. But the impossible was not to be achieved—Kiev was not recaptured. The offensive momentum of Fourth Panzer Army had spent itself. The Soviets were able to hold on to the core of their strategic bridge-head at Kiev. This bridge-head had a depth of just under 50 miles and a width of nearly 120 miles. All along this massive sector the German front had now been pushed away from the middle Dnieper. The Soviet bulge, presently replenished with offensive troops, was jutting out dangerously towards the west.

Colonel-General Hoth, a commander who had proved himself in a thousand battles, was made the scapegoat for a situation brought solely by Hitler's mistakes. He had to relinquish command of Fourth Panzer Army in favour of General Raus.

3. Zaporozhye

Fortress guarding the flank on the Dnieper–Six divisions and a heavy Panzerjäger regiment–Malinovskiy attacks with three armies–A sealed letter in a parachute dispatch-case–Stalin's black-white-red legion–Crisis at the hydro-power dam–"Henrici, you're risking your neck!"–Two hundred tons of dynamite–A far-reaching Russian victory.

DANGER was lurking not only in the Kiev area. At Kremenchug and Cherkassy the situation also looked grim: here Colonel-General Konev had been able to establish a strong bridge-head with parts of his second Ukrainian Front and with the active help of daring partisan detachments. Since mid-October the most dangerous spot, however, had been Zaporozhye. Zaporozhye with its gigantic dam and the huge "Lenin" power-station—a showpiece of the communist electrical industry—was, for the Soviet Command, an emotionally loaded objective. Something like the prestige of Stalingrad was at stake.

Zaporozhye also played a special part in Hitler's plan. He had good reasons when, about mid-September, he demanded that Manstein should form a large bridge-head to protect the city and the dam. The Field-Marshal had not been too pleased, because he needed every regiment on the western bank. But Hitler remained adamant. The generating capacity of half a million kilowatts was at stake—the power which kept the West Ukrainian industrial region alive. Work in the Kirovograd metallurgical plants and in the mines of Krivoy Rog was proceeding at full speed. Was all that to be threatened by the loss of electricity from Zaporozhye?

Economic considerations, however, were not the only reason for Hitler's insistence on Zaporozhye. Strategic considerations were equally important. So long as a bridge-head was maintained on the eastern bank at Zaporozhye, the Russians could not risk a thrust between the Dnieper bend and the Sea of Azov down to the lower reaches of the Dnieper in order to gain the approaches to the Crimea. The Zaporozhye bridge-head ideally covered the flank of Sixth Army and simultaneously threatened the Soviet forces operating towards Dnepropetrovsk from the north.

Even Manstein could not dismiss these arguments of Hitler's. And the Soviet history of the war confirms that the German bridge-head was a serious obstacle to Russian operations against the lower Dnieper. Zaporozhye, that fortress on the flank, prevented a strike at the Crimea. Hitler was therefore right to demand that the bridge-head should be defended tooth and nail.

The thankless task of "tooth and nail" was assigned to General Henrici's experienced XL Panzer Corps. From its three Panzer divisions and the infantry divisions of XVII Army Corps—under General of Mountain Troops Kreysing—the Army-sized Combat Group Henrici was formed. It was to stand guard at the Zaporozhye dam. Needless to say, these were not sufficient forces for securing both the western bank and the twenty-five by twelve-mile bulge on the eastern bank. This bastion, in fact, was defended by six divisions and one heavy Panzerjäger regiment. But the Soviet High Command employed against it an entire Army Group with three armies, one air fleet, and two tank corps—including such crack formations as Eighth Guards Army under General Chuykov, the defender of Stalingrad. Three armies and an air fleet against six and a half divisions. A superiority of ten to one.

Nevertheless, the first large-scale Soviet attacks were successfully repulsed. The success was due largely to the offensive fighting spirit of the Rhineland-Westphalian 16th Panzer Grenadier Division under Count Schwerin and the defensive strength of the 656th Heavy Panzerjäger Regiment under Lieutenant-Colonel von Jungenfeldt. The super-heavy Ferdinand assault guns, also known as the "Porsche Tigers", with their 8·8-cm cannon knocked out the T-34s one after another; the 15-cm howitzers carried by the forty-seven fighting vehicles of the Assault Panzer Battalion 216 were veritable mobile fortresses with devastating fire power.

Unfortunately, von Jungenfeldt's regiment had only one battalion of assault tanks and only two of Ferdinands. Twice or three times that number—together with a few replenished infantry and Panzer divisions—might well have changed the course of the battle of Zaporozhye. But with just one regiment of heavy anti-tank weapons that battle was not to be won.

General Henrici was a worried man. The front-line strength of the division was diminishing. Reinforcements were not arriving. Worst of all was the supply situation—ammunition was so low that since the beginning of October even enemy columns deployed within sight could no longer be shelled.

On the morning of 10th October Malinovskiy mounted another attack. He sent in his entire Army Group, with all its three armies. He had again chosen a Sunday for the attack in the hope that the Sunday atmosphere would make the German defenders less alert. The battle was opened with a massive artillery barrage from all guns. For the first time the Soviets were employing independent artillery divisions. These ensured a rapid concentration of fire at the focal points—a matter of crucial importance in these breakthrough battles. Not until later, after an experiment with 18th Artillery Division, did the German Command adopt a similar reorganization of its artillery by creating the artillery brigades and the people's artillery corps.

The intensity of the bombardment of the German lines at Zaporozhye had never before been equalled. With an unprecedented expenditure of ammunition Malinovskiy ploughed over the German main defensive line. Then he let loose his steam-roller.

On the southern sector of the attack, at Novo-Aleksandrovka, Major Horstmann's assault tanks hurled themselves against the Russians who had broken into the lines. Ahead of them all was Second Lieutenant Weisbach, upright in the turret. Second Lieutenant Hofer got as far as the anti-tank ditch. South of the main road Sergeant Leder and Corporal Habermann checked the Russian assault against Novo-Aleksandrovka and threw the Russians back to their jumping-off position. In the evening forty-eight wrecked enemy tanks were lying in front of the bridge-head.

The same happened the following day. Russian attack. German counter-attack. Henrici's infantry also held out gallantly in the face of undiminished enemy offensive activity on the second and third days of the battle. The Soviets kept feeding their large-scale attacks with fresh forces brought up from the rear. They charged. They were killed. They were scattered and fell back. They charged again.

On the morning of 12th October there was an intermezzo of interest to the history of the war. Lieutenant-General Rauch, commanding

123rd Infantry Division, sent General Henrici a Soviet parachute dispatch-case dropped over Rauch's sector. It contained a sealed envelope. The address was typed: General Erwin Rauch, commanding 123rd Infantry Division.

"Dear Rauch! I tried repeatedly to get in touch with you through bearers of a flag of truce but your men invariably fired at them. . . . I am therefore choosing this way. . . .

"I am sure you still remember the days when we were at the Military Academy together. . . .

"Your division is in a hopeless situation. . . . Your division is surrounded and faces a new Stalingrad. . . . Come over with your division to our side, in a body. . . . I have arranged with the Soviet High Command particularly honourable and favourable conditions for your division and yourself personally. . . . Decent treatment, the prisoners will keep their personal property, the officers will keep their personal arms. The division will remain together and will be employed for labour service in a body. . . . After the war the division will be the first to be allowed to return home." Signed: Von Seydlitz, General of Artillery.

This letter from General von Seydlitz, who had been taken prisoner by the Russians at Stalingrad, was a psychological warfare move on the part of the Soviets. But the men of 304th Infantry Division, employed north of the hydro-power dam to cover the western bank of the Dnieper, had a more drastic experience of the operations of the "Free Germany National Committee". The division commander reported that boats flying black-white-red flags and with crews singing the German anthem had tried to cross the Dnieper on the sector of the division but had been repulsed by fire.

The voice of Stalin's black-white-red legion was heard also over the radio receivers of the troops. Colonel Hans-Günther van Hooven, for many years in charge of the Panzer Corps Signals Battalion 440 and therefore familiar with the communications of his old battalion, addressed his young lieutenants over the air. Van Hooven had also been taken prisoner at Stalingrad, as Chief of Army Signals, and had joined the National Committee.

Hooven had been very popular in his battalion, and at XL Panzer Corps Headquarters his sound judgment had been much appreciated. His siren song, therefore, promising "honourable treatment and good food in captivity" appeared in a particularly questionable light. The overtures were passionately discussed, but generally rejected. The troops did not accept the argument that the fight against Hitler and his political system was being waged on the battlefield or by means of false arguments against one's own comrades.

On 13th October, the fourth day of the battle, the Soviets succeeded in making a massive penetration in the German defences. The crisis had come. The danger of a breakthrough to the dam had become real.

The war diary of XL Panzer Corps leaves no doubt about the seriousness of the situation that day. A mood of sudden alarm was produced at the Assault Panzer Battalion of the Heavy Panzerjäger Regiment by the radioed report of the Soviet penetration. Eight T-34s and two regiments of Soviet infantry were already three miles behind the German main defensive line. Once more the powerful assault tanks succeeded in saving the situation: three T-34s were knocked out and the rest turned tail. The Russian infantry was sprayed with airburst ricochets and fell back again. But it was obvious that, in view of the relative strength, these dangerous situations would recur again and again—and the firing power of von Jungenfeldt's Heavy Panzerjäger Regiment could not be everywhere.

Henrici's Army-sized Combat Group, to provide for just this emergency, had ordered the construction of small but effective covering positions on the approaches to the dam and to the railway bridge. These were to provide cover for the dynamiting. This work demanded considerable preparation—the water level above the dam had to be lowered by at least fifteen feet to prevent a sudden flood wave from endangering the downstream bridges in the sector of Sixth Army.

Moreover, the filling of the mine chambers would take twenty-four hours. Yet instead of leaving the decision on when to start preparations for the demolition to the responsible commander in the field, as General Wenck, chief of staff of First Panzer Army, had proposed, OKH expressly reserved for itself approval of all measures of this kind. Henrici felt like a cat on hot bricks.

On the morning of 13th October the dam came under deliberate Russian artillery fire for the first time. The general at once demanded a free hand from OKH. There was no reply. A few hours later the threat of a Soviet breakthrough was beginning to take clear shape. Another appeal to OKH. Henrici was at his command post on the eastern approach to the dam. Every five minutes he rang through to his signals centre: "Still no instructions from the Wolfsschanze?" "No, Herr General." Major Kandutsch, the intelligence officer, did not leave the telephone for a minute. The division commanders were asking for instructions. But the Wolfsschanze remained silent. Hitler was still sleeping. And no-one at the Führer's Headquarters had the nerve to wake him. General Henrici therefore got himself connected with Colonel-General von Mackensen, C-in-C First Panzer Army. "Herr Generaloberst, I am about to issue orders for the mine chambers to be filled and for the water level in the reservoir to be lowered—on my own responsibility."

Mackensen did not argue with him. He knew about Henrici's anxieties. He merely remarked laconically: "Henrici, you're risking your neck." Henrici risked his neck.

On 14th October the Soviets accomplished another deep tank penetration in the direction of the reservoir. At the last moment combat groups of 16th Panzer Grenadier Division and the 421st Grenadier Regiment of 125th Infantry Division managed to seal it off. Heavy artillery fire shattered the prepared fuse cables running to the mine chambers of the dam. Officers of the army engineer commander had to go forward again to mend the severed cables and lay new ones.

Two hundred tons of dynamite, the load of ten freight wagons, were stacked in the turbine hall of the power-station. Forty tons had been placed in the mine chambers of the dam itself, together with a hundred aerial bombs, all of them 1000-pounders, making another fifty tons.

Henrici ordered the demolition of the railway bridge for 1845 hours; the hydro-power dam was to be blown up at 2000. But the army engineer commander could not yet allow the firing buttons to be pushed. The 16th Panzer Grenadier Division, the rearguard protecting the bridge and the dam, still had to be notified. "Send a signal to the 16th to say demolition is in two hours," Major Braun, the chief of operations, instructed the signals officer. A little while later the signals officer returned uneasily: "We've got no contact with the 16th, Herr Major."

"Damn!"

Second Lieutenant Christian Stoeckle of the XL Panzer Corps Operations Staff was sent off in a jeep. "You've got to find Count Schwerin. How you do it is your business."

Lieutenant Stoeckle drove off. Zaporozhye was in flames from one end to the other. Even the trees along the road were blazing torches. A suspiciously large number of troopers were hurrying westwards in the direction of the railway bridge. But none of them knew where the command post of 16th Panzer Grenadier Division was at that moment. With an old soldier's instinct Stoeckle made for a peasant hut at the northern edge of the town. Right enough—there, in the gloomy hut, by the light of a candle and surrounded by his staff officers, sat the general, studying the map. The lieutenant handed him the message and reported on the situation. Count Schwerin made his plan at once. "We'll hold out until everything's across!" And 16th Panzer Grenadier Division held its lines in front of the two-tier rail and road bridge to the very last minute. Whatever had not got across by H hour was ferried in boats and on rafts to the mid-stream island of Khortitsa. For Jungenfeldt's assault tanks, which were still south of Zaporozhye on the Melitopol highway, covering the flank, a tank ferry was built.

During the night of 14th–15th October, just before midnight, the bridge and the hydro-power dam were blown up. It was like a crash of thunder. But in spite of the enormous quantity of high explosive only a few gaps were torn into the massive concrete wall of the 800-yard-long dam. With a roar the 60-foot-deep reservoir burst through the gaps. A swirling wave of water several feet high flooded the land and the villages in the river valley. Cautiously the Soviet advance detachments probed their way into the blazing town. Carefully they approached the eastern ramp of the dam.

Farther south the last heavy assault tanks were ferried across the river.

4. The Battle for the Wotan Line

Tolbukhin's steam-roller moves towards Melitopol–The Russians charge thirty times; thirty times they are repulsed–The German Sixth Army has twenty-five tanks left–A corps fights its way out–An army is saved–But the Crimea is cut off.

ZAPOROZHYE was no spectacular victory for the Russians. There were no huge German losses to be announced. Nevertheless, it may well have been one of the most important and most far-reaching victories achieved by the Soviet troops on the Dnieper in 1943. The *History of the Great Fatherland War* rightly observes: "With the liberation of Zaporozhye the situation in the southern Ukraine was fundamentally changed." That was perfectly true. For now the Russians were able to reach out for the lower Dnieper, for the Dnieper estuary and for the approaches to the Crimea. The Soviet High Command did not hesitate a moment to open its attack against Sixth Army.

No army in the world can carry on for a whole year in ceaseless and costly retreats and fierce defensive fighting, without reinforcements or adequate supplies of arms and ammunition. The law of numbers was making itself felt on the lower Dnieper as everywhere else. Six Soviet armies were facing a single German army. Colonel-General Hollidt had eleven and a half German and two Rumanian divisions—formations which had burnt themselves out in months of defensive fighting and retreats.

The divisions of XXIX Corps had pulled back to the Wotan Line. In the course of this difficult disengagement the 55th Grenadier Regiment of 17th Infantry Division had knocked out forty T-34s in the course

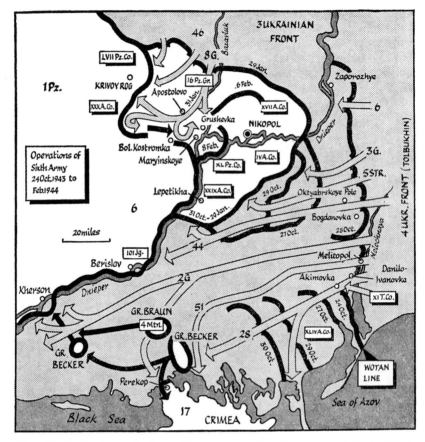

Map 41. The battle on the lower Dnieper resulted in the cutting of the land link with the Crimea. The Nikopol bridge-head was intended as a springboard for the re-establishment of that link in the future.

of three days. But even the most gallant formations could not in the long run stand up to and repulse the assault of six Soviet armies in a steppe providing no cover whatever. The Russian superiority exceeded anything experienced in the past. At the beginning of October they mounted their attack against the Wotan Line with forty-five rifle divisions, two motorized and three tank corps, as well as two cavalry corps.

Eight hundred tanks were on the move. Four hundred troops of artillery and 200 multiple mortars supported the attack. Sixth Army reeled under this blow. Its two Panzer divisions and three assault gun battalions hurled themselves into the path of the Russian steamroller with 181 tanks and assault guns. The weakened regiments of the Infantry divisions dug their heels into the arid soil of the Nogay

Steppe. Grenadiers, mountain Jägers, and the men of the Luftwaffe field divisions knew what was at stake. They had to hold that triangle of featureless steppe between Zaporozhye, the Sea of Azov, and the Dnieper estuary. Otherwise the Seventeenth Army in the Crimea would be lost.

But how were they to achieve this objective in this infernal steppe? There were no hard roads—only tracks and dirt roads from the Dnieper to the front, through an immense and boundless area. Now that it was autumn sandstorms swept the land with elemental force. Between the German troops and the sea there was not a single river behind which they might have dug in, not a single ridge of high ground to which they might have clung. Their artillery stood exposed on the flat ground. There was not a tree or a bush which might have hidden the guns from enemy observers.

The much-vaunted Wotan Line was a hurriedly dug anti-tank ditch, protected by a few infantry trenches along the edge of the steppe. Only the elevated banks of the Molechnaya stream represented a modest natural obstacle. This then was the arena in which the fate of the Crimea and of Rumania was to be decided.

For two weeks, from 27th September until 8th October, Sixth Army held its front. Then its turn came too. On 9th October at 1000 hours, an entirely unconventional hour, Tolbukhin opened the great battle. It began with an infernal artillery barrage. Within an hour 15,000 shells burst on a strip of land nine miles wide. One shell every three feet. Then came the Russian infantry. Confident of victory, arms linked. Shouting "Urrah!" After their artillery barrage the Russians did not expect any appreciable German resistance—but they had a nasty shock. From the ploughed-up steppe machine-guns raked the Soviet ranks. Field howitzers barked. Nebelwerfer mortars whined. Tolbukhin's assault regiments collapsed. They flooded back. They came again. They were again repulsed. They came again the next day, Sunday. And again on Monday. And Tuesday. And Wednesday. Every day. For two weeks.

"The objective is the annihilation of the German Sixth Army. Once that is defeated the door to the Crimea will be wide open," Colonel Tolbukhin lectured his commanders of the Fourth Ukrainian Front every morning. "The objective is decisive for the outcome of the war. It justifies any sacrifice."

The fiercest fighting flared up around Melitopol on the southern wing of the Wotan Line. The Soviet infantry lost mountains of dead, the Soviet XI Tank Corps lost hundreds of T-34s. Hollidt's Sixth Army was again fighting against the spectre of Stalingrad—for what Tolbukhin had in mind for Hollidt's divisions was a Stalingrad on the Dnieper. The fighting at Melitopol in no way yielded to that at Stalingrad in savagery.

Bogdanovka, Oktyabrskoye Pole, Akimovka, Danilo-Ivanovka, and the plantations south of Melitopol are names of battlefields less well-known in popular histories of the war than those associated with the drama of Stalingrad—nevertheless they are among the most blood-drenched localities of the last War. Thirty times the Russians charged against Oktyabrskoye Pole; thirty times they were repulsed. Those were bad days for the Jägers of 3rd Mountain Division, for the Grena-diers of 258th and 17th Infantry Divisions, and for the men of Major von Gaza's combat group of 13th Panzer Division. The Russians lost sixty-two tanks in these engagements.

Equally successful were the regiments in the plantations south of Melitopol. Many of the soldiers who were in action between Zapo-rozhye and the Sea of Azov at that time will have forgotten the num-bers of the divisions. But their tactical signs are still remembered. And when the men saw them on the signposts they knew on whom they could rely to their right or left—the Cross of Lorraine of 79th Infantry Division, the white diamond of 111th Infantry Division, the nine-pointed star of the Hessian 9th Infantry Division, the dog's head of the Westphalian 336th Infantry Division, and the fixed bayonet of the Franconian 17th Infantry Division.

On the northern wing the tanks of 17th Panzer Division, together with the Grenadiers of 101st Jäger Division and 302nd Infantry Divi-sion, were fighting just as fiercely. The Armoured Reconnaissance Battalion 13 under Captain Schütz protected the exposed flanks with its motor-cyclist riflemen and armoured scout parties. They were gallant units and disciplined ones. To the very end.

But the battle east of the lower Dnieper had been hopeless for Colonel-General Hollidt from the start. In the long run the law of numbers could not be disregarded.

Melitopol fell on 23rd October. That gave the Russians their oppor-tunity to thrust southwards towards the Crimea. Tolbukhin employed everything he had for a decisive breakthrough. He moved three fresh rifle corps to the front. He concentrated four hundred tanks at the penetration point.

On 24th October he charged the sector of XLIV Corps south-west of Melitopol with six rifle divisions and two waves of tanks. The German grenadiers were overrun in their firing pits. Alarm units and assault guns flung themselves against the enemy. Ninety-four of his tanks were destroyed and the attack was halted. Those were among the most savage days of the whole war.

They were the days of the Panzer Group von Hake. With the tanks, assault guns, and armoured infantry carriers of 13th Panzer Division, Colonel von Hake barred the enemy's advance. They were also the days when the 336th and 370th Artillery Regiments and the Heavy Panzerjäger Battalion 93 stood and fought to the end: they first resisted with their guns and assault guns, then with their sub-machine-guns, bayonets, trenching tools, and hand-grenades. They bled to death.

At noon on 27th October 73rd Infantry Division reported an effective strength of 170 men—one-hundredth of its nominal strength. And that was a division which had only been freshly assigned to Sixth Army on 4th October. The 111th Infantry Division was down to 200 men fit for action. The heavy equipment of the divisions and corps was 60 per cent destroyed. The entire army was down to 25 operational tanks and assault guns. True, their repair services were working feverishly to get the tanks and other equipment ready for action as quickly as possible, even while in retreat, but the losses were too great. The Russians too had suffered frightful casualties and lost hundreds of tanks. Yet always and everywhere the Russians had one battalion, one regiment, or one corps more than Hollidt. According to Soviet sources they had a ten-fold superiority at every moment of the battle.

Thus the armoured forces of Lieutenant-General Kreyzer's Soviet Fifty-First Army eventually succeeded in knocking northwards the right wing of the Franconian 73rd Infantry Division in the Melitopol area and in ripping open the German front along a nine-mile sector.

Colonel-General Hollidt was unable to free forces quickly enough to close the gap. Like a breached dam the edges of the gap crumbled more and more. The gap through which Tolbukhin's divisions poured grew wider and wider. To the right of the Soviet Fifty-First Army and its XIX Tank Corps, Lieutenant-General Zakharov's Second Guards Army now poured through the breach with a mechanized corps, swamped the small German combat group which had remained in their positions, and soon widened the gap to twenty-eight miles. A dam-burst of disastrous dimension was in the making. Was the bulk of Sixth Army, built up anew after Stalingrad, to be wiped out again—this time in the waterless, sand-swept Nogay Steppe?

It proved impossible to seal the twenty-eight mile gap. Sixth Army was cut in two—a weaker group in the south and a northern group, both of them fighting desperately against envelopment.

In the south General Angelis's XLIV Corps was facing a difficult situation. A greatly superior enemy stood in front of it and in its rear. Between the Corps and the lower Dnieper were thirty miles of water-less desert.

But now the troops showed their real spirit. Major-General Braun's 4th Mountain Division acted as the battering-ram for the withdrawing corps. The small armoured group of 13th Panzer Division under Colonel von Hake reinforced the striking group and with its few tanks covered the division's flank. Fighting all the way they made for the Dnieper. Immediately south of them the Group Becker with 370th Infantry Division, remnants of 336th Infantry Division, and Rumanian regiments fought its way westwards through enemy forces. The Soviet

Fifty-First Army, which was wheeling southwards, was pierced by both groups.

The Soviet Second Guards Army, meanwhile, had pushed on to the west and was racing towards the Dnieper estuary. But this dangerous enemy bolt was again forced back. At the beginning of November the Group Becker, the 13th Panzer Division, and the remnants of the Rumanian regiments passed through an intercepting position of 4th Mountain Division. The Dnieper was crossed at Kherson on ferries and by a pontoon bridge.

The XLIV Army Corps was saved. In addition to the troops, some 15,000 motor vehicles, the same number of horse-drawn transports, and a large number of heavy weapons were salvaged. The biggest Soviet breakthrough and pursuit of the war had failed to achieve its real objective. The German Sixth Army pulled its formations back to a new defensive position between the Crimea and Nikopol, in a body and ready for action, and set up a new front on the Dnieper.

But—and this was an important but—the approaches to the Crimea, which had been dominating Hitler's thoughts and the decisions of OKH throughout the past few months, were lost. The peninsula, where the German Seventeenth Army was still positioned, was now cut off from all land communications. A terrible drama began. Time was running out for Seventeenth Army.

The headlong development at Hollidt's southern group meant that the Russians were also able to dictate the course of operations for the two corps of the northern group. It proved impossible to restore the connection that had been lost at the northern approaches of the Crimea. Even OKH resigned itself to its loss. The corps of the northern group of Sixth Army hinged back their fronts. Their instructions were to establish an extensive bridge-head on the southern bank of the Dnieper in front of Nikopol, in order to protect the vital manganese ore deposits. But that was only half the objective. Hitler had more in mind. Just as important as the ore was the hope of going over to the offensive again very soon from this projecting salient, of striking towards the approaches of the Crimea, thus cutting off the strong Soviet forces which had advanced to the Dnieper estuary, and re-establishing contact with Seventeenth Army.

It was a good plan—on paper. But wishful thinking is not strategy. Nevertheless, the next few weeks were inspired by that hope.

5. West of Nikopol

Kalmyks against partisans–"Ladies' excuse me" for Group Schörner–Chuykov's Guards want a victory–Hand-to-hand fighting–Blizzard at Maryinskoye–Sixteen feet of straw between war and peace–Sixteen divisions save their bare skins–The Nikopol pocket has burst.

IN early February 1944, in a small township in Lower Bavaria, the parents of Mountain Jäger Gerhard Ertl received a field post letter from their son. In it he asked: "Do you know how far Nikopol is from Munich? One thousand and fifty-five miles! I know this from a sign-post which our gunners have put up at a gun position." Nikopol was 1055 miles east of Munich. By comparison, the famous Italian abbey of Monte Cassino, which likewise appeared just then in the German communiqués day after day, was considerably nearer. Only 440 miles separated Munich from Central Italy where German paratroops and grenadiers in that February of 1944 were holding the Americans back from the Alpine passes.

Strictly speaking, under the censorship rules, Private Ertl should not have mentioned that he was deployed in the Nikopol bridge-head. Or the censor should have cut it out. But by the beginning of 1944 the censorship had become rather slack. Besides, his parents already knew his whereabouts from a wounded comrade, and his remark was only a reply to a question asked in a letter from his mother.

It was hardly surprising that mothers in Munich, Vienna, Düsseldorf, Schwerin, Königsberg, Breslau, and Dresden were interested in Nikopol. Everyone in Germany knew the name of that Soviet nickel city on the Dnieper at the beginning of 1944. Throughout that first week of January every single High Command communiqué began with the words: "In the Nikopol bridge-head . . . "

In February the wording changed by a significant nuance. The High Command communiqués now began like this: On 4th February: "In the Nikopol area yesterday . . . "

On 5th February: "In the battle area of Nikopol the Soviets intensified . . . "

On 6th February: "In the Nikopol area our divisions continue to . . . "

On 7th February: "In the Nikopol area the enemy continues with strong forces . . . "

On 9th February: "Fired with exemplary spirit, our troops in heavy defensive fighting at Nikopol repulsed . . . "

And on 10th February: "On the Eastern Front enemy attempts west of Nikopol again failed . . ."

And finally on 11th February: "Our troops on the Eastern Front again repulsed numerous strong Soviet attacks in the area west of Nikopol and south of Krivoy Rog."

Then, for seven days, the name of Nikopol disappeared from the communiqués. There was silence about the bridge-head on the Dnieper. What was being hushed up?

In the morning of 15th February a blizzard sprang up on the lower Dnieper. The thermometer rapidly dropped to fifteen degrees below zero Centigrade. A cutting, icy wind and the darkness produced by driving snow were the setting for the final act of the drama of Nikopol.

The bridge-head positions south of the Dnieper had been lost for a fortnight. True, the Soviets had not succeeded in breaking through the German barrier positions. In heavy defensive fighting south of the river the East Prussian 24th Panzer Division, in particular, succeeded again and again in saving all critical situations by massive counter-blows with its armoured groups. The division had destroyed 290 enemy tanks, 130 anti-tank guns, 60 guns of all calibres, 31 mortars, and 25 aircraft, and taken over 800 prisoners. Its own casualties totalled 500 men, including an outstanding officer, Captain Georg Michael, bearer of the Oak Leaves, a native of Hamburg.

But gallantry alone cannot decide a battle. A Soviet thrust from the north by the Eighth Guards Army with concentrated employment of nine rifle divisions and several armoured brigades through the gaps in the front of 16th Panzer Grenadier Division into the rear of the bridge-head had drastically altered the situation at the end of January.

The commander of the German troops in the bridge-head was General of Mountain Troops Ferdinand Schörner. Here Hitler had entrusted a danger spot to a man who was ideally suited to this task. In 1942 Schörner still commanded the Austrian 6th Mountain Division which we have encountered at Murmansk; he was next commander of the XIX Mountain Corps on the Arctic Front, and since October 1943 he had been commanding the experienced XL Panzer Corps with whose headquarters personnel, renamed Group Schörner or Army Detachment Nikopol, he had been conducting the defence of the bridge-head since 25th November. Every General Staff officer knew this difficult field commander. He had a reputation for outstanding personal courage, toughness and resolution, great tactical skill, and a belief in iron discipline. He was utterly fearless. In the First World War, as a young lieutenant in the Bavarian Infantry Regiment of the

German Alpine Corps, he had stormed the controlling mountain fortress of Monte Kolowrat together with Rommel and his Württemberg Mountain Battalion, and taken Hill 1114 far behind the broken Isonzo front. On 24th October, 1917, in recognition of this feat, he was awarded the highest decoration for gallantry of the Imperial Army, the Pour le Mérite Order. Rommel, with his Württemberg Jägers, supported the frontal attack of the Bavarians and stormed the mountain massif of Monte Matajur thirty miles to the north-east, and for this achievement received the Pour le Mérite Order on 27th October. The two daredevil lieutenants of 1917 became outstanding and dashing commanders in the Second World War.

Ever since the end of 1943 Schörner had organized the defence of the Nikopol bridge-head against a vastly superior enemy with great energy and circumspection. It was a difficult task. The position across the arc was seventy-five miles long. With no depth at all. Six to nine miles behind the front ran the Dnieper, 650 to 1300 yards wide, and in front of it, moreover, lay the Plavna, the extensive, swampy lowlands which were swarming with partisans.

These clandestine forces in the inaccessible hiding places of the swamps would have been a serious danger to the German lines but for Senior Sergeant Willi Lilienthal. This man from Hamburg turned up at the end of November with the Kalmyk Major Abushinov. With him came five cavalry squadrons—1200 Kalmyk volunteers from the yurt villages of the Kalmyk Steppe. These mortal enemies of the Russians had been fighting on the German side since the summer of 1942. With their wives and families they had followed 16th Panzer Grenadier Division from the wide open spaces around Elista all the way to the west. There were no better scouts and no better hunters of partisans. They kept the *francs-tireurs* of the Plavna in check.

Two Corps—XXIX and IV—had been placed under the command of XL Panzer Corps at the beginning of the fighting, designated Group Schörner. Altogether there were nine infantry divisions, plus one Panzer division, the 24th, as the only tactical reserve. Later the group was joined by General Kreysing's XVII Corps. Schörner's shrewd chief of staff, Colonel von Kahlden, made an ideal team-mate for the tough and uncompromising commander. Schörner had yielded to Hitler's decision to defend the advanced frontal salient in spite of the difficult situation. But when General Chuykov's Eighth Guards Army on 31st January and 1st February delivered its death blow from the north against the rear of the bridge-head, Schörner did not hesitate for a moment or wait for any decisions from the Führer. Operation "Ladies' Excuse Me" was set in motion. That was on 2nd February and meant

Colonel-General Katukov (right) with his War Council member, General Popel. Russian infantry attacking, supported by trench mortars.

that, contrary to all orders from the Wolfsschanze, the positions across the Dnieper were being abandoned. The formations of the Southern Front crossed the river by the two hard-pressed bridges of Nikopol and Lepetikha and were switched against the IV Guards Mechanized Corps and other formations of the Soviet Eighth Guards Army which came charging down from the north.

The battle had once more been stabilized. At the last minute, the very last minute, a Soviet breakthrough to the Dnieper had once more been averted, and a small corridor between the river and the town of Apostolovo had been opened up and kept open. Schörner now executed his plan for a break-out from the all-but-closed trap against every attempt at interference from Hitler. "No dithering!" was his slogan, in contrast to Hitler's perpetual hesitation. Thus the general and his chief of staff accomplished a brilliant and daring break-out operation.

Schörner, always in the line with his troops, knew exactly how much he could expect of his weary formations. It was this judgment which enabled him at the last moment to prevent a confident enemy from accomplishing his final push to the river.

The 3rd Mountain Division, the first to be pulled out of the bridgehead by Group Schörner, was employed to provide flank cover west of Grushevka. It was followed by 17th Infantry Division which took over the sector as far as Maryinskoye. From there, on 8th February, the Combat Groups Zimmer and Lorch mounted an attack on Apostolovo with parts of 17th and 3rd Divisions under the direction of IV Corps. The objective of the attack was the railway line and Tok-Apostolovo station. The attack by Group Mieth succeeded but it made great demands on grenadiers and mountain Jägers—in particular on 17th Infantry Division which had to thrust deep into the enemy penetration area. The grenadiers had to tie strips of canvas round their boots in order not to lose them in the knee-deep mud. This Ukrainian mud was of an unimaginable viscosity. Not even ten horses were able to move a small anti-tank gun once it was bogged down.

With an enormous effort the protective front along the narrow corridor was reinforced. Under its cover the formations of XVII Corps moved westwards. Chuykov's Eighth Guards Army was contained west of Apostolovo.

Since 10th February the Advanced Detachment Lindenberg of 24th Panzer Division had been barring the way to the Russians who had pushed through the communications centre of Apostolovo, and had even forced them back into the town. This created the prerequisite for holding the narrow corridor open.

With small combat groups from the weakened regiments of 3rd Mountain Division, 97th Jäger Division, 17th Infantry Division, and General Bleyer's 258th Infantry Division, Schörner succeeded again and again in repulsing full-scale enemy attacks against the flanks of the narrow corridor. Lieutenant-General Chuykov's Eighth Guards Army furiously tried to burst through the German barrier holding open the Nikopol trap. In vain. The victor of Stalingrad this time overrated the strength of his famous army—originally the Sixty-Second Army but now since Stalingrad bearing the banner and title of Eighth Guards Army.

Schörner's divisions detached themselves from the Dnieper. While 125th Infantry Division was switched to reinforce IV Corps, the formations following it crossed the Bazavluk stream by the bridge at Grushevka and at Perevizskiye. The Soviets were pressing hard. At Grushevka the crossing was a single small bridge. Panic here might endanger the whole operation. General Schörner drove to the crossing-point. With some military police he stood at the approach to the bridge on 8th February. Now and again he ordered light flak to fire over the heads of the German transport units pushing towards the bridge—a brutal but effective reminder to them to keep in line.

The 97th Jäger Division and the most advanced parts of 24th Panzer Division meanwhile held the western corner-post of the escape hole—Bolshaya Kostromka. The fighting ebbed to and fro, man against man, with cold steel. On the far side stood the Carinthians and Styrians of 3rd Mountain Division and the Franconians of 17th Infantry Division. In spite of the difficult ground and the hostile weather they had dug in between Maryinskoye on the Dnieper and Verkhne-Mikhaylovka. The Lower Austrian 9th Panzer Division under General Jolasse was coming down from the north to meet the formations of Group Schörner as they broke out of the trap.

Corporal Bergmann of 138th Mountain Jäger Regiment, lying behind his machine-gun in biting frost on the morning of 15th February, 1944, knew nothing of the over-all situation. All he knew was that the line at Maryinskoye must be held unless the whole of Group Schörner was to be overtaken by disaster.

The Soviets came on again and again. They were determined to break through. The billowing veil of snow reduced visibility to ten yards. Bergmann fired belt after belt. Suddenly he fell over on his side. Blood jerked from a gaping head wound. His No. 2 took over the machine-gun. He fired over to the left, where the din of fighting came from in front of the neighbouring machine-gun. Now that machine-gun fell silent. "If they've been overrun the Reds will pour through that gap," the wounded Bergmann muttered. "I must go and see what's up." He crawled off. But half-way there he remained motionless. Face downward. Dead.

But Maryinskoye, the corner-post of the escape corridor, was held.

It was held because every man made super-human efforts—like Bergmann or like Second Lieutenant Holzinger, a man of twenty-four, who knocked out nine T-34s with two assault guns of the Mountain Panzerjäger Battalion near Verkhne-Mikhaylovka and thus prevented a penetration by a Soviet tank brigade.

In the evening the Mountain Jägers moved on. The 387th Infantry Division had arrived and, with 125th Infantry Division on its left, took over the cover of the corridor.

The blizzard raged. Muffled, the men trudged on. They moved by compass, because visibility was less than an arm's length. They had been continuously in action for two weeks. They were staggering. Some let themselves drop to the ground. But that meant death. And so their comrades urged them up again. In the blizzard they reached Bolshaya Kostromka. In the blizzard they bumped into a Soviet combat group which had burst through the weakened German strongpoint of 24th Panzer Division. Their rifle locks were frozen up and could not be worked. They had to use their bayonets. At least until the first few houses on the south-western edge were in their possession. Then the battle fell silent. The Russian's weapons and fighting spirit also froze under the icy breath of the steppe.

In the sector of 2nd Battalion, 144th Mountain Jäger Regiment, the thirty degrees below zero Centigrade even gave rise to a curious truce. Friend and foe had spotted a straw rick. They sought shelter in it simultaneously. They discovered each other. But they waved. "Nix voyna!" The Russians crept in among the bales on its eastern side and the Germans on the western. Sixteen feet of straw stood between war and peace. Sixteen feet of straw and an icy gale guaranteed a peaceful night. The next morning the two groups departed in silence, each in its own direction. Then they about-turned to make war again.

During the night of 15th–16th February the job was finished—the troops were out of the Nikopol trap. That was the night when British bomber fleets dropped 3300 tons of bombs on West Berlin. But two days later, on 18th February, Nikopol again appeared in the German High Command communiqué. "In the heavy fighting for Nikopol," it said—and then, in the euphemistic language of military communiqués, came the final announcement of the loss of the bridgehead.

The communiqué did not reveal what actually happened. But the methodical war diary kept for Sixth Army by Major Dr Martin Franck reveals it clearly. This is how he summed it up: "Sixteen of the divisions of Sixth Army had lost most of their vehicles. A large part of the *matériel* of the supply troops, in particular bakery and butchery companies, field kitchens, and also a good deal of heavy armament had to be left behind. But the manpower of the divisions had been saved."

The most impressive testimony to the precision of the retreat, however, is the fact that Schörner did not leave a single wounded man behind. More than 1500 of them were brought back and saved under the most difficult conditions on peasant carts protected by the Cossack Squadron of XL Panzer Corps. The intelligence officer, Major Kandutsch, made a more personal remark in his diary about the final act of Nikopol. He wrote: "The pocket is burst open. Schörner has been to say goodbye. Without him and his chief of staff we should probably all be marching towards Siberia at this moment. No-one who fought at Nikopol will ever forget what he owes Schörner."

6. Winter Drama on the Middle Dnieper

Crisis at Kirovograd–A general on patrol–Four divisions encircled–"I'm breaking out"–A broad wedge of tanks–Exemplary manoeuvre of 3rd Panzer Division–The great pincers–Sacrifice of Olympic medallist Hasse–Contact with Konev's 67th Tank Brigade–Rudel's merciless air strikes.

STALINGRAD is on the Volga. The Don marked the beginning of the German defeat. But the Dnieper became the blood-drenched watershed of the last War. Almost exactly to the hour as Schörner's Army-sized combat group saved itself through the hotly-contested escape corridor between Apostolovo and Maryinskoye, two hundred miles farther north, on the middle Dnieper, another winter drama was nearing its end.

The date was the 7th January, 1944, and the place the battle HQ of the Berlin 3rd Panzer Division at Lelekovka. It was high noon, but inside the little peasant hut it was so dark that the chief of operations had lit the oil lamp. Lieutenant-Colonel Wilhelm Voss had pulled his chair up to the stove. His map table was before him.

Voss was a busy man. The new commander of 3rd Panzer Division, General Bayerlein, spent most of his day with his troops in the line. He led according to the precepts of his teachers Guderian and Rommel. He had been out again with an armoured reconnaissance party since early morning in order to see the situation for himself. "A hell of a situation," he had observed.

Since 5th January the Soviets had been charging past Kirovograd in the north, across the Ingul river, with two mechanized corps, the VII and VIII Corps. Latest reports also confirmed a powerful armoured thrust south of the town. Were the Russians about to bring to a successful conclusion the heavy fighting which had been raging east of Kirovograd and all round it ever since mid-October? For two months the Soviets had tried to make headway on this sector—ever since they pushed across the Dnieper south of Kremenchug in October. But Konev had not been able to achieve the decisive breakthrough. At the last moment, invariably, some formation from some German division flung itself in his path. The 23rd Panzer Division had been one of them. The Panzer Regiment of "Grossdeutschland" Division inflicted a heavy defeat on Konev's armoured brigades. On one famous Monday, 18th October, Sergeant Sepp Rampel of 11th Company, in a Tiger which was really due for servicing, knocked out eighteen Russian tanks. He was awarded the Knight's Cross, but before it could be hung round his neck he was killed in the fighting for Kirovograd.

The 11th Panzer Division also fought a superior Russian force with cunning and every trick it knew. General von Wietersheim lured a Russian armoured brigade into an ambush which he had laid in a ravine with every available anti-tank gun and damaged tank. At the entrance to it Lieutenant-Colonel Lauchert's 15th Panzer Regiment was lying in wait. The moment the Soviet brigade was in the trap fire was opened. Three dozen Soviet tanks were destroyed.

Another unit in action at Kirovograd was the Saxon 14th Panzer Division. Hill 190 became the battlefield of Combat Group Domaschk.

The paratroopers of General Ramcke's 2nd Parachute Division spent a cruel December here and proved their worth as a "fire-brigade". One name in particular in that division was heard everywhere during those weeks at Kirovograd—Dr Schmieder, surgeon and deputy chief of 1st Medical Company. He enjoyed an almost legendary reputation among the paratroops: "Schmieder will put you right," became a slogan. His reputation was based on the knowledge that Schmieder would get every seriously wounded man back into hospital—even if he had to pack him in the general's car.

Kirovograd witnessed the whole tragedy and the whole misery of a great battle. Every tenth man who fought in Russia knows Kirovograd. It was one of those places to which the war clung. The Germans were determined not to give it up. But Konev would not let go. The grand design of STAVKA was driving him on inexorably. The decisive reasons were not only strategic. Konev's plan was to conquer the vital West Ukrainian industrial centre of Kirovograd. And in doing so he would encircle the four German divisions in that important area.

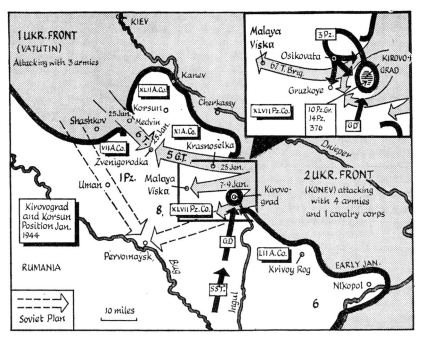

Map 42. Rendezvous at Pervomaysk: the armies of the First Ukrainian Front were aiming at the Bessarabian Bug in the rear of the German Eighth Army. The other jaw of the pincers was Konev's Second Ukrainian Front. But the grand plan misfired. Only a small pocket was formed—the Korsun pocket.

It was in order to reconnoitre this precarious position that General Bayerlein had been out with a patrol since daybreak.

Now the time was 1200 hours. The vast expanse of snow lay under a hazy light. The noise of engines approached. The clank of tank-tracks. Bayerlein's column was returning. The general climbed out of the armoured carrier. He beat his arms about his body a few times. Twenty degrees below zero Centigrade in a cold command vehicle was no fun. Then he stepped into the hut and joined Voss.

"Things are getting serious," he said. He bent over the map and explained: "The Russians are streaming past Kirovograd. They have already cut its supply route from the west. I've never seen anything like it. A huge caterpillar of supply vehicles, largely horse-drawn, is moving forward with the armoured columns."

Voss nodded. "Just as I thought, Herr General. Telephone communications to Corps have been lost. We've no radio contact either."

"And what news from our neighbouring divisions?"

"The same reconnaissance picture, Herr General. And they've no connections with Corps either. There's no doubt about it—we're already encircled. The trap is closed."

The trap was indeed closed, and in it were four divisions—3rd and 14th Panzer Divisions, 10th Panzer Grenadier Division, and 376th Infantry Division.

Bayerlein stepped up to the stove. He had only been on the Eastern Front for ten weeks. Before the first winter battle, in the autumn of 1941 at the peak of the German victories in the East, he had been transferred from the Russian frosts to the scorching sun of the African desert. There, in the German Afrika-Korps, he had been Rommel's chief of staff.

Thus he did not go through that notorious Russian winter of 1941–42. Nor through the retreats of 1942–43. He did not suffer from the trauma of Russian numbers or the Russian winter. And he had learnt from Rommel the principle that the judgment of a commander in the field was more important than hold-on orders on pieces of paper signed at a green-baize table at the Führer's Headquarters.

"We've got to get out," the general said. "Kirovograd sounds too much like Stalingrad to me."

"I'm all for it," Voss nodded. "But we've got the Führer's strict orders to hold the town at all costs."

Bayerlein waved the objection aside. "We're not going to hold it by sitting here inactive. In a few days our fighting strength will be spent, and there are no supplies coming through now. And we've next to no stocks left. But if we now seize the initiative, if we burst through the encirclement and operate against Kirovograd from outside, then we may possibly achieve something. We are still in a position to do it. And that is our task. The purpose of a Panzer division is mobile warfare, not defence of a fortified locality."

That was the credo of the German tank commanders of the Guderian school. Bayerlein had always practised it and was determined to continue to do so. He was fortunate in not having to ask for authority, since at that particular moment he had no contact with Corps or any other superior command. Teleprinter contact had also been lost; no response had been received from those at the other end for several hours. Here was a return to the ancient position of the commander in the field.

This raised an interesting question. The conduct of the last War was largely determined by the technological development of the means of communications. Great operational decisions could be set in motion or transmitted within minutes. The movements of large formations could be co-ordinated at lightning speed. Whereas formerly couriers and orderly officers had to spur their weary horses through all kinds of weather, only to find that they got there too late anyway, all that was now needed was a coded radio signal, a non-monitorable conversation on a decimeter wave across hundreds of miles, or a dialogue by teleprinter.

But the blessings of modern communications technique were frequently offset by its curse—there was now unlimited scope for interference by remote command authorities in the actual conduct of battle. Questions could be asked ceaselessly, commanders disciplined, and orders changed without knowledge of local conditions. Thus, both on the German and the Soviet side, the initiative of officers and commanders-in-chief in the field in the last War was kept on a tight rein. This circumstance had particularly disastrous consequences in critical situations. Stalingrad was the most spectacular illustration, but there were numerous other convincing instances. Thus the sudden silencing of telephone and radio might prove a lucky break for a commander in the field who would now have to rely solely on his own judgment and on the voice of his conscience as a soldier.

General Bayerlein had such a break at Kirovograd. The other divisions, with experienced Eastern Front commanders, did not feel able to follow him. But he remained undismayed.

He discussed his plan with General August Schmidt, the commander of 10th Panzer Grenadier Division, and arranged that the regiments of 10th Division should take over the defence sectors of 3rd Panzer Division.

Immediately after the issue of the midday meal Bayerlein summoned his officers. "We are breaking out tonight. Not in order to save us but in order to regain our freedom of action," the general announced. The officers were delighted. The battle order was laid down at once—all in an entirely unorthodox way, direct to the unit commanders.

Five combat groups were formed—A, B, C, D, E. Group A was to be the battering ram, with all available tanks, the armoured infantry carrier company, engineers, and armoured artillery on self-propelled carriages. Then came Combat Group B, consisting of engineers, artillery, and 3rd Panzer Grenadier Regiment under Colonel Wellmann. Group C comprised the supply columns and the damaged vehicles on tow, as well as the wounded with their medical units. Combat Group D was the reinforced 394th Panzer Grenadier Regiment under Lieutenant-Colonel Beuermann. Group E, the rearguard, consisted of Major Deichen's Armoured Reconnaissance Battalion. Flank cover was provided by Panzerjägers, and flak on self-propelled carriages. The assembly area was Lelekovka, a suburb of Kirovograd. Time of break-out: nightfall.

Never before had the division fallen in so quickly. Officers and men were in high spirits. At 1730 hours the division was ready. The signals commander sent off the last signal to Corps and Army: "3rd Panzer Division is bursting through the ring in a north-westerly direction in order to close gap in the front and to operate in the enemy's rear against the encircled town." Thereupon Bayerlein ordered radio silence. No countermanding order could now be received.

It was a dark moonless night. The sky was overcast. The temperature was twenty-five degrees below zero Centigrade. The snow crunched under their boots. The countryside was flat under the snow.

They moved off. Tanks forming a broad wedge. No lights. No open fires. Not a shot. The general was in his jeep with the leading group. Suddenly there were enemy muzzle flashes. Anti-tank guns! The lead tank was hit. It was blazing. The flames lit up the battlefield over a great distance. They lit up the approaching columns. But the darkness blurred all outlines and everything seemed bigger, more powerful, and more numerous. To the Russians the 3rd Panzer Division must have appeared like a ghost army. They were firing wildly and nervously with all weapons and thus betrayed their positions. The hatch-covers of the tanks slammed shut. Attack!

The tanks attacked. They had fire-cover from the artillery. Engineers and Panzer grenadiers followed. Within minutes the foremost tanks were in the Soviet positions and grenadiers and engineers mopped them up. Russian resistance collapsed rapidly. Anti-tank and flak guns were abandoned. The Russians everywhere were in full flight. Prisoners subsequently stated that the surprise assault in the eerie light had given the impression of a gigantic massed attack by at least one Panzer corps and had caused panic among the Soviets who had thought themselves entirely safe.

By daybreak the division had broken through the Russian ring, suffering only very slight losses—one tank with its crew. Vladimirovka was recaptured and the great breach was sealed up. The general immediately about-turned his division and in the morning of 8th January moved against Osikovata, against the rear of the Soviet ring round Kirovograd.

The full extent of the threat between Dnieper and Bug was clearly revealed by the operations map of XLVII Panzer Corps.

On 7th January General von Vormann had been forced to evacuate his advanced battle HQ on the northern edge of Kirovograd. Soviet tanks had suddenly disappeared outside. He moved his HQ to Malaya Viska, twenty-eight miles farther west. It was impossible for the general to conduct his exceptionally strong corps of seven divisions—almost an Army—from amidst the confusion of the main defensive line. A broad sector such as his demanded an over-all view, and that was to be obtained more readily at Malaya Viska. There his battle HQ was close to the supply railway from Pervomaysk and next to the large airfield of Fourth Air Fleet, where Lieutenant Colonel Rudel's Stuka *Geschwader* Immelmann was deployed, ready to intervene at any crisis point in the battle.

General von Vormann and Colonel Reinhard, his chief of staff, were bending over their maps by candlelight during the night of 8th–9th January. The major Soviet objective could be seen from them at a glance. The armies of the First Ukrainian Front, Vatutin's Army Group, having won their victory at Kiev and broken through in the Berdichev area, were now aiming towards the south-east, towards the Bessarabian Bug, in the rear of the German Eighth Army. Konev's breakthrough at Kirovograd represented a companion piece to Vatutin's offensive, the second jaw of the pincers, and was likewise aimed at the Bug. But this thrust was in a south-westerly direction. The two thrusts would meet in the Uman-Pervomaysk area. That was almost at the Rumanian frontier.

If this large-scale operation succeeded, then not only would Eighth Army be encircled but its annihilation would so advance Malinovskiy's moves that the German Sixth Army would also be inevitably doomed. Nothing could then save the German Seventeenth Army in the Crimea from annihilation. It was, in fact, the objective which Stalin had been pursuing for a long time—the annihilation of the German southern wing, the great victory.

In the flickering candlelight Vormann and his chief of staff realized the threatening catastrophe. To stop the breakthrough towards Uman from the north-west—that was the task of First Panzer Army whose command and Army troops Field-Marshal von Manstein had switched to that area. Would General Hube succeed? Vormann asked the question anxiously. But whatever happened there, his XLVII Panzer Corps had to seal off the breakthrough at Kirovograd. Feverishly Vormann and Reinhard made their plans. What was to be done?

South of Kirovograd things were looking very black. Soviet tanks were thirty miles south-west of the town and there was nothing between them and the Rumanian frontier. There was only one hope left—the "Grossdeutschland" Division had been brought up in forced marches, followed by parts of the SS "Totenkopf" Panzer Division. They had struck at the flank of the Soviet XVIII and XXIX Tank Corps and engaged them in battle. But would they succeed in halting them?

And what about Kirovograd itself? On 8th January three German divisions were still encircled in the town—10th Panzer Grenadier Division, 14th Panzer Division, and 376th Infantry Division. A renewed order from Hitler had nailed them to their positions. Kirovograd was to be defended to the end, as a "fortress".

Thus, thanks to its daring break-out, only Bayerlein's 3rd Panzer Division was now available for averting the worst danger north of Kirovograd. It had to smash the two Soviet mechanized corps which had already broken through and thus make possible the rescue of the encircled German divisions. That was how it had to be done. That was the only way it could be done.

Orders. Telephone calls. Radio signals. The time was 0200. Just then, right into the nocturnal planning and calculating, burst the rattle of rifle-fire and the hard crack of tank cannon. The flak batteries of the airfield barked. Tank alarm. At the HQ of XLVII Panzer Corps a prominent German sportsman was the adjutant—Major Hasse, the German show-jumper and gold-medallist of the Berlin Olympic Games in 1936.

As Hasse opened the door to the map room a draught blew out the candle. Into the darkness the Major said calmly: "We've got to get out, Herr General. Soviet tanks have broken into the village. I'm taking over the defence of the command post with the headquarters staff."

Fearlessly and coolly, as on a show jumping course, Hasse organized the clerks, the runners, the motor-cycle messengers, and the men of the Corps Signals Battalion for defence. With mines, high-explosive charges, and infantry weapons. The Panzer Corps had no armour-piercing weapons.

Russian tanks with mounted infantry were moving through the village, shelling the houses, setting vehicles on fire, and opening up at anything they saw. It was an entire tank brigade, the 67th of VIII Mechanized Corps. It turned the village into a heap of rubble and then attacked the airfield.

General von Vormann and his staff with their most important secret papers and situation maps only just managed to get out of the village. Major Hasse sacrificed himself. He was killed in action. And with him the first orderly officer, Lieutenant Becker, and many men of the Corps Signals Battalion.

Apart from two transmitters the Corps HQ's signalling apparatus, so valuable and indispensable in modern warfare, was lost. General von Vormann and his command staff were forced to move in on an Eighth Army telephone exchange at Novomirgorod until the most important communications equipment was replaced, to make sure that at this crucial period of operations he would be able to direct his Corps at least in an improvised manner.

The Soviet ghost brigade continued to haunt the rearward areas for some time. But in spite of these gloomy developments Vormann's plan succeeded. In bold attacks Bayerlein first struck at the Soviet VII and later at the VIII Mechanized Corps; he pinned the Soviets down in local fighting, stopping their further advance to the west and so bringing much-needed relief to the three German divisions encircled at Kirovograd-Lelekovka.

Twenty-four hours later Hitler's authority granting the group in Lelekovka freedom of movement was wrested from him. After a bold counter-attack during the night of 9th–10th January, the three divisions succeeded in withdrawing across the Ingul into the area west of Gruzkoye without further losses. There they established a strong barrier, linked up on the left with 3rd Panzer Division and on the right with the "Grossdeutschland" Panzer Grenadier Division. Clearly General Hoernlein's regiments had not disappointed Vormann's hopes.

Those experienced formations, together with the 3rd "Totenkopf" Panzer Division, had halted the Russians south of Kirovograd. The danger was over.

And what about the raid by Konev's 67th Tank Brigade? What was achieved by the combat groups of Rotmistrov's famous Guards Tank Army which was to be the trail-blazer of the boldly conceived Soviet link-up on the Bug? It was engaged in the hinterland by pursuit parties of XLVII Panzer Corps. Many of their T-34s fell victim to that feared "anti-tank gunner of the Luftwaffe", Lieutenant-Colonel Rudel. With his tank-busting *Staffel* he chased the Soviets across the snowy plain between Malaya Viska and Gruzkoye. Tank after tank was mercilessly hunted down. What Rudel and his *Staffel* were unable to knock out themselves they drove right across the sights of the tank-busting parties of XLVII Panzer Corps. None of them escaped.

In those critical days of January 1944 General von Vormann scored a very major defensive success at Kirovograd. The Russians did not accomplish their objective of encircling the German Eighth Army and thereby creating the prerequisite for the annihilation of the German southern wing. Daring and flexible operations with decimated but resolute divisions had inflicted heavy losses on the Russians by way of offensively conducted defence, halted their victorious advance, and frustrated Stalin's plan. The militarily correct action of a general, on the strength of sound judgment of the situation and against an express order from the Führer, had been the curtain-raiser for this success. As the success of the break-out of 3rd Panzer Division from the Kirovograd pocket became obvious, Bayerlein and his regiments were praised in the High Command communiqué. But for the time being no decoration came his way. A decoration for successful dis-obedience—that would have been too much for Hitler to swallow. Nevertheless, four months later, Bayerlein was put in charge of what was then the best-equipped armoured unit—the Panzer Lehr Division.

For two weeks the German High Command communiqué had been giving daily mention to the theatre of operations of Kirovograd. Always in connection with heavy fighting, serious threats, and costly critical situations. Now the name disappeared from the official chronicle of the war. Another name emerged. Almost daily the High Command communiqué began with the words: "South-west of Cherkassy". But south-west of Cherkassy was about thirty miles north of Kirovograd.

The names had changed, the theatre of operations had shifted, but the Soviets were still pursuing the same objective—the annihilation of the German Eighth Army.

The Soviet Command had not abandoned this objective after its failure at Kirovograd. It continued to pursue it, though no longer in the shape of a major strategic encirclement with a link-up in the Uman-Pervomaysk area, but on a smaller scale. The Russians intended to nip off a projecting salient of Eighth Army, a salient projecting far to the east and still reaching to the Dnieper at its apex at Kanev and south-east of Korsun. This salient was in the Russians' way. Like a wedge it divided the two Soviet Army Groups of Vatutin and Konev and thus represented a constant danger to their flanks.

For exactly that reason Hitler now insisted on holding on to it, on digging his heels in at this last piece of Dnieper frontage. He intended, at the first opportunity, to thrust forward again from this favourable position to Kiev, only 40 miles away, and to restore a defensive line on the Dnieper. The salient was about 60 miles deep, and the chord across the arc was about 80 miles. The area involved was about 5000 square miles.

This dangerous salient was defended by two corps—XI Army Corps under General Stemmermann and XLII Army Corps under Lieutenant-General Lieb, altogether six and a half divisions with roughly 56,000 men.

The Soviet objective did not remain a secret from the German Command. As long ago as 24th January, reconnaissance in force by 3rd Panzer Division had established the presence of massive enemy concentrations at Krasnoselka, thirty miles north of Kirovograd. Naturally, the reconnaissance did not discover the full extent of what Konev had massed at this point—four Soviet armies and one cavalry corps were deployed on the northern wing of the German Eighth Army, facing General Stemmermann's corps.

PART SEVEN:
Disasters on the Southern Wing

1. Cherkassy

56,000 men in a hopeless position–The trap snaps shut at Zvenigorodka–Army General Konev's costly error–Relief Group West takes Lysyanka–Ill-fated Hill 239–Another six miles to the front of the pocket–"Password Freedom, objective Lysyanka, 2300 hours"–Hell between Zhurzhintsy and Pochapintsy–Massacre at Hill 222–Drama on the Gniloy Tikich–Death of the corps commander–Balance-sheet of a battle.

KONEV attacked on 25th January. After a heavy artillery barrage the Soviet Guards charged. General Ryshov's Fourth Guards Army was to force the first breach. But the German defenders were ready for them. The infantry stood firm. The murderous fire of strong German artillery concentrations pinned Ryshov's regiments to the ground.

Konev had to move in his crack armour earlier than he had planned—Colonel-General Rotmistrov's famous Fifth Guards Tank Army. But even the heroes of Prokhorovka were unlucky this time. Rotmistrov's attack collapsed in the fire of heavy German anti-tank guns and the long-barrel cannon of the Panther battalions.

But the German jubilations did not last long. About nightfall the right wing of the Hessian 389th Infantry Division yielded to the persistent attacks of Rotmistrov's armoured brigades.

The god of war favoured Konev. He saw his chance and moved fresh forces into the breach. Stemmermann countered by sealing off the penetration with two Panzer divisions. He straightened his front. In this way he freed the Bavarian 57th Infantry Division under General Trowitz. He sent it into action against the enemy.

The focal point of the battle was at Kapitanovka on the left wing of the army. There on the 26th January the Silesian 11th and the Central German 14th Panzer Division were once more successful. But their numerically weak Panzer Grenadier regiments were no longer able to hold the sector.

The further course of the battle was determined by a dramatic measure of Konev's. This is how General von Vormann describes the situation: "Regardless of losses—and I really mean regardless of losses—masses of Soviets about midday streamed westwards past the German tanks which were firing at them with everything they had. It was an amazing scene, a shattering drama. There is really no other comparison—the dam had burst and a huge flood was pouring over the flat land, past our tanks which, surrounded by a few grenadiers, were like rocks towering from the swirling flood. Our amazement was even greater when, later in the afternoon, the cavalry formations of three Soviet divisions galloped through our defensive fire in close order. It was something I hadn't seen for a long time—it just seemed unreal."

This striking account by such an outstanding and experienced general as von Vormann sums up the dramatic character of the situation.

The front had been pierced at Kapitanovka. But catastrophes rarely come singly. The anxiety which all commanders in the field had felt in early January about the second jaw of the Russian pincers, the thrust made by strong parts of the First Ukrainian Front from Kiev via Belaya Tserkov towards the south-east, was becoming acute—three Soviet armies, including General Kravchenko's Sixth Tank Army, broke through the thin German defensive front of VII Corps on the western side of the German salient, in the sector of First Panzer Army.

The Bavarian 88th and the Baden-Württemberg 198th Infantry Divisions flung themselves against the Soviet tank packs. They were smashed. A wide breach was gaping in the front. There were no German reserves left to close the breach. Unopposed, the Red divisions moved towards the south-east, towards their link-up with General Konev's thrust to the north-west. Only sixty miles separated the two spearheads—no distance at all for an armoured formation. If they linked up the trap would spring shut around the two German Corps in the Kanev salient.

They did link up. Kravchenko's and Rotmistrov's tank crews met

Opposite, top: Return from a mission on the southern front: a Messerschmitt 110 and an Italian fighter over Budapest. *Opposite, bottom:* In the Caucasus: the Laba valley, the scene of fierce fighting by mountain Jägers.

Overleaf, top: The sector of 11th Panzer Division in the summer of 1943. *Overleaf, bottom:* Horse and "rhino": A signal for the commander of a heavy raiding tank.

at Zvenigorodka on 28th January. The disastrous battle of the Cherkassy pocket was about to begin.

Once more the Soviets had successfully applied the recipe of Stalingrad. By a double envelopment the German salient of Kanev, projecting eastwards to the Dnieper, had been nipped off. The XLII and XI Corps with six divisions and an independent brigade were surrounded and out-manoeuvred. A breach sixty miles wide had been ripped into the German front. Through that breach the Red flood could now pour towards Rumania, because there was no barrier left east of the Rumanian frontier.

The Soviet command was once again offered the same chance which it had won for itself three weeks earlier at Kirovograd but had then lost owing to General von Vormann's XLVII Panzer Corps and the heroically fighting divisions of Eighth Army. Would the Soviet High Command seize its opportunity this time? "What are the Russians going to do?" Manstein asked his commanders when he had summoned them at Uman on 28th January. "Are they going to sink their teeth into the pocket or are they going to push on?"

"What are the Russians going to do?" was also the question put by General von Vormann, commanding XLVII Panzer Corps, to his chief of staff Reinhard at Novomirgorod.

"Konev has a huge number of large formations already lined up. Is he going to by-pass the pocket, leaving it well guarded, and push down to the Bug with everything he has available? The way Yeremenko did at Stalingrad in 1942 when he raced past the city and on to the Don?"

From a strategic point of view the follow-up through the sixty-mile gap, into an entirely undefended area, seemed the obvious move. This was the bold, large-scale operation that must lead to the annihilation of the German southern wing. In fact, there really was no alternative—provided Konev and the great co-ordinator at Soviet Headquarters, Marshal Zhukov, correctly appreciated the situation on the Second Ukrainian Front.

But could anyone fail to appreciate it correctly? Could anyone overlook the disastrous situation of the Germans? If the reputation of the partisans was even half-way justified, then surely Soviet Headquarters must have been appropriately informed by their secret eyes. And

Previous page, top: A Soviet tank battalion thrusting into the German defences. *Previous page, centre:* Attack repulsed: a German assault party with a knocked-out "Joseph Stalin" tank. *Previous page, bottom:* Medical orderlies attending to a casualty.

Opposite, top: The land east of the Dnieper is being evacuated: mounted commandos setting fire to stooks of grain. *Opposite, bottom:* Herds of horses are driven to the west.

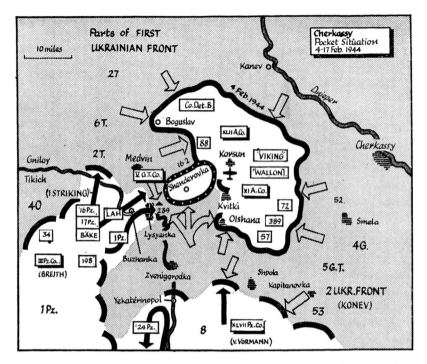

Map 43. Six and a half German divisions were surrounded in the Korsun pocket, also known as the Cherkassy pocket. The German High Command made a supreme effort to free them. The III Panzer Corps got within six miles of the ring surrounding the westward-facing pocket.

from 28th January, at any rate, the Soviet commanders in the field must have learnt from their own civilian population behind the pocket that there was no continuous German front left. In the summer of 1941, when the Soviets had been in exactly the same situation as the Germans were now, Guderian, Hoth, and Kleist had mounted their massive enveloping operation and smashed the Red Army in European Russia. Would the same fate now befall the Germans? No. The Soviet High Command did not exploit its opportunity for a large-scale, decisive operation.

To this day there is no satisfactory answer to the question of why, in the winter of 1943–44, STAVKA and in particular Marshal Zhukov and Army General Konev let slip through their fingers this unique opportunity of defeating the German southern front west of the Dnieper. Did they overrate German strength? Or did they misjudge the situation in the pocket? Whatever the reason—Konev and Zhukov opted for the lesser solution and concentrated the full power of their six and subsequently seven armies, including two outstanding tank armies and several independent tank corps, on the liquidation of the encircled six and a half German divisions.

It was an extravagant effort and comprehensible only on the assumption that the Soviets had a totally mistaken idea of German strength inside the pocket. All the evidence seems to point to the fact that the Soviet operation was based on a simple but grotesque error. The Soviets evidently believed that they had surrounded the bulk of the German Eighth Army, in particular its armoured units as well as the Army headquarters. This view is supported by a conversation which Colonel Kalinov, then a staff officer in the 6th Department of the Red Army General Staff, had with Colonel Kvach, the commander of Konev's command train, on 3rd February.

Kvach said to Kalinov: "The German Eighth Army under General Wöhler is surrounded in the pocket at Kanev. It comprises no fewer than nine of the best motorized divisions of the Wehrmacht as well as a division of the Waffen SS and the motorized "Wallonie" Brigade. Another Stalingrad is in the making."

Most interesting. But Kalinov not only spoke to Kvach; he also had a conversation with Konev himself. And the Army General confirmed the information of his headquarters commander. "We've done it this time," Konev said. "I've got the Germans in the pincers and I'm not letting them slip out again." There is no room for doubt—Konev believed that he had the entire Eighth Army together with its C-in-C and ten and a half divisions in his pocket. He thus estimated the number of the surrounded troops at over 100,000. This miscalculation in turn produced the figures about losses and prisoners which, even in Germany, have been appearing in print unquestioned to this day.

One reason for Konev's mistake was very probably the 112th Infantry Division. For camouflage purposes it bore the designation Corps Detachment "B" and had been formed from three badly-mauled infantry divisions. The remnants of the Silesian 332nd, the Saxon 255th, and the Saar-Palatinate 112th Infantry Divisions were lumped together as "divisional groups" under the headquarters staff of 112th Infantry Division. Their fighting strength was that of an infantry division. Corps Detachment "B" was commanded by Colonel Fouquet.

Another source of the Soviet error was probably the fact that the pocket also contained groups of the Silesian 417th Grenadier Regiment with parts of the Engineer Battalion, 168th Infantry Division, as well as the Bavarian 331st Grenadier Regiment of 167th Infantry Division. In the pocket there were, moreover, the 108th Panzer Grenadier Regiment of 14th Panzer Division, as well as a battalion of the Silesian 213th Local Defence Division and the Ski Battalion of 323rd Infantry Division. In recording prisoners of these units the Soviet authorities no doubt assumed that the divisions were complete and present as a body.

Whatever the cause of the mistake, the Russians attacked their "new Stalingrad" with a tremendous force, with the bulk of two Army Groups. Army General Konev, C-in-C Second Ukrainian Front, was put in command of the operation.

The German Command soon noticed the over-cautious moves of the Russians. On 31st January the monitoring platoon of XLVII Panzer Corps intercepted a radio signal from a Soviet engineer commander at Shpola. This garrulous engineer officer of the Soviet XX Tank Corps reported to his Army about the laying of his minefields.

Minefields meant that the Russians who had broken through were organizing themselves for defence on the southern edge of the pocket, even though for the time being there was no-one there against whom they needed to defend themselves. Indeed, rearward the pocket lay entirely open.

In fairness to Konev it must be stated that he could hardly have expected the German divisions to remain on the Dnieper. The logical thing would have been for them to turn about and try to regain contact with XLVII Panzer Corps. But Hitler stopped the logical move by issuing another hold-on order. Lieb and Stemmermann, the two corps commanders in the pocket, were ordered to hold on at all costs to their entire positions along a two-hundred-mile arc with their badly battered six divisions, and moreover to screen off their rear by establishing a new front there. Form hedgehog and stand fast! Hitler's prescription at Stalingrad! Just as then he had been reluctant to let go of the Volga, he now hung on grimly to that last stretch of the Dnieper. He did not want to give up his plan of using the Kanev salient as the jumping-off point for a new operation towards Kiev when the time came. As for the reality of the situation, Hitler refused to acknowledge that reality. "Reality, *c'est moi*" might have been his motto.

Hitler's hold-on order meant that General of Artillery Stemmermann, the Commander-in-Chief in the pocket since 31st January, had to extend his over-stretched two-hundred-mile front even farther so as to set up, at lightning speed, a new sixty-mile line to cover his open rear in the south. Considering the general situation this manoeuvre should not normally have succeeded. But it did succeed thanks to the indecision of the Russians.

On 1st February a blizzard was sweeping the frozen land between the Dnieper and the Bug. It was mid-winter in the Ukraine, with a temperature of fifteen degrees below zero Centigrade and two feet of snow. In the gap east of Uman the Reconnaissance Battalion, 1st Panzer Division, was detrained on the open line in order to reinforce the weak formations of 198th Infantry Division. Supply columns in the pocket drove their sleighs from combat group to combat group. The Soviet Air Force was quiet—the bad weather was keeping it grounded. True, German airborne supplies were similarly affected, but that seemed a small price to pay for this weather which favoured defence and made quick, unobserved moves possible. "Let's hope it holds," was the prayer of staff officers and troopers.

But during the night of 1st–2nd February, against all expectation, the weather broke. There was a thaw. And with the warm wind the *rasputitsa* came over the black earth. *Rasputitsa* was the spring mud, the Ukrainian "roadlessness", the period when everything was swallowed up in a sea of thick, sticky mud and when the peasants withdrew to their stoves. But Stemmermann's troops could not hide out by their stoves. They had to march, they had to switch positions, they had to repulse enemy formations which had broken in. All that in the knee-deep, black morass. It pulled the boots off the men's feet. It ripped the tracks of armoured carriers and tractors. It trapped the horses. Not a wheel turned. Only the tanks and assault guns of the 5th SS "Viking" Panzer Grenadier Division managed to get through the morass, though with a maximum speed of two to three miles per hour. And at an extravagant consumption of fuel. To complete the misfortune frost returned overnight. The tanks were concreted into the deep, hard-frozen mud. They had to be freed with blowtorches in the morning.

Nevertheless, Stemmermann regrouped continuously. He inter-cepted Russian attacks in the west and south-east. He shortened the fronts. He freed forces. He switched them to the critical points. XLII Corps abandoned the Dnieper. It pulled in its feelers in the north. In the south-east XI Corps pulled its main defensive line back step by step. In this way a battalion might be saved at one point, to reinforce a threatened sector elsewhere, or a combat group might be freed to seal a gap.

Only one thing mattered—the continuity of the front had to be preserved and the centre of the pocket, the village of Korsun with its forward airfield, had to be held as long as possible. It was for this focal point of Korsun that the battle raged during the first twelve days. The Russians are therefore quite right to speak of the "Korsun pocket". The term "Cherkassy pocket" was invented in the German High Command communiqué but is not really accurate.

This was how 56,000 men—Bavarians, Hessians, Franconians, Austrians, Saxons, men from the Saar-Palatinate, as well as Belgians, Dutchmen, and Scandinavians from the Waffen SS volunteer regiments —stood up to the assault of half a dozen Russian Armies.

The disaster of Stalingrad had been the result of "too little and too late". Too much time had been wasted in November 1942 on the relief preparations and too few forces had eventually been made available by the German High Command for the relief attack. The lesson of Stalingrad had been learnt not only by the HQ staffs in the field but also by the Führer's Headquarters. That was why Hitler reacted very quickly to the Cherkassy-Korsun crisis, and immediately after the encirclement authorized Field-Marshal von Manstein to concentrate two strong armoured groups to annihilate the enemy who had broken through the German front and re-establish contact with the Korsun group.

Hitler intended to employ nine Panzer divisions, concentrated in the III and XLVII Panzer Corps, and commanded by two experienced corps commanders—Generals Breith and von Vormann. This relief force included some outstanding formations, fully equipped and highly experienced divisions, each of them able to take on a Soviet tank corps. Among them were the 1st Panzer Division, the 16th Panzer Division, and the 1st SS "Leibstandarte Adolf Hitler" Panzer Division.

The relief plan was bold and far-sighted. Manstein intended not only to break open the pocket but also to annihilate the strong enemy forces which had broken through the front by taking them in his pincers. By means of an armoured strike in the Guderian manner the Soviets were to be intercepted north of Zvenigorodka, Kanev was to be defended, the encircled divisions were to be liberated, and the huge gap between First Panzer Army and Eighth Army was to be closed again. It was a good plan. The army commanders looked more hopeful again. And the officers and men in the pocket were confident. Their resolution to hold out was reinforced by the hope that they would only have to do so for five to ten days before the big operation outside got going.

But what use were the imperious signals from the Führer's Headquarters to armies and corps? Between Dnieper and Bug a general far more powerful than Hitler was in charge—his orders weighed a lot more on the Ukrainian battlefield than those of the restless spirit in the Rastenburg forests: *rasputitsa*, the spring mud, was holding sway. The best plans and the greatest courage were of no avail while the men were trapped in the mud, while guns were sinking into the mud, while armoured infantry carriers were immobilized by the mud. How was any movement to be carried out? But the units had to move, since most of the Panzer divisions had to be brought up over long distances and directed radially to the Korsun salient.

What these troop movements were like is not only very dramatically described in the chronicles of 1st, 14th, and 16th Panzer Divisions, but exemplified even more strikingly by the journey of 24th Panzer Division. At the beginning of 1944 that division was in the Apostolovo-Nikopol theatre of operations, where it was Schörner's only intact and fast reserve. The impending catastrophe of Korsun drew Hitler's attention to this battle-worthy formation. He decided to take the division away from Schörner and switch it to the north—a distance of two-hundred-odd miles. There it was to become the spearhead, the battering-ram, of the relief attack by XLVII Panzer Corps.

Tensely General von Vormann was waiting for his "steam hammer". He took off in his Storch aircraft to reconnoitre the route over which the division must come. At last he spotted the regiments of the distinguished East Prussian division below him on the ground. But it was no road along which tanks, vehicles, and grenadiers were advancing, but a bed of mud. During the day the columns were stuck fast and only during the few cold hours of the night, when the mud froze solid, were they able to make any headway. The tanks had to do service as tractors.

Indefatigably the columns pushed northwards, mile after mile, driven on by their officers who had a lecture each evening from Freiherr von Edelsheim, the division commander, on how the fate of 56,000 men in the Korsun pocket depended on the rate of progress of 24th Panzer Division. And the successors of the ancient East Prussian 1st Cavalry Division reached their target. In the evening of 3rd February General von Edelsheim reported that his division, with the most advanced parts of his armoured group, was ready for action the next morning. The spearheads were already directly south of Zvenigorodka, where the Russians had linked up five days earlier, thereby closing the pocket. In front of them was Rotmistrov's Tank Corps—not an insuperable opponent for the East Prussians.

Vormann's plan was clear and simple. Edelsheim's 24th Panzer Division was to drive through the Russians on the morning of 4th February and in doing so sweep along with it the combat groups of the corps' remaining four divisions which had been in action for the past four days and were, some of them, still tied down in defensive fighting farther east. In view of the over-extended enemy the plan appeared to be fool-proof and by all reasonable calculations should succeed. But matters turned out differently.

At the very time when the relief of the encircled units in the Korsun pocket was due to start the situation at Nikopol took a turn for the worse. The Russians had broken through in Schörner's rear and were threatening the entire Army Detachment. Since the departure of 24th Panzer Division the Sixth Army had no large-scale formations left in reserve. Naturally enough it asked for reinforcements. And Hitler, worried about the Nikopol group, decided on 3rd February that the 24th Panzer Division must return to Apostolovo at once.

All protestations, all arguments that the division was already deployed for attack in its jumping-off positions, that in view of the mud the armoured formations could not reach Apostolovo for several days anyway—all these arguments were in vain. Not even the point that what Sixth Army needed was not a Panzer division but infantry cut any ice with Hitler.

About-turn! Through the rivers of mud and then, in a huge detour by rail, the division was moved back. Needless to say, it arrived too late to bring about a decisive turn in the situation at Apostolovo or to save Schörner's bridge-head. Its armoured formations arrived just in time to play some part in holding open the narrow evacuation corridor —but they were unable to prevent the loss of the bridge-head.

At the Korsun pocket, on the other hand, the employment of the division would probably have drawn major Soviet forces and might well have enabled XLVII Panzer Corps to break through into the pocket. The two surrounded corps would have been set free and the prerequisites created for a decisive operation. But Hitler's stubbornness prevented all this. And that fine East Prussian Division had to act out a truly tragic role—at Zvenigorodka it was prevented from intervening decisively and at Apostolovo it arrived too late to avert disaster.

But this was not the end of a string of foolish decisions. Now, after the departure of 24th Panzer Division, after the failure of the planned combined relief attack of III and XLVII Panzer Corps, the correct decision would have been to employ III Panzer Corps, directly for a thrust against the pocket, without wasting any further time in pursuing secondary objectives—especially as 1st Panzer Division was now arriving from Berdichev with its advanced combat groups and was therefore able to take over protection of the wide-open flank south of 198th Infantry Division.

Nothing of the sort! The Führer's Headquarters insisted on the attack of III Panzer Corps being made first towards the north, in accordance with the old plan. On the high ground of Medvin, the corps was to wheel east in order to envelop and annihilate the Soviet forces between the pocket and XLVII Panzer Corps. It was a good plan, but based on a lot of "as ifs"—as if a Panzer corps could defeat five enemy armies one after another; as if the thick mud did not exist; as if the conditions of 1941 still applied. A frightening string of absurdity and foolishness!

General Breith launched his attack on the morning of 4th February. Only part of his forces were in position. Only the 16th and 17th Panzer Divisions as well as the Heavy Panzer Regiment under Lieutenant-Colonel Bäke were available. But they moved off all the same. Bäke's tanks were in front—a mighty phalanx of thirty-four Tigers and forty-seven Panthers. Their flanks were covered by the 34th and 198th Infantry Divisions as well as by advanced parts of SS "Leibstandarte" Panzer Division. The attack moved northwards through mud and enemy positions. One mile. Two miles. Six miles. But that was all. The *rasputitsa* and four enemy tank corps brought Breith to a halt.

The general did not give up. The bulk of the experienced "Leib-standarte" and the advanced parts of 1st Panzer Division had now arrived. Breith moved them into action. The two well-tried formations really succeeded in gaining the German formations some elbow-room and in enabling 16th Panzer Division to move the attack forward once more. By 8th February the Tigers and Panthers of Bäke's Heavy Panzer Regiment had reached the Gniloy Tikich stream with parts of 16th Panzer Division and "Leibstandarte". That stream was to play a decisive role in the fate of the Korsun pocket.

The regiments of III Panzer Corps made a supreme effort. But they did not get any farther. The northward thrust was bogged down. Nineteen miles from the edge of the pocket. Hitler at last realized his mistake and gave permission for the shortest way to the pocket to be taken, for a direct eastward thrust. The 1st Panzer Division, originally employed to protect the eastern flank was turned into the spearhead of "Relief Group West" on 11th February. In a bold raid General Koll's armoured group captured the village of Buzhanka on the Gniloy Tikich, and swiftly seized the bridge intact. He established a bridge-head. From there was the shortest way to the edge of the pocket. But the Soviets were aware of that. In consequence, the enemy and the rising ground towards the north compelled 1st Panzer Division to find another hiding-place—Lysyanka. This village was situated on the fly-path of the German Ju-52 and He-111 machines which operated to the Korsun pocket and kept Stemmermann's divisions supplied by air. And well supplied at that. General Seidemann's VIII Air Corps employed 1536 aircraft. The distance from Uman to Korsun was only 60 miles. On the other hand, the weather was bad and Soviet flak strong. Nevertheless, Major Knapp's operations staff ferried 2026·6 tons of supplies to the pocket over a fortnight, and the Junkers machines moreover evacuated 2825 wounded. Underneath the droning airbridge of Seidemann's transport squadrons the Panthers and grenadiers of 1st Panzer Division made a surprise penetration into the southern part of Lysyanka during the night of 11th–12th February.

The reinforced 1st Panzer Regiment thrust into the strung-out village through minefields and anti-tank defences.

Second Lieutenant Ciliox of 1st Panzer Regiment pressed his headphones closer to his ears when he heard his name on the R/T. It was his regimental commander, Lieutenant-Colonel Frank, speaking:

"Ciliox, quickly to the bridge."

With the tanks of 2nd Company Ciliox worked his way through to the eastern bridge, in the face of T-34s, anti-tank guns, and field guns.

"Get across!" Crash. The driver whipped the reeling Panther over to the side. Immediately in front of it the steel skeleton of the bridge blew up. Ciliox cursed and led his tanks of 1st Battalion down to the river. The Panzer grenadiers mopped up the southern part of the village. That was on 12th February.

On 13th February Sergeant Hans Strippel in his Panther forded the thirty-yard-wide river at a previously reconnoitred shallow spot. His troop under its experienced tank commanders followed. In the wake of the tanks Lieutenant Leben with grenadiers of 113th Regiment waded through the shoulder-deep, icy Gniloy Tikich. On the far side a dozen T-34s of the Soviet V Guards Tank Corps were waiting for them. But Strippel's Panthers got the better of them. Two Panther Companies of 1st Battalion under Captain Cramer followed up. By the late hours of the night the Germans had established a bridge-head over half a mile deep.

The 14th was on a Monday. The new week did not promise well. The temperature dropped—but not enough to let the river freeze over hard enough for the ice to bear. And no bridging materials arrived.

Abruptly the situation turned. At 1745 hours Sergeant Strippel with his troop seized the forty-ton bridge on the north-eastern edge of Lysyanka by a surprise coup in the gathering dusk. With his uncanny gift for anti-tank fighting he knocked out the two well-camouflaged T-34s guarding the approach—his fifty-ninth and sixtieth kills.

The news of the bridge spread like wildfire. No-one knew how. At first light the corps commander, General Breith, arrived by Fieseler Storch. At the battle HQ of 1st Panzer Division he met General Koll. If they were ever to succeed—now was the time. The main effort was switched to the right wing of Corps. Orders were: Next objective of the attack is Hill 239.

This hill was a commanding spot in the approaches to the pocket, two miles north-east of Lysyanka. If it could be captured, the relief operation was as good as accomplished. From there to the edge of the pocket was a mere six miles. Six miles or 10,000 metres—a mere thirty minutes for a runner on a cinder track in a stadium. For more than 10,000 men under the hazy winter sky of Cherkassy it was an eternity.

Hill 239. Just a geographical point. But the slopes and ravines around it were drenched with blood. The hill has a lasting place in the history of the war in Russia.

The Armoured Group Frank, reinforced by Tigers and Panthers of Bäke's Heavy Panzer Regiment, again attacked Hill 239. Meanwhile the 16th Panzer Division repulsed all enemy counter-attacks. But the commander of the Soviet V Guards Tank Corps also realized the value of that hill. Again and again he attacked from the north, down the main road from Medvin, and also made armoured thrusts from the woods in the south and east. Thus, on 16th February, he struck with 20 T-34s from the east and with 30 T-34s from the south-east. Colonel

Söth's artillerymen kept the Russian infantry down. The Panthers scattered the Soviet tank packs. Sergeant Strippel completed his triumph and with his seven Panthers knocked out 27 T-34s. It was a fantastic achievement, but it was no use.

Captain Ebeling with 70 Panzer grenadiers and three tanks under Second Lieutenant von Dörnberg succeeded in taking Oktyabr, half-way to Hill 239, but after that the attack got definitely stuck in the Russian defensive fire and in their counter-attacks.

Again and again the Soviets made massive thrusts from the thick forests along both sides of the road. Neither sacrifices nor incantations were any use now. Neither an attack by the reinforced Panzer Grenadier Battalion of "Leibstandarte" nor Rudel's Stukas could change the situation.

In the evening of 16th February the 2nd Battalion, 113th Panzer Grenadier Regiment, was down to 60 men. Sixty out of 600. Things were not much better with 1st Panzer Grenadier Regiment or with "Leibstandarte". When the companies numbered off they barely got to 10 or at the most 12. Company commanders and platoon commanders had been killed or wounded. The picture was the same with the Panzer engineer troops and the Panzer regiment. Only 12 Panthers and a few Mark-IVs were still battle-worthy. The 16th Panzer Division was pinned down in costly defensive fighting on the road from Medvin five miles north of Lysyanka. The 17th Panzer Division was still desperately fighting with a Soviet tank corps farther to the west. "Leibstandarte", the bulk of its units engaged in heavy defensive fighting at Vinograd, was at the end of its strength. The 198th Infantry Division was only a number on a sheet of paper. It was all too obvious—the relief attack by III Panzer Corps had failed. Five and a half miles from the Soviet ring around General Stemmermann's 56,000 men the rescue operation had got stuck. The chief of staff of First Panzer Army, General Wenck, arrived in the evening of 16th February on his motorcycle tractor to see if anything could be done with his old 1st Panzer Division. But he merely found that the strength of III Panzer Corps was insufficient to dislodge the strong Russian opposition.

And over there, in the pocket, the regiments were waiting in their jumping-off positions. They were listening to the crump of the tank cannon. They were watching the flashes of fire over to the west. And they were asking: "Aren't they coming yet?"

The man in the front line inevitably sees only a small sector of the battle—only as much as his own pair of eyes can see. He fights at his own post. In his tank or behind his gun. He charges or he resists the charge of the enemy. He sees the enemy charging up, yelling. He sees the whites of his eyes. He repulses him or he is overrun.

But the great tactical and strategic pattern of the battle remains hidden from him behind fire and smoke, in the ding-dong fighting for patches of woodland and small streams, for hills and ditches, for villages and ravines. Only the man who studies the daily situation map can feel the pulse-beat of the battle and discern plan or chaos.

The situation map of the fighting in the Korsun pocket reveals a bold and historically significant pattern, a plan impressed upon the gloomy and bloody events south-west of Cherkassy.

On 7th February the German High Command realized that in the long run the pocket could not be held and that a quick breakthrough from the outside to the encircled corps was becoming increasingly doubtful. The pocket was like a figure of eight around the two centres of Korsun and Gorodishche. Its twenty-eight-mile axis pointed from north-west to south-east. This was a favourable position for the relief attack of XLVII Panzer Corps from the south since the southern point of the pocket extended almost into the Shpola area from where General von Vormann intended to mount his thrust. But when, following the disastrous to-ing and fro-ing of 24th Panzer Division, a successful relief could no longer be expected from the south it became vital for the encircled troops to readjust themselves to a relief thrust from the west and therefore to reach out as far as possible towards III Panzer Corps. This meant changing the position and shape of the pocket so that its longitudinal axis should run from east to west. It was rather like turning a battleship in the midst of an enemy sea.

On 7th February at 1140 hours Eighth Army, under whose command the troops in the pocket were, instructed the two corps by radio: "Group Stemmermann will shorten the front lines and move the pocket in the direction of Shenderovka in order to be able, when the time comes, to break out towards the forces mounting a relief attack from outside."

General Stemmermann immediately embarked on the difficult task of moving the pocket about. In the east the battalions of the Waffen SS gave up Gorodishche and in the north the 88th Infantry Division evacuated the Yanovka area. Korsun with its airfield was the pivoting point, the tethering post to which the Group Stemmermann was tied because of supplies. This regrouping sounds easy enough but in fact was unbelievably difficult. All roads were deep in mud and the only practicable route was a railway embankment.

Within three days, from 11th to 13th February, a fundamental

Map 44. The Korsun pocket turned to face the forces trying to relieve it. To begin with, all went well. But a planning disaster in the relief attack resulted in disaster: Hill 239 remained in Soviet hands. III Panzer Corps was unable to take it.

7 Feb.1944

Yanovka

Co.Det.B

88   XLIIA.Co.

Korsun

FOUQUET   "VIKING"

XIA.Co.   "WALLON"

Shenderovka

Gorodishche

Zhurzhintsy

Pochapintsy   57   72

Lysyanka   389

10 miles   Olshana

Gniloy Tikich   Shpola

11-15 Feb.1944

10 miles   12 Feb.

13 Feb.

Zhurzhintsy   Korsun

Khilki   Komarovka

III Pz.Co.   Novaya-Buda

Lysyanka   Pochapintsy

16-17 Feb.1944

2 miles

Khilki   Shenderovka

Zhurzhintsy   72

16Pz.   B   389

BÄKE   239   Novaya-Buda

17Pz.   LAH   "VIKING"

Lysyanka   1Pz.

III Pz.Co.   Pochapintsy

Gniloy Tikich

regrouping took place in the pocket. The villages of Shenderovka, Novaya-Buda, and Komarovka had to be broken out of the Soviet encirclement front to provide a favourable springboard for a break-out towards the south-west.

The attack of the Moselle 72nd Infantry Division on Novaya-Buda was typical of the nature and the fierceness of this first phase of the break-out. The Russians were established in solidly built snow positions at the top of an entirely open slope. Without any cover, presenting a perfect target, the German troops would have to advance across crusted snow. The difficult task was assigned to 105th Grenadier Regiment. Major Kaestner decided on a night attack.

The plan was simple and based entirely on the fighting performance of each individual. It was war in its primal sense—man against man. In front was a ramming wedge with bayonets, trenching tools, sub-machine-guns, and machine-guns. They were followed by the bulk of the units with their heavy weapons—four guns of 172nd Artillery Regiment, each drawn by eight horses.

The date was 11th February and the time 2030 hours. There was no moon. The night was dark and cold. Noiselessly the men were advancing towards the Soviet position. Their white camouflage tunics made them invisible. Not a sound. No talking. No firing. They could hear the Russians talking at the first strongpoint. A Soviet sentry noticed something. He challenged them: "Stoy, parol!"

"Forward!" was Captain Roth's answer. They fired while still on the run. They jumped into the trenches. It was a case of cold steel. Whoever opposed them was battered down. Shock troops mopped up the trenches to both sides and provided flank cover.

The surprise succeeded. In one powerful leap the regiment pushed right through the deeply echeloned Soviet position. The horse-drawn units were following close behind. They drove through blizzard and enemy fire, and captured the ground around Hill 200. Shortly after midnight the Sukhiny–Shenderovka road was reached. From the east came an unsuspecting column of Russian trucks. They were making for Shenderovka. A few multiple mortars could be seen among them. "Flak forward!" At a range of two hundred yards the convoy came under fire from the German 2-cm flak guns on self-propelled carriages and was shot up. The trucks carrying motor fuel burst into huge sheets of fire, lighting up the snowscape. The attack on Novaya-Buda started at 0100 hours. By 0230 the village was in German hands. Soviet transport and cavalry units, snatched from their sleep, avoided the fighting and fled: 250 prisoners were taken.

To the right of 72nd Infantry Division the attack was also progressing. The Hamburg SS "Germania" Panzer Grenadier Regiment made a charge against Shenderovka, the second gate-post of a future break-out. Here too the hand-to-hand fighting was fierce and savage. Equally costly was the subsequent fighting for Komarovka, four miles from the edge of the pocket.

On 13th February, a Sunday, Korsun was evacuated in the east. In exchange, Komarovka was finally captured in the west by 72nd Infantry Division and held in savage fighting against furious enemy counter-attacks. At Novaya-Buda the "Wallonie" Assault Brigade, consisting of Belgian volunteers, with its six tanks, four anti-tank guns, and four companies of fifty to a hundred men repulsed all massed attacks by the Soviets. The brigade lost more than two hundred killed. Among them was its first commander, Lieutenant-Colonel Lucien Lippert, a former Belgian General Staff officer. The brigade's staff officer, Lieutenant Léon Degrelle, assumed command and held Novaya-Buda against all enemy counter-attacks.

On 15th February the 72nd Infantry Division captured the small village of Khilki, north of Komarovka. "The capture of this village is vital for the execution of the break-out from the pocket," Division had radioed to 105th Grenadier Regiment. Major Kaestner's men understood. Khilki was captured.

That was the moment when, outside the pocket, 1st Panzer Division and the Heavy Panzer Regiment Bäke were trying in vain to seize the commanding Hill 239 in order to mount their final push to reach Stemmermann's forward detachments. But they were unable to advance another step. A relief attack by Rudel's Stuka *Geschwader* helped them intercept the Soviet counter-attacks and pin the enemy down—but it was the same old story. They were a dozen tanks short, and half a dozen Grenadier battalions, and most of all they were short of fuel for Lieutenant-Colonel Bäke's Panthers which kept running out of juice.

Meanwhile in the pocket the troops were crowded dangerously close together in an area four by five miles around Shenderovka, ready to break out towards their liberators. They did not know yet that the relief attack had got bogged down and they were still wait-ing for the order which would spell freedom. If it did not come soon they would be doomed; for once the Soviets realized the position and started pounding the pocket with concentrated artillery the results would be catastrophic.

The Soviets meanwhile spared no trick to gain an idea of the situation inside the pocket. Men of the "Free Germany National Com-mittee" crossed the line in German officers' uniform in order to reconnoitre. Thus on 11th February one of these officers appeared at the position of Armoured Reconnaissance Battalion I and began to ask questions about strength, weapons, and objectives. A check with Division elicited the order: "Arrest him!" But by then the spy had disappeared. At certain division HQs Soviet officers appeared under a flag of truce, after a preliminary announcement over the radio, to offer the Germans conditions for their surrender.

On 10th February, according to the diary of III Panzer Corps, General von Seydlitz in his capacity of President of the "Association of German Officers" and Vice-President of the "Free German National Committee" addressed the troops in the pocket over the transmitter of the National Committee. He called for capitulation and promised them good food and accommodation, complete safety, and employment of units in a body under their own officers. The declaration had no effect on the morale of the troops. Most of the officers and men who heard the broadcast or read the leaflets which were dropped took little notice of them. Seydlitz's name did not weigh heavily enough among the troops for the offer to be seriously considered.

Meanwhile the 56,000 men in the minute pocket, bombarded by Soviet artillery as well as by leaflets, were awaiting their rescue. Their situation deteriorated from hour to hour. Finally Field-Marshal von Manstein decided to issue the break-out order without further reference to the Führer's Headquarters. His decision was based on a clear and frank report by Major-General Wenck, chief of staff of First Panzer Army.

On 15th February at 1105 hours Eighth Army radioed to the pocket: "Capacity for action of III Panzer Corps limited. Group Stemmermann must perform breakthrough as far as Zhurzhintsy/Hill 239 by its own effort. There link up with III Panzer Corps." This order contained the seed of subsequent tragedy. For it left unsaid one important fact—the fact that Hill 239, in spite of continuing attempts by the Heavy Panzer Regiment Bäke and the armoured combat group of 1st Panzer Division, was still not in the hands of III Panzer Corps. Stemmermann, on the other hand, was bound to conclude from the wording that when he reached that range of commanding hills he would find German troops there. In fact, when he got there, he was to encounter strong Soviet armoured forces. This fact was the root of the real tragedy of Cherkassy. On the morning of 15th February Eighth Army was still hoping that the spearheads of 1st Panzer Division or of Bäke's Heavy Panzer Regiment might after all gain the hill in the course of the 16th by employing their last Tigers. But a subsequent remark by Major-General Dr Speidel, chief of staff of Eighth Army, suggests that this possibility was not rated very high at Army HQ. It seems therefore that Army was deliberately vague about this important and dangerous circumstance so as not to discourage Stemmermann's battered divisions from the outset; they would need

Russian women and girls digging graves for German dead on the Zhizdra road. Cemetery at a base dressing station after a few days of heavy fighting near Rzhev.

all the courage and confidence they could muster in order to achieve their risky enterprise.

Stemmermann must have suspected something. He not only asked for an increased ammunition drop for the break-out but on the evening of 16th February also radioed to Eighth Army: "Group Stemmermann can break through the enemy along its own front but will not be able to force second breakthrough through enemy in front of III Panzer Corps."

That was clear enough. It meant: As a condition for breaking out I demand the liquidation of the Soviet positions on the range of high ground to both sides of Hill 239. It was a demand which the men of III Panzer Corps had been ceaselessly trying to meet but which, in the face of an unfavourable situation, was unrealizable. Would Stemmermann mount his break-out if he was told of this? Or would he hesitate and waver, just as Paulus had hesitated and wavered at Stalingrad fourteen months earlier?

The spectre of Stalingrad was raising its head. There, similar uncertainties had led to that fatal postponement of the break-out which finally ended in catastrophe. Another point was that the Führer's Headquarters had still not given its approval to the break-out. Any moment—as in the case of Stalingrad—it might issue a veto.

At that point Manstein, the C-in-C responsible, decided to cut the Gordian knot. Sweeping aside all conditions, considerations, and questions of responsibility, he radioed the following laconic but clear order to General Stemmermann on 16th February: "Password Freedom, objective Lysyanka, 2300 hours."

The radio station of XLII Corps received the signal. A few minutes later it was on the desk of Colonel Franz, chief of staff of Group Stemmermann. He heaved a sigh of relief. This was the clear order for action. There would be no Stalingrad. Feverishly the break-out plans, which for several days had been lying in the document boxes of the staff officers, were put into effect.

The battle HQ of XLII Corps, in charge of the break-out, was in a peasant hut on the north-western edge of Shenderovka. There were only three other villages in the pocket—it had shrunk so much. Of these, Novaya-Buda, until then defended by the gallant Walloons, was soon abandoned, while at Khilki and Komarovka resistance continued against furious Soviet attacks. The huts of Shenderovka were crammed with wounded. There were four thousand of them; they could no longer be flown out as since 10th February it had not been possible to land on the muddy airfield of Korsun. Four thousand bitter tragedies. Wedged in among them were the battle HQs of battalions, regiments, and divisions. In the village street, in the vegetable

One child of many—one house of many.

patches, and all round the huts stood guns, tanks awaiting repair, field kitchens, motor vehicles, horse-drawn carts. And all over the place small fires were being lit—in accordance with orders the troops were burning all documents, war diaries, and all expendable personal belongings such as letters, notebooks, souvenirs. Nothing was to be left except those few things which each man needed for hand-to-hand fighting and was able to carry on his own back. Nothing of any use was to fall into Russian hands. Only weapons, fighting vehicles, and field kitchens were to be evacuated. The girl signal auxiliaries were divided among the various units and experienced commanders were entrusted with their protection. Everyone knew what awaited these girls if they were captured. But in spite of all solicitude they were nearly all lost.

Major Hermani, the chief of operations of XLII Corps, had summoned the unit commanders to brief them about the break-out plan. There were no secrets now. Every man had to know exactly what was intended and what he had to do, even when there was no-one to ask.

The situation map was pinned to the wall. The light of a candle was flickering over the red and blue markings on it. "Here is the line Khilki–Komarovka. We are setting out in three ramming wedges. Deeply echeloned. Without artillery preparation. The first phase must be quite noiseless. The enemy must be dislodged at bayonet point. Break through to the area of Zhurzhintsy and Hill 239 in one swift movement. There we'll be met by III Panzer Corps."

Hermani lightly ran his hand over the map. His optimism wanted justifying. So he justified it. A few pencil lines clarified the situation:

Corps Detachment "B" to the right. 72nd Infantry Division in the middle. SS "Viking" Panzer Grenadier Division on the left. That was roughly 40,000 men. General Lieb was in command. Stemmermann would remain in the pocket with the rearguard. This was provided by the Bavarian 57th Infantry Division under General Trowitz and the Bavarian-Sudetenland 88th Infantry Division under General Count Rittberg. Parts of 389th Infantry Division, except the Panzerjäger Battalion, as well as splinter groups of 167th and 168th Infantry Divisions had been attached to 57th Infantry Division. In this way General Trowitz had another 3500 men. Count Rittberg's Division was somewhat weaker. Rear cover for the break-out was thus provided by 6500 men. Non-transportable wounded were to remain behind with their doctors and nursing staff to be handed over to the Soviets. That was the most painful aspect of the plan. Nor was it obeyed everywhere.

Then came the hardest part of the briefing. Officers were told to urge NCOs and men to write a few lines to their families and to exchange these letters among each other—to provide for the worst. To make sure a last line was received back home.

The chief of operations added a few serious words about the comradeship which would undergo its supreme test during the next few hours. Comradeship—a hard-worked word. Now it would become obvious how much this word and its underlying idea meant to each individual.

In the report of the chief of operations we read: "Thursday, 16th February, 2200 hours. We are sitting in our battle HQ, silent. There are no more orders to be given and no directives to be issued—for the first time since the encirclement twenty days ago. Every man is thinking of home. The last letter from 'outside' has been burnt and all those other things one had become so attached to in over four years of war—photographs of one's wife and children, Goethe's *Faust* or Eugen Roth's *Woman in World History!*"

At that moment, when it was clear that Stemmermann's break-out would encounter on Hill 239 not German patrols but Soviet tanks, III Panzer Corps decided to tell Stemmermann the full truth and inform him about the bridge-head at Lysyanka. Colonel Merk, the chief of staff of Group Breith, who only returned from Soviet captivity in 1955, told the present author that during the night of 16th–17th February, the attempt was made to inform Stemmermann by radio. But his signals station no longer answered. While the important signal was being pushed out into the ether the big break-out had already been set in motion inside the pocket.

Hell was let loose at Shenderovka. The approach route of three divisions led through that village. Down a narrow street. The only bridge over the ravine was blocked by a tank which had broken through the roadway. It took the engineers several hours of laborious work to push it into the gorge. Then they had to do a first-aid repair on the bridge.

Traffic meanwhile had got inextricably snarled up. Everybody was shouting. Soviet shells were bursting all over the place. Every shell hit a target. Wounded were dragged into the huts. At the door to Corps HQ lay a staff officer with his head torn off by a shell splinter.

The time was 2230. Low-flying He-111s were dropping boxes with ammunition and shells. With a crash they burst right among field kitchens and peasant carts. The enemy bombardment was getting fiercer. The bursts were right in front of Corps HQ. General Lieb arrived. He was wearing his favourite white fur cap. He was calm and optimistic. With him was the chief of staff of XI Corps, Colonel Gaedke, with whom he discussed the last details of the break-out.

The time was 2300. H-hour. The night was pitch dark. No moon. No stars. The thermometer stood at four degrees below zero Centigrade. But an icy wind was blowing from the north-east. Fortunately it was a tail wind for the marching columns and a head wind for the watching enemy. At times it was so fierce that it carried the snow before it. Favourable weather for an enterprise which hoped to escape the enemy's eyes and ears.

Corps Detachment "B" was moving on the right wing. Ahead of it were parts of 258th Regiment Group. On the left wing the 5th SS "Viking" Panzer Grenadier Division was attacking; its spearhead was Armoured Reconnaissance Battalion 5. Next to it came the Panzerjäger Battalion of the Hessian 389th Infantry Division, whose 3rd Company had been formed from the old Flak Battalion 66, which perished at Stalingrad. The Battalion was down to ninety-seven men, and 3rd Company to thirty. The centre of the break-out wedge was formed by 72nd Infantry Division, with 105th Grenadier Regiment in front.

Major Kaestner had a captured Soviet map which, on a scale of 1:10,000 showed his sector of attack very clearly. Together with his prismatic compass it made an excellent means of orientation. That was important because there were no roads: the troops' route lay across open country, across fields and pastures. Over frozen mud, covered by crusted snow. Kaestner had given his men explicit instructions: no unnecessary sound, no lighted cigarettes. More important still, he had ordered all rifles to be unloaded to make sure no nervous trooper opened up prematurely and so deprived the break-out of its element of surprise. The first Soviet position was taken at bayonet point. The second was overrun. Only at one point was there fierce fighting with enemy gun positions which had to be taken in hand-to-hand combat. The main part of the division was following. Was it all going to be as easy as that? The time was 0330. Kaestner, Captain Roth, and Lieutenant Bender were studying the map. They had reached the ravines south-east of Zhurzhintsy. Before them, on the ridge of high ground, was the road to Pochapintsy, running straight over Hill 239.

It was still dark. If everything had gone according to plan, the most advanced outposts of 1st Panzer Division should have reached the road by now. Nevertheless: careful—scouts forward! Lieutenant Bender was soon back. "Tanks all right," he said; "but not German ones. Half a dozen T-34s are stationed exactly at the southern exit from Zhurzhintsy. And a mile and a half farther to the south-east, on the same road, silhouettes of more T-34s."

That might mean that Hill 239 was occupied by the enemy. In spite of the radio silence Kaestner decided to pass on this surprising and dangerous piece of information to Division at once. Then he moved forward again silently. Once more he reminded his men: "No fire unless absolutely necessary."

In a narrow column but in wide-open formation, the regiment pushed forward across the road, precisely through the gap between the outpost tanks. The Russians did not notice anything. Careful now. Soft soles were more important than hand-grenades. They had got to two hundred yards beyond the road over Hill 239 when the point group stopped. A sergeant slipped alongside Kaestner. In a whisper he reported: "Enemy positions ahead, Herr Major. Facing westwards. But I think the Ivans are sleeping."

Facing westwards. That could only be the Soviet defensive line against the German relief forces. In other words, the last barrier. "Attack!" Kaestner commanded. Again they went in with rifle butt, trenching tool, bayonet. Silently, without any battle-cries. Doggedly. No-one suspected that the real drama of Cherkassy was only now beginning.

It was a brief engagement. The Russians fled. But they fired wildly in all directions. And the fire alerted the V Guards Tank Corps whose T-34s were covering the road from Zhurzhintsy to Pochapintsy. The Russian tanks switched on their headlights. They fired flares into the sky. And now they could see the bulk of 72nd Infantry Division approaching the road over open ground.

"Look out! Germans!" the tank commander shouted. "Otkryt ogon —open fire!" Abruptly, an unequal battle had begun. The main body of 72nd Infantry Division was forced down.

But the companies of 105th Grenadier Regiment hurried on. Again they spotted the outlines of three tanks in front. Kaestner himself crept closer. The silhouettes of Panthers! And now he could see the German cross. He leapt to his feet. And at the top of his voice, into the first light of the breaking day, he shouted the password: "Freedom! Freedom!"

The hatch-covers of the Panthers flew open. Kaestner's men had reached the outpost line of 1st Panzer Division, provided by 1st Company of the Erfurt 1st Panzer Regiment. Second Lieutenant Freiherr von Dörnberg climbed out of his tank and welcomed Kaestner. They had made it.

The 105th Grenadier Regiment had got out. Of the 27 officers and 1082 men which the regiment had when the pocket was closed three weeks before, only 3 officers and 216 men were left. A mere 216 men. But they had brought with them their 11 light and one heavy machine-guns, one mortar, and one infantry gun. And each man had brought his rifle or sub-machine-gun. The break-out itself had scarcely cost them two dozen casualties.

But how did the rest fare?

On the sector of the "Viking" Panzer Grenadier Division, to the left of 72nd Infantry Division, the Armoured Reconnaissance Battalion 5 under Lieutenant Debus also managed the first phase quickly. As soon as the last fighting vehicles of 5th Panzer Regiment had once more repulsed a nocturnal counter-attack against the eastern edge of Shenderovka, the Soviet encirclement front in the west was pierced at the first attempt and anti-tank and machine-gun positions were overrun. The first positions on high ground at Pochapintsy were taken by storm.

The SS Armoured Reconnaissance Battalion reached the highway close to Hill 239 at about the same time as Kaestner's 105th Grenadier Regiment. They were now facing the main enemy positions guarding the pocket. Lieutenant Debus distinguished the strong Soviet tank barrier on the high ground. But he decided to attack it.

The time was 0430 hours. The first charge collapsed in the Russian fire at the foot of the hill. Debus's men and the Wallonie Assault Brigade which followed them were caught in enfilading machine-gun fire. Four or five Panthers might have turned the tables, but the Reconnaissance Battalion had only one Mark III left. The rest of the Panzer Regiment had been involved at Shenderovka in a savage tank battle with pursuing T-34s and Joseph Stalin-IIs and had sacrificed itself. Debus tried once again. Again in vain. The Soviet defences, now fully awake, were too strong.

Meanwhile the bulk of the "Viking" Division was arriving. Moreover, waves of 72nd Infantry Division which had failed to get across the road farther north were flooding down. The men of Corps Detachment "B" had not fared much better. Colonel Viebig with 112th Division Group had overrun the first strongpoint and eliminated the first enemy machine-gun without firing a shot. The Division Group thrust towards the south-west, collided with the bulk of 72nd Infantry Division, and was deflected towards the south.

Day was breaking. Soviet shells from tanks and anti-tank guns were now crashing murderously into the German columns which had no cover at all on the featureless ground. Their anti-tank guns and field howitzers had got stuck on the icy flanks of the ravines, in spite of eight or ten horses being harnessed to each of them. Apart from *Panzerfaust* bazookas the units had no armour-piercing weapons left and could only save themselves from this enemy onslaught by evasive action. The masses welled towards the south. All hope of a planned operation was gone. Each man tried to find a way out of the chaos for himself.

In closed formations of a few hundreds, but also in smaller groups and even individually, they were all trying to get out of the range of the Russian fire. Finally they all turned west again, towards freedom. Soviet infantry was swept aside at bayonet point. Soviet cavalry was repulsed. But the Soviet tanks continued to fire unimpeded into the German columns.

The 3rd Company, Panzerjäger Battalion 389, had none of its 2-cm flak guns left. But the men were hauling along a handcart with twelve *Panzerfaust* bazookas. Staff Sergeant Krause was leading the company —if that handful of twenty men could still be called a company. They could not get through the ravine. It was blocked by tanks lined up on the slope above and pumping shells into the valley. "Follow me," Krause said to Corporal Fritz Hamann, the gun commander of No. 2 Troop. He picked up three bazookas from the handcart and pushed them under Hamann's arm. Then he helped himself to three. Cautiously they moved off across the dead ground to the lip of the ravine where the Soviet tanks were positioned. They charged over the edge. Crash. Crash.

The first two T-34s were on fire with smoke pouring from them. They provided ideal cover for the two men. Hamann knocked out two more, Krause knocked out another. At that the commanders of the remaining four or five became nervous and drove off. The road was clear. Instantly the ravine was filled with columns pressing forward. A new road had been opened to the shelter of the little beech-wood of Pochapintsy.

No High Command communiqué, no memorial scroll, no recommendation for an Order would report this feat—the gallantry of the anonymous heroes of the break-out battle.

The main part of Corps Detachment "B" under Colonel Fouquet, with parts of 188th Artillery Regiment in its first block of attack, seized a favourable moment for its forward-strike wedge to charge across the road to both sides of Hill 239. They succeeded. The regimental groups fought their way through the wood, where they were safe from tanks, and reached Oktyabr and Lysyanka—though without any of their heavy equipment.

Nothing of all this was known as yet back at Corps HQ. General Lieb and his headquarters personnel had followed the first phase of the break-out from Shenderovka. The chief of staff and the chief of operations were standing outside a peasant hut, listening.

Silently the columns moved past. The clatter of the horses' hooves on the frozen ground was swallowed up by the night and the wind. The corps commander joined them: "Any news from up front?" he asked. A routine question really. "Nothing, Herr General." There was no noise of battle to be heard either from Komarovka or from Khilki. But surely the spearhead of the break-out must have pushed through there by now? "What d'you make of this silence?" Lieb asked. Franz, his voice a little hoarse, answered: "It can mean only one thing— the first wave has got through and has opened the pocket at bayonet point."

"Then let's go, gentlemen," said Lieb. He pushed his tall, white fur cap firmly down on his head and strode across to the hut where his horse stood. He looked like a Grand Duke.

Shortly after midnight General Lieb set up his battle headquarters on the western edge of Khilki. The village formed the right corner-post of the German break-out corridor and had to be held at all costs. But the Russians were pressing furiously from the flank. They had already reached the eastern edge of the village. The situation was getting critical. If the Russians recaptured the village the corridor would collapse.

"I need a reliable combat group to hold up the Russians," Lieb groaned. "Whom have we left?"

An Austrian artillery commander stepped forward to the map table. Standing in the candlelight he said calmly: "I've only a hundred men left, but I'll hold this dump, Herr General—you may rely on it." He held it. Until the last man was through. And he even got himself and his rearguard out of the hot spot.

At 0600 Lieb's Corps HQ personnel rode out of Khilki with the last marching columns.

"Who's going to inform Stemmermann that we're breaking out and can no longer receive orders?" Lieb asked his chief of operations. Franz pointed to a horseman. Captain von Meerheimb, the intelligence officer, had volunteered. The steeplechase rider from Mecklenburg silently put his fingertips to his helmet. He wheeled his piebald round. A moment later he was seen chasing at a tearing gallop right through the enemy artillery fire.

Lieb's column cantered on. It was an eerie sight. A Napoleonic vision. On the outside was Major Ganschow, the quartermaster, on a powerful grey. His huge German mastiff was running alongside. "Give my love to my wife," Ganschow had said to Major Hermani at Khilki. "I won't get through." He had added softly: "Look after my dog—I don't want him to become a stray." Hermani could not get those words out of his mind as he was watching Ganschow cantering alongside the marching column. Were there premonitions of death? he wondered.

Dawn in the Western Ukraine at this time of year usually came towards 0600. But on 17th February, 1944, that bloody Thursday, the blizzard prevented the day getting properly light. The columns moved on, across the snow-covered, open ground. The farm carts creaked and the wounded men on them groaned. Most units had disregarded orders to abandon them. They had too much bad experience of the Soviets.

From afar came the noise of battle. The troops were getting jumpy. The enemy's artillery was intensifying its bombardment of the formations. It struck at the marching columns. Everybody scattered. The horses bolted. Hermani's roan was hit and collapsed. Dazed, the Major staggered on. He looked for his groom and for his map-case. But how was anyone to find a person, let alone a map-case, in that chaos? Machine-gun fire was now also coming from the right flank. They were up against the Soviet armoured barrier between Zhurzhintsy and Pochapintsy. And just as the columns before them, they too tried to turn away to the left.

Colonel Franz also had his horse shot from under him. The last vehicles and guns had got stuck on an icy slope leading up from a dip in the ground. Enemy anti-tank guns were firing at them. Horses complete with harness were bolting. Franz caught himself an artillery horse, flung himself in the saddle, and raced up the slope. He had a shock—about fifteen T-34s were approaching. They rumbled through the narrow gorge where a column of peasant carts with Red Cross flags had stopped. With their machine-guns the tanks mowed down the horses and then steam-rollered the carts. The tracks crushed everything into pulp.

"Swine! Swine!" Franz panted. He knew that the column was evacuating the serious casualties of "Viking" Division. General Gille had not wanted to leave them behind. About 140 had set out aboard tracked vehicles under the command of Dr Isselstein. The rest, 100 seriously wounded as well as about 30 lesser casualties from the main dressing station of Corps Detachment "B", had been loaded on peasant carts by Dr Thon, the chief of the Medical Company of "Viking" Division. For them the war ended then, right under Colonel Franz's eyes. Dr Thon managed to save a bare dozen of them. Dr Isselstein's column was shot up by tanks west of Shenderovka. He was killed by a burst from a T-34.

From amidst this inferno suddenly came the sound of a great many hoarse voices. Franz turned his head. Was it possible? Did this kind of thing still exist in 1944? Out of a ravine came a horseman leading a column of 3000 to 4000 men against a drawn-out line of enemy tanks and a position of anti-tank guns in a clearing on the edge of a wood, blocking the road to the shelter provided by the trees. It was Lieutenant-Colonel Müller who was leading this massed charge of parts of 72nd Infantry Division through the Russian lines into the wood where there was safety from tanks. Colonel Franz joined the column. It was being raked by Russian machine-gun fire. Gashes were being torn into it by the anti-tank guns.

Between a Stalin-II tank and a T-34 was a gap of 50 yards. No more than 50 yards. Into this gap Franz spurred his panting horse through the driving snow. There was only a field between him and the edge of the wood now. With a hiss a shell splinter struck the horse's head. Its forelegs gave. It turned a somersault on the frozen ground. Franz was lucky to slip out of the stirrups and remain unhurt. His sniper's rifle with its telescopic sights lay on the ground by the dead horse. He snatched it up and ran for the cover of the wood.

It is always interesting to see what can be achieved by determination, and it is militarily instructive to consider the limited effect of armoured fighting vehicles unsupported by infantry in the face of fanatic mass breakthroughs. On the German side it was long believed that in the battles of encirclement of the first years of the war enemy break-outs were unsuccessful against the German tank barriers. During the second half of the war the Soviets appeared to have held the same erroneous view. If the Soviet commander in charge of Hill 239 or Army General Konev himself had been able to watch events in the forest of Pochapintsy in the morning of 17th February they would have realized their mistake.

More and more groups of 72nd Infantry Division, of Corps Detachment "B", of "Viking" Division, and of 389th Infantry Division were rallying there. They had got through the line of tanks, even though the road over the hill seemed totally barred by the Russian fire. Admittedly, they had lost their last vehicles, their last assault guns and armoured infantry carriers, their last guns and horse-drawn peasant carts in the ravines outside Pochapintsy. Indeed, many men had not even been able to save their small arms. All they saved was their bare skins. They were soon to discover that worse was to come.

The wood in which Colonel Franz had found temporary shelter was suddenly full of shouting. There was the crack of shots. Two men of the Belgian Wallonie volunteer brigade appeared. "An enemy machine-gun is blocking the way out from the forest across a clearing. We can't get through. We've already suffered casualties—killed and wounded," the Walloons reported.

Colonel Franz picked up his sniper's rifle and cautiously accompanied the two men to the clearing. The machine-gun was on the far side. In his telescopic sights Franz could make out the Russians very clearly. Three men. Range 300 yards. Franz fired three times in rapid succession. Then he waved and ran forward through the shallow dip. The others waited until he had made the first five steps. When the Russian Maksim remained silent, everyone followed Franz. Forward. To the south-west.

The corps commander tried to get some kind of order into his column of 3000 to 4000 men. Officers and men were spent, both physically and psychologically, but they still realized that discipline was better than a chaotic "every man for himself". Suddenly Major Hermani was standing at Franz's side. "Herr Oberst," he said, "now we've met in this hell unscathed we're sure to get through all the way."

But misfortune continued to dog them. At Hill 222, immediately east of Lysyanka, they thought they had at last reached the German outposts. But the five or six armoured fighting vehicles on the slight hill turned out to be T-34s. Once more they suffered heavy losses. Hermani had his sub-machine-gun shattered in his hands.

The important thing was not to stop. Keep running! Keep running! And so, panting heavily, they raced all the way to the Gniloy Tikich.

Time was getting on for 1100. From a long way off they saw the surging crowd by the river. It was more than thirty yards wide and over six feet deep. The current was strong and the bank steep and icy.

And not a bridge as far as the eye could see.

The bridge of 1st Panzer Division and a temporary footbridge rapidly built by the Jena Armoured Engineer Battalion 37, under cover of the last grenadiers of "Leibstandarte", were a mile and a half to the north. A mere mile and a half! But no-one knew that. And they were all driven by only one desire—to get across the river, to the far bank, where the Soviet tanks could not follow them.

This overriding thought left no room for calm consideration. The great disappointment at Hill 239 had demoralized the men. They were feeling abandoned and betrayed. They were quarrelling and cursing. All they cared about was getting out of this hell.

The temperature was five degrees below zero Centigrade, and an icy wind was blowing. But what did it matter? Four T-34s drove up to within a few hundred yards of the dense crowds and opened up at them with high-explosive shells and ricochet air bursts. It was frightful. Groups of thirty or forty men jumped blindly into the icy water. Whole groups were drowned. The bodies of horses were drifting among the ice floes. Only thirty-odd yards across. But even thirty yards of icy current required strength and a clear head. That cursed panic!

Colonel Franz chose a clear spot and with a few forceful strokes glided to the far bank. Immediately under a willow whose branches were hanging into the water like helping arms. But what promised salvation very nearly meant his ruin. His greatcoat was caught in a branch. It pinned Franz down in the water. His fingers were going rigid. His body was beginning to feel heavy. Was this the end? But for young Lieutenant Güldenpfennig, who happened to see the Colonel's plight and helped him up the bank, it would have been the end of Franz as it was for so many others. Hermani got across the river safely.

At the point where the units of "Viking" reached the Gniloy Tikich General Gille prevailed on his men to organize the crossing sensibly. In a fur jacket and with his knobbly stick he stood on the bank. He had got 4500 men, 70 per cent of his Division, safely to this spot. He did not propose to suffer any big losses now. He ordered the last tractor to be driven into the river. It was to be a kind of make-shift pier for an emergency footbridge. But the current swept it away. Farm carts, pushed into the river, were also carried away by the swirling waters.

Gille had the non-swimmers sorted out. Human chains were formed with alternately one swimmer and one non-swimmer. The general himself stepped into the water at the head of the first chain. But half-way across the third man suddenly let go. The human bridge broke. Help! Screams and curses. Helplessly the non-swimmers were carried away. Lieutenant-Colonel Schönfelder, Gille's chief of operations, rallied the men. Another attempt. But again too many were drowned.

Captain Dorr of the "Germania" SS Regiment came up with the rearguard. On boards and cart shafts they were pulling the last survivors of the casualty transports through the snow. Dorr's grenadiers, together with a group of 14th Panzer Division which had got into the pocket, had been looking after the column of wounded. In repulsing the murderous tank attacks "Viking" suffered the heaviest casualties of the entire break-out.

And that group down there by the river? What were they up to? They were Belgians of the "Wallonie" Brigade. On a peasant cart with their wounded they had brought with them their former commander, Lieutenant-Colonel Lucien Lippert, killed in action on 13th February. After the column had been shot up by Soviet tanks, four men had carried the dead commander all the way to the river. They would not let the Russians have him. Wrapped in a sheet of tent canvas the body was piloted across the river by four men. On the far side they again pulled it through snow and up icy slopes—all the way behind the outposts of III Panzer Corps.

Captain Westphal, Gille's first staff officer, tried to get the last Mark III tank across the river. But it was impossible. Westphal had to swim across the Gniloy Tikich. His safe arrival on the far bank meant not only the rescue of another gallant officer, but also of an important witness to the fate of General Stemmermann.

Again and again one encounters the legend that Stemmermann was shot by the SS. But Stemmermann was not murdered; he was killed in action by a Russian anti-tank gun. The circumstances were as follows. In a hollow near Pochapintsy the general, who had lost his own car owing to an engine breakdown, came across the cross-country vehicle of the chief of operations of "Viking" Division. But this vehicle had burst a tyre. Schönfelder and Westphal therefore ran up the icy slope, the crest of which was raked by enemy fire, in order to observe. Just then Stemmermann arrived with his ADC; he was pretty well exhausted. He saw the vehicle and wanted to drive it up the slope without changing the tyre. But the driver could not manage it. He got stuck. At that moment a shell from an anti-tank gun hit the vehicle. It tore open the rear. Stemmermann and his ADC were killed by the fragments.

A Russian auxiliary and the driver managed to pull them clear of the vehicle. Then they ran up the slope and reported to Schönfelder and Westphal: "The general and his ADC are dead."

"Really dead, not just seriously wounded?"

"No Obersturmbannführer—direct hit in their backs. Finished instantly." Captain Schönfelder thereupon gave orders that no more vehicles were to be driven up that infernal slope.

This is the authentic account of General Stemmermann's death.

The Gniloy Tikich, that raging torrent, revealed the hidden aspects of the human soul—the precipices of fear, the caverns of cowardice, but also the shining peaks of heroism, comradeship, and self-sacrifice.

Sergeant Wohler, for instance, swam the river three times. With a kind of swimming harness, which he hurriedly contrived from belts and shoulder-straps, he got three non-swimmers to the safe bank. Two NCOs of 389th Infantry Division pulled wounded men, tied to planks, through the stream behind them. Five stragglers of 3rd Company, Panzerjäger Battalion 389, arrived at the river. Staff Sergeant Krause was one of them. They brought along half a dozen Russians who had been taken prisoner when their anti-tank gun position was overrun. As the Germans were taking off their greatcoats to get into the water the Russians vigorously shook their heads. Those nature boys did the job differently. They unbuttoned their greatcoats, slid down the bank to the water, and let their coats open out on the water like wings. They then started swimming.

Corporal Fritz Hamann had no faith in the Russian method. In a bend, where the river was frozen over almost to the middle, he saw some very young boys crawling over the ice on their stomachs. He tried to do the same. But the ice crackled and cracked. He broke through. He supported himself on his elbows. He broke through again. Thus, yard by yard, he struggled through the cracking ice. He clung to the ice floes. It took him half an hour. Utterly exhausted, he grabbed the carbine butt which a comrade held out to him to pull him up. Saved!

Where were the others? There was no-one in sight. Not even Krause. He staggered on. Don't look back. That river ran through the underworld of the war.

General Lieb tried to swim the stream on his horse. But the gelding could not keep it up. He was swept away and drowned. The general made it to the other bank.

Colonel Dr Hohn, the experienced commander of 72nd Infantry Division, also crossed the Gniloy Tikich by swimming, with most of his men from the Moselle. His uniform frozen hard as a board, he stood on the western bank, waiting until the last group was safely across.

Colonel Fouquet, the commander of Corps Detachment "B", did not get as far as the river. In an attack on a Russian anti-tank gun position he was seriously wounded. He later died in Soviet captivity.

As the first survivors, more dead than alive in their hard-frozen uniforms, staggered into the arms of outposts and pickets of "Leibstandarte" and 1st Panzer Division at Lysyanka, the units there instantly realized the desperate situation a mile and a half south of the bridge-head. Assault parties of Armoured Engineer Battalion 37 moved off downstream under cover of Panzer grenadiers and a troop of tanks. Piloting parties tried to wave the bulk of the break-out forces, as they arrived on the eastern bank, towards the north, towards the bridging-point of 1st Panzer Division at Lysyanka.

Some of the groups understood the shouts and signals from the western bank. But the increasingly widespread panic prevented a co-ordinated detour. Soviet tanks by the river made the chaos worse. Eventually, Thuringian Panzer engineers under Major Braun, each party covered by two Panthers of the Erfurt 1st Panzer Regiment, built a number of emergency footbridges at several points, and the river was now traversed by these. Thus at least the rearguards, similarly deflected southwards, were now able to cross over by these makeshift bridges without having to leap into the icy water.

General Trowitz led his Bavarian 57th Infantry Division and the remnants of 389th Division back as a coherent body, in spite of fierce rearguard fighting. He got more than 3000 men across the river—as well as all the wounded he had taken along, 250 men in all. With 3500 men he had defended the rearguard positions of Group Stemmermann. Trowitz himself was one of the last to limp out of the hell of Korsun; he had been wounded.

General Count Rittberg, commanding 88th Infantry Division, like-wise brought the bulk of his men to the crossing points on the Gniloy Tikich. The Bavarians, Palatinate men, and Swabians of 246th Grena-dier Regiment had held the northern front of the pocket along Hill 192 in hard fighting as recently as the night of 16th–17th February, and had only then fallen back step by step. Reduced entirely to its own resources the regiment fought its way back to the river. With the main part of the division there was also a strange marching column—Russian women, afraid of Soviet reprisals because of their auxiliary service for the Germans.

When Count Rittberg, an artilleryman from Verden and a well-known show-jumper, saw that even experienced officers lost their nerve at the crossing-points, became ruthless, and elbowed their way to get across more quickly, he asked with his proverbial sarcasm: "Since when have officers had precedence in flight?" From that moment on-wards everything went smoothly.

The last units of the "Wallonie" SS Volunteer Assault Brigade suc-cceded in reaching the bridge-head of 1st Panzer Division at Lysyanka by different routes. Until the morning of 17th February the rearguard of the Walloons had been holding Novaya-Buda. Then, according to orders, it had followed its first wave, passed the break-out columns, and found itself in the tank-trap north of Pochapintsy together with the men of "Viking" Division. The Walloons managed to reach a ravine and, having knocked out two T-34s, to gain the cover of a patch of woodland south of Hill 239, after fighting their way through swarms of Cossacks. In the wood Léon Degrelle rallied all his stragglers. He defended the wood a few miles east of Lysyanka till dusk. Quietly, without a single shot being fired, Degrelle got to the outposts of 1st Panzer Division on 18th February. With him were 3000 men, including many civilians and the last 632 Walloons of his brigade.

And Major Ganschow? The quartermaster of XLII Corps, who had ridden off to the Gniloy Tikich on his grey, with premonitions of death in his heart? He did not get through. His batman swam across the river with the mastiff. A little earlier the major had tried to reconnoitre a safe route for a group. But only his grey was sighted again, riderless by the river. After that even the horse's tracks were lost.

The accusation has been levelled at III Panzer Corps, and in particular at 1st Panzer Division, that when H-hour came for the Korsun divisions, its units failed to make an all-out effort to spare the break-out forces the calvary of Hill 239. This accusation is unfounded. The 1st Panzer Division held the Lysyanka bridge-head open for nine days with its very few soldiers and tanks. When Generals Lieb and Gille reached Lysyanka with their men on 17th February, twelve battle-worthy Mark IVs and Mark Vs, together with a few damaged tanks employed statically with eighty Panzer grenadiers and three groups of Panzer engineers, were keeping the road open across the Gniloy Tikich. The men under Major-General Koll, Colonel Söth, and Lieutenant-Colonel Dr Bäke struggled to the point of collapse to hold Lysyanka against furious Soviet counter-attacks. By doing so they enabled the break-out units to be led back through Buzhanka. The seriously wounded men were flown to Uman from Lysyanka and Buzhanka thanks to the solicitude of Captain Dr Königshausen.

The 1st Panzer Division held its bridge-head until the last rearguards had been received into it on the morning of 19th February. More than that it was unable to achieve. By mid-February 1944, given the greatly reduced strength of the German units, no amount of gallantry or sacrifice could undo the serious and fatal mistakes made by the top German Command on the battlefield between Kiev and Kirovograd over the last few months.

In the evening of 16th February, when the Heavy Panzer Regiment Bäke and the armoured combat group of 1st Panzer Division had been all but bled white in front of the woods and the hill road between Zhurzhintsy and Pochapintsy, General Breith during that very night of 16th–17th employed two battalions of "Leibstandarte" against the Soviet barriers in an attempt to break them. The entire division might have succeeded—if it had been available. But with two battalions? It was an insoluble task even for a crack force.

Having suffered heavy casualties the battalions got stuck on the icy slopes in front of Hills 239 and 222. It was hardly surprising. Konev had concentrated the mass of two tank armies in the break-out area. In addition he had a dozen divisions of two rifle armies, as well as independent cavalry formations.

Two battalions were facing the bulk of two armies.

Of course, the Russians were also exhausted and had long lost their full vigour. That presumably was the reason why the German break-out through the first ring of encirclement was accomplished so quickly and almost without losses. But the Soviet barrier on the ridge of high ground from Zhurzhintsy to Pochapintsy, commanding pathless and icy slopes, represented an ideal defensive position.

If the break-out of Group Stemmermann nevertheless resulted in the rescue of 60 per cent of the strength then this was an astonishing achievement. Nearly 35,000 men were brought back safely. They were led back into the assembly areas east of Uman. This is not to belittle the Russian victory. Its significance lay in the elimination of the fighting power of six and a half German divisions. Six and a half divisions which had lost all their weapons. True, the gap in the front between the German Eighth Army and First Panzer Army was temporarily sealed by a counter-attack of two Panzer divisions. But how long could that thin line hold?

Manstein's command train was steaming from Uman to Proskurov, along the Dnepropetrovsk–Lvov main line, across the white, wintery expanses of the western Ukraine.

The Field-Marshal had been visiting the survivors of the Korsun pocket in the hospitals and collection centres of Uman. He had spoken to officers and men. The Cherkassy chapter was finished. But he had new anxieties. Would the Russians keep quiet until the gaps in the front were somehow sealed again? That was one question. The other was: What were they to be sealed with? With the exception of the "Wallonie" Volunteer Assault Brigade none of the formations saved from the Korsun pocket was fit for action any longer. But that too had been transferred to the West with its last 632 men in order to be replenished. That meant that six and a half divisions were lost for the further conduct of operations. At the centre of his front Manstein was six and a half divisions short. A nasty situation.

It was this situation that demonstrated the importance of the Soviet successes at Korsun. The strategic consequences of that victory were vastly more important than the German losses, although to this day the Soviets, by means of a curious juggling with figures of casualties and prisoners, are making these losses the main feature of the Korsun battle. Professor Telpukhovskiy, the Soviet historian, for instance, lists the German losses as 52,000 killed and 11,000 taken prisoner. The Soviet *History of the Great Fatherland War* speaks of 55,000 killed and 18,000 prisoners.

These are absurd figures. They would imply that out of no more than 56,000 men surrounded, some 73,000 had been killed or captured. Documentary evidence discloses a different picture. The time has come to accept the evidence.

The daily report of Eighth Army for the evening of 11th February 1944 gives the ration strength of the two encircled corps including Russian volunteers as 56,000 men. Out of that total 2188 wounded were flown out. Nearly 35,000 men, according to the records of the chiefs of staff of the encircled corps, reached the German front and were there recorded as safely arrived at the reception points. The war diaries of the divisions and regiments involved moreover confirm these data. Their average losses were between 20 and 30 per cent. Hence the casualty balance-sheet of Cherkassy was 18,800 men. Needless to say, hardships, suffering, and death cannot be encompassed in any balance-sheet. The tragedy of that lonely Ukrainian Hill 239 and of that God-forsaken stream, the Gniloy Tikich, has gone down in history. And so have their strategic consequences.

2. Hube's Pocket

Report from "Foreign Armies East"–Zeitzler tries a ruse–Between Pripet and Carpathians–First Panzer Army surrounded–Manstein's ultimatum to Hitler–Clash at the Berghof–Telephone-call from Hube–Hitler gives in–"Western alternative; order follows"–Zhukov waits in vain–Across four rivers and through two enemy armies–Towards the moving pocket–Rendezvous at Buchach–Stalin's great trap is burst open–Exit of the saviour.

MANSTEIN'S command train was slowly rolling through Vinnitsa station. The station commandant and the transport controller were on the platform, saluting. The Field-Marshal was in his office carriage with General Busse and Colonel Schulze-Büttger, studying the maps. Lieutenant Stahlberg, the orderly officer, had a folder full of reports and signals by his elbow and was passing the papers across the desk, one by one.

One did not have to be a prophet to read a gloomy future from the situation maps and front reports. The reserves of the Army Group were spent. The fast divisions were badly mauled from ceaseless engagement. The infantry complement of the main defensive line, both at Eighth Army and at First Panzer Army on its left, was exceedingly thin on the ground. Only between the Dnieper estuary and Shepetovka was there anything like a continuous front left. From there to the Pripet marshes was a gap of over fifty miles, guarded by a single weak army corps, the Nuremberg XIII Corps under General Hauffe. His was the heavy responsibility of guarding the strategically vital strip of firm ground south of the Pripet marshes so as to bar it to the Russians. The threat at this point had been acute for several months, ever since the Soviet Thirteenth Army had got across the "wet triangle" between Dnieper and Pripet in mid-November.

Hauffe, a competent General Staff officer, had succeeded in slowing down the Soviet advance but had been unable to halt it. Now the Russians were on the strip of land in the Rovno area, hard in front of the old Polish frontier, in the strength of six armies. They were threatening the important railway centre of Kovel on the western edge of the swampy region, and a strike against Manstein's northern wing seemed imminent.

The Field-Marshal was viewing this dangerous development with anxiety. From his visits to the front of LIX Army Corps, which was under the command of his former chief of staff, Lieutenant-General Schulz, he knew how overstretched the formations were in the most forward strongpoints. Time and again he had warned the Führer's Headquarters. He had repeatedly asked for reinforcements and had proposed the assembly of an army behind the threatened Rovno area.

But Hitler had merely shrugged his shoulders: "Where am I to find an army?" So again it had all been a case of improvisation. Fourth Panzer Army, commanded by the Austrian Panzer General Raus since Hoth's dismissal, had taken over around Ternopol. First Panzer Army, in turn, had been moved into the area east of Shepetovka. All Manstein could do now to avert the threatening danger of envelopment was to weaken his own central sector by withdrawing strong armoured forces and positioning them behind the northern wing of his Army Group so as to be prepared for the worst at that spot. The "Leibstandarte Adolf Hitler" SS Panzer Division was assembled in the area south of Shepetovka, the 1st, 6th, and 16th Panzer Divisions were assembled on the Bug, and the 11th Panzer Division was pulled out.

So far so good. But these makeshift measures gave rise to a fresh danger—the withdrawal of more than half of the armour from Eighth Army further weakened that already weak force. And Eighth Army was just then faced by those Soviet armies of the Second Ukrainian Front which Konev had concentrated against the Korsun pocket and which, following a short period of rest, were now again ready for attack. Six armies! Wöhler, on the other hand, had next to no tanks and was moreover short of those six and a half divisions lost at Cherkassy. These facts spoke for themselves.

Konev, in consequence, had a very real chance of reaching that tempting objective of Bessarabia and Rumania. Yet it would have been so easy to hold that line if Hitler had deployed the available forces more effectively.

At no other period of the war in Russia had the Soviet strategic intentions been so manifest. The enemy's concentration of forces, as well as geography and politics, revealed the Soviets' plans clearly. Deserters and prisoners supplied the last details.

This is shown by an interesting document. At the beginning of March Reinhard Gehlen, then a colonel in the General Staff, produced an assessment of the situation in which the Russian intentions were clearly outlined. On the strength of espionage and reconnaissance data Gehlen analysed STAVKA's plans with great accuracy. He reported: The Russians are ready to mount a pincer operation against the German southern wing. For that purpose they will shortly get their First Ukrainian Front to launch a large-scale attack against our LIX Corps south of the Pripet marshes in order to strike towards Poland. Simultaneously they will wheel southwards towards the Dnestr, to turn the German southern wing. Konev's Second Ukrainian Front will strike

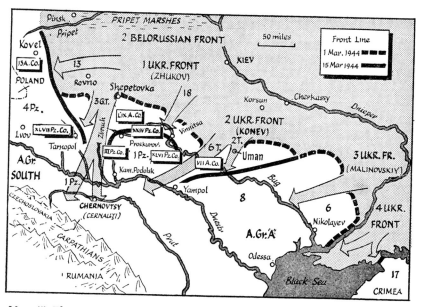

Map 45. The moment of danger on the German southern wing in the spring of 1944: Soviet forces thrusting towards the Carpathians, surrounding First Panzer Army. Only one loophole remained: in the south, on the Dnestr. But Manstein ordered: Break out to the west.

from the Zvenigorodka area to break through the weakened Eighth Army, thrust towards Rumania, and in co-operation with the First Ukrainian Front encircle the forces of our First and Fourth Panzer Armies which are still east of the Dnestr.

That was Gehlen's assessment.

But Hitler refused to acknowledge these manifest dangers. He was deaf to all proposals and placed his hope in the spring mud which, he believed, would paralyse all large-scale operations.

But the Russian "General Mud" did not feel he owed any obedience to Hitler and took his time. Snow and rain alternated, and temperatures fluctuated around freezing point, with the result that enemy movements, especially at night and in the morning, were by no means greatly impeded.

There was a mood of dejection at the Wolfsschanze. How was Hitler to be persuaded to make forces available for clearing up such a disastrous situation?

Zeitzler, the Chief of the General Staff of Land Forces, employed every trick he knew. Cunningly he would ask Hitler: "Supposing you were a Russian, my Führer, what would you do now?" The logical answer, the one which Zeitzler expected, was: "Attack". But Hitler sulkily replied: "Nothing at all!" That was against all reason, and Hitler knew it as well as Zeitzler. But with his "nothing at all" he was trying to cover up his bankruptcy. He did not want to yield an inch of soil. The Crimea? Must be held. Norway? Must be held. Hungary? Must be occupied. Italy? Must be defended. France? Nothing to be moved out from there—on the contrary, forces should be moved in to be ready for the invasion.

Hitler wanted to defend everything. He forgot the wisdom of Frederick the Great of Prussia, who had said: "He that would defend everything will defend nothing." Hitler insisted on his strategy of "fortified centres", and demanded the fanatical defence of these centres which he personally chose. He believed that such breakwaters could halt the Russian flood, in the manner of Kolberg in 1807.

It was on the morning of 4th March, 1944, a Saturday, that Adolf Hitler was proved terribly wrong. The First Ukrainian Front, Stalin's most powerful Army Group, attacked Manstein's left wing. The blow was directed by Marshal Zhukov. He had succeeded General Vatutin at the end of February, after Vatutin had been attacked and seriously wounded by Ukrainian irregulars. Vatutin, that dynamic Soviet general, died on 15th April. He was one of the best and one of the few modern commanders ever produced by the Red Army's academies. Now this outstanding general had faded out at a crucial point in the war. His place was taken by Zhukov, Stalin's intimate and until then the Soviet High Command's plenipotentiary and co-ordinator at the focal points of the fighting. This energetic and tough marshal was from now onward to impress his personality on all major military events on the Eastern Front.

The battle began. A savage battle between the Pripet and the Carpathians. The Soviet Thirteenth Army struck at General Hauffe's XIII Corps and dislodged its weak infantry forces in hard fighting. To the south of it, Zhukov with four armies struck at General Schulz's LIX Corps. With an infernal bombardment he hammered its positions and eventually ripped open the German front. Between the furiously resisting strongpoints of 7th Panzer Division and past the positions of 96th and 291st Infantry Divisions, the combat group of the Russian Tank Armies poured south-westwards through the gaping front. The "Leibstandarte" SS Panzer Division, employed for an immediate counterattack, was unable to prevent a deep penetration. Twelve hours later Zhukov raced his Eighteenth Army through the thirty-mile gap.

Thus the German Fourth Panzer Army was cut in two. The formations of XIII Army Corps were forced towards the west and north-west, while the 96th and 291st Infantry Divisions of LIX Army Corps were forced back on the sector of First Panzer Army.

But now Manstein's careful preparations were paying off. The two Panzer corps assembled behind his northern wing—the III under Breith and the XLVIII under Balck—were on the scene in time to prevent the worst. Balck intercepted the smashed German formations and fell back step by step towards Ternopol. The 7th Panzer Division, the "Leibstandarte" SS Panzer Division, and parts of 68th Infantry Division formed hedgehogs. Breith's III Panzer Corps sealed off enemy penetrations. The pierced LIX Corps managed to fight its way back under cover of a counter-attack by the bulk of 1st Panzer Division and the Heavy Panzer Regiment Bäke. But the price had now to be paid for the saving of the northern wing. It was paid by Eighth Army.

At first light on 5th March more than 1000 guns and mortars hammered its left wing in the Uman area. Then came Konev's armies of the Second Ukrainian Front—with 415 tanks and 247 guns on self-propelled carriages. General Wöhler had nothing to oppose this armada effectively. He was overrun. His armies were ripped to pieces. Five days later Konev's tanks stormed the fiercely defended town of Uman. They thrust through to the Bug. With a truly amazing skill at improvisation they crossed the river, even though it had burst its banks, and continued to race towards the Dnestr.

Simultaneously two more Soviet Guards Armies, the Fifth and the Seventh, mounted their attack on the lower Dnieper against Hollidt's Sixth Army, tied down its forces, and thus prevented Wöhler from receiving any help from that quarter. Every move was co-ordinated with every other, as indeed predicted by Colonel Reinhard Gehlen in his analysis of secret intelligence material.

On 16th March Konev cut the vital railway line between Lvov and

Odessa. Thus the principal supply route of the German southern wing was paralysed. By 17th March Konev's strike groups had crossed the 275-yard-wide Dnestr, the last Russian river before the Carpathians, and were simultaneously wheeling north-west to envelop the German First Panzer Army. Disaster was approaching at an uncanny speed. On 26th March Russian advance guards crossed the Rumanian frontier. The Red Army was stepping on the soil of south-east Europe.

Things were not going quite so fast for Zhukov as they were for Konev. The German armoured formations offered stubborn resistance to the armies of the First Ukrainian Front. The 1st Panzer Division succeeded in freeing the formations of 96th and 291st Infantry Divisions which had been forced back towards the south-east. Colonel Charly Neumeister, the well-known Austrian steeplechaser, with a battalion of the Weimar 1st Panzer Grenadier Regiment and with men taken straight off leave trains, defended Staro-Konstantinov with an obstinacy that made the Russians despair. But this did not change the fact that the front of LIX Corps was torn wide open between Shepetovka and Rovno.

The III Panzer Corps managed for the time being to hold the Bug by means of flexible defence. Armoured forces and infantry of LIX Corps at the last moment prevented a western envelopment of the forces falling back via Proskurov. But the fierce fighting for Staro-Konstantinov, Proskurov, and Gorodok could not change the situation. The endless crocodile of Soviet infantry and armour pushed on to the south through the mud and over the tributaries of the Dnestr.

On 29th March Zhukov forced the Dnestr and took the ancient Bukovina town of Cernauti, now known as Chernovtsy. His units were now on a broad front in the rear of Army Group South. From the east the spearheads of Konev's Second Ukrainian Front were approaching his own spearheads.

The nightmare which had been pursuing Manstein for a year and which he had been hoping to avert had now become reality. This was the catastrophe. The Fourth Panzer Army was ripped open and forced back to the west. The Eighth Army was smashed. The Sixth Army on the lower Dnieper was isolated and in several places pierced by Malinovskiy's armies of the Third Ukrainian Front. Worst of all, General Hube's First Panzer Army was trapped in a huge pocket between Bug and Dnestr, separated from the bulk of Fourth Panzer Army by a gap of over 50 miles. If the surrounded 22 divisions, which included the best Panzer divisions, suffered the fate of Stalingrad then nothing on earth could save the 500-mile-long southern front. The dam would burst and the Red Army would stream westwards, unopposed. Stalin was on the point of achieving his great triumph, of attaining the objective he had been steadily pursuing ever since Stalingrad. And Adolf Hitler had been his best ally.

His persistently excessive demands on the troops in the field, his stubborn hold-on orders, his fatal insistence on defending every inch of soil—all these had sapped the strength of the Eastern Front. Most of the divisions had completely burnt themselves out in the unremitting battles since the opening of "Citadel". Now the account was being presented.

This was the most exciting phase of the war. It held the secret of the German defeat, but it also revealed the tragic fact that on the Eastern Front there was a German general, tried in a hundred battles, who might have brought about a turn in military developments. At this black hour between Bug and Dnestr he once more proved his genius—for the last time. That too made this phase one of the great chapters of the Second World War.

On 23rd March Manstein, from his headquarters in Lvov—or Lemberg, as the Germans called it—asked Hitler for the speedy dispatch of reinforcements so that the connection could be re-established with the encircled First Panzer Army.

This army could now only be supplied from the air. But Manstein had had unfortunate experiences with supplies from the air. Stalingrad was one deterrent example. And the problems were no easier on the Dnestr. Blizzards were raging during the last week of March; moreover, as part of the withdrawal of the fighting formations, the airfields had to be moved almost every day. General Hube had already given orders for all superfluous ballast to be jettisoned so that every drop of fuel could be used for tanks and self-propelled guns. What mattered most at this moment of crisis was to keep the forces mobile, even at the cost of sacrificing *matériel*, base supplies, and staff files.

In this way Hube succeeded in maintaining mobility. By means of ceaseless German attacks the Russians were repulsed time and again, and their attempts at envelopment in the north and north-west were foiled. All this was achieved even though supply difficulties imposed the strictest economy even with small-arms ammunition. But, of course, this could not go on indefinitely.

The situation demanded one important decision to be taken speedily: when was the break-out to be made, and where to? Once again a vitally necessary decision by the Führer turned into a drama. For several days now Hitler had been conducting operations in all theatres of war from Berchtesgaden. With his closest staff of collaborators he was sitting in his Eagle's Nest at the Berghof. His gaze was turned south. There a crisis was looming. The European southern wing was rumbling—behind the lines of Germany's allies, in Bulgaria, in Rumania, and above all in Hungary. Germany's allies were getting restive. They sensed the approaching disaster.

On 24th March the reply to Manstein's demand came from the Berghof: The First Panzer Army will hold its front on the Bug and will re-establish its severed rearward communications by its own efforts.

The Field-Marshal in Lvov shook with anger as he read the order. This was Stalingrad all over again, this was the road to disaster. He immediately had a telephone communication made with the Berghof, over a special line with a scrambler to prevent tapping. The time was 1300 hours. General Zeitzler answered the call.

Manstein began: "The order to hold on and simultaneously to seal the big gap between First and Fourth Panzer Armies is unrealizable. Please inform the Führer that I shall give First Panzer Army the order to break out unless I have his binding assurance by 1500 hours that reinforcements will be sent to me."

It was an ultimatum. It was a clear threat of insubordination by a Field-Marshal *vis-à-vis* his Supreme Commander.

1500 hours. No answer from the Berghof.

The minutes ticked away. They ticked away against First Panzer Army and for Zhukov.

1530 hours. The chief of operations of Army Group South was formulating the preliminary order to First Panzer Army to break out. The objective of First Panzer Army had already been changed the previous day and General Hube had been ordered to restore connection with Fourth Panzer Army on the Seret. In plain language this meant: "Get ready to move off to the west."

1600 hours. A telephone message from the Berghof. An officer of the Operations Section had this to announce: The Führer agrees to First Panzer Army re-establishing its westward links, but he still demands that it should generally hold its entire front as hitherto.

When General Busse passed on the message to the Field-Marshal, Manstein observed coldly: "That's an elastic reply. Break out and hold at the same time. I'd like to know how that's to be done."

Busse nodded. "It's his attitude at Stalingrad all over again." Busse was right. Then too, in December 1942, Hitler had eventually agreed to authorize a break-out of Sixth Army provided it would simultaneously hold Stalingrad and its positions on the Volga. Because of this unrealizable condition the rescue of Sixth Army had proved impossible. Was this catastrophe now to be repeated with First Panzer Army? Manstein was firmly determined at all costs to oppose any such thing.

He got himself put through to Zeitzler once more. He said to the Chief of the General Staff: "The Führer's order is unrealizable. Is that really so difficult to see?"

"Not for me," Zeitzler replied. "But the Führer still does not realize the full gravity of the situation."

"Is that so?" said Manstein. "In that case I'll take whatever measures the situation demands."

By teleprinter signal No. 58683/10 at 1735 hours on 24th March,

Manstein transmitted to First Panzer Army the preliminary order for a breakthrough to the west. Half an hour later Hitler had been informed of the order. But he did not hurl his anathema at Manstein. At 1900 hours he summoned his Chief ADC Schmundt: "Send an urgent signal to Manstein to come here tomorrow to report on the situation." And Schmundt sent the Field-Marshal an urgent signal, received at Lvov at 1930 hours: The Führer orders Field-Marshal von Manstein to report to him at the Berghof tomorrow, 25th March.

The large window of Hitler's sitting-room at the Berghof turned the panelled room into an open stage. There was a long view across the Berchtesgaden landscape. On this stage Manstein was about to cross swords with Adolf Hitler. Here, in front of the primeval backdrop of the mountains, a battle was about to be fought in which the rescue or destruction of twenty-two divisions, or more than 200,000 men, were at stake.

Colonel Schulze-Büttger spread out the maps on the big map table by the window. Manstein explained the situation. With convincing logic he developed his demand: The First Panzer Army will thrust westwards with its armoured forces, through the two Soviet armies in the rear of the southern front, and so regain contact with Fourth Panzer Army. To achieve this, it must pull back its eastern and north-eastern fronts. However, with the forces available, this operation can succeed only if Fourth Panzer Army thrusts eastwards to meet the forces of First Panzer Army half-way along their break-out route. After all, nearly fifty miles of enemy-controlled country would have to be covered. For that purpose the Fourth Panzer Army, at present engaged in hard fighting in the Ternopol area, would have to receive fresh reinforcements amounting to at least one Panzer corps.

Hitler had listened in silence, his palms resting on the map table. Now he straightened up. He snapped at Manstein: "And where am I to find reinforcements for Fourth Panzer Army? In France, the invasion is imminent—I can't spare a single battalion from there. In Hungary, Horthy's unreliable attitude makes it necessary to hold the country in military occupation, and I can't take a single regiment away from there without running the risk of some political dirty business with Horthy jumping off our wagon. And since you yourself say that the break-out can succeed only if Fourth Panzer Army thrusts eastwards with fresh forces, the whole thing's pointless. First Panzer Army remains where it is, and must clear up its rear by its own efforts. There's no other choice."

Hitler barked these sentences out hard and fast. Now that he was in a temper he unleashed a whole avalanche of accusations against the Field-Marshal—about his using up his reserves, about his continuous demands for the formation of focal points and for evasive operations.

"You keep on wanting to operate. And all that happens is that you are falling back farther and farther."

Manstein turned purple. A shiver ran through those present. The great clash was about to take place. The Field-Marshal accepted the challenge. Icily, but with deliberate calm, he said: "You, my Führer, are to be blamed for what has happened. For eight months you have been presenting our forces on the southern wing with one strategically insoluble task after another. To cope with them you have granted me neither adequate reinforcements nor freedom of movement. If you had done so, you would not now be lamenting the disastrous situation. Responsibility for it lies at your door entirely."

Before Hitler could pull himself together and answer him, Manstein continued: "But no post-mortem now can change the situation. I must give First Panzer Army the order to break out this very day—otherwise it is lost. I'm asking for your agreement."

Before Zeitzler could intervene Hitler turned on his heel. On the way out he said: "I cannot agree with you. We'll discuss the other problems at the evening conference." He left the room. He left behind him an atmosphere of excitement. Calmly Manstein walked out into the small conservatory. He stepped up to General Schmundt, Hitler's ADC and military confidant, and said: "Kindly inform the Führer that he should entrust someone else with the command of the Army Group —if he finds he cannot agree with my views." He buckled up his belt. He put on his cap. He walked out.

Manstein was staying at the Berchtesgadener Hof Hotel. He had no sooner got to his room than the telephone rang. It was General Busse ringing from Lvov. After his argument with Hitler he was now to have trouble with General Hube. This outstanding one-armed commander-in-chief of First Panzer Army had been pestering Army Group, demanding permission to break out—not, however, to the west, but to the south, across the Dnestr, where along a line of roughly sixty miles the side of the pocket was formed only by the river and weak Soviet reconnaissance forces.

Hube had valid reasons for wanting to slip out of the trap towards the south, contrary to his original plan. As recently as 24th March he had given orders, in line with Manstein's concept, for a westward break-out north of the Dnestr, while the fronts towards the north and the east were to be covered. But on 25th March the situation took a turn for the worse. A deep enemy penetration south-west of Proskurov had made rapid headway towards the south and cut off parts of LIX Corps as well as III Panzer Corps. Kamenets Podolskiy and Khotin were threatened, and the westward withdrawal roads were blocked by the enemy.

The C-in-C First Panzer Army and his chief of staff, Colonel Carl Wagener, were unanimous—the changed situation had deprived the

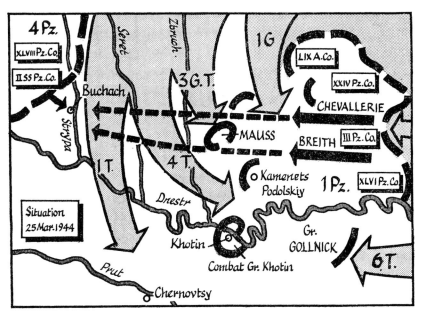

Map 46. Marshal Zhukov expected the First Panzer Army to break out towards the south, over the Dnestr. He therefore moved his main forces south to intercept Hube there. But the German corps struck to the west. Zhukov realized his mistake too late.

Army of its freedom of action. Now that the forces freed in the north had to be employed to cope with the threat south of Kamenets Podolskiy a breakthrough towards the west seemed too dangerous. A weighing-up of all possibilities suggested that the lesser risk was a withdrawal to the south, where all engineer battalions and bridge-building columns were already assembled on the Dnestr. These were the points which Hube had explained over the telephone to Manstein's chief of staff Busse, and which Busse was now passing on to the Field-Marshal in Berchtesgaden.

Of course it was a tempting idea to pull back the encircled army across the still open Dnestr, without costly fighting. More tempting, certainly, than a break-out to the west, where half a dozen rivers and two Soviet crack armies would have to be tackled. The break-out to the south was certainly the lesser risk. And Hube knew only too well the risks associated with breaking through a strong enemy. The tragedy of Cherkassy had taken place right under the eyes of First Panzer Army. Hube did not want his divisions to face that kind of disaster: that was why he was urgently demanding Manstein's immediate approval of a break-out to the south.

What Hube was not able to judge correctly was the overall development of the situation. If his Army were to fall back to the south, the gap between it and Fourth Panzer Army would become enormous and the Russians would at last have a clear run all the way to Galicia. All they would have to do was keep moving.

And what would First Panzer Army have gained? Nothing. By 25th March Zhukov's and Konev's armoured spearheads were already south of the Dnestr. The main parts of the First and Second Ukrainian Fronts were being brought up in forced marches.

Thus, First Panzer Army would escape encirclement north of the Dnestr but would be walking straight into another encirclement, in an even more dangerous pocket whose rear would be formed by the pathless Carpathians.

Manstein realized that danger. More important, he saw the strategic necessity of not allowing the gap between First and Fourth Panzer Armies to get any wider. What would be the use of the escape of First Panzer Army into the exitless slopes of the Carpathians if the Russians were thereby to gain an unimpeded advance through Galicia to Breslau and Prague?

No—Hube had to break out to the west. His route must lie straight through the two Soviet Armies which were moving south. This would entail fighting, but apart from the army's rescue it would produce the strategic advantage that Zhukov's armies would, for their part, be penetrated, cut off from their rearward communications, and paralysed. The rescue of First Panzer Army was to become, at the same time, the basis for a general clearing up of the situation. That was Manstein's plan.

The Field-Marshal has been accused that this plan was a gamble. Such criticism underestimates Manstein as a strategist. He never confused boldness with gambling, or shrewdness with recklessness. Army Group not only saw the need for a westward thrust but had moreover made sure that such a thrust had a realistic chance of success.

A decisive factor in ordering First Panzer Army to break out westwards north of the Dnestr, apart from strategic considerations, was the picture which Army Group possessed of the enemy's dispositions. Manstein was in the fortunate position of knowing Zhukov's intentions down to the last detail. Colonel von Blumröder, the Army Group intelligence officer, was listening in to the headquarters of the Soviet Armies which had broken through the German lines. Blumröder's monitoring staff had discovered the frequencies of the Russian forward transmitters and broken the code of the Army Staffs. Blumröder thus read all orders and reports of the Soviet First and Fourth Tank Armies in the breakthrough area south of Ternopol. The monitored signals revealed the movements, daily objectives, and, above all, the strength of the Red formations.

To complete their good fortune, Blumröder's men also succeeded in listening in to the quartermaster signals of Zhukov's First and Fourth Tank Armies and in decoding them. As a result, Manstein learnt as much about those two armies as Marshal Zhukov himself. Twice a day Manstein's HQ was kept accurately informed about the number of battleworthy enemy tanks possessed by each Red tank brigade. It was an ideal form of reconnaissance. Manstein, to all intents and purposes, was sitting at Zhukov's map-table.

Here was another illustration of where the most important and the most reliable sources of information are to be found in modern war— sources whose quantity and quality must make any agent or master spy go green with envy. Quite apart from the immediacy and speed with which such information crosses the frontiers! No master spy could compete with that technique. Manstein was in a superb position.

Zhukov commanded: First Tank Army will thrust to the Dnestr in the direction of Chernovtsy. "Good," acknowledged Manstein. Zhukov's next order was: Fourth Tank Army will wait until its infantry divisions have moved up. "Better still." It was now clear that the weak point of the Russians was north of the upper Dnestr, on the sector of the Soviet Fourth Tank Army—so long as its infantry had not yet caught up.

One other thing that emerged from the enemy's radio traffic was that Zhukov was firmly counting on a German break-out to the south across the unguarded area on the Dnestr bank. In fact he positively wanted to induce Hube to make just that move and had planned his own operations accordingly. But Manstein had no intention of doing Zhukov this favour. That was why, in spite of all Hube's arguments, Manstein gave orders for a westward break-out.

In Berchtesgaden on 25th March, as the Field-Marshal and his chief of staff were once more going over their notes of Busse's telephone message, Schulze-Büttger remarked: "One ought to explain our reasons to Hube in detail. Maybe someone should fly out to the pocket."

Manstein shook his head. "There's no time. No doubt Busse will have given Hube and Wagener a sufficiently clear idea of why we reject their assessment of the situation and why the withdrawal must be towards the west and on no account towards the south."

Towards 1930 hours the Field-Marshal once more set out for the Berghof, with a heavy heart.

"There's spring in the air," Schulze-Büttger attempted a conversation in the car. The Field-Marshal glanced up to the snow-capped mountains. Spring? Back east, where the fate of First Panzer Army now hung in the balance, winter had returned for a number of days, with icy winds, blizzards, and cutting cold. Would he succeed in leading Hube's divisions out of the white hell of Kamenets Podolskiy? Manstein did some mental calculations:

Just then the troops must be in process of regrouping in order to break out westwards in two parallel corps groups, to the Seret and the Strypa, as soon as the code-word was given. Manstein had the whole disposition in his head. It was a good plan. General Hube, the man who had stormed Stalingrad, was one of the most intrepid commanders in the field. And the troops themselves were ready for anything. It must be possible to get them out. Manstein was smiling. He felt good. In his mind he was making the moves which Hube would make: XLVI Panzer Corps holds the southern front of the pocket and repulses all Soviet attempts at envelopment. The III and XXIV Panzer Corps, as well as the LIX Army Corps, disengage step by step, and in two big wedges thrust through to the west to the Seret and then to the Strypa. There they should be met by the German relief thrust of First Panzer Army. That was how it must be done.

As General Schmundt, Hitler's chief ADC, welcomed the Marshal on the front steps of the Berghof he handed him a teleprinter message which had arrived a few minutes previously from General Busse in Lvov: First Panzer Army was again requesting "authority for break-out south". Hube had addressed the application to Army Group Head-quarters at 1920. The final sentence of the message ran: "Break-out west impossible for reasons of terrain."

Hube's reference was not only to the four major rivers running from north to south, but also to the fact that the Russians were in firm control of the main withdrawal highway and that the situation on the northern front of the pocket had further worsened owing to a deep enemy penetration. Forces earmarked for the break-out to the west had now to be employed to contain the Russians. The spectre of Stalingrad!

General Hube, as Busse now informed Manstein, had already sent his corps the preliminary orders for a break-out to the south and had cancelled the earlier directives for a westerly break-out. As soon as the code word "Litzmann" was issued the operation was to start. And Hube was now asking the Field-Marshal for his authority to issue the signal "Litzmann" at once.

Manstein read the urgent message in silence. He then passed it on to Schulze-Büttger. Without a word he followed Schmundt into the big room where Hitler was talking to Keitel by the fireplace.

As Manstein raised his hand in salute Hitler walked over to him with a smile and cordially welcomed him. There was nothing left now of his icy obstinacy. Hitler seemed a changed person. He said: "Manstein, I've thought the whole business over and I agree with your plan to let First Panzer Army break out to the west. With a heavy heart I have also decided to let Fourth Panzer Army have the II SS Panzer Corps with 9th and 10th SS Panzer Divisions from France, as well as 367th Infantry Division and the 100th Jäger Division from

Hungary. I'm transferring these formations at once so that Hube can be met by a counter-thrust in the area south-west of Ternopol."

Manstein listened in amazement. And with relief. He had won the day. Hitler had given in all along the line. He had yielded to reason. Of course, Manstein did not yet know the price which the Führer would exact from him for his victory. Manstein was wise enough not to show his triumph. He fell in with the pretence that the decision was the result of Hitler's careful consideration. The Field-Marshal now explained to Hitler the details of his break-out. The rescue of the twenty-two divisions was revealed as an integral part of the new strategic concept. Its objective was the restoration of a stable front between the Carpathians and Pripet marshes by means of First Panzer Army and the reinforced Fourth Panzer Army. Eighth Army must be moved alongside the Sixth Army of Army Group "A", as a shield to protect Rumania. The Carpathian passes must be held by the Hungarian Army. If this plan succeeded the main danger would be averted.

But for the moment everything depended on First Panzer Army getting out of its mortal stranglehold. It must break out to the west. Not, as Hube was planning, disengage towards the south. Forty minutes after midnight, at the end of a long day in Hitler's mountain fortress, Manstein had a signal sent to Hube: "Western alternative. Order follows. Manstein." The die was cast.

At 0250 hours Schulze-Büttger, Manstein's chief of operations, transmitted the final order to First and Fourth Panzer Armies by teleprinter. It was also sent to Eighth Army, for information. The great adventure was now set in motion—the transfer of an entire encircled army, still fighting, over a distance of some sixty miles to the west, straight through two enemy tank armies and across four major rivers.

It was long past midnight when Manstein, tired after his day's battle with Hitler, was driven down the hairpin bends from the Berghof to Berchtesgaden. On the following morning he flew back to Lvov. A few hours later he was with Fourth Panzer Army, at General Raus's headquarters. There, the relief attack towards the Seret was already being planned. True, Raus was rather worried about the surrounded garrison of Ternopol, but mounting the big blow was more important now.

Inside the pocket preparations were also going ahead for the break-out. General Dessloch's Fourth Air Fleet was making continuous supply runs. General Morzik, in charge of the transport planes, commanded these missions. On 26th and 27th March things were still a little uneven. But after that all went smoothly—fuel, ammunition, and foodstuffs were flown in and the wounded were flown out.

Zhukov's strong forces meanwhile were waiting for Hube south of Kamenets Podolskiy on the Dnestr. There, Zhukov intended to intercept the German formations if—as he believed they would—they tried to fall back over the Dnestr. And what a reception he had laid on for them! The remnants of the German southern front would be chased into the Carpathians. It was a clever plan. Except that the Germans were not going to oblige him.

But Zhukov was sure of himself. He switched his First Tank Army to the southern bank of the Dnestr with all its mobile corps. He attacked Chernovtsy, Kolomyya, and Stanislas. Thus, expecting a German break-out to the south—he committed his strong forces far away from the pocket. That was a disastrous mistake. When he needed them in the north, in the decisive theatre of operations, they were no longer available.

General Hube and his chief of staff, Colonel Wagener, meanwhile were sitting in a peasant hut at Dunayevtsy, north-east of Kamenets Podolskiy. They realized that things were not going too badly. Group Mauss with its three divisions had already very nearly linked up with Fourth Panzer Army. The 1st Panzer Division was continuing to hold the corner-post of Gorodok. The LIX Corps had gained the Frampol-Yarmolintsy area. The 17th Panzer Division was attacking Kamenets Podolskiy. Aerial supplies were working smoothly. Inside the pocket the commander of the transport planes had organized his so-called pocket parties—four men with all the equipment needed for laying out landing strips and dropping areas. They had everything necessary —radio beacons, emergency flare-path lights, and signal flares of all kinds. Each day, according to the army's movement, they reconnoitred landing strips and dropping areas. Things had changed since Stalingrad. The operation now was based on organization and not just on empty promises.

Hube and Wagener knew all that. But they also knew that the to-ing and fro-ing of break-out preparations—one moment to the west and the next to the south—had unnerved the troops. It was important now to restore their confidence. And so, during the night of 27th–28th March, the following signal was sent to all units in the pocket: "First Panzer Army will fight its way through the enemy and defeat him wherever he is encountered." That was the right note—a slogan for the troops.

Army had formed two break-out groups. The northern one, Corps Group von der Chevallerie, was to cover the northern flank, establish a bridge-head across the Zbruch by concentrating its forces, and then gain the main crossings over the Seret and keep them open. The southern break-out wedge, Corps Group Breith, was to dislodge the enemy in the Kamenets Podolskiy area and break out over the Zbruch at Okopy.

The grenadiers' "artillery": the *Panzerfaust,* a bazooka-type anti-tank weapon.
On the bank of the Dnieper. On the far side are the Russians.

Like a phantom hunt the advanced combat groups of the northern break-out wedge charged towards the Zbruch on 29th March. Advanced detachments of the Westphalian 16th and the Thuringian 7th Panzer Divisions steamrollered all enemy resistance. The 1st Panzer Division, pulled out of the front behind them, took over the rearguard of XXIV Panzer Corps.

The offensive also went well for the southern group. General von der Meden's 17th Panzer Division and the 371st Infantry Division thrust to the south-west. The East Prussian 1st Infantry Division and the Baden-Württemberg 101st Jäger Division acted as the rearguard of XLVI Panzer Corps, together with parts of "Das Reich" SS Panzer Division, and pinned down the northern wing of Konev's Second Ukrainian Front. The pocket was on the move. It changed its shape. The procedure of Cherkassy was repeated—the original north–south axis was turned to run east–west. What to the trooper in his combat group, in his platoon, or in his company must have seemed complete chaos or unplanned improvisation, was in fact on the situation map a miracle of strategic co-ordination. A testimony to skilful leadership at the top and perfect discipline lower down.

The initial success was encouraging. The Corps Group Chevallerie established some bridge-heads across the Zbruch—one at Skala even with an intact bridge. The first phase of taking the enemy by surprise had come off. It had come off because Zhukov had not closed his ring tightly enough in the west. And the reason why he had not closed it tightly was his firm belief that Hube would break out to the south. When the Marshal realized his mistake it was too late. He only managed to switch a single tank corps from the southern bank of the Dnestr into the decisive battle of the break-out operation, towards the flank of First Panzer Army. It was not enough.

In vain did Zhukov rant over the telephone at the corps commanders of his First Tank Army: "About-turn, back again to the north!" But weather and road conditions also operated against the Russians. It was not possible to bring enough forces over to the northern bank of the Dnestr again to block the crossings of the Zbruch and the Seret effectively or in time. Zhukov's measures came too late.

In this situation Zhukov tried to compensate for his disastrous error by a piece of poor and clumsy psychological warfare. Perhaps a trick would give him victory after all. The Marshal must have been very angry or surrounded by very bad advisers to expect any success from his venture. On 2nd April at 1000 hours, XLVI Panzer Corps, III Panzer Corps, and many divisional HQs in the pocket received an open

20th November, 1943: Zhitomir is recaptured.
Partisans being sworn in: solemnly they undertake to fight to the last drop of blood.

signal in German—at least the words were German—to the following effect:

(1)   In order not to make further sacrifice I propose you to finish pointless resistance to end of 2nd April and to capitulate with supporting units. You are encircled in all side, hope is pointless. You cannot get out of pocket.

(2)   If you not capitulate by end of 2nd April 44 then of all soldier who accept not this offer of ending pointless resistance every third will be shot. This is punishment for pointless resistance. You surrender in groups, you are encircled in three ring. All officer what stop resistance voluntarily will keep old rifle, decoration, and transport.

Zhukov, Commander of the Front and Marshal of
the Soviet Union.

The German commanders had barely recovered from their amazement at this barbarous piece of nonsense when at 1300 hours a supplementary signal arrived from the Russians. Evidently some linguistically more qualified advisers had been informed of Zhukov's panic action and had somehow brushed up the quaint double-Dutch of the original signal. The new signal ran:

At 1100 hours a distorted translation was transmitted of the following proposal by the Commander of the Front, Marshal of the Soviet Union Zhukov. It should read as follows: German soldiers and officers who lay down their arms voluntarily may expect good treatment. Only those commanders will be shot, and moreover in front of their units, who, though the Marshal's offer is addressed to them, refuse to cease their pointless resistance by this evening. They will be shot as a punishment for pointlessly shedding the blood of the troops entrusted to them.

Zhukov, Commander of the Front and Marshal of
the Soviet Union.

The signal now was linguistically unexceptionable but still highly questionable in terms of usages of war. In point of fact, the threat heightened rather than weakened the fighting spirit of the German troops.

A blizzard was sweeping the land between Dnestr and Seret. The roads were blocked by drifts. But the spirit of the troops was indestructible. Of course, there was some cursing and short temper, and bad officers had a rough time. But the weather had one advantage—the Red Air Force did not turn up, or only occasionally. All the more impressive was the achievement of the German Luftwaffe which, in spite of the weather, kept up its supply missions. There was rarely any shortage of fuel or ammunition—the machines of General Morzik, in charge of the transport flights, brought in sufficient supplies night after night. Night after night, because that was when they made their runs. At night visibility was better and at night there were no Soviet fighters about. The Soviets were not in a position to put up night fighters.

However, not a crumb of food was flown in. That the troops had to find for themselves. They had to live off the land and on the army's resources. The latter also included the unfortunate horses, nearly all of which had to be killed.

The 4th April was a lucky day. After a night frost the roads were frozen hard. All movements went smoothly. All the divisions received adequate supplies of ammunition and fuel. Aerial supplies were working perfectly. The rearguards of Corps Group Breith were already falling back to the Zbruch. The 1st Panzer Division was making good headway with its attacks. The 7th Panzer Division was thrusting towards the important road from Chortkov to Buchach.

"No sign of the relief thrust?" the soldiers and officers were asking. No sign as yet on the 4th. But the staffs had already received a signal from Army Group, setting out exactly how the link-up with the relief forces of Fourth Panzer Army was to be accomplished at Buchach on the Strypa. Corps Group Chevallerie would bar the Seret to the enemy at Chortkov and cover the northern flank west of the river. Strong advanced formations were to seize the Chortkov–Buchach road and keep it open. Meanwhile, the Corps Group Breith would gain the crossings over the Strypa and open up the crossing at Buchach from the south. In order to protect the southern flank, the Dnestr crossings would be blocked and the bridge blown.

The plan succeeded. It sounds easy enough. But behind the success of the plan lay a vast amount of work and fighting. The anonymous heroism of a modern battle of annihilation has nothing romantic about it. The achievement of the men at the time makes one shudder when reading about it today.

Major Udo von Alvensleben, the intelligence officer on the staff of 16th Panzer Division, describes in his diary the coup by which 1st Panzer Division seized two sixty-ton bridges over the Seret on 2nd April.

It was like the old days of the blitzkrieg—fast, bold, hard-hitting. But under what conditions were these deeds accomplished? Alvensleben writes: "The men have tied their soles to their uppers with string; for marching is half the victory. Food is less than meagre. A handful of snow is often the only refreshment. Worst of all is the situation of the wounded. Vehicles are available only for the serious cases; everybody else, even casualties with leg injuries, have to march along with the troops. Many give up. Many are not found again and die, alone, by the side of a muddy road or choose the grim lot of captivity." Alvensleben's picture applied to all the divisions in Hube's pocket.

On 5th April tension ran high at the HQs of First Panzer Army. Would the relief group of Fourth Panzer Army manage to break through the Soviet barrier from the west? Thirty miles was the distance it had to cover. A mere thirty miles. The II SS Panzer Corps, which Manstein had extorted from Hitler for the relief attack during his dramatic encounter at the Berghof, was moving up to meet Hube's divisions with two SS Panzer Divisions—"Frundsberg" and "Hohen-staufen"—and with 100th Jäger Division which had been put under its command. They were pushing ahead through the mud and the Russian lines. Towards midday Hube received Manstein's signal: "II SS Panzer Corps thrusting from north to west in direction Buchach, at present bridging difficulties."

Bridging difficulties. Hube swore.

Zhukov meanwhile was trying desperately to strike at the flank of Corps Group Breith with his XI Guards Tank Corps which he had raced back northwards over the Dnestr again. But things did not go well for him. Breith's Corps Group knocked out thirty-five tanks, badly mauled the corps, and threw it back over the Dnestr. This time Zhukov was the victim of "too little and too late".

The 6th April dawned after a night of frost and blizzard. The grenadiers of the Rhineland-Westphalian 6th Panzer Division were fighting their way to Buchach. The Russian brigades of Fourth Tank Army were resisting stubbornly. But the men of Major Stahl's 114th Panzer Grenadier Regiment knew that now was the time for a supreme effort. They fought like men possessed. They took the town. Hausser's divisions also knew what mattered most—not to let the enemy recover his breath, and not to let one's own momentum spend itself.

It was the 10th SS Panzer Division, the "Frundsberg" Division under Lieutenant-General von Treuenfeld, which broke the last Soviet resistance at Buchach at 1700 hours and moved into the town. Five minutes later the men of "Frundsberg" and of 6th Panzer Division were slapping each other's backs: "We've done it!" Contact with the rest of the front, severed for a fortnight, had been re-established. The pocket which held 200,000 men had been slit. Stalin's trap had been burst open.

But the man who had conceived the plan, who had broken Hitler's obstinacy, and had once more averted the great catastrophe on the southern wing, was no longer there to receive the joyful signal: "Contact re-established." Manstein had been dismissed. The best strategic brain of the German Wehrmacht had been sent into the wilderness. On 30th March Hitler had summoned him to Berchtesgaden. After pinning on him the Swords to the Knight's Cross, he informed him: "I have decided to part company with you and to appoint someone else to the Army Group." After an embarrassed pause he added: "The time for operating is over. What I need now is men who stand firm."

That was Hitler's revenge for his defeat at the Berghof on 25th March.

The time for operating was over! Hitler might as well have said: "The war is lost." For when was a war ever brought to a satisfactory conclusion without operations? Two "firm standers", the well-tried and tough defensive leaders Model and Schörner, took over from Manstein and from Field-Marshal von Kleist, who had likewise been dismissed. Model took over Manstein's command, but Army Group South was simultaneously renamed "Army Group Northern Ukraine". Schörner took over the former Army Group "A", now renamed "Army Group Southern Ukraine".

Colonel-General Hube, the C-in-C of First Panzer Army, survived his army's rescue by only a fortnight. He lost his life under tragic circumstances. Having received from Hitler the Swords to the Knight's Cross, he was killed when his aircraft crashed near Berchtesgaden. A melancholy end for a courageous officer and outstanding commander in the field.

The link-up of Buchach, of course, was only the beginning of the break-out operation proper. The combat groups of General von Waldenfels's 6th Panzer Division at Buchach were in an exposed position and had been cut off again from Breith's Corps by the headlong advance of the Soviet Fourth Tank Army. The following divisions of the corps were bogged down on the muddy roads. The "Frundsberg" Division likewise had lost contact with its corps. And 600 tons of supplies which followed Hausser's corps for First Panzer Army were still a long way back. The columns were making painfully slow progress on the terrible roads.

Zhukov did not yet give up hope of once more severing the newly restored contact between the German formations. But the fortunes of war were again on Model's side. By bold and far-ranging operations, after a regrouping of his Army Group, he succeeded not only in completing the liberation of First Panzer Army but also in stabilizing the front on the southern wing.

It must have been a big surprise for Zhukov when, right in the middle of his triumphal advance, he had crushing blows dealt to him. Breith's III Panzer Corps smashed the Soviet forces on the northern bank of the Dnestr and chased four Russian rifle divisions back over the river. The II SS Panzer Corps attacked over the Strypa, gained nearly ten miles of ground, and forced five Soviet tank corps and four rifle divisions on to the defensive north-east of Buchach.

The XXIV and XLVI Panzer Corps and the LIX Army Corps were pulled back by Model to the Strypa. In this way the First Panzer Army was again fitted into a continuous front and the biggest break-out battle of the Second World War had come to an end. Hube's army had not only been saved but was already in action again, both in defence and counter-attack. The dangerous gap north of the Dnestr had been sealed.

For the Russians this outcome of the great battle between Dnieper and Seret was a bitter disappointment. Zhukov's offensive, begun so promisingly, had got stuck. In spite of the huge superiority of the armies of his First Ukrainian Front, the Soviet Marshal not only failed to reach his objective but also suffered heavy losses during the final phase of the fighting. He had overreached himself, been to confident of victory, and underestimated the still considerable strength and military skill of the Germans. He was to take his lesson to heart.

3. The Battle in the Crimea

Politics and strategy–Forbidden evacuation–The Navy guarantees 50,000 tons–Stalin's fear of the Stukas–Seventeenth Army waits–Action at the Tartar Ditch–Codeword "Eagle"–Successful retreat to Sevastopol–"The fortress will be held"–The Sapun hills are lost–Last front on the Kherson peninsula–Everyone is waiting for the Navy–The last 10,000 men–A sorry ending.

WHOM God would destroy he first sends mad. The battle in the Crimea, the third catastrophe on the German southern wing in the spring of 1944, is the best illustration of the old adage. If anything was ever unnecessary then it was the disaster which befell the Seventeenth Army on that ill-fated peninsula in the Black Sea between 20th April and 12th May, 1944.

Until then everything had worked out moderately well on the southern flank of the Eastern Front. The Seventeenth Army had left the Asian mainland at the beginning of September 1943 as part of the general German withdrawal movement, evacuating the Kuban bridgehead and crossing over to the Crimea without appreciable losses. OKH had given the operation the code-word "Krimhild", making a punning connection between the 10,000-square-mile peninsula—whose German name is Krim—and the blonde heroine of the Nibelungen saga.

The ferrying of Seventeenth Army across the Strait of Kerch was a complete success. Over a period of 34 days naval and engineering craft transferred 227,484 German and Rumanian troops, 72,899 horses, 28,486 non-German auxiliaries and other manpower, 21,230 motor vehicles, 27,741 horse-drawn vehicles, and 1815 guns. All that was done under the eyes of the Soviet Black Sea fleet whose heavy units were lying in the Caucasian ports of Batumi and Poti but, for fear of the German Stuka *Geschwaders* did not make a single serious attempt to interfere with Operation Krimhild from the sea.

It is arguable whether it was correct, after the evacuation of the Kuban, to leave half of Seventeenth Army in the Crimea instead of transferring all its forces—and not just parts—to the threatened German southern wing on the mainland—*i.e.*, to the Sixth Army's front on the Mius or to Army Group South on the Dnieper. With its sixteen divisions Field-Marshal von Manstein might have been able to cope more successfully with many a critical situation between Melitopol and Kiev. Alternatively, keeping all the divisions of Seventeenth Army in the Crimea would have made possible a more effective defence. Once again neither the one nor the other was done, but both were attempted at the same time.

Hitler's reasons for defending the "Crimean fortress" were not to be dismissed out of hand. About mid-August he had himself toyed with the idea of switching Colonel-General Jaenecke's sixteen German and Rumanian divisions from the Kuban bridge-head over to the Dnieper, to the new East Wall. Sixteen divisions! Just about the formations which Manstein lacked to prevent the Soviet leap across the Dnieper.

But Hitler had to abandon the tempting idea. Marshal Antonescu, the Rumanian Head of State, violently opposed such a denuding of the eastern Black Sea bastions for fear for the safety of the Rumanian coast. The King of Bulgaria likewise opposed the surrender of the Kuban. Consideration had finally to be given to Turkey, that important neutral on the southern coast of the Black Sea.

When the course of military events made the evacuation of the Kuban inevitable, political and military considerations concerning Germany's Balkan allies and neutral Turkey immediately concentrated on the Crimea.

The Seventeenth Army, together with the German naval units and Luftwaffe formations, was keeping the Russians in the Black Sea in check. Until the beginning of April 1944 they prevented the Crimea from becoming a Soviet air base for attacks against the Rumanian oil-fields or a jumping-off base for landings on the Rumanian or Bulgarian

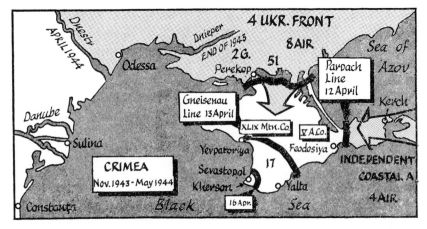

Map 47. Hitler was motivated by political and economic considerations in defending the Crimea even after it had been severed from all landward communications. He feared that the evacuation of the Crimea and the consequent loss of German control of the Black Sea would drive Turkey into the enemy camp. He also wanted to prevent the peninsula from becoming a Soviet air base for attacks on the Rumanian oilfields.

coast. Turkey was being kept neutral by the German show of force in the Black Sea and, in spite of Western pressure, had to allow the merchant ships of Germany's allies to pass through the Dardanelles. And, finally, a German force in the Crimea continued to represent a threat to the Soviet southern wing on the mainland.

All this changed dramatically, facing the German Command with a new and unexpected situation, when Tolbukhin's Army Group on 24th October, 1943, broke through the front of the German Sixth Army north of Melitopol and raced across the Nogay Steppe towards the lower reaches of the Dnieper. Once it thrust past the Perekop isthmus the Seventeenth Army would be completely cut off from the mainland. Stalingrad!

Colonel-General Erwin Jaenecke, the C-in-C Seventeenth Army, was particularly sensitive to this situation since he had been in command of IV Corps at Stalingrad until the middle of January 1943. Jaenecke had seen the danger approaching and made a contingency plan, called "Study Michael". Its subject was the timely break-out of the army through the Perekop isthmus and its wheeling round into the German positions on the Lower Dnieper. The operative word was "timely".

The Army's break-out had been prepared for 29th October and orders issued to this effect. But on 28th October at 2100 hours Hitler prohibited the operation. Whether it would have succeeded is another question—Soviet tanks of Tolbukhin's Second Guards Army appeared at Perekop by the 30th. What would have happened if they had struck at Seventeenth Army while it was breaking out? Struck at an Army whose heavy anti-tank capability was down to two assault gun brigades and a few troops of 8·8-cm flak, and which largely consisted of horse-drawn formations?

But Hitler's prohibition was not based on these considerations. He continued to be motivated by the political and strategic arguments in favour of the defence of the Crimea, even after all land communications had been cut. He was confirmed in this view by the C-in-C of the German Navy, Grand Admiral Dönitz. The surrender of the Crimea, he warned Hitler, would have dangerous consequences for the naval situation in the Black Sea. As for keeping Seventeenth Army supplied, that was no problem; the Navy could guarantee 50,000 tons of supplies per month. And should evacuation become necessary after all, the Navy could accomplish that as well. With the shipping available it would be possible to take off 20,000 men with all their equipment in four days. That meant that the whole of Seventeenth Army with its 200,000 men, complete with horses and *matériel*, could be evacuated within forty days, or in case of bad weather in no more than eighty days.

Was it surprising that, in the face of these assurances in October 1943, Hitler issued orders to hold on to the Crimea in spite of the lost land communications, and to defend it?

To begin with, events proved him entirely right. Jaenecke's German and Rumanian divisions repulsed all Russian attempts to get into the peninsula at Perekop and at Kerch. True, the Soviets succeeded in establishing small bridge-heads at Kerch and on the Sivash—the Putrid Sea—but they did not achieve any decisive penetrations. Supplies for the Army also functioned smoothly. A steady stream of them reached Sevastopol and Yevpatoriya from the ports of Odessa and Constanta. Shipping space was adequate. Urgent transport was handled by a *Staffel* of large, six-engined Gigant aircraft—evacuation of wounded, flying in of important reinforcements. Everything worked smoothly. Rumanian destroyers and German E-boats carried their flags and their transports over the Black Sea as though there were no Soviet battleships, cruisers, or destroyers lying in the naval bases on the Caucasian coast.

Today we know why Stalin's heavy ships lay low in their ports, like bears in their lair during hibernation. Fear of the German Stukas and ground-support aircraft in the Crimea held them firmly by their anchor chains. Stalin did not want to risk any of his big ships and, as has since been confirmed by Admiral Oktyabrskiy, had made each naval operation subject to his own personal authorization.

The control of the Black Sea by the German Navy was therefore based on General Deichmann's I Air Corps and on the ground-support formations based on the Crimea. These 120 to 160 Stukas, ground-support aircraft, and fighters of Colonel Bauer's operations staff of I Air Corps were the Alpha and Omega of the defence of the Crimea. In spite of the achievements of the Navy, the supplies and hence the fate of Seventeenth Army—as indeed in all pocket operations of the war in the East—depended ultimately on the Luftwaffe, on having a secure roof overhead, on German control of the Russian skies. We shall presently see how tragically this thesis was to be proved.

General Jaenecke was holding the Crimea with thirteen divisions—six German infantry divisions, of which only one and a half were available to start with, three Rumanian mountain divisions, two Rumanian cavalry divisions and two Rumanian infantry divisions. Following the transfer of 13th Panzer Division to Sixth Army there were no tanks; on the other hand, there were two excellent assault gun brigades, the 191st under that dare-devil Major Alfred Müller and the 279th under Captain Hoppe, as well as the Mountain Jäger Regiment "Krim" and the Army Flak Battalions 275 and 279. Among special formations there was further the 9th Flak Division under General Pickert which effectively guarded the Perekop isthmus with its 8·8-cm guns. If one considers that these formations represented an appreciable threat to the Soviet flank on the mainland, it cannot be denied that the Crimean bastion had a certain strategic value, certainly while the German bridge-head at Nikopol, east of the Dnieper, held out, and the Soviets were therefore in danger of a thrust being mounted for the re-establishment of land communications with the Crimea. While this threat existed the Russians were forced to station strong forces around the exits from the Crimea and in front of Kerch. Eventually these forces assembled around the Crimea amounted to three armies plus a tank corps, several independent brigades, and altogether thirty rifle divisions. The six German and seven Rumanian divisions were thus tying down a massive enemy force.

On 29th November Captain Hans Ruprecht Hensel, an officer in the operations staff of Seventeenth Army, noted in his diary: "The Crimea is like an island well outside the breaking surf." But the alert young officer also recorded that many HQs had but one idea—to get out of the Crimea. Yet no-one seemed to take the war seriously in the Crimea. Engineer units were employed by many HQs on beautifying staff quarters instead of building fortifications. Entire houses were rebuilt and converted into traditional German peasant interiors when the men would have been far better employed in repairing and strengthening the shattered Russian defences.

This atmosphere sprang from an understandable anxiety, from the knowledge that the Army's strength was not up to a Soviet full-scale attack from the north and east, let alone a strike anywhere along the four hundred miles of coastline. Any officer could see that—and of course every division commander and, even more so, the Army C-in-C and his able chief of staff, Major-General Ritter von Xylander, realized it only too well. Their efforts were therefore aimed at getting Hitler to revoke his order to defend the Crimea and at preparing for a systematic and timely evacuation of Seventeenth Army by sea.

In November 1943 the contingency plan "Rowing Boat" was prepared. Then came "Skim Boat" and finally, in early April, the contingency plan "Eagle". The basic idea was that within six or seven days the troops from all sectors on the peninsula would pull back into the fortified area of Sevastopol. From there they would be evacuated by sea. In order to intercept the pursuing Russian armoured formations during this disengagement towards Sevastopol, blocking positions and switchlines with anti-tank ditches were established in the wide open spaces of the Crimea. The most important of these, the "Gneisenau Line", in an arc round Simferopol, covered the main roads converging on the city. Sevastopol was to be held for about three weeks. During that time the Army was to be embarked in the ports and from the jetties.

Thus Seventeenth Army waited. It waited for the Russians and it waited for the evacuation order. There was General Allmendinger's V Corps with 73rd and 98th Infantry Divisions as well as the Rumanian 6th Cavalry Division and the Rumanian 3rd Mountain Division far over in the east, on the Kerch Strait. General Konrad's XLIX Mountain Corps was blocking the Perekop isthmus in the north and along the Sivash dam; it consisted of 50th and 336th Infantry Divisions as well as the Rumanian 10th and 19th Infantry Divisions and the Rumanian 9th Cavalry Division. The Rumanian I Mountain Corps with two divisions was covering the coastal regions and was also employed in fighting the partisans in the interior of the peninsula. The 111th Infantry Division, switched to the Crimea at the beginning of March 1944, was the army's reserve. One assault gun brigade each had been assigned to the northern and eastern fronts.

Since mid-March 1944 anybody could see the moment of the Soviet large-scale attack drawing nearer. The Nikopol bridge-head had fallen. The German front of Army Group "A" on the mainland had been forced back behind the Dnestr. Odessa, the supply base of Seventeenth Army, was exposed and on 10th April was taken by the Russians. The Russian southern wing had got out of its pinched position between the Dnieper bend and Perekop and now enjoyed freedom of movement. The strike against the Crimea was now the logical strategic move. And Stalin made it.

It started on the afternoon of 7th April. Seven to eight battalions struck at the strongpoints of the Rumanian 10th Infantry Division on the Sivash. The full-scale attack on the northern front of the Crimea began towards 0900 hours the following day. The Fourth Ukrainian Front under Army General Tolbukhin moved in with two armies. After heavy artillery preparation a tank corps with nearly five hundred tanks and eighteen infantry divisions charged the positions of three divisions of General Konrad's XLIX Mountain Corps.

The East Brandenburgers of 50th Infantry Division stood firm on the Tartar Ditch and together with parts of the Lower Saxon 111th Infantry Division cleared up Soviet penetrations by a counter-attack. The Saxon 336th Infantry Division on the western side of the Sivash front also held. But the Rumanian 10th Division, which suffered the whole brunt of the armoured thrust from the Soviet bridge-head on the Sivash, faltered. After stubborn resistance the regiments were crushed at many points.

On 9th April Captain Hensel, having seen the situation reports which arrived at Army HQ, noted in his diary: "The northern front reports a large-scale enemy attack on the Tartar Ditch with exceedingly heavy artillery and mortar fire. The 5th Infantry Division is forced to fall back to a new line. Even more critical is the situation with the Rumanian 10th Infantry Division on the Sivash front. The Army requested Army Group to authorize 'Eagle'. That means retreat to Sevastopol. The decision came during the night. 'Eagle' is starting."

On 10th April he recorded: "The northern front can no longer be held. The 50th Infantry Division just about managed to withdraw to the A-1 line, though with heavy losses. But strong Russian armoured formations are now advancing through the gap on the Rumanian sector, threatening the rear of the other combat groups. We are working frantically to prepare for the manning of the Gneisenau Line. I was ordered to fly out to the Kerch front, to V Corps, as the courier carrying the plans for Sevastopol. A 'most secret' document. Our Storch wobbled alarmingly among the gusty down-draughts of the Yayla mountains. We landed at Leninskoye. I reported to Colonel Bruhn, the corps artillery commander, and handed him the documents. V Corps has been ordered to disengage during the coming night and fall back to Sevastopol."

The 73rd and 98th Infantry Divisions and the two Rumanian divisions of V Corps received the code-word "Eagle" on Easter Sunday. Combat formations to start moving at 1900 hours. It was high time. The distance back to the west, via the Parpach Line to the Gneisenau Line, was 150 miles.

A dramatic race began. No sooner had the German formations evacuated a position than the Soviets followed up. And they pressed very vigorously. We have met their commander-in-chief before— Army General Yeremenko. He was now commanding the independent Coastal Army: twelve rifle divisions, one tank brigade with one hundred tanks, and an Air Army was what he now flung at the rear-guards of the yielding German V Corps.

Yeremenko knew what was happening the moment the German disengagement began. The move was being signalled to him in a way he could not miss. Not by scouts or by spies, but by nervous and now frequently undisciplined formations. Certain Rumanian units, and units of the German Luftwaffe and Navy, disregarded security orders. Instead of observing radio and telephone silence there was soon a great deal of senseless telephoning. The Rumanians, as well as the German naval gunners, "used up" their ammunition which they could not take back with them; they set fire to troop quarters and observation towers, they carried out demolitions at Bagerovo airfield. Furiously HQs and commanders watched this dangerous display of indiscipline but were unable to do anything about it.

As a result, the Russians were alerted about the withdrawals before they actually began. Thus, when the last combat units abandoned their positions at the scheduled time the Russians followed up immediately. A terrible race began between the motorized Soviets and the troops of V Corps who, after prolonged positional warfare, had lost the habit of swift movement and whose transport in any case was largely horse-drawn. It could only be a hopeless race provided that Yeremenko fully exploited his technical superiority.

The Russian armoured and motorized troops were faster. Nevertheless, the German 73rd and 98th Infantry Divisions reached the Parpach Line by 12th April, though at the cost of considerable losses. The enemy was held up until nightfall. The guns of the artillery regiments were employed in the main defensive line. Their fire had a devastating effect among the Russian tank packs.

Since the Russians had already thrust into Simferopol from the north and—if they were daring enough—might turn up in the rear of V Corps at any moment, the corps wheeled south with a view to continuing its westward withdrawal along the coastal road via Sudak and Yalta.

On 13th April the corps reached the foot of the pass into the Yayla mountains north of Saly. Two combat groups of 98th Infantry Division, one under Colonel Faulhaber and the other under Colonel Schmidt, dug themselves in for defence even before daybreak. The columns moved through the pass.

At 0900 hours the first Soviet tanks appeared from the direction of Staryy Krym. The tail-end of the column of Group Allmendinger was just moving into the pass. An anti-tank gun of Panzerjäger Battalion 198 engaged the Soviet advanced detachment. The gun commander and his crew worked as on a gunnery exercise. Eventually nine enemy tanks were lying at the foot of the pass, immobilized or in flames, blocking the road to the Russians pressing behind. That saved the German column.

In vain did General Reinhardt, the commander of 98th Infantry Division, propose the gun commander for the Knight's Cross. If anyone deserved it, this NCO did. But he did not get it. Field-Marshal Keitel later explained to Reinhardt: No decorations for retreating troops!

However, it proved impossible to get the artillery's guns over the pass. The teams of six horses to each gun just could not manage it. Guns and vehicles had to be dynamited and the horses shot. By the evening of 13th April V Corps reached Sudak. By the morning of 14th April they reached Alushta. Along the roads running into the coastal road from the mountains small combat groups provided cover, protecting the corps against unpleasant surprises from partisans. Once the marching column had passed, these covering parties rejoined it at the tail-end, reinforcing the rearguard.

On 15th April the corps made an early start in order to reach Yalta. The rearguard was provided by 98th Infantry Division. Since General Gareis's illness at the beginning of February 1944, the division had been commanded by Major-General Reinhardt. The division commander was riding in a signals vehicle with the rearguard. Now and again the column came under rifle fire from partisans. At 1300 the rearguard reached Yalta. In the main street the V Corps chief of staff, Colonel Hepp, was waiting. Reinhardt greeted him and reported: "98th Infantry Division present without incidents; it will take on food supplies and refuel, and be ready to move off again at 1500 hours."

But the corps chief of staff had different instructions: "Herr General, the corps commander requests you to come to the Rumanian generals' club. He intends to rest here until tomorrow morning."

"What? Rest here till tomorrow morning?" Reinhardt grumbled. "But we can't defend ourselves here! Just look around you! These steep Yayla mountains come right down to the edge of the town. And this narrow beach. Our men are dead beat. They'll fall asleep and we'll be killed like dogs. Well, come along then!"

Together with Hepp, Reinhardt strode across to the Rumanian generals' club. He entered the dining-room, strictly according to etiquette—wearing gloves, his cap under his arm. He made his report to the corps commander, General Allmendinger: "98th Division present without incident; it will take on food supplies and re-fuel, and be ready to move off again at 1500 hours."

Allmendinger waved the formalities aside: "Take your things off, Reinhardt, and have lunch with us. We'll rest here till tomorrow morning."

But Allmendinger, though himself from Württemberg, did not know the Swabian Reinhardt. "No, Herr General," was all he said. Allmendinger looked at him in surprise. But Reinhardt gave him no chance: "Herr General, if we're attacked we can't defend ourselves here. And our men are finished—we've got to keep them moving. If we make a stop here they'll fall asleep and before we can offer any resistance we'll be done in. I therefore request, with respect, resumption of movement at 1500."

A German-speaking Rumanian general intervened, pointing out the risk of being attacked by partisans at night. But Reinhardt did not let up. And in the end Allmendinger agreed. The march was resumed at 1500 exactly. At the head was Colonel Faulhaber with his combat group. Behind him the quadruple flak guns. Then the German and Rumanian HQ staffs and the signals troops, as well as supply units. Then Lieutenant-Colonel Göttig's combat group, followed in turn by German and Rumanian supply units, and finally the combat group under Major Mez whose task it was, as the rearguard point, to cover the column against attacks from the rear. With it were the last assault guns of Assault Gun Brigade 191.

All combat group commanders had orders to dispose their men on their vehicles so that they could fire to both sides with their small arms. On no account was the column to stop if it came under fire. Immobilized vehicles were to be pushed down the precipice at once and their crews to be picked up by the following vehicles. Movement would continue until 2200 hours. Then the column would halt. It would wait for the moon to rise, towards 0200 hours. Then it would move on.

No sooner was the Combat Group Faulhaber out of the town than it came under fire from the mountains. As ordered, the men opened up with all they had, without stopping. The four-barrel flak guns joined in, their tracer pointing the direction. This proved effective. The partisans left the column alone. They gave no more trouble until Sevastopol.

On 16th April between 1000 and 1100 hours the last parts of V Corps arrived in the fortress area of Sevastopol. Some 10,000 men of the corps, who had boarded naval vessels in the ports on the south coast, had already been put ashore in Balaclava harbour by Lieutenant Giele's 1st L-Flotilla. The task was accomplished. The 150-mile race against a ten-fold superior enemy had been won. It had been won thanks to sound and cool leadership and to the discipline and high morale of the troops. Everyone was now hoping for an early evacuation from the doomed peninsula. They were to be disappointed. The V Corps moved into its sector in the fortress front. The curtain was going up on the final act.

And what had happened meantime to General Konrad's XLIX Mountain Corps? On 12th and 13th April his shrunken regiments had reached the Gneisenau Line after a counter-thrust by parts of Assault Gun Brigades 191 and 279 and had temporarily relieved pressure on them. They dug in. Soviet armoured formations followed up and thrust past their blocking positions. The Luftwaffe and General Pickert's flak combat parties brought temporary respite. A group of bomber *Geschwader* 27, whose operations were directed by Air General Deichmann from the foremost infantry strongpoints, made a low-level bombing attack on Soviet armoured formations and knocked out more than fifty tanks. But what was the use of it? On 13th April the Soviets were in Simferopol. Twelve hours previously Colonel-General Jaenecke had still had his HQ there. That was how fast the battle developed.

On 14th April the bulk of Konrad's Corps, fortunately with its heavy artillery saved, moved into the northern part of the Sevastopol fortified area. It was presently followed by the combat group under Lieutenant-General Sixt who, with a motley collection of flak units, transport units, and parts of 50th Infantry Division, had defended the forward airfield of Satabus against all Russian attacks. Soviet tanks were following up furiously, but Colonel Betz, the fortress commandant of Sevastopol, pinned them down at Bakhchisaray with a blocking formation of two battalions of infantry, six troops of flak, and half a dozen assault guns. The nucleus of this blocking formation was a makeshift armoured flak train organized by General Pickert; this train had already been successfully employed at the Tartar Ditch in October 1943. It gave the XLIX Mountain Corps the vital twelve hours it needed to move into the fortifications. By 16th April the Seventeenth Army was already in action in the fortress area of Sevastopol against Russian attacks. When Betz abandoned his barrier at Bakhchisaray and fell back into the fortress, his retreat was already being covered from inside the fortress by the guns of 336th and 111th Infantry Division.

It was a miracle that this withdrawal operation under pressure from a superior enemy should have succeeded. Clearly the Soviets themselves had thought it could not possibly succeed, and for that reason had failed to take any exceptional measures. They had made no landings with their vastly superior fleet on the south coast of the Crimea in order to cut off the retreat of V Corps. Nor had they, as one would have expected, used their Air Force to attack the two crowded roads along which the German and Rumanian columns were retreating. No daring move whatever had been made from the Soviet side. General Konrad made the most of his opportunities in the north just as V Corps did on the coast in the south.

Of course, the divisions were in bad shape when they reached the fortress. The Rumanian formations were near dissolution and the German divisions were no more than reinforced regiments. The combat strength of the Army on 16th April was down to 19,500. German losses totalled 13,131 men, and Rumanian losses 17,652. The ration strength of the Army on 18th April had dropped to 124,233.

The evacuation by naval units had been running smoothly since 12th April. Rearward services, transport units, Eastern Legion members, prisoners of war, and non-combatants were being evacuated currently. By 20th April the total was 67,000 men—a daily performance of over 7,000. Given another eighteen days the task could be completed. Could! But this optimistic "could" marked the crucial point of the Crimean disaster.

Since 12th August the evacuation had been running smoothly and without any losses. The German Luftwaffe was still established on the Crimea with *Geschwaders* of I Air Corps, it still had runways and air-strips within the fortified area, and it was still keeping the Red Air Force in check. Tolbukhin's and Yeremenko's long-range and ground-support formations were only hesitantly beginning to attack German airfields, ports, and the main defence zone. Attacks on German-Rumanian convoys were also over-cautious and produced scant results. The offensive formations of the Soviet Eighth and Fourth Air Armies were clearly lacking tactical experience.

Even more important was that throughout the whole of April the Soviet Black Sea Fleet failed to mount any decisive strikes against the German convoy traffic. Its submarine operations were slight. There were never more than five to eight submarines in action at any one time, and these were prevented from achieving any success by the heroic struggle of German anti-submarine units. Soviet motor torpedo-boats as a rule attacked only at night, and invariably without success. The nucleus of the Soviet Black Sea Fleet continued to stay in its hiding places. As a result, the well-equipped port of Sevastopol could be used to the limit for trans-shipment to the mainland.

Everything looked hopeful. The defensive and blocking positions in the fortified belt could be held successfully for at least two or three weeks. Until that time, therefore, the forward airfields in the fortified area were safe against Soviet artillery fire. Everything hung together: as long as the fortified belt around Sevastopol held out, the Luftwaffe could stay put; as long as the Luftwaffe was present the evacuation could continue. It was an optimistic picture. The Seventeenth Army could be saved, every one of its units could be saved, even—given clever and courageous action—the rearguards of the final engagement. Seventeenth Army was convinced of this—as testified by an essay of Lieutenant-Colonel Freiherr von Weitershausen, its chief of operations at the time.

But its doom had already been sent out into the ether. All hope was shattered. At this most promising hour Hitler once again made one of his incomprehensible decisions. On 12th April he ordered: "Sevastopol

will be defended indefinitely. No fighting troops will be evacuated."
On the contrary, fighting battalions were to be switched to the fortress.
Sevastopol must hold out! Here, and only here, began the tragedy of
six German divisions, many of them with long and famous traditions.

Jaenecke, as well as Schörner who had been commanding Army
Group Southern Ukraine since Kleist's dismissal on 31st March, and
indeed also Zeitzler, the Chief of the OKH General Staff, all tried in
vain to get Hitler to rescind his senseless order. Allmendinger repeated
the attempt on the occasion of a visit to the Führer's Headquarters.
Hitler's argument that the loss of the Crimea would shake Turkey and
undermine the reliability of the Rumanians and Bulgarians certainly
had some substance until the withdrawal of Army Group "A" to the
Dnestr west of Odessa. But what use were correct arguments when
the hard facts of relative strength in the field ruled out all possibility
of holding Sevastopol for more than three weeks?

The dramatic tug-of-war between Hitler and the command in the
field is reflected in Schörner's endeavours to get the Führer's order
revoked. Schörner, this much-maligned man, used the right tactics
with Hitler: on 18th April at 1030 hours he put a call through to
Zeitzler. His argument was as follows: "The Führer's order to hold
Sevastopol will of course be carried out. But I would like to point out
that any weapon which is sent to the Crimea, and any ammunition
shipped to the Crimea, will be missed in the vital operation of Army
Group Southern Ukraine on the Dnestr—the decisive encounter which
must be won at all costs."

Zeitzler's reply showed that Schörner had struck the right note: "I
entirely agree with you," he said, "but in order to get the Führer to
authorize the evacuation of Sevastopol it would be helpful for me
to have more precise data about Seventeenth Army."

At 2205 Schörner, in another telephone conversation with Zeitzler,
emphasized that "the decision concerning Sevastopol must be taken
by 20th April because by that date all dispensable transport formations will have left Sevastopol." Schörner explained his timetable to
Zeitzler: In the evening of the 19th the evacuation of non-combatant
Wehrmacht personnel would be completed; after that it would be the
turn of the Rumanians. The daily capacity was 7000 men. However,
the situation in the air over the Crimea was getting more unfavourable
all the time. Enemy artillery was now covering the entire fortified area
with the exception of the tip of the Kherson peninsula. "The fate of
the Army Group will be decided on the mainland, at Wöhler's Army
Group, and not at Sevastopol," Schörner concluded.

The following day Schörner continued to urge Zeitzler in another
long-distance telephone-call at 2130 hours: "The decision about the
Crimea must be taken now. Aerial and naval transport space has
already suffered some losses, our Navy now has to go into action on

both outward and inward crossings, and the losses of the Luftwaffe are difficult to make good. Evacuation will take at least two weeks. That's why an immediate start is necessary. And don't forget one thing. We don't really have five divisions for defence—in fact they are just five German regiments. The Rumanians have practically no fighting value left."

In spite of these weighty appeals Hitler at the evening conference on 19th April turned down Schörner's proposition. Again he prohibited the evacuation of fighting troops. But Schörner did not give up.

On 21st April he flew to the Berghof to persuade Hitler in person to countermand his hold-on order. Colonel-General Schörner proved to his Supreme Commander that Sevastopol could not be defended in the long run.

Hitler argued against him with honeyed words. Turkey's attitude, he said, had become uncertain since the collapse of the front at Perekop and Kerch, and now depended on whether the Crimea, in other words Sevastopol, was held. That was the decisive factor in his decision to defend Sevastopol. "There are two things I need for the war above everything else—Rumanian oil and Turkish chrome ore. Both will be lost if I abandon the Crimea." Then he qualified his statement: The Crimea need not, of course, be held indefinitely, but just for eight or ten weeks. Once the expected invasion in the West was successfully repulsed, Sevastopol could be quietly evacuated after a few weeks, without any political risk.

Other men before had succumbed to Hitler's eloquence. In his endeavour to achieve the evacuation of the Crimea, Schörner now made a mistake. He knew that there were no reserves available, least of all for the Crimea, and so he tried to bluff Hitler by saying: "My Führer, Sevastopol can only be held if you let Seventeenth Army have reinforcements."

That was a mistake. Schörner had underestimated Hitler. Hitler now had his general's "if" and he immediately seized on it. "Very well, I'll send you reinforcements."

Schörner was outmanoeuvred. Hitler, of course, did not keep his word and did not send Schörner anything apart from two foot battalions with 1300 men, fifteen anti-tank guns, ten mortars, and four field howitzers. But he had made his promise and thus Schörner's hopes of getting the directive for Sevastopol's defence countermanded were gone. So in the Crimea too the law of Hitler's hold-on strategy now took its course.

In July 1942, when Field-Marshal von Manstein attacked Sevastopol, the fortress was defended by seven Russian rifle divisions, four naval brigades, and one cavalry division. The Soviets were established in concrete bunkers and deep concreted saps; the most up-to-date big-calibre fortress artillery was installed in underground forts. Even so the Russians were unable to hold Sevastopol. It took Manstein exactly a month to capture the fortress.

In April 1944 the fortress was being defended by virtually five German regiments. Their artillery consisted of the salvaged equipment of one corps. True, the main defensive line was well established, the positions were protected by wire obstacles, but properly constructed strongpoints in depth existed only at a few tactically important points. A second or third line, manned by reserves, just did not exist. The old Soviet bunkers and forts had not been repaired and could only be used as hospitals or assembly positions. The positions south-east of Sevastopol were poorly built. Infantry trenches were not deep enough. The V Corps had no heavy artillery left and scarcely any heavy infantry weapons. The 98th Infantry Division did not even have trenching tools. General Reinhardt had to issue orders for picks and shovels to be collected throughout the fortified area. Army engineers had to manufacture handles for them. Only then did the building of earthworks begin. And this "fortress" was now being assaulted by twenty-nine Soviet divisions, one tank corps, three artillery divisions, and a dozen independent brigades with altogether 470,000 men. It was being bombarded by more than 6000 guns. It was being charged by 600 tanks.

At the last moment, on 27th April, when catastrophe had become inescapable, Colonel-General Jaenecke sent a teleprinter message, intended for Hitler, to Army Group. Schörner immediately passed it on to the Führer's Headquarters. Jaenecke, who on 24th April had asked for information about the two divisions promised him as reinforcements, was now categorically demanding one division at once. In addition he demanded "freedom of action".

Freedom of action! A phrase which Hitler hated like the very devil. Colonel-General Jaenecke was summoned to Hitler to report. He was dismissed from his post. General of Infantry Allmendinger was put in charge of the army. The general commanding the XLIX Mountain Corps, General Konrad, was also relieved. He was succeeded by General Hartmann, bearer of the Oak Leaves, a man of outstanding bravery but with considerable physical handicaps—he had only one arm and one leg.

The full-scale Russian attack began on 5th May at 0930. The battle was opened by 400 heavy guns and 400 multiple mortars. The thrust of five Soviet rifle divisions fell upon the 336th Infantry Division. But General Hagemann's Saxons stood unshakable. They held out for twelve hours. Twenty-four hours. Thirty-six hours. On 7th May the northern front was still holding.

But now Yeremenko struck at the southern and eastern fronts of V Corps. The Coastal Army had moved into action 320 guns for each mile of front. They battered the German strongpoints and gun positions. Then came Yeremenko's brigades. They charged the weak regiments of 73rd, 111th, and 98th Infantry Divisions.

The front of 73rd Infantry Division was ripped open. Deep penetrations were achieved at 111th Infantry Division. By 1800 hours the German losses on both frontal sectors amounted to 5000. The men of V Corps were fighting at all the ancient, well-known landmarks— Sapper Gorge, the British cemetery, the Sapun hills, all of them known from the Crimean War of 1855.

Fort Maksim Gorkiy II, destroyed in 1942, served as a field hospital. The wounded lay there in long rows. There was moaning and stench. A ditch had been cut into the steep coast to allow the casualties to be brought down to the jetties for evacuation. The water below was covered with strange objects bobbing up and down.

What had happened there was described by Captain Hensel in his diary under the date of 22nd April: "In accordance with the evacuation order all horses were shot and tipped into the sea. There was a long queue of them, each horse waiting patiently for its turn to come. A glance down into the bay shows it crammed with thousands of dead bodies of horses. They rise and fall in the rhythm of the swell." This slaughter of the horses was one of those senseless things done in the Crimea. The Rumanians thought it too time-wasting to shoot each of their old equine friends individually. Instead they drove the animals to the edge of the cliff and opened up at them with machineguns. For hours on end.

The crisis came on 8th May. The Russians broke through on the high ground of Sapun. All attempts to intercept them and to recapture the hill with the notorious vineyard, the Nikolayevka hill, and the cemetery were in vain. Desperately the army fought at the Sapun hills. For a while Captain Dr Finke succeeded with 2nd Battalion, 282nd Grenadier Regiment, in regaining the ridge of high ground, but he had to yield again. Dr Finke was killed. Army ordered renewed attacks. What else could it do? No evacuation order was coming through. So Sevastopol had to be defended. But without the Sapun hills that was impossible. What would happen if they were lost?

In that case only remnants of the army would succeed in escaping to that last position, the tip of the Kherson peninsula. And if they did not find any ships there—what then?

When the Sapun hills were lost, Seventeenth Army rallied all its reserves and mounted a counter-attack. At noon Lieutenant-Colonel Freiherr von Weitershausen, the chief of operations, reported to Army Group by radio that the counter-attack had come to a halt. "We'll do everything to recapture that vital high ground." But in spite of all their bravery they did not succeed. The crucial blocking position was lost.

In that situation, at 2115 hours on 8th May, Colonel-General Schörner had a teleprinter signal telephoned to the Führer's Headquarters. It ran: "Request evacuation since further defence of Sevastopol no longer possible."

Now Hitler had to yield to the facts. Within an hour and three-quarters, by 2300 hours, his agreement arrived. Bitterly he remarked to the Chief of the General Staff: "The worst thing about this enforced evacuation, to my mind, is that the Russians can now pull out their Crimean armies and employ them against Army Group Southern Ukraine." No mention now of Turkey.

By 0215 on 9th May General Allmendinger had the order for the evacuation of the fortress on his hands. The army immediately pulled back to its last redoubt—the Kherson position on the most westerly tip of the coast.

Towards 1600 hours the last combat groups of 50th Infantry Division pulled out from the ruins of Sevastopol and moved into the northern part of the new defensive line. In the evening Colonel Betz, the gallant fortress commandant, was killed; since 1st May, when General Sixt was wounded, Betz had been commanding 50th Infantry Division with prudence and boldness.

The Kherson position was efficiently laid out and well built. The main defensive line was formed by a continuous infantry trench with communication trenches. There was also concreted dug-outs for the troops, for ammunition, and for foodstuffs. That was good for morale. There were ample stores of good food. Since there was no water in the Kherson peninsula, supplies of soda water had been laid in. Experienced grenadiers and infantry officers were in command of small combat groups composed of the remnants of all branches of the Wehrmacht. On the sector of 98th Infantry all the personnel that could be scraped together behind the strongpoints of the grenadiers, as long as they had any front-line experience at all, were organized into a striking and tactical reserve and held in readiness. They amounted to 250 men. At that time that was a considerable force.

Needless to say, the Russians followed up vigorously and tried to break through the last bridge-head of Seventeenth Army, push it in, and mop up the positions. But in spite of an enormous superiority they did not at first succeed in doing so.

But what use was courage? The moment had now come when Seventeenth Army was losing the main trump card of its defence—General Deichmann's air formations on the peninsula were out-manoeuvred. The last airfield in the Kherson peninsula was being accurately shelled by the Russians who, from the Sapun hills, had a clear view of the tip of the peninsula. In the evening of 9th May, when the field was pitted with craters, Deichmann was forced to

order his last thirteen fighter aircraft: Evacuation—back to the mainland! The air umbrella over the peninsula was lost. The mainland was
too far away for more than very limited operations by German fighters
or ground support aircraft.

Such twin-engined fighters as were available were required for
convoy escort duties. Only the truly intrepid pilots of the old Ju-52
Geschwaders would put down after dark on the last makeshift landing
strip in the Kherson peninsula from now on, in order to evacuate the
wounded. During the night of 10th May a thousand wounded were
flown out in this way.

The final act of the tragedy opened on 10th May, 1944, with a
shattering blow. A blow which testified to the close links between
aerial, naval, and land warfare.

As soon as Hitler had authorized the evacuation, the Navy set in
motion its carefully prepared, large-scale ferrying operation. Would
it succeed? Upon the answer to this question depended the salvation
or destruction of Seventeenth Army. The first convoys put to sea at
once. The voyage from Constanta to the Crimea took one or two nights
plus a day. That was the great difference compared with Dunkirk,
where the British succeeded in ferrying an entire army across the
Channel in 1940 because the crossing took only a few hours.

On 10th May, towards 0200 hours, the two transports *Totila* and *Teja*
appeared off the Crimea. They hove to two nautical miles north of
Kherson point because otherwise they would have been within range
of Soviet artillery. Motor ferries and engineer craft performed the
embarkation. The *Teja* took on board 5000 men and the *Totila* 4000.
And then came disaster. Soviet ground support aircraft and bombers
came roaring over with fighter escort. There were no German fighters
about. At 0545 *Totila* received three direct hits and began to drift in
the sea, ablaze. Two and a half hours later she sank. Only a few hundred men were saved. *Teja* suffered the same fate. Soviet torpedo aircraft damaged her so heavily that towards 1500 hours she sank. In
her case 400 men were saved—400 out of 5000. Eight thousand men
drowned at one blow. What would happen next?

Seventeenth Army intended to embark during the night of 10th–11th
May. There were roughly 30,000 men left in the Kherson position.
The Navy agreed. Dönitz intervened personally. Anything seaworthy
was sent across. Over 190 German and Rumanian warships and mer-
chantmen were at sea. They had a total ferrying capacity of 87,000
men. That was more than adequate. Especially as, by 8th May, more
wounded and non-combatants had been shipped to the mainland, so
that the army had barely more than 50,000 men left in the peninsula.

The plan worked. Things were not looking too bad. But man pro-
poses and God disposes. Suddenly the heavens conspired against the

Crimean Army. A storm blew up. The timetable was upset. The
Naval Commander, Crimea, Rear-Admiral Schulz, was working feverishly with his officers. But what could they do against a Force 8 gale?
Many convoys with not entirely seaworthy craft were forced to turn
back or to heave to. Other convoys were delayed. It was soon clear
that the ships could not reach Kherson before 11th May. Embarkation
therefore had to be postponed until the following night, the night of
11th–12th May. But that meant that Seventeenth Army HQ could not
carry out its plan to evacuate the remaining parts of the army in one go
during the night of 10th–11th and that therefore, unless the whole
army was to be sacrificed, the Kherson position had to be held for another twenty-four hours.

The battalions held their line. The full horror of this improvised
operation emerges from a report by General Reinhardt, the commander
of 98th Infantry Division. On 10th May, 1944, the Russians attacked
furiously, seven times, each time in several waves. And each time they
were repulsed. One tank which had broken through was knocked out
right in front of the foremost trench and remained there immobilized.
It provided a good screen against bullets.

Towards evening, as Reinhardt returned from the main defensive line
to division HQ, the general commanding the XLIX Mountain Corps,
General Hartmann, was on the telephone. Hartmann, General Konrad's
successor, was known to the men as "Iron Gustav".

"Reinhardt," Hartmann was saying; "Reinhardt, you're the focal
point. If your front should break—it'll be everybody for the ships!"

The staff officers were listening in on the conversation and that was
why Reinhardt replied: "But, Herr General, there's no cause for anxiety.
The Russians made seven attacks on my sector today and they were
kicked back seven times. They've made no penetration anywhere.
And besides—what ships? I don't see any ships. We can manage to
hold our sector for another twenty-four hours—so long as the ships get
here."

Thereupon General Reinhardt stretched out on a wooden bench to
snatch a few hours' sleep. About the same time, rescue came for another chronicler of the battles in the Crimea. Captain Hensel gives the
following account in his diary of the evacuation of the headquarters
personnel of Seventeenth Army: "10th May, 1944. The fort was under
continuous artillery and mortar fire. But the subterranean passages
opened out into the cliff face on the coast. So we climbed down in
the dark, on rope ladders, and from 0100 hours onwards waited among
the cliffs. Two hours passed without any sign of life. Only the Russian
shells whined overhead, towards the sea. We were in dead ground
under the cliffs. We had almost given up hope. Once dawn came it
would be too late. But suddenly they were here. Over a loud-hailer

the voice of a commander called on us to embark. They were two motor torpedo-boats. Because of the rocky coast they could not come right in. Fortunately, the sea was quite calm. So we rowed out in small boats, eight men to each boat. It was a slow business and by then it was getting light. But at last we were ready to put out to sea. Each boat had taken aboard 50 men. In line astern, on a south-westerly course, we were off at full speed. Had we really escaped from hell? We had 250 miles ahead of us still, with all kinds of hazards such as submarines and enemy aircraft. The coast of the Crimea slowly disappeared in the pale light of a hazy day. Below deck the men were crowded together. I remained up on deck. Only when I was flung against the rail, together with the heavy steel box I was clinging to, did I leave my airy spot in the stern. I presently found a slightly more sheltered spot alongside a spare torpedo. Eight hours passed before we entered the calm waters of the port of Constanta. We were saved."

Meanwhile, the fighting continued for the last bastions. The Russians renewed their attacks on 11th May. At 2000 hours they concentrated their heavy fire on the landing points. A little while later they shortened their range and again pounded the main defensive line; thereupon they mounted an attack along the entire front. They achieved a penetration on the sector of 98th Infantry, near "Battery Hill". It was cleared up by an immediate counter-attack.

In the course of 11th May all units received orders to fall back to their various embarkation points at 2300 hours and to dig in there for local defence. Orders were issued simultaneously to the effect that, in the event of the ships not arriving at their appointed embarkation points, the troops should get on board whatever other ships they could find. It was a necessary order in view of the situation, but also one which opened the door wide to chaos and panic.

The Russians fortunately noticed nothing of the final disengagement. Telephone communication between HQs was still working and Reinhardt called up the regimental adjutants. The pre-arranged game of question and answer followed: "Well, how are things? Everything OK?" Answer: "Everything OK, all quiet in front." Reinhardt: "Fine, then I can have a quiet cup of tea." That was the code word and meant: back to the embarkation points.

Time was getting on for 2400 hours. Reinhardt was in radio contact with the embarkation points of the division. Repeated questions always elicited the same answer: there were no ships.

No ships. What had gone wrong? The ships were there all right; the evacuation fleet was lying in the roadsteads in sufficient strength—but it could not find its way inshore.

At 2130 Admiral Schulz went on board the command craft of 1st MTB Flotilla. He intended to guide the convoys to their anchorage in person as the radio command apparatus had broken down. The frequencies of the only available channel were being jammed so that orders could not be transmitted any longer to the individual ships. But that was not the end of the disaster. The devil seemed to be fighting on the Russian side. Schulz sent out a signal to all ships, instructing them to sail as close as possible to the mouth of Kamyshevaya Bay. From there he would pilot them to the embarkation points. But this radio order, personally handed in by the Admiral at the signals centre, never arrived. It was either not transmitted, or it just disappeared, or it was lost on the jammed wavelengths.

It was a black night. But Admiral Schulz had placed his hopes in just that blackness. In the dark the Soviet artillery was unable to pinpoint any targets and the Red Air Force had no experience of night raids.

The motor torpedo-boat swished through the sea. Anxiously the officers raised their night glasses to their eyes. What on earth was that? "Fog," said the First Officer. They were aghast. "But where's it coming from?" A thick white fog bank was drifting out to sea from the peninsula. It was getting denser and denser. Jetties and landing piers were visible only at close range now. But that was no fog bank—incredible though it seemed, it was a smokescreen. How was that possible?

In the course of the past few months the Navy had installed a smokescreen system along the port installations and the bays, with several hundred smoke drums. In the event of major attacks by enemy air formations the military objectives, and in particular the anchorages and jetties, were to be hidden from enemy eyes by smokescreens, so as to make deliberate bombing impossible. Now, by an unhappy chance, these smoke drums had been set off by enemy artillery fire. Surprised and delighted to find themselves thus hidden from enemy eyes, a few German formations had moreover set off the still intact smoke generators to ensure, as they thought, their greater safety. Little did they suspect what they were doing.

The disaster was not now to be undone.

True, Schulz found the transport *Dacia* and had it guided inshore. He also found a few other ships. But there were sixty of them lying in the roadsteads, and most of them he did not find. Besides, they did not wait. At daybreak many of them returned to Constanta, empty.

There would have been one possibility of intensifying the search for them—if the admiral could have seen his way to sending out the remaining boats of his MTB flotilla with orders to seek out other ships and pilot them to the landing points. But that flotilla was the only operational unit left to the admiral for warding off attacks by Soviet surface units. Was he to deprive himself of that possibility? What would he then do in the event of a Soviet attack? In that case all ships would have been in the most dire danger. Who can blame the admiral for keeping his only weapon intact?

Thus came the great disaster for the last 10,000 men of the Crimean Army. The very men who had fought to the end.

Partly by soldier's instinct and partly through good luck General Reinhardt found five flat-bottomed ferries on a lonely spot on the coast. Their gallant commander had manoeuvred these shallow craft right up to the shore. Reinhardt also found ten small escort vessels. By runners and loud-hailers he rallied his division and all units of 117th Grenadier Regiment of 111th Infantry Division who were within reach and got them on board these craft.

The general kept back the last ferry. He ordered its commander not to cast off until he himself was on board. And he did not go on board because, once on board, he would no longer have any power of command. He wanted to wait as long as possible in the hope that stragglers might still arrive. Sure enough, quite a few of them turned up, including Colonel Haidlen, chief of staff of XLIV Corps, and Lieutenant-Colonel Becker, the chief of operations of 73rd Infantry Division. And a lot of other officers and men. At 0300, at daybreak, Reinhardt ordered his last ferry to cast off. The convoy put to sea. The remnants of 98th Infantry Division were saved.

The drama enacted at the embarkation point of 50th Infantry Division is reported in a cool, matter-of-fact manner in the divisional history. The regiments had held their lines to the last moment. Here too the Russians failed to notice their withdrawal to the embarkation points.

The 121st Regiment embarked. But at the embarkation point of 123rd Grenadier Regiment there was only one ferry. It was able to take a few hundred men on board. Another ferry arrived. The men formed two ranks and went on board.

Halt. A few more wounded were carried on board. No more room.

Major Teschner ordered the officers back on shore. Silently, as though this were the most natural thing, the officers all disembarked again. The major led the remaining men under cover. They dug in for their last action. Their backs to the water, the small combat group of 50th Infantry Division took up a defensive position. It held out for another six hours. Then it was overpowered. But 2800 men of the divisions had been evacuated. The rest remained on the peninsula.

Things were similar with 336th Infantry Division, whose gallant commander had been seriously wounded and flown out. As for 73rd Infantry Division, most of the men were rescued by ferries, and the rest on board a submarine chaser. General Böhme, the division commander, was taken prisoner at his battle HQ.

Thirty-nine thousand eight hundred and eight men were embarked from the Kherson peninsula during the last three days. Thirty-one thousand seven hundred and eight of them arrived at their destination.

And what about 111th Infantry Division, the regiments which had been switched to the Crimea in March to reinforce the units there? It was this division which suffered the heaviest blow. Not one of the sixty transports which were moving about the roadsteads in darkness and fog found its way inshore to the division's embarkation points. Not one.

The day was breaking—the 12th May. There was a blue sky. T-34s were attacking the last line of outposts guarding the embarkation points of the Lower Saxons. The men only had their rifles and a few machine-guns. Their heavy equipment had already been destroyed.

Lieutenant-Colonel Franz, the intelligence officer, was burning the secret documents on the beach. Resistance collapsed. Panic broke out Lieutenant Gottlieb, the adjutant of 117th Artillery Regiment, found himself a plank and with it ran into the water to paddle himself out to sea. Under a burst of machine-gun fire from a Soviet fighter aircraft he drowned. Barely four weeks ago this young officer had brought back the body of his dead brother under heavy enemy fire to bury it behind the German lines.

Suddenly a few German assault boats arrived. A sergeant asked: "Herr Oberstleutnant, which way to Turkey?" Then he jumped aboard the already crammed army engineer craft. They cast off.

The Russian tanks kept their distance. Their artillery was shelling the beach. The barrage crept slowly forwards. Closer and closer. The strip of ground between cliff and water's edge was less than thirty yards. And a few thousand men were crammed together on the few square yards of earth among mud and shingle and rocks.

Then the tanks moved in slowly. Their hatch covers were open. General Gruner walked towards a T-34, erect. Its cannon barked. Slowly the general sagged to the ground.

The Soviet infantrymen accompanying the tanks seemed furious about something or other. They were shouting. They were firing. Hitting out with rifle butts. A German sergeant refused to hand over his German Cross in Gold. "Khoroskiy soldat"—and then he was mown down.

The officers were picked out and led away. Bursts of fire and screams. Fritz Niedszwedski, a company runner and formerly a much-travelled waiter from the Eden Hotel in Berlin, together with Sepp Prötzner, the intelligence officer's driver, grabbed Lieutenant-Colonel Franz and pulled him into a group of rankers. They pressed close around him. They hid his red staff officer's stripes from the eyes of the Russians.

The Russian auxiliaries were lined up against the cliff and put to death. A savage end.

Six months later Lieutenant-Colonel Franz was facing a Soviet interrogation officer in a Moscow prison. The Russian was correct, polite, and curious. He was particularly interested in the operation of 111th Infantry Division in the Crimea. And he said: "We were in no hurry to take the Crimea. After all, it was our biggest POW cage. The Germans were virtually prisoners on the peninsula since November 1943. They supplied themselves. They guarded themselves. They went off on leave. And even returned on their own account."

If the end in the Crimea had not been quite so macabre one might agree with the Russian officer. But the balance-sheet was too grim to dismiss it with a *bon mot*.

The number killed and wounded between 8th April and 13th May was 57,500—31,700 Germans and 25,800 Rumanians. Moreover, comparison of evacuation figures revealed that the fate of a further 20,000 men remained unknown. It was a disaster on the scale of Stalingrad.

The small peninsula had been a kind of microcosm of the whole war. Everything that had happened in this area of roughly one hundred miles square was typical of the entire Eastern front—from Petsamo in the extreme north down to the Caucasus.

Discipline and gallantry, obedience and self-sacrifice, as well as meanness, brutality, and savagery were present there, as were foolishness and error, ambition and fear, fanaticism and drunkenness. The entire war in Russia was reflected in this peninsula.

But so also were the imponderables—strategic mistakes, economic and political considerations, and the laws of land, sea, and aerial warfare. They all played their part in this confined place, but what happened here affected the big over-all development.

Hitler and Stalin clashed on this restricted battlefield. Here they revealed their weaknesses and here they played their trump cards.

And the men who determined or suffered the course of the battle between the Putrid Sea and the beaches of Yalta were typical of the men anywhere in the East, of the men fighting in the line or planning operations at the map table. The battle of the Crimea was a genuine microcosm of all the theatres of operation during the latter half of the war in Russia.

PART EIGHT:

The Cannae of Army Group Centre

1. Deployment

An example from ancient history–Hitler expects a Galician offensive–Stalin chooses the weakest point–A tenfold superiority–Arguments in the Kremlin–Rokossovskiy gets his way.

ON 2nd August in the year 216 B.C. the Carthaginian army under Hannibal was facing the Roman army under the Consul Terentius Varro near the village of Cannae in the Apulian plain in southern Italy. The Romans had a numerical superiority, but Hannibal's superb cavalry more than offset the difference in numbers.

The battle began. The two armies moved towards each other. Hannibal played his trump: with his powerful cavalry Hasdrubal, the commander of his horse, struck at the weaker Roman cavalry on the right wing of the Roman army. The Roman horsemen were thrown into the Aufidus river. Moving behind the rear of the Roman infantry, Hasdrubal now raced across to the left wing where a second group of 3000 Roman horsemen were skirmishing with Carthaginian light cavalry. He attacked them from behind. He defeated the Roman horse. And he then attacked the Roman infantry from the rear.

What did it avail Terentius Varro that his heavily armed infantry were superior to the Carthaginian auxiliaries? With Hasdrubal's horse in the rear and the Carthaginian infantry on the flanks, the doom of the Romans was sealed. The first battle of annihilation was reaching its end—envelopment of the enemy's main forces by fast formations, followed by a pincer attack by the infantry against both enemy flanks.

Count von Schlieffen, the Prussian Field-Marshal, has left a brilliant study of the battle. The Romans, he explained, were being progressively compressed. They were making their final fighting effort. Hannibal rode about the bloody battlefield, encouraging the eager warriors and scoffing at the lax ones. Tired of the butchery they eventually took the surviving 3000 Romans prisoner. There were 48,000 dead bodies lying in that narrow space, piled up in heaps. The Consul Aemilius Paulus and the Proconsul Servilius were among the killed. With a few horsemen and some heavy infantry Varro succeeded in escaping. In the village of Cannae and in the two Roman camps further thousands of men fell into the hands of the victors.

This is what Schlieffen wrote in 1909: "This was a perfect battle of annihilation. Weapons and fighting methods have totally changed over the past two thousand years. Troops no longer tackle one another with short swords but fire at each other over thousands of yards; the place of the bow has been taken by the recoil gun and that of the sling by the machine-gun. Instead of butchery we now have surrender. But the over-all pattern of battle has remained unchanged. A battle of annihilation can be fought to this day according to the same plan—the plan thought up by Hannibal in a long-forgotten age."

Count Schlieffen was right. In the summer of 1944 the Cannae of the Romans was re-enacted in Russia, on the Berezina.

Just as the course of the German-Russian war was all along signposted by mistaken decisions, the final act of the campaign similarly opened with a tragic error by the German High Command. From it sprang the all-decisive defeat in the East, the disaster on the central front in the summer of 1944.

Who would have thought it possible in 1941 that the proud armies of Army Group Centre would suffer the greatest disaster in military history within a mere three years, a battle of annihilation, a Cannae without parallel?

The German Army Group Centre had been the spearhead of Operation Barbarossa. With its two Panzer groups and three powerful infantry armies it was to have smashed the main Soviet forces west of the Dnieper and then made a lightning-like thrust at the heart of the Soviet Union, Moscow.

The Army Group had raced at a breathtaking speed through Brest-Litovsk to Minsk and across the Dnieper to Smolensk. Then came Hitler's disastrous hesitation. His departure from the "Moscow plan". His wheeling down to Kiev in order first to capture the Ukraine. Only after weeks in the mud at the onset of winter was the thrust against

"I'm breaking out": Major-General Bayerlein at Kirovograd. 24th Panzer Division struggling against the *rasputitsa*, the Ukrainian spring mud.

Moscow finally revived. By then it was too late. The Russian winter with its Siberian frosts and fresh Siberian troops had been too much for the German troops and their weapons. Army Group Centre was defeated at the approaches to Moscow.

This event in the winter of 1941 resulted in a decisive turn in the whole war in Russia. The focus of German strategy was shifted from the centre and from purely military considerations, aiming at the enemy's capital with its central communications, to economic objectives in the south of the Soviet Union, objectives which Hitler, unlike his generals, considered decisive for the outcome of the war—coal, steel, and oil. The Donets region and the Caucasus were regarded as the decisive battlefields. There the big blows were dealt. There the dice were cast for victory or defeat.

Army Group Centre, following its retreat from the approaches to Moscow, remained in the eyes of the German High Command a "secondary theatre of war". Guderian's bold Second Panzer Army, which according to the Barbarossa schedule was to envelop Moscow from the south and capture it, remained for a period of twenty months, until August 1943, in its blocking position around Orel, to which it had fallen back after the tragedy of Tula. One more indication that, after his victory on the Volga, Stalin intended to smash the German front not at the centre but in the south.

In vain had Field-Marshal von Manstein urged the Führer's Head-quarters ever since Stalingrad: "The decision will come in the south—that's where we've got to be strong." Time and again he had asked for the southern wing to be reinforced, if necessary at the expense of other Army Groups. Hitler failed to do so.

Thus, one battle after another was lost in the south. Lost, also, was the conquered wealth of iron and coal, nickel and manganese ore, as well as the granaries of the Ukraine—not to mention that flanking bastion of the Crimea. Lost because of an error!

The situation map of June 1941 clearly revealed the tragic developments in the south of the Eastern Front. The Soviets had pushed far to the west. Their line now ran from Odessa on the Black Sea along the northern slopes of the Carpathians to Kolomyya and there turned abruptly towards the north, to the edge of the Pripet marshes north of Kovel. From there the big bulge of Army Group Centre projected eastward over 250 miles, and at Orsha and Mogilev even to 30 miles across the Dnieper. The rearward communications of this projecting salient were already being threatened from the south at the western edge of the Pripet marshes.

The Korsun pocket: This is how they broke out.
The heavy Panzer Regiment Bäke preparing its relief attack from outside.
This is what was left behind.

This threat, mercifully, got most literally bogged down in the Russian spring mud, and the German High Command as a result gained some much-needed breathing space. And with it a chance of stabilizing, even if on a makeshift basis, the dangerously threatened frontal sector between the Carpathians and the Pripet marshes.

The problem which worried the Wolfsschanze and the Mauerwald was: What was Stalin going to do after the mud? Where would he mount his summer offensive? That was the great, the all-decisive problem of 1944.

The answer which Hitler and his advisers worked out was wrong. And that wrong answer, based on a wrong assessment of the situation, led to disaster.

For eighteen months Hitler had refused to acknowledge that Stalin was clearly trying to force a decision on the southern wing. For eighteen months he had underrated the Red Army and its increasing military experience. Now he committed a new error. He believed that Stalin could seek the decision nowhere but in the south—simply because in Galicia he had a great strategic opportunity of advancing towards Warsaw and the Vistula and hence into the rear of Army Group Centre. Hitler dismissed all doubts: the Russians, he said, will strike between the Pripet marshes and the Carpathians! They must strike there!

Night after night he pored over the situation map. Studying and planning. And in every plan he made he attributed his own thoughts to his opponent. Of course it would be tempting to seize a projecting bulge in a huge pair of pincers and thus to cut off two Army Groups with seven armies. After all, from the sources of the Pripet to the Baltic Coast was a mere 280 miles, with no appreciable obstacles. A perfect run. It was without any doubt a bold and tempting idea for a daring general with adequate forces. It is interesting that not only Hitler but also his advisers, such as Colonel-General Jodl and General Heusinger, that shrewd chief of the Operations Department, succumbed to the fascination of that plan. That fascination was so strong that the Führer's Headquarters continued to believe in an operation based on Galicia even when, after 10th June, more and more reports were coming in about enemy preparations in front of Army Group Centre. All these were discounted as Russian feints. The phantom of a

Map 48. Four Soviet Army Groups with 2,500,000 men were lined up against the projecting salient of Army Group Centre, ready for attack. To defend this salient, Field-Marshal Busch had four armies with roughly 400,000 men. But Hitler did not believe in a Russian frontal attack; he was afraid of an enveloping operation from Galicia via Lvov to Königsberg. He therefore weakened Army Group Centre even further and switched nearly all his armoured forces in Russia to the area of Army Group Northern Ukraine.

STOCKHOLM

HELSINKI
Gulf of Finland
TALLINN
Leningrad
LENINGRAD FRONT
Novgorod
Lake Peipus
Baltic
18
Pskov
3 BALTIC FRONT
A.Gr. NORTH
RIGA
2 BALTIC FRONT
Dvina
Dvinsk (Daugavpils)
16
1 BALTIC FRONT
Niemen
Polotsk
Vitebsk
3 BELORUSS. FR.
Königsberg
Kaunas
VILNIUS
3 Pz.
Smolensk
Danzig
Molodechno
Borisov
Orsha
2 BELORUSS. FRONT
A.Gr. CENTRE
Minsk
4
Mogilev
Bialystok
Stolbtsy
Bobruysk
Rogachev
Vistula
Bug
Baranovichi
Slutsk
9
1 BELORUSSIAN FRONT
WARSAW
Brest-Litovsk
2
Pinsk
PRIPET
Gomel
MARSHES
Pripet
1 BELORUSSIAN FRONT
Baranow
Kovel
4 Pz.
A.Gr. NORTHERN UKRAINE
Rovno
Zhitomir
Kiev
1 UKRAINIAN FRONT
Dnieper
GALICIA
Lvov
Ternopol
CARPATHIANS
1 Pz.
4 UKRAINIAN FRONT
100 miles
Kolomyya
Dnestr
Chernovtsy
2 UKR. FRONT
FRONT LINE on 22 June 1944
8
3 UKR. FRONT
6
Odessa
A.Gr. SOUTHERN UKRAINE
Galician operation expected by Hitler

Vistula-Baltic operation so enthralled the Führer's Headquarters that there was never any shadow of doubt that the Russians might, after all, be planning something different. All warnings and appeals by army commanders were in vain.

The result was that OKH concentrated all available reserves in Galicia. Above all its Panzer divisions. Four Panzer corps with eight Panzer and two Panzer Grenadier divisions. A considerable force.

The other fronts, in particular Army Group Centre, were ruthlessly denuded. Confidently the German High Command was looking forward to the expected encounter along the front of Army Group Northern Ukraine. And its new commander-in-chief, Field-Marshal Model, was almost as optimistic as OKH itself: for the first time, he pointed out, a concentrated Soviet effort would be matched by a concentrated German effort.

It was a vain hope. It showed how poorly the German High Command was informed, how little it knew of the actual facts. For years the Führer's Headquarters had underrated the Soviets; now it overrated their strategic daring.

In the summer of 1944 the Soviet High Command had no such far-reaching strategic plans in mind as Hitler was crediting it with. His experiences on the Donets and on the Dnieper made Stalin recoil from such great projects. The catastrophe of Popov's armoured group and of Sixth Army in the battles at Krasnoarmeyskoye and Kharkov had made him careful. Besides, he very rarely attacked the enemy at his strongest point. And a brilliant reconnaissance effort enabled him to base his plans on an accurate knowledge of the enemy's situation. In the summer of 1944 this method achieved the very opposite of what the Germans expected. Stalin did what Manstein had wanted to do in the Kursk salient at the very last moment, when he appreciated the very strong Russian defences along its flanks—attack the salient frontally at the point where the enemy was weak, or at any rate weaker than at the corner-posts.

For precisely that reason Stalin set in motion his plan of operation against the salient of Army Group Centre. The Führer's Headquarters, unfortunately, had no "Werther" at STAVKA to supply them with information.

The disastrous extent to which the German High Command remained rooted in its strategic error to the very last minute is shown by a lecture given by Field-Marshal Keitel, the Chief of OKW, on 20th June, 1944, about the general military situation. He explained that the Russians would not attack until the Western Powers had achieved some major successes with their invasion forces which had landed in Normandy on 6th June. And the focal point of the Soviet effort would then be in Galicia and not against Army Group Centre.

Forty-eight hours later the Chief of the German High Command was given the lie in a most alarming manner. The Russians attacked. But not in Galicia.

The 22nd June, 1944, was the anniversary of Operation Barbarossa —the third anniversary of the German attack on Russia. With his infallible feeling for the effect which such anniversaries had on the Russian mind, Stalin exploited the sensations and passions aroused by them for a fanatical boosting of the morale of his troops. Just as he had ordered Kiev to be captured for the Revolution Anniversary, on 7th November, 1943, so he now made the anniversary of the German attack against the Soviet Union his D-day for the decisive offensive of the summer of 1944.

In order to keep the German Command guessing as long as possible about the focal point of that summer offensive, Marshal Zhukov, one of the two STAVKA plenipotentiaries for the over-all operation, decided on a phased opening along the 450 miles of weakened front of Army Group Centre. The great moment had come.

The first act belonged to the partisans. During the night of 19th–20th June the territory behind the front was rocked by sabotage on a vast scale. By daybreak 10,500 explosions had severed all railway lines from the Dnieper to west of Minsk. The principal bridges were blown up. Supply traffic was interrupted, often for more than twenty-four hours.

Not only were the railways paralysed—much worse, the telephone cables along the railways had been cut in several thousand places. And since in 1944 there was no such thing as railway traffic control by radio, the entire command apparatus of the "General in command Transport, Centre", was paralysed. This total paralysis of all rail traffic was a decisive cause of the catastrophic development during the next forty-eight hours. Railway transport, after all, was the life-blood of military organization. Once that circulation was interrupted a dangerous paralysis must set in.

Colonel Teske, the "General in command Transport", realized the completeness of this collapse when he flew over the territory in his Storch. All the stations and sections of rail were congested. Engines were moving only yard by yard. The few trains still functioning had clusters of people hanging from them, even from the engine—mostly casualties from the threatened areas.

The following figures illustrate the problem. On 1st July some 8000 wounded had to be evacuated from Minsk. On 7th July there were 98 transport trains moving towards the Army Group. On the same day there were altogether 216 trains in the area of Army Group, namely 138 troop transports, 59 supply trains, 12 trains for the Luftwaffe, and seven for the railway engineers. They encountered the greatest difficulty in making any headway at all. The urgently needed supplies did not reach the front—neither troops nor ammunition.

The second act of the great battle opened on 22nd June. Colonel-General Reinhardt's Third Panzer Army was attacked on both sides of Vitebsk on the Dvina by the First Baltic Front and parts of the Third Belorussian Front. Twenty-four hours later the offensive spread to the sector of General von Tippelskirch's Fourth Army. Here the Soviet Second Belorussian Front was attacking the section of the Dnieper between Orsha and Mogilev. Finally, on 24th June, STAVKA unleashed the First Belorussian Front under Rokossovskiy against General Jordan's Ninth Army. This thrust was aimed at Bobruysk on the Berezina.

Thus it was not until 24th June that the German Command realized that the Russians had mounted their big, decisive blow along the entire front of Army Group Centre. On 23rd June the Führer's Headquarters still indulged itself in the delusion that the Russian attacks in the centre were no more than a diversion for the expected operation from Galicia. Twenty-four hours later Hitler realized his fatal mistake.

The weight of the Soviet offensive, the crushing superiority of artillery, tanks, and ground-support aircraft was obvious after the first forty-eight hours. Aghast, Hitler and his advisers stared at the alarming reports from the front. Horrified, they realized what German reconnaissance had quite clearly failed to discover—the deployment of an unprecedented Soviet offensive force, an irresistible tidal wave which swept away within hours what had stood up to all Russian attacks through a year of six heavy defensive battles.

Field-Marshal Busch defended the eastern sector of Army Group Centre, a front nearly 450 miles long, with three armies of altogether thirty-four divisions. His weak Second Army on the Pripet was covering the southern flank and the link with Army Group Northern Ukraine. A single Panzer division, the 20th Panzer Division, had been deployed behind Ninth Army at Bobruysk for a number of days. Nearly all the other Panzer divisions on the Eastern Front were in Galicia or in the area west of Kovel, waiting for an enemy who was not attacking there. And what other reserves were there? Behind the Fourth Army Busch only had the 14th Infantry Division; on the right wing of Third Panzer Army he had the 95th Infantry Division. At Mogilev—i.e., on the sector of Ninth Army—was the "Feldherrnhalle" Panzer Grenadier Division, but this was still being replenished, and on the left wing was the 707th Infantry Division. And that was all. Or not quite all—there was also the Sixth Air Fleet under Colonel-General Ritter von Greim. But all it had left on the day of the attack was forty operational fighters. A mere forty. Everything else was in Germany or in France, where barely three weeks earlier, on 6th June, the Allied invasion had begun with a crushing superiority in the air. It was the Second Front which Stalin had for years been urging the Allies to open. Stalin waited another sixteen days to make sure this was in fact the massive, hoped-for, and successful support of the Western Powers. When it was clear that the operation in Normandy was not just another Dieppe, but the invasion proper, mounted with all the military weight the West could summon, Stalin struck as well. Now he could be sure that Hitler would not withdraw from France a single division, a single tank, or a single aircraft to help his hard-pressed Army Group Centre.

Marshal Zhukov and Marshal Vasilevskiy, two Red Army aces, commanded the Soviet forces now facing Busch's thirty-four divisions. The Russians had a numerical superiority of six to one, but in terms of weapons it was more than ten to one. Four Russian Army Groups with fourteen armies, reinforced by armoured formations, and five air armies were deployed for action. That came to nearly 200 divisions with 2,500,000 men. And what equipment! Altogether 6000 tanks and assault guns, 45,000 guns and mortars, and 7000 aircraft not counting long-range formations. Not to mention automatic weapons, explosives, and motor vehicles.

In the face of such superior forces, the German armies which throughout the winter of 1943–44 had stood up to all Soviet attacks, were now in a hopeless position. Hopeless not only because of their material inferiority, but also because Hitler's rigid hold-on orders were depriving them of all strategic latitude and seriously impeded even their tactical operations. A third handicap, finally, was the fact that many of their divisions were tied to the so-called "fortified localities". Fortified localities, indeed! On the lines of the fortresses and forts of past wars, these had been conceived from Hitler's experience in the First World War, notably the tactics of Verdun and Douaumont. On this outdated experience Hitler based a new hold-on strategy—the strategy of a numerically inferior force—and in this way he was hoping to outmanoeuvre the Russian large-scale offensives.

The idea was simple enough. Important communication centres, supply centres, and places of political and historical prestige, would be defended in every possible way, to the last round. In this way these "fortresses" would tie down such large enemy forces that supplies to the formations which had broken through the line would be seriously disrupted and the enemy's striking power broken.

In the area of Army Group Centre the towns of Slutsk, Bobruysk, Mogilev, Orsha, Vitebsk, and Polotsk were declared such "fortified localities"; one front-line division each was earmarked for their defence, with the exception of Vitebsk which was assigned three.

It was a plausible plan but it had one snag. The idea would work only if the enemy really attacked those "fortified localities" and concentrated his forces there. But supposing he did not do so? Supposing he did not attack them at all, but merely by-passed them, leaving a sentry outside, without allowing himself to be slowed down in his advance?

And there was something else. In the event of an enemy break-through the German armies and corps could not hope to seal off the pierced front again because all available divisions were tied down in the "fortified localities".

But Hitler dismissed all these objections by his army commanders. He refused to see that an entirely new Red Army had appeared on the battlefields in the summer of 1944. That was no longer the Red Army of 1941 or 1942. Staffs and troops in the field had learnt important lessons from the operations of 1943. They had learnt, above all, how to concentrate their efforts at focal points, how to use mobile troops to the best effect, and how to employ large-scale, formations of armour.

Moreover, the Russians were generously equipped with weapons and ammunition. The Soviet war economy had reached its zenith in 1944. By its appeal to Russian patriotism, the Bolshevik system had inspired a quite astonishing effort among the Soviet population. Military successes in the liberation of extensive areas and Hitler's disastrous occupation policy with its philosophy of "inferior races" further emphasized this trend. And finally there was every kind of American aid, which by 1944 had reached its peak: many divisions of the Red Army moved on American trucks, fired American shells, lived on Canadian wheat, and wore uniforms of American cloth.

The decisive battle of the Soviet summer offensive was thus fought at the height of the Soviet Union's war effort, both economic and in terms of morale. Germany, on the other hand, had reached its lowest point. As the 20th July, the date of the attempt on Hitler's life, was casting its shadow forward over the Third Reich, the Soviet Union experienced a powerful upsurge of patriotic sentiment. Hundreds of thousands of solemn pledges were being taken; hundreds of thousands of Soviet citizens swore to fight to their last drop of blood.

To quote just one instance among many: at a mass rally Vera Proshina, a girl radio operator in the 103rd Tank Brigade, expressed her thoughts and feelings in this way: "Today my dream is coming true—to kill the Hitlerites from inside a tank, to avenge the sufferings of the people, to avenge my own sorrow. The Fascists have killed my father and mother. I will therefore destroy them mercilessly and thus show what a Soviet girl is capable of. Death to the accursed conquerors!"

This public fighting oath, together with other similar obligations undertaken by soldiers and officers, was distributed on the front in millions of leaflets and was emulated a thousandfold. It produced nationwide support for the devotion, the courage, and the effort of the fighting forces.

As for the strategic decisions behind the "Belorussian operation", as the big summer offensive was called, we have a more distinguished witness than Vera Proshina. Marshal Rokossovskiy, the Commander-in-Chief of the First Belorussian Front, which attacked on the sector of the German Ninth Army, has written an exceedingly instructive essay disclosing various hitherto unknown facts about the dramatic struggle which the generals had with Stalin about the plan of the operation.

Rokossovskiy, twice Hero of the Soviet Union, at one time a stonemason and a sergeant in the Dragoons of the Tsar's army, was a typical general produced by the Revolution—courageous, cool, with a natural gift for strategy and a dash of Dragoon bravado. A man with an easy manner, and indeed charm—the legacy perhaps of the Polish side of his ancestry. In many respects Rokossovskiy was not unlike Manstein.

The objective of liberating Belorussia, Rokossovskiy reports, had been set to the Fronts concerned as early as the autumn of 1943, "when we were pushing towards the Dnieper. But the task proved impossible then, because we had suffered too heavy losses in the course of the summer's fighting. As the troops of our Front reached the Sozh and the Dnieper, the enemy's resistance increased markedly and we had to make an all-out effort to get across the Sozh and move our armies into the ground between the two rivers, the Dnieper and the Pripet. For anything more our strength was inadequate. We had to make a pause to rally our strength again." That was Rokossovskiy's account.

About the middle of March 1944 Rokossovskiy received a telephone call from Stalin. Stalin acquainted him with the outlines of his Front's tasks. At the beginning of May 1944 the plan of operations began to be worked out in detail. Rokossovskiy's sector was to be the focal point of the battle. Its first phase was to involve the capture of Bobruysk, the road and rail centre in the middle of the forest and swamp country of the Berezina lowlands.

Bobruysk was vital for the farther operation towards Brest-Litovsk. Rokossovskiy and his staff came to the conclusion that the attack must be mounted in the form of a pincer movement, with two armies and a tank corps for each jaw—the one moving towards Bobruysk from the north-west, from the Rogachev area, and the other from the south, aiming at Bobruysk and Slutsk. But the Soviet generals too had to deal with a dictator who had his own strategic ideas—ideas frequently as obstinate as Hitler's.

The conference to discuss the plan was held at Stalin's Headquarters on 22nd and 23rd May. Rokossovskiy's decision gave rise to violent argument. Stalin and several STAVKA members demanded that he should concentrate all his forces for a single offensive thrust from the Dnieper bridge-head. The experienced general's arguments that for such a move the operations area was too small and the ground too difficult, and that the attack would expose its flank to the north, were all dismissed. Stalin stubbornly insisted on a single offensive thrust. Just as Hitler had his "fortified localities", so Stalin had his theory of concentrated thrusts, a theory he stubbornly wanted to see applied everywhere. He was, of course, right in principle, but in this particular case the situation called for a departure from the rule. But Stalin refused to acknowledge that. It is interesting to see by what method he tried to force his will upon his marshals and army group commanders. Here is Rokossovskiy's account:

"Stalin ordered me to go to the next room and think over STAVKA's proposal for twenty minutes. Then I was to come back. But there was nothing for me to think over. When the time was up I returned and continued to stick to my view. I was sent back to the next room. Again for twenty minutes. During this second confinement Foreign Minister Molotov and Stalin's right-hand man Malenkov joined me. They disapproved of my quarrelling with the Supreme Commander. They asked me to accept STAVKA's proposal. I replied that I was convinced of the correctness of my view and that, if STAVKA ordered me to mount an offensive according to its own plan, I would have to ask to be relieved of the command of the Front. I returned to the conference room. But again I failed to convince Stalin and his advisers. I was sent next door for a third time. But when I returned for the third time and still stuck to my view my plan was approved."

Not, however, without a biting remark by Stalin about the army general's obstinacy or with the warning that he would be held responsible for the operation. Rokossovskiy accepted the responsibility. He had saved his plan of operation.

2. Attack

"Storm five, five, five"–Fatal hesitation–The Bobruysk trap–Bloodthirsty Berezina–Vitebsk in the grip of the pincers–"Personally vouch for struggle to the end"– A mystery solved: Soviet command of the air.

AT their very first attempt the Soviets achieved deep penetrations on the left wing of the Army Group's front, on the sector of Third Panzer Army. Within twenty-four hours the "fortified locality" of Vitebsk was in the grip of the Red pincers.

Things were the same with Fourth Army. The divisions of the Soviet Second Belorussian Front struck towards Orsha and Mogilev and soon tore a wide gap into the front of General Tippelskirch's army east of Mogilev. Behind Mogilev stood the "Feldherrnhalle" Panzer Grenadier Division, the former 60th Motorized Infantry Division from West Prussia and Danzig; it owed its new name to the SA Guards Regiment which had been added to it.

Its first action in the battle of the summer offensive was typical of the kind of thing that was happening between Dnieper and Berezina. Since the middle of May, following some tough fighting north of Vitebsk, the division had been in its reserve position, for rest and replenishment. Parts of its artillery regiment and the panzer battalion were still in Germany. Some of their replacements were coming from Norway; they were used to the quiet life of an occupied country, not to the rigours of the war in the East. The last transport arrived about mid-June, eight days before the offensive. Without any combat experience the men went into this merciless battle.

On the evening of the first day of battle "Feldherrnhalle" received orders to stop "the hole east of Mogilev". When the division commander, General von Steinkeller, reported to the general commanding XXXIX Corps, General Martinek shook his head. "Precisely what hole are you supposed to stop? We've got nothing but holes here. Your place is back on the Berezina, so that we should have an interception line there for when we can't hold out on the Dnieper any longer. And that'll be pretty soon."

Martinek was right. The Berezina runs about forty-five miles west of the Dnieper. If "Feldherrnhalle" had in fact been employed there, alongside the 18th Panzer Grenadier Division at Berezina, with the idea of intercepting the mixed-up divisions of Fourth Army, a good many things might have been avoided. For it was on the Berezina that the great catastrophe occurred soon afterwards.

But orders were otherwise. "Feldherrnhalle" went into action some sixty miles east of the Berezina, beyond the Dnieper. In a hopeless position. A drop in the ocean. "During the night of 25th–26th June," General von Steinkeller later reported, "I succeeded, more by good luck than good management, in getting my divisions back across the Dnieper at Mogilev."

While the general was leading the division's armoured formations against the Soviet tanks, its chief of operations, Lieutenant-Colonel Felsch, received the following signal from XII Army Corps at 1400 hours on 24th June: "Troops fighting their way through to the west; 12th Infantry Division defending Mogilev." From that moment onwards there was virtually no control left in the area of operations. The roads to the west were congested by baggage vehicles and units of the most varied divisions, streaming back with no clear objective in

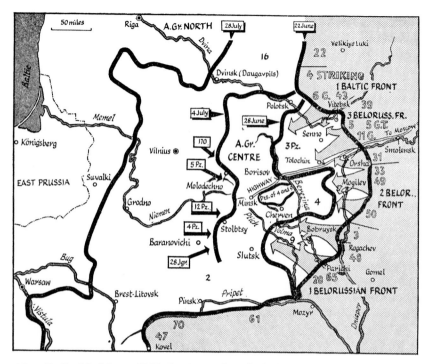

Map 49. On 22nd June, 1944, the Soviets launched their all-out offensive against the salient of Army Group Centre. The "fortified localities" of Vitebsk, Orsha, Mogilev, and Bobruysk were encircled by pincer movements, but the bulk of the Soviet offensive forces swept on towards the west. Thus, Hitler's strategy of "fortified localities" collapsed: the weak front crumbled, and the bulk of Fourth and Ninth Armies was trapped between Minsk and the Berezina. Model, the newly appointed Army Group commander, tried in vain to stabilize an interception line between Baranovichi and the Dvina by means of counter-attacks by hurriedly brought-up divisions. Five weeks after the start of their offensive the Soviets were on the Vistula and on the border of East Prussia.

any direction that was possible. And every now and again Soviet tanks thrust into these columns.

Just then the Soviets delivered their main blow on the right wing of the Army Group—Rokossovskiy's First Belorussian Front mounted its attack against Bobruysk.

General Batov, the C-in-C of the Soviet Sixty-Fifth Army, had chosen for his armoured thrust at Bobruysk a spot where General Jordan and his German Ninth Army had least expected a tank attack—across five hundred yards of swamp believed impassable. It was a masterly operation. Prepared mats of twigs and sticks were laid across the swamp by army engineers under cover of smoke screens, in much the same way as an army bridge is pushed across a river.

"Storm five, five, five," squeaked the RT receivers of the tank commanders. It was the code-word for the attack by the Don Tank Corps across the four hundred yards of corduroy road on 24th June. The infantry too received its signal for attack. They too got across the treacherous swamp which was guarded only by a thin line of German pickets from 36th Motorized Infantry Division. They crossed the swamp like skiers crossing an expanse of new snow—on their feet were home-made skis of plaited willow wands. It was another instance of the Russian's talent for improvisation. Swamp, primeval forest, and night were their favourite elements and they coped with their difficulties superbly.

The XLI Panzer Corps was completely taken by surprise. What was General Hoffmeister to do? His corps was a Panzer corps in name only —apart from 36th Motorized Infantry Division it consisted of only two infantry divisions. The obvious counter-blow against the enemy's surprise tank thrust towards the Mogilev–Bobruysk highway would have been the employment of 20th Panzer Division which was in an exceedingly favourable reserve position near Bobruysk. But General Jordan, hoping no doubt that XLI Corps would be able to cope with the critical situation on its own, hesitated a whole day before making a clear decision. It was a fatal hesitation. But then this kind of failure by normally experienced commanders was typical also of this disastrous battle. And it was such an obvious opportunity.

East of the Bobruysk bridge over the Berezina was the reinforced 2nd Battalion, 21st Panzer Regiment, of the Hessian 20th Panzer Division. It was well placed. It could be employed against either a northerly or a southerly thrust by the Russians. The battalion was superbly equipped. It had about a hundred battleworthy Mark IVs. But it received no orders. Finally its commander, Major Paul Schulze, acting on his own initiative hurled himself with three of his companies against the tank attack of the Soviet Forty-Eighth Army north of Bobruysk. But he could not prevent a tank corps of the Soviet Third Army achieving a breakthrough farther north, along the junction with Fourth Army. Schulze left a company with about twenty Mark IVs behind as a tactical reserve and with the rest of his tanks moved off again to strike at the flank of the Russians who had broken through.

No sooner had he mounted his attack than a contrary order arrived from Army: Employment south of Bobruysk. Ninth Army HQ had at last realized that the main danger threatening it was from Batov's Don Tank Corps thrusting towards the north–south highway. Even so it was a major blunder to snatch Schulze's tanks away from the attack they had just mounted in order to send them to the south. In consequence, the strong German armoured forces were unable to intervene effectively at any of the threatened points.

Major Schulze quite rightly observed: "While we were travelling from north to south the Russians smashed the strongpoints of our infantry divisions and overran them. Thus, all along my move to the southern sector of Ninth Army, I encountered only formations in flight."

Nevertheless, the counter-attack by the armoured group made quite good progress to start with. But while the tanks were still clearing up Russian penetrations at the front, the villages in their rear were already in flames. The Russians had broken through in the north-west and were threatening the rear of Schulze's Panzer combat group.

The major pulled Lieutenant Begemann's Panzer company out of the operation and made it race back to the north in order to keep open the crossroads and bridge east of Bobruysk.

It was astonishing to see what a single, strong, armoured formation under bold and resolute leadership was able to achieve. But unfortunately it was the only such formation in that area. Indeed the whole of Army Group Centre only had another two Panzer battalions and a few assault gun formations. Of these more than a third were again positioned in the wrong place—*i.e.*, at the front of Second Army. With such modest forces, no matter how well equipped and brilliantly led, it was impossible to break up the attack of fourteen Russian armies and half a dozen independent tank corps.

General Jordan's irresolute leadership earned the Army Group its first decisive defeat. It cost the general his command. This otherwise outstanding officer became the first scapegoat of the great summer battle. He was dismissed and replaced by General von Vormann, an experienced and energetic leader. But he could not have taken over the Ninth Army at a worse moment.

By the morning of 28th June, 1944, the situation reports from the corps no longer left any doubt about the extent of the disaster. The major part of Ninth Army was surrounded at Bobruysk on the eastern bank of the Berezina and Soviet advanced formations were moving across the river to the west.

On 29th June the "fortified locality" of Bobruysk fell. In a desperate break-out during a clear night the Panzer grenadiers and Panzer companies of 20th Panzer Division fought their way out of the town and through the Soviet blocking formations. Coolly the commanders of three hard-hit infantry divisions, and the chief of operations of 20th Panzer Division, Lieutenant-Colonel Schöneich, organized the final break-out.

In front were the Panzer grenadiers. They were followed by the last few tanks under Major Schulze. Then came ten assault guns under Captain Brade. In bitter fighting the break-out succeeded. Thus at least a part of XLI Panzer Corps and XXXV Army Corps had re-established contact with the main front. But 5000 wounded remained in Bobruysk. Roughly 30,000 men had escaped from the Bobruysk trap

when on 4th July Colonel Demme, commanding 59th Panzer Grenadier Regiment, reached Ninth Army's interception line with the rearguard of 20th Panzer Division. Thirty thousand out of roughly 100,000.
No-one knows how many troops were drowned in the treacherous,
bloodthirsty Berezina, or lost their lives in the vast forests and swampy
lowlands.

Rokossovskiy's blow on the southern wing, against the German
Ninth Army, had been successful. He had fulfilled his plan ahead of
schedule: the encirclement of Bobruysk had been envisaged by
STAVKA for the eighth day of the summer offensive, but was in fact
achieved on the fourth.

And what was the situation on the Third Belorussian Front and the
First Baltic Front, on the northern wing of Army Group Centre, where
the German Third Panzer Army was resisting the Russian attack? Here
the town of Vitebsk was the first strategic objective of the Russians.
The "fortified locality" on the Dvina was enveloped by two massive
pincer jaws but was not directly attacked. Another illustration of the
ineffectiveness of Hitler's strategy of "fortified localities".

This powerful thrust also took the command of Third Panzer Army
by surprise. True enough, Colonel-General Reinhardt, its C-in-C, had
repeatedly drawn attention to the danger along his sector. About the
middle of May in an appreciation of the situation he had referred
Field-Marshal Busch to the massive deployment of enemy formations
in front of the Army's left wing, and had therefore concluded that the
main defensive effort should be concentrated in the area north of
Vitebsk. But Field-Marshal Busch and OKH had not gone along with
Reinhardt's assessment of the situation. They did not believe in a
pincer operation aiming past Vitebsk into the depths of the German
rear; they clung to their wishful thinking that a powerful thrust would
be made against Vitebsk itself and would doubtless be stopped by the
garrison acting as a breakwater.

"What can I do?" Busch more than once asked his chief of staff,
Lieutenant-General Krebs, at his headquarters in Minsk. "What can
I do?" What he meant was that it was impossible to upset Hitler's
assessment of the situation. And since there was no answer to his
question he had been consoling himself with the assurance that his
experienced Third Panzer Army would surely discharge its breakwater
task in one way or another.

But Reinhardt's army no longer possessed its former fighting power.
Nearly a third of its divisions had been sent to other sectors of the
front. Of its powerful army artillery it had kept less than half. The
only reserves it had was the 14th Infantry Division and a few engineer
battalions. In the rearward army area there was only the 201st Local

Defence Division and a local defence battalion. But the Führer's Headquarters was acting as if nothing had changed. All right, so there were fewer forces and bigger tasks—but to the German soldier nothing was impossible!

Thus, acting upon Hitler's directives, Busch moreover had ordered Third Panzer Army to concentrate three to four divisions, in other words more than one-third of its entire fighting power, inside the "fortified locality" of Vitebsk. Protestations were in vain. It was a grotesque order.

But what could Reinhardt do? He had received an order. A controversial order, but an order none the less. And that order demanded that Vitebsk was to be made as strong as possible and an entire corps with four divisions was to be stationed inside the fortress. The Führer's Headquarters were convinced that the Russians would attack the town and find themselves pinned down in front of it with twenty to thirty divisions. But the Russians did not attack. They simply by-passed the fortress with its four divisions and thereby upset the entire German defensive concept.

The question arises: How was it possible for the German command to be so totally mistaken about the enemy's strength and intentions?

That the German side should have no insight into the major strategic intentions of the Soviet High Command was nothing out of the ordinary—there simply was no German intelligence service inside the senior Soviet commands. Germany had no Dr Sorge and no "Werther". But that even the intentions of the lower enemy commands in the frontal area should have remained concealed from the Germans—that surely was most unusual. As a rule aerial reconnaissance, deserters, local scouts, tapped telephone cables, and intercepted radio signals provided a fair idea of the enemy's tactical intentions. Monitoring and radio intelligence had frequently achieved considerable successes in that respect. Why did all that fail with Army Group Centre in the summer of 1944?

The answer to that question is supplied by Lieutenant-General S. Pokrovskiy, then chief of staff of the Soviet Third Belorussian Front. In an interesting account he reveals astonishing details of Russian methods of deception and camouflage. The troops, for instance, were made to dig trenches and build defences until a few days before the offensive. In this way they were themselves made to believe that the divisions were getting ready for a protracted period of positional warfare. And all that was done solely in order to deceive German aerial reconnaissance, agents, and the carriers of news. In order to keep their planning secret, strict security rules were imposed even on senior staffs. Written documents concerning the operation could be prepared only by certain listed officers and had to be passed on by hand. There was a strict ban on transmitting any information connected with the operation by mechanical means—by telephone, teleprinter, or radio. The written directives were issued separately for each army and not until 20th June—*i.e.*, two days before the start of the offensive. These were draconian, inhibiting, and entirely exceptional measures, but they undoubtedly bore fruit and paid off.

Since the gigantic deployment of more than twenty armies with 207 divisions could not be entirely concealed in the Russian hinterland, the Soviet General Staff took special measures to keep German aerial reconnaissance at bay. Special fighter commandos were continually in action in order to engage German reconnaissance machines. Of course, these measures were not a hundred per cent successful but they sufficiently obstructed German reconnaissance to prevent the collection of conclusive evidence.

But it is always the little things that go wrong and no plan is ever perfect. At the beginning of June a Russian "sewing machine", one of those slow, old-fashioned reconnaissance planes, was shot down in the zone of operations of the Silesian 252nd Infantry Division. In it was a Soviet major from the staff of an air division, and he was captured almost unscathed. In his document case were some exceedingly interesting hand-written papers of the Third Air Army, papers allowing far-reaching conclusions to be drawn about the threatening offensive. The division commander, Lieutenant-General Melzer, passed the matter on to IX Corps. But what use are discovered secrets if no-one wants to believe them?

Colonel-General Ivan Danilovich Chernyakhovskiy, the Commander-in-Chief of the Third Belorussian Front, was one of the most gifted Soviet generals. Not a grey-haired warrior grown old in the service of the Revolution, but a man of the younger generation, only thirty-eight. A bold commander in the field, passionately interested in all modern weapons and technical achievements. Also in terms of character the ideal type for the Soviet system of command, based as it was on team work between Commander-in-Chief, chief of staff, and Military Council member—the so-called collective. He was killed in action in East Prussia in 1945.

Chernyakhovskiy and his right-hand neighbour, the bald and cautious Army General Bagramyan, proceeded according to the STAVKA recipe. First, a tremendous artillery barrage from 10,000 guns. Then aerial bombardment by two air armies with more than 1000 bombers. Then the troops moved in. With four rifle armies in its first block, the Third Belorussian Army attacked the German VI Corps south of Vitebsk. The main weight fell upon the 299th Infantry Division. It collapsed. Then came the second blow. Chernyakhovskiy had a tank corps and another fast group composed of mechanized formations and cavalry ready to pounce from a concealed position. No sooner was the German front ripped open than the tanks and mechanized brigades rushed into the gap, overrunning the last German centres of resistance and racing past Vitebsk in the south.

North of the town Bagramyan's First Baltic Front followed the same pattern with three rifle armies and one tank corps. Bagramyan struck at General Wuthmann's IX Corps north of Vitebsk. There was violent fighting in the area of the Silesian 252nd Infantry Division. The Russians made a penetration. A German counter-attack. A tank thrust. A bombing raid. After twelve hours the Silesians had to give ground. The IX Corps pulled back to a protective position twenty miles behind Vitebsk. There, for the moment, General Wuthmann was able to re-establish a line.

But what use was that? Bagramyan and Chernyakhovskiy wheeled their inner wings to left and right. Within three days the "fortified locality" of Vitebsk was surrounded. The great hope that Vitebsk would be a barrier, to be defended to the last round by General Gollwitzer with the four divisions of his LIII Corps in order to pin down the main Soviet forces—that hope had gone.

Colonel-General Reinhardt realized the disaster and at the last moment snatched one of those divisions, the 4th Luftwaffe Field Division, out of Vitebsk. But on 24th June in the early morning this move was no longer of any use. It came too late. Already Rotmistrov's Fifth Guards Tank Army was about to pounce on the lower end of the firm strip extending between Dnieper and Dvina through the swamps towards Minsk. Once the Soviet breakthrough was accomplished, Rotmistrov's army was to achieve the real strategic objective in the sector of the Third Belorussian Front—the thrust down the motor highway towards Minsk. That great highway along which Guderian's Panzer divisions had once raced in the opposite direction from Brest-Litovsk to the Dnieper, in a mere fifteen days.

By 24th June the Soviet armies had thrust deep into the German rear, past Vitebsk, and the "fortified locality" had lost its meaning. The divisions inside it were doomed. And meanwhile, at the pierced front, they were badly missed. By now this was obvious even to a child. But the Führer's Headquarters refused to have it so and decided on a half-hearted measure. At 1830 hours Hitler sent a signal to Gollwitzer authorizing the break-out of LIII Corps. But simultaneously he ordered: "One division will remain in Vitebsk and continue to hold out. The name of the commander is to be reported to me."

So one division was now to defend what four divisions had not been able to hold! With a heavy heart Army chose Lieutenant-General Hitter's 206th Infantry Division for this death-and-glory assignment. But nothing had been gained. Permission for the break-out of the other divisions arrived too late anyway—on the evening of 24th June. On 25th June at 1312 a signal from General Gollwitzer was received at Third Panzer Army: "Situation drastically changed. Totally encircled. 4th Luftwaffe Field Division no longer exists. 246th Infantry Division and 6th Luftwaffe Field Division engaged in heavy fighting in several directions. Fierce fighting in the built-up area of Vitebsk."

The LIII Corps with its 35,000 men went to its death. At 1930 the corps commander signalled from Vitebsk: "Personally vouch for struggle to the end. Gollwitzer." This was a deliberate allusion to the historic signal sent to Kaiser Wilhelm on 23rd August, 1914, by the commander of Tsingtao in East Asia. Captain Meyer-Waldeck then signalled from his fortress, 7000 miles from home: "Personally vouch for fulfilment of duty to the end." The "end" was two and a half months away when he decided to defend Tsingtao with his 4000 men against 40,000 Japanese.

Gollwitzer's strength lasted barely two days. His signal was the last signal out of the town. On the morning of 26th June he got ready for a break-out towards the south-west. With parts of his units he reached an area twelve miles south-west of Vitebsk on 27th June. What happened then is reported by the Soviet chronicler of the *History of the Great Fatherland War*: "One German group of about 8000 men succeeded in breaking out of the Vitebsk pocket but it was soon encircled again. On the morning of 27th June the remnants of the enemy divisions accepted an ultimatum of the Soviet Commander-in-Chief and surrendered. The enemy lost 20,000 killed, and more than 10,000 soldiers and officers were taken prisoner. Among the prisoners was the commander of the LIII Army Corps, General of Infantry Gollwitzer, and his chief of staff, Colonel Schmidt."

And what about the East Prussian 206th Infantry Division which was to have held Vitebsk? What became of it? The continuous stream of radioed orders from the Führer's Headquarters, "206th Infantry Division will hold the town until relieved," could not in any way alter the fact that against the floodwave of the Soviet offensive there was nothing to hold. The divisions in the penetration area on the left wing of Army Group were crushed. Vitebsk was a grave. On 26th June at 1645 hours, therefore, Lieutenant-General Hitter ordered a break-out on his own responsibility. It was mounted about 2200 hours. The wounded had been loaded on horse-drawn carts and on an artillery tractor.

The shock groups made about nine miles' headway. Then they were pinned down. They were intercepted and encircled by formations of the Soviet Thirty-Ninth Army. One last attempt to charge through the Russian lines with fixed bayonets and yells of "Urra" failed. That was the last action of the ancient East Prussian 301st, 312th, and 413th Grenadier Regiments. The few survivors were killed or captured in a small patch of forest. Only a few groups of tough and desperate officers and troops saved themselves along adventurous routes. After a great deal of marching they reached the German lines and told the story of the extinction of their division.

A demobilization office was set up at Rudolstadt in Thuringia. Not in East Prussia, the division's home ground, because that was already threatened by the enemy. In laborious, painstaking work the names of the twelve thousand men who had been with the division had to be established—the catastrophe of Vitebsk had also resulted in the loss of all papers and documents. Twelve thousand notifications eventually went out to the next-of-kin of the missing men. On 18th July the division was officially declared dead and the order was given for its disbandment. The demobilization staff used the official date of the division's death for its new field post number: 18744. It was like engraving the date of death on a tombstone.

Among the files of the Rudolstadt demobilization office the question crops up again and again: How was it possible for an entire division to perish so swiftly and so terribly?

How was it possible for the Russians to have swept away from the battlefield so many gallant, experienced, and tough East Front divisions and within forty-eight hours hurled Army Group Centre into disaster?

To ask these questions means looking for the factors behind the Soviet victory. Was it their vast superiority? Yet the German front in the East had frequently stood up to a numerically superior enemy. Was it the fire power of the Soviet artillery? But that was nothing new and certainly not the key to the catastrophe. German divisions had been faced with that kind of concentrated artillery more than once before. The decisive factor was something entirely different—apart from the huge numerical superiority and the astonishingly good equipment of the Red Army, it was above all the appearance of a superior Red Air Force which brought the decisive shift in the balance of power. The Soviet superiority in the air was probably the nastiest surprise of all for the German troops in the East, and also the most decisive one. The long years of German command of the air over the Russian battlefields were suddenly at an end. The Allied Air Forces had swept the Russian skies clear for the Russians. None other than the Allied Air Forces in the West! After the first forty-eight hours of the invasion of France it became clear that the decision in the West would depend on whether Eisenhower's command of the air could be broken. This command of the air paralysed all effective counter-attacks by German armoured forces, it smashed the motorized divisions while they were still moving towards the coast, it shattered the Atlantic Wall and put Hitler's European Fortress out of action from above. Hermann Göring had made no provision for this contingency. Hence, during those early days of June 1944, Hitler had no choice but radically to denude his Eastern Front of all Luftwaffe *Geschwaders* and to switch them to the West.

The situation on the Eastern Front on 22nd June was characterized by the fact, already mentioned above, that the Sixth Air Fleet had a mere forty fighters available when the Soviet offensive began. Forty fighters against five Soviet air armies with seven thousand operational aircraft. Of course, the Luftwaffe hurriedly switched all available machines in the East to the threatened part of the front, but this was a drop in the ocean. The disaster in the air was complete. In the West the German *Geschwaders* were insufficient to challenge Eisenhower's command of the air, and in the East the German troops found themselves at the decisive moment without a roof, without any protection against an arm of vital importance in modern war. Thus the Soviets achieved mastery of the air, and this proved the principal factor in the catastrophic defeat of Army Group Centre.

The decisive role of the air force in ground operations was clearly revealed in the fighting on the central sector of the Soviet offensive, on the sector of the German Fourth Army. There, Army General Zakharov was leading his Second Belorussian Front against the last German positions on the Dnieper. The main Russian thrust was aimed across the Dnieper at Mogilev. Here too a Soviet army group with three armies and an air army was facing a single German army. In other words, twenty-two Soviet rifle divisions and four independent tank and mechanized brigades were lined up against ten German divisions, which admittedly included such experienced formations as 78th Storm Division, 18th Panzer Grenadier Division, and 12th Infantry Division.

The balance of forces was dangerous, but it was by no means such that catastrophe was inevitable. One handicap, certainly, was the fact that just before the Soviet offensive there had been several changes in senior German commands. General Tippelskirch had assumed command of what used to be Kluge's Fourth Army as recently as the first week of June; his XII Corps had gone to Lieutenant-General Vinzenz Müller. There was also a change of command at XXXV and XLI Corps after the dismissal of Generals Wiese and Weidling. There were consequential changes in division commands. None of that enhanced the fighting spirit of the troops. Worst of all, the responsibility for the central sector of the Army Group, with Orsha and the fortified Mogilev, had been entrusted to a new Commander-in-Chief who had not previously commanded an army. Moreover, he had an especially difficult task. He had orders to hold on in all circumstances to the position on the Dnieper which projected like a spearpoint in the flesh of the enemy. Admittedly, Tippelskirch had the support of two assault gun brigades and one Panzer battalion. An appreciable force —but not enough to offset the weakness of the German position.

It was obvious to Marshal Zhukov that the German Fourth Army would be a particularly tough nut to crack. For that reason he employed Air Marshal Verzinin's Fourth Air Army primarily against this sector. The Air Force was to beat Tippelskirch's trump cards. And it beat them all right. Verzinin had carefully reconnoitred the Fourth Army's system of defences over a depth of twenty miles. In particular, the German gun positions had been accurately pinpointed.

Simultaneously with the first charge by Zakharov's infantry, the Red ground-support aircraft appeared. They bombed the German positions. With their machine-guns they swept empty all approach roads. With their cannon they drilled the bunkers of the command posts. Bridges were destroyed by pinpoint-bombing. Minefields and wire obstacles were cleared by carpet-bombing. And then came something entirely new—special units swept over the battlefield at low altitude, attacking the feared German assault guns. It was the technique developed by Rudel. Marshal Verzinin had set up special ground-support air divisions for the purpose. Again the Russians had been quick to learn. There was no defence against those Red hawks. The sky was empty of German fighters.

But the Russian trump card was their air operation against the German artillery. This became a decisive phase of the battle between Dnieper and Berezina. Because of the low combat strength of the German infantry and the shortage of tanks, the artillery had become the backbone of the German defence. Many of its guns had been posted on forward slopes or in open positions to reinforce anti-tank defences. Army Group, armies, and corps expected decisive help from the gunners against the dangerous Soviet tank corps and mechanized brigades. The Soviet High Command had recognized these tactics in good time, or perhaps had been informed about them by their secret service. In any case, the Red Air Force countered successfully.

By means of well-prepared air strikes, the Russians succeeded in eliminating the previous reconnoitred or rapidly pinpointed gun positions of the German artillery. The backbone of the German defence was broken. The German infantry was helpless against any motorized or mechanized enemy. The same dilemma arose as in the West. Soviet ground-support aircraft bombed the retreating columns of the German rearward services and reserve units at bridges and road bottlenecks. The effect was devastating. There was chaos on the roads. No switching of units was possible, no movement was feasible. Faced with this sudden enemy superiority in the air, the German divisions were desperate and, in view of their defencelessness, frequently panicked. There was nothing the German command could do.

Nothing revealed more strikingly the turn in the military situation on the Eastern Front than the crushing superiority of the Soviet Air Force. Thanks to Eisenhower, Stalin had conquered the Russian skies. Without a protective roof overhead no front on earth could be held in the long run. The Russians had learnt this in 1941 and 1942. Now this law of modern warfare was being proved against the German armies—in both East and West.

3. Breakthrough

The situation map at Army Group HQ in Minsk–Model is appointed to save the situation–A gigantic pocket–Zhukov reprimands his generals–"Every man for himself"–Thirty-one generals killed or captured–The war reaches the East Prussian frontier–Diercks's group fights its way back.

THE 28th June, 1944, was a Wednesday. It was the thirtieth anniversary of the assassination of the Austrian heir to the throne, Franz Ferdinand, by the Serb anarchist Princip. That assassination triggered off the First World War. But German headquarters between Minsk and the Berezina had other things than historical reminiscences to worry about. The situation map at the Army Group's HQ at Minsk looked terrible. No solid, coherent front left. Breakthroughs everywhere. After a great many telephone-calls all efforts by Field-Marshal Busch to get Hitler to abandon his rigid hold-on strategy and permit the armies of the Army Group to go over to a flexible defence had come to nothing. Field-Marshal Busch was an excellent commander in the field—but he was not a strategic genius in the Manstein class. Besides, the northern front, where he successfully commanded an army for a number of years, had offered little opportunity to display his skill as a general. But above all, he was not the man to stand up to Hitler. He had yielded too often to Hitler's orders. Time and again Busch's superior military grasp and his incipient opposition had collapsed in the face of Hitler's eloquence and political arguments. Now that the Führer's orders had hurled the Army Group into disaster, Busch was given the blame and kicked out. Justifiably offended and deeply hurt, he silently left his headquarters. His successor was that great "firm stander", Field-Marshal Walter Model. He took over the central front and simultaneously retained his command of Manstein's old Army Group South, now Army Group Northern Ukraine. As a result, Model's command covered more than half of the Eastern Front. Never before in the war had Hitler entrusted so much military responsibility to one man. This was very nearly Manstein's old dream of a Commander-in-Chief, East. But this measure, too, came too late.

We have encountered Model as an inspired improviser, as a fearless man with iron nerves who had mastered the great crises of Rzhev, Orel, and the Leningrad area. Would he be able to avert the disaster threatening Army Group Centre?

He tried to do so in every possible way. But even Model could not raise armies from nothing. Without an effective Luftwaffe, without adequate anti-tank weapons, without a minimum of mobile reserves and infantry, even a general as bold and as favoured by the fortunes of war as Model could not stand up to the Soviet onslaught.

On 27th June Zhukov let Rotmistrov's Fifth Guards Tank Army off the leash and raced it across the strip of land between Dvina and Dnieper. Through Tolochin and Senno it thrust along the motor highway to Borisov on the upper Berezina. There the 5th Panzer Division, which had been brought up from Kovel, was just then being detrained. Together with police formations, Lieutenant-General Decker checked Rotmistrov's advanced formations. That same day the communication centre of Orsha fell to the Russians on the sector of Fourth Army.

In view of the situation Model, immediately upon assuming command, decided to go over to a flexible type of warfare. The 5th Panzer Division was employed as the nucleus of the Group von Saucken to cover the wide gap north of Minsk; 12th Panzer Division and 4th Panzer Division, which was being brought up, were switched to the Stolbtsy area south of Minsk in order to keep open the Berezina crossings for Fourth Army. Second Army was instructed to thrust in the direction of Ninth Army with its assault gun brigades and cavalry formations and also to re-establish contact with Fourth Army. In vain. Everything was in vain. The Soviet advance was no longer to be halted.

Minsk, the capital of Belorussia and the location of Army Group Centre HQ, fell on 3rd July. The city had been in German hands for three years. From Minsk ran the motor highway to Moscow, the fast road into the heart of the U.S.S.R. The expulsion of the Germans from this vital centre of Belorussia was therefore of symbolic importance. Minsk had been the first big city to be captured by the German Panzer blitzkrieg in 1941. Now this metropolis of western Russia was liberated. Small wonder that salutes were fired in Moscow on 3rd July, 1944.

But this was not just the liberation of a city. The major part of Fourth Army and parts of Ninth Army were surrounded in a huge pocket south-east of Minsk. In order to save what could be saved Model tried to build up a new front a long way behind Minsk, in front of the Baranovichi–Molodechno line, and meanwhile to halt the enemy with freshly brought up forces from the sectors of Army Groups North and Northern Ukraine. The intersections of the main roads through the huge forest areas of central Russia, the narrow strips of land between swamps, and the river crossings became the focal points of this defensive battle. The objective was to intercept the enemy by flexible operations. On this phase of the battle depended the fate of the last formations of Fourth and Ninth Armies which were still fighting at Minsk and were trying to fight their way back. Model brought up three Panzer divisions for this rescue operation, as well as a Jäger division and two infantry divisions.

The Silesian–Sudeten 5th Panzer Division north of Minsk cleared the important Minsk–Molodechno–Vilnius railway line and highway along which the reinforcements from Army Group North were arriving. The Pomeranian 12th Panzer Division flung itself in the path of the advanced detachments of the Soviet I Guards Tank Corps south-east of the city. The Würzburg 4th Panzer Division and the Silesian 28th Jäger Division defended the interception positions on the Niemen to both sides of Stolbtsy, holding open the only road of retreat to Baranovichi. The North German 170th Infantry Division was moved to Molodechno.

That was Model's method. He stopped the most dangerous holes, stiffened the collapsing front, and constantly moved among his units, encouraging, intervening, and even leading them into battle.

Zhukov soon noticed the new style of command on the German side. He knew from Rzhev and Orel what this man Model was capable of. He saw the danger of this Marshal snatching from him what he regarded as his certain prey.

It was a clash between two men charged with energy, between two forceful characters. The battle became personified in the two Marshals. Their duel was to be fought at Baranovichi.

Ceaselessly Zhukov spurred on General Batov's Sixty-Fifth Army: "Don't give them any respite, keep fighting, and take that rail centre Baranovichi!"

For a whole week Batov and his HQ personnel had been with the troops in the front line. On 7th July, when General Frolenko's division was already fighting on the edge of Baranovichi and the Sivash Division had almost reached the town from the east, the general, tired and filthy, drove back to Army HQ at the village of Velke to get some proper sleep again, have a wash, and eat a hot meal. But Batov had made his plan without Marshal Zhukov. He had just finished shaving, his mud-caked boots had been polished again after a long time, and a steaming glass of tea was on the table before him. Just then a car stopped outside, its brakes screeching.

Batov's chief of staff glanced out of the window. Zhukov! The two men hurriedly thrust their feet into their boots and went out on the landing to report their latest successes outside Baranovichi to the STAVKA representative. But Batov was given no chance of saying anything. Hands planted on his hips, Zhukov stood at the bottom of the stairs. "You are shaving! Perfuming yourself?" he roared without a word of greeting. "Why haven't you taken Baranovichi?" Then he asked coldly: "Where is the situation map?" They stepped into the room. Zhukov was in no way placated by Batov's detailed report but continued to blame him for not yet having taken Baranovichi.

Radetskiy, the Military Council member, pale with anger, tried to come to the aid of his Commander-in-Chief. He declared that at any moment he was expecting the news that the troops had entered the town. "And what makes you so sure?" the Marshal asked with a sneer. "There's only one way to be sure," he added. "You'll drive over to Baranovichi now and you won't come back until the town's been taken." He turned brusquely, fiercely kicked a footstool into the corner, slammed the door, and disappeared. Twenty-four hours later the Soviet Army communiqué announced: "Baranovichi has been liberated." Zhukov had won.

A sultry heat with large swarms of midges hung over the lowlands between Berezina and Volma. General von Steinkeller sat under a willow by a small stream, his map-board on his knees. The war was revolving around three names—Minsk, Cherven, and Borisov. They were trapped in this accursed bloody triangle. There the greater part of two armies died like cattle. The remnants of five corps of Ninth and Fourth Armies were caught in that scorching pocket. They were trying to get out towards the west, past Minsk, to reach some German interception line.

"Have you any news about the situation, Ratzel?" Steinkeller asked the commander of the artillery regiment. "Nothing beyond what it says in the communiqué!" the lieutenant-colonel replied. What it said in the communiqué! Beyond that they knew nothing. That was the information on which they had to base their moves. According to which they chose the direction of their break-out. But the High Command communiqué was no situation report. On the contrary— it glossed over the situation to boost morale and promote optimism. But there was no ground for optimism in the hot triangle of Minsk-Cherven-Borisov.

The artillery regiment of the "Feldherrnhalle" Division was its most experienced formation. Its NCOs were nearly all old front-line soldiers. For that reason the artillerymen with the guns of the 1st Light Battalion—the only one left of the regiment—were invariably the spearhead of any break-out attempt. The division, moreover, consisted of a few hundred grenadiers, six tanks, about sixteen armoured scout cars, and a dozen trucks crammed full with wounded.

A situation conference of all available unit commanders with the corps commanders had arrived at the opinion that the break-out should be made to the north-west. But then they learnt from the High Command communiqué that German Panzer divisions were thrusting towards Minsk. Surely that meant they must now change the direction of their break-out? They decided to make for the west or the south-west.

The men drew fresh hope. The HQ of the Munich XXVII Corps, parts of 78th Storm Division, 14th Infantry Division, the Silesian 18th Panzer Grenadier Division, and the 57th Infantry Division moved westwards. "Feldherrnhalle" kept a little more to the south-west. But the road was not clear. In vain did General Trowitz with combat groups of 57th Infantry Division and the units placed under it charge the blocking positions of the Soviet I Guards Tank Corps.

On 5th July at 1930 hours General Völckers disbanded his corps by radio signal and commanded: "Fight your way out westwards, every man for himself. Start at 2230 hours." Painful as the decision was, it came as a relief. Orders were quickly issued. At 2220 hours the artillery fired its last salvoes. The roar of the guns drowned the blowing up of the vehicles; the guns themselves were blown up with the last shells. With the determination of desperate men the regiments embarked on their break-out. Anything dispensable was left behind. Sick and wounded men, not capable of walking, were assembled at the centre of the pocket, to be left behind and handed over to the Russians.

At 2300 hours they assembled for the charge. The general objective was Baranovichi. A few units intoned "Deutschland über Alles". Villages were in flames. Shells were crashing all over the place. There was small-arms fire. And among it all the shrill, blood-chilling shouts of "Urra" as the desperate units made their charges. This display of furious courage took the Russians by surprise. The break-out succeeded. But it was not a break-out to freedom. The columns merely found themselves in a new pocket. The Russians had been in Minsk for three days, they had been in Slutsk for the past five days, and they were already twenty miles east of Baranovichi. And Baranovichi was still 105 miles away.

As the troops continued to move west many divisions still stuck together. But north of the Cherven–Minsk road strong Russian forces had dug in and repulsed all German attempts to push southwards across the road in daylight. Ceaseless heavy attacks by Russian ground-support aircraft wrought havoc among the German columns. It was the end of all co-ordinated action.

Many groups tried to make their retreat away from the big main roads. One such combat group was led by General Traut, the experienced commander of 78th Storm Division. Lieutenant-General Vinzenz Müller tried to lead some remnants of the Wiesbaden XII Corps out of the trap. Since the deaths of Generals Martinek and Schünemann he had assumed command also of XXXIX Panzer Corps and was now trying in vain to force a break-out to the west. It was no longer possible. Famous divisions with ancient traditions, divisions which we have encountered on the endless roads of Russia and at the focal points of battle, were bleeding to death. Traut's group was decimated in strenuous fighting with troops of the Soviet Forty-Ninth Army. Only a few tankmen of Panzer Battalion 5 under Major Rette-meier succeeded in getting through. On 8th July Vinzenz Müller ceased resistance at Chalin and surrendered to the HQ of a rifle corps of the Soviet Fiftieth Army. When he capitulated the German front had been flung back far beyond Minsk.

Three weeks later the Soviets had passed Brest and were standing on the Memel and the Vistula, where German blocking formations had only just managed, for the moment, to check their advance. In five weeks they had covered 435 miles, fighting all the way, which was almost exactly the blitzkrieg tempo of Guderian's and Hoth's Panzer groups along the Brest–Smolensk–Yelnya road in 1941.

But the territorial gains were not the decisive factor. Decisive was the annihilation of Army Group Centre, the loss of irreplaceable men. Out of 38 German divisions in action 28 were smashed. Some 350,000 to 400,000 men had been wounded or killed, or were missing. Of these, according to Soviet reports, 200,000 were killed and 85,000 taken prisoner.

The most striking illustration of the catastrophe was the fact that out of 47 generals employed at the front as corps commanders or division commanders, 31 remained on the battlefield, killed or captured. Of these 31, 10 were killed in action or missing, and 21 went into captivity. The terrible balance-sheet for the various corps was as follows:

Third Panzer Army

LIII Army Corps	General of Infantry Gollwitzer	prisoner
246th Infantry Div.	Major-General Müller-Bülow	prisoner
4th Luftwaffe Field Div.	Lieutenant-General Pistorius	killed in action
6th Luftwaffe Field Div.	Lieutenant-General Peschel	killed in action
206th Infantry Div.	Lieutenant-General Hitter	prisoner
VI Army Corps	General of Artillery Pfeiffer	killed in action
197th Infantry Div.	Colonel Hahne	missing
256th Infantry Div.	Major-General Wüstenhagen	killed in action

Fourth Army		
XXXIX Panzer Corps	General of Artillery Martinek	killed in action
110th Infantry Div.	Lieutenant-General von Kurowski	prisoner
337th Infantry Div.	Lieutenant-General Schünemann	killed in action
12th Infantry Div.	Lieutenant-General Bamler	prisoner
31st Infantry Div.	Lieutenant-General Ochsner	prisoner
XII Army Corps	Lieutenant-General Vinzenz Müller	prisoner
18th Panzer Grenadier Div.	Lieutenant-General Zutavern	suicide
267th Infantry Div.	Lieutenant-General Drescher	killed in action
57th Infantry Div.	Major-General Trowitz	prisoner
XXVII Army Corps	General of Infantry Völckers	prisoner
78th Storm Div.	Lieutenant-General Traut	prisoner
260th Infantry Div.	Major-General Klammt	prisoner
Ninth Army		
Senior Engineer Commander	Major-General Aurel Schmidt	prisoner
XXXV Army Corps	Lieutenant-General Freiherr von Lützow	prisoner
134th Infantry Div.	Lieutenant-General Philipp	suicide
6th Infantry Div.	Major-General Heyne	prisoner
45th Infantry Div.	Major-General Engel	prisoner
XLI Panzer Corps	Lieutenant-General Hoffmeister	prisoner
36th Infantry Div.	Major-General Conrady	prisoner
Among the reserves in action:		
95th Infantry Div.	Major-General Michaelis	prisoner
707th Infantry Div.	Major-General Gihr	prisoner
"Feldherrnhalle" Panzer Grenadier Div.	Major-General von Steinkeller	prisoner
Bobruysk garrison commander	Major-General Hamann	prisoner

No elaborate analysis is needed. Stalin had accomplished his hoped-for Cannae. Explanations are possible, and so are excuses, but the facts cannot be denied.

The collapse of Army Group Centre was not an isolated military event, not an unfortunate incident brought about by a concatenation of adverse circumstances, but a reflection of the excessive military demands made on the troops, of the waning potential of the German war economy, and of the approaching collapse of the Reich. That was the measure of the German catastrophe. And that was also the measure of the Russian victory. In point of fact, the Russians themselves were astonished at the magnitude of their victory. They had not expected such far-reaching success in so short a time. The depth of the operation planned for the Third Belorussian Front was 112 miles—as far as the upper Berezina. On 28th June, therefore, STAVKA hurriedly issued another directive on the crossing of the Berezina and the continuation of the thrust towards Minsk. The extent of the confusion reigning at STAVKA over its own successes is shown by the fact that the Second Belorussian Front received orders to occupy

Minsk not later than 8th July; it had in fact been taken by troops of the First and Third Belorussian Fronts as early as 3rd July.

Events were developing at avalanche speed, outstripping all planning.

By the end of July 1944 the war had reached the East Prussian frontier. It had also reached the Vistula. The curtain was being rung up over the last act. The battle for Germany was beginning.

In enormous columns the Soviet armies of four army groups were moving from Belorussia along the dusty, sun-parched roads to the west, towards the Vistula. "We're off to Berlin," the Red Army men laughed.

"We're off to Berlin!"

But at night, when the Red Army men sought shelter in the villages or rolled up in their blankets by some camp fire, another army was setting out on its march. Softly, in small groups of twenty or thirty, frequently fewer, sometimes in pairs or even singly, thousands of German soldiers were moving westwards through enemy territory. They were the tough and fearless ones, the ones who did not relish Soviet captivity. Most of them were young men. And experienced regulars. Experts have put their number at 10,000 to 15,000. Their trek started on the Berezina; it aimed westward to where the men were hoping to find a German defensive line. During the day they lay low, lurking by the highways. They raided badly-guarded supply vehicles and field kitchens. They crossed impenetrable forests. They hunted and were hunted. They lived on unripe bilberries, they ate the grain from the ears of corn in the fields, or half-rotten potatoes from old clamps. They stole sheep from pens and slaughtered them. They caught chickens, cows, and calves. They drank from brooks and puddles. During the day they hid out. At night they went out in search of food, and trekked to the west.

The Russians soon discovered this nocturnal movement through their country. Many of the Germans wore civilian clothes, but some were in full uniform, with or without weapons. The Russians organized special commandos to hunt for the Germans. They mobilized their partisans. German-speaking officers in German uniforms turned up and pretended to be rallying stragglers. In fact they led them into the arms of Soviet hunting commandos. Low-level aircraft swept over forests and fields day after day, looking for the hideouts of the German ghost army. A merciless battle began, a battle unrecorded in the official communiqués. No scroll of honour records the furious struggle waged by the last survivors of Ninth and Fourth Armies for their freedom and their lives. They knew what they were in for if caught. Anyone found by the search commandos was shot or beaten to death—only on the rarest of instances were men taken prisoner.

Not many of them got through. Eight hundred altogether. They made their way back to the German front on the Vistula, in East Prussia, or in Rumania—and it took them seven or eight weeks of foot-slogging. Eight hundred out of at least 10,000.

One such group on a hopeless trek was Diercks' group. At Parichi on the Berezina the No. 8 Troop of 36th Army Artillery Regiment, forming part of 20th Panzer Division, had covered the retreat across the river by the infantry of XXXV Corps. The troop had held the bridge and the highway. Then, suddenly, it had found itself in the midst of the Bobruysk disaster. Assigned to 383rd Infantry Division, the troop experienced the grim break-out battles.

The odyssey of Corporal Johannes Diercks began in a thorn thicket. At first he was alone. Then he was joined by Corporal Brixius with four men. Thus they moved off into the first night.

During the day they hid out in the swamps. They were hungry. In their ears rang the rumble of the Soviet columns moving westwards along the nearby highway. Diercks had a map. Brixius had a compass. On that basis they planned their route.

At first the bilberries were still green. But each day they got riper and riper. They judged the time by the colour of the berries.

They had skirmishes with Russian patrols and search commandos. They met other German groups. They came across the crew of a shot-down He-III. They joined up. They parted again. On an old tree-trunk they paddled their non-swimmers across the Ptich. They crossed the highway from Minsk to Brest-Litovsk, the road they used to take when going on leave. Pistol in hand they requisitioned bread and now and again a few field-flasks full of milk. Much more difficult was a handful of salt and a box of matches. They encountered a larger group of escapers—forty men led by a colonel. But they parted again. Each group had its own law.

A platoon of 52nd Nebelwerfer Regiment joined Diercks. Its lieutenant placed himself under the corporal. Leadership now went with personality, not with rank. That kind of life-and-death trek needed an objective. "What's our objective, Diercks?"

They studied the map. They were lying in a drizzly forest. They decided to make for East Prussia.

They crossed the Memel. They were as cunning as old poachers. Noiselessly, in a matter of minutes, Jakobs, a master-butcher, killed a sheep in a stall. They tied up its legs. They slipped a pole through to carry it. And they moved on. In the forest they carved up the carcass.

Week after week passed. Their uniforms were in tatters. Their bodies were emaciated. Their faces were covered with beards. Only their eyes showed, and those were hard. Their mouths were hard. They all looked the same, the men trekking from Minsk to the west.

The men returning from the German pockets on the Berezina. The Pripet marshes were far behind them, and so was Novo-Gorodok. They had passed through the catchment area of the Niemen in the sparsely inhabited Lithuanian countryside with its peaceful natives. On they went. This was their seventh week.

Where was the German main defensive line? They came across traces of recent fighting. But invariably the war had been there before them, it was running ahead of them. They were unable to catch up with it. But now and again it hit out at them. Corporal Rall and Corporal Hummel became casualties. They were seriously wounded and were left dying. Then suddenly the men heard the voices of the front, the crash of guns, the rattle of machine-gun fire. It was like the sounds of home.

Mangel-wurzels were their main meal. Grains of rye were their dessert. In front of them was a Russian mortar position. They tried to slip past it. But they were spotted. They came under fire. Every one of them was hit. None, fortunately, in the legs. They took refuge in a field of rye. Their nerves were taut to breaking point. They were between a Russian observer post and the main Soviet line. All round them on the high ground were Russian gun positions. The day was the 14th August, 1944.

The night was chilly. Bauer and Diercks had huddled close together for warmth. Sergeant Seitz groaned with pain. He was feverish. The hours seemed endless. They could not sit up. All around them were swarms of Russians. They picked some ears of rye to pieces and ate the grain. "Shall we manage it tomorrow night?" whispered Bauer.

Diercks nodded. "I know one thing for certain," he said softly. "There's no going back. Either we make it—or . . . "

They made it. Their last move was forced upon them by fate. A Soviet sentry discovered them. Diercks felled him. "Forward!"

The Russians put up a barrage with their mortars. Good! That showed that there was no Russian trench in front of them. But there was a trench all the same. Empty. They got across. And another. Empty. At last German voices.

"We're back!"

Nine miles east of Suwalki, on 14th August, Diercks' group rejoined the German front of 170th Infantry Division. Two hundred and eighty miles as the crow flew, four hundred miles on the ground, allowing for their detours. That was the distance they had covered. And all of it in enemy territory.

The crew of an anti-tank gun were their welcoming committee. They

They fought their way through the Russian encirclement back to the German lines:
men reporting to General Lang.
They escaped annihilation: wounded men from the Minsk pocket.

directed them to the advanced regimental HQ. The adjutant was sitting at a table. Diercks pulled himself up, straight as a ramrod: "Five German soldiers from the pockets on the Berezina reporting back to the German Wehrmacht after forty-nine days!"

A lot had happened between 27th June and 14th August. The men had come a long way. A longer one still lay ahead.

Russian assembly position: "Forward to the Vistula!"

Documents

Document No. 1: Operation Order for the Battle of Kursk

Operation Order No. 6 (Citadel) of 15.4.1943

The Führer   Führer's HQ, 15th April, 1943
OKH, Gen.St. Land Forces, Ops, Gr. (I)
No. 430246/43 m. secr., sen. cmdrs.

Most Secret   13 copies
Senior Commanders Only   Copy No. 4
By Hand of Officer Only

Second Army HQ, Chief of Ops. 591/43
Most Secret, Senior Commanders Only
Recd. 17.4.43 (two enclosures) ditto

Operation Order No. 6

I have decided to launch Operation Citadel, as the first of this year's offensive blows, as soon as the weather situation permits.

This attack therefore acquires vital importance. It must succeed rapidly and completely. It *must* give us the initiative for this spring and summer. For that reason, all preparations must be carried out with greatest circumspection and vigour. The best formations, the best weapons, the best commanders, and large quantities of ammunition must be used at the focal points. Every commander and every man must be deeply convinced of the decisive importance of this offensive. The victory of Kursk must be like a beacon fire to the world.

I therefore command:

(1) *The objective of the offensive* is to encircle the enemy forces in the Kursk area by means of strongly concentrated, merciless, and rapid thrusts by one offensive army each from the areas of Belgorod and south of Orel, and to annihilate them by concentric attack.

In the course of this offensive a shortened manpower-saving front is to be established along the line Nezhega–Korocha sector–Skorodnoye–Tim–east of Shchigry–Sosna sector.

(2) *It is vital*

(a) to preserve *the element of surprise* as far as possible and in particular keep the enemy guessing about the timing of the offensive;

(b) *to concentrate the attacking forces to the greatest possible extent on a narrow sector* in order to strike through in *one move* until the link-up of the two attacking armies in the enemy zone and thus to close the pocket; for this purpose an overwhelming local superiority must be achieved in respect of *all* means of attack (tanks, assault guns, artillery, *Nebelwerfer* mortars, etc.);

(c) to keep the attacking wedges supplied, as fast as possible, with forces brought up *from the rear* in order to cover their flanks, so that the assault wedges themselves need thrust only *forwards*;

(d) by an early *thrust into the pocket* from all sides not to allow the enemy any respite and thus accelerate his annihilation;

(e) to perform the attack *so rapidly* that the enemy can neither pull out from the encirclement nor bring up strong reserves from other fronts;

(f) by means of rapidly *establishing the new front* to free forces, especially mobile formations, for further tasks as soon as possible.

(3) *Army Group South* will jump off with strongly concentrated forces from the Belgorod–Tomarovka line, break through across the Prilepy–Oboyan line, and link up with the attacking army of Army Group Centre at and east of Kursk. In order to cover the offensive *against the east* the line Nezhega–Korocha sector–Skorodnoye–Tim must be reached as quickly as possible, without however jeopardizing the massive concentration of forces in the direction of Prilepy–Oboyan. To cover the offensive *against the west* partial forces are to be employed, whose task it will be to thrust simultaneously into the pocket as it is formed.

(4) *Army Group Centre*, with its attacking army jumping off from the line Trosna–north of Maloarkhangelsk after the strongest concentration of forces, will break through across the Fatezh–Vereytenovo line, with the main effort on the eastern wing, and will link up with the attacking army of Army Group South at and east of Kursk. In order to cover the attack *against the west* partial forces are to be employed.

The forces of Army Group Centre employed west of Trosna as far as the boundary with Army Group South must tie down the enemy by means of local attacks by specially composed offensive groups, right from the start of the offensive, and at an early stage thrust into the pocket as it is formed. Continuous reconnaissance on the ground and observation from the air must ensure that the enemy does not disengage unnoticed. In that event an attack must be launched at once along the entire front.

(5) *The deployment of the forces of both Army Groups* must take place at a great distance from the jumping-off positions and under application of all possible measures of camouflage, blinds, and deception, in such a way that, as from 28.4., the offensive can be mounted on the sixth day after issue of orders by OKH. Earliest date of offensive therefore 3.5. Movement to the jumping-off position must only take place at night and with every possible camouflage.

(6) In order to *deceive the enemy,* preparations for Operation Panther are to go ahead in the *zone of Army Group South.* They are to be emphasized in every possible way (conspicuous reconnaissance, appearance of tanks, deployment of bridging equipment, radio, agents, creation of rumours, employment of Luftwaffe, etc.) and kept up as long as possible. These deception measures, moreover, will be effectively supported by the measures necessary in any case for increasing the defensive strength of the Donets front (see under 11). *In the zone of Army Group Centre* no major deception measures need be taken, but every effort is to be made to confuse the picture of the situation for the enemy (counter-movements and wrong movements, as well as day-time transports, dissemination of false information suggesting dates of attack not until June, etc.)

In *both Army Groups* the formations to be newly brought up for the attacking armies must observe radio silence.

(7) *To ensure security,* these intentions are to be disclosed only to persons indispensably requiring this information. This briefing is to be extended phase by phase, as late as possible. This time we *must* ensure at *all* costs that nothing leaks out of these intentions through carelessness or negligence. Enemy espionage must be continually countered by an intensified counter-espionage effort.

(8) *The attacking forces,* in view of the limited space and the accurately known objective of the offensive, in contrast to earlier operations, must *leave behind* all vehicles of all kinds not absolutely necessary for the attack, as well as all encumbering *ballast!* Everything else is only an impediment and is apt to impair considerably the momentum of the attack and the rapid bringing forward of the follow-up forces. For that reason every commander must be determined to carry with him only what is essential for battle. Corps commanders and division commanders must strictly and ruthlessly supervise

execution of this directive. Strict traffic control must be instituted. It must act ruthlessly.

(9) *Directives concerning supplies* and the immediate complete round-up of *prisoners, inhabitants, and booty,* as well as for *propaganda* directed to the enemy are set out in appendices 1–3.

(10) *The Luftwaffe* will likewise employ all its available forces by concentration against focal points. Talks with Luftwaffe commands are to start at once. The need for security (see under 7) is particularly emphasized.

(11) The success of the offensive will depend vitally on the enemy not succeeding, by attacking at other points of Army Group South and Centre, in forcing us to postpone Citadel or prematurely to withdraw attacking formations.

For that reason both Army Groups, simultaneously with the offensive battle Citadel, must systematically prepare for *defensive operations* along the remaining parts of the front which are particularly threatened; these preparations to be carried out with all means by the end of the month. It is particularly important to speed up in every possible way the construction of defences, generously to furnish the tank-threatened sectors with anti-tank defences, to deploy local tactical reserves, to spot enemy focal points in good time by lively reconnaissance activity, etc.

(12) *The final objective* following completion of the operation envisages:

(a) The shifting of the boundary between Army Groups South and Centre to the general line Konotop (South)–Kursk (South)–Dolgoye (Centre);
(b) *The transfer of Second Army HQ* with three corps HQs and nine infantry divisions, as well as army troops yet to be designated, from Army Group Centre to Army Group South;
(c) *The deployment* of three further infantry divisions of Army Group Centre, to be available to OKH in the area north-west of Kursk;
(d) *The pulling out of all fast formations* from the front for employment elsewhere.

Movements, in particular by formations of Second Army, are to be adapted to these intentions.

I reserve the right to subordinate the HQs and formations referred to under paragraph (12) (b) to Army Group South, even during the course of the operation, phase by phase, in accordance with the progress of the fighting.

I similarly reserve the right, given the progress of the operation according to plan, to mount an attack towards the south-east (Panther) in one continuous movement, in order to exploit the enemy's confusion.

(13) *The Army Groups will report* the measures taken by them for attack and defence, on the basis of the present operation order, enclosing maps 1:300,000 with explanations and details of disposition of army troops, as well as of arrangements made with Fourth Air Fleet of Luftwaffe HQ East for support of the offensive and deception measures.

To be handed in by 24.4.

(Signed)	Adolf Hitler
	For accuracy:
(Signed)	Heusinger,
	Lieutenant-General

Document No. 2: Observations by Army Group South in August 1943, concerning Maintenance of Morale

On 5.8 the Commander-in-Chief of the Army Group made the following observation to Army Detachment Kempf: "The mood of panic among the troops must be cleared up. The 198th and 168th Infantry Divisions are holding frontages on which enemy attacks can be repulsed. There must be no retreat." The Commander-in-Chief of Army Detachment Kempf replied that the two divisions in the line had on the whole held their positions but were encircled. "If we had not fallen back during the night there would have been far greater trouble." He reported that the enemy was again "bringing up strong infantry and armoured forces from the north". At 1630 hours the Commander-in-Chief of the Army Group ordered the following signal to be sent: "It is incomprehensible that the battleworthy 198th Infantry Division should let itself be pushed out of Belgorod." The Army Detachment reported to Army Group (1735 hours) that it was considering the "establishment of a reconnoitred line" (from south of Belgorod to east of Bessonovka). Army Group replied (1805 hours) that "an attempt must be made to stop this evasive action"; the new line was to be prepared, and if the situation so required evasive action would be taken the next day. (On the extreme left wing of XI Army Corps the troops were in that line by the evening of 5.8.)

On 5.8 the Commander-in-Chief of Army Group ordered: "I request information as to what circumstances led to the fact that 167th Infantry Division, which was on the high ground of Visloye on 3.8., could only be rallied in its remnants twenty miles south-west of Bessonovka on 4.8." and "I request information on why 6th Panzer Division, which had invariably defeated the enemy no matter how strong he was and how reduced its own numbers, has been dislodged by every enemy attack since 4.8. I also request a report on which formations of the division were in action on 3.8."

(The reports by Fourth Panzer Army HQ in reply to these questions are not contained in the documents available.)

On 10.8 Army Detachment Kempf reported to Army Group (1840 hours) that the situation of 282nd Infantry Division, whose front had been repeatedly pierced, inevitably required a further pulling back of the northern front during the coming night (to a line north of Chuguyev–Dergachi).

According to Document No. 44701/12, the Army Group (12.8.) was considering "draconian measures (shooting of one man in every 10) for 282nd Infantry Division". These were judged inappropriate by the HQ of Army Detachment Kempf.

Document No. 5: Reports by Eighth Army HQ of 22.8. and 2.9. 1945 concerning the Morale of the Troops

A report submitted by Eighth Army HQ to Army Group on 22.8. states: "... so long as other parts and branches of the Wehrmacht continue to be given priority in the allocation of highly-qualified drafts, the infantry will always be short of the required percentage of valuable human material. In consequence, this principal arm will never have a sufficient number of rankers fit to become leaders and sub-leaders."

A report by the C-in-C Eighth Army of 2.9. (Document No. 44701/12), which points to "the dwindling strength of the troops, especially the infantry", throws a striking light on the situation. The report states:

"(1) While we are forced to conduct the most difficult ammunition tactics, the enemy has unlimited artillery and mortar ammunition available to him. With these weapons he creates focal points and thins out our ranks to such an extent that the manning of the main defensive line can no longer be ensured and local defence groups, linked by patrols have to be formed. Whenever the enemy has broken in he can then only be dislodged by locally scraped-up reserves. Casualties are exceptionally high. This morning the combat strength of 39th Infantry Division was down to six officers and roughly 300 men.

"(2) Baggage units have already been vigorously combed out. The men left in them now are mostly the last surviving sons or the fathers of large families. I request a decision from above on whether the operational employment of these troops is to be ordered. In my opinion a sound ratio between troops and baggage can be achieved only by the merger of divisions.

"(3) Apart from their dwindling strength, the men's state of fatigue gives rise to great anxiety. I am informed by unit commanders that, owing to excessive fatigue, such a state of apathy has arisen among the troops that draconian measures do not at this moment produce the desired results, but only the good example of officers and 'kindly persuasion'. Both these, however, depend very greatly on the dwindling number of officers.

"(4) I realize that newly arrived formations lack the necessary steadfastness. Thus 223rd Infantry Division has not so far in its battle performance squared up to the situation. In 10 days it suffered more than 1100 casualties and yesterday alone its losses of heavy equipment consisted of 126 machine-guns, 28 mortars, three infantry guns, one anti-tank gun, three light and one heavy field howitzer. Measures have been put in hand to clarify the question of responsibility, if necessary by court martial inquiry.

"(5) In connection with solicitude for and inquiries about the strength of units, commanders and troops resent the fact that each report from above is followed by protracted investigations while there is little evidence of practical help for the troops. I am mentioning this point because it might undermine confidence between commanders and troops. . . ."

Document No. 4: Re. "Scorched Earth"

Appendix 2 of No. 9 War Diary of XXIII Army Corps, Ops. Group (1.11.1941 to 31.1.1942), contains the following order:

Most Secret!
Copy
Ninth Army HQ
Ops. Gr. No. 4534/41 m. secr.

Army HQ 21.12.41
11 copies
Copy No. 2

Copy of teleprinter message from OKH/General Staff of Land Forces/Ops. Gr. (IM) to Army Group Centre.

In connection with a briefing on 20.12. the Führer made the following observations by way of reconfirming his ideas expressed in Directive OKH/General Staff of Land Forces/Ops. Gr. (IM) No. 1736/41 m. secr., point 1:

(1) A fanatical will to defend the ground on which they stand must be instilled in the troops with every means, including the most drastic. Provided all troops are equally inspired with that determination, the enemy's attacks, even if they lead to penetrations in a few points, must in the end be doomed to failure. But where that resolution is not present to its full extent, the front will begin to waver, without a prospect of stabilizing it again in prepared positions. Every officer and man must realize that evasive action by the troops must expose them to a far greater degree to the dangers of the Russian winter than holding on to a position, however scantily established—quite apart from the inevitable considerable losses of *matériel* entailed by such an evasive movement. The Russians will immediately follow up any withdrawing troops, they will not allow them any respite, they will time and again attack and assault them, and in the absence of prepared positions in the rear these troops would not find a foothold. The catchword of a Napoleonic retreat would then threaten to become reality. For that reason evasive movement must only be carried out where a prepared position exists further rearward. Only when a soldier sees that, after disengagement from the enemy, he will find another position, even though scantily established, will he understand the withdrawal. Only then will such a retreat not undermine the confidence between troops and commanders. If, however, the troops find that they have to leave a position in which they had tolerably well settled down, without being offered an appropriate substitute, then any retreat represents a danger of leading to a crisis of confidence in the leadership.

(2) The dwindling combat strength . . .

(3) All territory which the troops are forced to yield to the enemy must, as far as possible, be made useless to him. Every village must be burnt down and destroyed, without consideration for the population, in order to deprive the enemy of possible shelter. Preparations must be made accordingly. Should such destruction not succeed, any villages which have remained undestroyed must subsequently be destroyed by Luftwaffe operation, remembering that the enemy, just as our own troops, will, in view of the cold, depend on the settlements. These difficulties will be even greater for him, as the attacker, than for our own troops provided they are in a tolerably well-equipped position.

(4) ...

The above considerations are being sent out with the request that they be brought to the notice of subordinate command authorities.

The Army will justify the Führer's confidence.

OKH/General Staff of Land Force/Ops. Gr. (IM) No. 3208/41, m. secr.

Addendum by Army:
Re clause (3): Areas not destroyed, requiring Luftwaffe operation, must be reported to Ninth Army HQ in good time.

> On behalf of Army HQ
> The Chief of Staff:
> By order
> (Signature)
> Colonel

For the accuracy of the copy:
(Signed) Freiherr von Seckendorf

Document No. 5: Re. "Scorched Earth"

Chief of the General Staff of Land Forces No. I/5705/43, m. secr.	OKH/HQ, 30.8.43 50 copies Copy No. 17
Re: Evacuation of Donets Region	Eight sub-copies Sub-copy No. 2

The Führer has ordered:

General of Infantry Stapf, Chief of Economic Staff, East, is authorized as the representative of the Economic Directorate to organize and carry out the reception of evacuated population groups and economic assets of all kinds arriving in the domestic theatre of operations as well as in the occupied eastern territories as a result of the evacuation of the Donets region.

To this end he is authorized to issue binding directives within the scope of his task to all competent military and non-military authorities.

	By command of the Führer
	(Signed) Zeitzler
For accuracy:	General of Infantry
(illegible signature)	and Chief of the General Staff of
Lieutenant	Land Forces

Document No. 6: Re. "Scorched Earth"

Most Secret

The Reich Marshal	Leipziger Strasse 3
of the Greater German Reich	Berlin W.8, September 7, 1943
Commissioner for the	Most Secret (political)
Four-Year Plan	40 copies
Economic Directorate, East	Copy No. 13
	Eight sub-copies
V.P. 11207/6/3 m. secr. (pol.)	Sub-copy No. 2

Re: Evacuation of stored harvest and destruction of production facilities of agriculture and food industry in parts of the occupied eastern territories.

By order of the Führer I direct:

(I) The following measures are to be taken in the areas east of a line laid down by the Supreme Military Command in accordance with the military situation at the time, and carried out sector by sector. The sectors are to be determined by the Commanders-in-Chief of the Army Groups:

(1) All agricultural produce, facilities, and machinery will be evacuated from agricultural and food industry enterprises;

(2) production and processing facilities of the food industry are to be destroyed;

(3) the production base of agriculture, in particular basic facilities and installations (stores, etc.) of food supply and collecting organizations, are to be destroyed;

(4) the population employed in agriculture and the food industry is to be taken to areas west of the designated line.

(II) The direction of these measures is entrusted to the Chief of Economic Staff, East, General of Infantry Stapf, as the representative of the Economic Directorate. Execution of the measures is the responsibility of the highest military command authorities, upon whom the expert instructions of the appropriate departments of the economic authorities are binding.

(III) In the performance of his task General Stapf is subject to the instructions of the Head of my Working Party for Food Supplies, Under-Secretary of State Backe. He is authorized, for the purpose of discharging his tasks and receiving evacuated property in the occupied areas and in the domestic theatre of war, to issue binding directives to all military and non-military authorities.

For accuracy: (Signed) Göring
(Signature illegible)   Witnessed:
Lieutenant   (Signed) Schwinge
                                       Ministerialregistrator

Document No. 7: Re. "Fortified Localities"

The Führer
High Command of Land Forces
General Staff of Land Forces/Ops. Gr. (I) No. 2434/44 m. secr.

Führer's Headquarters,
March 8, 1944

Most Secret!

Führer Order No. 11
(Commandants of fortified localities and battle commandants)

In view of various incidents I order:

(1) A distinction must be made between:

"Fortified localities", each under a "commandant of fortified locality" and "local strongpoints", each under a "battle commandant". The "fortified localities" are meant to discharge the same functions as fortresses in the past. They must prevent the enemy from taking possession of these strategically vital localities. They must allow themselves to be encircled and in this way tie down the largest possible number of enemy forces. In this way they will play a part in creating the prerequisite for successful counter-operations.

The "local strongpoints" are envisaged as stubbornly defended strongpoints in the depth of the battle zone in the event of enemy breakthroughs. By incorporation in the main defensive line they are to provide the backbone of defence and, in the event of enemy penetrations, the pivot points and corner-posts of the front, as well as jumping-off bases for counter-attacks.

(2) The "commandant of a fortified locality" should be a specially selected tough soldier, if possible of general's rank. His appointment will be made by the Army Group concerned. The commandant of a fortified locality is to be personally entrusted with his tasks by the Commander-in-Chief of the Army Group.

The commandant of a fortified locality vouches with his soldier's honour for the implementation of his task to the very end.

Only the Commander-in-Chief of the Army Group in person, acting with my approval, can relieve the commandant of a fortified locality of his tasks and, if necessary, order the abandonment of a fortified locality.

The commandant of a fortified locality comes under the orders of the Commander-in-Chief of the Army Group or of the Army in whose zone the fortified locality is situated. He must not be further subordinated to corps commanders.

The authority of the commandant of a fortified locality extends, in addition to the local defence and total garrison, to all persons present or assembling at the fortified locality, whether military personnel or civilian, and irrespective of their service rank or official position.

The commandant of a fortified locality has the Wehrmacht authority and disciplinary powers of a corps commander. For the discharge of his tasks, flying courts martial and summary courts are to be made available to him.

The staff of the commandant of a fortified locality is to be set up by the Army Group concerned through command channels. The post of chief of staff will be filled by OKH upon proposal by Army Group.

(3) The garrison of a fortified locality consists of

> the local defence garrison and
> the total garrison.

The local defence garrison must be permanently present in the fortified locality. Its strength is to be laid down by the Commander-in-Chief of the Army Group. It will depend on the size of the locality and the tasks entrusted to it (preparation and construction of defences, holding of the fortified locality against enemy coups or lesser local attacks).

The total garrison must be made available to the commandant of a fortified locality in such good time that it can properly take up its defensive positions and be briefed before a threatening systematic attack by the enemy. Its strength is to be laid down by the commandant of the Army Group according to the size of the fortified locality and the tasks assigned to it (decisive defence of the fortified locality).

(4) The "battle commandant" is an officer under the commander in the field. He is appointed by him, comes under his command, and receives from him his objective and briefing. His rank will depend on the importance of the locality in the zone of operations and the strength of the garrison. His tasks demand particularly energetic officers who have proved their worth in critical situations.

(5) The strength of the garrison of a "local strongpoint" depends on the significance of the locality and the forces available. It is to be laid down by order of the service authority superior to the battle commandant.

(6) The tasks of the "commandants of fortified localities" and of the "battle commandants", as well as a list of fortified localities and of the reports to be submitted by Army Groups, are set out in the appendices.

(7) The above supersedes all previous orders issued concerning battle commandants.

(Signed) Adolf Hitler

General distribution

Bibliography

I. Books and Periodicals

ACCOCE, PIERRE; QUET, PIERRE: *La guerre a été gagnée en Suisse, 1939–1945, L'affaire Roessler* (Libr. Acad. Perrin, Paris, 1966).

BÄCHINGER, KONRAD; FISCH, JOSEF; KAISER, ERNST: *Laßt hören aus alter Zeit; General Guisan: Haltet durch!* (Arbeitsgem. f. prakt. Unterr. St Gallen, 1963).

BAILEY, GEOFFREY: *The Conspirators* (Victor Gollancz, London, 1961).

BAUER, E.: *Der Panzerkrieg*. Bd. I und II (Offene Worte, Bonn, n.d.).

BEKKER, CAJUS: *Angriffshöhe 4000* (Stalling, Oldenburg, 1964).

BENARY, ALBERT: *Die Berliner 257. Bären-Division* (Podzun, Bad Nauheim, 1957).

BIDERMANN, G. H.: *Krim-Kurland mit der 132. Infanterie-Division 1941–1945* (privately published, Hanover, n.d.).

BÖHMLER, RUDOLF: *Fallschirmjäger* (Podzun, Bad Nauheim, 1961).

BRAUN, J.: *Enzian und Edelweiß, 4. Geb. Div.* (Podzun, Bad Nauheim, 1955).

BREITH, H.: *Der Angriff des III. Pz. Korps bei Zitadelle im Juli 1943* (Wehrkunde, 1958).

BREITHAUPT, HANS: *Die Geschichte der 30. Infanterie-Division* (Podzun, Bad Nauheim, 1955).

BUCHNER, ALEX: *Gebirgsjäger an allen Fronten* (Sponholz, Hanover, 1954).

BÜCHMANN, GEORG: *Geflügelte Worte* (Haude & Spener, Berlin, 1964).

FREIHERR VON BUTTLAR: *Ehrenbuch der deutschen Wehrmacht* (Riegler, Stuttgart, 1954).

BUXA, WERNER: *Weg und Schicksal der 11. Infanterie-Division* (Podzun, Bad Nauheim, 1963).

CARELL, PAUL: *The Foxes of the Desert* (translated by Mervyn Savill; Macdonald, London, 1960).
　Invasion – They're Coming! (translated by Ewald Osers; Harrap, London, 1962).
　Hitler's War on Russia (translated by Ewald Osers; Harrap, London, 1964).

CARIUS, OTTO: *Tiger in Schlamm* (Vowinckel, Neckargemünd, 1960).

CONZE, W.: *Die Geschichte der 291. I.D.* (Podzun, Bad Nauheim, 1953).

DAHMS, HELMUT GÜNTHER: *Geschichte des zweiten Weltkrieges* (Wunderlich, Tübingen, 1965).

DALLIN, ALEXANDER: *Die Sowjetspionage* (Politik und Wirtsch., Cologne, 1956).

DEAKIN, F. W.; STORRY, G. R.: *The Case of Richard Sorge* (Chatto & Windus, London, 1966).

DEGRELLE, LEON: *Die verlorene Legion* (Veritas, Stuttgart, n.d.).

DENZEL, EGON: *Die Luftwaffen-Felddivisionen 1942–1945* (Vowinckel, Neckargemünd, 1963).

DIECKHOFF, G.: *Die 3. I. D. (mot.)* (Börries, Göttingen, 1960).

DINGLREITER, JOSEPH: *Die Vierziger* (privately published, Augsburg, n.d.).

VON DONAT, HANS: "Eisenbahn-Pioniere", in *Deutsches Soldatenjahrbuch, 1966* (Schild, Munich/Lochhausen, 1966).

ERLAU, PETER: *Flucht aus der weißen Hölle* (Riegler, Stuttgart, n.d.).

VON ERNSTHAUSEN, A.: *Wende im Kaukasus* (Vowinckel, Neckargemünd, 1958).

ESTEBAN-INFANTES, GENERAL: *Blaue Division* (Druffel, Leoni, 1958).

FEY, WILLY: *Panzer im Brennpunkt der Fronten* (Lehmann,Munich, 1960).

FLICKE, F. W.: *Agenten funken nach Moskau* (Welsermühl, Wels/Munich, 1957).

FOERSTER, WOLFGANG: *Kämpfer an vergessenen Fronten* (Dtsch. Buchvertr., Abt. f. Veröff. a. Amtl. Arch., Berlin, 1931).

FOLTTMANN, JOSEF; MÖLLER-WITTEN, HANNS: *Opfergang der Generale* (Bernard & Graefe, Berlin, 1952).

FORSTMEIER, FRIEDRICH: *Die Räumung des Kuban-Brückenkopfes im Herbst 1943* (Wehr und Wissen, Darmstadt, 1964).

FRETTER-PICO, MAXIMILIAN: *Mißbrauchte Infanterie* (Bernard & Graefe, Frankfurt/M., 1957).

FULLER, JOHN F.: *The Second World War* (Eyre and Spottiswoode, 1948).

GACKENHOLZ, HERMANN: "Der Zusammenbruch der Heeresgruppe Mitte 1944" in *Entscheidungsschlachten des zweiten Weltkrieges* edited by DR HANS-ADOLF JACOBSEN and DR JÜRGEN ROHWER; Bernard & Graefe, Frankfurt/M., 1960).

GAREIS, MARTIN: *Kampf und Ende der Fränkisch-Sudetendeutschen 98. Infanterie-Division* (Podzun, Bad Nauheim, 1956).

GARTHOFF, RAYMOND L.: *Die Sowjetarmee, Wesen und Lehre* (Markus, Cologne, 1955).

GÖRLITZ, WALTER: *Keitel, Verbrecher oder Offizier?* (Musterschmidt, Göttingen, 1961).

Der zweite Weltkrieg 1939–1945, Bd. I und II (Steingrüben, Stuttgart, 1951, 1952).

GRAMS, ROLF: *14. Panzer-Division* (Podzun, Bad Nauheim, 1957).

GRASER, G.: *Zwischen Kattegat und Kaukasus*, 198. I. D. (privately published, Tübingen, 1961).

GRÖSSEL, EMIL: *Grenadiere*, I. R. 530 (privately published, o. Ersch.-Ort, n.d.).

GROSSMANN, H.: *Geschichte der 6. I. D.* (Podzun, Bad Nauheim, 1958).

Rschew, Eckpfeiler der Ostfront (Podzun, Bad Nauheim, 1962).

GRUBE, RUDOLF: *Unternehmen Erinnerung;* Eine Chronik über den Weg und den Einsatz des Grenadierregiments 317 in der 211. Infanteriedivision 1939–1945 (Gieseking, Bielefeld, 1961).

GRUBER, ANTON: *Das Infanterie-Regiment 213* (privately published, Nürnberg, 1963).

GSCHÖPF, R., DR: *Mein Weg mit der 45. I. D.* (Oberöster. Landesvlg., Linz, 1955).

GUDERIAN, HEINZ: *Erinnerungen eines Soldaten* (Vowinckel, Heidelberg, 1951).

HALDER, FRANZ: *Kriegstagebuch*, Bd. 1, 2 und 3 (revised by DR HANS-ADOLF JACOBSEN, Kohlhammer, Stuttgart, 1963–66).

HAUCK, FRIEDRICH WILHELM: "Der Gegenangriff der Heeresgruppe Süd im Frühjahr 1943", in *Wehrwissenschaftliche Rundschau*, 1962, Nos. 8, 9.

"Warum der Angriff im Frühjahr 1943 im Donez-Becken nicht zu Ende geführt wurde", in *Wehrwissenschaftliche Rundschau*, 1964.

HAUPT, WERNER: *Demjansk, ein Bollwerk im Osten* (Podzun, Bad Nauheim, 1963).

HAUSSER, PAUL: *Waffen-SS im Einsatz* (Plesse, Göttingen, 1953).

HEIDKÄMPER, OTTO: *Witebsk* (Vowinckel, Heidelberg, 1954).

HEILBRUNN, OTTO: *Der sowjetische Geheimdienst* (Bernard & Graefe, Frankfurt/M., 1956).

HEINRICI, GOTTHARD; HAUCK, FRIEDRICH WILHELM: "Zitadelle", in *Wehrwissenschaftliche Rundschau*, 1965, Nos. 9, 10.

HENNECKE, KARDEL: *Die Geschichte der 170. I. D.* (Podzun, Bad Nauheim, 1952).

HERMANN, WALTER: *Die Geschichte des Infanterie-Regiments 51* (privately published,Munich, 1964).

HERTEL, WERNER: *Beobachtungsabteilung 6, 1936–1945* (Laumann, Dülmen, 1965).

HILLGRUBER, ANDREAS: "Die Raümung der Krim 1944", in *Wehrwissenschaftliche Rundschau*, supplement 9, 1959.

HOFFMANN, KARL-OTTO: *Geschichte der Luftnachrichtentruppe* (Manuscript in preparation, Vowinckel, Neckargemünd).

HOTH, HERMANN: *Panzer-Operationen* (Scharnhorst Buchkameradschaft, Heidelberg, 1956).

HUBATSCH, WALTER: *61. Infanteriedivision* (Podzun, Bad Nauheim, 1958).
  Hitlers Weisungen für die Kriegführung (Bernard & Graefe, Frankfurt/M., 1962).

INTERNATIONALER MILITÄRGERICHTSHOF: *Der Prozeß gegen die Hauptkriegsverbrecher vor dem Internationalen Militärgerichtshof Nürnberg* (I.M.G., Nürnberg, 1947–49).

JACOBSEN, HANS-ADOLF: *1939–1945, Der zweite Weltkrieg in Chroniken und Dokumenten* (Wehr und Wissen, Darmstadt, 1959–60).

JACOBSEN, HANS-ADOLF; ROHWER, JÜRGEN: *Entscheidungsschlachten des zweiten Weltkrieges* (Bernard & Graefe, Frankfurt/M., 1960).

KARB, HERBERT: *Erinnerungen der Pz.-Aufklärungsabteilung 12;* (privately published, Bonn-Lengsdorf, 1965).

KELLIG, WOLF: *Das deutsche Heer 1939–1945* (Podzun, Bad Nauheim, 1956).

KERN, ERICH: *Kampf in der Ukraine, 1941–1944* (Plesse, Göttingen, 1964).

KESSELRING, ALBERT: *Kesselring: A Soldier's Record* (translated by Lynton Hudson; Morrow, New York, 1954).

KIMCHE, JON: *General Guisans Zweifrontenkrieg* (Ullstein, Frankfurt/M./Berlin, 1962).

KLATT, PAUL: *Die 3. Gebirgsdivision 1939–1945* (Podzun, Bad Nauheim, 1958).

VON KLEIST, HEINRICH: *Die Hermannsschlacht*, Werke: 1. Bd. (Lolls Nachf., Elberfeld, n.d.).

VON KNOBELSDORF, O.: *Geschichte der 19. Panzer-Division* (Podzun, Bad Nauheim, 1959).

KONRAD, R.: *Kampf um den Kaukasus* (Copress, Munich, n.d.).

KRÜGER, HEINZ: *Bildband der Rheinisch-Pfälzischen 263. Infanterie-Division* (Podzun, Bad Nauheim, 1962).

KALLINOW, KYRILL D.: *Sowjetmarschälle haben das Wort* (Hansa, Hamburg, 1950).

LANGE, WOLFGANG: *Korpsabteilung C* (Vowinckel, Neckargemünd, 1961).

LANZ, HUBERT: *Gebirgsjäger* (Podzun, Bad Nauheim, 1954).

LEMELSEN, JOACHIM: *29. i. D. (mot.)* (Podzun, Bad Nauheim, 1960).

LIDDELL HART, BASIL HENRY: *The Soviet Army* (Edited by B. H. L. Hart; Weidenfeld & Nicolson, London, 1956).
The Other Side of the Hill (Hamilton & Co. Ltd, London, 1956).
LOHSE, G.: *Geschichte der 126 I. D.* (Podzun, Bad Nauheim, 1957).
LUBS, GERHARD: *I. R. 5. Aus der Geschichte eines Pommerschen Regiments, 1920–1945* (privately published, Bochum, 1965).
LUSAR, RUDOLF: *Die deutschen Waffen und Geheimwaffen des zweiten Weltkrieges* (Lehmann, Munich, 1962).
MADER, JULIUS; STUCHLIK, GERHARD; PEHNERT, HORST: *Dr. Sorge funkt aus Tokio* (Dtsch. Milit. Vlg., Berlin, 1965).
VON MANSTEIN, ERICH: *Lost Victories* (Edited and translated by Anthony G. Powell; Methuen, London, 1958).
VON MANTEUFFEL, HASSO: *Die 7. Panzer-Division im zweiten Weltkrieg* (privately published, Diessen am Ammersee, 1965).
VON MELLENTHIN, F. W.: unter Mitarbeit von ROLF STOVES: *Panzerschlachten* (Vowinckel, Heidelberg, 1963).
MENEDETTER, H. K.: *Chronik des Artillerie-Regiment 188* (privately published, Bayreuth, 1960).
MELZER, W.: *Geschichte der 252. I. D. 1939–1945* (Podzun, Bad Nauheim, 1960).
VON METZSCH, F. A.: *Die Geschichte der 22. I. D.* (Podzun, Bad Nauheim, 1952).
MEYER-DETRING, WILHELM: *Die 137. Infanterie-Division* (privately published, Petzenkirchen, Niederösterreich, 1962).
MIDDELDORF, EIKE: "Das Unternehmen Zitadelle", in *Wehrwissenschaftliche Rundschau*, 1955, Nos. 8, 9, 10.
MÜLLER, VINZENZ: *Ich fand das wahre Vaterland* (Berlin, 1963).
MUNZEL, OSKAR: *Panzer-Taktik* (Vowinckel, Neckargemünd, 1959).
Die deutschen gepanzerten Truppen bis 1945 (Maximilian, Herford, 1965).
NEHRING, WALTER: "Der Einsatz russischer Fallschirmverbände im Kampfraum des XXIV. Panzerkorps zwischen Tscherkassy und Kiew bei Kanew am 24./25. September, 1943", in *Deutsches Soldatenjahrbuch, 1963* (Tettnang, 1963).
NITZ, GÜNTHER: *Die 292. Infanteriedivision* (Bernard & Graefe, Frankfurt/M., 1957).
PAYK, ERNST: *Die Geschichte der 206. Infanterie-Division, 1939–1945* (Podzun, Bad Nauheim, 1952).
PHILLIPPI, A.; HEIM, F.: *Der Feldzug gegen Sowjetrußland* (Kohlhammer, Stuttgart, 1962).
PICKERT, WOLFGANG: "Ein sowjetischer Ausbruch", in *Allgemeine Schweizerische Militärzeitschrift*, June, 1953.
Vom Kuban nach Sewastopol (Vowinckel, Neckargemünd, 1955).
PLOETZ, A. G.: *Geschichte des zweiten Weltkrieges* (Ploetz, Würzburg, 1960).
POHLMANN, HARTWIG: *Geschichte der 96. Infanterie-Division* (Podzun, Bad Nauheim, 1959).
900 Tage im Kampf um Leningrad (Podzun, Bad Nauheim, 1962).
POTTGIESSER, HANS: *Die Reichsbahn im Ostfeldzug* (Vowinckel, Neckargemünd, 1960).
PRAUN, ALBERT: *Soldat in der Telegraphen- und Nachrichtentruppe* (privately published, Würzburg, 1965).
RAUS, ERHARD: "Winterkämpfe an der Bistraja und Kalitwa", in *Allgemeine Schweizerische Militärzeitschrift*, January, 1954.

"Zweimal Charkow", in *Allgemeine Schweizerische Militärzeitschrift*, December, 1964.

REBENTISCH, ERNST: *Zum Kaukasus und zu den Tauern, 23. Pz. Div.* (privately published, Eßlingen/N., 1963).

REHM, WALTER: *Jassy* (Vowinckel, Neckargemünd, 1959).

REDELIS, VALDIS: *Partisanenkrieg* (Vowinckel, Neckargemünd, 1958).

RENDULIC, LOTHAR: *Gekämpft – gesiegt – geschlagen!* (Welsemühl, Wels, 1965). *Soldat in stürzenden Reichen* (Damm, Munich, 1965).

REINICKE, ADOLF: *Die 5. Jäger-Division* (Podzun, Bad Nauheim, 1962).

RIECKER, KARLHEINRICH: *Ein Mann verliert einen Weltkrieg* (Friedericus, Frankfurt/M., 1955).

RÖHRICHT, EDGAR: *Probleme der Kesselschlacht* (Condor, Karlsruhe, 1958).

RÖHRS, HANS-DIETRICH: *Hitlers Krankheit* (Vowinckel, Neckargemünd, 1966).

SAINT-LOUP: *Les volontaires* (Presse de la Cité, Paris, 1963).

SCHAUB, OSKAR: *Aus der Geschichte Panzer-Grenadier-Regiment 12* (privately published, Bergisch-Gladbach, n.d.).

SCHEFFLER, KURT: *Das A. R. 268 im Kampf gegen den Bolschewismus* (privately published, Regensburg, n.d.).

SCHEIBERT, HORST: *Zwischen Don und Donez* (Vowinckel, Neckargemünd, 1961).

SCHELM, WALTER; MEHRLE, DR HANS: *Von den Kämpfen der 215. Württemberg-Badischen Infanterie-Division* (privately published, Stuttgart, n.d.).

VON SCHLIEFFEN, ALFRED: *Cannae* (Mittler & Sohn, Berlin, 1936).

SCHMIDT, AUGUST: *Geschichte der 10. Division* (Podzun, Bad Nauheim, 1963).

SCHMIDT, GERHARD: *Regimentsgeschichte des Panzer-Artillerie-Regiment 73* (Boettcher, Bremen, n.d.).

SCHRAMM, PERCY ERNST; JACOBSEN, HANS-ADOLF; HILLGRUBER, ANDREAS; HUBATSCH, WALTER: *Kriegstagebuch des Oberkommandos der Wehrmacht*, Bd. I–IV (Bernhard & Graefe, Frankfurt/M., 1961–65).

SCHRÖDER, JÜRGEN; SCHULTZ-NAUMANN, JOACHIM: *Die Geschichte der Pommerschen 32. Infanterie-Division* (Podzun, Bad Nauheim, 1956).

SCHULZ, HEINZ: *34. Infanterie-Division* (privately published, Baden-Baden, n.d.).

SCHWARZ, DR A.: *Datentafel 323. Infanteriedivision* (privately published, Bayreuth, 1966).

VON SEEMEN, GERHARD: *Die Ritterkreuzträger 1939–1945* (Podzun, Bad Nauheim, 1955).

VON SENGER UND ETTERLIN, FRIDO: *Krieg in Europa* (Kiepenheuer & Witsch, Cologne, 1960).

VON SENGER UND ETTERLIN JR., DR F. M.: *Die deutschen Panzer 1926–1945* (Lehmann, Munich, 1959).
Die deutschen Geschütze 1939–1945 (Lehmann, Munich, 1960).
Der Gegenschlag (Vowinckel, Neckargemünd, 1960).
Die 24. Panzer-Division, vormals 1. Kavallerie-division (Vowinckel, Neckargemünd, 1962).

SPAETER, HELMUTH: *Geschichte des Panzerkorps Großdeutschland* (privately published, Duisburg-Ruhrort, 1958).

STEINER, FELIX: *Die Freiwilligen* (Plesse, Göttingen, 1963).

STOVES, ROLF: *Die 1. Panzerdivision* (Podzun, Bad Nauheim, 1962).

STRAUSS, FRANZ JOSEPH: *Friedens- und Kriegerlebnisse einer Generation, Panzerjäger-Abteilung in der ehemaligen 2. (Wiener) Panzerdivision* (privately published. Kitzingen, 1960).

TELPUCHOWSKI, BORIS S.: *Die sowjetische Geschichte des großen Vaterländischen Krieges 1941–1945* (edited with critical commentary by ANDREAS HILLGRUBER and HANS-ADOLF JACOBSEN; Bernard & Graefe, Frankfurt/M., 1961).

TESKE, HERMANN: *Die silbernen Spiegel* (Vowinckel, Heidelberg, 1952).

"Die Bedeutung der Eisenbahn bei Aufmarsch und Rückzug einer Heeresgruppe", in *Allgemeine Schweizerische Militärzeitschrift, 1955.*

"General Ernst Köstring", in *Profile bedeutender Soldaten,* Bd. 1 (issued by Bundesarchiv/Militärarchiv Koblenz; Mittler & Sohn, Frankfurt/M., 1965).

VON TIPPELSKIRCH, KURT: *Geschichte des zweiten Weltkrieges* (Athenäum, Bonn, 1951).

TIEMANN, R.: *Geschichte der 83. Infanteriedivision* (Podzun, Bad Nauheim, 1960).

TORNAU, G.; KUROWSKI, F.: *Sturmartillerie, Fels in der Brandung* (Maximilian, Herford, 1965).

TRESS, KARL; U. A.: *Das Infanterie- und Sturmregiment 14 im zweiten Weltkrieg;* (Kameradschaft ehemaliger 114er, Constance, 1959).

VEALE, J. P.: *Der Barbarei entgegen* (Nölke, Hamburg, 1954).

VON VORMANN, NIKOLAUS: *Tscherkassy* (Scharnhorst Buchkameradschaft, Heidelberg, 1954).

WAGENER, CARL: "Der Vorstoß des XXXX. Panzerkorps von Charkow zum Kaukasus, Juli–August 1942", in *Wehrwissenschaftliche Rundschau,* 1955, Nos. 9, 10.

"Der Gegenangriff des XXXX. Panzerkorps gegen den Durchbruch der Panzergruppe Popow", in *Wehrwissenschaftliche Rundschau,* 1957, No. 1.

"Der Ausbruch der 1. Panzerarmee aus dem Kessel von Kamenez–Podolsk, März/April 1944", in *Wehrwissenschaftliche Rundschau,* 1959, No. 1.

WARLIMONT, WALTER: *Im Hauptquartier der Deutschen Wehrmacht 1939–1945* (Bernard & Graefe, Frankfurt/M., 1962).

WEIDINGER, OTTO: *Kameraden bis zum Ende* (Plesse, Göttingen, 1962).

WEINMANN, WILLI: *Die 101. Jäger-Division, Dokumente, Berichte und Bilder* (privately published, Offenburg, 1966).

WENSAUER, MATTHIAS: *Chronik des Infanterie-Regiments 246* (privately published, Göttingen, 1962).

WERTH, ALEXANDER: *Rußland im Krieg 1941–1945* (Droemer, Munich, 1965).

WERTHEN, WOLFGANG: *Geschichte der 16. Panzer-Division* (Podzun, Bad Nauheim, 1958).

WICH, RUDOLF: *Baden-Württembergische Divisionen im 2. Weltkrieg* (Braun, Karlsruhe, 1957).

VON ZYDOWITZ, KURT: *Die Geschichte der 58. Infanterie-Division* (Podzun, Bad Nauheim, 1958).

ZWEIG, STEFAN: *Sternstunden der Menschheit* (Fischer Bücherei Nr. 595, Frankfurt/M., 1964).

534   *Bibliography*

II. Private Publications

Geschichte der 21. Infanterie-Division (Hamburg, 1960).

Geschichte der 24. Infanterie-Division (Study Group of the Division, Stolberg, 1956).

Die 50. Infanterie-Division, 1939–1945 (Göttingen, 1965).

Geschichte der 56. Infanterie-Division 1938–1945 (Study Group of the Division, Hann. Münden, n.d.).

Das Buch der 78. Sturm-Division (Tübingen, n.d.).

Der Weg der 93. Infanterie-Division, 1939–1945 (Weinheim a. d. B., 1956).

Taten und Schicksale der 197. Infanterie-Division (n.d.).

Geschichte der 207. und 281. Infanterie-Division mit ihren Zwischengliederungen 1939 bis 1945 (Kiel, n.d.).

Festschrift zum 1. Treffen der Angehörigen der 225. Inf. Div. (Hamburg, 1956).

290. Infanterie-Division (Delmenhorst, 1960).

Geschichte des Artillerie-Regiments 129, 1940–1945 (Bremen, 1962).

Tagebuch der Sturmgeschütz-Brigade 190 (Neuß, n.d.).

Pionier Bataillon 240 (Hamburg, n.d.).

Die Flut verschlang sich selbst, nicht uns! Tscherkassy (Truppenkameradschaft "Wiking", Hanover, 1963).

Der Kessel von Tscherkassy (Kartenwerk nach Originalkarten, Truppenkameradschaft "Wiking", Hanover, 1963).

Südlich des Ladoga Sees, Winter 1943 (published by the Army at Leningrad).

Vom Tschir zum Mius (published by Sixth Army HQ, 1943).

Die Abwehrschlachten der 6. Armee im Donezbecken und in der Nogaischen Steppe vom 18. 8. – 3. 11. 1943 (published by Sixth Army HQ, 1943).

Die Winterschlachten der 6. Armee im großen Dnjepr-Bogen, im Brückenkopf Nikopol und im Raum Nikopol-Apostolowo-Kriwoi Rog vom 10. 1. – 18. 2. 1944 (published by Sixth Army HQ, 1944).

Die zweite Winterschlacht der 6. Armee zwischen Dnjepr, Ingulez und Bug vom 3. bis 23. 3. 1944 (published by Sixth Army HQ, 1944).

Abwehrschlacht der 6. Armee zwischen Bug und Dnjestr vom 28. 3. – 12. 4. 1944 (published by Sixth Army HQ, 1944).

Abwehrkämpfe der 6. Armee am Dnjestr und Pruth vom 20. 4. – 31. 5. 1944 (published by Sixth Army HQ, 1944).

Ln-Truppe schafft sichere Fernmeldeverbindungen nach Demjansk (essay by Karl-Otto Hoffmann).

Die Durchbruchsschlacht der 1. Panzerarmee (edited in the field for the Chief of Staff of First Panzer Army, 1944).

SS-Panzerkorps in der Schlacht zwischen Donez und Dnjepr (published for SS-Panzer Corps HQ, 1943).

Chronik SS-Pz.Rgt. 5 "Wiking" (1964).

Kriegstagebuch der 15. I. D.

Gefechtsbericht der 20. Pz.Div. Juni/Juli 1944.

Kriegstagebuch der 223. I. D., 1. 4. 43 – 30. 9. 43.

III. Archives and Other Sources

MICROFILMS of the National Archives and Records Service, General Services Administration, Washington, D.C., U.S.A.

ORIGINAL RECORDS and excerpts from war diaries concerning Army Group Centre, Federal German Archive/Military Archive, Koblenz.

DITTRICH, HELMUT: *Die Entwicklung des sowjetischen Kräfteeinsatzes von Ende März 1943 bis zum Angriffsbeginn Zitadelle am 5. Juli 1943* (Military History Research Office, 1964).

SECRET REPORTS of the Swiss Bureau Hausamann to the Swiss High Command, microfilms, Federal German Archive/Military Archive, Koblenz.

IV. Unpublished Essays and Manuscripts

AUGUSTIN, HANS, Senior Public Prosecutor
BÄKE, FRANZ, DR, Major-General (Reserve)
BALCK, HERMANN, General of Armoured troops (rtd.)
BAYERLEIN, FRITZ, Lieutenant-General (rtd.)
FREIHERR VON BÖNNINGHAUSEN
BRASSAT, JULIUS
BUSSE, THEODOR, General of Infantry (rtd.)
DEBUS, Lieutenant of Waffen SS (rtd.)
DEINHARDT, HERBERT, Colonel (rtd.)
DIERCKS, JOHANNES
DIESENER, K. Lieutenant-Colonel
REICHSFREIHERR VON EDELSHEIM, MAXIMILIAN, Major-General (rtd.)
FRANZ, ALEXANDER, Colonel
FRANZ, GERHARD, Major-General (rtd.)
FRANTZ, PETER, Major (rtd.)
GILLE, General of Waffen SS (rtd.)
GRAF, SEPP
GROSSMANN, HORST, General of Infantry (rtd.)
HEINRICI, GOTTHARD, Colonel-General (rtd.)
HENSEL, HANS RUPRECHT, Dr
HESSE, JOACHIM, Colonel (rtd.)
HOENICKE, ALEXANDER
HOFFMANN, KARL-OTTO, Lieutenant-Colonel
HORSTMANN, KARL, Major (rtd.)
HOTH, HERMANN, Colonel-General (rtd.)
KAESTNER, ROBERT, Colonel (rtd.)
VON KAHLDEN, WOLF, Brigadier-General (rtd.)
KANDUTSCH, HERMANN, Major (rtd.)
KIRCHENBAUER, FRIEDRICH, Dr, Captain (rtd.)
KITTEL, HEINRICH, Lieutenant-General (rtd.)
KRÄTSCHMER, GÜNTHER
KÜHN, WALTER, Dr, Major-General (rtd.)
KÜHNE, KLAUS, Captain (rtd.)
LAHMEYER, Major (rtd.)
VON MANTEUFFEL, HASSO, General of Armoured Troops (rtd.)
MEMMIGER, FRITZ, Captain (rtd.)

536 *Bibliography*

MERCK, ERNST, Major-General (rtd.)
MILDEBRATH, WERNER, Colonel (rtd.)
VON MITZLAFF, BERND, Colonel
MÜLLER, WOLFGANG, Lieutenant-Colonel
MUSCULUS, FRIEDRICH,Major (rtd.)
NEHRING, WALTHER K., General of Armoured Troops (rtd.)
VON OPPELN-BRONIKOWSKI, HERMANN, Major-General (rtd.)
PHILIPPI, ALFRED, Major-General (rtd.)
PICKERT, WOLFGANG, General of Flak Artillery (rtd.)
PINGEL, HERMANN
VON PLATO, ANTON-DETLEV,Major-General
RATZEL, Lieutenant-Colonel (rtd.)
REINHARDT, ALFRED, Lieutenant-General (rtd.)
REINHARDT, HEINZ, Lieutenant-Colonel (rtd.)
RENZ, MANFRED, Dr, Captain of Waffen SS (rtd.)
RÖNNEFARTH, HELMUT K. G., Dr
SANDER, K. J., Dr, Major
GRAF SCHIMMELMANN VON LINDENBERG, Colonel (rtd.)
SCHMAGER, GERT, Major of Waffen SS (rtd.)
SCHÖRNER, FERDINAND, Field-Marshal
SCHÖTTL, OSKAR, Dr
SCHULZE, PAUL, Major (rtd.)
SCHWARZENBERGER, HORST
SEIDEMANN, HANS, Air Force General (rtd.)
SÖTH, WILHELM, Major-General (rtd.)
STAHL, PAUL, Dr, Lieutenant-Colonel (Reserve, rtd.)
STEINER, FELIX, General of Waffen SS (rtd.)
VON STEINKELLER, F. K.,Major-General (rtd.)
STOVES, ROLF, Lieutenant-Colonel
TEBBE, GERHARD,Major (rtd.)
THOMALE, WOLFGANG, Lieutenant-General (rtd.)
THRÄN, EMIL
TROWITZ, ADOLF, Major-General (rtd.)
WEBER, RENATUS, Dr, Ministerialdirektor
WENCK, WALTHER, General of Armoured Troops (rtd.)
WESTHOVEN, FRANZ, Lieutenant-General (rtd.)
WESTPHAL, WERNER,Major of Waffen SS (rtd.)
WIENER, FRITZ, Dr, Lieutenant-Colonel (rtd.)
WIESE, FRIEDRICH, General of Infantry (rtd.)
VON WIETERSHEIM, WEND, Lieutenant-General (rtd.)
WILLEMER, W., Brigadier-General (rtd.)
WINTERFELD, KURT, Dr
WÖRNER, AUGUST
WOTHE, WILLY
ZIMMER, RICHARD, Lieutenant-General (rtd.)

V. Soviet Sources

ABSALYAMOV, M.; ANDRIYANOV, V.: "Lessons of Co-operation between Airborne Troops and Partisans in the Great Fatherland War", in *Voyenno-istoricheskiy zhurnal*, No. 11, 1964.

BACHURIN, A.: "In Action on the Berezina", in *Voyenyy vestnik*, No. 8, 1964.

BATOV, P. I.: *Campaigns and Battles* (Publ. House of the U.S.S.R. Ministry of Defence, Moscow, 1962).

BIRYUZOV, S. S.: *The Soviet Soldier in the Balkans* (Publ. House of the U.S.S.R. Ministry of Defence, Moscow, 1963).
"The Search for the Right Decision", in *Voyenno-istoricheskiy zhurnal*, No. 5, 1963.

BLINOV, S. I.: *From the Vistula to the Oder* (Publ. House of the U.S.S.R. Ministry of Defence, Moscow, 1962).

CHUYKOV, V. I.: *The Beginning of the Road* (Deutscher Militär-Verlag, Berlin, 1961).

DEBORIN, G. A.: *The Second World War* (Publ. House of the U.S.S.R. Ministry of Defence, Moscow, 1960).

DZENIT, Y.: "The Annihilation of the Encircled Enemy Force", in *Voyenno-istoricheskiy zhurnal*, No. 2, 1965.

GRECHKO, A.: "The Fighting for the Capital of the Ukraine", in *Voyenno-istoricheskiy zhurnal*, No. 2, 1963.

KARAVAN, A.: "Towards Minsk", in *Voyenno-istoricheskiy zhurnal*, No. 6, 1964.

KAZAKOV, M.: "The Great Victory at Leningrad", in *Voyenno-istoricheskiy zhurnal*, No. 1, 1964.

KONEV, I.: "The Completion of the Liberation of the Soviet Ukraine and the Reaching of the Vistula", in *Voyenno-istoricheskiy zhurnal*, No. 7, 1964.

KRASOVSKIY, S.: "The Second Air Army in the Sandomierz-Lvov Operation", in *Voyenno-istoricheskiy zhurnal*, No. 7, 1964.

KRAVCHENKO, A.: "Tank Men Cross a River", in *Voyenno-istoricheskiy zhurnal*, No. 9, 1963.

KRIVOSHEIN, S.: "War Report", chapter *In the Kursk Salient* (Molodaya Gvardiya Publ. House, Moscow, 1962).

KUROCHKIN, P.: "The Breakthrough through the Enemy's Defences in the Direction of Lvov", in *Voyenno-istoricheskiy zhurnal*, No. 7, 1964.

LUCHINSKIY, A.: "The Fighting at Sevastopol", in *Voyenno-istoricheskiy zhurnal*, No. 5, 1964.

MARKIN, I. I.: *The Battle of Kursk* (Publ. House of the Ministry of National Defence, Berlin, 1959).

MOROZOV, V.: "Why the Spring 1943 Offensive in the Donets Basin was not brought to its Conclusion", edited by F. W. Hauck, *Wehrwissenschaftliche Rundschau*, Nos. 7 and 8, 1964.

MOSKALENKO, K.: "The Commanders of the Main Blow", in *Komsomolskaya Pravda*, No. 89, 1964.

PANTELEYEV, V.: *The Front at Sea* (Publ. House of the U.S.S.R. Ministry of Defence, Moscow, 1965).

PLATONOV, S. P.; PAVLENKO, N. G.; PAROTKIN, I. V.: *The Second World War 1939–1945*, Vol. 1 of text and Vol. 1 of maps (Moscow, 1958).

POKROVSKIY, A.: "On the Third Belorussian Front", in *Voyenno-istoricheskiy zhurnal*, No. 6, 1964.

POPEL, N. K.: *The Tanks are Turning West* (Publ. House of the U.S.S.R. Ministry of Defence, Moscow, 1960).
The Tanks Are Attacking (Deutscher Militär-Verlag, Berlin, 1964).

POSPELOV, P. N.; and others: *History of the Great Fatherland War of the Soviet Union 1941–1945*, Vols. 1–4 (Institute for Marxism-Leninism under the CPSU Central Committee, Moscow, 1960).

ROKOSSOVSKIY, K.: "The Two Main Offensives," in *Voyenno-istoricheskiy zhurnal*, No. 6, 1964.

ROTMISTROV, R.: "The Speed of Attack of a Tank Army", in *Voyenno-istoricheskiy zhurnal*, No. 6, 1964.

SAMSONOV, A. M.: *From the Volga to the Baltic* (Publ. House of the U.S.S.R. Academy of Sciences, Moscow, 1963).

SOFRONOV, G. P.: *Air Landings in the Second World War* (Publ. House of the U.S.S.R. Ministry of Defence, Moscow, 1962).

Soviet War News; published by the Press Department of the Soviet Embassy in London; bound vols. 1, 2, 3, 4, 5, 6, 7, 8, 9, 10, 11, 13, 14, 15.

STALIN, I. V.: *War Speeches – Orders of the Day* (Hutchinson, London).

SYCHEV, K. V.; and others: *Combat Operations by Rifle Units* (Publ. House of the Ministry of National Defence, Berlin, 1958).

UMANSKIY, T.: "The Occupation of the Lyutezh Bridge-head", in *Voyenno-istoricheskiy zhurnal*, No. 9, 1963.

VERSHININ, K.: "The Fourth Air Army in the Belorussian Operation", in *Voyenno-istoricheskiy zhurnal*, No. 6, 1964.

VORONOV, N. N.: *On Active Service* (Publ. House of the U.S.S.R. Ministry of Defence, Moscow, 1963).

VYSOCHKIY, F. I.; MAKUKHIN, M. E.: *The Guards Tanks* (Moscow, 1963).

YAKOVLEV, V.: "The Black Sea Fleet in the Fighting for the Liberation of the Crimea", in *Voyenno-istoricheskiy zhurnal*, No. 5, 1964.

YEREMENKO, A. I.: *Stalingrad; the Notes of a Front Commander* (Publ. House of the U.S.S.R. Ministry of Defence, Moscow, 1961).

YUSHCHUK, I. I.: *The XI Tank Corps in the Fighting for the Homeland* (Publ. House of the U.S.S.R. Ministry of Defence, Moscow, 1962).

ZAKHAROV, M.: "A Lightning-Like Operation", in *Voyenno-istoricheskiy zhurnal*, No. 8, 1964.

ZAVYALOV, A. S.; KALIYADIN, T. Y.: *The Battle for the Caucasus* (Publ. House of the U.S.S.R. Ministry of Defence, Moscow, 1956).

ZHILIN, F. A.: *The Most Important Operations of the Great Fatherland War 1941–1945* (Moscow, 1956).

ZHUKOV, YU.: *The Taming of the Tigers* (Moscow).

Abbreviations and Symbols used in the Text and on the Maps

A. Co.	Army Corps; several infantry divisions under the command of a corps commander
Pz. Co.	Panzer Corps; several Panzer divisions, or several Panzer and infantry divisions, under the command of a corps commander
Mtn. Co.	Mountain Corps; several mountain divisions, or several mountain and other divisions, under the command of a corps commander
Flak	Anti-aircraft gun; used also for anti-aircraft units
A. Gr.	Army Group; several armies
He	Heinkel aircraft
Hs	Henschel aircraft
Ju	Junkers aircraft
Me	Messerschmitt aircraft
OKH	Oberkommando des Heeres = German High Command of Land Forces
OKW	Oberkommando der Wehrmacht = German High Command of the Armed Forces
STAVKA	Soviet High Command
Stuka	German dive-bomber

German Units and their Allies

18	Eighteenth Army
3 Pz.	Third Panzer Army
A. Det.	Army Detachment
XXIII A. Co.	XXIII Army Corps
XLVI Pz. Co.	XLVI Panzer Corps
XLIX Mtn. Co.	XLIX Mountain Corps
XLIV Jg. Co.	XLIV Jäger Corps

SS Pz.Co.	SS Panzer Corps
III Lw.F.Co.	III Luftwaffe Field Corps
Rum. Cav. Co.	Rumanian Cavalry Corps
11 Pz	11th Panzer Division
31	31st Infantry Division
36 mot.	36th Motorized Infantry Division
213 L. Def.	213th Local Defence Division
Pts. 20 mot.	Parts of 20th Motorized Infantry Division
3 Mtn.	3rd Mountain Division
10 Pz. Gr.	10th Panzer Grenadier Division
97 Jg.	97th Jäger Division
21 Lw.F.	21st Luftwaffe Field Division
"GD"	"Grossdeutschland" Panzer Grenadier Division
"LAH"	"Leibstandarte Adolf Hitler" Panzer Division
SS'T'	"Totenkopf" SS Panzer Division
SS'R'	"Das Reich" SS Panzer Division
SS'V'	"Viking" SS Panzer Grenadier Division
Gr. Renz	Combat Group Renz
Pz.J.Rgt	Panzer Jäger Regiment
401 Rgt.	401st Infantry Regiment
II/374	2nd Battalion, 374th Infantry Regiment
Bäke	Heavy Panzer Regiment Bäke
Ca. Det. B	Corps Detachment "B"
Wallon	"Wallonie" SS Volunteer Brigade

Russian Units

65	Sixty-Fifth Army
5 G.	Fifth Guards Army
1 T.	First Tank Army
5 G.T.	Fifth Guards Tank Army
1 STR.	First Striking Army
XVIII R.Co.	XVIII Rifle Corps
XXXV G.R.Co.	XXXV Guards Rifle Corps
XXXI T.Co.	XXXI Tank Corps
V G.T.Co.	V Guards Tank Corps
III Mech.Co.	III Mechanized Corps
III G.Mech.Co.	III Guards Mechanized Corps
305 R.	305th Rifle Division
81 G.R.	81st Guards Rifle Division
9 Mtn.	9th Mountain Division
122 T.Brig	122nd Tank Brigade
125 G.R.Rgt	125th Guards Rifle Regiment
Popov	Armoured Group Popov
	Airfield
	Boundaries between Army Groups
	Boundaries between Armies

INDEX

Officers' rank as of 1st July, 1944. Figures in italics refer to photographs.

SCORCHED EARTH

Front Line Nov.1942

1937 Frontiers − − − −

Printed in Great Britain

Inset map (top right)

NORWAY
Barents Sea
Kirkenes
Petsamo
Murmansk
KOLA PENINSULA
Salla
FINLAND
Kiestinki
White Sea
Lake Onega
100 miles
Lake Ladoga

Main map

burg
chvin
ay
ansk
eliger
n
hev
Volga
Moscow
Kaluga
Tula

Orel
Kursk
Oboyan
Belgorod
ov
Izyum
epropetrovsk
Stalino
orozhye
Taganrog
Rostov
of Azov
Kerch
Novorossiysk
Tuapse
Sochi
Sea

100 miles

Voronezh
Kalach
Don
Donets
Mius
Marych
Salsk
Elista
Kuban
Krasnodar
Armavir
Maykop
CAUCASUS
Mt Elbrus
Sukhumi
Batumi

Saratov
Stalingrad
Volga
Astrakhan
Caspian
Mozdok
Terek
Groznyy
Tiflis